IT Audit, Control, and Security

IT Audit, Control, and Security

ROBERT MOELLER

WILEY

John Wiley & Sons, Inc.

For general information on our other products and services or for technical support, please contact our Customer Care Department within the United States at (800) 762-2974, outside the United States at (317) 572-3993 or fax (317) 572-4002.

Wiley also publishes its books in a variety of electronic formats. Some content that appears in print may not be available in electronic books. For more information about Wiley products, visit our web site at www.wiley.com.

Library of Congress Cataloging-in-Publication Data:
Moeller, Robert R.
   IT audit, control, and security / Robert Moeller.
        p. cm.
   Includes bibliographical references and index.
   ISBN: 978-0-471-40676-1 (cloth); 978-0-470-87741-8 (ebk); 978-0-470-87767-8 (ebk); 978-0-470-87768-5 (ebk)
   1.   Information technology—Auditing.   2.   Electronic data processing departments—Auditing.   3.   Computer security.   4.   Computer networks—Security measures.   I.   Title.
   T58.5.M645 2010
   658.4'78–dc22   2010013505

10 9 8 7 6 5 4 3 2 1

Dedicated to my best friend and wife, Lois Moeller.
Lois has been my companion and partner for over 40 years,
whether we are on our Lake Michigan sailboat,
skiing in Utah or elsewhere,
traveling to interesting places in the world,
gardening in the backyard,
or cooking its produce.

Contents

Introduction: Importance of IT Auditing

W ELCOME TO THE WORLD of *IT Audit, Control, and Security*. Much has changed in information technology (IT) auditing since we published our first edition of this book when we were then called *Computer Auditors*. Back in those days, traditional mainframe or legacy computer systems were still common, we had difficulty envisioning laptop systems as serious business information systems tools, and the Internet was little more than an e-mail and text document communications tool for many. Computer security then was largely based on locked, secured mainframe facilities, and we were just seeing the very first computer viruses. Many auditors, both internal and external, typically had only limited knowledge about IT systems controls, and there were wide knowledge gaps among auditors, systems security specialists, and developers. It is hard to focus on just one development or event that has turned our view of IT audit controls into a separate discipline. However, the overall influence of the Web along with audit, security, and internal controls concerns has made IT controls more important to many today.

This book focuses on both the technical and professional issues facing today's audit, security, and internal control specialists in an information systems environment, with the goal of providing an understanding of key IT audit security and internal controls issues. We have expanded our audience beyond just auditors to include IT security and internal control specialists as well. Although some may not have not have specific job titles covering these audit, security, and internal controls disciplines, many professionals in today's enterprises have a responsibility to ensure that good IT controls have been installed and are operating. IT auditors are key persons responsible for assessing these controls. Although the individual chapters of this book, outlined next, cover a broad range of technical and audit-related topics, each of the chapters focuses on three broad IT audit topic areas:

1. Technology-driven audit and internal controls. The effective IT auditor today needs to have a good understanding of a wide range of IT technologies as well as appropriate related audit, security, and control issues and techniques. As our first broad concentration area, the text addresses some of the more significant technology changes today along with their audit, security, and internal control implications. This book is not a detailed technology tutorial, but we describe important IT issues and introduce their IT control procedures in the following broad areas:

- Electronic commerce systems, including the use of the XBRL protocol as well as wireless and cloud computing. This area generally goes under the name of "e-business" with evolving standards and good practices.

- Modern application implementation processes, including the use of comprehensive enterprise resource planning (ERP) software packages, software as a service (SAAS) implementation approaches and object oriented-application development processes.
- Effective IT continuity planning processes. Because virtually all enterprise operations today are tied to often interlocking IT processes, facilities must be in place to restore them to normal operations if some unexpected event arises.
- Systems infrastructure controls for managing existing applications and operations. Configuration management, service-level agreements, and effective customer service functions are all important in today's modern IT environment.
- Effective IT governance procedures. Whether Sarbanes-Oxley Act (SOx) rules or international standards guidelines, all IT organizations today must understand and comply with the many new rules covering all aspects of IT governance and operations.
- The importance of storage management. Effective processing rules and IT governance requirements require that we keep backup copies of much of the data we use in IT operations as well as database operations to allow an enterprise to search for and retrieve that data easily. IT storage audit, security and internal control issues, and newer concepts such as virtualization are important IT concerns.
- Modern computer security procedures, including trusted networks and firewall-protected systems. Enterprises need to protect their data in light of ever-increasing threats in today's Web and wireless environments.

This list is not all-encompassing but highlights the overall topics in these chapters. Although some of these expressions may seem like buzzwords or techno-jargon to some readers, the chapters to come introduce many technical concepts with an emphasis on their related audit, security, and internal control concepts and procedures.

2. Security, privacy, and continuity issues. As the second broad topic area in this book, we discuss disaster recovery planning as well as effective continuity and information systems security processes in a modern IT environment. The emphasis is more on getting the business back in operation rather than just getting the IT resources working again. Closely related to security matters, privacy is another issue facing IT auditors. We are increasingly seeing legislation mandating privacy protections over multiple types of information systems data, such as medical records, financial data, and other areas. These new rules have encouraged many enterprises to install strengthened internal controls.

3. Auditing legislative and governance changes. Professionals constantly face legal and other changes that impact their work. Understanding and developing appropriate procedures is this book's third broad objective. Although it occurred years ago now, the catastrophic failure of the then-prominent corporation, Enron, introduced a raft of new issues. Based on its stock market capitalization, Enron was then a rapidly growing large company engaged in trading oil, gas, and other commodities. Enron's financial reports, in retrospect, contained many red-flag warnings of possible troubles. Despite these warning signs, Enron's external auditors seemingly looked the other way.

Enron subsequently collapsed, hurting many and leaving a trail of recriminations and questions about the overall independence and objectivity of its external auditors. As a result, the U.S. Congress passed the Sarbanes-Oxley Act (SOx), which changed the process of auditing internal accounting controls for financial management as well as for external and internal auditors. The text discusses how SOx rules continue to impact auditors and financial management with a focus on internal controls, security, and IT auditing.

The worldwide market meltdown starting in 2008 has caused a series of other concerns when what were then major financial and other enterprises worldwide either totally failed or lost value to investors. Audit, security, and internal control issues and concerns do not just arise because of a single event, such as the 9/11 terrorism attack or the Enron bankruptcy. Our third focus area, auditing legal and governance changes, evolves over time, and we will discuss newer issues and what we feel are evolving concerns. Our emphasis over these next chapters is on newer rules, evolving technologies, and their combined impact on today's IT audit professional.

Our text covers a blend of audit, internal control, and security issues that are key knowledge areas for IT auditors. These are also topics where financial (often external) auditors, internal audit management, and other professionals who are not IT audit specialists should have at least some general understanding. IT security and controls issues have become so pervasive today that enterprise professionals at many levels should have a general knowledge of them.

An overall objective of this book is to highlight areas that are the most important, from an internal controls risk perspective, for today's IT auditors. These chapters present a high-level overview of each of the three broad objective areas just discussed. No matter what the technical topic, there are always opportunities to present even more detailed technical information. However, we focus on areas that we feel are important to today's professional, whether an enterprise IT audit staff member, a manager, or a student learning more. In summary, the chapter-by-chapter IT audit, control, and security topics discussed in this book include:

Chapter 1, SOx and the COSO Internal Controls Framework. The Sarbanes-Oxley Act and its internal controls assessment rules have been the biggest regulatory changes in decades, and they have impacted both auditors and enterprise management in the United States and worldwide. This chapter summarizes the SOx Section 404 requirements for internal control reviews to support an enterprise's financial reports. Our emphasis, however, is on internal accounting controls reviews of primarily IT applications. The chapter also discusses the newer financial audit AS5 rules released in late 2008.

In addition, we discuss the Committee of Sponsoring Organizations (COSO) framework on internal controls as well as some the newly released COSO guidance materials for monitoring internal control systems. This chapter emphasizes an IT auditor's responsibility for understanding and using the COSO internal controls framework.

Chapter 2, Using CobiT to Perform IT Audits. A more IT-oriented internal controls framework, called Control *Objectives* for *Information* and related *Technology* (CobiT), was in place even before SOx, and many enterprises began to use CobiT when SOx became the law as a preferred tool for complying with its Section 404 internal controls procedures. The CobiT framework provides guidance on evaluating and understanding internal controls, with an emphasis on enterprise IT resources. CobiT is not a replacement for the COSO internal controls framework but is a different way to look at internal controls in today's IT-centric world.

Although originally launched as a tool to help specialist internal and external auditors who reviewed IT-related internal controls, CobiT today is a helpful tool for evaluating all internal controls across an enterprise. It emphasizes the linkage of IT with other business resources to deliver overall value to an enterprise. This chapter provides an overview of the CobiT framework and its key components. More important, the chapter describes the relationship between CobiT objectives and the COSO internal control framework for use in internal audit reviews. Even if an internal auditor does not use the CobiT framework in reviews of internal controls, all internal and IT auditors should have a high-level knowledge of the basic CobiT framework. Knowledge of CobiT and the COSO internal controls framework will help an IT auditor to better understand the role of IT controls and risks in many enterprise environments.

Chapter 3, IIA and ISACA Standards for the Professional Practice of Internal Auditing. Every profession requires a set of standards to govern their practices, general procedures, and ethics. The key standards for all internal auditors are the Institute of Internal Auditors' (IIA's) Professional Standards for the Practice of Internal Auditing, a set of guidance materials that were most recently revised in 2009. This chapter summarizes the current IIA standards and provides guidance on how to apply them. The chapter also introduces the IIA's Global Technology Audit Guide (GTAG) series IT guidance materials. An understanding of the IIA's International Standards is an absolute must for all internal and IT auditors. These standards provide the support for many if not nearly all internal audit professional activities.

This chapter also revisits the IIA Code of Ethics, an important supporting foundation for internal and IT auditors, as well as the Code of Ethics for the Information Systems Audit and Control Association (ISACA). ISACA members are often IIA members or Certified Public Accountants, but the ISACA Code of Ethics places a special emphasis on IT-related activities. Although ISACA does not have the same type of standards as the IIA, its CobiT IT internal control framework provides standards guidance for IT auditors. The chapter also highlights ISACA's standards and guidelines. These are particularly important for IT auditors.

In addition, Chapter 31 introduces another very important set of internal audit standards, the quality audit standards from the American Society for Quality (ASQ). ASQ's internal audit standards and its quality auditors represent a different dimension and discipline when contrasted with the IIA's and ISACA's approaches and standards. They also represent an area that must be better represented and understood in the overall world of internal auditing.

Chapter 4, Understanding Risk Management through COSO ERM. Although the term *enterprise risk management* (ERM) is frequently used, many IT auditors do not have a consistent understanding of and how to use it as a tool for effective internal audit reviews. This chapter introduces the COSO Enterprise Risk Management (COSO ERM) framework and its elements. Although their basic framework models look similar, COSO ERM is different from the COSO internal controls framework discussed in Chapter 1. COSO ERM is an important reference to better understand and evaluate the risks surrounding internal controls at all levels. This chapter describes the major elements of the COSO ERM framework and looks at how IT auditors can better build

COSO ERM into their review processes as well as steps for auditing the effectiveness of an enterprise's risk management processes.

Every IT auditor needs to have an understanding of risk assessment approaches and the overall risk management process, with an emphasis on COSO ERM. This chapter presents IT audit techniques for understanding and assessing risks in many areas, from selecting items to review to evaluating risks as part of IT audit reviews.

Chapter 5, Performing Effective IT Audits. This chapter describes basic processes for performing an effective IT audit. Basic reviews can be performed by many specialists in an enterprise, but this chapter focuses on basic audit steps for performing an IT internal audit review, ranging from risk-based audit planning to preparing effective internal audit reports.

This chapter does not describe the overall internal audit review process but emphasizes some of the key elements necessary to perform effective IT-related reviews.

Chapter 6, General Controls in Today's IT Environments. IT processes and systems today range from an application to control an enterprise's accounting general ledger to the all-pervasive Internet. Although the lines of separation are sometimes difficult, we can generally think of IT controls on two broad levels: application controls that cover a specific process—such as an accounts payable application to pay invoices from purchases—and what are called general IT controls. This latter category covers internal controls that do not relate just to specific IT applications but are important for all aspects of an enterprise's IT operations.

The concept of IT general controls goes back to the early days of centralized, mainframe computers. At that time, internal auditors sometimes looked for such things as an access control lock on a computer center door as a general control that covered all processes and applications operating from within the centralized IT operations center. Today, we often think of the processes that cover all enterprise IT operations as the IT infrastructure, a concept further discussed in Chapter 7.

This chapter discusses reviews of IT general controls from an IIA standards and CobiT perspective. Although general controls were once considered in terms of centralized mainframe computer center operations in an earlier era, today we should think of them as those controls impacting any set of similar IT machine resources. For example, an internal audit function may equip its entire staff with laptop computers, and good general controls are necessary in this environment to encourage all internal and IT auditors to use common software control procedures on those assigned laptops. General controls weaknesses can impact all IT processes.

Chapter 7, Infrastructure Controls and ITIL Service Management Best Practices. This chapter looks at IT general controls based on the worldwide recognized set of best or good practices called the Information Technology Infrastructure Library (ITIL). These ITIL recommended best practices outline the type of framework an IT auditor should consider when reviewing IT internal control risks and recommending effective IT general controls improvements.

ITIL processes cover what we frequently call the IT infrastructure—the supporting processes that allow IT applications to function and deliver their results to systems users. For example, an ITIL process outlines best practices for installing an effective IT help desk operation for all systems users. All too often, auditors have focused their attention on the application development side of IT and ignored important service delivery and support IT processes. An enterprise can put massive efforts into building and implementing a new budget forecasting system, but that application will be of little value unless there are good problem and incident management processes in place to allow the users of this budget forecasting system to resolve systems difficulties. Also needed are good capacity and availability processes to allow the new application to run as expected. ITIL processes are part of what is called the IT infrastructure. IT auditors should have a good understanding of these enterprise processes, and they should be covered in IT audit general controls reviews.

Chapter 8, Systems Software and IT Operations General Controls. Whether it is a Microsoft Windows operating system on a laptop computer or Linux controlling an office server, the operating system (OS) and its supporting software are key components to any computer system operation. This chapter discusses some of the various OS types and the supporting systems software that are essential in an IT operation. IT auditors should have a very general understanding of the purposes and importance of these types of IT software and should look for effective general controls when performing reviews in this important general controls area.

Chapter 9, Evolving Control Issues: Wireless Networks, Cloud Computing, and Virtualization. New IT technologies make many processes easier to use or more efficient, but they often introduce new internal control concerns. This chapter has selected three of these newer areas and considers internal control risks and potential audit procedures for each. Wireless networks is the first topic here. Although it is certainly convenient to not have to connect IT terminals and other devices through a formal cable network, the very open environment of using wireless technology approaches introduces some security and control risks. The chapter looks at wireless networks from an audit, security, and control perspective.

As a second topic area, the chapter introduces the rapidly evolving IT configuration called cloud computing. Although the term sounds almost exotic to many, it has become a significant concept today with our growing dependence on using Web-based applications for many business processes rather than applications downloaded to home office servers. Cloud computing processes are also called web services, software as a service (SaaS), or service-oriented architecture (SOA). In cloud computing, many different Internet applications—supported by multiple vendors and operating on multiple servers—operate together out of what looks like a large fuzzy Internet cloud. This chapter introduces cloud computing concepts and discusses some security and controls concerns that may impact IT auditors in their assessments of IT general controls.

This chapter's third topic is virtualization. With the massive amount of data and information that most enterprises retain, storage management is very important for almost all IT operations. Whether it is the very high-capacity miniature USB devices so common today or new database tools, there is a need to install appropriate controls in these storage management environments. In virtualization, any device can be defined to look like another. This concept can create a challenging environment for an IT auditor, and the chapter provides some introductory internal controls guidance to these evolving areas.

Chapter 10, Selecting, Testing, and Auditing IT Applications. In order to perform internal controls reviews in specific areas of enterprise operations, such as accounting, distribution, or engineering, IT auditors must have the skills to understand, evaluate, and test the controls over their supporting IT applications. Reviews of specific application controls often are more critical to achieving overall audit objectives than reviews of general IT controls.

This chapter discusses approaches to review internal accounting controls in IT applications, using several different types of applications as examples. The chapter also discusses audit approaches for evaluating and testing those application controls as well as techniques for reviewing new applications under development. We focus on the internal control characteristics of different types of applications and then discuss how to select appropriate applications in internal controls reviews. There are many differences from one application to another; this chapter focuses on how an IT auditor should select higher-risk applications as candidates for IT audit reviews; the tools and skills needed to understand and document application internal controls; and, finally, processes to test and evaluate those applications.

Chapter 11, Software Engineering and CMMi. The Carnegie-Mellon University Software Engineering Institute's IT-based Capability Maturity Model for integration (CMMi®) is an effective approach for an enterprise and its IT software development functions to assess how well they are organized. It is a measure on whether processes are well managed, repeatable, or even unpredictable. IT auditors can use CMMi as a tool to measure how well they are doing, and it can serve as a guide for process improvements. The chapter provides an overview of how IT audit specialists can use CMMi in their assessments of internal controls and in organizing their own IT projects.

Chapter 12, Auditing Service-Oriented Architecture and Record Management Processes. SOA is an IT systems approach where an application's business logic or individual functions are modularized and presented as services for consumer/client applications. This chapter introduces SOA concepts for the IT auditor and discusses internal control and IT auditor issues surrounding the development and operations of IT applications using this technology. The chapter also reviews the importance of effective records management systems in today's enterprises from an internal controls and IT audit perspective. Today, almost all business records are created and most live their entire lives electronically. Failure to manage electronic records and physical records in accordance with established records management principles ignores potential risk.

Chapter 13, Computer-Assisted Audit Tools and Techniques. IT auditors test and review the internal controls surrounding their IT systems, and they often need tools to better understand and evaluate the completeness and accuracy of the data stored in the IT applications' files and databases. This chapter reviews approaches to retrieving data through computer-assisted audit tools and techniques (CAATTs), the use of independent auditor–controlled software to assess organization IT files and documents. Whether purchased software administered by an IT auditor or an operational procedure to better analyze IT data, many tools and techniques can help make audit reviews of IT-supported systems more efficient and effective. The chapter provides IT auditors with a basic understanding on the general use of CAATTs to access and review automated data to support IT audits.

Chapter 14, Continuous Assurance Auditing, OLAP, and XBRL. Continuous assurance auditing (CAA) is the process of installing control-related monitors in automated systems such that these monitors will send messages to internal auditors if the system's processing signals a deviation from an established audit limit or parameter. This chapter discusses CAA as an improved alternative approach for reviewing automated systems as well as an overview of continuous monitoring (CM), business controlled procedures that can be subject to periodic internal IT audits.

The chapter also introduces XBRL, the extensible business reporting language developed by the American Institute of Certified Public Accountants. XBRL is a standards-based way to communicate business and financial information across multiple enterprises. IT auditors should have a basic understanding of XBRL, a methodology that is growing in recognition and use, and its necessary supporting internal controls.

Chapter 15, IT Controls and the Audit Committee. The management or supervisory authority of enterprise's internal audit function is the board of directors' audit committee. This committee is responsible for approving internal audit plans, reviewing audit reports, hiring internal audit management, and taking other actions as appropriate. Although historically much of an audit committee's interests have been based on audited financial statements and an enterprise's financial audit, IT audit has an important role here as well. This chapter examines planning and reporting key IT audit activities to the enterprise's audit committee.

Chapter 16, Val IT, Portfolio Management, and Project Management. This chapter looks at three knowledge areas that are important to IT auditors: (1) ISACA's enterprise value initiative, called Val IT, to better manage and understand IT investments; (2) portfolio management approaches to better deal with the large number of diverse applications and IT resources in the typical enterprise; and (3) project management good practices to better control and manage many IT activities. Internal audit functions normally should develop an audit universe list, a compilation of all potential auditable entities for that enterprise. The chapter also looks at audit universe portfolio management from an IT audit perspective.

The chapter also discusses the importance of effective project management procedures. Audits and internal control activities should be planned and performed in a well-organized manner. The program and project management procedures described in the chapter will aid in this process.

Chapter 17, Compliance with IT-Related Laws and Regulations. Both in the United States and worldwide, a wide range of laws and regulations impact enterprise IT operations. Some of these have direct IT connections, such as the U.S. Computer Fraud and Abuse Act (CFAA), while others, such as SOx, are not really IT-related laws but nevertheless have multiple IT relationships. This chapter reviews a series of primarily U. S. IT-related laws and regulations, highlighting areas that should be considered in IT audit reviews.

Chapter 18, Understanding and Reviewing Compliance with ISO Standards. The International Standards Organization (ISO) has guidance that covers a wide range of areas, such as defining fastener screw threads in an automobile engine, the thickness of a personal credit card, and IT quality standards. This chapter provides an overview and introduction to several of the many ISO standards that are particularly important for IT auditors, with a focus on ISO 27001 and 27002 computer security standards. The chapter also provides an introduction to several other ISO standards, including international standards for IT management systems and for quality management. Enterprise compliance with appropriate ISO standards is important worldwide today, as they establish benchmarks for worldwide compliance.

Chapter 19, Controls to Establish an Effective IT Security Environment. Effective IT security is very important in all enterprises. Beyond password controls and backup processes discussed in other chapters, an enterprise needs a high-level enterprise commitment to IT security as well as strong procedures to build effective IT security processes. These procedures can range from such matters as a strong enterprise code of conduct setting the rules for enterprise associates to overall management policies promoting the need for an effective security environments. This chapter outlines some techniques as well IT audit procedures to review enterprise-wide IT security effectiveness.

Chapter 20, Cybersecurity and Privacy Controls. In our Web-dominated world today, IT security or cybersecurity and privacy controls over data and information are very important. This chapter discusses these controls from two focus areas: (1) some of the many cybersecurity and privacy concerns that IT auditors should consider in their reviews of systems and processes and (2) IT privacy issues. We have limited our focus to only some cybersecurity areas because the field of IT security controls is vast and sometimes very technical, beyond the skills of many auditors. Regarding IT privacy, there is a growing set of issues about how much personal data and information individuals should allow to be given to interested enterprises, government authorities, and even other individuals.

Chapter 21, IT Fraud Detection and Prevention. An effective auditor needs to recognize potential fraudulent business practices as part of any IT audit and then should recommend controls and procedures to limit exposure to the fraudulent activity. This chapter outlines some of the red flags—common conditions that an IT auditor might encounter when faced with a potential fraud as well as steps to identify, test, and properly process fraudulent activities. Fraud investigation can be a very detailed and specialized activity, but IT auditors should have a high level understanding of how to audit for potentially fraudulent activities as well as of processes for investigating and reporting fraud. Fraudulent activities represent a breakdown in a wide range of good practices and procedures, but IT auditors must recognize that fraudulent activities always may exist.

Chapter 22, Identity and Access Management. With all of the personal data stored in so many IT databases and systems, there is always a major concern that some perpetrator will hijack and steal someone's personal information to use for improper purposes. The concern that someone will steal this personal information is called identity management. Although certain laws are in place to prohibit such actions, an enterprise needs to establish strong procedures to discourage such improper activities. Starting with effective IT password access controls and the monitoring of potential password violations, an enterprise needs to have strong identity and access management processing in place. This chapter outlines procedures that are effective for IT security management and provides guidance for performing effective IT audits.

Chapter 23, Establishing Effective IT Disaster Recovery Processes. This chapter introduces what is called IT disaster recovery planning processes. (Chapter 25 discusses business continuity controls, which are similar but very different.) IT disaster recovery includes effective backup processes for restoring all aspects of IT operations, whether a classic server-based data center or a network of laptop or desktop system operations. The chapter briefly introduces some of the technical tools, such as data mirroring, that improve IT disaster recovery procedures today. The chapter concludes with guidance on testing disaster recovery plans as well as steps for auditing such plans. Because of our massive dependence on IT operations, effective disaster recovery plans are key components in IT operations.

Chapter 24, Electronic Archiving and Data Retention. Because so much data and supporting documentation is recorded on databases or other IT media formats, it is important to preserve backup copies in separate, independent locations. This is as true for an enterprise with massive business transactions as it is for an IT auditor. The chapter discusses some best practice approaches for saving and archiving data as well as control procedures for its access. In addition, the chapter outlines steps for an audit of data retention processes.

Chapter 25, Business Continuity Management, BS 25999, and ISO 27001. This chapter introduces best practices for effective enterprise IT continuity and disaster recovery planning processes including establishing enterprise internal controls in enterprise-critical areas. Going beyond Chapter 24's disaster recovery backup procedures, continuity planning is based on the concept that an enterprise needs to have processes in place to resume normal business operations in the event of a major disruption in IT services. This major task involves restoring business process operations beyond just the IT applications.

This chapter also discusses BS 25999, a U.K.-based standard for business continuity management as well as the ISO 27001 international standards. The chapter uses BS 25999 to describe the processes necessary for effective continuity planning for a sample enterprise.

Chapter 26, Auditing Telecommunications and IT Communications Networks. Moving beyond the wireless networks discussed in Chapter 9, enterprise IT systems typically are tied to vast telecommunications networks, internally or through the Web. This chapter provides an introduction to the wide variety of network topologies in place today and outlines processes surrounding IT network controls and tools such as scanners and sniffers. The chapter outlines approaches for an IT auditor's internal controls and security-related review of an enterprise's telecommunications including its wireless operations.

Chapter 27, Change and Patch Management Controls. Enterprises can be exposed to major security vulnerabilities in the event of unauthorized or inappropriate changes to its IT systems and programs. Strong IT change management processes are always needed. This chapter discusses effective IT change and patch management controls and introduces procedures for auditing internal controls in these areas.

Chapter 28, Six Sigma and Lean Technologies. Enterprise operations managers, at all levels, are regularly looking for ways to improve their operations, whether in shop-floor production processes, office administrative procedures, or elsewhere. Many have found six sigma processes to be effective here. This chapter provides a high-level introduction to six sigma concepts and how they can be applied to enterprise IT operations. We provide an overview of six sigma and the lean approaches to implementing it. Even though an internal or IT audit function may not be using six sigma concepts as part of their overall operations, IT auditors should have a basic understanding of this important quality improvement concept.

Chapter 29, Building an Effective IT Internal Audit Function. Other chapters have discussed many aspects of IT audits. This chapter steps back and looks at some the requirements for an enterprise to build an effective IT audit function as part of their overall internal audit group. The chapter reviews IT audit positions descriptions, audit planning, workpapers, audit reports, and other factors needed to build an effective IT internal audit function.

Chapter 30, Professional Certifications: CISA, CIA, and More. IT auditors have a need for strong and well-recognized professional certifications. Many have joined the profession with no specific certification requirements beyond their undergraduate college degrees; others attained accounting degrees and prepared for the Certified Public Accountant (CPA) examination. Today, an IT auditor can take a qualifying examination and complete other requirements to become a Certified Information Systems Auditor (CISA), a Certified Internal Auditor (CIA), a Certified Fraud Examiner (CFE), or any of a series of other certifications. This chapter discusses the professional designations that are important to the IT auditor, with an emphasis on the CIA and CISA certifications, including their qualification and examination requirements. In addition, the chapter considers some other certification options available to IT auditors, including the Certified Information Systems Security Professional (CISSP) requirements.

Chapter 31, Quality Assurance Auditing and ASQ Standards. This chapter reviews the role of quality auditors in an enterprise, their practices and standards. There are many similarities between the activities of quality auditors and the IT auditors that are the main focus of this book. With a growing convergence of enterprise activities to improve governance, IT processes, and internal controls, we can expect to see these internal audit groups become more closely aligned. Although we focus more on IIA and ISACA types of IT internal auditors, there also is a need for a general understanding of the roles, responsibilities, and activities of quality auditors. In addition, we also consider internal audit Quality Assurance (QA) reviews of an IT audit function performed by members of the internal audit team themselves or by contracted outside reviewers.

HOW TO USE THIS BOOK

The role of an IT auditor is changing now and will change even more in the future. The internal control SOx, COSO, and CobiT models presented in Chapters 1 and 2 suggest a much broader role for the IT audit and internal controls specialist of the future. In addition, technology changes and new concepts, such as many of the newer issues introduced throughout this book, will require that IT auditors develop expanded knowledge needs. An overall objective of this book is to introduce some of these newer concepts. Our objective is not to provide an exhaustive tutorial in each subject area but to discuss concepts and related IT audit, security, and internal controls issues.

The chapters throughout this book contain many suggested audit programs—the steps necessary to perform actual IT audits. There is an increasing need for persons with a broad knowledge of IT audit, security, and internal controls. Although there is also a need for some with very specialized skills, such as a computer crime investigator or a financial auditor with detailed knowledge of a specialized area, such as bond indentures, today's IT auditor should have good skills in the overall areas of audit, control, and security. Providing an overview and some background guidance is a goal of this edition. The author hopes that this edition and potentially more frequent updates will help to provide both new and experienced audit and internal control specialists with information to help them become more effective professionals.

IT Audit, Control, and Security

PART ONE

Auditing Internal Controls in an IT Environment

CHAPTER ONE

SOx and the COSO Internal Controls Framework

THE CONCEPT OF INTERNAL controls assessments has been around since the inception of auditing and has been an important concept going back to the early days of information technology (IT) auditing. Although there have been many definitions of internal controls, a good one for IT auditors is that internal control is a process, affected by an entity's board of directors, management, and other personnel, that is designed to provide reasonable assurance regarding the achievement of objectives in the categories of effectiveness and efficiency of operations, reliability of an enterprise's financial reporting, and an enterprise's systems and process compliance with laws and regulations. This well-recognized definition was established by the U.S. Committee of Sponsoring Organizations (COSO), an internal controls standards-setting authority that we will be discussing further in this chapter.

Audit professionals are responsible for reviewing and assessing enterprise management controls. Internal auditors do not construct and administer these controls—that is the responsibility of management. Auditors, acting as independent parties, both review and perform tests of enterprise internal controls to report to management and other parties whether they are adequate. These reviewers consist of both internal and external auditors, with external auditors in the United States following the rules and standards of the American Institute of Certified Public Accountants (AICPA). Internal auditors follow a similar but different set of standards and generally subscribe to the guidelines of the Institute of Internal Auditors (IIA), their international professional organization.

Both of these audit organizations have heritages going back to paper-and-pencil days, before today's pervasive use and reliance on IT systems and processes. Over the years, the Information Systems Audit and Control Association (ISACA) and its IT audit professionals have provided guidance for IT-related internal controls. IT auditors serve in both external and internal audit roles, although most professionals may serve as internal auditors for their enterprises.

This chapter outlines the role of an IT auditor, particularly an IT internal auditor, in today's business enterprise. In addition, the chapter discusses two important IT audit concepts: the COSO internal control standards and the Sarbanes-Oxley Act (SOx) internal control review rules. Both COSO internal controls and SOx started as U.S. internal controls guidance rules but have become worldwide standards. They both had their origins as general financial and operations review standards and are now very applicable to IT audit environments as well.

Today's IT auditor must understand and use the COSO internal controls framework and SOx internal controls review procedures. Although these rules and procedures have origins in financial reporting and auditing, in today's IT-centric world, COSO internal controls and SOx are equally important to IT auditors. Enterprises need to follow these rules in order to assert or attest to regulators that their organizations have effective internal controls in place and that they are operating in compliance with those newer rules. The chapters in this volume rely on the internal control rules and procedures as we discuss a wide range of other IT audit, control, and security topics.

 ## ROLES AND RESPONSIBILITIES OF IT AUDITORS

Much of this chapter and others focuses on the roles and responsibilities of an internal audit specialist, whom we call an IT or information systems auditor. Although sometimes serving as a member of a public accounting firm or outside consulting organization, IT auditors are generally members of an enterprise internal audit organization. An internal audit group is led by a manager with the title of chief audit executive (CAE) and is staffed by internal auditors with skills in reviewing and understanding operational and financial controls as well as compliance and regulatory issues impacting the enterprise. With IT processes and tools so pervasive in today's enterprise, all internal auditors should have a good understanding of IT controls and processes, but many internal audit functions require the skills of what we are calling an IT auditor.[1]

Traditional internal auditors always have had skills in understanding, testing, and evaluating what were once traditional paper-based controls and procedures. Starting in the 1970s, as enterprises started to build and implement more and more computer-based applications, they needed internal audit specialists who understood the new systems. Thus the role of the IT auditor was born.

The field once was called electronic data processing (EDP). Auditors are now sometimes known as information systems (IS) auditors or computer audit specialists; however, we are using the expression *IT auditor* throughout this book. An IT auditor is a specialist who follows the standards and principles of the IIA and often is a member of ISACA as well. There are many recognized specialist skills here, including the IT security procedures discussed in Chapter 19 and IT auditors skilled in computer-assisted audit tools and techniques (CAATTs), but most IT auditors are expected to have a strong

---

Auditor, Information Systems
JOB DESCRIPTION
Job Summary: Under direction of the Chief Audit Executive (CAE) and internal audit management, audits, reviews, tests, and evaluates IT-based applications and control procedures and reviews electronic security over the enterprise IT services network.

CHARACTERISTIC JOB TASKS AND RESPONSIBILITIES
May include any and/or all of the following:

1. Designs a technology-based audit approaches; analyzes and evaluates enterprise IT processes to assess internal controls and minimize risks; performs risk analysis of the enterprise's information technology infrastructure and services network; evaluates the possible risks of various computer systems; prepares reports documenting findings and risk assessment; evaluates management responses to findings and risk assessment.
2. Works independently or with other members of internal audit to review enterprise internal controls, following the COSO internal controls framework.
3. Examines the effectiveness of the information security policies and procedures; identifies inadequacies within the existing security program and possible action to be taken.
4. Develops and implements computer-assisted audit tools and techniques (CAATTs) to assist overall internal audit efforts and performs other IT-related tests of controls, as appropriate.
5. Develops and presents training workshops for audit staff on security controls and risk concepts.
6. Conducts and oversees investigation of inappropriate computer use.
7. Performs special projects and other duties as assigned; provides input on departmental administrative activities.

KNOWLEDGE, SKILLS, ABILITIES, AND PERSONAL CHARACTERISTICS
- Knowledge of auditing, information systems, and network security
- Investigation and process flow analysis skills
- Interpersonal/human relations skills
- Verbal and written communication skills
- Ability to exercise good judgment
- Ability to maintain confidentiality
- Ability to use IT desktop office tools, vulnerability analysis tools, and other IT tools

MINIMUM QUALIFICATIONS
Education and experience equivalent to:
- Bachelor's degree in computer science, computer programming, or accounting
- Certified Information Systems Auditor (CISA) credentials or candidate
- Certified Internal Auditor credential preferred

EXHIBIT 1.1 IT Auditor Job Description

---

general set of skills in evaluating IT-based internal controls. Exhibit 1.1 is a position description for a typical senior IT auditor.

This chapter emphasizes the importance of IT audit processes in performing internal controls reviews in today's heavily IT powered enterprises. IT audit specialists also have important key roles in the corporate governance of today's enterprise. They have skills that are unique but certainly should be adopted by all members of an internal audit team in expanding their IT knowledge and internal controls review procedures.

IMPORTANCE OF EFFECTIVE INTERNAL CONTROLS AND COSO

Internal control is one of the most important and fundamental concepts that external and internal auditors and business professionals at all levels must understand. The business professional builds and uses internal controls; auditors review and test the operational, IT, and financial systems and processes with a goal of evaluating their internal controls. Although internal and external auditors have different objectives, most of our references in this chapter apply to IT auditors, who have a major responsibility to understand and assess IT-related internal controls.

Although there have been many slightly different definitions of internal controls in the past, of COSO standards provides an appropriate definition. It recognizes that internal control extends beyond just accounting and financial matters and includes all enterprise processes. Also, because IT is so embedded into almost all business processes, IT-related internal controls are a major portion of our overall understandings of internal controls. An enterprise unit or process has good internal controls if it:

1. Accomplishes its stated mission in an ethical manner
2. Produces accurate and reliable data
3. Complies with applicable laws and enterprise policies
4. Provides for economical and efficient uses of its resources
5. Provides for appropriate safeguarding of assets

All members of an enterprise are responsible for the internal controls in their area of operation and for operating them effectively.

Despite or perhaps because of this broad and wide-reaching internal controls definition, many business professionals have had problems in fully understanding and applying internal control concepts. Looking at our definition a bit differently, the concept of an internal control and supporting control processes goes back to the basic mechanical and paperwork procedures that once existed throughout everyday life. Control processes are necessary for activities inside and outside today's enterprise, and many basic concepts and principles are the same no matter where the control is implemented. An automobile provides some basic controls examples. When the accelerator—a speed control—is pressed, the automobile goes faster. When the brake— another control—is depressed, the automobile slows or stops. When the steering wheel is turned, the vehicle turns. The driver *controls* the automobile, and all three of these represent the car's basic internal control system. If the driver does not use or improperly uses the accelerator, brake, or steering wheel, the automobile will operate *out of control*.

Expanding this concept just a bit, a stop sign, traffic direction sign, or gate crossing barriers all represent external controls to the auto and its driver. The driver is the operator of the automobile-based internal control process or system but has little decision authority over the message delivered from a traffic light external control.

From an internal control perspective, an enterprise can be compared to our automobile example. There are many enterprise systems and processes at work, such as accounting operations, sales processes, and IT systems. If management does not operate or direct these processes properly, the enterprise may operate out of control. All members of an enterprise should develop an understanding of the appropriate control systems and then determine if they are properly connected to manage the enterprise. These systems are referred to as the enterprise's *internal control* systems.

Internal Controls Standards Background

Although the concept and definition of internal controls is fairly well understood today, this was not true until the late 1980s. The general concept may have been understood, but there was no consistent agreement among many interested about what was meant by "good internal controls." Early definitions that first came from the AICPA and were used by the U.S. Securities and Exchange Commission (SEC) for the Securities Exchange Act of 1934 provide a good starting point. Although there have been changes over the years, the AICPA's first codified standards, called the Statement on Auditing Standards[2] (SAS No. 1) defined the practice of financial statement external auditing in the United States for many years. This AICPA definition of internal control has been subject to changes and reinterpretations over the years. Throughout the 1970s, the SEC and AICPA released many internal control definitions, and the major external auditing firms developed voluminous interpretations and guidelines.

Things changed in the late 1970s and early 1980s, a period when there were many major U.S. enterprise failures due to factors such as high inflation and the resultant high interest rates. Many times enterprises reported adequate earnings in their audited financial reports, only to suffer a financial collapse shortly after the release of favorable audited financial reports. A few of these failures were caused by fraudulent financial reporting, although many others were due to high inflation or other enterprise instability issues. Nevertheless, several members of Congress proposed legislation to "correct" these potential business and audit failures. Bills were drafted and congressional hearings held, but no legislation was passed.

In response to these concerns as well as the lack of legislative action, the National Commission on Fraudulent Financial Reporting was formed. It consisted of five professional organizations: the IIA and AICPA, mentioned previously; the Financial Executive International (FEI), an association of senior financial managers; the American Accounting Association (AAA); and the Institute of Management Accountants (IMA). The AAA is a professional organization for the academic accountants, and the IMA is the professional organization for managerial or cost accountants.

The National Commission on Fraudulent Financial Reporting came to be called the Treadway Commission after the name of its chairperson. Its major objectives were to identify causal factors that allowed fraudulent financial reporting and to make recommendations to reduce their incidence. The Treadway Commission's final report, issued in 1987, included recommendations to management, boards of directors, the public accounting profession, and others.[3] It also called for management reports on the effectiveness of their internal control systems and emphasized key elements in what it felt should be a system of internal control, including a strong control environment, codes of conduct, a competent and involved audit committee, and a strong internal audit function.

The Treadway Commission report again pointed out the lack of a consistent definition of internal control, suggesting further work was needed. The same Committee of Sponsoring Organizations that managed the Treadway report subsequently contracted with outside specialists and launched a project to define internal control. Although it issued no standards, the Treadway Commission released the COSO internal control framework, discussed in the next sections and referenced throughout this book.

COSO Internal Control Framework

As mentioned, COSO refers to the five professional auditing and accounting organizations that formed a committee to develop this internal control report; its official title is *Integrated Control–Integrated Framework*.[4] Throughout this book, we refer to it as the *COSO internal controls report* or *framework*. This is in contrast to COSO enterprise risk management (COSO ERM) enterprise resource management framework introduced in Chapter 4. First released in September 1992, the COSO internal controls report proposed a common framework for the definition of internal control as well as procedures to evaluate those controls. In a very short number of years, the COSO internal controls framework has become the recognized worldwide standard for understanding and establishing effective internal controls in virtually all business systems. The next paragraphs provide a fairly detailed description of the COSO internal controls framework and its use by internal auditors and business professionals for internal controls assessments and evaluations.

Virtually every public corporation has a complex control procedures structure. Following the format of a classic organization chart, there may be levels of senior and middle management in multiple operating units or within different activities. In addition, control procedures may be somewhat different at each of these levels and components. For example, one unit may operate in a regulated business environment where its control processes are very structured, while another unit may operate almost like an entrepreneurial start-up with a far less formal structure. Different levels of management in these enterprises will have different control concern perspectives. The question "How do you describe your system of internal controls?" might receive different answers from persons in different levels or units in each of these enterprise components.

COSO provides an excellent description of this multidimensional concept of internal controls, defining internal control in this way:

> Internal control is a *process*, affected by an entity's board of directors, management, and other personnel, designed to provide reasonable assurance regarding the achievement of objectives in the following categories:
>
> ▪ Effectiveness and efficiency of operations
> ▪ Reliability of financial reporting
> ▪ Compliance with applicable laws and regulations[5]

Using this very general definition of internal control, COSO uses a three-dimensional framework to describe an internal control system in an enterprise. Exhibit 1.2

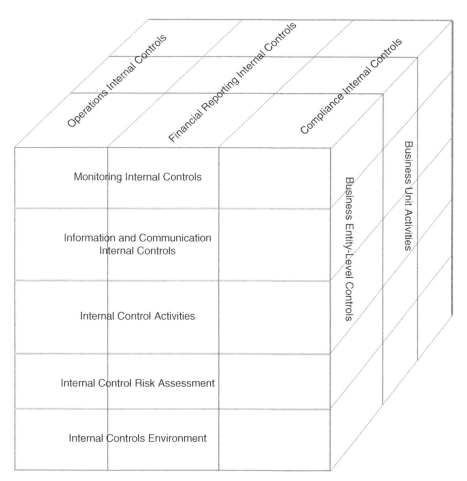

EXHIBIT 1.2   COSO Internal Controls Framework

describes this COSO internal control framework as a three-dimensional model with five levels on the front-facing side and the three major components of internal control—effectiveness and efficiency of operations, reliability of financial reporting, and compliance with applicable laws and regulations—taking somewhat equal segments of the model with slices across its top. The right-hand side of the exhibit shows three segments, but there could be more, depending on the structure of the enterprise.

Each of the COSO internal control framework's levels, from Monitoring on top down to the Internal Controls Environment, is discussed in greater detail in the sections to come. The idea here is that when we look at the middle internal control activity layer—such as the period-end financial close—we should consider that control in terms of the business unit or entity or the multiple divisions on the side of the framework where that control has been installed. However, in this three-dimensional model, each control is related to all others in the same row, stack, or column.

The point of the COSO internal controls framework is that we should always consider each identified internal control in terms of how its components relate to other associated internal control elements in the framework. In an example of end-of-period financial close internal controls, the enterprise should have information and communication links attached to the financial close processes, and the control should be monitored. Dropping down a level, there should be risk assessment activities associated with that financial controls process, and it should operate in an appropriate internal controls environment. Compliance and operations issues also contain factors for specific internal controls that may function at any level in the enterprise organization.

All IT auditors should have a strong understanding of the COSO internal controls framework. No matter what area is under review, IT auditors always need to review and consider internal controls in this type of a multilevel and three-dimensional manner. Starting with the first or bottom front-facing level, our text describes the COSO internal controls framework in greater detail.

Control Environment

The foundation of the COSO internal controls framework is what COSO calls the internal control environment, the foundation for all other components of internal control. It has an influence on each of the three objectives and all unit and entity activities. The control environment reflects the overall attitude of, awareness of, and actions by the board of directors, management, and others concerning the importance of internal controls in the enterprise. There are many fundamental concepts here, and each enterprise will have its own unique internal control foundation.

Enterprise history and culture often play a major role in forming this internal control environment. When an enterprise historically has had a strong management emphasis on producing error-free products and when senior management communicates the importance of high-quality products to all levels of the organization, the COSO control environment becomes a major enterprise internal control factor. The content and format of messages from the chief executive officer (CEO) or other senior managers are known as the tone at the top—management's messages to all stakeholders. However, if senior management has a reputation of looking the other way at policy violations, this same negative message will be communicated to other levels in the enterprise. A positive tone at the top by senior management is a key element of a strong enterprise control environment.

IT auditors should always try to understand and evaluate the overall control environment when performing virtually all reviews. When the internal control environment is weak, auditors almost certainly will find additional control concern areas. The control environment consists of the following components.

Integrity and Ethical Values.   If the enterprise has developed a strong code of conduct that emphasizes integrity and ethical values, and if stakeholders appear to follow that code, all stakeholders will have assurances that the enterprise has a good set of values. A code of ethics or conduct is an important component of organizational governance. Internal audit codes of conduct are discussed in Chapter 3. However, even if an enterprise has a strong code of conduct, its principles can be violated through ignorance rather than by deliberate employee malfeasance. In many instances, employees may not know that they are doing something wrong or may erroneously believe that their actions are in the enterprise's best interests. This ignorance often is caused by poor senior management moral guidance rather than by any individual employee intent to deceive. The enterprise's policies and values must be communicated to all organization levels. Although there can always be bad apples in any enterprise, strong moral messages will encourage everyone to act correctly. The objective should always be to transmit appropriate messages or signals throughout the enterprise.

All stakeholders, and certainly all internal auditors, should have a good understanding of their enterprise's code of conduct and how it is applied. If the existing code is out of date, if it does not appear to address important ethical issues facing an enterprise, or if management does not appear to be communicating the code to all stakeholders on a recurring basis, management needs to wake up and correct this deficiency. The code of conduct describes the rules for ethical behavior, and senior management should transmit a proper ethical message throughout the enterprise. Other incentives and temptations, however, can erode this overall control environment. Individuals may be tempted to engage in dishonest, illegal, or unethical acts if their enterprise gives them strong incentives or temptations to do so. For example, an enterprise may establish very high, unrealistic performance targets for sales or production quotas. If there are strong rewards for the achievement of these performance goals—or, worse, strong threats for missed targets—employees may be encouraged to engage in fraudulent or questionable practices to achieve those goals.

A strong internal audit function is a major component of the COSO control environment. If internal audit finds that management is placing constraints on the audit function, the CAE should remind senior management of internal audit's importance as part of the enterprise's overall internal control structure and, more important, should communicate these concerns to the board of director's audit committee.

Commitment to Competence. An enterprise's control environment can be seriously eroded if a significant number of positions are filled with persons lacking required job skills. An enterprise needs to specify the required competence levels for its various job tasks and to translate those requirements into necessary levels of knowledge and skill. By placing the proper people in appropriate jobs and giving adequate training when required, an enterprise is satisfying this important COSO control environment component.

Board of Directors and Audit Committee. The control environment is very much influenced by the actions of an enterprise's board of directors and its audit committee. An active and independent board is an essential component of the COSO control environment. By setting high-level policies and reviewing overall enterprise conduct, the board and its audit committee have the ultimate responsibility for setting this tone at the top.

Management's Philosophy and Operating Style. The philosophy and operating style of senior management has a considerable influence over an enterprise's control environment. Some top-level managers frequently take significant enterprise-level risks in their new business or product ventures while others are very cautious or conservative. Some managers seem to operate by the seat of their pants while others insist that everything must be properly approved and documented. Some may take very aggressive approaches in their interpretations of tax and financial reporting rules while others go by the book. These comments do not necessarily mean that one approach is always good and the other bad.

These management philosophy and operational style considerations are all part of an enterprise's control environment. Although no one set of styles and philosophies is best for all enterprises, these factors such as a strong organization structure and effective human resource policies are important when considering the other components of internal control in an enterprise.

Organizational Structure.   The organizational structure internal control component provides a framework for planning, executing, controlling, and monitoring activities to help achieve overall objectives. This control environment factor relates to how functions are managed and organized. Organizational structure is an important aspect of the enterprise's control environment, but no one structure provides any preferred internal controls environment.

An organizational structure is the manner or approach for individual work efforts to be both assigned and integrated for the achievement of overall goals. Every enterprise needs an effective plan of organization, and a weakness in organizational controls can have a pervasive effect throughout the total control environment. Despite clear lines of authority, however, enterprises sometimes have built-in inefficiencies that can become greater over time as they expand, causing control procedures to break down.

Assignment of Authority and Responsibility.   The assignment of authority and responsibility in the control environment is similar to the organizational structure component just discussed. An enterprise's organizational structure defines the assignment and integration of the total work effort. The assignment of authority is essentially the way responsibilities are defined in terms of formal job descriptions and are structured in terms of enterprise organization charts. Although job assignments can never fully escape some overlapping or joint responsibilities, the more precisely these responsibilities can be stated, the better. The failure to clearly define authority and workplace responsibility often causes confusion and conflict between individual and group work efforts.

Human Resources Policies and Practices.   Human resources (HR) practices cover personnel hiring, orientation, training, evaluating, and counseling, promoting, compensating, and taking appropriate remedial actions. Although the enterprise HR function should have adequate published policies and guidance materials, its actual practices should send strong messages to employees regarding expected levels of internal controls compliance, ethical behavior, and competence. The higher-level employee who openly abuses or ignores an HR policy quickly sends a message to other levels in the enterprise. The message grows even louder when a lower-level employee is disciplined for violating that same policy while everyone looks the other way at the higher-level violator.

Effective HR policies and procedures are a critical component in the overall control environment. Messages from the top of strong enterprise structures will accomplish little if the enterprise does not have strong HR policies and procedures in place. IT audit should always consider the HR element of the control environment when reviewing other parts of the internal control framework.

Summary. Just as a strong foundation is necessary for a multistory building, the control environment provides the foundation for the other components of internal control. An enterprise that is building a strong internal control structure should give special attention to placing solid foundation bricks in this control environment foundation. Of course, IT auditors should keep these concepts, such as effective HR policies, in mind when assessing internal controls. The COSO internal control environment does not require just a series of "do the debits equal the credits?" types of accounting rules but strong overall enterprise-wide policies that are effective.

Risk Assessment

The next level above the control foundation on the COSO internal control framework is risk assessment. An enterprise's ability to achieve its objectives can be at risk due to a variety of internal and external factors. Understanding and managing the risk environment are basic elements of the internal control foundation, and an enterprise should have a process in place to evaluate the potential risks that may impact attainment of its various objectives. This risk assessment component has its focus on internal controls within an enterprise and has a much narrower focus than the COSO ERM framework discussed in Chapter 4.

COSO internal controls risk assessment should be a forward-looking process that is performed at all levels and for virtually all activities within the enterprise. COSO describes risk assessment as a three-step process:

1. Estimate the significance of the risk.
2. Assess the likelihood or frequency of the risk occurring.
3. Consider how the risk should be managed, and assess what actions must be taken.

This COSO risk assessment process places the responsibility on management to assess whether a risk is significant and, if so, to take appropriate actions. COSO internal controls also emphasizes that risk analysis is not a theoretical process but often is critical to an entity's economic and operational success. As part of its assessment of internal control, management should take steps to assess the risks that may impact the overall enterprise as well as the risks over various enterprise activities or entities. A variety of risks, caused by either internal or external sources, may affect the enterprise.

The risk assessment element of the COSO internal controls Framework is an area where there has been much misunderstanding and confusion because of the similarly named COSO ERM framework discussed in Chapter 4. The risk assessment component of the COSO internal controls framework includes risk assessments for *within* an individual enterprise. The COSO ERM framework covers the entire entity and beyond. These are really two separate but related issues, and one is not a replacement for the other.

Control Activities

The next layer up in the COSO internal control framework is called control activities. These are the processes and procedures that help ensure that actions identified to address risks are carried out. Control activities exist at all levels and, in many cases, may overlap one another. They are essential elements to building and then establishing effective enterprise internal controls. The COSO internal controls framework identifies a series of these activities that are generally classified as manual, IT, or management controls; they are also described in terms of whether they are preventive, corrective, or detective control activities. Although no one set of internal control definitions is correct for all situations, COSO internal controls recommends these control activities for an enterprise:

- **Top-level reviews.** Management and internal auditors, at various levels, should review the results of their performance, contrasting those results with budgets, competitive statistics, and other benchmark measurements. Management actions to follow up on the results of these top-level reviews and to take corrective action represent a key control activity.
- **Direct functional or activity management.** Managers at various levels should review operational reports from their control systems and take corrective action as appropriate. Many management systems have exception reports covering these control activities. For example, an IT security system should have a mechanism to report unauthorized access attempts, with a control activity to follow up on reported events and take appropriate corrective action. Some of these activities link closely with the information technology infrastructure library (ITIL) best practices discussed in Chapter 7.
- **Information processing.** IT systems often contain controls to check for compliance in certain areas and then report any internal control exceptions. Those exception items should receive corrective action by automated systems procedures, by operational personnel, or by management. Other control activities include controls over the development of new systems or over access to data and program files.
- **Physical controls.** An enterprise should have appropriate control over its physical assets, including fixtures, inventories, and negotiable securities. An active program of periodic physical inventories represents a often significant control activity here, and IT auditors can play a major role in monitoring compliance here.
- **Performance indicators.** Management should relate sets of data, both operational and financial, to one another and take appropriate analytical, investigative, or corrective actions. This process represents an important enterprise control activity that can also satisfy financial and operational reporting requirements.
- **Segregation of duties.** Duties should be divided or segregated among different people to reduce the risk of error or inappropriate actions. This basic internal control procedure should be on almost every IT auditor's radar screen.

The control activities highlighted here represent only a small number of the many control activities performed in the normal course of business but involve policies establishing what should be done and procedures to affect them. Even though control activities sometimes may be communicated only orally, they should be implemented thoughtfully, conscientiously, and consistently. This recognition and communication of control activities is a strong message for internal auditors reviewing such internal control activities. Even though an enterprise may have a published policy covering a given area, there should be established internal control procedures to support that policy. Procedures are of little use unless there is a sharp focus on the condition to which the policy is directed. All too often, an enterprise may establish an exception report as part of an automated system while that exception report receives little more than a cursory management review by its recipients. However, depending on the types of conditions reported, those exceptions should receive appropriate follow-up actions, which may vary depending on the size of the enterprise and the activity reported in the exception report.

These control activities should be closely related to one another to identify risks from the COSO internal controls risk assessment component. Internal control is a process, and appropriate control activities should be installed to address identified risks. Control activities should not be installed just because they seem to be the right thing to do, even if there are no significant risks in the area where the control activity would be installed. Sometimes control activities may be in place that perhaps once served some control risk concern, although the concerns have largely gone away. A control activity should not be discarded because there has been no recent history of control violations, but management needs to reevaluate these relative risks periodically. All internal control activities should contribute to the overall control structure, and IT auditors should keep this concept in mind as they review internal controls and make recommendations.

The COSO internal controls framework emphasizes that control procedures are needed over all significant IT systems: operational, financial, and compliance related. COSO internal controls breaks down information systems controls into the well-recognized general and application controls. General controls apply to much of the information systems function to help ensure adequate control procedures over all applications. A physical security lock on the door to the IT server center is such a general control for all applications running within that facility. IT general controls are discussed in Chapter 6. Application controls, discussed in Chapter 10, are also important IT control areas for evaluating the overall adequacy of internal controls. The COSO internal controls framework document concludes with a discussion of the need to consider the impact of evolving technologies; it should always be considered when evaluating IT control activities. Due to the rapid introduction of new technologies, what is new today will soon be replaced by something else.

Communications and Information

The COSO internal controls framework in Exhibit 1.2 describes most internal control components as layers, one on top of another, starting with the control environment as the foundation. As another way to look at the framework, Exhibit 1.3 describes the COSO framework as a pyramid-shaped model with the information and communication component as a side element that spans across other components. As important portions

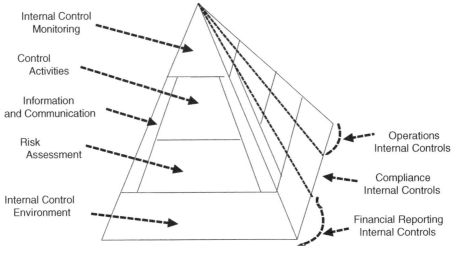

EXHIBIT 1.3 COSO Internal Controls Foundation Components

of the internal control framework, information and communications are related but distinct components. Appropriate information, supported by IT systems, must be communicated up and down the enterprise in a manner and time frame that allows people to carry out their responsibilities. In addition to formal and informal communication systems, enterprises must have effective procedures in place to communicate with internal and external parties. As part of any evaluation of internal controls, there is a need to understand these information and communication flows in the enterprise.

An enterprise needs information at all levels to achieve its operational, financial, and compliance objectives. For example, the enterprise needs information to prepare financial reports that are communicated to outside investors as well as internal cost and external market preference information to make correct marketing decisions. This information must flow both from the top levels of the enterprise on down to lower levels as well from lower levels back to upper levels. COSO internal control takes a broad approach to the concept of information systems, recognizing that they can be manual, automated, or even conceptual. Any of these information systems can be either formal or informal. Regular conversations with customers or suppliers can be highly important sources of information and are an informal type of an information system. The effective enterprise should have information systems in place to listen to customer requests and/or complaints and to forward that customer-initiated information to appropriate personnel.

COSO internal controls also emphasize the importance of keeping information and supporting systems consistent with overall enterprise needs. Information systems adapt to support changes on many levels. IT auditors, for example, often encounter cases where an IT application was implemented years earlier to support different needs. Although its controls may have been good, the system may not support the enterprise's current needs. COSO internal controls take a broad view of these types of systems and point to the need to understand both manual processes and automated technologies.

Monitoring

The pyramid view of COSO internal controls shows the monitoring component as the capstone, upper level of the COSO internal control components. Although internal control systems will work effectively with proper support from management, control procedures and both information and communication linkages must be in place to monitor all of these other activities. Monitoring has long been the role of IT auditors, who perform reviews to assess compliance with established procedures; however, COSO now takes a broader view of this control procedures monitoring. COSO internal control recognizes that control procedures and other systems change over time. What appeared to be effective when it was first installed may not be that effective in the future due to changing conditions, new procedures, or other factors.

A monitoring process should be in place to assess the effectiveness of established internal control components and to take corrective action when appropriate. This internal control component cannot be relegated just to the internal audit while management seems to remain oblivious to other potential control problems. An enterprise needs to establish a variety of monitoring activities to measure the effectiveness of their established internal controls as well as through separate evaluations of ongoing internal control activities to monitor performance and take corrective action when required.

Many routine business functions can be characterized as monitoring activities, and COSO internal control gives examples of this important component of internal control:

- **Operating management normal functions.** Normal management reviews over operations and financial reports are an important ongoing monitoring activity, but special attention should be given to reported exceptions and internal control deviations. Internal control is enhanced if reports are reviewed on a regular basis and corrective action initiated for any reported exceptions.
- **Communications from external parties.** External communication monitors, such as a customer complaint telephone number, are important, and the enterprise needs to monitor closely the messages from these calls and initiate corrective actions based on the calls when appropriate.
- **Enterprise structure and supervisory activities.** Senior management should always review summary reports and take corrective actions, but the first level of supervision often plays an even more significant role in monitoring. Direct supervision of clerical activities, for example, should routinely review and correct lower-level errors and assure improved clerical employee performance. This is also an area in which the importance of an adequate separation of duties is important, and dividing duties between employees allows them to serve as a monitoring check on one another.
- **Physical inventories and asset reconciliation.** Periodic physical inventories, whether of storeroom stock, negotiable securities, or IT assets, are an important monitoring activity. An annual inventory in a retail store, for example, may indicate a significant merchandise loss. A possible reason for this loss could be theft, pointing to the need for better security controls.

These are just a few examples of COSO internal controls monitoring activities. These types of procedures are often in place in many enterprises but are not thought of as ongoing monitoring activities. Any function or process that reviews enterprise activities on a regular basis and then suggests potential corrective actions can be thought of as a monitoring activity.

The COSO internal control framework points out the importance of ongoing monitoring activities and also suggests that "it may be useful to take a fresh look from time to time" at the effectiveness of internal controls through separate evaluations. The frequency and nature of these separate reviews greatly depend on the nature of the enterprise and the significance of the risks it must control. Management may want to initiate periodic evaluations of its entire internal controls, but most evaluations should be initiated to assess specific control areas. Often these reviews are initiated when there has been an acquisition, a change in business, or some other significant activity.

COSO also emphasizes that these evaluations may be performed by direct line management through self-assessment reviews. IT audit does not have to perform these reviews unless requested, and considerable time may pass before internal audit may schedule a self-assessment type of review in areas of operations. However, responsible management should consider scheduling and performing self-assessments on a regular basis. This type of internally generated review can point out potential control problems and cause operating management to take corrective action. Because these self-assessment reviews typically are not as comprehensive as normal internal audits, follow-up reviews should be launched if potentially significant problems are encountered through limited self-assessment reviews.

Internal Control Evaluation Process.   The COSO internal controls guidance materials outline an evaluation process for reviewing internal controls. The evaluator should first develop an understanding of the system design, test key controls, and then develop conclusions based on the test results. This is really the IT audit process. COSO internal control also mentions *benchmarking* as an alternative approach. Benchmarking is the process of comparing an enterprise's processes and control procedures with those of peer enterprises. Comparisons are made with similar enterprises or against published industry statistics. This approach is convenient for some measures but filled with dangers for others. For example, it is fairly easy to benchmark the size, staffing levels, and average compensations of a sales function against comparable enterprises in the same general industry; however, the evaluator may encounter difficulties in trying to compare other factors due to the many small differences that make all enterprises unique.

Evaluation Action Plans.   COSO internal control recognizes that many highly effective procedures are informal and undocumented. Many of these undocumented controls, however, can be tested and evaluated in the same manner as documented ones. An appropriate level of documentation makes any evaluation of internal control more efficient and facilitates employees' understanding of how the process works, but such documentation is not always essential. IT auditors reviewing an enterprise's internal financial controls systems always request to see systems documentation as part of their review work. If an existing process is informal, undocumented, but recognized as effective, the review team will need to prepare its own action documentation to explain how the process works and the nature of its internal controls.

Reporting Internal Control Deficiencies. When internal control deficiencies are identified—whether through processes in the internal control system itself, monitoring activities, or other external events—they should be reported to appropriate levels of enterprise management. The key question for the IT audit evaluator is to determine what should be reported, given the many details that may be encountered, and to whom the reports should be directed. COSO internal control states that "all internal control deficiencies that can affect the entity's attaining its objectives should be reported to those who can take necessary action." This COSO internal control statement makes sense but often is difficult to implement. The modern enterprise, no matter how well organized, is often guilty of a variety of internal control errors or omissions. COSO internal control suggests that all of these should be identified and reported and that even seemingly minor of errors should be investigated in order to understand if they were caused by overall control deficiencies. The COSO internal controls report uses the example of an employee's taking a few dollars from the petty cash fund. Although this could be viewed as a minor matter due to the small size of the theft, it still should be viewed as an overall control breakdown on several levels.

The monetary amount may not be significant, but COSO internal control urges that the matter be investigated rather than ignored, since "such apparent condoning of the personal use of the entity's money might send an unintended message to employees." Prior to SOx, external auditors regularly applied the concept of materiality when performing reviews and decided that some errors and irregularities were so small that they were not material to the external auditor's overall conclusion. In the first years of SOx compliance reviews with the original Auditing Standard No. 2 (AS 2) guidelines, the message from many external auditors was that materiality issues should not be considered—an error is an error. This approach caused many managers to wonder why their external auditors were raising issues on what they felt were minor matters. With the AS 5 rules discussed later in the chapter, materiality and relative risk now must be considered when evaluating the efficiency and effectiveness of internal controls.

The COSO internal controls guidance concludes by discussing to whom to report internal control deficiencies in the enterprise. In one paragraph, COSO internal control provides guidance that is useful for evaluations:

> Findings on internal control deficiencies usually should be reported not only to the individual responsible for the function or activity involved, who is in the position to take corrective action, but also to at least one level of management above the directly responsible person. This process enables that individual to provide needed support or oversight for taking corrective action, and to communicate with others in the enterprise whose activities may be affected. Where findings cut across organizational boundaries, the reporting should cross over as well and be directed to a sufficiently high level to ensure appropriate action.

The enterprise should also develop reporting procedures such that all internal control deficiencies encountered through IT audit reviews of ongoing operations are reported to appropriate levels of the enterprise. Management reporting and monitoring is a highly important aspect of internal control. Internal audit has a lead role in that process through IT audit reviews and should be aware of the need for other monitoring processes when reviewing and evaluating internal controls.

Other Dimensions of the COSO Internal Controls Framework

We sometimes forget that the COSO internal controls framework should be reviewed and evaluated as the three-dimensional model, shown in Exhibit 1.2. In addition to the front-facing dimension of that model covering control activities, the right side covers entities or activities, and the top side or dimension of the framework cube covers the three dimensions of all internal controls:

1. Effectiveness and efficiency of operations
2. Compliance with applicable laws and regulations
3. Reliability of financial reporting

Each of the control areas just discussed—from the control environment to monitoring—should also be considered with respect to those other two dimensions.

Regarding the right side dimension, internal controls should be installed and evaluated across all units in the enterprise. This does not mean that a control activity, such as an expense approval process, must be identical in all units, such as at corporate headquarters or a sales office in a remote geographic location. However, there should be a consistent set of control processes throughout the enterprise with consideration given for the relative risks and scopes of operations. Internal controls should be consistent, but they should be applied appropriately in individual operating units.

The top dimension of the COSO internal controls framework is even more significant. It says that internal control activities should be installed in all enterprise operating units with respect to the three factors of internal controls: reliability of operations, regulatory compliance, and financial reporting effectiveness. Looking at internal controls from this three-dimensional viewpoint, there may always be some variations but the framework should be under a basic and consistent internal controls. Consider the example of a subsidiary facility in a central Asian nation, far away from its U.S. headquarters. Country expense approval procedures may be subject to local laws, and other processes may be somewhat different due to communication distances or differences in local IT systems. However, those internal controls still should be implemented in a manner that ensures reliability in financial reporting as results are reported to corporate headquarters.

All internal control considerations must be considered in terms of the COSO three-dimensional cube. That is, the control must be considered in terms of where it fits in the overall enterprise and its relationship to the three control objective areas just discussed. This concept provides IT auditors with a powerful way of looking at internal controls from a total perspective. The COSO internal controls framework continues to be an important standard and set of guidance materials for measuring and evaluating internal controls.

The COSO internal control framework is becoming the worldwide standard for building and developing effective internal controls. It is a continuous process in each of its three dimensions. On the front-facing side of the model, the monitoring component on top is of little value unless internal control processes are in place all the way down to the internal control environment foundation. Similarly, effective internal controls must be installed in all levels of organizational units, and each of those controls must be sensitive to the three top-facing internal control elements.

COSO INTERNAL CONTROL SYSTEMS MONITORING GUIDANCE

Extensive guidance materials on the COSO internal controls framework have been available with sources ranging from AICPA auditing standards, various ISACA materials, and our own additional guidance materials.[6] However, many professionals had been seeking more specific guidance on how to implement COSO internal controls in business operations. A three-volume set of internal controls guidance materials was published by COSO in 2009.[7]

These volumes emphasize the importance of establishing processes to monitor the effectiveness and efficiency of established internal controls. Our previous description of the COSO internal controls framework, as shown in Exhibit 1.1, suggests that enterprises implement internal control monitoring processes in a manner similar to the way in which a manufacturing organization monitors the continued effectiveness and efficiency of its manufacturing procedures. The materials suggest that enterprises establish a four-phase or -stage monitoring process, as shown in Exhibit 1.4, where

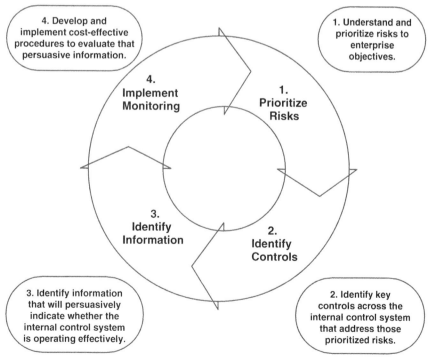

EXHIBIT 1.4 Monitoring Design and Implementation Process

an enterprise should first prioritize and understand the risks to its organizational objectives, then identify the controls that address those prioritized risks. IT auditors play a key role in the third step: identifying information that will persuasively indicate that the internal control system is operating effectively. The model calls for implementing cost-effective procedures to evaluate the information gathered through monitoring processes. The internal controls evaluation process is also very similar to the continuous assurance auditing procedures discussed in Chapter 14.

SARBANES-OXLEY ACT

The Sarbanes-Oxley Act (We will refer to the Act as SOx) is a U.S. law enacted in 2002 as a response to a series of accounting misdeeds and financial failures with an objective to improve public company financial reporting, audit, and enterprise governance processes. It first had a major impact on businesses in the United States and now is recognized worldwide. Although SOx's auditing and internal control rules have directly changed many external auditor practices, the act has also had a major impact on IT auditors. A general understanding of SOx, with an emphasis on its Section 404 internal accounting control rules, is a key knowledge requirement for all IT auditors.

Here we provide a high-level overview of SOx today with an emphasis on its Section 404, the rules that are most important to IT auditors. We summarize SOx requirements for reviews of internal accounting controls—a process important for IT auditors. In addition, we summarize the relatively new external auditing standards called Auditing Standard No. 5 (AS 5), a set of risk-based auditing approaches that also emphasize the importance of internal audit's work in performing financial reporting internal control reviews. IT auditors should have general knowledge and understanding of SOx internal control rules.[8]

Key Elements

The official name of SOx is the Public Accounting Reform and Investor Protection Act. It became law in August 2002 with most of the final detailed rules and regulations released by the end of 2003. Business professionals refer to it as the Sarbanes-Oxley Act, from the names of its principal congressional sponsors, which is shortened to SOx, SOX, or Sarbox, among many other variations.

SOx introduced a series of totally changed processes for external auditing and gave new governance responsibilities to senior executives and board members. SOx also established the Public Company Accounting Oversight Board (PCAOB), a rule-setting authority under the SEC that issues financial auditing standards and monitors external auditor governance. As happens with all financial and securities-related federal laws, an extensive set of specific regulations and administrative rules has been developed by the SEC based on the SOx legislation.

U.S. federal laws are organized and issued as separate sections of legislation called titles, with numbered sections and subsections under each. Much of the SOx legislation contains rules that are not that significant for most internal auditors and business

Title	Subject	Rule or Requirement
101	Establishment of PCAOB	Overall rules for the establishment of the PCAOB, including its membership requirements.
104	Accounting Firm Inspections	Schedule for PCAOB inspections of registered public accounting firms.
108	Auditing Standards	The PCAOB will accept current but will issue its own new auditing standards.
201	Out-of-Scope Practices	Outlines prohibited accounting firm practices, such as internal audit outsourcing, bookkeeping, and financial systems design.
203	Audit Partner Rotations	The audit partner and the reviewing partner must rotate off an assignment every five years.
301	Audit Committee Independence	All audit committee members must be independent directors.
302	Corporate Responsibility for Financial Reports	The CEO and CFO must personally certify their periodic financial reports.
305	Officer and Director Bars	If compensation is received as part of fraudulent/illegal accounting, the benefiting officers or director is required to personally reimburse funds received.
404	Internal Control Reports	Management is responsible for an annual assessment of internal controls.
407	Financial Expert	One audit committee director must be a designated financial expert.
408	Enhanced Review of Financial Disclosures	The SEC may schedule extended reviews of reported information based on certain specified factors.
409	Real-Time Disclosure	Financial reports must be distributed in a rapid and current manner.
1105	Officer or Director Prohibitions	The SEC may prohibit an officer or director from serving in another public company if guilty of a violation.

EXHIBIT 1.5   Sarbanes-Oxley Act Key Provisions Summary

professionals. For example, Section 602(d) of Title I states that the SEC "shall establish" minimum professional conduct standards or rules for SEC practicing attorneys. Although this rule perhaps is good to know, it does not have any IT audit impact. Exhibit 1.5 summarizes the major titles of SOx, although our focus is on Titles I and IV. Our intent is not to describe all of these sections or to reproduce the full text of this legislation—it can be found on the Web[9]—but to highlight portions of the law that are more significant to internal audit and business professionals. Of interest, even though internal control processes very much rely on both external and internal auditors, the original SOx legislation makes almost no direct references to the important roles and responsibilities of internal auditors. The importance of internal audit's role in SOx internal control reviews was highlighted subsequently in the AS 5 rules, released in mid-2007 and discussed later in this chapter. Our emphasis throughout is on the role of internal audit in today's SOx environment.

Title I: Public Company Accounting Oversight Board

SOx introduced significant new rules for external auditors. Prior to SOx, the AICPA had guidance-setting responsibility for all external auditors and their public accounting firms through its overall responsibility for the Certified Public Accountant (CPA) certification. Although state Boards of Accountancy actually license CPAs, the AICPA previously had overall responsibility for the profession. External audit standards were set by the AICPA's Auditing Standards Board (ASB). Although basic standards—called generally accepted auditing standards (GAAS)—have been in place over the years, newer auditing standards were released as numbered Statements of Auditing Standards (SASs). Much of GAAS was just good auditing practices—for example, accounting transactions must be backed by appropriate documentation—while the SASs covered specific areas requiring better definition. SAS No. 99, for example, covered the consideration of fraud in a financial statement audit. The AICPA's code of professional conduct required CPAs to follow and comply with all applicable auditing standards.

The AICPA's GAAS and its numbered SAS standards were accepted by the SEC, and these auditing rules defined external auditing standards and the tests necessary for an audited financial statement. However, the accounting scandals that led to the passage of SOx signaled that the AICPA-led process of establishing auditing standards was "broken"; SOx took this audit standards-setting process away from the AICPA, which was dominated by major public accounting firms, and created the PCAOB, a nonfederal, nonprofit corporation with the responsibility to oversee all audits of corporations subject to the SEC.

The PCAOB does not replace the AICPA but assumes responsibility for the external auditing practices for AICPA members. The AICPA continues to administer the CPA examination, with its certificates awarded on a state-by-state basis, and sets auditing standards for U.S. private, non-SEC organizations. SOx Title I defines PCAOB auditing practices for external auditors; other audit process and corporate governance rules have changed how internal auditors coordinate their work with external auditors. Although SOx Title I contains many new rules, perhaps the three most important to IT auditors are that the PCAOB now has both major responsibility for public accounting firms, sets their external auditing standards, and sets audit standards rules such as workpaper retention. The next paragraphs briefly describe these SOx Title I external audit process rules.

- **PCAOB administration and public accounting firm registration.** The PCAOB is administered through an SEC-appointed board with required membership that is not dominated by CPA and public accounting firm interests. The PCAOB is responsible for overseeing and regulating all public accounting firms that practice before the SEC and for establishing auditing standards.
- **Auditing, quality control, and independence standards.** The PCAOB has the authority to establish auditing and related attestation standards, quality control standards, and ethics standards for registered public accounting firms. SOx recognizes previously issued AICPA auditing standards and has issued a limited number of new standards to date, such as AS 5 for the review and evaluation of internal controls. SOx rules further specify that an external auditor's evaluation must

contain a description of material weaknesses as well as any material non-compliance matters found. External auditors are required to update the effectiveness of internal controls, and an absence of this documentation should be considered a weakness of internal controls.

- **Audit workpapers retention.** PCAOB standard AS 3, *Audit Documentation*, mandates that audit workpapers and other supporting materials should be maintained for a period of not less than seven years. This requirement is in response to an infamous event just prior to the fall of the corporation that prompted SOx, Enron, and its auditor, Arthur Andersen. Enron was still in operation but was under some financial pressures when the SEC announced that it was going to conduct an on-site investigation. Enron's external auditors, Arthur Andersen, used an internal firm policy to justify destruction of all but the most current of their Enron audit documentation. This was a factor that led to the establishment of this SOx rule.
- **Scope of internal control testing.** PCAOB rules require external auditors to describe the scope of both their testing processes and their test findings. Prior to SOx, external auditors sometimes used internal firm policies to justify the smallest test sizes, and they frequently tested only a very small number of items despite being faced with very large test populations. If no problems were found, they expressed an opinion for the entire population based on the results of a very limited sample. External auditors now must pay greater attention to the scope and reasonableness of their testing procedures, and the supporting documentation must clearly describe the scope and extent of testing activities.

Title IV: Enhanced Financial Disclosures and Section 404

SOx Title IV is designed to correct some financial reporting disclosure problems, to tighten up conflict of interest rules for corporate officers and directors, to mandate a management assessment of internal controls, to require senior officer codes of conduct, and other matters. There is a lot of material here, but the most significant nugget for internal auditors is Section 404, Management's Assessment of Internal Controls. SOx requires that all annual 10K reports must contain an internal controls report stating management's responsibility for establishing and maintaining an adequate system of internal controls as well as management's assessment, as of the fiscal year ending date, of the effectiveness of those installed internal control procedures. These are what have popularly become known as the Section 404 rules. Internal and IT audit, outside consultants, and even the management team—but not the external auditors—have the responsibility to review and assess the effectiveness of their internal controls, and external auditors are then to attest to the sufficiency of the internal control reviews built and controlled by management.

Section 404 reviews are supported by the AS 5 standards discussed later in this section and are particularly important to internal auditors because the rules specify that external auditors may elect to use the work of internal auditors in their internal controls reviews. All IT auditors should have a basic understanding of SOx Section 404, whether they are acting as consultants in helping to build these internal accounting controls or acting in support of enterprise external auditors by auditing those internal accounting controls.

SOx Section 404 rules state that an enterprise is responsible for reviewing, documenting, and testing its own internal accounting controls, with those review results then passed on to the enterprise's external auditors, who are charged with reviewing and attesting to that work as part of their review of the reported financial statements. When SOx first became the law, Section 404 reviews were a major pain point for many enterprises because external auditors were required to follow a very detailed set of AS 2 financial accounting audit procedures that did not give any allowance for small errors or omissions. Section 404 auditing rules have changed with the release of AS 5 in 2007; a more risk-based audit approach also allows external auditors to better use the work of internal auditors in their assessments.

Section 404 Internal Controls Assessments

Management always has had the overall responsibility for designing and implementing internal controls over an enterprise's operations. Although the standards for what constituted good internal controls were not always that well defined in the past, they have remained a fundamental management concept. SOx Section 404 requires an annual internal control report, with these information elements, as part of an enterprise's SEC-mandated Form 10K annual report:

- A formal management statement acknowledging the enterprise's responsibility for establishing and maintaining an adequate internal control structure and procedures for financial reporting
- An assessment, as of the end of the most recent fiscal year, of the effectiveness of the enterprise's internal control structure and procedures for financial reporting

In addition, the external audit firm that issued the supporting audit report is required to review and report on management's assessment of its internal financial controls. Simply put, management is required to report on the quality of its internal controls, and its public accounting firm must audit or attest to that management developed an internal controls report in addition to the normal financial statement audit. Management has always been responsible for preparing periodic financial reports, and external auditors then audited those financial numbers and certified that they were fairly stated. With SOx Section 404, management is now responsible for documenting, testing and reporting on their internal financial controls effectiveness. External auditors then review the supporting materials leading up to that internal financial controls report to assert that the report is an accurate description of the internal control environment.

To the non–financial statement auditor and for some IT auditors, this might appear to be an obscure or almost trivial requirement. Even some IT auditors who perform operational audits primarily may wonder about the nuances in this process. However, this process follows a basic internal control on the importance of maintaining a separation of duties where the person who develops transactions should not be the person who approves them. Under Section 404 procedures, the enterprise builds and documents its own internal control processes, then an independent party such, as internal audit, reviews and tests those internal controls. Finally, the external auditors review and attest to the adequacy of this process. Their financial audit procedures will be based on these internal controls. This Section 404 process improves things from pre-SOx days when external auditors frequently built, documented, and then audited their own internal controls—a separation-of-duties shortcoming.

Identifying Key Processes to Launch a Section 404 Compliance Review

Whether based on IT systems or even manual procedures, the basic processes for every enterprise should normally be considered in terms of some basic accounting cycles:

- **Revenue cycle.** Processes dealing with sales or other enterprise revenue.
- **Direct expenditures cycle.** Expenditures for material or direct production costs.
- **Indirect expenditures cycle.** Operating costs that cannot be tied directly to production activities but are necessary for overall business operations.
- **Payroll cycle.** Covers all personnel compensation.
- **Inventory cycle.** Although inventory eventually will be applied as direct production expenditures, time-based processes are needed for holding inventory until applied to production.
- **Fixed assets cycle.** Property and equipment require separate accounting processes, such as periodic depreciation accounting over time.
- **General controls IT cycle.** This set of processes covers IT controls that are general or applicable to all IT operations and are discussed in Chapter 6.

We will discuss some of these processes in Chapter 5 in the context of planning and performing effective IT audits. The identification of these key enterprise processes is an initial Section 404 compliance step, and an enterprise should document, understand, and test all of these "key processes." IT audit often can be a major help here, as it may have already reviewed the prime systems and supporting IT processes through its annual audit reviews and documentation.

Internal Audit's Role

Even though SOx does not give specific responsibilities to internal audit, IT auditors are an important enterprise resource for the completion of Section 404 internal controls assessments. Under SOx, a separate and independent function within the enterprise—often internal or IT audit—reviews and documents the internal controls covering key processes, identifies key control points, and then tests those identified controls. External audit then reviews that work and attests to its adequacy. For many enterprises, IT audit can be a key resource for performing these internal controls reviews for technology-based processes. When SOx first became the law, internal audit functions often distanced themselves from Section 404 reviews because of potential internal auditor independence standards. The IIA Standards, as discussed in Chapter 3, now allow internal auditors to act as consultants to help document and establish effective internal control processes.

The CAE, financial management, and the audit committee should work with the enterprise's external auditors to define responsibilities for their Section 404 internal

1. Determine status of review: Is this the first round of Section 404 reviews for the entity or a subsequent-year follow-up?
2. If a new review, follow the work steps to understand, document, and test key processes. Otherwise, plan for a subsequent-period review.
3. Review the detailed documentation covering prior 404 reviews, including process flow charts, internal control gaps identified and remediated, as well as overall project planning documentation for prior review.
4. Review any recently published PCAOB rules covering Section 404 reviews and related auditing changes, and adjust review procedures to reflect those changes.
5. Meet with the external audit firm responsible for the current Section 404 attestations and determine if there are any changes in documentation and testing philosophy, with an emphasis on AS5 rules, from that prior review.
6. Consider any organization changes since the past review, including acquisitions or major reorganizations, and modify review coverage, if necessary.
7. Through meetings with senior and IT management, identify if new systems or processes have been installed over the past period and if those new changes have been reflected in updated documentation.
8. Review any internal control weaknesses identified in the past review, and assess whether internal control corrections reported as installed appear to be working.
9. Assess the status of existing Section 404 documentation, and determine the extent of new documentation preparation necessary.
10. Assuming the prior Section 404 review was done by internal audit, determine that appropriate knowledgeable, trained resources are available to perform the upcoming review.
11. Interview all parties involved in the prior Section 404 review exercise to assess any lessons learned and develop plans for corrective actions in the upcoming review.
12. Based on discussions with external auditors and senior management, determine scope materiality parameters for the upcoming review.
13. Determine that the software, if any, used to document prior review is still current, and make any changes necessary to have adequate tools in place to perform the upcoming review.
14. Prepare a detailed project plan for the upcoming Section 404 review, with consideration given to coordination of review activities at business entity units and external auditors.
15. Submit plan for approval by senior management.

EXHIBIT 1.6   Planning Considerations for a Section 404 Internal Controls Review

control reviews. These reviews are performed on an annual process, with documentation prepared and tested in the first year updated and retested in future periods. All parties should develop a cost-effective approach to achieve these SOx requirements and assess their IT applications and controls.

IT audit–led SOx Section 404 reviews should be planned and conducted like any new IT audit project as discussed in Chapter 5 on planning and developing effective IT audits. Exhibit 1.6 outlines some planning considerations for an IT audit–led Section 404 internal controls review. Internal audit can play a major role in helping senior management establish Section 404 compliance. Based on the internal audit standards discussed in Chapter 3, internal audit should recommend internal control improvements as the new processes are being developed, or internal audit can act as consultants for installing those new internal control processes.

AS 5 Rules and Internal Audit

Shortly after SOx became law in the United States, the PCAOB released its AS 2 guidance, which called for external auditors to take very conservative and detailed approaches on their audits of financial statements. AS 2 mandated a "look at everything" detailed audit approach, and enterprise external audit bills became much more expensive in those first SOx years. However, there were frequent complaints by industry leaders and others with a general consensus that AS 2 needed some revisions. The SEC and the PCAOB agreed to revise AS 2, and AS 5 was issued in late May 2007.

AS 5 is a set of standards for external auditors who review and certify published financial statements. The new rules are also important for internal auditors. AS 5 introduces risk-based rules with an emphasis on the effectiveness of internal controls, oriented to enterprise facts and circumstances. In addition, AS 5 calls for external auditors to consider including reviews of appropriate internal audit reports in their financial statement audit reviews. It allows external auditors to place more emphasis on management's ability to establish and document key internal controls.

AS 5 rules are particularly important for IT auditors because external auditors can rely on the work of internal auditors in their Section 404 assessments. AS 5 has three broad objectives:

1. **Focus internal control audits on the most important matters.** AS 5 calls on external auditors to focus their reviews on areas that present the greatest risk that an internal control will fail to prevent or detect a material misstatement in financial statements. This approach calls for external auditors to focus on identifying material weaknesses in internal control in their audits, before material misstatements of financial statements arise. AS 5 also emphasizes the importance of auditing higher-risk areas, such as the financial statement period-end close process and controls designed to prevent fraud by management. At the same time, the new standard provides external auditors a range of alternatives for addressing lower-risk areas, such as by more clearly demonstrating how to calibrate the nature, timing, and extent of testing based on risk, as well as how to incorporate knowledge accumulated in previous years' audits into the auditors' assessment of risk. Also very important to internal auditors, AS 5 allows external auditors to use the work performed by an enterprise's internal auditors, when appropriate.

2. **Eliminate audit procedures that are unnecessary to achieve their intended benefits.** AS 5 does not include the previous AS 2 standard's detailed requirements to evaluate management's own evaluation process and clarifies that an internal control audit does not require an opinion on the adequacy of management's processes. For example, AS 5 focuses on the multilocation dimensions of risk in an enterprise and reduces requirements that external auditors should test a "large portion" of an enterprise's operations or financial positions. This should allow a reduction in financial audit work.

3. **Make the financial audit clearly scalable to fit the size and the complexity of any enterprise.** In order to provide guidance for audits of smaller, less complex companies, AS 5 calls for tailoring internal control audits to fit the size and

complexity of the enterprise being audited. The standard has guidance on how to apply AS 5 to smaller, less complex enterprises as well as the units of larger enterprises.

Following AS 5, external auditors may consider using the work of others to help perform their SOx financial statement internal control audits. Although it was not as well defined under previous AS 2 rules, AS 5 now explicitly states that an external auditor may use the work performed by, or receive direct assistance from, internal auditors, other company personnel, or third parties working under the direction of management or the audit committee, to provide evidence about the effectiveness of financial reporting internal controls. This is a major change for internal auditors.

Of course, external auditors are signing off on or attesting to the audit results, and they must assess the competence and objectivity of the persons whose work they plan to use. The higher the degree of competence and objectivity of others, the greater use an auditor may use their work. In particular, AS 5 calls for an assessment of the competence and objectivity of internal auditors. *Competence* means the attainment and maintenance of a level of understanding and knowledge that enables persons to perform the tasks assigned to them, and *objectivity* means the ability to perform those tasks impartially and with intellectual honesty. To assess competence, an external auditor should evaluate the qualifications and ability of the internal auditors or others to perform the work the external auditor plans to use. To assess objectivity, AS 5 calls for an external auditor evaluation of whether factors are present that either inhibit or promote a person's ability to perform with the necessary degree of objectivity the work the auditor plans to use.

AS 5 goes on to state that external auditors should not use the work of persons who have "a low degree of objectivity, regardless of their level of competence," and also should not use the work of persons who have a low level of competence regardless of their degree of objectivity. Personnel whose core function is to serve as a testing or compliance authority at an enterprise, such as internal and IT auditors, normally are expected to have greater competence and objectivity in performing the type of work that will be useful to the external auditor. This may be an area where the CAE, as well as the audit committee and senior management, may want to challenge external auditors if they see no role for internal audit in this financial statement audit planning process.

Although AS 5 talks about internal auditors in an almost generic fashion, the role of the professional IIA member IT auditor is important here. Based on the IIA's International Professional Practice of Internal Auditing standards, as summarized in Chapter 3, an IT auditor can be expected to have the competence and objectivity necessary for help in supporting an external auditor's review of Section 404 internal controls. Although other persons, such as outside consultants, can be used to assist external auditors in their financial statement internal control reviews, IT auditors should have a major role here in assisting with Section 404 and AS 5 audit compliance.

Internal audit's ongoing role here should be viewed with a level of caution. We have discussed how IT auditors often are excellent resources to identify, document, and test key Section 404 internal control processes. They could do this in a support role for the external auditor's attestation reviews. However, pure separation-of-duties independence rules say that they cannot perform these reviews, as internal auditors, within the enterprise and then act as a third-party helpmate for the external auditors to help attest to that same work. This conflict of duties should be clearly understood by all parties, and internal auditors and management should exercise care to prevent it.

WRAPPING IT UP: COSO INTERNAL CONTROLS AND SOx

This chapter has introduced two important concepts for IT auditors: the COSO internal controls framework and SOx internal controls standards. IT auditors work in a variety of enterprise environments, but today they will almost always encounter COSO internal control framework rules and SOx internal control review requirements under AS 5. Although this chapter provides just a summary description of each of these standards, and many auditors will require a greater understanding, all IT auditors should have a general knowledge and understanding of the COSO internal controls framework and SOx rules for understanding internal controls. These are worldwide standards requirements for today's effective IT auditor.

NOTES

1. More information on the total roles and responsibilities of internal audit in today's enterprise can be found in Robert Moeller, *Brink's Modern Internal Auditing*, 7th ed. (Hoboken, NJ: John Wiley & Sons, 2009).
2. Statement on Auditing Standards No. 1, *Codification of Auditing Standards and Procedures*, AICPA, Professional Standards.
3. *National Commission on Fraudulent Financial Reporting*, Report of the National Commission on Fraudulent Financial Reporting (1987).
4. *Internal Control—Integrated Framework*, www.coso.org/publications.htm Note: This reference is for the COSO internal controls report, which can be ordered through the AICPA at www.cpa2biz.com.
5. AICPA-published COSO internal control standards are described in the Statement on Auditing Standards (SAS) numbers 103, 105, 106, 107, 109, 110, and 112.
6. See Robert Moeller, *Sarbanes-Oxley Internal Controls: Effective Auditing with AS5, CobiT, and ITIL* (Hoboken, NJ: John Wiley & Sons, 2008).
7. COSO, *Guidance on Monitoring Internal Control Systems* (2009). www.coso.org/documents/COSO_Guidance_On_Monitoring_Intro_online1.pdf.
8. Here we are presenting only a high-level summary of SOx requirements. See Moeller, *Sarbanes-Oxley Internal Controls*, for much more information.
9. As a public document, the text of the law can be found in many Web locations. One source is http://fl1.findlaw.com/news.findlaw.com/hdocs/docs/gwbush/sarbanesoxley 072302.pdf.

CHAPTER TWO

Using CobiT to Perform IT Audits

THE COMMITTEE OF SPONSORING Organizations (COSO) internal controls framework, as introduced and discussed in Chapter 1, has become the standard tool for measuring and evaluating internal accounting controls for a wide span of systems and processes since the 1990s and under the Sarbanes-Oxley Act (SOx). However, some professionals, and information technology (IT) auditors in particular, have expressed concerns about using the COSO internal controls framework in today's IT-oriented world. The concern is that the published COSO internal controls guidance just does not give enough emphasis to IT tools and processes. For example, the published COSO internal controls guidance materials (see Chapter 3) look at IT application internal controls only at a very high level, when there appears to be a need for more IT-specific internal control guidance.

A more IT-oriented internal controls framework, called CobiT (*Control Objectives for Information and related Technology*), was in place long before SOx; it was first released in 1996. Although earlier CobiT versions were more oriented to providing IT auditor and controls guidance, CoboT has became a preferred tool for complying with SOx Section 404 internal controls procedures for many enterprises. CobiT provides guidance on evaluating and understanding internal controls, with an emphasis on enterprise IT resources. CobiT is not a replacement for the COSO internal controls framework but is a different way to look at internal controls in today's IT-centric world.

Although originally launched as guidance to help those professionals once called computer auditors—specialist internal and external auditors who reviewed IT-related internal controls—CobiT has evolved into a helpful tool for evaluating all internal controls across an enterprise. CobiT emphasizes the linkage of IT with other business resources to deliver overall values to an enterprise today. This chapter provides an overview of the CobiT framework and its key components. More important, the chapter describes the relationship between CobiT objectives and the COSO internal control framework for use in all internal audit reviews.

CobiT and its related principles can be used or mapped to other IT initiatives as well. For example, Chapter 11 on software engineering and Capability Maturity Model for integration (CMMi) highlights CMMi linkages to CobiT, as does Chapter 25's discussion on the ISO 17799 standards. In addition, Chapter 16 introduces the related Val IT, an approach to better recognize the value of all IT assets in the enterprise. Val IT addresses assumptions, costs, risks, and outcomes related to a balanced portfolio of IT-enabled business investments.

Even if an internal auditor does not use the CobiT framework in reviews of internal controls, all IT and internal auditors should have a high-level knowledge of the basic CobiT framework. As mentioned, CobiT had its origins as an IT audit guidance tool, but it is much broader today. In addition to the COSO internal controls framework, knowledge of CobiT will help an internal auditor to better understand the role of IT controls and risks in many enterprise environments.

INTRODUCTION TO CobiT

An unusual word for many, CobiT is an acronym that is becoming increasingly recognized by auditors, IT professionals, and many enterprise managers. CobiT is an important internal control framework that can stand by itself but is an important support tool for documenting and understanding COSO and SOx internal controls and recognizing the value of IT assets in an enterprise. A general or working knowledge of CobiT should be an IT auditor requirement.

The CobiT standards and framework are issued and regularly updated by the IT Governance Institute (ITGI) and their closely affiliated professional organization, the Information Systems Audit and Control Association (ISACA). ISACA is more focused on IT auditing while ITGI's emphasis is on research and governance processes. ISACA also manages the Certified Information Systems Auditor (CISA) examination and professional designation as well as its newer Certified Information Systems Manager (CISM) and the Certified in the Governance of Enterprise IT (CGEIT) certification and examination. The Certified Information Security Manager (CISM) certification targets IT security managers and promotes the advancement of professionals who wish to be recognized for their IT governance-related experience and knowledge. These audit-related professional certifications are discussed in Chapter 30. ISACA was originally known as the EDP Auditor's Association (EDPAA), a professional group begun in 1967 by internal auditors who felt that their then current professional organization, the Institute of Internal Auditors (IIA), was not giving sufficient attention to the importance of IT systems and technology controls as part of internal audit activities. We have almost forgotten that EDP once stood for electronic data processing, today an almost archaic term for IT. Over time, this professional enterprise broadened its focus and became ISACA, while the IIA has also long since embraced strong technology issues.

The EDPAA, originally an upstart IT audit professional organization, began to develop IT audit professional guidance materials shortly after its formation. Just as the

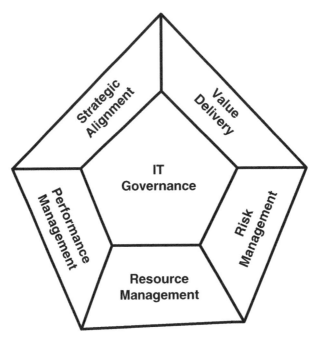

EXHIBIT 2.1   CobiT IT Governance Focus Areas

EDPAA evolved into the well-respected ISACA and now the ITGI, its original IT audit standards became an excellent set of internal control objectives that evolved to CobiT, now in its 2007 version 4.1 edition.[1] With virtually all enterprise processes today tied to IT-related facilities, an understanding of the overall area of IT governance is critical. The CobiT framework is often described as a pentagon covering five broad and interconnected areas of internal controls, as illustrated in Exhibit 2.1. The exhibit shows CobiT's major areas of emphasis arranged around the important core concept of IT governance:

1. **Strategic alignment.** Efforts should be in place to align IT operations and activities with all other enterprise operations. These efforts include establishing linkages between enterprise business operations and IT plans as well as processes for defining, maintaining, and validating quality and value relationships.
2. **Value delivery.** Processes should be in place to ensure that IT and other operating units deliver promised benefits throughout a delivery cycle and with a strategy that optimizes costs while emphasizing the intrinsic values of IT and related activities.
3. **Risk management.** Management, at all levels, should have a clear understanding of an enterprise's appetite for risk, compliance requirements, and the impact of significant risks. Both IT and other operations have their own and joint risk management responsibilities that may individually or jointly impact the entire enterprise.
4. **Resource management.** With an emphasis on IT, there should be an optimal investment in, and the proper management of, critical IT resources, applications,

information, infrastructure, and people. Effective IT governance depends on the optimization of knowledge and infrastructure.

5. **Performance measurement.** Processes should be in place to track and monitor strategy implementation, project completions, resource usage, process performance, and service delivery. IT governance mechanisms should translate implementation strategies into actions and measurements to achieve these goals.

These five CobiT internal control concerns are the elements of the CobiT framework and define IT governance. The CobiT framework is an effective tool for documenting IT and all other internal controls. This chapter looks this framework in the broader perspective of using CobiT to assist in the IT governance processes of management, enterprise, and internal auditing.

The following sections provide an overall description of the CobiT framework and its key elements to link business with IT goals through key controls and effective measurement metrics. In addition, the chapter describes mapping CobiT standards with the COSO internal control framework, discussed in Chapter 1, with the information technology infrastructure library (ITIL) best practices introduced in Chapter 7, and for overall IT and corporate governance. Elements and key components of IT governance are discussed as well. The CobiT framework is an effective mechanism for documenting and understanding internal controls at all levels. Although CobiT first started primarily as a set of "IT audit" guidance materials, it is a much more powerful tool today.

CobiT FRAMEWORK

IT processes and their supporting software applications and hardware devices are key components in any enterprise today. Whether a small retail business with a need to keep track of its inventory and pay employees, or a large Fortune 50 corporation, all need a wide set of interconnected and often complex IT processes that are closely tied to their business operations. That is, enterprise business processes and their supporting IT resources should work in a close information-sharing relationship. IT cannot and certainly should not tell business operations what types of IT processes and systems to implement, but IT provides information to help influence business decisions. In the very early days of computer systems, often IT managers felt they had lots of answers and promoted systems solutions to their businesses, sometimes with very counterproductive results. However, this relationship has changed today; IT and business operations generally should have a close mutual relationship of shared requirements and information. Internal auditors must understand the needs and information-sharing requirements on both sides. As discussed in Chapter 1 in the COSO internal controls framework, IT has responsibilities over a series of other related process areas that are audited by or through established audit guidelines, are measured by a series of performance indicator measures and activities, and are made effective through activity goals. All of these can also easily become part of CobiT, a control framework including both IT and business processes.

Chapter 1 described the COSO internal control framework and its importance in defining SOx internal controls. An IT auditor might ask, "I understand and use COSO

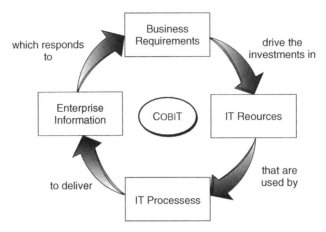

EXHIBIT 2.2　Basic CobiT Principles
Source: COBIT 4.1 © 1996–2001 IT Governance Institute. All rights reserved. Used by permission.

internal controls. Why another framework?" The answer here is that CobiT provides *an alternative* approach to define and describe internal controls that has more of an IT emphasis than the pure COSO internal controls framework. Information and supporting IT processes often are the most valuable assets for all enterprises today, and management has a major responsibility to safeguard its supporting IT assets, including their automated systems. Management, users, and IT auditors all need to understand these information-related processes and the controls that support them. This combination of IT processes amd internal controls focuses on the effectiveness and efficiency of IT resources, processes, and overall business requirements. Exhibit 2.2 describes these basic CobiT principles, with business requirements driving the demand for IT resources and those resources initiating IT processes and enterprise information in a continuous, circular manner. Management should be interested in the quality, cost, and appropriate delivery of its IT-related resources whose control components are the same as the COSO internal control elements discussed in Chapter 1. Internal controls over IT resources are very much based on the effectiveness and efficiency interdependencies of these IT components.

IT governance is a key concept that was not strongly emphasized as a CobiT element prior to SOx. It is an important internal control concept today with the ITGI playing a strong leadership role. As described in the IT governance pentagon in Exhibit 2.1, CobiT defines IT governance as a series of key areas ranging from keeping focus on strategic alignments to the importance of both risk and performance measurement when managing IT resources. We refer to this IT governance pentagon again as we navigate through the CobiT framework.

CobiT looks at internal controls from three IT dimensions: resources, processes, and information criteria, described in the CobiT Cube illustrated in Exhibit 2.3. Similar to the COSO internal controls framework cube discussed in Chapter 1 and Chapter 4 on the COSO ERM framework, this CobiT model looks at IT controls from a three-dimensional perspective. That is, each component on one surface relates to the two other connecting dimensions. However, CobiT's front-facing dimension with its pictorial descriptions of

Business Requirements

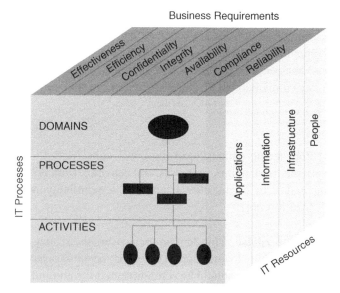

EXHIBIT 2.3 CobiT Cube
Source: COBIT 4.1 ©1996–2001 IT Governance Institute. All rights reserved. Used by permission.

process flow diagrams sometimes scared off non-IT people from considering CobiT. The non–IT savvy professional—and there are many—may look at the process diagrams on the face of the CobiT cube and decide this approach must be too technical. This is not at all correct. We describe and explain the CobiT framework and why it can be valuable for understanding SOx internal controls and improving both IT audit and governance practices in the next sections.

CobiT Cube Components

IT Resources

The IT resources side of the three-dimensional CobiT cube framework represents all of an enterprise's IT assets, including its people, the application systems, installed technology, IT facilities, and the value of data. The right-hand side of the framework cube represents the necessary concerns and considerations for all of the resources necessary for the control and administration of enterprise IT resources. Either individually or as groups, these resources should be considered when evaluating controls in an IT environment:

- Applications consisting of both automated user systems and manual or automated procedures to process information
- Information, including input, output, and processed data, for use by business processes
- Technology and facility infrastructure components including hardware, operating systems, databases, networks, and the environments that house and support them
- Key and specialized personnel to plan, organize, acquire, implement, support, monitor, and evaluate IT services

We have started our CobiT description from the right-hand side of the CobiT cube, but internal control considerations always must be considered in terms of how they relate to other components on that side of the CobiT cube as well as with others in this three-dimensional perspective. The point here is that IT resources should always be considered as a key component to IT governance and internal controls.

IT Processes

The second and front-facing dimension of the CobiT cube refers to IT processes and consists of three segments: domains, processes, and activities. Domains are groupings of IT activities that match to organizational areas of responsibility, with four specific domain areas defined in CobiT:

1. **Planning and enterprise.** This domain area covers the strategy and tactics that allow IT to best contribute to and support enterprise business objectives. This type of IT strategic vision message should be communicated throughout the enterprise—the message of IT's mission and what it is trying to accomplish for the overall enterprise.
2. **Acquisition and implementation.** IT solutions need to be identified, developed, or acquired and both implemented and integrated with business processes. This domain area covers changes and maintenance of existing systems.
3. **Delivery and support.** This domain area covers the actual delivery of required services, both application and infrastructure tools. The actual process of application data and controls is covered within this domain.
4. **Monitoring and evaluation.** This area includes control processes, including quality and compliance monitoring, as well as external and internal audit evaluation procedures.

Within an IT enterprise, the process to identify and build new applications—traditionally called systems development life cycle (SDLC) procedures—could be viewed as part of the CobiT implementation domain, and quality assurance could be viewed as part of the monitoring domain. For the planning and enterprise domain, CobiT suggests these specific processes:

■ Define a strategic IT plan.
■ Define the information architecture.
■ Determine technological direction.
■ Define the IT enterprise and relationships.
■ Manage the IT investment.
■ Communicate management aims and direction.
■ Manage human resources.
■ Ensure compliance with external requirements.
■ Assess risks.
■ Manage projects.
■ Manage quality.

Individual processes are the next level down. They are a series of joined activities with natural control breaks. Finally, activities are the actions needed to achieve measurable results. Activities have a life cycle whereas tasks are discrete. We can think of the systems development life cycle (SDLC) process as a cycle where a new application is designed, implemented, operated over time, and then replaced with an improved process.

Business Requirements

The third dimension of the CobiT model consists of business requirements. These seven components should be considered when evaluating all business requirements and with consideration given to the following necessary IT resources and process criteria elements:

1. Effectiveness
2. Efficiency
3. Confidentiality
4. Integrity
5. Availability
6. Compliance
7. Reliability

All IT overall systems or processes should be evaluated with consideration given to one or more of these seven criteria areas. Emphasis will vary, but all IT processes should have elements of one or more of these criteria. For example, for a given IT application, an IT auditor may be concerned about its confidentiality and integrity controls. Business functions typically establish such requirements for their general business needs. For IT applications, each of these attributes is discussed in more detail in the next section as well as in Chapter 8 on planning and performing IT general controls audits.

Similar to the COSO cube internal control model from Chapter 1 and the COSO enterprise risk framework discussed in Chapter 4, the CobiT cube presents an effective way to understand the relationships among business requirements, IT processes, and IT resources. The three-dimensional nature of the model emphasizes the cross relationships and interdependencies between business and IT processes. In our IT-dependent world, this is a useful way for an IT auditor to look at and understand internal controls. CobiT is a rich—sometimes almost too rich—set of processes for focusing on business and IT goals and key controls, and for identifying key measurement metrics. The next sections discuss CobiT in some detail, but the reader is encouraged to consult the ITGI's CobiT reference materials at www.isaca.org for further information.

 ## USING CobiT TO ASSESS INTERNAL CONTROLS

Besides the CobiT cube, with its forward face showing process flow diagrams to emphasize relationships, the published CobiT guidance materials[2] can look formidable to many internal auditors and other business professionals as well as even some IT professionals. The basic CobiT reference material is published in a nearly 200-page manual filled with an array of charts and tables. It is a useful set of materials, but some study may be required to fully understand the concepts behind the CobiT framework. The following sections should help an IT auditor to navigate through the published CobiT framework, and more importantly, use it to develop and assess enterprise internal controls.

Although any dimension of the CobiT cube can be used to understand control environments, the four previously discussed domains, starting with Planning and Enterprise, is an effective first step in the CobiT cube diagram. Based on these initial three CobiT control cube dimensions, each IT process should be evaluated through these five navigation steps:

    I. The control of [*Process Name*]
      II. Which satisfy [*List of Business Requirements*]
        III. By focusing on [*List of important IT goals*]
          IV. Is achieved by [*List of Control Statements*]
            V. And is measured by [*List of key metrics*]

This five-step process dialogue can go from number I on down or can start at the base level and navigate up. In either case, the CobiT framework says that the control of any process should be satisfied by a list of supporting business requirements and that those business goals should focus on important IT goals. This only makes sense. A designated process would just be an idle name unless supported by specific business and IT requirements to drive and govern that process. Each of those requirements should be defined by one or more control statements with specific control practices. Finally, we must assess whether matters are operating effectively, and key measurement metrics are necessary. Although CobiT's emphasis historically has been on IT, this type of analysis should be used for a wide range of internal control–related audits, IT related or not.

Each major control objective described in the published CobiT guidance material is based on the ITGI's navigation framework shown in Exhibit 2.4. The upper left corner of that exhibit shows business requirements. While this is a blank sample, in the published CobiT guidance, each of these requirements are marked with a P to indicate a primary requirement, S for a secondary, or left blank for a not applicable control objective. The lower right-hand corner lists the IT resource areas. If any are applicable, they are noted with a check mark. The lower left-hand corner shows the same pentagon diagram we saw in Exhibit 2.1. Here sections are shaded or marked if they are of primary or secondary importance.

The center of each of the CobiT guidance pages has the "Control over the IT Process of . . . " series of statements completed for each control objective. We will show examples of completed statements as we review the CobiT domains. Even though the CobiT navigation and supporting documentation is thorough and somewhat elegant, it can scare away first-time some auditors. The next sections look at CobiT navigation across various selected domains to give a feel for its organization. Even if auditors are accustomed to using the COSO internal controls framework, they should at least experiment with using CobiT in selected reviews. This chapter provides an introduction and overview to CobiT, its supporting ITGI professional organization has a wide variety of published and educational offerings on the use of CobiT that can be found on previously referenced Web site www.isaca.org.

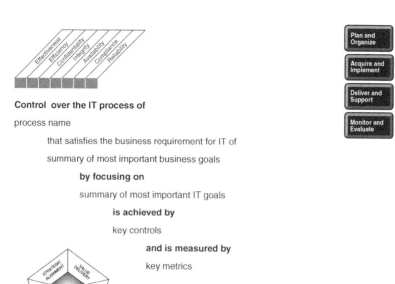

EXHIBIT 2.4 Navigating the CobiT Framework
Source: COBIT 4.1 ©1996–2001 IT Governance Institute. All rights reserved. Used by permission.

Planning and Enterprise

CobiT calls for a high level group of processes that set the direction for the enterprise and its IT resources. For this domain, CobiT has 10 high-level Planning and Organizing (PO) control objectives, defined and numbered as follows:

PO1	Define a Strategic Plan
PO2	Define the Information Architecture
PO3	Determine Technological Direction
PO4	Define IT Process, Enterprise, and Relationships
PO5	Manage the IT Investment
PO6	Communicate Management Aims and Direction
PO7	Manage IT Human Resources
PO8	Manage Quality
PO9	Assess and Manage IT Risks
PO10	Manage Projects

These are all very high-level concepts. Many IT professionals and other managers might say "Of course!" when an internal auditor asks whether they have such a strategic plan, have defined their information architecture, or are in compliance with any of the other high-level PO objectives. However, CobiT drills down into its defined control objective areas in greater detail. While many of the issues are similar, this is in strong contrast to the monitoring element of COSO internal controls as discussed in

Chapter 1. There, the concepts are only at a fairly high level; CobiT is much more specific. For example, using the PO1 control objective on defining a strategic plan, CobiT then expands this to six more detailed objectives:

PO1.1   IT Value Management
PO1.2   Business-IT Alignment
PO1.3   Assessment of Current Performance
PO1.4   IT Strategic Plans
PO1.5   IT Tactical Plans
PO1.6   IT Portfolio Management

The numbering here is important as the published CobiT guidance materials references each of these and other objectives in terms of references to their inputs and outputs. CobiT's published materials provides a high-level description for each of these objectives. For example, the PO1.4 objective on strategic plans states:

Create a strategic plan that defines, in co-operation with the relevant stakeholders, how IT will contribute to the enterprise's strategic objectives (goals) and related costs and risks. It includes how IT will support IT-enabled investment programs and operational service delivery. It defines how the objectives will be met and measures and will receive formal sign-off from the stakeholders. The IT strategic plan should cover investment/operational budget, funding sources, sourcing strategy, acquisition strategy, and legal and regulatory requirements. The strategic plan should be sufficiently detailed to allow the definition of tactical IT plans.

This paragraph is an example of one of the many control objectives outlined throughout the CobiT guidance. All are covered elsewhere. The objectives here do not tell the professional *how* to write an IT strategic plan but do provide excellent guidance to build such a plan, no matter the size or status of the enterprise. These general objectives are also good tools for internal auditors in their needs to build review criteria in any of these areas. IT auditors can develop those audit objectives by taking each sentence of the objectives and developing audit review areas.

For each of the CobiT objectives, the guidance material also contains what is called a supporting RACI chart. A tool that evolved from quality initiatives in the 1960s, RACI charts are good tools to identify roles and responsibilities. Using a spreadsheet format, activities are identified in a side column and functions or position descriptions are located in cells across the top. Responsibilities for those activities are identified in intersecting cells through one or several of the RACI initials:

R = **Responsible** (who owns the problem or process)
A = **Accountable** (who must sign off on the activity before it is effective)
C = **Consulted** (who has the information and/or capability to complete the work)
I = **Informed** (who must be informed of the results but need not be consulted)

This type of chart can be useful in many areas to help identify responsibilities over multiple areas. Exhibit 2.5 is a RACI chart, adapted from CobiT materials, on the PO1 objective to define a strategic IT plan. Going down the column of responsibilities, in this

CobiT PO1 Activities	CEO	CFO	Business Executive	CIO	Process Owner	Head of Operations	Head IT Admin.	Internal Audit
Link Business Goals to IT Goals	C	I	A/R	R	C			
Identify Critical Dependencies and Current Performance	C	C	R	A/R	C	C	C	C
Build an IT Strategic Plan	A	C	C	R	I	C	C	C
Build IT Tactical Plans	C	I		A	C	C	C	I
Analyze Program Portfolios and Manage Service Portfolios	C	I	I	A	R	C	C	I

EXHIBIT 2.5   RACI Chart Example

example, the Business Process Owner acts as a **C**onsultant on linking business goals, building tactical plans, and identifying critical dependencies; is **I**nformed on processes for building the strategic plan; and is **R**esponsible for analyzing program portfolios. The chart outlines responsibilities for such people as the enterprise's head of IT or chief information officer (CIO), the process owner, and internal audit. This type of RACI chart appears in the published guidance for each of the CobiT control objectives.

The CobiT material concludes with a summary analysis of the control objective. This is a metrics-based set of considerations that outlines the activity goals for a given control objective that are measured by key performance indicators (KPIs) that drive process goals and are measured by process-related key goal indicators. The latter drive IT goals that are measured by IT key goal indicators. This CobiT documentation is explained in more detail as we review the other CobiT control objectives.

For the major control objective, the guidance material discusses each PO control objective in the same manner and following the same approach with suggested high-level controls review approaches. However, many of these CobiT items may be found only in larger IT enterprises, although the CobiT guidance material has a range of approaches for each objective. For example, the CobiT objective PO3.5 calls for the need for an enterprise IT architecture board or function. This is valuable guidance, but many smaller IT functions do not have the resources to establish such a formal IT architecture board function. Managers who use CobiT and auditors who evaluate compliance should always remember that CobiT is a set of best practices *guidance* materials, not mandatory requirements. Internal auditors should always use the CobiT guidance with some level of caution, recognizing that CobiT often only specifies some very high-level ideal environments. An auditor reviewing IT general controls in a smaller enterprise who follows CobiT guidance to the letter and recommends such a formal "IT Architecture" board could get laughed out of someone's office.

Acquisition and Implementation

Each of the CobiT high-level control objectives discusses the control procedures in the same general format. Whether it is in-house software development efforts or purchased

IT components, the recommended high-level CobiT acquisition and implementation (AI) objectives are:

AI1   Identify Automated Solutions
AI2   Acquire and Maintain Application Software
AI3   Acquire and Maintain Technology Infrastructure
AI4   Enable Operation and Use
AI5   Procure IT Resources
AI6   Manage Changes
AI7   Install and Accredit Solutions and Changes

Each of the detailed objectives in this domain covers control procedures over the implementation of new tools. Although the emphasis is on IT software, the internal control concepts also can be applied to the acquisition and implementation of many new enterprise tools.

Space does not allow complete coverage of each control objective, but we will examine AI6 on managing change as an example of how CobiT uses its basic framework to outline the importance of this control area. For example, earlier we outlined CobiT's five-step process for evaluating control objectives. The outline for these steps appears in the center of the Exhibit 2.4 navigation page. The AI6 objectives on managing changes follow the same five-step process and are outlined in this way:

I. Control over the IT Process of managing changes
   II. That satisfies the business requirement for IT of responding to business requirements in alignment with business strategy, while reducing solution and delivery defects and rework
   III. By focusing on controlling impact assessment, authorization, and implementation of all changes to the IT infrastructure, applications, and technical solutions, minimizing errors due to incomplete request specifications and halting implementation of unauthorized changes
   IV. Is achieved by
      ▪ Defining and communicating change procedures, including emergency changes
      ▪ Assessing, prioritizing, and authorizing changes
      ▪ Tracking status and reporting on changes
   V. And is measured by
      ▪ Number of disruptions or data errors caused by inaccurate specifications or incomplete impact assessment
      ▪ Application or infrastructure rework caused by inadequate change specifications
      ▪ Percent of changes that follow internal change controls processes.

This series of statements, taken from the CobiT guidance materials, describes the control requirements and measure for this AI6 control objective. The CobiT guidance materials have a similar set of statements for each control objective. This summary of control considerations is useful when attempting to better understand the characteristics of each control.

That same guidance material looks at how each control objective relates to the other two sides of the CobiT cube. For the AI6 managing changes control objective, it indicates that on the IT Resources side, all CobiT defined internal controls are important or have a check mark to help in in understanding this control objective. That is, the control object impacts applications, information, infrastructure, and people. Turning to the upper left side of the navigation sheet business requirements dimension, the guidance material indicates objectives of whether they are of primary, secondary, or of no significant importance. For this AI6 example control objective, the business requirements of effectiveness, efficiency, integrity, and availability are of primary importance while reliability is of secondary importance. The remaining two business requirements, confidentiality and compliance, however are not considered significant to this control objective.

For each control objective, the CobiT guidance material is based on an image of the Exhibit 2.1 focus areas pentagon for the AI6 control objective, and value delivery is of prime importance with resource management secondary. The CobiT guidance material does not provide detailed discussion of the reasons for that designation. Professionals working with the CobiT control objectives usually can deduce why a given IT governance area has been designated as of primary or secondary significance.

Delivery and Support

Following the same general format, the third high-level CobiT control objective is called Delivery and Support (DS). This control objective largely covers service management issues related to the ITIL business process objectives, as discussed in Chapter 7, and highlights some of the changes to our understandings of internal controls that have evolved since the enactment of SOx in 2002. Both CobiT and ITIL were in existence at that time, but the SOx Section 404 emphasis on effective internal controls has brought things together. The CobiT DS control objectives are also similar to the ITIL internal controls to enhance business processes. Both cover the important area of what is known as IT service management, the processes required to ensure efficient IT operations and to deliver these services.

In earlier days, concerns about IT internal controls focused on individual application-by-application controls. Much attention was paid to the higher-level general controls, such as perimeter security or disaster recovery planning, but financial auditors often focused on computational and balancing controls in specific applications. However, no matter how well designed, all such IT applications must operate in an efficient and almost automated process. There will always be smaller problems, such as a legitimate systems user becoming locked out by entering incorrect passwords, and there is a need for efficient service and problem management processes to report and resolve such matters. The CobiT DS control objectives cover many of these important areas:

DS1   Define and Manage Service Levels
DS2   Manage Third-Party Services

DS3   Manage Performance and Capacity
DS4   Ensure Continuous Service
DS5   Ensure Systems Security
DS6   Identify and Allocate Costs
DS7   Educate and Train Users
DS8   Manage Service Desk and Incidents
DS9   Manage the Configuration
DS10   Manage Problems
DS11   Manage Data
DS12   Manage the Physical Environment
DS13   Manage Operations

These control objectives represent important areas of IT operations that historically have not received sufficient attention from IT auditors. The CobiT material looks at each of these objectives in the same general format, summarizing how each control objective is achieved and measured as well as the relationships and interdependencies across all three sides of the CobiT cube.

Many of these control objective areas did not receive sufficient attention in internal controls reviews prior to SOx Section 404 and its Auditing Standard No. 5 (AS 5) rules. COSO objectives address internal controls at a high level but sometimes does not address more detailed service management–related internal control issues. The CobiT DS10 control objective for problem management is an example:

> Effective problem management requires the identification and classification of problems, root cause analysis and resolution of problems. The problem management process also includes identification of recommendations for improvement, maintenance of problem records and review of the status of corrective actions. An effective problem management process improves service levels, reduces costs, and improves customer convenience and satisfaction.

IT users have had problems over the years in reporting problems and seeking resolutions with various systems and applications. Insensitive IT operations staffs frequently did not do an appropriate job in resolving reported problems efficiently. All too often, if an application totally failed, there would be a strong effort to get it back in operation; smaller, less critical problems would be brushed off in a cavalier manner as something to be "considered in the next update."

The published CobiT guidance material links this control objective to others that provide for its inputs as well as outputs. For example, the objectives of AI6 on change authorization, DS8 for incident reporting, DS9 for IT configuration management, and DS13 on error logs all provide inputs to the DS10 control objective. Our purpose is to not reproduce the full contents of all of the published CobiT control objectives but to give the IT auditor a feel for CobiT's approach. Here and for all of the domains and objectives, CobiT provides a powerful way to look at the breadth and depth of these IT-related internal controls and their relationships.

We have discussed how each CobiT control has a series of detailed objectives, has other control inputs and outputs, and has a RACI chart balancing functions and

---

Activity Goals and Metrics

Assigning sufficient authority to problem manager

Performing root cause analysis of reported problems

Analyzing terms

Taking ownership of problems and problem resolution

      are measured by **Key Performance Indicators**

      Average duration between the logging of a problem and identification of root cause.

      % of problems for which root cause analysis was undertaken

      The frequency of reports or updates to an ongoing problem based on its severity.

        drive **Process Goals**

        Record and track operational problems through resolutions.

        Investigate the root cause of all significant problems.

        Define solutions for identified operations problems.

          are measured by **Process Key Goal Indicators**

          % of problems recorded and tracked

          % of problems that recur by time and severity

          % of problems resolved with required time period

          # of open, new, and closed problems by severity

          Average and standard deviation of time lag between problem identification and resolution

          Average and standard deviation of time lag between problem resolution and closure

            drive **IT Goals**

            Ensure satisfaction of end users with service offerings and service levels.

            Reduce solution and service delivery defects and rework.

            Protect the achievement of IT objectives.

              are measured by **IT Key Goal Indicators**

              # of recurring problems with impact on business

              # of business disruptions caused by operational problems

EXHIBIT 2.6   CobiT Example: DS10 Manage Problems Goals and Metrics

---

responsibilities for each control. In addition, the published CobiT guidance materials have a goals and metrics section for each control objective. Exhibit 2.6 shows this goals and metrics chart for the DS10 Manage Problems control objective. Each published CobiT control objective has a similar set of these very useful analyses. With problem management, for example, three suggested measurement metrics should be considered. One is performing root cause analyses of reported problems, which is an important goal that is sometimes missed. The related RACI chart highlights that the problem manager is responsible for this activity with others given a consulting role.

Under each activity goal, a table of KPIs follows that drive a set of process goals. With different specific content for each CobiT control, this type of analysis provides all parties with a good set of standards for measuring the performance of control areas and establishing metrics to assess achievement of these goals. This analysis for our selected control objective of problem management is a good example of the power of the published CobiT materials. Many IT operations have some types of help desk function to report and resolve problems. Here, CobiT provides some good suggestions for the types of measures and metrics that can be used to evaluate the achievement of this control objective.

Similar tables of goals and objectives as well as detailed control objectives exist for each CobiT control objective. These are requirements similar to the SOx Section 404 auditing procedures discussed in Chapter 1 or the internal audit professional practice standards referenced in Chapter 3. However, this set of CobiT materials provides excellent guidance materials for establishing and then measuring effective internal controls. IT auditors should become familiar with CobiT,

Monitoring and Evaluation

The fourth CobiT domain is called Monitoring and Evaluation (ME). This set of control objectives emphasizes CobiT as a closed loop process that effectively never ends. CobiT calls for establishing baseline measures to allow an enterprise to measure how it is performing and to provide the enterprise with future opportunities. This domain area covers quality assurance areas that are traditionally more common to manufacturing and other operations areas than they have been to IT. Although not discussed in the CobiT guidance materials, the pioneering quality assurance work of Edward Deming provides a way of considering this CobiT domain area.

A consultant helping to rebuild Japan in the aftermath of World War II, Deming developed quality standards and approaches that helped Japan rebuild and establish the quality practices that are used worldwide today. Among his approaches, Deming developed a quality system that called for business processes to be analyzed and measured to identify the sources of variations that cause products to deviate from customer requirements. He proposed that business processes be viewed or defined in a continuous feedback loop so that managers could identify and change any parts of the process that needed improvement. This concept defines a continuous, never-ending cycle where we should always monitor current process performance and take actions to implement improvements to that process. Deming called this the Plan, Do, Check Act cycle (PDCA), as shown in Exhibit 2.7. The steps here are:

Step 1. Plan. Business processes should be designed or revised to improve results.
Step 2. Do. Implement to plan and measure its performance.
Step 3. Check. Assess the measurements and report the results.
Step 4. Act. Decide on needed changes to improve results.

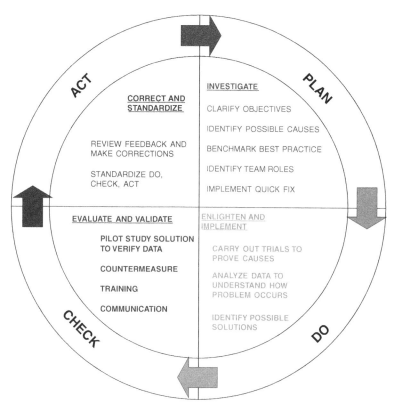

EXHIBIT 2.7 Deming's PDCA Cycle

Source: Robert R. Moeller, *Sarbanes-Oxley Internal Controls: Effective Auditing with AS5, CobiT, and ITIL* (Hoboken, NJ: John Wiley & Sons, 2008). Copyright © 2008 John Wiley & Sons. Reprinted with permission of John Wiley & Sons, Inc.

Although Deming's focus was on postwar reconstruction and on industrial production, his concepts have been carried forward and are very appropriate for today's business environments, including IT operations and SOx internal control monitoring. Chapter 1 discussed the status of SOx today and its continuing monitoring requirements. This CobiT monitoring and evaluation component calls for such continuous monitoring processes.

Following the same format as the other CobiT domains, the ME domain component has four principal control objectives:

ME1   Monitor and Evaluate IT Performance
ME2   Monitor and Evaluate Internal Controls
ME3   Ensure Regulatory Compliance
ME4   Provide IT Governance

This area is of particular interest to internal auditors as well as other members of an enterprise. The control material for ME2 on monitoring and evaluating internal controls is a good example of CobiT's strength. It states that the process of monitoring and evaluating internal control is achieved by defining the system of IT controls embedded in the IT process framework, by monitoring and reporting on the effectiveness of these internal controls, and by reporting exceptions to management for corrective action. This is really the Deming PDCA process just discussed, and it should be measured by:

- ▪ Number of internal control breaches
- ▪ Number of control improvement initiatives
- ▪ Number and coverage of control self-assessments

As with most of the CobiT framework, the material here focuses on IT controls, but many of these concepts can be generalized to an overall internal controls review process. The term *control self-assessments* refers to the process of ongoing internal reviews on the completeness and effectiveness of internal controls.

This CobiT controls objective has seven detailed supporting objectives. These detailed controls have been somewhat abbreviated from the CobiT guidance materials to describe their essence. Although CobiT is oriented to internal reviews of these primarily IT resource areas, this guidance is particularly important for internal auditors in their reviews of IT and all other internal controls:

ME2.1. Monitoring of the Internal Control Framework. IT auditors should continuously monitor the control environment and framework using industry best practices and benchmarking to improve the control environment and framework.

ME2.2. Supervisory Review. In addition to auditor reviews, CobiT calls for management to monitor and report on the effectiveness of IT internal controls through supervisory reviews, including compliance with policies and standards, information security, change controls, and controls established in service-level agreements.

ME2.3. Control Exceptions. Record information regarding all control exceptions and ensure that it leads to analysis of the underlying cause and to corrective action. Management should decide which exceptions should be communicated to the individual responsible for the function and which exceptions should be escalated.

ME2.4. Control Self-Assessments. IT management should evaluate the completeness and effectiveness of the internal controls over IT processes, policies, and contracts through a continuing program of self-assessment.

ME2.5. Assurance of Internal Control. IT operations should obtain, as needed, further assurance of the completeness and effectiveness of internal controls through third-party reviews by the corporate compliance function, internal audit, outside consultants, or certification bodies.

ME2.6. Internal Control at Third Parties. Assess the status of each internal external provider's internal controls and confirm they comply with legal and regulatory requirements and contractual obligations.

ME2.7. Remedial Actions. Identify and initiate remedial actions based on the controls assessments and reporting. This includes follow-up of all assessments including: (1) review, negotiation, and establishment of management responses; (2) assignment of responsibility for remediation or risk acceptance; and (3) tracking the results of the actions taken.

These CobiT control objectives are described as "detailed" but provide openings for a wide range of even more detailed control procedures. For example, ME2.1 on Monitoring the Internal Control Framework requires IT auditors or other internal controls specialists to develop detailed control procedures that typically may result in a program of many more tests or steps.

This CobiT control objective, as well as all of the others in the supporting documentation, has a section on assessing the maturity of each internal control. *Maturity* here refers to the Capability Maturity Model for Integration (CMMI), introduced in Chapter 11, and a five-level assessment measure designed and developed by Carnegie Mellon University.[3] The model has defined levels for when controls can be assessed from a CMMI level 1 of nonexistent, level 2 as initial or ad hoc controls all the way to level 5, called optimized controls. CobiT rates each of its controls against this CMMI measure. For example, CobiT defines that an enterprise will be at level 3, defined process controls for ME2, Monitor and Evaluate Internal Controls, when management supports and has institutionalized internal control monitoring. The guidance goes on to say that policies and procedures should have been developed for processing and reporting internal control monitoring activities. To achieve this CMMI level, an educational and monitoring program for internal control evaluations should have been defined. CMMI is discussed in greater detail in Chapter 11.

We have shown this limited extract for ME2, but the published CobiT materials also have a similar limited set of CMMI maturity level guidance materials for each of their internal controls. Although summarized at a very high level, these maturity model guidelines allow an enterprise to assess how it is doing with regard to each of CobiT's internal controls.

 ## USING CobiT IN A SOx ENVIRONMENT

When SOx first became effective in the United States, there was little guidance on how to implement and manage its Section 404 internal controls reviews. The Public Company Accounting Oversight Board initially indicated that they were going to establish some specific standards but initially left enterprises and their external auditors on their own. With its heavy emphasis on high-level IT-oriented internal controls, many enterprises adopted CobiT as the internal control framework of choice. This section reviews using the CobiT framework to help achieve SOx compliance.

Chapter 1 discussed SOx Section 404 internal controls assessment requirements and highlighted risk-based approaches for evaluating internal controls with an emphasis on the COSO internal controls framework. CobiT is a powerful alternative internal controls assessment framework, particularly in environments with a heavy concentration of IT processes and resources. As discussed, both COSO internal controls and CobiT use three-dimensional frameworks to describe their internal control environments. Each is similar,

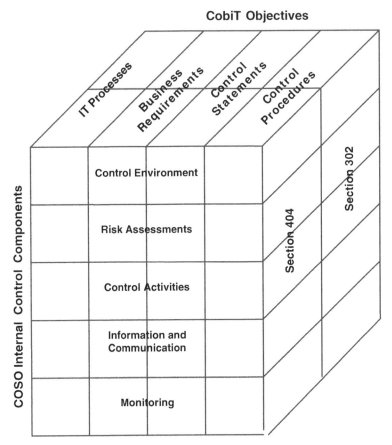

EXHIBIT 2.8   Relationship between COSO Components and CobiT Objectives

but with slight differences in classifications and terminology. Exhibit 2.8 shows how the CobiT framework maps to the COSO internal controls model. CobiT's prime objectives, from Planning and Enterprise to Monitoring and Evaluation, can be used to understand and evaluate internal controls through COSO's five internal control components. Whether considering COSO internal controls in general or when using CobiT, an internal auditor should move through a series processes from planning to performing risk assessments and on to identifying, documenting, and evaluating key internal controls.

With SOx, the industry-wide increased emphasis on IT governance and the recognition of the criticality of IT in most internal control decisions, CobiT has gone through multiple revisions up through its current 4.1 edition. CobiT's sponsoring IT Governance Institute has been doing an excellent job releasing publications that map the CobiT framework to these other standards. For example, a very detailed study maps the CobiT framework to SOx audit requirements.[4] Exhibit 2.9 is an extract of this published CobiT guidance showing how major CobiT control objective areas links with the major COSO components of internal control. This link-up ties together even better by going a level lower. For example, CobiT objective AI6, Managing Changes, under the Acquire and

	COSCO Components				
	Control Environment	Risk Assessment	Control Activities	Information and Communication	Monitoring
Plan & Organize COSO Control Objective					
Define a strategic IT plan		X		X	X
Define the information architecture			X	X	
Determine technological direction					
Define the IT organization and relationships	X			X	
Manage the IT investment					
Communicate management aims and directions	X			X	X
Manage human resources	X			X	
Ensure compliance with external relationships			X	X	X
Assess risks		X			
Manage projects					
Manage quality	X		X	X	X
Acquire and Implement COSO Control Objective					
Identify automated solutions					
Acquire and maintain application software			X		
Acquire and maintain technology infrastructure			X		
Develop and maintain procedures			X	X	
Install and accredit			X		
Manage changes			X		X
Deliver and Support COSO Control Objective					
Define and manage service levels	X		X		X
Manage third-party services	X	X	X		X
Manage performance and capacity	X		X		
Ensure continuous service	X		X		X
Ensure systems security	X		X	X	X
Identify and allocate costs	X		X	X	X
Educate and train users	X		X		
Assist and advise customers					
Manage the configuration	X		X	X	
Manage problems and incidents			X	X	X
Manage data			X	X	
Manage facilities			X		
Manage operations			X	X	
Monitor and Evaluate COSO Control Objective					
Monitor the processes				X	X
Assess internal control adequacy					X
Obtain independent assurance	X				X
Provide for independent audit					

EXHIBIT 2.9   COSO and CobiT Relationships

Implement control domain impacts the COSO components of Control Activities and Monitoring. The current published CobiT detailed control objectives tie to each of these COSO components and the current version of CobiT is in draft form at this time of publication.

There is a close relationship between these CobiT and COSO control objectives and components.

The full set of CobiT control objectives materials will provide strong support for an internal auditor performing a SOx Section 404 internal controls assessment review. Although the concepts can be used in any internal control area, the emphasis is on IT applications and processes. For many enterprises, an understanding and assessment of those IT-associated internal controls is key to achieving SOx compliance. CobiT has been around for some years now, but too many have viewed it as just a specialized IT audit tool, and not a more general help for other internal audit work. Although CobiT's emphasis continues to be on IT, all internal auditors should explore the CobiT framework as a tool for helping with current and evolving SOx compliance requirements.

CobiT ASSURANCE FRAMEWORK GUIDANCE

The CobiT framework provides guidance for establishing effective internal controls with an emphasis on IT resources. In 2008 the ITGI released its Information Technology Assurance Framework (ITAF^{TM})[5] guidance, a good-practice-setting model to provide guidance on the design, conduct, and reporting of IT audit and assurance assignments. The objective of this guidance is to establish standards that address IT audit and assurance professional roles and responsibilities; knowledge and skills; and diligence, conduct, and reporting requirements. This new CobiT guidance focuses on another perhaps soon to be common audit-related word, *assurance*.

This term is also found in IIA basic references that state: "Internal auditing is an independent, objective assurance and consulting activity designed to add value and improve an organization's operations. It helps an organization accomplish its objectives by bringing a systematic, disciplined approach to evaluate and improve the effectiveness of risk management, control, and governance processes." Assurance services cover all forms of internal auditing, risk management, and compliance services. This CobiT guidance covers a wide range of reviews performed by an internal auditor.

The overall objective of ITAF is to define a set of standards to help ensure the quality, consistency, and reliability of IT assessments, based on a set of good-practice-setting guidelines and procedures. Although the ITAF document refers to its guidance as "standards," CobiT's ISACA professional organization is not recognized as widely as the IIA's International Standards for the Professional Practice of Internal Auditing. Chapter 3 outlines the IIA Standards and summarizes the CobiT-related ITAF Standards. We mention the new ITAF Standards to highlight the fact that internal auditing standards are being developed to help with reviews in a CobiT environment. However, internal auditors should understand that ITAF is new; and it may achieve more recognition as it becomes better accepted and perhaps fine-tuned.

CobiT IN PERSPECTIVE

Whether operational, financial, or IT specialists, all internal auditors should have at least a high-level understanding of the CobiT framework. It is a particularly useful tool for assessing internal controls in a more IT-oriented environment—the type of environment that we almost always encounter today. The decision to use CobiT in internal audits should not be a one-time or individual audit–level decision. Rather, internal audit should train key members of the audit team in the use of CobiT and then try using it to assess internal controls on some other audit currently being developed and documented using the IT audit techniques discussed in Chapters 8 and 10.

Unfortunately, the IIA hasn't really given proper reference to CobiT and its IIA members. Although the IIA now has some good internal audit standards for its members, as discussed in Chapter 3, the IIA Standards do not come close to CobiT as a tool for helping to define and understand IT controls. All IT auditors should understand and use CobiT.

If internal audit feels that CobiT will offer some improvements to ongoing audit processes, the concept should first be discussed with the audit committee to explain reasons for changing internal audit approaches. If the enterprise places a heavy reliance on IT systems and processes, using CobiT seems to be a good logistical move. However, an overall internal audit function should avoid having IT internal audit specialists use CobiT assessment processes while the rest of internal audit uses established operational/financial internal audit standards.

CobiT is an elegant—sometimes even too elegant—internal control framework and evaluation tool for assessing internal controls. Perhaps the largest impediment to its overall use is that CobiT was originally constructed as primarily an IT audit tool. Although the move from ISACA to the ITGI sponsorship has broadened its appeal and focus, the published CobiT guidance materials have a very heavy IT focus. This focus sometimes scares away some potential users.

The real strength of CobiT is its IT governance focus, as described in Exhibit 2.1. That exhibit illustrates the importance of the strategic alliance of business and IT resources with value delivery, resource management, risk management, and performance measurement processes. All five of these areas allow an enterprise to establish effective IT governance, and CobiT should help in managing and understanding these concepts. We can expect CobiT published standards and practices to continue to broaden and go beyond just "IT audit" special concepts. All internal auditors should learn to use and understand the CobiT internal controls assessment framework.

 ## NOTES

1. IT Governance Institute, *CobiT—Governance, Control and Audit for Information and Related Technology*, 4th ed. (Rolling Meadows, IL: Author, 2000).
2. IT Governance Institute, *CobiT 4.1* (Rolling Meadows, IL: Author, 2007).
3. Capability Maturity Model® Integration (CMMI) is a Carnegie Mellon University–developed process improvement approach that provides organizations with the essential

elements of effective processes. It can be used to guide process improvement across a project, a division, or an entire organization.

4. IT Governance Institute, *IT Control Objectives for Sarbanes-Oxley,* 2nd ed. (Rolling Meadows, IL: Author, September 2006).

5. IT Governance Institute, *ITAFTM: A Professional Practices Framework for IT Assurance* (Rolling Meadows, IL: Author, 2008).

CHAPTER THREE

IIA and ISACA Standards for the Professional Practice of Internal Auditing

E VERY PROFESSION REQUIRES A set of standards to govern its practices, general procedures, and ethics. These standards allow specialists performing similar work to call themselves professionals in their area of expertise. The key standards for all internal auditors are the Institute of Internal Auditors' (IIA's) International Professional Standards for the Practice of Internal Auditing, a set of guidance materials that in the pre-Web paper-document days were known as the *Red Book* by many internal auditors. These standards have gone through multiple revisions over the years and more recently have been issued in a set of internal audit mandatory and guidance materials known as the International Professional Practices Framework (IPPF).

Although the IIA Standards have been in place for many years, 2008 brought some significant new changes to internal audit standards. Standards that in the past were more guidance directed, stating that an internal auditor "should" do something, now are far more definitive and specify practice areas where an internal auditor "must." This chapter summarizes the current IIA Standards and provides guidance on how they apply to today's information technology (IT) auditor. An understanding of the IIA's *International Standards for the Professional Practice of Internal Auditing* is an absolute *must* requirement for IT and all other internal auditors. These standards and the IPPF provide the support for many if not nearly all internal audit professional activities.

We also summarize the IT auditing standards of the Information Systems and Control Association (ISACA). As discussed in Chapter 2 on the Control Objectives for Information and related Technology (CobiT) framework, ISACA is the leading professional organization for IT auditors. ISACA's IT audit standards complement the IIA Standards but are much more technically specific. These standards are relatively new, compared to the IIA Standards; the first ISACA standards were released in the late 1990s. A full set of these IT audit–specific standards now exists, which is essential for IT auditing activities.

This chapter focuses on these important IIA and ISACA standards for IT auditing. Some other, but often less significant, IT audit–related standards in place that are not included in this chapter. For example, Chapter 31 outlines the American Society for Quality (ASQ) internal audit standards; the guidance is important but is effectively subservient to the IIA international standards. ASQ's internal audit standards and its quality auditors represent a different dimension and discipline from the IIA's approaches and standards. It also represents an area that must be better represented and understood in the overall world of internal auditing.

Of course, a different set of standards also impacts auditors involved in external auditing—public accountants—whether financial or IT audit related. Outside of the Sarbanes-Oxley Act (SOx) rules highlighted in Chapter 1, public accounting IT audit standards are beyond this book's scope.

We also visit the IIA code of ethics for internal auditors, an important supporting foundation for internal auditors in today's world of frequent questions regarding professional ethics. And we also consider the ISACA's code of ethics. Most ISACA members are IT audit specialists who are often IIA or Certified Public Accountants (CPAs). The ISACA code of ethics places a special emphasis on their IT-related activities.

The IIA's *International Standards for the Professional Practice of Internal Auditing* represent a must-know set of information for all internal auditors today, whether they are IT specialists or not. Similarly, IT auditors should have a good understanding of the very complementary ISACA standards. Although any standards are evolving sets of rules that may not exactly reflect all industry practices at a point in time, the IIA and ISACA standards define a set of guidelines for internal auditors worldwide to follow in their service to management. The new IIA *International Standards for the Professional Practice of Internal Auditing*, summarized here, are available from the IIA.[1] They represent important guidance for today's internal auditor and should be in every internal auditor's professional library.

INTERNAL AUDITING'S INTERNATIONAL PROFESSIONAL PRACTICE STANDARDS

Internal auditors work in a large variety of enterprises and are asked to perform internal audit reviews in a number of operational, financial, and IT-related areas. Despite this diversity, an enterprise audit committee and senior management expects internal auditors to perform reviews in a competent and consistent manner. Internal audits performed using a set of recognized standards are a key approach to meet those management expectations. As the premier and leading worldwide internal audit professional enterprise, the IIA develops and issues standards that define the basic practice of internal auditing. Its *International Standards for the Professional Practice of Internal Auditing* is designed to:

▪ Delineate basic principles for the practice of internal auditing.
▪ Provide a framework for performing and promoting a broad range of value-added internal audit activities.

■ Establish the basis for the measurement of internal audit performance.

■ Foster improved organizational processes and operations

The IIA Standards aid in this process; they provide a guideline both for the audit committee and management to measure their internal auditors as well as for internal auditors to measure themselves. Although the overall emphasis of this book is on IT audit, security, and control issues, because the IIA Standards and the ISACA standards set some constraints on all internal audit activities, whether IT related or not, they both are discussed here.

Background of the IIA Standards

Internal auditing is a profession that developed its own standards and processes over the years. Its professional organization, the Institute of Internal Auditors, first issued standards for what was called the Professional Practice of Internal Auditing in 1978 with an objective "to serve the entire profession in all types of business, in various levels of government, and in all other enterprises where internal auditors are found . . . to represent the practice of internal auditing." Prior to these 1978 Standards, the most authoritative document was called the Statement of Responsibilities of Internal Audit, a statement originally issued by the IIA in 1947 and revised many times over the years.

The IIA Standards are developed by the IIA's Professional Standards Committee based on members' own professional expertise as well as comments from IIA members and other interested parties. Because of the diverse group of participants who developed the earlier Standards, their final language often had some overlap, compromise, and incompleteness. The early IIA Standards were often weak in IT-related audit issues; that area has been strengthened through supporting practice advisories and guides.

All internal auditors today, as IIA members, are expected to follow these standards. Internal auditors may also come from other professional areas, such as banking or external audit firms, and many disciplines have their own professional standards that, generally, are not in conflict with the IIA Standards. They may use slightly different terminology, as will be discussed with the ISACA code of ethics, but must follow audit practices that generally fit under the IIA Standards. As a matter of practice, however, the IIA's *International Standards for the Professional Practice of Internal Auditing* governs the work of internal auditors worldwide, and it is important to understand them. When there appears to be a conflict and when the individual questioning that conflict is working as an internal auditor, the IIA's Standards take precedence over any other professional standards.

The IIA has historically published its standards in a small publication known as the *Red Book*. With a changing world and impressions of the role of internal auditors, these Standards have changed. The older IIA Standards, up through the year 2004 releases, contained an almost impossible level of detail. For example, an older general auditing standard on audit follow-up procedures guidance for completed audits had 23 individual sub- or sub-subclarifying standards. The IIA Standards have always contained good general guidance, but those older Standards were often far too specific. For example, a substandard of that older section 440.01.12.a stated: the "Director of Internal Audit must establish the procedures for the time frame in which audit report responses are required." Although certainly a valid guideline, it does little good to tell an auditee that IIA Standards "require" that audit report responses must be delivered in 7 days if the response is that it will take 10 days. This is just one small example. Many of the older IIA Standards were almost too detailed for effective internal audit management. In addition, those older standards had little to say about IT-related internal controls issues. The IIA Standards of past years were complex, sometimes difficult to implement, and often followed only in a broad, haphazard manner. The current IIA Standards provide a much more realistic set of guidance materials to allow an internal audit function to perform effectively and efficiently.

There was a major change to the IIA Standards in 2004 with revisions that permitted internal auditors to act as in-house consultants as well as in their traditional attest role as auditors. These changes codified the supporting role of many IT auditors who, because of their specialized IT security and control knowledge, often acted as internal IT consultants to their enterprises. Earlier Standards, going back to the first days of internal auditing, prohibited internal auditors from acting as consultants. This prohibition was often ignored, but the 2004 revisions clarified this issue and divided IIA Standards into those covering internal audit assurance activities and others for internal audit consulting work.

IIA's Current Standards: What Has Changed

IIA Standards are updated regularly to reflect current needs by both business and practicing internal audit professionals. For example, because of expressed professional concerns about the quality of some internal audit functions, in 2007 the standards were revised to add Attribute Standard 1312 on External Assessments:

> External assessments must be conducted at least once every five years by a qualified, independent reviewer or review team from outside the organization. The potential need for more frequent external assessments as well as the qualifications and independence of the external reviewer or review team, including any potential conflict of interest, must be discussed by the CAE [chief audit executive] with the Board. Such discussions must also consider the size, complexity and industry of the organization in relation to the experience of the reviewer or review team.

This was a *significant change* to internal auditing standards. This new standard calls for a qualified external reviewing to visit an internal audit function to review its quality procedures and standards. The IIA publishes practice advisories on all of its standards, including this change. For external reviews, two practice advisories outline detailed requirements for reviewers; one requirement is that an external review team should consist of individuals who are competent in the professional practice of internal auditing and the external assessment process. The advisories cover all aspects of this significant change to internal audit practices.

This 2007 IIA Standards requirement for independent quality assurance reviews was a major change to internal audit practices. Nevertheless, at the time of this publication, it has not been actively embraced by all internal audit functions. The once-every-five-year requirement does not have strong beginning and end date requirements; nor does it make any allowances for the size of the enterprise. For example, when the SOx Section 404 requirements were first released, compliance dates were staggered by the size of the enterprise and whether it was domestic or foreign. However, the IIA has established peer review processes. Other internal auditors have volunteered to conduct independent quality assurance reviews, and an increasing number of consulting firms advertising through the Web are offering these services. All internal auditors should be aware of the quality review requirements.

In January 2009, the IIA released a major revision to its standards. These changes are significant in that they revise the standards requirements from stating practice areas that an internal auditor *should* do to stating that an internal auditor *must* do something. For example and with the change emphasized in bold italics, the older Standard 1100 on internal auditor Independence and Objectivity stated: "The internal audit activity ***should*** be independent, and internal auditors ***should*** be objective in performing their work."

The new revisions state: "The internal audit activity ***must*** be independent, and internal auditors ***must*** be objective in performing their work." The required change is significant whenever IT internal auditors state that their work is in compliance with internal auditing standards. The next sections provide a summary of the IIA international standards, with an emphasis on those have the most impact on IT auditors. These standards set the rules for all internal audit activity, whether the auditor is performing internal audits, serving as an internal consultant, or managing the overall internal audit function.

CONTENT OF THE IPPF AND THE IIA INTERNATIONAL STANDARDS

The IIA's IPPF, as shown in Exhibit 3.1, is divided into sets of mandatory and strongly recommended guidance materials. The mandatory standards are the upper three sectors of this diagram starting with audit definitions, the International Standards, the IIA code of ethics all on top. These top segments define the he basic definition of internal auditing:

> Internal auditing is an independent, objective assurance and consulting activity designed to add value and improve an organization's operations. It helps an organization accomplish its objectives by bringing a systematic, disciplined approach to evaluate and improve the effectiveness of risk management, control, and governance processes.

This definition defines what internal auditors do on a very high level. Although this basis standard has been in place for many years, some managers historically looked at their internal auditors as little more than accounting clerks or assistants to their external auditors. With its emphasis on being an objective assurance and consulting activity, this definition defines internal auditor tasks and expectations.

Mandatory Guidance

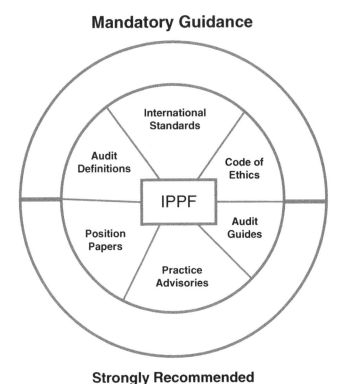

Strongly Recommended

EXHIBIT 3.1   IIA International Professional Practices Framework

The lower three segments of the exhibit show three strongly recommended internal audit standards: position papers, practice advisories, and practice guides. These IIA published materials describe approaches to assist internal auditors in employing IIA Standards.

The internal audit International Standards consist of Attribute and Performance Standards. The Attribute Standards address the characteristics of enterprises and parties performing internal audit activities, while the Performance Standards describe the nature of internal audit activities and provide quality criteria against which the performance of these services can be evaluated. These Attribute and Performance Standards apply to all internal audit services; other assurance and consulting Implementation Standards apply to specific types of engagements. This split in types of internal audit standards reflects the fact that internal auditors sometimes do strictly audit assurance projects, such as reviewing internal control effectiveness in some area, and sometimes do work related to internal audit consulting.

The Attribute Standards are numbered in sections as part of the number 1000 Series of Standards, while Performance Standards are classified in the 2000 Series. Implementation Standards, further designated as (A) for assurance and coded with an "A" following the standard number (e.g., 1130.A1) or (C) for consulting and noted by a "C" following the standard number (e.g., nnnn.C1), are organized under each of these

Attribute and Performance standards. The next sections describe the Attribute and Performance standards in some detail as well as some of the descriptive Implementation Standards. Recognizing that internal auditors may be asked to review internal controls or to act more as internal consultants, multiple sets of Implementation Standards may apply: a set for each of the major types of internal audit activity.

Exhibits 3.2 and 3.3 summarize the IIA Attribute and Performance standards by their numbers along with brief descriptions. Our objective here is not to just reproduce all of these IIA published standards but to describe some that are more significant to IT auditors. All internal auditors, however, should obtain a copy of the standards from the IIA and develop a good understanding of their contents. Knowledge of these standards is a requirement for all internal auditors, and the IIA Web site (theiia.org) is an official source for these IIA internal audit standards.

Internal Audit Attribute Standards

Attribute Standards address the characteristics of enterprises and individuals performing internal audit activities. Numbered from paragraph 1000 to 13000, they cover broad areas that define the attributes or characteristics of today's internal auditor. Here, and for the Performance Standards later in the chapter, we list and describe selected standards (listed by their standards paragraph numbers), and offer comments when appropriate.

1000—Purpose, Authority, and Responsibility. The purpose, authority, and responsibility of the internal audit activity should be formally defined in an internal audit charter, consistent with these standards, and approved by the board of directors. Separate Implementation Standards state that internal auditing assurance and consulting services must be defined in the internal audit charter. This standard is supported by substandards defining an internal auditor's purpose, authority, and responsibility roles when serving in assurance and in consulting roles.

    1010—Recognition of the Definition of Internal Auditing. This standard was released in 2009 and emphasizes the importance of the IIA Standards, the code of ethics, and an internal audit charter in outlining internal audit's roles and responsibilities. This is the type of standard that an internal auditor can use when about defining internal audit's role in an enterprise. Audit charters are a key component that defines an internal audit group.[2]

1100—Independence and Objectivity. The internal audit activity must be independent, and internal auditors must be objective in performing their work. Subsections discuss the importance of both individual and organizational objectivity as well as the need to disclose any impairment to internal audit independence or objectivity.

    1110—Organizational Independence. Although the IIA International Standards do not specify that internal audit should report to the audit committee, that reporting relationship must be free from any interference in determining the scope of internal auditing, performing work, and communicating results. We often think of internal audit as a key component in today's SOx-defined

Standard #		Description
1000		Purpose, Authority and Responsibility
	1000.A1	Purpose, Authority and Responsibility for Assurance
	1000.C1	Purpose, Authority and Responsibility for Consulting
1010		Recognition of the Definition of Internal Auditing, the Code of Ethics, and the Standards in the Internal Audit Charter
1100		Independence and Objectivity
1110		Organizational Independence
	1110.A1	Interference
1111		Direct Interaction with the Board
1120		Individual Objectivity
1130		Impairment to Independence or Objectivity
	1130.A1	Impairment due to former responsibilities
	1130.A2	Audit of functions for which CAE is responsible
	1130.C1	Scope of impairment for consulting
	1130.C2	Disclosure of impairment when consulting
1200		Proficiency and Due Professional Care
1210		Proficiency
	1210.A1	CAE acquiring necessary assurance engagement competencies
	1210.A2	Identification of fraud indicators
	1210.A3	Information technology risk controls and tools
	1210.C1	CAE acquiring necessary consulting engagement competencies
1220		Due Professional Care
	1220.A1	Scoping for assurance engagements
	1220.A2	Use of technology-based audit techniques
	1220.A3	Risk identification
	1220.C1	Scoping for consulting engagements
1230		Continuing Professional Development
1300		Quality Assurance and Improvement Program
1310		Requirements for Quality Assurance and Improvement Program
1311		Internal Assessment
1312		External Assessment
1320		Reporting on the Quality Assurance and Improvement Program
1321		Use of conformance with IIA Standards
1322		Disclosure of Nonconformance

EXHIBIT 3.2　IIA Attribute Standards Summary

	Standard #		Description
2000			Managing the Internal Audit Activity
	2010		Planning
		2010.A1	Annual risk assessment
		2010.C1	Acceptance of consulting engagements
	2020		Communication and Approval
	2030		Resource Management
	2040		Policies and Procedures
	2050		Coordination
	2060		Reporting to Sr. Management and the Board
2100			Nature of Work
	2110		Governance
		2110.A1	Evaluation of ethics programs
		2110.A2	Assessing information technology governance
		2110.C1	Consistency of ethics and values when consulting
	2120		Risk Management
		2120.A1	Evaluating organization's risk exposure
		2120.A2	Evaluating fraud risks
		2120.C1	Reviewing risks during consulting
		2120.C2	Risk knowledge obtained during consulting
		2120.C3	Limitations of involvement in risk management
	2130		Control
		2130.A1	Evaluating the adequacy and effectiveness of controls
		2130.A2	Assessing achievement of goals and objectives
		2130.A3	Assessing consistency of results with goals and objectives
		2130.C1	Reviewing controls when consulting
		2130.C2	Knowledge of controls gained from consulting engagements
2200			Engagement Planning
	2201		Planning Considerations
		2201.A1	Planning engagements with external parties
		2201.C1	Agreement with clients on engagement scope and objectives
	2210		Engagement Objectives
		2210.A1	Preliminary assessment of risks
		2210.A2	Probability of significant errors and other exposures
		2210.A3	Setting criteria to evaluate controls
		2210.C1	Focusing consulting on governance, risk management and control
	2220		Engagement Scope
		2220.A1	Scope of assurance engagement
		2220.A2	Consulting opportunities during assurance engagement
		2220.C1	Scope of consulting engagement
	2230		Engagement Resource Allocation

(Continued)

EXHIBIT 3.3   IIA Performance Standards Summary

	Standard #		Description
	2240		Engagement Work Programs
		2240.A1	Procedure for managing information
		2240.C1	Work program for consulting engagements
2300			Performing the Engagement
	2310		Identifying Information
	2320		Analysis and Evaluation
	2330		Documenting Information
		2330.A1	Controlling access to engagement records
		2330.A2	Retention requirements
		2330.C1	Information retention and release policies for consulting
	2340		Engagement Supervision
2400			Communicating Results
	2410		Criteria for Communicating
		2410.A1	Final communications of engagement results
		2410.A2	Acknowledgement of satisfactory performance
		2410.A3	Releasing results to parties outside the organization
		2410.C1	Communicating results of consulting engagements
	2420		Quality of Communications
	2421		Errors and Omissions
	2430		Use of conformance with IIA Standards
	2431		Engagement Disclosure of Nonconformance
	2440		Disseminating Results
		2440.A1	CAE responsibility for communication of results
		2440.A2	Assessment of conditions for releasing results to outsiders
		2440.C1	CAE responsibility for communication of consulting results
		2440.C2	Communication of significant issues identified when consulting
2500			Monitoring Progress
		2500.A1	Establishing a follow-up process
		2500.C1	Monitoring exposition of results for consulting engagements
2600			Resolution of Senior Management's Acceptance of Risk

EXHIBIT 3.3   (*Continued*)

corporate world with board audit committees, but internal audit can operate in many different international locations or for many different types of enterprises. Whether serving a not-for-profit organization in the United States or a governmental agency in a developing country, internal audit always must exhibit organizational independence.

1120—Individual Objectivity. This standard repeats a basic principle of internal auditing: Internal auditors must have an impartial, unbiased attitude and avoid conflicts of interest.

1130—Impairments to Independence or Objectivity. If internal audit's independence or objectivity is impaired in fact or appearance, the details of the impairment must be disclosed as part of the audit work. The impairment could be a management-imposed impairment or one due to the background of or other circumstances regarding an individual internal auditor. There are several Assurance and Consulting attribute standards here, but one summarizes this standard:

> **1130.A1 and 1130.C1**—Internal auditors should refrain from assessing specific operations for which they were previously responsible. Objectivity is presumed to be impaired if an internal auditor provides either assurance or consulting services for an activity for which the internal auditor had responsibility within the previous year.

These first standards are important. Because of their specialized knowledge, internal auditors sometimes are asked to go back to the group where they once worked to audit it or act as a consultant. No matter how impartial they may try to act, others will not view them as objective.

1200—Proficiency and Due Professional Care. Engagements must be performed with proficiency and due professional care. There are two important proposed new Implementation Standards here:

> **1210.A1**—The chief audit executive should obtain competent advice and assistance if the internal audit staff lacks the knowledge, skills, or other competencies needed to perform all or part of the engagement.

> **1210.A2**—An internal auditor must have sufficient knowledge to identify the indicators of fraud and the manner in which it is managed by the organization, but the auditor is not expected to have the expertise of a person whose primary responsibility is detecting and investigating fraud.

Even though many IT auditors are not regularly involved in fraud-related issues, this fraud-related guidance is weak. The American Institute of Certified Public Accountants (AICPA) Statement of Accounting Standards No. 99 external audit standard requires external auditors to aggressively think about "red flags," that are indicators that might include the possibility of fraud, as well as to look for potential fraud in the course of their audits. Although this AICPA guidance is certainly not an IIA professional standards decision, internal auditors should maintain a greater awareness about the possibility of fraud in the course of their internal audits. IT internal auditors are often the best investigators to find these circumstances. Chapter 21 discusses such fraud detection and prevention activities from an IT audit perspective.

> **1210.A3**—Internal auditors must have sufficient knowledge of key IT risks and controls and available technology-based audit techniques to perform their assigned work. However, not all internal auditors are expected to have the expertise of an IT or technical auditor whose primary responsibility is IT auditing. This standard on the importance of IT auditing provides support to many other issues discussed throughout this book.

> **1210.C1**—The CAE must decline consulting engagements or obtain competent advice and assistance if the internal auditors lack the knowledge, skills, or other competencies needed to perform all or part of a consulting engagement. Recognizing there is a need for IT audit specialists, the A1 and A3 Assurance

Standards as well as C1 covering consulting are all important in IT-related environments.

This standard says that *all* internal auditors *must have sufficient knowledge of key IT risks and controls* and available technology-based audit techniques to perform their assigned work (emphasis added). All internal auditors should have some level of IT-controls related knowledge and should reserve their more technical issues for IT audit specialists. If an internal audit function lacks sufficient technical knowledge, the CAE should ensure that all members have that knowledge, through training, or bring in consultants to provide support.

1220—Due Professional Care. Internal auditors must use due professional care and act in a reasonably prudent and competent manner when performing all internal audit activities. Due professional care does not imply infallibility. Another section of this standard states that in exercising due professional care, an internal audit must consider:

- ▪ Extent of work needed to achieve the engagement's objectives.
- ▪ Relative complexity, materiality, or significance of matters to which assurance procedures are applied.
- ▪ Adequacy and effectiveness of risk management, control, and governance processes.
- ▪ Probability of significant errors, irregularities, or noncompliance.
- ▪ Cost of assurance in relation to potential benefits.

This IIA standard really says that an internal auditor must be cautious in beginning and performing an internal audit. The first of the previous bullet points regarding the extent of work says that an internal auditor, for example, must perform an adequate level of investigation and testing before making a final audit recommendation. Computer-assisted audit tools and techniques are discussed as part of the new standards released in 2004:

1220.A2—In exercising due professional care, the internal auditor must consider the use of technology based audit tools and other data analysis techniques. This guidance very much relates to the importance of computer-assisted audit tools and techniques discussed in Chapter 13.

1220.A3—The internal auditor must be alert to the significant risks that might affect objectives, operations, or resources. However, assurance procedures alone, even when performed with due professional care, do not guarantee that all significant risks will be identified. As discussed in Chapter 4 on risk management, an understanding of risk assessment techniques is an important knowledge area for internal auditors. This guidance has been part of the IIA Standards going back to the early versions and should be part of an internal auditor's procedures.

The standards continue in this section with 1230—Continuing Professional Development, a standard on the requirement for continuing professional education and development.

1300—Quality Assurance and Improvement Program. An internal audit function must develop and maintain a quality assurance and improvement program that covers all aspects of activities and continuously monitors its effectiveness. The quality assurance and improvement program must be designed to enable an evaluation of the internal audit activity's conformance with Internal Auditing Standards as well as an evaluation of whether internal auditors apply the code of ethics. The program also assesses the efficiency and effectiveness of the internal audit activity and identifies opportunities for improvement.

The standards here call for both internal and external quality reviews and emphasize the importance of good-quality assurance processes within internal audit. Quality assurance activities as well as quality audits are discussed in Chapter 31. Six supporting standards follow 1300, but the two more important of these standards for IT auditors here are:

1311—Internal Assessments—Internal audit management must have internal assessment processes in place that include both the ongoing monitoring of the performance of the internal audit activity and periodic reviews performed through self-assessment or by other persons within the enterprise with sufficient knowledge of internal audit practices.

1312—External Assessments—As discussed previously, external assessments must be conducted at least once every five years by a qualified, independent reviewer or review team from outside the organization. The CAE must discuss this need for more frequent external assessments with the board audit committee and the qualifications and independence of the external reviewer or review team, including any potential conflicts of interest.

There are four additional substandards under 1300 defining other areas on the quality of internal audit work. For example, 1321 provides guidance on what an internal auditor can report regarding conformance these IIA Standards.

Internal Audit Performance Standards

Performance standards describe the nature of internal audit activities and provide quality criteria against which these services can be measured. There are six Performance Standards, outlined in Exhibit 3.3, along with substandards and Implementation Standards that apply to compliance audits, fraud investigations, and control self-assessment projects. We are only summarizing the standard here for the purpose of describing internal audit processes. Interested IT audit professionals should contact the IIA Web site to obtain these full standards.

2000—Managing the Internal Audit Activity. The CAE must effectively manage the internal audit activity to ensure it adds value to the enterprise. This standard covers six sub-Standards covering Planning, Communication and Approval, Resource Management, Policies and Procedures, Coordination, and Reporting to the Board and Senior Management. These sub-Standards generally describe such good internal audit management practices as 2040 on Policies and Procedures stating that the CAE must establish such guides.

2060—Reporting to the Board and Senior Management. This substandard contains guidance applicable to today's SOx rules: "The chief audit executive should report periodically to the board and senior management on the internal audit activity's purpose, authority, responsibility, and performance relative to its plan. Reporting must also include significant risk exposures and control issues, corporate governance issues, and other matters needed or requested by the board and senior management. Reporting must also include significant risk exposures and control issues, including fraud risks, governance issues, and other matters needed or requested by senior management and the board."

2100—Nature of Work. Internal audit activity includes evaluations and contributions to the improvement of risk management, control, and governance systems using "a systematic and disciplined approach." Earlier IIA Standards did not really address the important area of risk management, further discussed in Chapter 4 and outlined next.

2110—Governance. Internal audit must assess and make appropriate recommendations for improving the governance process in its accomplishment of these objectives:

- Promoting appropriate ethics and values within the enterprise
- Ensuring effective organizational performance management and accountability
- Communicating risk and control information to appropriate areas of the enterprise
- Coordinating the activities of and communicating information among the board, external and internal auditors, and management

2120—Risk Management. Internal audit must assist the enterprise by identifying and evaluating significant exposures to risk and contributing to the improvement of risk management and control systems. Determining whether risk management processes are effective is a judgment resulting from an internal auditor's assessment that:

- Organizational objectives support and align with an enterprise's mission.
- Significant risks are identified and assessed.
- Appropriate risk responses are selected that align risks with the enterprise's risk appetite.
- Relevant risk information, enabling staff, management, and the board to carry out their responsibilities, is captured and timely communicated across the enterprise.

Risk management processes should be monitored through ongoing management activities, separate evaluations, or both.

2120.A1—Internal audit activity must monitor and evaluate the effectiveness of the enterprise's risk management system.

2120.A2—The internal audit activity must evaluate risk exposures relating to the enterprise's governance, operations, and IT regarding the Committee of Sponsoring Organizations (COSO) standards of internal control.

2120.C1—During consulting engagements, internal auditors must address risk consistent with the engagement's objectives and must be alert to the existence of other significant risks.

2120.C2—Internal auditors must incorporate knowledge of risks gained from consulting engagements into the process of identifying and evaluating significant risk exposures of the enterprise.

2120.C3—When assisting management in establishing or improving risk management processes, internal auditors must refrain from assuming any management responsibility by actually managing risks.

Substandard 2130 on Control follows. Although not summarized here, this IIA control standard is very consistent with the SOx internal controls review requirements discussed in Chapter 1. A major function of internal audit activities includes evaluating the effectiveness and adequacy of internal controls.

2200—Engagement Planning. Internal auditors must develop a plan for each audit engagement, including the scope, objectives, timing, and resource allocations. An important aspect of all internal audits, planning is discussed in Chapter 5 on the key elements for performing effective IT audits.

2201—Planning Considerations. In planning an audit engagement, internal auditors should consider:

- The objectives of the activity being reviewed and the means by which the activity controls its performance.
- The significant risks to the activity, its objectives, resources, and operations and the means by which the potential impact of risk is kept to an acceptable level.
- The adequacy and effectiveness of the activity's risk management and internal control processes compared to a relevant control framework or model.
- The opportunities for making significant improvements to the activity's risk management and control processes.

2201.A1—When planning an engagement for parties outside the enterprise, internal auditors must establish a written understanding with those outside parties about objectives, scope, respective responsibilities and other expectations, including restrictions on distribution of the results of the engagement and access to engagement records.

2201.C1—Internal auditors must establish, and generally document, an understanding with consulting engagement clients about objectives, scope, respective responsibilities, and other client expectations. For significant engagements, this understanding must be documented.

2210 Engagement Objectives. This almost naturally *assumed* requirement states that the objectives must be established for each audit engagement. Internal auditors should never go on fishing expeditions, looking around for problems with no clear objectives.

2210.A1—Internal auditors must conduct a preliminary assessment of the risks relevant to the activity under review, and engagement objectives must reflect the results of this assessment.

2210.A2—The internal auditor must consider the probability of significant errors, irregularities, noncompliance, and other exposures when developing the engagement objectives. The standard relates to the risk assessment considerations discussed previously.

2210.A3—Adequate criteria are needed to evaluate controls. Internal auditors must ascertain the extent to which management has established adequate criteria to determine whether objectives and goals have been accomplished. If adequate, internal auditors must use such criteria in their evaluation. If inadequate, internal auditors must work with management to develop appropriate evaluation criteria.

2210.C1—Consulting engagement objectives must address risks, controls, and governance processes to the extent agreed on with the client.

2220—Engagement Scope. The established audit scope must be sufficient to satisfy the objectives of the engagement.

2220.A1—The scope of the engagement must include consideration of relevant systems, records, personnel, and physical properties, including those under the control of third parties.

2220.A2—If significant consulting opportunities arise during an assurance engagement, a specific written understanding as to the objectives, scope, respective responsibilities, and other expectations must be reached and the results of the consulting engagement communicated in accordance with these consulting standards. This substandard says that an internal auditor can begin an audit as a strictly assurance level of review but may expand it to a consulting-level audit if there is a need or management request.

2220.C1—In performing consulting engagements, internal auditors must ensure that the scope of the engagement is sufficient to address the agreed-on objectives. If internal auditors develop reservations about the scope during the engagement, they must discuss these reservations with the auditee to determine whether to continue with the engagement.

2230—Engagement Resource Allocation. Internal auditors must determine the appropriate resources necessary to achieve the audit engagement objectives. Staffing must be based on an evaluation of the nature and complexity of each engagement, time constraints, and available resources.

2240—Engagement Work Program. Internal auditors must develop and document work programs that achieve the engagement objectives. These work programs must establish procedures for identifying, analyzing, evaluating, and recording information during the engagement. They must be approved prior to their implementation, and any adjustments must be approved promptly. Work programs for consulting engagements may vary in form and content depending on the nature of the engagement.

2300—Performing the Engagement. Internal auditors must identify, analyze, evaluate, and record sufficient information to achieve an audit engagement's objectives and must base conclusions and engagement results on appropriate analyses and evaluations.

2310—Identifying Information. Internal auditors must identify sufficient, reliable, relevant, and useful information to achieve the engagement's objectives.

Sufficient information is factual, adequate, and convincing so that a prudent, informed person would reach the same conclusions as the auditor. *Reliable information* is the best attainable information through the use of appropriate engagement techniques. *Relevant information* supports engagement observations and recommendations and is consistent with the objectives for the engagement. *Useful information* helps an enterprise meet its goals.

2320—Analysis and Evaluation. Internal auditors must base conclusions and engagement results on appropriate analyses and evaluations.

2330—Recording Information. Internal auditors must record relevant information to support the conclusions and engagement results.

2330.A1—The CAE must control access to engagement records and must obtain the approval of senior management and/or legal counsel prior to releasing such records to external parties, as appropriate.

2330.A2—The CAE must develop retention requirements for engagement records, regardless of the medium in which each record is stored, that are consistent with the enterprise's guidelines and any pertinent regulatory or other requirements.

2330.C1—The CAE must develop policies governing the custody and retention of engagement records as well as their release to internal and external parties. These policies must be consistent with the enterprise's guidelines and any pertinent regulatory or other requirements.

2340—Engagement Supervision. Engagements must be properly supervised to ensure that objectives are achieved, quality is assured, and staff is developed. The extent of supervision required will depend on the proficiency and experience of internal auditors and the complexity of the engagement. The CAE has overall responsibility for supervising the engagement, whether performed by or for the internal audit function, but may designate appropriately experienced members of the internal audit function to perform the review. Appropriate evidence of this supervision is documented and retained.

2400 and 2410 Communicating Results. Internal auditors must communicate their engagement results including the audit's objectives and scope as well as applicable conclusions, recommendations, and action plans as well as the internal auditor's overall opinion and or conclusions.

2410.A1—Final communication of engagement results must, where appropriate, contain the internal auditor's overall opinion and/or conclusions.

2410.A2—Internal auditors are encouraged to acknowledge satisfactory performance in engagement communications.

2410.A3—When releasing engagement results to parties outside the enterprise, the communication must include limitations on distribution and use of the results.

2410.C1—Communication of the progress and results of consulting engagements will vary in form and content depending on the nature of the engagement and the needs of the client.

2420—Quality of Communications. Communications must be accurate, objective, clear, concise, constructive, complete, and timely.

2421—Errors and Omissions—If a final communication contains a significant error or omission, the CAE must communicate corrected information to all parties who received the original communication.

2430—Use of the expression "Conducted in conformance with the *International Standards for the Professional Practice of Internal Auditing."* Internal auditors are encouraged to report that their engagements are "conducted in conformance with the *International Standards for the Professional Practice of Internal Auditing."* However, internal auditors may use that statement only if the results of the quality assurance and improvement program demonstrate that the internal audit activity conforms to the standards.

2431—Engagement Disclosure of Noncompliance with IIA Standards—When noncompliance with the Standards impacts a specific engagement, communication of the results must disclose the:

- Principle or rule of conduct of the code of ethics or standard(s) with which full conformance was not achieved.
- Reason(s) for noncompliance.
- Impact of noncompliance on the engagement.

2440—Disseminating Results. The CAE is responsible for communicating the final results of audit work to appropriate parties who can ensure that the results are given due consideration.

2440,A1—The CAE is responsible for communicating the final results to parties who can ensure that the results are given due consideration.

2440.A2—If not otherwise mandated by legal, statutory, or regulatory requirements, prior to releasing results to parties outside the enterprise, the CAE must:

- Assess the potential risk to the enterprise.
- Consult with senior management and/or legal counsel as appropriate.
- Control dissemination by restricting the use of the results.

2440.C1 and C2—The CAE is responsible for communicating the final results of consulting engagements to clients. During consulting engagements, risk management, control, and governance issues may be identified. Whenever these issues are significant to the enterprise, they must be communicated to senior management and the board.

2500—Monitoring Progress. The CAE must establish and maintain a system to monitor the disposition of results communicated to management as well as a follow-up process to monitor and ensure that management actions have been effectively implemented or that senior management has accepted the risk of not taking action.

2600—Resolution of Management's Acceptance of Risks. When the CAE believes that senior management has accepted a level of residual risk that *may be* unacceptable to the enterprise, the CAE must discuss the matter with senior management. If the decision regarding residual risk is not resolved, the CAE and senior management must report the matter to the board for resolution.

The current IIA Standards represent a significant improvement over the older and very lengthy standards that were in place through the 1990s. The Standards conclude with a glossary of terms to better define the roles and responsibilities of internal auditors. Various glossary terms are introduced in other chapters but one that is important for internal auditors is the definition of *independence*. The word frequently appears in internal auditing literature, but the IIA's official definition of internal auditor independence is:

Independence is the freedom from significant conflicts of interest that threaten objectivity. Such threats to objectivity must be managed at the individual auditor level, the engagement level, and the organizational level.

This is an important concept for today. We again emphasize that these past paragraphs are *not the verbatim IIA Standards* but an edited and annotated version.

Some of the more minor standards statements have been eliminated in this chapter, a few words in some cases have been slightly changed, and descriptive comments have been added. As previously stated, internal auditors are advised to obtain the official version of these standards through the Institute of Internal Auditors.

STRONGLY RECOMMENDED IIA STANDARDS GUIDANCE

IIA Standards as well as the code of ethics are not optional or best practices recommendations, such as the information technology infrastrucuture library IT service life cycle best practices discussed in Chapter 7. Professionals who are members of the IIA are expected to follow these standards as a condition of their professional IIA membership. As discussed, in the early days of the IIA Standards, they were often just sort-of followed. Newly revised and streamlined, they represent mandatory standards for the completion of internal audits today.

As shown in Exhibit 3.1, the IPPF framework has both a mandatory section—the upper three segments of the chart—and also a section called "Strongly Recommended," consisting of position papers, practice advisories, and practice guides. These materials provide guidance and interpretations for IIA members.

IIA Standards Practice Advisories

IIA practice advisories are designed to assist internal auditors in applying the definition of internal auditing, the code of ethics, and the standards and promoting good practices. Practice advisories address internal auditing approaches, methodologies, and other considerations, but not detailed processes or procedures. They include practices relating to international, country, or industry-specific issues; specific types of engagements; and legal or regulatory issues.

The practice advisories take the often very general words found in the standards and add some interpretations and clarifications. Exhibit 3.4 shows an example practice advisory for substandard 2130.A1-1 on Information Reliability and Integrity. These practice advisories are updated and released from time to time when the IIA membership raises questions about some matter.

IIA Standards Position Papers

The objective of the standards position papers is to assist a wide range of interested parties, including those not in the internal audit profession, in understanding significant governance, risk, or control issues and delineating related roles and responsibilities of internal auditing. This is a new standards initiative; to date, only two papers have been issued.

The objective of these position papers is to describe the role of internal auditing in some specialized area. For example, a position paper on the role of internal auditing in enterprise in risk management (ERM) outlines areas that should be core internal audit roles with regard to ERM, areas that can be legitimate areas for internal audit concern, and other roles in this area that internal audit should not undertake. This position paper is referenced in Chapter 4 on understanding risk management, and it contains some good guidance materials.

Practice Advisory 2130.A1-1:
Information Reliability and Integrity

Primary Related Standard

2130.A1—The internal audit activity must evaluate the adequacy and effectiveness of controls in responding to the risks within the organization's governance, operations, and information systems regarding the:

Reliability and integrity of financial and operational information;

Effectiveness and efficiency of operations;

Safeguarding of assets; and

Compliance with laws, regulations, and contracts.

1. Internal auditors determine whether senior management and the board have a clear understanding that information reliability and integrity is a management responsibility. This responsibility includes all critical information of the organization regardless of how the information is stored. Information reliability and integrity includes accuracy, completeness, and security.

2. The chief audit executive (CAE) determines whether the internal audit activity possesses, or has access to, competent audit resources to evaluate information reliability and integrity and associated risk exposures. This includes both internal and external risk exposures, and exposures relating to the organization's relationships with outside entities.

3. The CAE determines whether information reliability and integrity breaches and conditions that might represent a threat to the organization will promptly be made known to senior management, the board, and the internal audit activity.

4. Internal auditors assess the effectiveness of preventive, detective, and mitigation measures against past attacks, as appropriate, and future attempts or incidents deemed likely to occur. Internal auditors determine whether the board has been appropriately informed of threats, incidents, vulnerabilities exploited, and corrective measures.

5. Internal auditors periodically assess the organization's information reliability and integrity practices and recommend, as appropriate, enhancements to, or implementation of, new controls and safeguards. Such assessments can either be conducted as separate stand-alone engagements or integrated into other audits or engagements conducted as part of the internal audit plan. The nature of the engagement will determine the most appropriate reporting process to senior management and the board.

EXHIBIT 3.4 IIA Practice Advisory Example: Information Reliability and Integrity
Source: Issued January 2009, PA 2130.A1-1 Revised. © 2009 The Institute of Internal Auditors.

IIA Standards Practice Guides

Practice guides provide detailed guidance for conducting internal audit activities. They include detailed processes and procedures, such as tools and techniques, programs, and step-by-step approaches, as well as examples of deliverables. At the time of this publication, these guides are published as a series of Global Technology Audit Guides, with multiple titles relating to IT audit, such as "Developing the IT Audit Plan."

 ## ISACA IT AUDITING STANDARDS OVERVIEW

It has been mentioned several times how the IIA has released standards-related guidance since its founding in the mid-twentieth century but that guidance and even the emphasis of that professional organization was perceived to be weak in IT audit and control related areas, at least in its early years. The launch of what is now ISACA corrected matters for IT audit professionals. Almost from its start, this organization started releasing IT audit guidance first as audit checklists, established the Certified Information Systems Auditor certification discussed in Chapter 30, and then the CobiT framework discussed in Chapter 2.

ISACA has published extensive IT audit guidance materials in addition to ongoing updated versions of the CobiT framework, but until 2008, it never published any auditing standards. Beginning in that year, ISACA began to issue preliminary standards, which have now evolved into a full suite of IT audit standards. In many respects, the specialized nature of IT auditing and the skills necessary to perform appropriate IT audits require standards that go beyond the IIA Standards just discussed and apply specifically to IT auditing. As a result, ISACA has since issued standards, guidelines, and procedures that define mandatory requirements for information systems (IS) auditing and reporting. These standards provide IT auditors with a minimum level of acceptable performance required to meet the professional responsibilities set out in the ISACA code of professional ethics, discussed in the next section, and provide management and other interested parties with the profession's expectations concerning the work of IT audit practitioners.

Just as compliance with the IIA Standards is mandatory for IIA members, CISA holders are expected to comply with these ISACA standards. Failure to comply may result in an investigation into the CISA holder's conduct by the ISACA board of directors or appropriate ISACA committee and, ultimately, in disciplinary action.

Exhibit 3.5 is a list of the ISACA audit standards at the time of publication. The standards cover the overall internal audit process with an emphasis on IT-specific areas. Copies of these standards are available through the ISACA Web site (www.isaca.org), and the standards will be referred to in many specific audit areas throughout this book. To provide an example of the ISACA audit standards, Exhibit 3.6 is the standard on IT

S1	Audit Charter 1
S2	Independence
S3	Professional Ethics and Standards
S4	Competence
S5	Planning
S6	Performance of Audit Work
S7	Reporting
S8	Follow-Up Activities
S9	Irregularities and Illegal Acts
S10	IT Governance
S11	Use of Risk Assessment in Audit Planning
S12	Audit Materiality
S13	Using the Work of Other Experts
S14	Audit Evidence
S15	IT Controls
S16	E-Commerce

EXHIBIT 3.5 ISACA IT Audit Standards Summary

Introduction

01   ISACA standards contain the basic, mandatory principles and essential procedures together with related guidance.

02   The purpose of this ISACA standard is to establish standards and provide guidance regarding IT controls.

Standard

03   The IT auditor should evaluate and monitor IT controls that are an integral part of the internal control environment of the organization.

04   The IT auditor should assist management by providing advice regarding the design, implementation, operation, and improvement of IT controls.

Commentary

05   Management is accountable for the internal control environment of an organization including IT controls. An internal control environment provides the discipline, framework, and structure for the achievement of the primary objective of the system of internal control.

06   CobiT defines control as "the policies, procedures, practices and organizational structures, designed to provide reasonable assurance that business objectives will be achieved and that undesired events will be prevented or detected and corrected." Also, CobiT defines a control objective as "a statement of the desired result or purpose to be achieved by implementing control procedures in a particular process."

07   IT controls are comprised of general IT controls, which include pervasive IT controls, detailed IT controls, and application controls, and refer to controls over the acquisition, implementation, delivery, and support of IT systems and services.

08   General IT controls are controls that minimize risk to the overall functioning of the organization's IT systems and infrastructure and to a broad set of automated solutions (applications).

09   Application controls are a set of controls embedded within applications.

10   Pervasive IT controls are general IT controls that are designed to manage and monitor the IT environment and, therefore, affect all IT-related activities. They are a subset of general controls, being those general IT controls that focus on the management and monitoring of IT.

11   Detailed IT controls are made up of application controls plus those general IT controls not included in pervasive IT controls.

12   The IT auditor should use an appropriate risk assessment technique or approach in developing the overall IT audit plan and in determining priorities for the effective allocation of IT audit resources to provide assurance regarding the state of IT control processes. Control processes are the policies, procedures, and activities that are part of a control environment, designed to ensure that risks are contained within the risk tolerances established by the risk management process.

13   The IS auditor should consider the use of data analysis techniques including the use of continuous assurance, which allows IT auditors to monitor system reliability on a continuous basis and to gather selective audit evidence through the computer when reviewing IT controls.

14   When organizations use third parties, they can become a key component in an organization's controls and its achievement of related control objectives. The IT auditor should evaluate the role that the third party performs in relation to the IT environment, related controls, and IT control objectives.

EXHIBIT 3.6   ISACA IT Audit Standards Example: S15 IT Controls
Source: IT Standards, Guidelines, and Tools and Techniques for Audit Assurance and Control Professionals. © 2008 ISACA. All rights reserved. Used by permission.

---

15 The following ISACA and IT Governance Institute (ITGI) guidance should be referred to for further information regarding IT controls:
- ■ Guideline G3 Use of Computer-Assisted Audit Techniques (CAATs)
- ■ Guideline G11 Effect of Pervasive IS Controls
- ■ Guideline G13 Using Risk Assessment in Audit Planning
- ■ Guideline G15 Planning
- ■ Guideline G16 Effect of Third Parties on an Organization's IT Controls
- ■ Guideline G20 Reporting
- ■ Guideline G36 Biometric Controls
- ■ Guideline G38 Access Controls
- ■ COBIT Framework and Control Objectives

Operative Date

16 This ISACA standard is effective for IS audits beginning 1 February 2008.

EXHIBIT 3.6 *(Continued)*

Controls. Although a general internal audit standard, it has a heavy emphasis on IT and relies frequently relies on CobiT framework.

ISACA guidelines are similar to the IIA Standards practice advisories discussed earlier. They provide very specific guidance for IT audits in special areas, are released fairly regularly, and provide specific guidance in various more technical areas. In order to strengthen the ISACA IT audit standards process, these guidelines are referenced in specific ISACA standards. For example, Exhibit 3.6 on IT Controls concludes with a list of applicable guidelines, such as a reference to Guideline G16, "Effect of Third Parties on an Organization's IT Controls."

The ISACA Auditing Procedures are similar to the IIA's IPPF Position Papers, except that the ISACA documents tend to be much more technical and IT related, covering specific areas. For example, the ISACA Guideline P9 is titled "Evaluation of Management Controls over Encryption Methodologies" and covers a very specific and specialized IT controls area. Materials in these ISACA will be referred to in other chapters. For example, topics in this audit procedure will be referenced in Chapter 20 on cybersecurity.

CODES OF ETHICS: THE IIA AND ISACA

Codes of ethics are key elements in both the IIA and ISACA Standards. The purpose of the IIA's code of ethics is to promote an ethical culture in the profession of internal auditing. This code of ethics is displayed in Exhibit 3.7. It is necessary and appropriate for a profession that depends on the trust placed on users of internal audit services on objective assurances about risk management, control, and governance. The IIA's current code of ethics was released in 2009 and is based on the principles of internal auditor integrity, objectivity, confidentiality, and competency.[3] These are the behavioral norms expected of internal auditors and are intended to guide the ethical conduct of all internal auditors.

Introduction to the Code of Ethics

The purpose of The Institute's Code of Ethics is to promote an ethical culture in the profession of internal auditing.

Internal auditing is an independent, objective assurance and consulting activity designed to add value and improve an organization's operations. It helps an organization accomplish its objectives by bringing a systematic, disciplined approach to evaluate and improve the effectiveness of risk management, control, and governance processes.

A code of ethics is necessary and appropriate for the profession of internal auditing, founded as it is on the trust placed in its objective assurance about governance, risk management, and control. The Institute's Code of Ethics extends beyond the Definition of Internal Auditing to include two essential components:

1. Principles that are relevant to the profession and practice of internal auditing.
2. Rules of Conduct that describe behavior norms expected of internal auditors. These rules are an aid to interpreting the Principles into practical applications and are intended to guide the ethical conduct of internal auditors.

"Internal auditors" refers to Institute members, recipients of or candidates for IIA professional certifications, and those who perform internal audit services within the Definition of Internal Auditing.

Applicability and Enforcement of the Code of Ethics

This Code of Ethics applies to both entities and individuals that perform internal audit services. For IIA members and recipients of or candidates for IIA professional certifications, breaches of the Code of Ethics will be evaluated and administered according to The Institute's Bylaws and Administrative Directives. The fact that a particular conduct is not mentioned in the Rules of Conduct does not prevent it from being unacceptable or discreditable, and therefore, the member, certification holder, or candidate can be liable for disciplinary action.

EXHIBIT 3.7   IIA Code of Ethics
Source: Issued January 2009 Code of Ethics Revised. © 2009 The Institute of Internal Auditors.

The IIA code of ethics replaces an earlier and also a rather lengthy 1988 version that had 11 specific articles defining preferred practices; that version, in turn, replaced a 1968 version with eight articles. The current 2000 version, with its highlighted emphasis on integrity, objectivity, confidentiality, and competency becomes much easier to understand and recognize than the rather detailed articles in the prior version. Any person performing internal audit services, whether or not a member of the IIA, should follow this code of ethics. Professional certificates, including the Certified Internal Auditor (CIA) designation, are discussed in Chapter 30.

The IIA code of ethics applies to both individuals and entities that provide internal auditing services. For IIA members and recipients of or candidates for IIA professional certifications, breaches of the code of ethics will be evaluated and administered according to IIA bylaws and administrative guidelines. The IIA goes on to state that even if a particular conduct is not mentioned in this code, this does not prevent the conduct or practice from being unacceptable or discreditable. Violators of this code, whether an IIA member, a CIA, or a candidate, can be become liable for professional disciplinary action.

As discussed, ISACA, as well as its affiliated research arm, the IT Governance Institute, is the professional audit enterprise that represents or speaks primarily for IT auditors. ISACA currently leads the IIA on technology-related issues. With its IT audit

The Information Systems Audit and Control Association, Inc. (ISACA) sets forth this *Code of Professional Ethics* to guide the professional and personal conduct of members of the Association and/or its certification holders.

Members and ISACA Certification holders shall:

1. Support the implementation of, and encourage compliance with, appropriate standards, procedures and controls for information systems.
2. Perform their duties with due diligence and professional care, in accordance with professional standards and best practices.
3. Serve in the interest of stakeholders in a lawful and honest manner, while maintaining high standards of conduct and character, and not engage in acts discreditable to the profession.
4. Maintain the privacy and confidentiality of information obtained in the course of their duties unless disclosure is required by legal authority. Such information shall not be used for personal benefit or released to inappropriate parties.
5. Maintain competency in their respective fields and agree to undertake only those activities, which they can reasonably expect to complete with professional competence.
6. Inform appropriate parties of the results of work performed; revealing all significant facts known to them.
7. Support the professional education of stakeholders in enhancing their understanding of information systems security and control.

Failure to comply with this *Code of Professional Ethics* can result in an investigation into a member's or certification holder's conduct and, ultimately, in disciplinary measures.

EXHIBIT 3.8   ISACA Code of Professional Ethics
Source: IT Standards, Guidelines, and Tools and Techniques for Audit Assurance and Control Professionals. © 2009 ISACA. All rights reserved. Used by permission.

and IT governance orientation, ISACA represents a somewhat different group of auditors. Historically, ISACA drew a large number of members from IT audit specialists and public accounting external audit firms, and it has had a very strong international membership in some areas of the world. Many IIA members are also ISACA members, and while the two groups do not have many joint meetings or other endeavors, each represents an important segment of the audit community.

Just as the IIA and ISACA each has its own audit standards, ISACA also has a code of ethics, as shown in Exhibit 3.8. Because of its IT heritage, the ISACA code is more oriented to technology-related issues. It is a set of professional standards that applies to and should be of particular value to IT audit professionals. Although the wording is different, there is nothing in the ISACA code that is really contrary to the IIA code. Internal auditors, whether working primarily in IT areas or with a more general internal controls orientation, should exercise strong ethical practice in their work.

 NOTES

1. Institute of Internal Auditors, *Standards for the Professional Practice of Internal Auditing* (Altamonte Springs, FL: Author, 2004).
2. Robert Moeller, *Brink's Modern Internal Auditing*, 7th ed. (Hoboken, NJ: John Wiley & Sons, 2009).
3. www.theiia.org.

CHAPTER FOUR

Understanding Risk Management through COSO ERM

NFORMATION TECHNOLOGY (IT) AND other internal auditors need to identify all of the business risks they face in their review activities—IT, financial, and operational as well as social, ethical, and environmental risks—and to assess that these risks are managed at an acceptable level. Understanding risks is a major component of achieving Sarbanes-Oxley (SOx) compliance, as discussed in Chapter 1, and is part of the international audit standards of the Institute of Internal Auditors (IIA) and the Information Systems Audit and Control Association (ISACA) discussed in Chapter 3. *Risk* has too often been one of those terms where IT auditors and internal control specialists often say "Yes, we must consider risks!" even though their understandings and assessments of risk are not well understood or defined. One professional's concept and understanding of risk may be very different from another's, even though they are both working for the same enterprise and in similar areas.

IT auditors need to have an understanding of risk management and how it impacts their approaches for assessing or developing effective internal controls. This chapter begins by discussing some of the fundamental concepts behind risk management for IT auditors, considers the various types of risk facing an enterprise, and then looks at quantitative approaches for assessing risks.

We then introduce internal audit risk management standards, tools, and approaches as defined in ISACA and IIA guidance materials and standards. An ongoing problem in an IT auditor's use and understanding of the concept of risk had been the lack of a consistent definition of what is really meant by *risk*. The word has some origins in the insurance industry, but the concept of risk has not been consistently used even in insurance areas, let alone by IT auditors or other business professionals. Many have talked about how they had "considered risk" when implementing a control or process, but they often had no consistent definitions here. The question of what steps were followed in such a risk consideration might produce a wide range of answers.

This all changed when the Committee of Sponsoring Organizations (COSO) released its enterprise risk methodology, COSO Enterprise Risk Management Integrated Format standards (COSO ERM).[1] This is a framework to allow an enterprise to consider and assess its risks at all levels, whether it is in an individual area, such as for an IT development project, or for global risks regarding an international expansion. Because it was released by the same COSO guidance-setting function that is responsible for the COSO internal controls framework, COSO ERM sometimes looks like its internal controls "brother." However, COSO ERM has a much different feel and approach.

This chapter introduces the COSO ERM framework and its elements, with an emphasis on why COSO ERM can be an important tool to better understand and evaluate the risks surrounding internal controls at all levels, but with an emphasis on IT resources. We describe major elements of the COSO ERM framework and also look at how IT auditors can better build COSO ERM concepts into their internal controls audits and reviews of IT resources. Although the basic framework models look similar to the COSO internal controls framework, COSO ERM, with its emphasis on enterprise-wide risks, is different.

RISK MANAGEMENT FUNDAMENTALS

Every enterprise makes business decisions and invests in resources to provide value for its stakeholders, but these investments and other activities have uncertain outcomes and are always subject to uncertainties or risks—whether the failure of a key IT business process, the challenge caused by a new and aggressive competitor, or the damage and even loss of life caused by a major weather disturbance. Risk management is a concept where an enterprise should use insurance mechanisms to provide a shield or protection from those risks. We make these decisions based on assessments of relative risks and the costs to cover them through the purchase of insurance. These risks and insurance costs also change over time. Fire insurance to cover an individual's home is an example of this evolving change. Back in the days of oil lanterns as a source for light and straw stored in a nearby stable, there was always a high risk of fires. We need only to think of the great Chicago fire of 1871 where, as legend suggests, a cow kicked over a lantern and caused a fire that devastated the city. The risk of fires in the typical building is not that great today, and fire insurance is not too expensive, in a relative sense. However, there is always the possibility of a lightning strike or electrical malfunction causing a fire in a structure, and mortgage finance companies require fire insurance coverage. Even if there is no mortgage, all prudent persons today purchase such fire insurance even if not required. A destructive fire to one's home presents a low-level but consistent risk. An individual homeowner might assess other potential risks, such as for earthquakes, and not purchase insurance for that type of risk. In a given geographic area, the possibility of an earthquake may appear so low that an owner would not consider purchasing any insurance, despite its low cost. In another situation, an individual may live by a body of water where there are damaging floods every several years. Even if one can purchase flood insurance in such an environment—and most insurance companies will not even offer it—the cost of flood insurance here will be very expensive. Some people may decide to accept the risk of a flood in future years and go without insurance coverage. In all of these cases, there has been an insurance purchaser risk management decision.

Starting with these insurance-buying foundations, enterprise risk management, as it is practiced today, is essentially a post-1960s phenomenon. Moving beyond concerns about natural weather-related events, risk management began to emphasize protecting enterprises against a major catastrophe, such as the risks surrounding a computer system back in the mainframe days, when most information systems assets were stored in centralized facilities. The concern about managing risks surrounding that one centralized computer system moved to a general concern about managing a wide range of other business risks. (IT disaster recovery planning is discussed in Chapter 23.)

Risk assessment, in combination with other audit techniques, should be considered in making such planning decisions, with consideration given to the nature, extent, and timing of any planned audit procedures; the areas or business functions to be audited; and the amount of time and resources to be allocated to an audit. A key risk assessment and audit planning concept, IT auditors should understand and make their assessments in terms of the levels of what are known as inherent, control, and detection risks.

- **Inherent risk.** As defined by the U.S. government's Office of Management and Budget (OMB), *inherent risk* is the "potential for waste, loss, unauthorized use, or misappropriation due to the nature of an activity itself." Inherent risk is the susceptibility of an audit error to occur in a way that could be material, individually or in combination with other errors, assuming that there were no related internal controls. Major factors that affect enterprise inherent risk are the size of its budget, the strength and sophistication of management, and the very nature of its activities. Inherent risk is outside the control of management and usually stems from external factors. For example, the major retailer Wal-Mart is so large and dominant in its markets that it faces various inherent risks due to its sheer size. Inherent risk for most IT audit areas is usually high, since the potential effects of errors ordinarily span several business systems and many users.
- **Control or residual risk.** This is the risk that remains after management responses to risk threats and countermeasures have been applied. There is virtually always some level of residual risk. These are also the risks of an error occurring in an audit that could be materially significant, individually or in combination with other errors, but that will not be prevented or detected and corrected on a timely basis by the internal control system. For example, the control risk associated with manual reviews of computer system activity logs can be high because activities requiring investigation can be easily missed, owing to the volume of logged information. The control risk associated with IT data validation procedures is ordinarily low because the processes are consistently applied.
- **Detection risk.** This is the risk that the IT auditor's substantive procedures will not detect an error that could be material, individually or in combination with other errors. For example, the detection risk associated with identifying breaches of

security in an application system is ordinarily high because logs for the whole period of the audit may not be available at the time of the audit. The detection risk associated with identifying a lack of disaster recovery plans is ordinarily low, since existence is verified easily.

Inherent, control, and detection risk are fundamental risk assessment concepts. IT auditors should have a general understanding of these concepts and how they will help an IT auditor to review and assess controls.

Enterprises today face a wide variety of IT-related risks. Management needs to assess these risks in order to make rational decisions related to cost and risk avoidance. This is the process of risk management. Although an enterprise today can just make seat-of-the-pants decisions to assess a potential threat as high, medium, or low risk and then make quick insurance or risk protection decisions based on those options, more sophisticated qualitative or quantitative tools are available to help them understand and evaluate these risks. IT auditors should have a general understanding of these processes as well. The next sections briefly survey some fundamental modern risk management approaches with the aim of helping to establish more effective IT risk management procedures in an enterprise.

An effective risk management process typically requires four steps:

1. Identify the relevant potential risks facing an activity.
2. Quantitatively or qualitatively assess those identified risks.
3. Prioritize risk and response planning.
4. Perform ongoing risk status monitoring.

There is always a need to identify and understand the various risks facing an enterprise, to assess those risks in terms of their cost or impact and probability, to develop responses in the event of a risk occurrence, and to develop documentation procedures to describe what happened as well as corrective actions going forward. This is true for specific IT-related risks as well as for other enterprise-wide non-IT risks.

The four-step risk management process should be implemented at all levels of an enterprise and is particularly useful for IT systems and related resources. Whether the company is a smaller one operating in a limited geographic area or a larger, worldwide enterprise, these risk management approaches should be developed for the entire enterprise. Doing so is particularly important for the worldwide enterprise with multiple operating units engaged in different business operations and with facilities in different countries. Some risks in one unit may directly impact or be related to risks in another, while other risk considerations may be independent from the whole. Although the overall focus of this book is on the activities of IT auditors, risk management should be an enterprise-wide responsibility, managed by risk management specialists in the enterprise. Many have established a chief risk officer (CRO) to take responsibility for these activities.

Risk Identification

As the first step in the previously outlined four-part risk management process, the enterprise's CRO or a supporting team should try to identify all possible risks that may impact the success of their enterprise, ranging from the larger significant risks to the overall business down to lesser risks associated with individual projects or smaller business units. This type of risk identification process requires a studied, deliberate approach to looking at potential risks in each area of operations and then identifying the more significant risk areas that may impact each operation in a reasonable time period. The idea here is not to list every possible risk but for an enterprise to identify those that might have a major impact on operations within a reasonable time period. This exercise can be difficult; it requires estimating the probabilities of various identified risks occurring or the nature of the consequences if the enterprise has to face the risk. This risk identification process should occur at multiple levels, with an understanding that a risk that impacts an individual business unit or project may not have that great of an impact on the entire enterprise or beyond. Conversely, a major risk that impacts the entire economy will flow down to the individual enterprise and its separate business units. Some major risks are so infrequent but can be so cataclysmic that it is difficult to identify them as possible future events.

For a larger enterprise, a good way to start a risk identification process is to begin with a high-level organization chart that lists corporate-level as well as operating units. Each of those units may have facilities in multiple locations and may also consist of multiple and different types of operations. Each separate facility will then have its own departments or functions. Some of these separate business units may be closely connected to one another while others represent little more than corporate investments. An enterprise-wide initiative, which is a difficult and sometimes complicated task, should be launched to identify all significant risks in these individual areas. This type of exercise can have interesting and sometimes troubling results. For example, a corporate-level senior manager may be aware of some product liability risks, but a front-line supervisor in an operating unit may look at the same risks from an entirely different perspective.

A marketing manager, for example, may be concerned about a competitor's pricing strategies or the risk of pricing activities that would put the enterprise in violation of restraint of trade laws. An IT manager may be concerned about the risk of a computer virus attack on application systems but will have little knowledge of pricing issue risks. More senior management typically will be aware of a different level and set of risks than would be on the minds of the operations-oriented staff. Still, all of these risks should be identified and considered on an operating unit–by–operating unit basis and over the entire enterprise.

To be effective, this risk identification process requires much more than just sending out an e-mail to all operating units with a request for recipients to list the key risks in their units. Such a request typically will result in a wide range of inconsistent answers with no common approach. A better method is to ask people at all levels of the enterprise to serve as risk assessors. Within each significant operating unit, key people should be identified from operations, finance/accounting, IT, and unit management. Their goal should be to identify and then help assess risks in their units built around a risk identification model framework. This type of initiative can be led by the CRO or a designated risk assessment team. IT auditors often play a key role here because of their ongoing understandings of IT disaster recovery risks.

Enterprise-Wide Strategic Risks	
External Factors Risks	**Internal Factors Risks**
▪ Industry Risk ▪ Economy Risk ▪ Competitor Risk ▪ Legal and Regulatory Change Risk ▪ Customer Needs and Wants Risk	▪ Reputation Risk ▪ Strategic Focus Risk ▪ Parent Company Support Risk ▪ Patent/Trademark Protection Risk

Operations Risks		
Process Risks	**Compliance Risks**	**People Risks**
▪ Supply Chain Risk ▪ Customer Satisfaction Risk ▪ Cycle Time Risk ▪ Process Execution Risk	▪ Environmental Risk ▪ Government Rules and Regulatory Risk ▪ Policy and Procedures Risk ▪ Litigation Risk	▪ Human Resources Risk ▪ Employee Turnover Risk ▪ Performance Incentive Risk ▪ Training Risk

Finance Risks		
Treasury Risks	**Credit Risks**	**Trading Risks**
▪ Interest Rate Risk ▪ Foreign Exchange Risk ▪ Capital Availability Risk	▪ Capacity Risk ▪ Collateral Risk ▪ Concentration Risk ▪ Default Risk ▪ Settlement Risk	▪ Commodity Price Risk ▪ Duration Risk ▪ Measurement Risk

Information Risks		
Financial Risks	**Operational Risks**	**Technological and IT Risks**
▪ Accounting Standards Risk ▪ Budgeting Risk ▪ Financial Reporting Risk ▪ Taxation Risk ▪ Regulatory Reporting Risk	▪ Terrorist Attack ▪ Pricing Risk ▪ Performance Measurement Risk ▪ Employee Safety Risk	▪ Information Access Risk ▪ Business Continuity Risk ▪ Availability Risk ▪ Infrastructure Risk

EXHIBIT 4.1   Types of Enterprise Risks

An effective idea here is to outline some high-level "straw man"[2] risks that may impact various operating units. Knowledgeable people can then look at these lists and modify them as appropriate. Exhibit 4.1 shows some types of major risks that may impact an enterprise, including various strategic, operations, and finance risks. A chief executive officer (CEO) might use such a high-level list to respond to a shareholder annual meeting question "What worries you at the end of the day?" This is the type of first-pass list that an enterprise can use to get started on a detailed risk identification. Other senior managers in the enterprise—often the CEO and supporting staff—can meet with senior management and ask some of these types of questions to identify such high-level risks.

This very general, high-level risk model can serve as a basis to better define the broad range of specific risks facing various units of an enterprise. An IT auditor should be able to expand an entry, such as Business Continuity Risk listed under Technological Risks, into a long list of detailed technology-related risks associated with business continuity. An operations manager who is the user of IT resources might look at business continuity risks from a different perspective and may introduce other risks associated with what happens if IT services are not available. In order to have a better understanding of the risks facing an enterprise, it is often best to expand these lists to establish a more complete set of risks.

An enterprise management team should then use this more complete list of potential enterprise risks and ask themselves such questions as:

- Is the risk common across the overall enterprise or unique to one business group?
- Will the enterprise face this risk because of internal or external events?
- Are the risks related, such that one risk may cause another to occur?

The idea is to gain a strong understanding of the nature of enterprise-level risks and then to highlight major risks, including, for example, the risks of: a significant fall in customer satisfaction ratings, a new and very large competitor entering the market, and an identified significant internal control weakness as part of the financial statement close. Any of these major risks could present significant challenges to an enterprise.

Enterprise management should review their risks and highlight those that appear to be most critical in order to prepare a final set of risks by the overall enterprise and by specific operating units. Because viewpoints and perspectives will vary across the enterprise, these identified risks should be shared with responsible operating, IT, and financial management, giving them opportunities to provide feedback. The idea here is to identify the population of risks that threaten an enterprise, both at an individual unit level and on a total enterprise basis. These risks will not necessarily be the enterprise's core risks but they often are a starting point for enterprise risk assessments.

Key Risk Assessment Principles

After the significant enterprise risks are identified, a second important step is to assess their likelihood and relative significance. A variety of approaches can be used here, ranging from best-guess qualitative conjectures to detailed mathematical quantitative analyses. The idea is to help decide which of a series of potentially risky events management should worry the most about.

A simple but often effective approach is to take the list of identified risks and circulate them to key managers with a questionnaire asking for each risk:

- What is the likelihood of this risk occurring over the next one-year period? Using a range of 1 to 9, assign a best-guess score as follows:
  - Score 1 if you see *almost no chance* of that risk happening during the period.
  - Score 9 if you feel the event will *almost certainly happen* during the period.
  - Score 2 through 8 depending on how you feel the likelihood the event will fall between these two ranges.
- What is the significance of the risk in terms of cost to the enterprise? Again using the same 1 to 9 scale, scoring ranges should be set depending on the financial significance of the risk. A risk whose costs could lower earnings per share by perhaps 1 cent might qualify for the maximum score of 9.

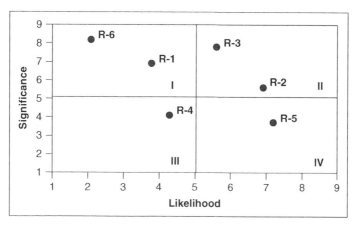

EXHIBIT 4.2 Risk Assessment Analysis Map
Source: Robert R. Moeller, *COSO Enterprise Risk Management: Understanding the New Integrated ERM Framework* (Hoboken, NJ: John Wiley & Sons). Copyright © 2007 John Wiley & Sons. Reprinted with the permission of John Wiley & Sons, Inc.

Questionnaires here should be circulated independently to knowledgeable people to score each of the identified risks per these two measures. As an example, assume that an enterprise has identified six risks, R-1 through R-6, and four managers are asked to separately evaluate each risk in terms of its likelihood and significance. These scores can be averaged by both factors and plotted on a risk assessment analysis chart as shown in Exhibit 4.2. R-1 had an average Likelihood score of about 3.75 and a Significance score of 7.00, and this score is plotted in quadrant I of the chart. For example, R-1 is relatively significant but not that likely to occur. After all identified risks are plotted in this manner, the high-likelihood and more significant risks in quadrant II should receive immediate management attention. This type of chart provides a good qualitative measure to understand some of the significant risks surrounding an enterprise.

This high-risk assessment process works well when an enterprise has identified a relatively small number of risks. It is fairly easy to look at the analysis chart and focus on remediation planning for the high-likelihood and significant risks in the upper left-hand quadrant. Often, however, an enterprise may identify a much larger set of risks, with risk ranges of only 1 to 9 as well as plots on the example chart will not provide sufficient detail. It is often a better approach to express risk significance and impact estimates in terms of two-digit percentage estimates (e.g., 72%) of achieving some risk or as a probability. However, just increasing the number of digits, from a 7% to a full 72%, does not increase the accuracy of the assessment. More attention should be given to better understanding the relationship between probabilities covering independent and related risk events.

Combined estimates of likelihood and significance are key factors in any risk analysis assessment. The combination of two probabilities requires one to go back to some basic mathematical concepts. A basic rule of probability is that we cannot add up independent probability estimates to develop a joint estimate. If the probability of risk A occurring is 60% and the probability of a separate but related risk B is also 60%, we *cannot* say that the probability of both occurring is $0.60 + 0.60 = 1.20$. This 120% does not make sense! Rather, the joint probability of two independent events is the product of the two separate probabilities:

$$\text{Pr(Event 1)} \times \text{Pr(Event 2)} = \text{Pr(Both Events)}$$

That is, if Event 1 has a probability of 0.60 and Event 2 is also 0.60, the combined probability of both events occurring is $(0.60) \times (0.60) = 0.36$. In terms of the assessments, if a risk has a 60% significance estimate or we are 60% certain that the risk will occur, and if the impact has been rated at 60%, there is a 36% probability that we will achieve both of those risks. We can also call this the risk score for the individual risk.

An accurate risk assessment process, however, requires more than just top-of-the-head estimates stated in percentage estimates. Enterprise management should take a hard look at identified risks and gather more information, if required. For example, during the risk identification process, one manager may have identified the consequences of a new tariff law as a serious risk. However, responsible managers may want to better understand its actual consequences. Perhaps the law is not applicable to the unit in question, or it often does not go in to effect until some years in to the future. The point here is that all identified risks may need some additional information before they can be assessed accurately.

Risk independencies must always be considered and evaluated throughout the organizational structure. Although any entity should be concerned about risks at all levels of the organization, it really has control over only the risks within its own sphere. The 2002 example of the fall of the major public accounting firm Arthur Andersen in the wake of the Enron collapse is an example. Each city-by-city and country-by-country unit of that once esteemed public accounting firm had its own risk assessment procedures, following firm-wide standards. However, a risk event at one operating office, in Houston, Texas, caused the firm to collapse worldwide. An operating office in another area, such as Toronto, might not have even have fully anticipated such risks in a far-away Houston. The point here is that risks within an enterprise are often very interdependent. Each operating unit is responsible for managing its own risks but may be subject to the consequences of risk events on units above or below it in the organization structure.

The examples used in this chapter show a short list of identified risks, but a typical enterprise will end up with a very long list of potential risks. A next step is to take the established significance and likelihood estimates, calculate risk rankings, and identify the most significant risks across the entity reviewed. Exhibit 4.3 is an example of this type of analysis. Based on the likelihood and significance scores from Exhibit 4.2, the product of these two values gives relative risk rankings. Risks C and G have the highest risk rank scores and would be plotted in the upper right-hand quadrant as the most significant risks in this sample. These risks would be called the risk drivers for this set identified risk. That is, these are the key risk areas requiring attention. An organization should focus its attention going forward on these primary risks. These risk-ranked schedules should be organized on a unit-by-unit basis and adjusted to accommodate all related risks in parallel with as well as above or below the entity being evaluated.

Identified Risk	Significance Probability	Likelihood Probability	Risk Score (P × I)	Rank
A	0.55	0.30	0.17	8
B	0.88	0.24	0.21	7
C	0.79	0.66	0.52	1
D	0.77	0.45	0.35	4
E	0.35	0.88	0.31	5
F	0.54	0.49	0.26	6
G	0.62	0.72	0.45	2
H	0.66	0.20	0.13	9
I	0.90	0.45	0.41	3
J	0.12	0.88	0.11	10

EXHIBIT 4.3   Risk Scoring Schedule

This analysis requires that a risk management team identify its unit-by-unit assessed risks to make certain that risk likelihood and significance estimates are appropriate throughout. All too often, risk events that occur far away from corporate headquarters can cause major problems. An example from nearly 30 years ago can be drawn from a risk event at Union Carbide, a U.S. corporation. On the night of December 2, 1984, over 40 tons of poisonous gases leaked from a pesticide factory owned by Union Carbide in Bhopal, India, killing more than 20,000 residents.[3] After much legal wrangling, Union Carbide, which had built the plant in 1969, settled a civil suit brought by the Indian government by agreeing to pay US$470 million for damages suffered by the half-million people who were exposed to the gas. The company maintained that this payment was made out of a sense of "moral" rather than any "legal" responsibility since the plant was operated by a separate Indian subsidiary, Union Carbide India Limited (UCIL), but court proceedings revealed that senior management's cost-cutting measures had effectively disabled safety procedures essential to prevent such disasters or alert employees to problems. Dow Chemical has since taken over Union Carbide and also denies responsibility for this disaster. However, because of the tremendous loss of life in Bhopal and because Dow Chemical is much larger than what Union Carbide and its UCIL subsidiary had been, ongoing actions haunted Dow Chemical over many years.

The Bhopal gas leak is an example of how a risk event at a distant and relatively small unit can have disastrous consequences for a major corporation. The risk identification and assessment rules outlined in this chapter would not have accounted for a catastrophe of this magnitude, and each unit in an enterprise needs to recognize the likelihood and consequences of risks at individual unit levels. As noted, a risk event at a small foreign subsidiary can bring down the entire enterprise. Risk management at all levels should recognize that catastrophes can happen, although we never can predict risks of this major consequence; an enterprise should always be aware of the worst disaster that can happen.

This Bhopal incident was much more than an IT-related matter; we have cited it as the type of a major risk that can impact an enterprise. Risk assessment at all levels should be based on two estimates: the relative significance probability and the likelihood of the risk event occurring.

 QUANTITATIVE RISK ANALYSIS TECHNIQUES

There is little value in identifying significant risks unless an enterprise has at least some preliminary plans in place for the action steps necessary if one of the risks is incurred. The idea is to estimate the cost impact of incurring some identified risk and then to apply that cost to a risk factor probability to derive an expected value or cost of the risk. Often this exercise that does not require detailed cost studies with lots of supporting historical trends and estimates. Rather, expected cost estimates should be performed by front-line people at various levels of the enterprise who have a good level of knowledge of the area or risk implications.

The idea here is to go through each of the identified risks—or, if time is limited, only the key risks—and estimate the costs of incurring the risk. Because the kinds of risks discussed involve such matters as the failure of an IT hardware component, the drop in market share, or the impact of a new government regulation, typically they are not the types of costs that one can just look up in a current vendor catalog. Some typical risks, arbitrarily labeled A, B, and C, illustrate this type of thinking:

Risk A: Loss of up to x% market share due to changing consumer tastes

- Estimate the reduction in sales and loss of profits due to the x% drop.
- Estimate how much will it cost to begin to restore the lost market position.

Risk B: Temporary loss of major manufacturing facility for zz days due to major database failure

- Estimate the best- and worst-case costs to get the database temporarily repaired and back in operation within zz days.
- Estimate the extra labor and production costs incurred during the interim.

Risk C: Loss of information systems for two days due to pernicious IT network virus

- Estimate the business and profitability loss during the down period.
- Estimate the cost to transfer operations to the business continuity site.

The above factor examples illustrate the type of thinking needed to estimate the costs of recovering from some risk event. It is often difficult to determine what it would cost to recover from these risks. There is no need to perform detailed, time-consuming analyses. Knowledgeable people who understand the risk area often can provide good estimates on the basis of:

1. What is the best-case cost estimate if it is necessary to incur the risk? This is an assumption that there will be only limited impact if the risk occurs.

2. What would a sample of knowledgeable people estimate for the cost? For Risk A mentioned earlier, the director of marketing might be asked to supply an estimate.
3. What is the expected value or cost of incurring the risk? This is the type of risk that might include some base costs as well as other factors, such as additional labor requirements.
4. What is the worst-case cost of incurring the risk? This is a what-if-everything-goes-wrong type of estimate.

We have suggested using four estimates as an idea of the ranges of costs. However, one best-guess estimate should be selected from the four estimates—usually something between estimates 2 and 3. These estimates and supporting work should be documented, with the selected cost estimate entered as the cost impact on the risk response planning schedule in Exhibit 4.4. These are the same risks that were identified in Exhibit 4.3, but here they are ordered by risk rank. This reordering is important when an enterprise has a long list of identified risks.

The expected value or cost values in Exhibit 4.4 are just the products of the cost impacts and their risk scores. Exhibit 4.4 shows an estimate of what it would cost an enterprise to incur some risk. Although the numbers selected for these samples are very arbitrary, they show how a risk management specialist should interpret this type of analysis. Risk C, for example, has a high likelihood and significance as well as fairly high expected cost to correct. This is the type of risk that management should identify as a candidate for corrective actions. However, the next risk on the schedule, Risk G, also belongs in the upper left-hand quadrant but with a relatively low cost to implement. Management may decide to accept this risk or to develop some other form of remediation plan. Risk H is an example of another risk with a high cost to accept that risk, with its fairly high significance and a low likelihood of occurrence. The numbers shown for Risk H are the kinds where management frequently decides to hope for the best and live with the risk. It will be expensive if management incurs the risk, but it also would be expensive to install corrective action facilities.

Identified Risk	Significance Probability	Likelihood Probability	Risk Score (P × I)	Rankings	Cost Impact	Expect Cost (Cost × Score)
C	0.79	0.66	0.52	1	$ 120,600	$ 62,881
G	0.62	0.72	0.45	2	$ 785,000	$350,424
I	0.90	0.45	0.41	3	$ 15,000	$ 6,075
D	0.77	0.45	0.35	4	$ 27,250	$ 9,442
E	0.35	0.88	0.31	5	$ 52,350	$ 16,124
F	0.54	0.49	0.26	6	$ 1,200	$ 318
B	0.88	0.24	0.21	7	$ 12,650	$ 2,672
A	0.55	0.30	0.17	8	$ 98,660	$ 16,279
H	0.66	0.20	0.13	9	$1,200,980	$158,529
J	0.12	0.88	0.11	10	$ 88,600	$ 9,356

EXHIBIT 4.4   Risk Ranking Expected Cost Estimate

IIA AND ISACA RISK MANAGEMENT INTERNAL AUDIT GUIDANCE

Risk management and understanding risks are important elements in both the standards and supporting guidance materials released by the IIA for all internal auditors and ISACA, with its more IT audit focus. Chapter 3 reviewed many of the internal audit standards. This section examines the levels of guidance available to assist IT auditors in their risk-related reviews. Each of these important IT audit professional organizations provides both standards and supporting guidance to help IT auditors to consider risks in their IT audit review activities.

Which standards should the IT audit professional follow? This question was answered somewhat in Chapter 3. The IIA International and ISACA IT Audit Standards are not in conflict with each other and are very similar with regard to risk management. Some chief audit executives (CAEs) and audit committee members are more familiar with the IIA offerings, and that will dictate the standards selection approach. However, if the enterprise has selected Control Objectives for Information and related Technology (CobiT) as its guidance framework for SOx compliance work, the ISACA standards are the better approach.

IIA Risk-Related International Standards and Management Guidance

The need to understand and assess risks has been part of the IIA International Standards going back to their earliest versions. Risk concepts are part of both the IIA's Attribute and Performance Standards. For example, the supporting Attribute assurance standard 1220.A3, titled Risk Identification, states:

> Internal auditors must be alert to the significant risks that might affect objectives, operations, or resources. However, assurance procedures alone, even when performed with due professional care, do not guarantee that all significant risks will be identified.

The problem with this standard, however, is that it really does not give much guidance on what is meant by a "significant risk." This lack of definition is one of those issues that has led to the COSO ERM framework and its definition of risk management. Without a clear and consistent understanding, internal auditors may miss key areas of audit risk in their review work.

As discussed in Chapter 3, the IIA International Standards for the Professional Practice of Internal Auditing consist of Attribute Standards that define areas of internal audit activity at a high level and Performance Standards that define minimum requirements for performing all levels of internal audits. There is a full Performance Standard, 2120, along with several assurance and consulting substandards on risk management.

International Professional Practice Standard 2120 on risk management says: "The internal audit activity must evaluate the effectiveness and contribute to the improvement of risk management processes." With a bit more guidance than Assurance substandard 1220.A3, this risk-related IIA International Standard is supported by two Assurance and three Consulting Standards related to risk management:

2120.A1. The internal audit activity must evaluate risk exposures relating to the organization's governance, operations, and information systems regarding the:

- Reliability and integrity of financial and operational information;
- Effectiveness and efficiency of operations;
- Safeguarding of assets; and
- Compliance with laws, regulations, and contracts.

2120.A2. The internal audit activity must evaluate the potential for the occurrence of fraud and how the organization manages fraud risk.

2120.C1. During consulting engagements, internal auditors must address risk consistent with the engagement's objectives and be alert to the existence of other significant risks.

2120.C2. Internal auditors must incorporate their knowledge of risks gained from consulting engagements into their evaluation of the organization's risk management processes.

2120.C3. When assisting management in establishing or improving risk management processes, internal auditors must refrain from assuming any management responsibility by actually managing risks.

The Assurance substandard A1 gives a broader picture of the areas an internal auditor should review and consider with regard to risks. Whether the review is IT related or in other areas, an internal auditor should take a wide view regarding risk exposures. Substandard A2 on fraud risks is the only place where the topic of fraud appears in the IIA international standards. IT audit fraud detection and prevention issues are discussed in Chapter 21.

Chapter 3 discussed the mix of IIA mandatory and strongly recommended guidance materials. One of the recommended guidance materials is an IIA publication in their Guides to the Assessment of IT (GAIT) series titled *GAIT for Business and IT Risk.*[4] This useful guide is available to IIA members. Many of its concepts appear later in this chapter on considering risk when auditing IT-related controls.

ISACA Audit Risk-Related Standards and Management Guidance

With its focus more on IT audit-related issues, ISACA has taken a stronger position on considering risk issues through its CobiT framework, discussed in Chapter 2, and the ISACA IT Audit Standards. Exhibit 4.5 is the ISACA Audit Standard S11 on the use of risk assessment in audit planning. The exhibit shows the full standard with only a few minor changes (American versus English spelling). It also follows the ISACA format where standards items in bold type are considered to be mandatory for ISACA member IT auditors.

Similar to the IIA International Standards, this standard says that IT auditors should follow a consistent risk evaluation process to plan areas for their audit reviews. ISACA also has a companion audit guideline, G13, with the same title. A fairly detailed guide, it advises that there are many risk assessment methodologies available from which the IT auditor may choose. These range from simple classifications of high, medium, and low, based on the IS auditor's judgment, to complex calculations to

---

Introduction

01 ISACA IT Auditing Standards contain the basic principles and essential procedures, identified in bold type, that are mandatory, together with related guidance.

02 The purpose of this standard is to establish standards and provide guidance regarding the use of risk assessment in audit planning.

Standard

03 The IT auditor should use an appropriate risk assessment technique or approach in developing the overall IT audit plan and in determining priorities for the effective allocation of IT audit resources.

04 When planning individual reviews, the IT auditor should identify and assess risks relevant to the area under review.

Commentary

05 Risk assessment is a technique used to examine auditable units in the IS audit universe and select areas for review to include in the IT annual plan that have the greatest risk exposure.

06 An auditable unit is defined as a discrete segment of every organization and its systems.

07 Determination of the IT audit universe should be based on knowledge of the organization's IT strategic plan, its operations, and discussions with responsible management.

08 Risk assessment exercises to facilitate the development of the IT audit plan should be carried out and documented at least on an annual basis. Organizational strategic plans, objectives, and the enterprise risk management framework should be considered as part of the risk assessment exercise.

09 The use of risk assessment in the selection of audit projects allows the IT auditor to quantify and justify the amount of IT audit resources needed to complete the IT audit plan or a particular review. Also, the IT auditor can prioritize scheduled reviews based on perceptions of risk and contribute toward the documentation of risk management frameworks.

10 An IT auditor should carry out a preliminary assessment of the risks relevant to the area under review. IT audit engagement objectives for each specific review should reflect the results of such a risk assessment.

11 Following the completion of the review, the IT auditor should ensure that the organization's enterprise risk management framework or risk register is updated, if one has been developed, to reflect findings and recommendations of the review and subsequent activity.

12 The IT auditor should refer to IT auditing guideline G13, Use of Risk Assessment in Audit Planning, and the IS auditing procedure P1, IS Risk Assessment Measurement.

EXHIBIT 4.5   ISACA Standard S11 Use of Risk Assessment in Audit Planning

Source: IT Standards, Guidelines, and Tools and Techniques for Audit Assurance and Control Professionals. © 2005 ISACA. All rights reserved. Used by permission.

---

provide numeric risk ratings. IT auditors should consider the level of complexity and detail appropriate for the activity being audited.

IT auditors should include, at a minimum, an analysis, within their methodology, of the risks to the enterprise resulting from the loss of and controls supporting system availability, data integrity, and business information confidentiality. In developing an appropriate risk assessment methodology, IT auditors should consider such things as:

- The type of information required to be collected and the extent to which the information required is already available
- The cost of software licenses required to use the methodology

- The amount of additional information required to be collected before reliable output can be obtained, and the cost of collecting this information (including the time required to be invested in the collection exercise)
- The opinions of other users of the methodology, and their views of how well it has assisted them in improving the efficiency and/or effectiveness of their audits
- The willingness of management to accept the methodology as the means of determining the type and level of audit work carried out

No single risk assessment methodology can be expected to be appropriate in all situations, but IT auditors should reevaluate the appropriateness of their chosen risk assessment methodologies and make changes the can justify as appropriate.

 ## COSO ERM: ENTERPRISE RISK MANAGEMENT

COSO ERM is a framework to help enterprises have a consistent definition of their risks. It is also an important tool for understanding and improving SOx internal controls. COSO ERM was launched in a manner similar to the development of the COSO internal control framework, as discussed in Chapter 1. Just as there had been no consistent definition of internal controls, industry accounting professionals felt there had been no consistent enterprise-level definition of risk. For example, assessing risks by their likelihood and probability of occurrence is important for IT auditors and other professions, but this method was not universally accepted elsewhere. Similarly, our discussion of IIA and ISACA standards for considering risk really do not fully define what is meant by this concept of enterprise-wide risk for IT auditors and others.

Until recently, there was no commonly accepted definition of *risk management* and no comprehensive framework outlining how the process should work, which made risk communication among board members and management difficult and sometimes frustrating.[5] Similar to the manner in which the COSO internal controls framework was developed, COSO developed an enterprise risk management framework. It was first published just after the enactment of SOx in September 2004. Just as the COSO internal controls framework started by proposing a consistent definition of its subject, the COSO ERM framework document starts by defining enterprise risk management:

> Enterprise risk management is a process, effected by an entity's board of directors, management and other personnel, applied in a strategy setting and across the enterprise, designed to identify potential events that may affect the entity, and manage risk to be within its risk appetite, to provide reasonable assurance regarding the achievement of entity objectives.

This definition is rather academic sounding. Professionals should consider the key points supporting this COSO ERM framework definition, including:

- **ERM is a process.** An often misused word, the dictionary definition of a *process* is a "set of actions designed to achieve a result." Although this definition does not provide much help for IT audit professionals, the idea here is that a process is not a static procedure, such as the use of an employee badge to allow only certain authorized persons to enter a locked IT server facility. Such a badge procedure—like a key to a lock—only either allows or does not allow someone entry to the facility. A process tends to be a more flexible arrangement. In a credit approval process, for example, acceptance rules are established with options to alter them, given other considerations. An enterprise might bend the credit rules for an otherwise good credit customer that is experiencing a short-term problem. ERM is that type of process. An enterprise often cannot define its risk management rules through a small, tightly organized rule book. Rather, there should be a series of documented steps to review and evaluate potential risks and to take action based on a wide range of factors across the entire enterprise.

- **ERM process is implemented by people in the enterprise.** An ERM will not be effective if it is implemented only through a set of rules sent in to an operating unit from a distant corporate headquarters, where the people who drafted the rules may have little understanding of the various decision factors that arise. The risk management process must be managed by people who are close enough to the risk situation to understand the various factors surrounding and implications of that risk.

- **ERM is applied through the setting of strategies across the overall enterprise.** Every enterprise is constantly faced with alternative strategies regarding a vast range of potential future actions. Should the entity acquire another complementary business to expand growth or just build internally? Should it adopt a new technology in its manufacturing processes or stick with the tried and true? An effective ERM set of processes should play a major role in helping to establish those alternative strategies. Since many enterprises are large with varied operating units, ERM should be applied across that entire enterprise using a portfolio type of approach that blends a mix of high- and low-risk activities.

- **Concept of risk appetite must be considered.** A newer concept for many, risk appetite is the amount of risk, on a broad level, that an enterprise and its individual managers are willing to accept in their pursuit of value. Risk appetite can be measured in a qualitative sense by looking at risks in such categories as high, medium, or low; alternatively, it can be defined in a qualitative manner. The basic idea behind risk appetite is that every manager and, collectively, every enterprise has some appetite for risk. Some will accept risky ventures that promise potentially high returns while others prefer a more guaranteed-return, low-risk approach. One can think of this appetite for risk concept in terms of an example of two investors. One may prefer to invest in very-low-risk but typically low-return money market or index funds; another may invest in low-cap start-up technology stocks with expectations of very high returns. That latter investor can be described as having a high appetite for risk. As another example, on a street intersection with a Walk or Don't Walk crossing lights, the person who keeps crossing the intersection when the light begins to flash "Walk," meaning it will soon change to "Don't Walk," has a higher appetite for risk.

- **ERM provides only reasonable, not positive, assurance on objective achievements.** The idea here is that an ERM, no matter how well thought out or implemented, cannot provide management or others with any assured guarantee of outcomes. A well-controlled enterprise, with people at all levels consistently working toward understood and achievable goals, may achieve those objectives period after period, even over multiple years. However, an unintentional human error, an unexpected action by another, or even a natural disaster can occur. Despite an effective ERM process, an enterprise can experience a major and totally unexpected catastrophic event. Reasonable assurance does not provide absolute assurance.

▪ **ERM is designed to help attain the achievement of objectives.** An enterprise, through its management, should work to establish high-level common objectives that can be shared by all stakeholders. Examples here include such matters as achieving and maintaining a positive reputation within an enterprise's business and consumer communities, providing reliable financial reporting to all stakeholders, and operating in compliance with laws and regulations. The overall ERM program for an enterprise should help it to achieve those objectives.

ERM-related goals and objectives are of little value unless they can be organized and modeled together in a way that management can look at the various aspects of the task and understand—at least sort of—how they interact and relate in a multidimensional manner. This is a real strength of the COSO internal controls framework. It describes, for example, how an enterprise's compliance with regulations impacts all levels of internal controls, from monitoring processes to the control environment, and how that compliance is important for all enterprise entities or units. The COSO ERM framework provides some common definitions of risk management and can help to achieve SOx internal control objectives as well as better risk management processes throughout the enterprise.

Although COSO ERM is designed to provide guidance to the total enterprise, auditors should consider its concepts when performing reviews and assessments at multiple levels. The next sections describe the COSO ERM framework in greater detail. The ERM framework looks very similar to the COSO internal controls framework discussed in Chapter 1, but it has different objectives.

Key Elements

The COSO internal control framework, has become a worldwide model for describing and defining internal controls and has been the basis for establishing SOx Section 404 compliance. Perhaps because some of the same team members were involved with both COSO internal controls and ERM, the COSO ERM framework—at first glance—looks very similar to the COSO internal controls framework. The COSO ERM framework is also shown in Exhibit 4.6 as a three-dimensional cube with the components of:

▪ Four vertical columns representing the strategic objectives of enterprise risk.
▪ Eight horizontal rows or risk components.
▪ Multiple levels to describe any enterprise, from a "headquarters" entity level to individual subsidiaries. Depending on organization size, there can be many "slices" of the model here.

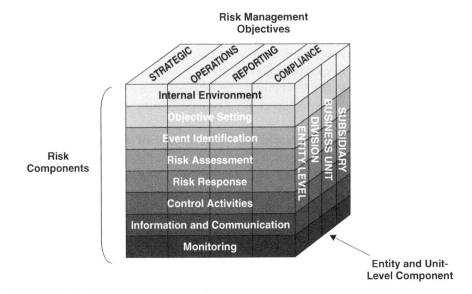

EXHIBIT 4.6 COSO ERM Framework
Source: Robert R. Moeller, *COSO Enterprise Risk Management: Understanding the New Integrated ERM Framework* (Hoboken, NJ: John Wiley & Sons). Copyright © 2007, John Wiley & Sons. Used with permission of John Wiley & Sons.

This section focuses on the front-facing horizontal components of COSO ERM, with brief discussions on COSO ERM's other two dimensions and how they all relate to one another. The concept behind the ERM framework is to provide a model for enterprises to consider and understand their risk-related activities at all levels as well as how these risk components impact one another. An objective of this chapter is to help internal auditors at all levels—from from the CAE to staff IT auditors—to better understand COSO ERM and learn how it can help manage a wide range of risks facing enterprises.

Because the COSO ERM framework diagram looks very similar to the COSO internal controls framework, some have incorrectly viewed COSO ERM as just a new update to their familiar COSO internal controls framework. However, COSO ERM has different objectives and uses. *COSO ERM should not be considered just a new and improved or revised version of the COSO internal control framework.* It is much more. The next sections outline this framework from a risk components perspective.

- **Internal environment component.** Looking at the front of the COSO ERM cube, there are eight levels, with the internal environment component located at the top of ERM framework. The internal environment may be thought of as the capstone to COSO ERM. It holds the framework together. This capstone component is similar to the box at the top of an organization chart that lists the CEO as the designated head of a function. This level defines the basis for all other components in an enterprise's ERM model, influencing how strategies and objectives should be established, how risk-related business activities are structured, and how risks are identified and acted on. The COSO ERM internal environment component consists of these elements:

- **Risk management philosophy.** These are the shared attitudes and beliefs that characterize how the enterprise should consider risk in everything it does. More than a message in a code of conduct, a risk management philosophy is the attitude that should allow stakeholders at all levels to respond to high-risk proposals with an answer along the lines of "No, that's not the kind of venture our company will be interested in."

- **Risk appetite.** Appetite is the amount of risk an enterprise is willing to accept in the pursuit of its objectives. An appetite for risk can be measured in either quantitative or qualitative terms, but all levels of management should have a general understanding of their enterprise's overall risk appetite. The term *appetite* was not often used by internal auditors prior to COSO ERM, but it is a useful expression that describes an overall risk philosophy.

- **Board of director attitudes.** The board and its committees have a very important role in overseeing and guiding an enterprise's risk environment. The independent, outside directors in particular should closely review management actions, ask appropriate questions, and serve as a check and balance control for the enterprise.

- **Integrity and ethical values.** This ERM element requires more than just a published code of conduct and includes a well-thought-out mission statement and integrity standards. There should be a strong corporate culture to guide the enterprise, at all levels, in helping to make risk-based decisions. This area should be an essential component in every ERM framework today.

- **Commitment to competence.** *Competence* refers to the knowledge and skills necessary to perform assigned tasks. Management decides how these critical tasks will be accomplished by developing strategies and assigning the proper people to perform them. With a strong commitment to competence, managers at all levels should take steps to achieve their promised goals.

- **Organization structure.** An enterprise should develop an organization structure with clear lines of authority, responsibility, and appropriate reporting. Every professional has seen situations where an organization does not allow for appropriate lines of communication. There can be many situations in which the organization structure needs improvement to achieve effective ERM.

- **Assignments of authority and responsibility.** This ERM component refers to the degree to which authority and responsibility is assigned or delegated. The trend in many enterprises today is to flatten organizations by eliminating middle management levels. These structures usually encourage employee creativity, faster response times, and greater customer satisfaction. However, this type of customer-facing organization requires strong procedures and rules for the staff as well as ongoing management processes so that lower-level staff decisions can be overruled if necessary. All individuals should know how their actions interrelate and contribute to the overall objectives of the enterprise.

■ **Human resource (HR) standards.** Practices regarding employee hiring, training, compensating, promoting, disciplining, and all other actions send messages to staff regarding what is favored, tolerated, or forbidden. When management winks at or ignores some gray-area activities rather than taking a strong stand, that message is usually informally and quickly communicated to others. Strong standards are needed to ensure that HR rules are both communicated to all stakeholders and are enforced.

Other COSO ERM guidance materials include examples of the components necessary to build an effective internal environment. Many refer to the standards and approaches an enterprise should implement to accept and manage various levels of risk; others refer to just good business practices. No matter whether an enterprise has a high or low appetite for risk, it needs to establish control environment practices to manage those risks. For example, the enterprise can give its sales force rather free rein to do deals without much management supervision and approval. Yet everyone should know the legal, ethical, and management policy limits of those free-rein practices. Processes should be in place such that if anyone steps over the line regarding these limits, swift remedial actions are taken and communicated.

The COSO ERM internal environment components of the enterprise's risk management philosophy and its relative appetite for risk feed other elements of the COSO ERM framework. A risk management philosophy is often defined by the board of directors' attitudes and their policies, and the concept risk appetite is often a softer measure, where an enterprise has determined that it will accept some risks but reject others in terms of their likelihood and impact. Exhibit 4.7 shows a risk appetite map illustrating where an enterprise should recognize the range in which it is willing to accept risks in terms of their likelihood and impact. This exhibit says an enterprise may be willing to get involved in a high-negative-impact project if there is a low likelihood of an occurrence. There is a third dimension to this chart as well. An enterprise sometimes will have a greater appetite for a more risky endeavor if there is a higher potential return.

Objective-Setting Components

Ranked below the internal environment in the COSO ERM framework, objective setting outlines important conditions to help management create an effective ERM process. This emphasizes that an enterprise mission statement is a crucial element for setting objectives; it is a general, formal statement of purpose and a building block for the development of specific functional strategies. COSO ERM calls for an enterprise to formally define its goals with a direct linkage to its mission statement, along with measurement criteria to assess whether it is achieving these risk management objectives.

The COSO ERM's objective-setting component should formally define the enterprise's risk appetite in terms of risk tolerance and guidelines whether to accept these risks or not. Establishing and enforcing risk tolerances can be very difficult, if these rules are not clearly defined, well understood, and strictly enforced. An enterprise should

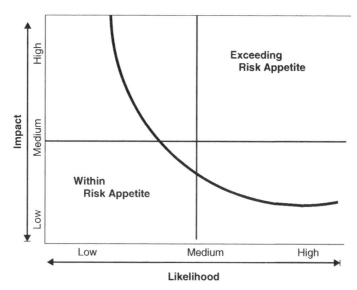

EXHIBIT 4.7   Risk Appetite Map
Source: Robert R. Moeller, *COSO Enterprise Risk Management: Understanding the New Integrated ERM Framework* (Hoboken, NJ: John Wiley & Sons, 2007). Copyright © 2007, John Wiley & Sons. Used with permission of John Wiley & Sons.

establish tolerable ranges of acceptable risks in many areas. For example, products coming off production lines might have acceptable preestablished error rates of no greater than 0.005%. That is an acceptably low error rate in many areas, and production management here would accept the risk of any product warranty claims or damage to the enterprise's reputation if there were errors within that relatively narrow limit. Of course, today's quality assurance emphasis on six sigma programs, as discussed in Chapter 28, brings those tolerance limits much tighter.[6]

The point here is that an enterprise should define its risk-related strategies and objectives and should decide on its appetite and tolerances for these risks. That is, it should determine the level of risks it is willing to accept and, given those risk tolerance rules, how far it is willing to deviate from these preestablished measures. In order to manage and control risks at all levels, an enterprise needs set its objectives and define its tolerances for engaging in risky practices and for adherence to these rules. Things will not work if the enterprise establishes some risk-related objectives but then proceeds to ignore them.

Event Identification

Events are enterprise incidents or occurrences—external or external—that affect the implementation of an ERM strategy and the achievement of its objectives. Although our tendency is to think of events in a negative sense—determining what went wrong—they can be positive as well. Many enterprises today have strong performance monitoring tools in place, monitoring costs, budgets, quality assurance, compliance, and the like. However, going beyond activities on a production assembly line, monitoring processes should include external economic, natural environmental, and political events.

An enterprise needs to clearly define its significant risk events and then have processes in place to monitor them in order to take any necessary appropriate actions. This is a forward-thinking type of process that is often difficult to recognize in many enterprises. Looking at these internal and external potential risk events and deciding which ones require further attention can be a difficult process. Some are immediate needs, and others very future directed. An enterprise should establish processes to review potentially significant risks and then take action.

Risk Assessments

While the internal environment component is COSO ERM's cornerstone, risk assessment processes allow an enterprise to consider the extent to which these potential risk-related events may be considered as part of an enterprise's achievement of its objectives. These risks should be assessed from the likelihood of the risk occurring and its potential impact. A key part of this risk assessment process, however, is the need to consider the inherent and residual risks, as discussed previously.

These two concepts imply that an enterprise will always face some risks. After management has addressed the risks that came out of its risk identification process, some residual risks to remedy still will exist. In addition, there are always some inherent risks where management can do little. As mentioned previously in our discussion of inherent risk, Wal-Mart can take some steps to reduce its inherent risks related to market dominance but can do essentially nothing regarding the inherent risk of a major earthquake.

Risk likelihood and impact are two other key components necessary for performing risk assessments. *Likelihood* is the probability or possibility that a risk will occur. In many instances, this can be a key management assessment stated in the terms of a high, medium, or low likelihood of the risk occurring. There are also some good quantitative tools to develop likelihood estimates, but it does little good to estimate the likelihood of a risk occurring unless there is strong supporting data.

Estimating the *impact* if a risk event occurs is a bit easier. Examples include, for IT-related risks, the impact of a data server and network center catastrophic loss or failure. An enterprise can develop some relatively accurate estimates such as the cost of replacing facilities and equipment, the cost of restoring systems, and the cost of lost business due to the failure. However, the whole concept behind ERM is not to develop precise, actuarial-level calculations regarding these risks but to gain some measure to provide for an effective risk management framework. Those detailed calculations can be delegated to insurance estimators and others.

Risk likelihoods and potential impacts can be analyzed through a series of quantitative and qualitative measures. The idea, however, is to assess all of the identified risks and to rank them in terms of likelihood and impact in a consistent manner. That is, each identified risk can be ranked on an overall relative scale of perhaps 1 to 10, with consideration given to the impact and likelihood of each. Then one can identify the risks that should receive the most thorough management attention.

Overall approaches to reviewing these various likelihood and impact risks need to be considered. Risk assessment is a key component of the COSO ERM framework.

This is where an enterprise evaluates all of the identified risks that might impact its various objectives, considers their potential likelihoods and impacts, considers their interrelationship on a unit-by-unit or total enterprise basis, and then develops strategies for appropriate responses. In some respects, this COSO ERM risk assessment process is not too different from the classic risk assessment techniques that have been used over the years. What is unique is that COSO ERM suggests that an enterprise should take a total approach, across all units and covering all major strategic concerns, to identify its risks in a consistent and thorough manner.

Risk Response Strategies

Having assessed and identified its more significant risks, COSO ERM risk response calls for measured actions to these various identified risks. There should be a careful review of estimated risk likelihoods and potential impacts, with consideration given to associated costs and benefits, to develop appropriate risk response strategies. These risk responses can be handled in any of four basic approaches:

1. Risk **Avoidance.** This is a strategy of walking away from a risk—such as selling a business unit that gives rise to a risk, exiting from a risky geographic area, or dropping a product line. The problem is that enterprises often do not drop a product line or walk away until *after* the risk event has occurred with its associated costs. Unless an enterprise has a very low appetite for risk, it is difficult to walk away from an otherwise successful business area or product line on the basis of a potential future risk. Avoidance can be a costly strategy if investments were made to get into an area with a subsequent pull-out to avoid the risk.

    A collective lessons-learned understanding of past activities often can help with this strategy. If the enterprise had been involved in some area in the past with unfavorable consequences, this may be a good way to avoid the risk once again. With the tendency of constant changes and short employment tenures, this collective history is too often lost and forgotten. An enterprise's well-understood and communicated appetite for risk is perhaps the most important consideration when deciding if a risk avoidance strategy is appropriate.

2. Risk **Reduction.** A wide range of business decisions may be able to reduce certain risks. Product line diversification may reduce the risk of too strong of a reliance on one key product line, or splitting IT operations into two geographically separate locations will reduce the risk of some catastrophic failure. There exists a wide range of often-effective strategies to reduce risks at all levels, going down to the obvious and mundane, such as cross-training employees to reduce the risk of someone departing unexpectedly.

3. Risk **Sharing.** Virtually all enterprises regularly share some of their risks through the purchase of insurance, but other risk-sharing techniques are available as well. For financial transactions, an enterprise can engage in hedging operations to protect from possible price fluctuations, or an enterprise can share potential business risks and rewards through corporate joint venture share-the-risk agreements. The idea is to have another party accept some of a potential risk as well as to share in any resultant rewards.

4. Risk **Acceptance.** This is a strategy of taking no action, such as when an enterprise self-insures by taking no action to reduce a potential risk. Essentially, an enterprise should look at a risk's likelihood and impact in light of its established risk tolerance and then decide whether to accept that risk or not. Acceptance is often an appropriate strategy for some of the risks that an enterprise faces.

Management must develop a general response strategy for each of its risks using an approach built around one or a mixture of the risk avoidance strategies. In doing so, it should consider the costs versus benefits of each potential risk response as well as strategies that best align with the enterprise's overall risk appetite. For example, an enterprise's recognition that the impact of a given risk is relatively low would be balanced against a low risk tolerance that suggests that insurance should be purchased to provide a potential risk response. For many risks, appropriate responses are obvious and almost universally understood. An IT operation, for example, spends the time and resources to back up its key data files and implements a business continuity plan. There are typically no questions regarding the need for these basic approaches, but various levels of management may question the frequency of backup processes or how often the continuity plan needs to be tested. That is, they may question the extent and cost of planned risk prevention measures.

An enterprise should go back to its established risk objectives as well as the tolerance ranges for those objectives. Then it should readdress both the likelihoods and impacts associated with each to develop an overall set of the planned risk responses. This is perhaps the most difficult step in building an effective COSO ERM program. It is comparatively easy to identify a 5% likelihood risk that there will be a fire in the scrap materials bin and then to establish a risk response remedy to install a nearby fire extinguisher. However, responses to most risks are much more complex and require fairly detailed planning and analysis. If there is a risk that an enterprise could lose an entire manufacturing operation due to a key but old equipment plant production failure, potential risk responses might include:

- Acquire backup production equipment to serve as spare parts for cannibalization.
- Shut down the manufacturing production line with plans to move it elsewhere.
- Arrange for a specialized shop to rebuild/reconstruct the old equipment.
- Reengineer the manufactured product along with plans for new product introduction.

Developing risk responses requires a significant amount of planning and strategic thinking. For example, one of the response strategies just mentioned is to acquire a set of backup equipment. If that is to be the approved strategy, action must be taken to acquire the backup equipment before this activity can even be identified as an actual risk response strategy. The idea is that all risks listed on such an analysis should be measured against the same impact factors, based on an accept, avoid, share, or reduce risks strategy.

COSO ERM calls for risks to be considered and evaluated on an entity- or portfolio-wide basis. This can be a difficult process in a large, multi-unit, multiproduct enterprise, but it provides a starting point in getting the various risks organized for identification of more significant risks that may impact the enterprise. The idea here is to look at these various potential risks, their probability of occurrence, and the impacts of each. A good analysis here should highlight areas for more detailed attention.

Control Activities

COSO ERM's control activities are the policies and procedures necessary to ensure action on identified risk responses. Although some of these activities may relate to an identified and approved risk response in only one area of the enterprise, they often overlap across multiple functions and units. The control activities component of COSO ERM should be tightly linked with the risk response strategies and actions previously discussed.

Having selected appropriate risk responses, an enterprise should select control activities necessary to ensure that these control activities are executed in a timely and efficient manner. The process of determining if control activities are performing properly is very similar to completing SOx Section 404 internal control assessments, as discussed in Chapter 1. COSO ERM calls for approaches of identifying, documenting, testing, and then validating these risk protection controls. Many control activities under the COSO internal controls framework are fairly easy to identify and test, including these internal control areas:

- **Separation of duties.** Essentially, the person who initiates a transaction should not be the same person who authorizes that transaction. This area is discussed in Chapter 6 on IT general controls.
- **Audit trails.** Processes should be organized such that final results can be easily traced back to the transactions that created them. This area is particularly important for reviews of IT applications, as discussed in Chapter 10.
- **Security and integrity.** Control processes should have appropriate control procedures such that only authorized persons can review or modify them. IT security controls are discussed in Chapter 19.
- **Documentation.** Processes should be appropriately documented. Chapter 12 discusses the importance of IT documentation and records management systems.

These well-recognized control procedures are applicable to all IT internal control processes and apply to many risk-related events. Many IT professionals—whether they have an accounting and auditing background or not—often can easily define some of these key controls, which are necessary in most business processes. For example, if asked to identify the types of internal controls that should be built into an accounts payable system, many would identify the significant control points that checks issued from the system must be authorized by independent persons, that accounting records must be in place to keep track of the checks issued, and that the check-issuing process should be such that only authorized persons can initiate such transactions. These are generally well widely understood internal control procedures. An enterprise often faces a more difficult task in identifying control activities to support its ERM framework. Although there is no accepted or standard set of ERM control activities at this time, the COSO ERM documentation suggests several areas:

- **Top-level reviews.** Senior management should be very aware of the identified risk events within their organizational units and perform regular top-level reviews on the status of identified risks.
- **Direct functional or activity management.** In addition to top-level reviews, supporting unit managers should have a key role in risk control activity monitoring.
- **Information processing.** Whether it is IT systems and processes or softer forms such as paper-based or messages, information processing represents a key component in an enterprise's risk-related control activities. Appropriate control procedures should be established with an emphasis on enterprise IT processes and risks.
- **Physical controls.** Many risk-related concerns involve physical assets, such as IT equipment, inventories, securities, and physical plants. Whether it is dealing with physical inventories, inspections, or plant security procedures, an enterprise should install appropriate risk-based physical control activity procedures.
- **Performance indicators.** The typical enterprise today employs a wide range of financial and operational reporting tools that can also support risk event–related performance reporting. Where necessary, performance tools should be modified to support this important COSO ERM control activity component.
- **Segregation of duties.** Segregation of duties is a classic control activity: The person who initiates certain actions should not be the same person who approves them.

These control activities can be expanded to cover other key areas. Some will be specific to individual units within the enterprise, but each control activity, singly and collectively, should be important components of supporting the enterprise's ERM framework. The next sections describe control activities from many perspectives of IT operations.

Information and Communication

This COSO ERM component links together each of the other components. For example, the risk response component receives residual and inherent risk inputs from risk assessment as well as risk tolerance support from the objective-setting component. COSO ERM risk response then provides risk response and risk portfolio data to control activities as well as feedback to the risk assessment.

Although it is relatively easy to describe how information should be communicated from one COSO ERM component to another in a simple flow diagram, in practice the process is far more complex. Many enterprises have a complex web of operational and financial information systems for their basic processes that often are not very well linked. These linkages become even more complex for many ERM processes, given that many basic enterprise applications do not lend themselves directly to processes for risk identification, assessment, and risk response. Going beyond a comprehensive ERM information application for an enterprise, there is a need to develop risk monitoring and communications systems that link with customers, suppliers, and other stakeholders.

The information half of the ERM information and communication component is normally thought of in terms of IT strategic and operational information systems. ERM communication is the second aspect of this component. It talks about communication beyond just IT applications, such as the need for mechanisms to ensure that all stakeholders receive messages regarding the enterprise's interest in managing its risks abs using a common risk language throughout the enterprise. COSO ERM will be of little value to an enterprise unless the overall message of its importance is communicated to all stakeholders in a common and consistent manner.

Monitoring Component

Placed at the base of the stack of ERM framework model components shown in Exhibit 4.6, monitoring processes are necessary to determine that all installed ERM components work effectively. People in the enterprise change, as do supporting processes and internal and external conditions, but the monitoring component helps ensure that ERM is working effectively on a continuous basis. The monitoring component should include processes to flag exceptions or violations in other components of the ERM process. For example, an IT accounts receivable billing system should identify the overall financial and operational risks if customer bills are not paid on a timely basis. An ongoing—almost real-time—credit collections monitoring tool could provide senior management with day-to-day and trending data on the status of collections. Dashboard monitoring tools, discussed in Chapter 14, are types of ERM monitors that can work on a continuous basis.

Going beyond IT dashboard tools, enterprise management should take an overall responsibility for ERM monitoring. In order to establish an effective ERM framework, monitoring should include ongoing reviews of the overall ERM process, ranging from identified objectives to the progress of ongoing ERM control activities.

Separate or individual evaluation monitoring processes refers to detailed reviews of individual risk processes by a qualified reviewer, such as internal or IT audit. Here the review can be limited to specific areas or cover the entire ERM process for an enterprise unit. Internal audit is often the best internal source to perform such specific ERM reviews. The role of internal audit in the ERM process and its role in monitoring, in particular, is discussed in the next sections.

Other Dimensions of COSO ERM: Risk Management Objectives

Although much of our COSO ERM discussion here is on the front-facing side of the three-dimensional framework, the two other dimensions—the operational and organizational levels—should always be considered as well. Each component of COSO ERM operates in this three-dimensional space, where each must be considered in terms of the other related categories. The top-facing components of strategic, operations, reporting, and compliance risk objectives are important for understanding and implementing COSO ERM. In addition, although Exhibit 4.6 shows each of these top-facing risk objectives as having the same relative size, the category of operations-level risk objectives is often viewed as a much broader and higher-exposure risk category than the others.

As an example, the top-facing component of the three-dimensional ERM framework, the operations-level risk objective, calls for the identification of risks for each enterprise unit or component. Identification of these risk objectives often requires detailed information gathering and analysis, particularly for a larger enterprise covering multiple geographic areas, product lines, or business processes. Of course, IT operations are usually a major component here. In order to gather more detailed background information on potential operations risks, an internal audit survey of direct on-the-floor members of the enterprise, along with follow-up questions, should survey potential operations risks across all levels of the enterprise. This type of survey is similar to the types of questions often used in other IT audit internal control assessments.

With COSO ERM's portfolio view of risks, an enterprise should avoid rolling things up to too much of a summary level, missing or rounding off important lower-level risks. Managers at all levels should be aware that they are responsible for accepting and managing the risks within their own operational units. Too often, unit managers believe that risk management is of concern only to some senior-level, headquarters type. The importance of COSO ERM and operations risk management should be communicated to all levels of an enterprise. Internal and IT auditors should act as eyes and ears here and report all observed operations risks.

Reporting Risk Management Objectives

This risk objective covers the reliability of an enterprise's reporting, including the internal and external reporting of financial and nonfinancial data. Accurate reporting is critical to an enterprise's success in many dimensions. News reports often relate the discovery of inaccurate corporate financial reporting and the resultant stock market repercussions for the offending entity; that same inaccurate reporting can cause problems in many areas.

No matter what the industry, an enterprise faces major risks from inaccurate reporting. Operating units must make certain that reported results are correct before they are passed up to the next level in the organization, and consolidated numbers must be accurate, whether on financial reports, tax returns, or any of a myriad of other areas. Although good internal controls are necessary to ensure accurate reporting, COSO ERM is concerned about the risk of authorizing and releasing inaccurate reports. Strong internal controls should minimize the risk of errors, and an enterprise should always consider the risks associated with inaccurate reporting. Small errors and discrepancies can be ignored over time until a major error needs to be disclosed. The risk of such inaccurate reporting should be a concern at all levels of the enterprise.

Legal and Regulatory Compliance Risk Objectives

Every enterprise has requirements to comply with a wide range of laws, government-imposed regulations, or industry standards. Although compliance risks can be monitored and recognized, legal risks are sometimes totally unanticipated. In the United States, for example, an aggressive plaintiff legal system can pose a major risk to otherwise well-intentioned enterprises. Asbestos litigation during the 1990s and beyond is an example. A fibrous mineral, asbestos has three extraordinary characteristics: It works as an insulator for heat and electricity; it resists other dangerous chemicals; and, when inhaled, it has been found to cause illnesses that may take decades to develop. Asbestos is a natural insulation material that previously was used extensively in building materials and was considered totally benign. Too much direct contact with asbestos fibers over time, however, can cause severe lung problems and even death. Underground miners extracting asbestos have met that fate. However, in the past, asbestos was used in many products, such as wrappers to insulate heating pipes or as fire protection wall barriers. The risks to persons working or living in a structure with these asbestos-sealed pipes are minimal, but aggressive litigators have brought actions against corporations, claiming that anyone who could have had any contact, no matter how minimal, with a product that used asbestos could be at risk sometime in the future. The result was litigation directed against companies that had manufactured products containing some asbestos, calling for damages based on potential human risks in future years. Because of huge damage awards, virtually all major corporations that once used asbestos have gone bankrupt or out of business, or have had to pay huge court-imposed damage losses. This is the type of legal risk that is very difficult to anticipate but that can be disastrous to an enterprise.

COSO ERM recommends that compliance-related risks be considered for each of the risk framework components, whether in the context of the internal environment, objective setting, or risk monitoring, as well as across the enterprise. The COSO ERM guidance material does not offer much additional material on this compliance objective other than to state that it refers to conformance with applicable laws and regulations. These COSO ERM elements are important components of the risk management framework that need to be communicated and understood.

All enterprises face a wide range of legal and regulatory compliance requirements; some impact virtually all enterprises, and others are related to only single business units in a specialized industry sector. The nature of those compliance risks needs to be communicated and understood through all levels of an enterprise. This is an area where an enterprise may accept a certain level of risk in terms of its concerns regarding legal compliance. Although an enterprise should not deliberately ignore a major law because of a feeling it never will be caught, it should always take a reasoned approach to risks in conjunction with its overall philosophy and risk appetites. For example, many regulatory rules specify that all expenditures over US$25 must be supported by a receipt. Although there usually are no reasonableness guidelines here, another enterprise could decide that "all expenditures" goes down to an employee travel expenses of less than $1.00, while another will require receipts for anything above $25.00. The latter enterprise has made a decision that the costs of documenting small expenditures is greater than any fine it might receive if caught in a regulatory compliance issue. This type of a risk-related decision is similar to the SOx Auditing Standard No. 5 on financial internal controls rules discussed in Chapter 1. In order to manage and establish legal and regulatory risk objectives, the board of directors, the CEO, and members of management need to have an understanding of the nature and extent of all of the regulatory risks the enterprise faces. The legal department, key managers, internal audit, and others can help in assembling this information. There are many regulatory enterprise-level risks ranging from major to minor, but regulatory risks are never "minor" when an enterprise is found to be in violation of one or another of them.

Another Dimension of COSO ERM: Entity-Level Risks

The third dimension of the COSO ERM framework calls risks to be considered on an organization or entity level. Exhibit 4.6 shows four divisions in this framework diagram: entity level, division, business unit, and subsidiary risks. This is not a prescribed company-type division, and COSO ERM suggests that risks should closely follow the official organization chart. COSO ERM risks should be identified and managed within each significant organizational unit, including risks on an entity-wide basis through individual business units.

Consider an enterprise with four major operating divisions and with multiple business units or subsidiary units under which each would have an ERM framework that reflects all of these units. These risks are important on an overall organizational level, but there should be some consideration of these risk crossing unit boundaries on a unit-by-unit basis to as low a level as necessary to allow the enterprise to understand and manage its risks. COSO ERM does not specify how thinly these unit-level risks should be sliced, and the criticality and materiality of individual business units should be given consideration. For a major fast-food restaurant chain with thousands of units, it almost certainly would not be reasonable to include each individual unit as a separate component in the risk model. Rather, management should define its organizational-level risks at a level of detail that will cover all significant, manageable risks.

Entity Risks Encompassing the Entire Enterprise

Multiple business unit–level risks should roll up to their entity-level risks. It is easy for an enterprise to consider some unit-level risks using pre-SOx public accounting terminology as being "not material," an enterprise has to think of all risks as potentially significant. For example, consider a relatively small subsidiary in a developing country that is manufacturing casual clothing. Often, such a subsidiary unit would be so small in terms of total corporate revenue contributions or its relative size that it can easily slip under the radar screen on a senior corporate level. However, due to political or social issues at the host country, the enterprise may soon find itself at the center of attention regarding this small subsidiary operation. In such a situation, journalists may ask the CEO to publicly comment on policies and procedures at that operation, even though the CEO may only vaguely know of its existence.

The point here is that both major as well as seemingly small risks can impact an entire enterprise. The delivery of tainted food produced at one small unit of a large fast-food chain can impact the prospects and reputation of the total enterprise. Although it is relatively easy to identify high-level, entity-wide risks, such as compliance with SOx Section 404, and to identify and monitor these local unit are part of the COSO ERM process as well, and care must be taken that smaller potential risks are not ignored. As risks are identified through organization-wide objective setting, they should be considered on an entity-wide basis as well as by individual operating units. Those individual unit risks should be first reviewed and consolidated to identify any key risks that may impact the overall organization.

Business Unit Entity-Level Risks

Entity risks must be considered for each significant organizational unit, whether a major production division with multiple plants or a small IT service unit. Even the risks identified in the minority ownership position in a foreign country sales company—risks unique to that unit—should roll up to the operating division and then to the entity. An example here could be entity-level risks that might result from failures in manufacturing or human rights standards from a small subsidiary in a developing country. Risk events here can cause an embarrassment to the overall enterprise, but they should have been controlled all the way down to that small company unit. The previously discussed Bhopal, India, plant disaster brought down the parent corporation.

Depending on the complexity and number of operating units, risk responsibility often can best start as a push-down process where corporate-level management formally outlines its major risk-related concerns and asks responsible management at each major division to survey risk objectives through the operating units within that division. In this manner, significant risks can be identified at all levels and then managed at levels where they can receive the most direct, local support.

A major concept surrounding COSO ERM is that an enterprise faces a wide range of significant risks at all levels. Some may be significant while others may be just troubling annoyances and viewed as minor. The COSO ERM framework provides a mechanism to consider these risks; it is an important tool to help an IT auditor identify and assess effective internal controls.

 ## IT AUDIT RISK AND COSO ERM

The COSO ERM framework addresses a risk management approach that is very useful for IT auditors. It is applicable to all industries and encompasses all types of risk. With its focus on recognizing an enterprise's appetite for risk and the need to apply risk management within the context of overall strategy setting, COSO ERM presents IT auditors with a risk management methodology that is specified by but unfortunately undefined in the IIA and ISACA auditing standards.

COSO ERM is an important tool for understanding the multiple risks an enterprise faces today and is particularly useful in an IT internal controls environment. IT auditors will encounter risk and risk management issues in many areas where they are performing reviews, and the effective IT auditor should understand risk management processes. All too often, an IT auditor performing an internal controls review in some area is told that the area was or was not selected because of "risk considerations." IT Auditors should understand basic risk management processes in order to ask the right questions and to review the adequacy of those risk management processes.

COSO ERM is an area where an IT auditor can improve the overall internal controls processes in the areas reviewed. With a focus on the COSO ERM framework as well as general good risk management practices, IT auditors can provide a service to their enterprise by planning and performing reviews of enterprise risk management processes. Of course, to review COSO ERM practices and implementation procedures, IT auditors need to develop a strong understanding of ERM controls and processes.

The idea for IT auditors is to establish some high-level review objectives for the effectiveness of COSO ERM, gather detailed implementation data, and then assess the effectiveness of COSO ERM in an enterprise and as a tool to support and enhance SOx compliance. Exhibit 4.8 provides guidance for auditing COSO ERM IT audit procedures.

Step	Audit Procedure
1	Meet with appropriate managers to gain an understanding of the enterprise's ERM implementation strategy, its planned scope, and current implementation status.
2	Develop a strategy for reviewing ERM processes, perhaps with a focus emphasizing all internal environment processes on an entity level as well as the status of all components for a selected subsidiary or business unit.
3	Develop detailed internal audit plans for the components selected for review, and publish engagement letters announcing the planned audits.
4	Review enterprise-wide ERM guidance materials in place to assess whether ERM objectives are being adequately communicated and assess areas where communication may be lacking.
5	Risk management philosophy and appetite
5.1	Meet with appropriate members of management to assess whether a risk management philosophy has been defined and communicated.
5.2	Through surveys or interviews, meet with selected members of the enterprise to determine if the risk appetite has been communicated.
6	Risk management integrity and ethical values
6.1	Review published codes of conduct and other materials to determine if risk-related ethical values are being communicated.
6.2	Review a sample of enterprise communications and assess whether attention is given to ERM philosophies.
7	Risk management organization structure
7.1	Meet with human resources management to assess whether processes are in place to communicate the ERM philosophy to enterprise.
7.2	Review the code of conduct records to determine that it has been periodically updated, that all stakeholders have acknowledged it, and that code compliance records are in place.
7.3	Based on a review of organization charts and other documentation, assess whether the ERM philosophy appears to be in place throughout selected units in the enterprise.
8	Select one subsidiary or enterprise unit to determine if enterprise-wide ERM objectives and risk components are in place for the selected unit
8.1	Assess compliance with ERM internal objectives for the selected business unit.
8.2	Assess compliance with ERM objectives-setting processes for the selected business unit.
8.3	Assess compliance with ERM event notification processes for the selected business unit.

EXHIBIT 4.8 Auditing COSO ERM IT Audit Procedures

8.4	Assess compliance with ERM risk assessment for the selected business unit.
8.5	Assess compliance with ERM risk response processes for the selected business unit.
8.6	Assess compliance with ERM control activity processes for the selected business unit.
8.7	Assess compliance with ERM information and communication processes for the selected business unit.
8.8	Assess compliance with ERM risk monitoring processes for the selected business unit.

EXHIBIT 4.8 (Continued)

Because the two framework models look quite similar, it is very easy to miss thinking about the unique characteristics of COSO ERM as compared to COSO internal controls. As discussed in Chapter 1, it took many years for the COSO internal controls framework to be recognized as more than an interesting technical study. COSO internal controls has now been codified as an auditing standard by the American Institute of Certified Public Accountants' Auditing Standards Board, and the Public Company Accounting Oversight Board mandated that COSO internal controls should be the internal controls standard. Arriving after SOx, COSO ERM does not yet have that same level of recognition. The IIA was an important early proponent. Elements of ERM can be seen in the new version of the ISACA control objectives for IT (CobiT) framework, as discussed in Chapter 2, but it still does not have the same importance for an enterprise as do COSO internal controls.

This recognition may take some time. The facts that the two frameworks look alike and both have COSO in their names have caused some confusion. However, the risk-related emphasis on the new auditing standards as well as an increasing recognition of risk issues in professional literature has somewhat increased professional interest in enterprise risk management. The three-dimensional ERM framework helps to place risk and internal control issues in a better perspective when evaluating IT internal controls.

Risk management and COSO ERM, in particular, are standards that should be part of every IT and internal auditor's tools. IT auditors should use risk management principles when deciding which areas to select for their reviews and then use risk principles when assessing audit evidence. Perhaps even more important, COSO ERM will grow in importance and recognition as more enterprises understand and adopt the ERM framework. IT auditors should understand COSO ERM to both audit compliance to these identified processes and should act as consultants to management to help with more effective implementations.

NOTES

1. COSO Enterprise Risk Management—Integrated Framework, COSO.
2. A straw man is an old military term meaning that a man or an idea that is filled only with straw is easy to attack or refute.
3. "Bhopal Faces Risk of Poisoning," November 14, 2004, http://news.bbc.co.uk/2/hi/south_asia/4010511.stm Note: This one of many references on this issue. A search for "Bhopal, India" and "Dow Chemical" will yield a large amount of information.

4. Institute of Internal Auditors, *GAIT for Business and IT Risk* (Altamonte Springs, FL: www.theiia.org.

5. "COSO Releases a New Risk Management Framework," *Accounting Today*, October 25, 2004.

6. Six sigma is a disciplined methodology for eliminating defects (driving toward six standard deviations between the mean and the nearest specification limit) in any process, from manufacturing to transactional and from product to service.

5

Performing Effective IT Audits

NFORMATION TECHNOLOGY (IT) AUDITORS have many roles and responsibilities in today's IT-centric enterprises, but the most important of these is to perform effective IT audits, under the overall supervision of their audit committee. To be effective, it is important that an IT auditor has a good understanding of the Committee of Sponsoring Organizations' (COSO) internal controls framework and the Sarbanes-Oxley (SOx) internal controls assessment standards discussed in Chapter 1. Perhaps even more important for any auditor reviewing IT controls is an understanding of the IT Governance Association's control objectives for IT (CobiT) framework introduced in Chapter 2. An understanding of the risk management concepts discussed in Chapter 4 is another essential key IT audit knowledge requirement. In addition, every IT internal auditor is expected to follow the appropriate audit standards as issued by the Institute of Internal Auditors (IIA) as well as the Information Systems Audit and Control Association (ISACA).

The preceding four chapters have outlined some of these essential tools necessary for performing effective IT audits and reviewing enterprise IT security and internal controls. This chapter brings these IT audit building blocks together to discuss what it takes to perform effective IT audits. With IT-related internal control and security issues so pervasive in all enterprises today, skilled resources should be in place to assess enterprise IT security and control issues and then to independently report the results of those reviews to appropriate levels of management and the board of directors' audit committee.

For most enterprises today, IT audit is a specialized skill that is an essential element of the overall internal audit function. Sometimes IT audit processes are performed by a separate group of specialists, and in other cases it is an additional skill performed by the regular operational and financial internal auditors. The chapter discusses this internal audit organization structure, including position descriptions for IT audit specialists. In addition, we discuss approaches for organizing and planning IT audits, including reviews of general IT controls, specific applications, and specific IT areas, such as security and privacy controls. In addition, this chapter highlights techniques for developing audit programs for performing consistent IT audits and approaches for developing IT audit workpapers.

The chapter then goes through the activities necessary to perform an effective IT audit, including steps to gather and assess audit evidence. Although it is a major subject itself, we also look at approaches for pulling samples of audit evidence and then evaluating those sample results to extract audit conclusions. We then discuss the full circle of IT audit activities, including reporting results through effective internal audit reports.

An effective IT audit group is usually a key component of an overall enterprise internal audit function. The chapter concludes with a discussion of coordinating IT audits with other financial and operational internal audit activities. From an overall enterprise perspective and certainly from a board of directors' audit committee view, IT audit should be a key resource in assessing and helping to improve the overall security and control environment in an enterprise.

IT AUDIT AND THE ENTERPRISE INTERNAL AUDIT FUNCTION

IT auditors generally operate on several different levels. Sometimes they are a special audit group that provides IT-related support to a public accounting firm's financial attest audit function, or they may serve in an independent consulting firm providing IT audit services. Most commonly, however, they act either as IT audit specialists within an enterprise's internal audit function or serve as internal auditors with strong IT functions. Our objective here is not to discuss all of the requirements to build a successful internal audit function in today's enterprise; other reference sources for building an overall internal audit function are available.[1] However, as a key element, every internal audit function needs to have an internal audit charter, approved by its audit committee and senior management.

An internal audit charter is a formal document to describe the mission, independence and objectivity, scope and responsibilities, authority, accountability, and standards of the enterprise's internal audit function. Because internal audit is a function that has free rein to look at a wide range of records and to ask questions at all levels, some type of enterprise-level authorizing authority is needed. Since the internal function reports to the audit committee of the board in a corporate structure, that audit committee should authorize internal audit's rights and responsibilities through a formal authorizing document or resolution—usually called an internal audit charter.

There are no fixed requirements for such an authorizing document, but an internal audit charter should affirm internal audit's:

- ▪ Independence and objectivity
- ▪ Scope of responsibility
- ▪ Authority and accountability

This charter, then, is the authorizing document that an internal auditor can use when a manager in a separate and sometimes remote organizational unit questions why an internal auditor is asking to see or review certain documents or to gain access to some enterprise facility. The charter says that senior management—the board of directors' audit committee—should have access to enterprise records. More important, the charter provides a high level of authorization for the enterprise's internal audit function.

There is no fixed format for the contents of an audit charter. The IIA's international internal audit standards, as discussed in Chapter 3, refer to the need for an internal audit charter, but the IIA does not provide that much specific format guidance. Exhibit 5.1 is an example internal audit charter from Global Computer Products, an example company that we will be using in other chapters. This example charter clearly outlines internal audit's authority as well as such responsibilities as developing a risk-based audit plan and issuing timely audit reports. It also makes appropriate high-level references to the role of IT audit as part of the company's internal audit functions.

 Global Computer Products

Internal Audit Department
Authorizing Charter

Internal Audit's Mission
The mission of Global Computer Products Internal Audit is to ensure that company operations follow high standards both by providing an independent, objective assurance function and by advising on best practice. By using a systematic and disciplined approach, Internal Audit helps Global Computer Products accomplish its objectives by evaluating and improving the effectiveness of risk management, internal control, information technology systems, and governance processes.

Independence and Objectivity
To ensure independence, Internal Audit reports directly to the Board of Directors' Audit Committee, and to maintain objectivity, Internal Audit is not involved in day-to-day company operations or internal control procedures.

Scope and Responsibilities
The scope of Internal Audit's work includes the review of risk management procedures, internal control, information systems, and governance processes. This work also involves periodic testing of transactions, best practice reviews, special investigations, appraisals of legal and regulatory requirements, and measures to help prevent and detect fraud.
To fulfill its responsibilities, Internal Audit shall:
- Identify and assess potential risks to Global Computer Product's operations.
- Review the adequacy of controls established to ensure compliance with policies, plans, procedures, and business objectives.
- Assess the reliability and security of financial and management information and supporting systems and operations that produce this information.
- Assess the reliability and integrity of information systems controls, including installed applications, server-based computer hardware, and connecting networks.
- Assess the means of safeguarding assets.
- Review established processes and propose improvements.

EXHIBIT 5.1 Internal Audit Charter Example (Continued)

- Appraise the use of resources with regard to economy, efficiency, and effectiveness.
- Follow up recommendations to make sure that effective remedial action is taken.
- Carry out ad hoc appraisals, investigations, or reviews requested by the Audit Committee and Management.

Internal Audit's Authority

In order to promote effective controls at reasonable cost, Internal Audit is authorized, in the course of its activities, to:

- Enter all areas of Global Computer Products operations and have access to any documents and records considered necessary for the performance of its functions.
- Require all members of staff and Management to supply requested information and explanations within a reasonable period of time.

Accountability

Internal Audit shall prepare, in liaison with management and the Audit Committee, an annual audit plan that is based on business risks, the results of other internal audits, and input from management. The plan shall be presented to senior management, including the General Counsel, for approval by the Audit Committee. Any needed adjustments to the plan should be communicated to and approved by the Audit Committee.

Internal Audit is responsible for planning, conducting, reporting, and following up on audit projects included in the audit plan, and deciding on the scope and timing of these audits. The results of each internal audit will be reported through a detailed audit report that summarizes the objectives and scope of the audit as well as observations and recommendations. In all cases, follow-up work will be undertaken to ensure adequate response to internal audit recommendations. Internal Audit also will submit an annual report to senior Management and to the Audit Committee on the results of the audit work including significant risk exposures and control issues.

Standards

Internal Audit adheres to the standards and professional practices published by the Institute of Internal Auditors as well as the appropriate standards issued by the Information Technology Governance Institute for information technology-related reviews.

EXHIBIT 5.1   *(Continued)*

An internal audit charter would be little more than a nice-sounding document unless there is a strong internal audit function in place to launch and perform these key internal audit activities. These include understanding the areas in any enterprise that should be candidates for internal audit reviews, building an effective internal audit organization and team, and establishing supporting procedures to allow those internal audits. Although an internal audit charter is an essential authorization to launch a new internal audit function, many if not most internal audit functions today have a charter that may have been developed and approved in the past. If one is already in place, it is often a good idea for the chief audit executive (CAE) to revisit that charter and present it to the audit committee to reaffirm their understanding of the role and responsibilities of internal audit. In particular, the charter should include some clear authorizing language for IT audit activities.

An approved charter gives internal audit, including its IT audit function, the authority to begin its audit assurance activities throughout the enterprise. There are many ways to organize an internal audit function, and its IT audit resources are often established as a separate group of internal audit specialists, performing their own

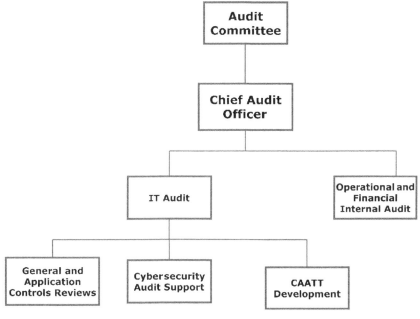

EXHIBIT 5.2 Internal Audit IT Audit Organization Chart

reviews but closely coordinated with the normal financial and operational internal audit activities. In this arrangement, IT auditors frequently report to an IT audit manager under the CAE with an organization structure where IT audit operates separately from the operational and financial internal auditors but closely coordinates their work under the CAE. There are many variations possible here, but Exhibit 5.2 shows an internal audit organization chart with IT audit as a separate unit under the CAE.

No matter where this internal audit resource fits in the internal audit department, IT auditors should have a minimum level of special IT-related skills. These skills go beyond such basic skills as knowing how to construct a complex database retrieval request program or understanding IT network security risks, reaching into such areas as how to build and run an effective enterprise IT operation. If he or she does not aspire to become a senior internal audit manager or even the CAE, the effective IT auditor should have many of the overall skills and knowledge to be a potential chief information officer (CIO), the head of an enterprise IT function.

Many IT auditors have a broad, general level of IT knowledge and skills; others specialize in such IT knowledge areas as having strong skills in developing computer-assisted audit tools and techniques (CAATTs), as discussed in Chapter 13, or as an IT audit security specialist, discussed in Chapter 19. However, Exhibit 5.3 outlines the overall skill requirements for most IT auditors. This exhibit summarizes key IT audit skill requirements, and some internal auditors performing reviews in operational or financial areas may have some of the same skills. An IT auditor should be able to understand and assess a wide range of IT controls.

IT systems and knowledge areas are pervasive in all aspects of business and span a wide range of options and technologies. However, an IT internal auditor should be expected to have at least a high-level working knowledge of these areas:

- Business application systems—whether for accounting, business or other purposes—and the basic balancing and integrity controls surrounding all automated systems
- Data management processes—whether a formal database or spreadsheet data—and the importance of validating and maintaining that data
- Systems development life cycle (SLDC) processes to implement and build business application systems, including both in-house development projects and purchased software packages
- Storage management and the importance of backup and recovery processes, including such concepts as storage virtualization an storage networks
- Computer operating systems basic functions—whether on a hand-held wireless device, a laptop system or larger system—and the potential risks and vulnerabilities if such IT systems are not updated or maintained
- Computer systems architectures, with an emphasis on Web, client-server configurations, and telecommunications
- IT service operations processes, with an emphasis on problem management, access controls, and general application management
- IT service design processes, including continuity, capacity, and information security management processes
- Governance and service strategy processes as well as essential IT financial management processes
- Programming or coding techniques sufficient to construct and implement computer-assisted audit procedures appropriate to the enterprise environment
- Ongoing interest and curiosity to understand and explore newer and evolving technology concepts, such as storage management virtualization

EXHIBIT 5.3   IT Internal Auditor Basic Knowledge Requirements

ORGANIZING AND PLANNING IT AUDITS

Using IT applications controls over a system installed at a server processing facility, this section walks us through the steps necessary to conduct an IT audit of application controls at such a facility. Of course, the overall IT audit process requires a well-organized and managed internal audit function, led by an involved and effective CAE and a committed audit committee. IT auditing requires a wide range of interrelated skills and knowledge domains that cannot be just described as one sequential set action steps but includes many interrelated activities.

This section outlines general steps for performing any IT audit, but it focuses on an IT internal controls review of the purchasing and accounts payable server-based IT application installed at our example company, Global Computer Products. Our hypothetical company has installed a vendor-supplied software package to purchase goods, through formal purchase orders in its production cycle and to recognize their receipt and pay for them through supporting accounting processes.

Establishing IT Audit Objectives

An effective IT audit function cannot just say "We haven't been to our Muddville plant in years. Let's visit them and schedule an audit." Rather, internal audit candidate selections should require risk-based assessments, a formal management request, or an audit committee directive to perform a review. Potential audit candidates would be assembled in an IT audit plan and approved by the CAE and audit committee. IT audit must clearly establish some objectives for a planned review.

A high-level objective statement should be established for each individual planned IT audit. The statement does not have to consist of detailed lists of requirements but should be an objective statement with sufficient information to tell the auditee (the function to be audited), management, and others what IT internal audit is trying to accomplish when launching an audit in some area. Some examples of internal audit objective statements are:

■ . . . to assess the adequacy of purchasing system internal accounting controls at the Global Computer Products Minneapolis facility as well as the purchasing processes at multiple branch facilities, interfaces to the accounts payable system at corporate headquarters, and automated systems to support these processes.
■ . . . to update documented IT processes and test internal controls, as necessary, for fixed asset management processes to satisfy their Sarbanes-Oxley Act (SOx) Section 404 requirements.
■ . . . to review the internal controls in place over maintenance for the IT configuration management database and supporting procedures.

Each of these fairly brief statements describes what IT audit is planning to accomplish in an upcoming review. The project can be expanded as the reviews get started, but these objective statements get an internal audit started or launched.

Closely tied to the objective statement, a scope statement is sometimes a valuable addition. For example, an objective statement can identify a planned review of quality management production processes in international operations, and a scope statement would limit the review to only Australia/New Zealand operations. The scope statement better defines what the new audit is trying to accomplish. These IT audit preliminary objective and scope statements should be reviewed with management or others requesting the audit.

An effective way to describe these internal audit plans is through an audit planning memo. This document is not presented directly to the auditee yet, but is an internal planning document that describes what IT audit is planning to accomplish, who will be doing the review, and its approximate timing. Such a memo is an essential starting document for initiating an internal audit. Exhibit 5.4 shows a sample audit planning memo where an internal audit supervisor outlines the objectives of a planned internal audit, who will be assigned to do the work, and its estimated timing. Of course, even though our exhibit shows this as a "memo" from the old hard-copy paper days, today's planning memo would almost certainly be an electronic document.

In this example, assume that internal audit has decided to launch a review of the Muddville Division facility operations and that IT audit has decided to coordinate its work at that same facility with others in the internal audit team. We will assume that IT audit has established general guidance audit programs for reviews of these areas and has enough general knowledge about the operations to get started in launching the IT audit.

Global Computer Products   February 2, 20xx

To: Workpaper Files

From: L. C. Tuttle, Audit Supervisor

Subject: Accounts Payable Systems IT Audit Planning Memo

This memo is to document the planned review of key IT purchasing and accounts payable systems processes at Global Computer Products manufacturing facility at, Muddville, MN. The review will be performed by two members of our IT audit staff with L. C. Tuttle as project leader and Herman Hollerith providing support for our review of network and IT systems controls.

The objective of this review will be to assess the adequacy of purchasing system internal accounting automated controls at the Global Computer Products Muddville facility as well as the purchasing processes at multiple branch facilities, interfaces to the accounts payable system at corporate headquarters, and automated systems to support these processes.

The audit is scheduled to begin on about March 15, 20xx, and has been budgeted for a total of XX hours of time from the on-site audit team. A detailed plan, including expected hours by each auditor, will be prepared prior to the start of this review.

The review will emphasize controls over linkages from the purchasing system to other enterprise manufacturing database systems. In addition, the review will update documentation and perform tests, as necessary, to support SOx Section 404 requirements covering this process. All recommendations and audit findings will be reported in a normal internal audit department report.

L. C. Tuttle, IT Audit Supervisor

W. J. Rawdon, IT Audit Manager

EXHIBIT 5.4   Audit Planning Memo Example

Sometimes, when IT audit has only limited knowledge of some area, auditors will schedule a preliminary review or request documents for review to gain some general knowledge about the facility. Depending on the role of IT audit in the enterprise, these reviews may be coordinated with regular internal audit activities or may be separate, IT-only reviews. For many audits, it is often best to coordinate IT audit reviews with any other organization internal audit activities.

Establishing Preliminary IT Audit Plans

A good early IT audit step is to look at other IT and general internal audits either in process or planned for the short term, to consider the availability of internal audit resources, and then to prepare a preliminary internal audit plan. Let us assume that our example Muddville facility is out of town but will not require any long-distance, international travel to visit the location. We also assume that although the IT audit team has an understanding of the general IT operations there, it has little information about the planned application to be reviewed. Based on the information available, IT

Date: March 15, 20XX

To: Workpaper Files

From: L.C. Tuttle, IT Audit Manager

Subj: IT Accounts Payable Systems Application Audit Planning Memo

This memo is to document the planned review of the IT accounts payable application at the Global Computer Products Muddville distribution facility. The review is planned to begin on about April 15, 20XX and will be staffed with two members of the IT audit organization, Herman Hollerith and Susan Smyth.

The review will include financial transaction testing procedures with key corporate data center financial systems as well as linkages with the Muddville materials purchasing and receiving systems.

In addition, we will review IT software change management controls over system components at the Muddville facility as well as attached corporate systems. We are anticipating using our computer-assisted audit software as part of our review here. This software accesses some of your Accounts Payable database files for analysis and recalculations. We will advise you of these software requirements when we arrive for the review.

Our review will emphasize controls over your recently implemented auto-pay process and its linkages to your distribution database systems. All audit concerns from this review will be discussed with you prior to any release of our audit reports. Please contact us with any questions.

_____
L. C. Tuttle, IT Audit Supervisor

EXHIBIT 5.5   Preliminary Applications Review IT Audit Plan

audit would prepare a preliminary plan for the upcoming Muddville IT applications review audit.

Exhibit 5.5 is an example of the type of preliminary IT audit plan that might be developed for such an applications controls review. Because the information here is only very preliminary, the plan does not use specific dates but assumes that two IT audit staff members will be assigned to do the work. The preliminary plan shown only uses approximate estimated hours at this time. Care should always be taken not to seal such preliminary plans in stone, as more information may force all planned estimates up or down.

Annual IT Audit Plans

Having developed preliminary plans for this audit, IT audit needs to assess other IT audit needs or audit requests for the period, match its plans with regular internal audit review work, assess its budgets and resources, and develop an IT audit plan for the upcoming, often annual period. This would be a high-level plan indicating relative risks and showing audit start and end dates. Exhibit 5.6 is an example of such an annual IT audit plan. Although this plan document shows only IT audit-related projects, normally it would be merged with plans for other operational and financial internal audit activities to show total planned internal audit activities for an upcoming period.

IT audit plans, following a format similar to Exhibit 5.6, should be approved by both the audit committee and the CAE. These types of plans should be updated as

Global Computer Products IT Audit Department April to June, 20XX IT Audit Project Schedule						
Project #	Audit	Auditor	Activity	April	May	June
A23-C06	Muddville AP IT Application Review	H. Hollerith	Document System Controls	80	20	20
A23-C06	Muddville AP IT Application Review	H. Hollerith	Develop and Implement CAATT	0	30	20
A23-C06	Muddville AP IT Application Review	H. Hollerith	Tests of Transactions	16	16	12
A23-C06	Muddville AP IT Application Review	S. Smyth	Tests of Transactions	12	8	8
A23-C06	Muddville AP IT Application Review	S. Smyth	Other Location Coordination	0	10	20
A23-C06	Muddville AP IT Application Review	L. Tuttle	Manage IT Audit	12	12	12
A28-378	Storage Mgmt. Virtualization Review	E. Zimbalist	Document Key Audit Points	60	36	12
A28-378	Storage Mgmt. Virtualization Review	E. Zimbalist	Develop Testing Approach	0	10	10
A28-378	Storage Mgmt. Virtualization Review	H. Hollerith	Perform Storage Tests	0	8	36
A28-378	Storage Mgmt. Virtualization Review	L. Tuttle	Manage IT Audit	12	8	8
E04-000	Firewall Security Review	S. Smyth	Test and Document Controls	0	36	40
E04-137	Firewall Security Review	E. Zimbalist	Review Security Procedures	60	20	18

EXHIBIT 5.6   IT Audit Annual Plan Example

required, but they would provide a basis for launching and monitoring IT audit activities. Going beyond the Exhibit 5.5 preliminary individual audit plan and the approved Exhibit 5.6 IT audit function plan, there are many other documents and procedures necessary to launch a program of IT audits. These include engagement letters that formally announce to an affected management, IT audit's plans to begin a review in some area.[2]

Starting with steps for planning an internal audit and then continuing through a variety of audit processes, the next sections outline the steps necessary for an IT audit applications review at a unit of our sample company, a representative IT internal audit. Our objective here, and in other supporting chapters, is to suggest a series of internal audit procedures for performing reviews. Whether as an individual professional or as the enterprise's IT audit department or function, internal audit will be more effective if all members of the IT audit staff follow consistent, professional procedures in performing their reviews. They will become a strong enterprise resource in the eyes of management, which should expect consistent, quality approaches from the internal audit resources.

DEVELOPING AND PREPARING AUDIT PROGRAMS

IT audits should be organized and performed in a consistent manner with an objective of minimizing arbitrary or unnecessary auditor procedures. To help achieve this goal of audit consistency, IT and all internal auditors use what are called *audit programs* to perform their audit procedures in a consistent and effective manner for similar types of audits. The term *program* refers to a set of auditor procedures similar to the steps in a computer program, instructions that go through the same program instructions every time the process is run. For example, a computer program to calculate pay includes instructions to read the time card file of hours worked, look up the employee's rate stored in another file, and then calculate the gross pay. The same steps apply for every employee unless there are exceptions, such as overtime rates, coded into the payroll program. Similarly, an audit program is a set of preestablished steps an internal auditor performs. An audit program is a tool for planning, directing, and controlling audit work and a blueprint for action, specifying the steps to be performed to meet audit objectives. It represents the auditor's selection of the best methods for getting the job done and serves as a basis for recording the work steps performed.

Effective IT auditors should have a series of generalized audit programs prepared for most of their recurring IT audit activities. Many of these programs, such as one covering an observation of logon practices for visiting a server processing facility, often are used from year to year and from one computer hardware center to another with little change. In other situations, an IT auditor may have to modify a standard program to the unique aspects of a particular audit. In some situations, a standard audit program will not be applicable. For example, an IT auditor may want to review IT controls for a new business entity with some unique control characteristics, or audit management may want to take a different approach because of problems encountered with similar previous reviews. Based on planned audit objectives and data gathered in the preliminary and field surveys, the in-charge IT auditor may want to prepare a customized audit program to guide the review. This may be little more than a standardized program with minimal local changes, or it may be a unique set of audit procedures based on the preliminary planning and the results from the field survey. In order to prepare this program, auditors first should have an understanding of the characteristics of what constitutes an adequate audit program.

IT Audit Program Formats and Their Preparation

An audit program is a procedure describing the steps and tests to be performed by an IT auditor when actually visiting an IT operations facility, reviewing an application, or performing some other audit review process. The program should be finalized after the completion of the preliminary and field surveys and before starting the actual IT audit. It should be constructed with several criteria in mind, the most important of which is that the program should identify the aspects of the area to be further examined and the sensitive areas that require audit emphasis.

A second important purpose of an internal audit program is that it should guide both less and more experienced IT internal auditors. For example, management may request that IT audit observe perimeter physical security controls at a data center. This type of review consists of fairly standard procedures to ensure, among other matters, that all visitors present valid badges to gain entry and that any entry monitor does not just wave people through with no checking. A less experienced IT auditor may not be aware of these procedure steps, and even experienced internal auditors may forget one or another. An audit program outlines the required audit steps for this type of procedure. An established IT audit department should build a library of audit programs, established over time, for tasks such as an audit of small system general controls or a review of program change management. When planning a review where such established audit programs exist, IT audit management needs only to use these established programs with consideration given to any changed conditions that have been discovered through the preliminary or field surveys. The audit program is revised as necessary, with the changes approved by audit management prior to the start of the review.

For many IT audit departments, appropriate established audit programs may not be available for many areas. This is because IT auditors typically face a wide and diverse set of areas for review, but they will not have the time or resources to review every area on a frequent basis. Established programs prepared for prior audits, such as specialized application reviews, often become out of date due to new systems or changed technologies. The IT auditor responsible for the field survey or another member of audit management should update any existing audit program or prepare a revised set of audit program steps for the planned review. Depending on the type of planned IT audit, programs usually follow one of three general formats: (1) a set of general audit procedures, (2) audit procedures with detailed instructions for the auditor, or (3) a checklist for compliance reviews.

The next examples illustrate these audit program types. Exhibit 5.7 contains a few general audit program steps for an IT applications controls review. The program steps

Note: These IT audit program steps represent a limited set of IT audit procedures from what would be a much larger set of audit steps for a review of extended application controls.			
Step	**Review Area**	**Control**	**Audit Tests**
	Application Audit Trails	Application should contain automated tracking of changes made to data, indicating the time of the change and specific user.	Select a sample of changes from change log files and trace to log files and determine if there is evidence of change reviews.
	Application Audit Trails	Application should provide automated tracking and highlighting of overrides to normal processing parameters.	Document the nature of override procedures and determine that there is evidence of management reviews and corrective actions when needed.
	Interface Application Balancing	Application should have automated checking processes in place to balance key control balances between systems.	Review and document balancing processes, and select a sample of processes to determine that balancing is working correctly.
	Automated File Functionality Calculations	Master files or rating tables should be in place to provide consistent values to all applications.	Compare key input values for all impacted applications through walk-through review.

EXHIBIT 5.7 Application Processing Controls Sample Audit Program Extract

#	Audit Steps: Data Center Petty Cash Review	Initial & Date	W/P Ref.
	Audit:_____ Location:_____ Date:_____		
1	Assess the need for a petty cash facility within the IT operations area. Determine if alternative procedures might be available through the corporate finance office or other area.		
2	Prior to review, determine who in the IT facility is responsible for the petty cash fund balances, receipt requirements, replenishment procedures, and guidelines for authorized disbursements.		
3	Perform this petty cash review on a surprise basis. Identify yourself to cashier, request that the cashier function be closed but observe audit during your initial review, and make a detailed count of cash in the account as well as any included personal checks.		
4	Having performed the cash count in presence of cashier, ask cashier to acknowledge results of the auditor's cash count.		
5	If any personal checks found in the cash count were over one day old, ask why they were not deposited or if they are being held as collateral for an employee short-term loan fund. If such a fund, assess propriety of this practice.		
6	Reconcile the audited cash count with the fund's disbursement register, noting any differences.		
7	Determine that all cash disbursements recorded have been made to valid employees for authorized IT-specific purposes.		
8	Observe office security procedures covering the fund and determine that funds are locked or otherwise secured.		
9	Review procedures for fund replenishments. Select a prior period, review its supporting documentation, and reconcile activity to purchase journal.		
10	Assess the overall control procedures, propriety, and efficiency of this petty cash process. Comment as appropriate.		
11	Determine that the petty cash function is used only for authorized IT facility small cash disbursements rather than a general change or short-term loan fund.		
12	Document the results of the review, and take steps to initiate immediate corrective actions if any problems were encountered during this review.		

Signature _____ Date _____

EXHIBIT 5.8　Audit Program: Data Center Petty Cash Review

define high-level audit objectives as well as internal audit procedures to test compliance with those objectives. An actual audit program would be much more detailed and extensive, but the exhibit shows the theme of this form of audit program. The program outlines the high level or general audit steps that IT auditors will need to follow, and IT audit should tailor its library of general audit programs covering reviews of major IT applications and data centers to the specific unit or facility that it is reviewing.

Exhibit 5.8 is an example of a more detailed audit program covering audit steps for a review of petty cash controls at a data center. It consists of general audit procedures to review cash at any unit of a multifacility organization. Petty cash controls are one of the smaller, less critical internal control concerns for many operational and data center operations, and an IT auditor often ignores this area when reviewing data center general controls. IT audit often elects to make detailed audit programs even more specific or detailed. The program shows the steps that should be included in any such audit and illustrates an example audit program.

Exhibit 5.8 represents a typical IT audit program format where audit tasks are broken into numbered steps with space on the form allowed for the initials and date of the auditor completing the audit step as well as a column for a reference to the workpaper that describes the audit step. For example, for step 2 the start of this process, the IT auditor performing the procedure would document data center cashier responsibilities. Typically, an established internal audit function would have developed these types of audit programs for many of its regular or periodic audits. The IT audit team visiting an organizational unit could then use standard programs to review general and application internal controls in a consistent manner from one unit to the next. This is particularly important in a larger multi-unit enterprise where IT audit management wants to have assurance that controls over the area were reviewed and evaluated in a consistent manner, no matter who is the assigned auditor or the location. This sample audit program is shown as a printed document that could be developed and controlled by internal audit. Of course, such a document would typically be located in the auditor's laptop system. In some instances, the in-charge auditor might prepare a custom program to evaluate certain special procedures encountered during the field survey.

At one time, the checklist-format audit program was internal audit's most common format. Often a more junior internal auditor was given an audit program composed of a long list of questions requiring "yes," "no," or "not applicable" responses and would complete these program steps either through examinations of documents or through interviews. Exhibit 5.9 is an example of a checklist-format audit program for reviewing ethics and code of conduct policies. The program steps here cover more than just the IT function and can be applied to the total enterprise. Yes-and-no responses, when asked in an information-gathering context, are often appropriate. A checklist-format audit program has two weaknesses, however. First, while a series of yes-or-no interview responses can lead an experienced IT auditor to look at problem areas or to ask other more probing questions, these same points may be missed when a less experienced auditor just completes the questionnaire and does not go beyond the yeses and nos, nor dig a bit deeper as to where those responses might lead. A procedures-oriented audit program better encourages follow-up inquiries in other areas where information gathered may raise questions.

Checklist-format IT audit programs were also very common in the early days of IT auditing general controls reviews, when many operational internal auditors did not have extensive IT controls backgrounds and needed detailed checklists as support. They were often called "Control Objectives" with survey statements requiring a yes-or-no auditor response. ISACA's predecessor organization, the EDP Auditors Organization, was very successful at publishing those checklist documents in the early days of IT auditing. Rapidly changing technology has reduced the importance of IT audit checklists today.

The questionnaire-format IT audit program also tends to cause auditors to miss examining necessary evidential matter while asking only the checklist questions. An

Audit Controls Step	YES	NO	N/A
1 Does the enterprise have a written code of business conduct?			
2 Does the code clearly apply to the IT organization?			
3 Is the code distributed to all stakeholders?			
4 Are new employees given an orientation to this code of conduct?			
5 Are all employees required to acknowledge that have read, understand and agree to abide by this code?			
6 Are training programs periodically delivered to all employees regarding compliance with the code?			
7 Does the code address standards that govern employee conduct in their dealings with suppliers and customers?			
8 Is there an effective mechanism in place to follow up on reports of suspected violations of the code?			
9 Is there an effective mechanism in place to allow employees to confidentially report suspected violations of the code?			
10 Is there a mechanism in place to allow employees to be informed of the results of their reported ethics concerns?			
11 Is compliance with the code's provisions a standard used for measuring employee performance at all levels?			
12 Is there a procedure in place to update the code on a periodic basis?			

EXHIBIT 5.9   Checklist Format Audit Program for Business Ethics Procedures

inexperienced IT auditor can too easily check "yes" on the questionnaire without determining, for example, whether that response is properly supported by audit evidence. An example would be a question regarding whether some critical document is regularly approved. It is easy to ask the question, receive an answer of "yes," and never follow up to see if those documents actually were approved. Each of these audit program formats works for different types of reviews, provided the IT auditor gives some thought to the program questions. The key concern is that all audits should be supported by some type of audit program that documents the review steps performed. This approach allows audit management to recognize what procedures the auditors did or did not perform in a given review. Strong and consistent audit programs are an important step to improving the overall quality of the IT audits performed.

The reliability of the materials and processes to be reviewed and internal audit's other understandings about an operation should also be considered when developing audit program for a specific facility or resource. There is little value in developing an IT audit program at a facility that calls for a review of systems and procedures that are no longer in use. In developing an audit program, an IT auditor should try to select audit steps that are meaningful and that will produce reliable forms of audit evidence. For example, the audit program often calls for detailed tests in a given critical, high-risk area rather than suggesting that the information can be gathered through interviews.

Advanced audit techniques should also be incorporated into audit programs wherever practicable. For example, CAATTs, discussed in Chapter 13, can perform selected audit steps, and the use of procedures such as statistical sampling allow an IT internal auditor to extract data easily from larger populations. Members of the audit staff who have IT audit or other technical skills should be consulted when preparing these audit program steps. There is no single best or set format for an IT audit program; however, the program should be a document that IT auditors can use to guide their efforts as well as to record activities.

 ## GATHERING AUDIT EVIDENCE AND TESTING RESULTS

Identifying higher-risk areas, developing audit programs to support consistent results, and planning IT audits are just preliminary steps to performing IT audits. An IT auditor must review a variety and sometimes a vast amount of materials to develop audit conclusions. Known as audit evidence, these materials can be database file records, paper documents, the auditor's observation of staff member actions, or any information that will support an audit objective. An IT auditor should assemble this audit evidence to develop an audit conclusion.

In many cases, there is a vast amount of audit evidence to help support developing an audit conclusion. For example, an IT auditor may be interested in how an automated quality assurance process is recording incoming materials receipts, as recorded on a large enterprise resource planning (ERP) systems database. For a larger enterprise, there could be several million database records of interest. A very important way to review these large volumes of data is to pull a representative sample of them and draw the audit conclusion from that sample data. In addition to gathering supporting audit information, audit sampling is an important IT auditor skill.

Types of Audit Evidence

As discussed in Chapter 3, both IIA and ISACA audit standards state that an IT auditor should examine and evaluate information on all matters related to the planned audit objectives. This information is called audit evidence and covers everything an IT auditor reviews or observes. An auditor should gather evidence in support of his or her evaluation—what is known as *sufficient, competent, relevant,* or *useful* audit evidence. A well-constructed audit program should guide an IT auditor in this evidence-gathering process. Multiple types of evidence—stronger or weaker—can be useful in developing audit conclusions. For example, actually observing some activity or obtaining an independent confirmation of that activity is one of the strongest forms of evidence. However, a casual response to an IT auditor's question covering that same activity will be weaker. It is not that an auditor thinks the IT staff member responding to the question is not telling the truth, but an IT auditor's actually observing some event is far superior to just hearing about it. Internal auditors will encounter different levels of audit evidence and should attempt to design their audit procedures to look for and rely on the best available audit evidence. Exhibit 5.10 provides some ranges of best evidence for different classifications of materials. The idea that a written, signed document is better evidence than a casual response should be no surprise to an IT auditor, but it is always good to keep these concepts in mind.

Evidence Classification	Strongest	Weakest
Audit Technique	Observation/Confirmation	Casual Inquiry
IT File or Database Materials	Auditor-Controlled CAATT Results	Printed Extract from File Data
Origin of the Evidence	Corroborative Materials	Underlying Statistics
Relationship of the Auditee	External Document	Auditee Internal Document
IT Data Repository	Enterprise-Controlled Data Center	Outside Service Provider
Form of Audit Evidence	Written with Signatures	Oral Comments
Sophistication of Evidence	Formal Documentation	Informal such as Notes
Location of Evidence	Connected to Area Reviewed	Derived/Supporting Materials
Source of Audit Evidence	Product of Internal Audit Work	Other Supporting Materials

EXHIBIT 5.10   IT Auditor "Best Evidence" Classification

The audit field survey and the subsequent development of an audit program are just preliminary activities to performing the actual IT internal audit. It is often more efficient to have supervisory personnel complete these preliminary steps before assigning staff IT auditors for the actual review. These supervisory auditors, either audit management or experienced in-charge auditors, usually have the experience to make quick assessments of field situations and to fine-tune the overall audit approach. However, once the survey and the completed audit programs have been reviewed and approved by IT audit management, the next challenge is performing the actual IT audit to meet its desired audit objectives. The preparatory work from the survey will play an important role in ensuring the audit's success; however, the IT auditor now faces the day-to-day challenges of performing the actual IT audit.

The actual audit steps performed will depend on the characteristics of the entity audited. A financially oriented audit of a credit and collection function will be quite different from an operational review of a design engineering department. The financial audit might include independent confirmations of account balances; the operational audit typically includes extensive interviews with management and supporting documentation to assess key internal controls. Despite these differences, all internal audits should be performed and supervised following a general set of principles or standards. This will ensure that internal audits are properly directed and controlled.

Audit Sampling Approaches

The IT audit process begins with first establishing audit objectives, then planning and preparing for the audit, and finally evaluating the audited results to determine if the audit objectives have been satisfied, if supporting internal controls are adequate, if the materials reviewed are sufficient to develop an audit conclusion, and if there is a need for corrective action–based audit recommendations. This process of testing, assessing, and then evaluating audit evidence is often a challenge for many IT auditors. For example, an auditor can review a sample of 100 items and find no problems with 99 of them. Should that one internal control problem exception cause the IT auditor to highlight this matter as an exception, or should the auditor give that single exception a pass and go forward? There often are no easy answers, but an IT auditor should evaluate this audit evidence and try to make the appropriate decision.

Audit sampling is a key approach for IT auditors, when faced with a large volume of audit evidence, to select a sample from that data and to make an overall audit assessment based on the results of the sampled data. That is, rather than looking at every item in an area of audit concern to develop evidence to support an audit, an IT auditor can examine a limited set of sample items to develop audit conclusions over the entire set or population of data.

An IT auditor has a challenge here to extract a sample of items that will be representative of the entire population. If there are 100,000 file record transactions on a data file and if an IT auditor looks at only 50 of them, finding 10 exceptions (20% of the sample), can the auditor conclude that 20% of the entire population of transactions, or 20,000, are exceptions? This audit conclusion is true only if the sample of 50 drawn is representative of the entire population. Audit sampling techniques can help an IT auditor determine an appropriate sample size and develop an opinion for this type of audit task.

Audit sampling has two major branches: statistical and nonstatistical. Statistical sampling is a mathematical-based method of selecting representative items that reflect the characteristics of the entire population. Using the results of audit tests on the statistically sampled items, an audit opinion can be developed for the entire group. For example, an IT auditor could develop a statistical sample of items in an inventory system, test those sample items for their physical quantity or value, and then express an opinion on the value or accuracy of the entire inventory. Nonstatistical sampling, also called judgmental sampling, is not supported by mathematical theory and does not allow an internal auditor to express *statistically precise* opinions on the entire population. Nevertheless, nonstatistical or judgmental sampling is often a useful audit tool.

When planning any audit that includes the examination of a large number of transactions or other evidence, an IT auditor should always ask "Should I use audit sampling?" The correct answer here is often not just a simple yes or no but may be complicated by such factors as the number or nature of items to be sampled, a lack of technical expertise or IT software availability to do the sampling, a sometimes fear of the mathematical focus of sampling, and the potential nonacceptance of the sampling results by management. *Sampling* is also a word that is frequently misused by many internal auditors. All too often, an operational internal auditor, faced with a file cabinet filled with hundreds of documents to review, will pull out one or two items from the front and perform audit procedures based on this limited selection. Although this examination of two items may be appropriate for an audit observation, an internal auditor *should not* try to draw conclusions for the entire population based on that limited a potentially nonrepresentative sample. To develop this type of conclusion effectively, IT auditors need to:

- Understand the total population of items of concern and develop a formal sampling plan regarding those items.
- Draw a sample from the population based on that sample selection plan.
- Evaluate the sampled items against audit objectives.
- Develop conclusions for the entire population based on audit sample results.

These steps represent the process of audit sampling, an IT audit procedure to examine less than 100% of the items within a class of transactions for the purpose of drawing a conclusion for the entire population based on the sample audit results.

Why use audit sampling? We often hear reports on the results of statistical sampling techniques in consumer research, government studies, or quality-control testing on a production assembly line, and audit sampling can be a very effective tool for IT auditors as well. Although 100% examinations work for limited amounts of audit evidence, an IT auditor using CAATTs almost always looks at a sample—either very large or small—of the audit evidence. The IT auditor then draws an audit conclusion based on the results of that sample. With formal audit sampling, an auditor can draw a conclusion along the lines of "Based on the results of our audit sample, we are 98% certain the true inventory balance is between X and Y." This type of statement and process is discussed in greater detail in the next paragraphs.

Audit sampling is more frequently used by operational or financial internal auditors rather than by IT auditors because of the challenges presented by reviews of large populations of data, such as in physical inventories or financial transactions. However, these techniques are also useful for IT auditors who often examine large amounts of IT file or database data.

Whenever an IT auditor needs to draw conclusions based on a population of multiple items but does not want to examine the entire population, audit sampling can often introduce better and more efficient audits. Reasons encourage the use of audit sampling include:

- **Conclusions may be drawn regarding an entire population of data.** When statistical sampling is used, the sample results can be accurately projected over the entire population without performing a 100% review of that population, no matter how large. For example, an IT auditor interested in the occurrence of some error condition in a large volume of log file error records could select a statistical sample of these documents, test the sample for the error condition, and then make a perhaps 98% certain type of estimate about the occurrence of that error condition in the entire population of the log file records. This will provide a strong audit position with significant audit savings.
- **Sample results are objective and defensible.** Internal control errors often occur on a random basis over the total items subject to error, and each error condition should have an equal opportunity of selection in an audit sample. An audit test based on random selection is objective and even defensible in a court of law. Conversely, a sample based on auditor judgment could be distorted due to intentional or unintentional bias in the selection process. An IT auditor looking for potential problems might examine only the larger or sensitive items, ignoring others.
- **Less sampling may be required through the use of audit sampling.** Using statistics, IT auditors need not increase the size of a sample directly in proportion to increases in the size of the population to be sampled. Although a sample of 60 items may be sufficient to express an audit opinion over a population of 500 items, that same sample of 60 still can be sufficient for a population of 5,000. An auditor who

does not use statistical approaches will often oversample large populations because of the incorrect belief that larger populations require proportionately larger samples. By using statistics-based sampling procedures, less testing may be required.

▪ **Statistical sampling may provide for greater accuracy than a 100% test.** When voluminous amounts of data items are counted in their entirety, the risk of significant clerical or audit errors increases. However, a small sample typically receives very close scrutiny and analysis. The more limited sample would be subject primarily only to sampling errors resulting from the statistical projection.

▪ **Audit coverage of multiple locations is often more convenient.** Audits can be performed at multiple locations with small samples taken at individual sites to complete an overall sampling plan. In addition, an audit using comprehensive statistical sampling may be started by one IT auditor and subsequently continued by another. Each of their sample results can be combined to yield one set of audit results.

▪ **Sampling procedures can be simple to apply.** In years past, an internal auditor often was required to use either tables published in sampling manuals or complex computer systems to develop a sampling plan and sample selection. With the availability of software packages for laptop computers, audit sampling today has become much more simplified.

Despite the advantages of audit sampling, an IT auditor must keep in mind that *exact information* cannot be obtained about a population of items based on just a sample, whether it is judgmental or statistical. Only by making a 100% test and following good audit procedures can an auditor obtain *exact* information. With statistical sampling, regardless of the number of items examined, positive information can be obtained about all of the items in the population within a level of statistical confidence.

There are three common audit sampling approaches depending on the audit's objectives: attributes, variables, and discovery sampling. Attributes sampling is an approach used to measure the extent or level of occurrence of various conditions or attributes—in other words, to assess internal controls. For example, an IT auditor might want to test for the attribute of whether invoice documents have received proper approval signatures. An invoice will either be correctly approved or not—a "yes" or "no" qualitative condition. Normally, the attribute measured is the frequency of an error or other type of deficiency. The extent of the existence of the particular deficiency, such as improperly approved documents, determines the seriousness of the situation and how internal audit will report its findings and recommendations. Attributes or characteristics can be applied to any physical item, financial record, internal procedure, or operational activity. Attributes sampling often measures compliance with a designated policy, procedure, or established standard and is an effective test for internal controls. A control is determined to be working or not working. Sort-of working is not an appropriate conclusion. An IT auditor tests conditions in the selected items and then assesses whether the overall population is in compliance with the control attribute.

Variables sampling deals with the size of a specified population, such as account balances or tests of individual sample items. Here the auditor's focus is on how much as opposed to the yes-or-no focus of attributes sampling. The objective of variables sampling is to project total estimated quantities for some account or adjustments to the account on the basis of the auditor's statistical sample. Illustrative would be a sample to estimate the total value of an inventory based on sample results. Variables sampling is concerned with absolute amounts as opposed to the number or extent of a particular type of error. This approach is more common for financial internal auditors.

The third type of statistical sampling, discovery sampling, is used when an auditor wants to pull a sample from a large volume of data without the statistical processes associated with variables and attributes sampling.

The next sections discuss attributes sampling methods in some detail but because of space limitations do not provide an IT auditor with enough information to become an expert in these statistical sampling techniques. All IT auditors should have a general understanding of audit sampling techniques, with an emphasis on attributes sampling. IT auditors will find this useful in their own work as well as when they work with operation and financial internal auditors.

Attributes Sampling Procedures

Attributes sampling is the process of pulling a sample to estimate the *proportion* of some characteristic or an attribute of interest in a population. For example, an IT auditor may be interested in the rate of occurrence of some monetary error or compliance exception that might exist in a population of accounts payable disbursement vouchers. The auditor here would test for the number of items that have some type of error condition, not the total monetary value of all of the errors. This type of test is very appropriate for assessing the level of internal control in some specific account, and can be a very important approach for SOx Section 404 internal controls tests. The starting point in attributes sampling is to estimate an expected rate of errors (i.e., how many errors can the IT auditor and management tolerate?). Depending on the items sampled and the culture of the enterprise, this expected error rate could be as little as 0.01% or as large as 5% or even more. Even if senior management states that no errors will be allowed in some highly critical operation, all parties often recognize that there may be a small or very small possibility of an error, and depending on the criticality of the operation, such a very small error rate will be accepted. An expected error rate is the recognition that certain types of operations contain errors no matter how good the other controls and procedures are. If IT audit were to perform a 100% examination of an account but find only a small number of errors—say, 0.5%—it might be difficult to convince management that its controls are weak. Management might expect and tolerate a 1% error rate here and not express much concern at audit's findings. In an attributes sampling test, the IT auditor must estimate the expected rate of errors in the population sampled, based on management's stated expectations, other audit tests, or just internal audit assumptions.

Along with estimating the expected error rate, an IT auditor must decide on the acceptable precision limits and the degree of desired confidence for the sample. In other words, an IT auditor would like to be able to say "I am 99% confident that the error rate of this account is less than 1%." These estimates will allow an auditor to determine the size of a sample that will provide a reliable conclusion regarding the condition tested.

This determination is made through statistical methods and can be obtained from common statistical software packages, Web resources, or even from manual tables found in the old statistical sampling books. These factors provide an initial basis for the size of the sample to be reviewed. The auditor now selects this sample and examines the items sampled to determine the number of errors that exist in them.

As can usually be expected, the error rate in a sample is normally higher or lower than the previously estimated acceptable error rate. If lower, the auditor has established that the condition tested is safely within the limits selected. If the sample shows a higher error rate, the auditor must determine whether the results are satisfactory and what further action, if any, is needed. Conceivably, the sample can be expanded, but IT audit will often feel that there is an adequate basis for arriving at a conclusion. The key to meaningful attributes sampling is to take an appropriate sample and properly develop an audit conclusion based on the sample results.

Attributes sampling, once commonly used by both internal and external auditors, is now used less frequently by auditors because of its sometimes difficult computational requirements and the auditor statistical knowledge required. However, there are good IT audit sampling tools available, and attributes sampling is an effective tool to assess the status of some control procedures.

Performing an Attributes Sampling Test

Attributes sampling is useful when an auditor is faced with a rather large number of items to be examined and wants to test whether certain controls are working. An IT auditor must first define the specific nature of the compliance tests to be performed, the nature of the sampling units, and the population characteristics. Attributes sampling is a yes-or-no type of audit test where the item or attribute sampled must either be correct or incorrect; there can be no measures of almost correct or close enough. In a test of the completeness of travel report approvals, for example, enterprise procedures may state that the responsible manager must approve all travel reports greater than $100. Thus any voucher not approved by the responsible manager would be considered a compliance error. Internal audit should carefully define the types of tests to be performed as well as the acceptance and rejection rules. Although it is possible to separately sample for two or more different attributes, each statistical test should concentrate on compliance with one such test criteria. If multiple criteria are used in a single test, the failure of any one would mean that the entire item sampled is out of compliance.

The size of the population as well as the auditor's tolerance for errors will impact the number of items to be sampled. If an auditor is testing for travel policy compliance and if there is a requirement for manager approval for vouchers over a $25.00 limit, should internal audit treat a nonapproved $25.01 item as an error, or should it allow for a perhaps 5% or 10% exception rate? As much as possible, these items should be defined in advance.

In addition, IT audit should have a clear understanding of the number and location of the items to be sampled. If initial plans are to sample *all* travel accounting reports, those reports must be available or readily accessible. If some items are filed at a remote, international location, internal audit may not be able to sample *all* such reports unless it gains access to the remote, international reports as well as the national items filed centrally. Otherwise, internal audit should reduce the scope of the population sampled and look only at domestic travel accounting reports.

An auditor must first make some preliminary estimates, based on observations and other audits, of what is expected from the sample results and then pull an actual audit sample based on those expectations. For example, if an auditor expects a fairly high level of errors in the population, the auditor's sample should be sufficient to confirm or refute those initial expectations. Internal auditors need to estimate such things as the maximum tolerable error rate, and then the initial sample size. Other key attributes for sampling are:

- Maximum tolerable error rate
- Desired confidence level
- Estimated population error rate
- Initial sample size
- Selecting the sample to perform audit procedures
- Evaluating the results of the attributes sampling test

Maximum Tolerable Error Rate

Statisticians also call the maximum tolerable error rate estimate the *desired upper precision limit*. This is the error rate an internal auditor will allow while still accepting the overall internal controls. The idea is that a typical population may have some errors. In the previously discussed audits of travel expense reports that were reviewed for departmental management approvals, a realistic internal auditor recognizes that there may be *some* errors, such as the $25.01 vouchers that are above the $25.00 requirement. This is an error an internal auditor might accept but still feel that internal controls are generally adequate.

The maximum tolerable error rate is normally expressed as a percentage that can vary based on the nature of the items reviewed. In the previous example, an auditor might accept a 5% tolerable error rate or upper precision limit. In other instances, a smaller or larger estimate can be used, but this estimate should never be more than 10%. Such an estimate indicates major internal control problems, and the resultant attribute sample may provide little further information. If an internal auditor knows that internal controls are very bad, it is of little value to take an attribute sample to verify what he or she has already determined through other audit procedures. Similarly, an internal auditor should normally expect some errors and establish some reasonable value for this rate, perhaps 1% or 2%.

Desired Confidence Level

The desired confidence level is a measure of an auditor's confidence in the results of a sample. That is, internal auditors generally would like 95% or 98% certainty that the results of their sample are representative of the actual population. An internal auditor will never be 100% certain that a condition exists unless he or she reviews essentially 100% of the items in the population. If a population of 100 items contains one error, an auditor might look at a sample of 10 items and find no errors. The auditor may look at 20, 30, 50, or even 90 items and still not find more than that one error. The only way to be 100% certain that the population contains a 1% error rate is to look at 100% of the items. However, an internal auditor typically should look at a much smaller sample and still be able to state that he or she is 95% or 98% certain that the error rate is no more than 1%.

The assumed confidence level value, usually 95% or 98%, along with the estimated population size, will determine the size of the sample needed to test the estimated population. Too large of a confidence level may require too large of a sample. Too low of a confidence level may reduce the size of the sample, but the results may be questionable. Management typically would not accept an internal audit finding that states the auditor is "75% confident" that some condition is true.

Estimated Population Error Rate

In attributes sampling, an internal auditor estimates the level of errors in a population and then takes a statistical sample to confirm or refute those assumptions. In order to calculate the sample size, an auditor also needs to estimate the expected rate of occurrence of errors in that same population. This estimate, together with the confidence level and the maximum tolerable error rate, determines the size of the sample. For example, if the confidence level is 95% and the maximum tolerable error rate is 5%, the auditor should select a sample of 1,000 items in a very large population if the estimated population error rate is 4%. A smaller estimated population error rate will reduce the sample size. Given the same parameters, an estimated population error rate of 1% will drive the sample size down from 1,000 to 100 items. If the expected population error rate is very large—greater than 50%—the required sample size will become very large. Generally, the larger the difference between the maximum tolerable error rate and the estimated population error rate, the smaller the necessary sample size.

Initial Sample Size

The preceding three factors determine the necessary sample size. Although calculation formulas can be found in statistics textbooks, IT auditors normally use audit software to develop attributes sampling plans. A Web search for *attributes sampling software* will provide a wide range of options where an IT auditor only needs to provide (1) the maximum tolerable error rate, (2) the confidence level, (3) the estimated population error rate, and (4) the approximate sample size. The software then provides the required sample size for the attributes test. For example, if the confidence level is 99%, the maximum tolerable error rate is not over 5%, and the estimated error rate is 4%, an auditor should examine 197 items for an attributes test over a population of about 1,000 items.

Attributes sample sizes tend to be large—a problem for many auditors—and it often is difficult to justify the larger sample sizes needed to perform a statistically correct attributes test. In some instances an internal auditor can modify the sample size by modifying sampling assumptions. For example, the previously mentioned sample of 197 for a 1,000 items population will become much smaller if the confidence level is lowered from 99% to 95%.

Selecting the Sample to Perform Audit Procedures

Having made some audit sample assumptions and determined the sample size, the next step is to pull the actual items for review. Random sampling procedures can be used to select items to review, and multiple attributes also can be tested using the same set of sample items. The concept to remember is that the internal auditor will be performing a separate yes-or-no type test for each of the individual attributes on each of the items in the sample.

Workpaper documentation should describe all items selected as part of the attributes test. Spreadsheet software is useful here for recording the results of the audit tests, but the internal audit procedures should be performed with great care. If an audit fails to recognize an error condition in the selected sample items, that fact will throw off the conclusions reached as part of the overall sample. With a large population, each sample item may speak for hundreds or even thousands of actual items. Each sample item should be evaluated carefully and consistently against the established attributes. An assessment of "close enough" should not be used. If some attribute measurement is too stringent for certain items, internal audit should consider reevaluating the entire sample set. An IT auditor may be looking for several error conditions but then find another error not included in the original test design. If significant, internal audit may then want to redefine the overall attribute test.

Evaluating the Results of the Attributes Sampling Test

As discussed, prior to actually selecting and evaluating the sample items, an IT auditor will have made initial assumptions regarding the maximum tolerable error rate, the reliability, and the level of confidence as well as about how many compliance errors would be tolerated to assess whether the controls are adequate. The next key step is to evaluate the sample results against those assumptions to determine if an internal control problem exists. Recall that an upper precision limit or maximum tolerable error rate and a confidence level formed the standards used to determine the sample size and perform the sampling test. An internal auditor should now assess the actual error rate of the sampled items and calculate an upper precision limit based on those sample errors. That precision limit, computed on the basis of the actual sample, should be less than or equal to the desired precision limits established at the beginning of the sample exercise in order for the auditor to report favorable results from the sample.

There can be a major audit finding if the results of an audit sample do not meet the preliminary criteria. Although these audit criteria should have been well thought out and approved before beginning the test, sometimes internal audit or management may decide that the original assumptions were too conservative. A new upper precision limit or confidence level could be used and the sample results measured against it. This approach should be used only with the greatest caution. In effect, the auditor here is attempting to justify some bad results. Were the matter ever to reach a court of law, internal audit would have a tough time justifying why it had altered its assumptions to make the sample results look good. A better approach when the results are unfavorable is to expand the sample size.

When attributes sampling results turn out unfavorably, management sometimes claims that internal audit only looked at some *very unusual* items and that the remainder of the population is not that bad. An increase in the sample size will have the effect of decreasing the computed upper precision limit, assuming that the auditor does not find a substantial number of additional errors. However, internal audit should weigh the relative costs and benefits of this approach. A better approach is to report the internal control problem based on the current results and to expand the sample size in a subsequent audit review. Management should, it is hoped, take steps during the interim to improve internal controls in the area of interest.

Attributes sampling is a very useful technique for assessing one or several internal controls in an area of audit interest. Because estimates of such things as the maximum tolerable error rate are made in advance, it is difficult to dispute the audit test assumptions when compared to sample results. Similarly, because random number or similar techniques typically are used to select the sample items, it would be difficult to claim auditor bias in the selections. This discussion presents attributes sampling only on a very high level. An IT auditor needs more study and experience to use it successfully, but attributes sampling is a technique that many IT auditors will find useful.

Attributes Sampling Advantages and Limitations

Whenever there is an audit need to review a large number of items, attributes sampling procedures can provide a statistically accurate assessment of selected control features. Although statistical theory requires a relatively large sample size, an IT auditor can review some control or condition within a sample of that data and then can state, within a preestablished confidence value or percentage, that the number of errors in a total population will not exceed a designated value or that the control is working. Attributes sampling is not useful for determining the estimated correct value on an account such as an inventory book value but is an extremely useful tool for reviewing control procedures in a variety of operational areas.

Attributes sampling equips an IT auditor with a very powerful tool to assess internal controls in a large population of data through the evaluation of a limited sample. Although the technique often is too time consuming or complex for many audit tests over paper-based records, an IT auditor should develop a basic understanding of attributes sampling to use when appropriate. The technique is particularly appropriate when an auditor is sampling from IT files or records and using automated tools. It also provides support if the initial, judgmental results of an internal controls review indicate problems in an area and when management disputes the preliminary results from audit's limited, judgmental sample as being "unrepresentative." A follow-up attributes sample will allow IT audit to take another look at the data and come back with a stronger statement about the status of internal controls surrounding the area in dispute.

 ## WORKPAPERS AND REPORTING IT AUDIT RESULTS

This chapter has presented some fundamental techniques that are essential for all IT and other internal auditors, including audit planning preliminary surveys, audit programs, and attributes statistical sampling. The next sections outline two other important skills for performing effective IT audits: the development of audit workpapers and preparing effective audit reports. There is much more content in each of these areas for an IT auditor, but the next sections discuss the preparation of audit workpapers, to document ongoing audit endeavors and the preparation of audit reports. Each of these is not just an IT audit technique but essential components of the overall internal audit process.

Preparing IT Audit Workpapers

Workpapers are the written records kept by an IT auditor to document review materials, notes, and other sample material—the evidential matter—gathered or accumulated during an audit. The term *workpaper* is a rather archaic auditor expression that describes a physical or computer file that includes the various schedules, analyses, memoranda prepared, and, in many cases, copies of documents secured as part of an audit. The common characteristic of all workpapers, however, is that they describe the results of the internal audit work performed and should be formally retained for subsequent reference and substantiation of reported audit conclusions and recommendations. Workpapers are the bridge between actual internal audit procedures and the audit reports issued. Not an end in themselves but a means to an end, workpapers are created to fit particular audit tasks and are subject to a great deal of flexibility. They must support and document the purposes and activities of an IT auditor, regardless of their specific form. Thus, workpaper principles and concepts are more important than any specific formats.

Internal audit workpapers also can have considerable legal significance. In certain investigations, they have been handed over, through court orders, to government, legal, or regulatory authorities. When scrutinized by outsiders in this context, inappropriate workpaper notes or schedules can easily be taken in the wrong context. They form the documented record of both who performed the audit and who reviewed that work. IT audit workpapers are the only record of that audit work performed, and they may provide future evidence of what did or did not happen in the area of audit interest at some point in time.

This section provides general guidance for preparing, organizing, reviewing, and retaining workpapers. Once organized in bulky legal-size paper folders, audit workpapers today are usually stored as computer-based folders or a combination of paper and computer format documents. As a side note, we use the term *workpaper*, although many have used *working paper* or *work paper*. All mean the same thing.

The objective of audit workpapers is to document that an adequate audit was conducted following professional standards. The IT auditor can perhaps better understand the overall role of workpapers in the audit process by considering the major functions these documents serve:

- ▪ **Basis for planning an audit.** Workpapers from a prior audit provide an IT auditor with background information for conducting a current review in the same overall area. They may contain descriptions of the entity, evaluations of internal control, time budgets, audit programs used, and other results of past audit work.
- ▪ **Record of audit work performed.** Workpapers describe the current audit work performed and reference it to an established audit program, discussed previously. Even if the audit is of a special nature, such as an IT network fraud investigation

where there may not be a formal audit program, a record should be established of the actual audit. This workpaper record should include a description of activities reviewed, copies or Web links to representative files, the extent of the audit coverage, and the results obtained.

■ **Use during the audit.** In many instances, the workpapers prepared play a direct role in carrying out the specific audit effort. For example, the workpapers can contain control logs for such areas as the responses received as part of an accounts receivable customer balance independent confirmation audit. Similarly, a flowchart might be prepared and then used to provide guidance for a further review of the actual activities in some process. Each of these would have been included in the workpapers in a previous audit step.

■ **Support for specific audit conclusions.** The final product of most internal audits is a formal audit report containing findings and recommendations. The findings may be actual evidence, such as a copy of a purchase order lacking a required signature, or derived evidence, such as the output report from a computer-assisted procedure against a data file or notes from an interview. The workpapers should provide sufficient evidential matter to support the specific audit findings that would be included in an audit report.

■ **Reference source.** Workpapers can answer additional questions raised by management, the operational or financial internal audit group, or external auditors. Such questions may be in connection with a particular audit report finding or its recommendation, or they may relate to other inquiries. For example, management may ask IT audit if a reported systems weakness problem also exists at another location that is not part of the current audit. The workpapers from that review may provide the answer. Workpapers also provide basic background materials that may be applicable to future audits of the particular entity or activity.

■ **Staff appraisal.** The performance of an IT audit staff member during a review—including that auditor's ability to gather and organize data, evaluate it, and arrive at conclusions—is reflected in the workpapers.

■ **Audit coordination.** Internal auditors on occasion exchange workpapers with external auditors, each relying on the other's work. In addition, government auditors, in their regulatory reviews of internal controls, may request to examine the internal auditor's workpapers.

In some respects, audit workpapers are no different from the formal files of correspondence, e-mails, and notes that are part of any well-managed organization. A manager would keep files of incoming and outgoing correspondence, notes based on telephone conversations, and the like. However, these files are based on just good practices and may vary from one manager to another in an organization. The manager may never be called on to retrieve these personal files to support some organization decision or other action.

Internal audit workpapers are different in that they may also be used to support or defend the conclusions reached from the audit. They may be reviewed by others for various reasons. Members of an internal audit organization may work on common projects and need to share workpapers to support their individual components of a larger

AR-2-5'1	Global Computer Products IT Audit General IT Controls Review of MUDDVILLE Server Operations	RRM yy/mm/dd

The IT audit team, led by L.C. Tuttle, began an IT general controls review at the Muddville distribution facility in Muddville, MN. After informing the IT manager, W.J. Rawdon, of the planned review, the assigned audit team met and visited with Rawdon on March 15, 20xx. He informed us of recent supervisor changes in server maintenance operations but otherwise provided assurances that there had been no significant changes in controls since our most recent review at the facility, yy/mm/dd.

IT Audit also informed Rawdon of our plans to review controls over the storage virtualization project in place at the facility. The manager in charge of the project met with IT audit and gave an overview of this project. We requested a current project plan for that effort and were advised it was currently being updated, with a completion date of the following week. We requested a copy of the most recent plan and were told it was not available.

IT audit then requested a walk-through tour of the server physical facilities. Pending more detailed tests, the audit team observed generally poor, sloppy physical housekeeping in many of the areas visited. Rawdon observed our concerns and claimed the problem was due to the inexperience of the new supervisor.

We informed Rawdon that our detailed review would begin at 9:00 the following morning.

EXHIBIT 5.11 IT Audit General Controls Review Workpaper Example

audit project or to take over an audit performed previously by another member of the audit staff. It is essential that an internal audit department have a set of standards to ensure consistent workpaper preparation.

Workpaper Documentation Organization

Most IT auditors prepare workpapers on their laptop computers, where they maintain many commentaries and schedules on secure files and folders. Regardless of page size or media, the purpose of a workpaper sheet is to provide a standard framework for documenting IT audit activities. Workpaper pages should be titled, dated, initialed by the preparer, and prepared in a neat and orderly manner. Exhibit 5.11 is an example workpaper page from an IT audit general controls review illustrating substance and format standards. The next paragraphs expand on that same basic workpaper format.

A typical IT audit gathers a large amount of materials to document the audit process. With the wide range of IT activities reviewed and the equally wide range of audit procedures, the form and content of those individual workpapers may vary greatly. The major categories depend on the nature of the audit materials and the work performed. For IT internal audits, workpapers can be separated into these broad audit areas:

- Permanent files
- Administrative files
- Audit procedures files

Permanent Files

Many audits are performed on a periodic basis and follow repetitive procedures. Rather than capture all of the data necessary every time each audit is performed, certain data can be gathered from what is called a permanent workpaper file, which contains data of a *historical or continuing nature* pertinent to current audits. Some of this data may include:

- Overall organization charts of the audit unit
- Charts of financial accounts (if appropriate for audit) and copies of major policies and procedures
- Copies of the last audit report, the audit program used, and any follow-up comments
- Financial statements about the entity, if appropriate, and any other potentially useful analytical data
- Information about any unique aspects of the IT hardware and software environment
- Information about the audit unit (descriptions of major products, production processes, and other newsworthy matters)
- Logistical information to help the next auditors, including notes regarding travel arrangements

A permanent file is not meant to be *permanent* in that it will never change; rather, it provides an IT auditor starting a new assignment a source of background material to help plan the new audit. Over the course of a new audit, an IT auditor may come across other materials to update or include in the permanent file. The permanent file is a source of continuity to tie audits together over time. Exhibit 5.12 shows an index from an audit permanent file binder.

In the past, internal auditors sometimes loaded up their audit permanent files with materials that do not deserve permanent file status—for example, copies of various procedures that will have changed by the time of the next scheduled audit. Materials readily available at the time of the next audit need not be retained in permanent files unless certain ongoing procedures were based on those earlier materials. This administrative planning audit workpaper material should be kept to a minimum.

Administrative Files

Although separate workpaper administrative files may not be necessary for a smaller audit, the same general administrative workpaper materials should be incorporated

Global Computer Products IT Audit Permanent File Index		
INDEX	**PERMANENT FILE**	**DATE**
A-13	Corporate Data Center IT General Controls	02/01/2012
A-24	Brussels Distribution Operations IT General Controls	05/11/2012
A-25	Muddville Operations IT General Controls	03/15/2011
B-17	Corporate ERP CAATTs	06/30/2005
B-38	Financial Systems CAATTs	09/30/2011
C-92	Corporate IT Service Delivery Controls	03/15/2013
C-04	Corporate Service Delivery Controls	06/05/2012

EXHIBIT 5.12 IT Workpaper Permanent File Index Example

somewhere in all audit workpaper sets. If only a single auditor or limited review, this material may be incorporated into the single workpaper.

Audit Procedures Files

Audit procedures files and folders record the actual audit work performed and vary with the type and nature of the audit assignment. That is, this is the documentation covering the actual audit. For example, the workpapers for an IT applications audit may contain interview notes and auditor observations and these workpaper documentation elements:

- **Listings of completed audit procedures.** Workpapers are a central repository documenting the IT audit procedures and include copies of the audit programs along with the signed initials of the auditors and the dates of the audit steps. Commentary notes may be on the programs or attached as cross-referenced supplementary notes.
- **Descriptions of operational procedures.** Workpapers should briefly describe the nature and scope of the specific IT activity reviewed. This description can be in flowchart or narrative form. The auditor should always note on the workpaper the source of information to develop this description. For example, a member of auditee management may have described the process or the auditor may have gathered this information through observation.
- **Review activities.** Many IT audit workpapers cover specific investigations that appraise selected activities. These can include testing of data, observations of performance, inquiries to designated individuals, and the like. This is perhaps the most common type of workpaper prepared by the internal auditor. It follows no one form but serves only to describe the audit activities performed and the results.
- **Organization documents.** Basic documents here include organization charts, minutes of meetings, policy statements, contracts, and the like. Although some of these might be more appropriate for the permanent file, others are unique to a particular audit. Sometimes it may be valuable to retain a limited set of hard-copy documents, but file records should retain active Web links to audit-related reference materials. The purpose of these documents is to provide references to audit decisions or processes.
- **Findings point sheets or drafts of reports.** Point sheets are review documents, normally prepared by in-charge audit supervisors or responsible audit management, that reflect an audit's supervisory review and any questions or review points that may have been raised as a result of that audit. The idea is that these point sheets allow the audit supervisor to raise questions about the audit along with appropriate IT auditor responses. The format of these documents can vary. Exhibit 5.13 is an example of a workpaper review point sheet. In addition, for smaller audits that do not have an administrative file, several draft versions of the written report should be included either as copies or references. These drafts can be annotated to show major changes, the persons responsible for authorizing those changes, and in some cases the reasons for the changes. The review functions of a software product, such as Microsoft Word, can be very useful here.

Global Computer Products Workpaper Review Notes—Muddville Storage Management General Controls		
yy/mm/dd		Prepared by: JAS
W/P Ref.	Audit Procedure	Disposition
A-13	Manager approval message missing for SystemMatic consulting reference.	corrected—DSA mm/dd
A-14	Workpapers should note date and time of server center walk-through.	
B-02	Documentation for yymmdd continuity test inadequate—describe Day 2 wrap-up.	
C-03	Workpaper cross-reference missing.	corrected—DSA mm/dd
C-15	ERP Firewall tests missing.	
G-02	Audit program step 4.7 does not appear complete—review assessments.	

EXHIBIT 5.13　Workpaper Point Sheets Example

▪ **Audit bulk files.** Internal audits often produce large amounts of evidential materials, which should be retained but not included in the primary workpapers. For example, an IT audit may perform a survey that results in a large number of returned questionnaires. These materials should be classified as workpapers but should be retrieved from the bulk file as necessary.

Workpapers are the method of documentation of communications within an internal audit department, from one IT audit or auditor to the next. They are also a means of communication with the enterprise's external auditors. An internal audit department should establish overall workpaper standards covering their style, format, and content. Some specific details do not need to be frozen, given the various types of audits performed and evolving audit automation procedures. However, workpaper contents should be prepared consistently for all audits. The audit procedures workpaper file, for example, should contain materials covering each of the listed areas.

PREPARING EFFECTIVE IT AUDITS

This chapter has summarized some the key elements that are necessary to perform any internal audit, with an emphasis on IT audits. Although IT audit is often a unique and very special function within an enterprise's internal audit function, IT auditors should follow many of the same procedures and processes as the other operational and financial internal auditors within an internal audit organization. IT auditors have a unique role in an internal audit organization, but they must work with other members of the internal audit team to perform effective audits.

This chapter has talked about many of the tasks necessary to perform effective IT audits, but there are many other details necessary. Performing effective IT audits is a comprehensive and important process. Exhibit 5.14 shows some of the steps necessary

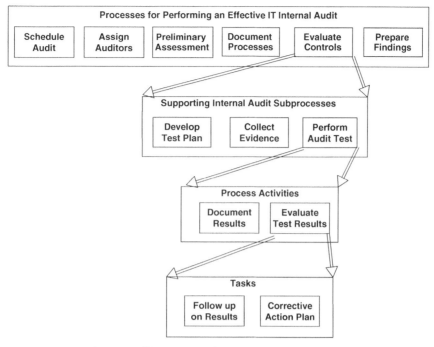

EXHIBIT 5.14   Performing Effective IT Audits Process Steps

to perform any IT audit. This exhibit provides just one path in what is normally a much larger process requiring many steps and going much beyond this chart. The overall process described here should be considered while reading the next chapters, which discuss the many and varied tasks and opportunities for IT auditors.

This chapter has described key processes for performing effective IT audits. The overall message here is that IT audits are in many respects not that different from many other internal audits. However, they always should be integrated with other enterprise internal audit processes, be consistent with other enterprise internal audit standards, and emphasize the unique risks and concerns associated with enterprise IT controls.

Even though an IT audit group may perform many very specialized IT security and control reviews, this work always should be coordinated with other enterprise internal audit activities. Whether IT audit or the operational and financial internal audit team members, all are reporting to the enterprise's audit committee. Satisfying audit committee key goals is the key element to performing effective IT internal audits.

NOTES

1. For an overall description of a successful internal audit function, see Robert Moeller, *Brink's Modern Internal Auditing: A Common Body of Knowledge*, 7th ed. (Hoboken, NJ: John Wiley & Sons, 2009).
2. Descriptions of these supporting documents and discussion on their use can be found in ibid.

PART TWO

Auditing IT General Controls

CHAPTER SIX

General Controls in Today's IT Environments

NTERPRISE INFORMATION TECHNOLOGY (IT) processes and systems cover many areas, ranging from an IT application to control an enterprise's accounting general ledger, file server devices to manage enterprise data, and connections to the all-pervasive Internet. An IT auditor should have a strong understanding of IT internal control techniques covering many of these technologies and processes. Although the lines of separation are sometimes difficult, we generally think of IT controls on two broad levels: application controls that cover a specific process, such as an accounts payable system to pay invoices from purchases, and what are called IT general controls. IT general controls cover all aspects of IT operations and are necessary in order for specific application controls to be effective.

Although many types of application-specific controls are discussed here and in later chapters, an example application control is a self-balancing routine in an accounting-related system that flags an error or stops processing if the accounts are out of balance for that specific application. An important control for that specific accounting application, it assumes that no one can inappropriately alter this application, by changing a parameter file or otherwise bypassing things, to override these self-balancing controls. A process to prevent unauthorized changes to all such applications is called a general control.

IT general controls cover broad areas of the overall IT environment, such as computer operations, access to programs and data, program development and program changes, network controls, and many others. In order for specific application controls to be effective, there must also be strong overriding effective IT general controls in place.

The concept of IT general controls goes back to the early days of centralized, mainframe computers. Before there were many specialized IT auditors, internal auditors sometimes looked for such things as an access control lock on a computer center door as a general control that covered all processes and applications operating within that centralized IT operations center. Today, we often think of the set of processes that cover all IT enterprise operations as the IT infrastructure. Because of the many possible variations in techniques here, no one technique is really right or wrong here. An enterprise should establish and implement a set of best practices that will serve as guidance for establishing IT general controls best practices.

This chapter looks at IT general controls from an IT auditor's perspective. Using the control classification hierarchy from Exhibit 6.1, this chapter reviews some key governance, management, and technical IT general controls. Many IT general controls also cover specific specialized areas, discussed in other chapters (such as Chapter 20 on cybersecurity and privacy controls), and this chapter discusses many IT general control procedures as they apply to enterprises of all sizes. Our overall focus, however, is on effective IT audits of these general controls.

 ## IMPORTANCE OF IT GENERAL CONTROLS

IT auditors became involved with early IT procedures—then called data processing controls—when accounting applications were first installed on punched-card accounting systems on very early computer systems. Those systems of long ago were often installed in glass-walled rooms within corporate lobbies to impress visitors with the enterprise's "sophistication." However, those same early computer systems were not particularly sophisticated and internal auditors, who were often unfamiliar with data processing technology, would audit around the computer. That is, they might look at input controls procedures and the application's outputs to check whether the inputs balanced to the output reports. At this time, there was little question about accuracy and controls when a report was produced by an IT system. An auditor would just go around the actual computer program processing procedures, assuming them to be accurate.

Things changed in the early 1970s when a California-based insurance company, Equity Funding, seemed to be almost growing too fast. Its external auditors decided to run their own audit software programs against Equity Funding's files, an almost unheard-of audit procedure at the time. The result was the discovery of a massive fraud with invalid data recorded on system files. Under management direction, fictitious insurance policy data had been entered on these computer files. Equity Funding's external auditors had previously audited around that computer system, relying on printed output reports, with no supporting procedures to verify the correctness of supporting computer programs and files. A massive fraud was discovered. In the aftermath of the Equity Funding affair, organizations such as the American Institute of Certified Public Accountants (AICPA) and the Institute of Internal Auditors (IIA) began to emphasize the importance of reviewing data processing operations and application controls. A new professional specialty, *computer or IT auditing*, was launched.

In those early days of business data processing, most IT systems were considered to be "large," and standard sets of auditor control objectives and procedures were developed for reviewing controls. Many are still applicable today, but IT auditors must look at these control objectives from a somewhat different perspective in today's

IT environments. The profession began to think of IT controls in terms of the controls within a specific application and what are called general controls, pervasive controls surrounding all information systems operations. IT general controls cover all information systems operations and include:

- **Reliability of information systems processing.** Good controls need to be in place over all IT systems operations. Discussed throughout this chapter, these controls often depend on the nature and management of the specific size and type of systems used.
- **Integrity of data.** Processes should be in place to ensure a level of integrity over all data used in various application programs. This is a combination of the general operations controls discussed in this chapter as well as specific application controls discussed in Chapter 10.
- **Integrity of programs.** New or revised programs should be developed in a well-controlled manner to provide accurate processing results. These control issues are part of the overall process of application program development and discussed in Chapter 7 on information technology infrastructure library (ITIL) best practices.
- **Controls over the proper development and implementation of systems.** Controls should be in place to ensure the orderly development of new and revised information systems. These control issues are discussed in Chapter 11.
- **Continuity of processing.** Processes should be in place to back up key systems and to recover operations in the event of an unexpected outage—what was once called disaster recovery planning and today is often known as business continuity planning. These control issues are discussed in Chapters 23 and 25.

This chapter discusses general controls over in-house IT operations ranging from client-server systems to desktop operations as well as older, larger mainframe computer systems. Although there are differences in size and management of these different systems, all should be subject to the same general control needs.

IT auditors should follow the general audit steps outlined in Chapter 5 for their reviews of IT general controls as well as for many types of IT audits:

- Develop the objectives of the area or function to be reviewed or audited.
- Assess the area being audited to determine if the audit objectives are being met.
- If the controls assessed do not appear to meet audit objectives, perform a formal test of these controls to better understand compliance.
- Evaluate the results of audit tests and the resulting risks of internal control failures.
- Develop recommendations for corrective actions based on these test results, and report them as part of the internal IT audit reporting process.

This basic audit process is described in more detail in Chapter 5 and is used in IT audit exercises in other chapters. IT auditors always should develop control objectives for the area reviewed, review the supporting materials, test the control objectives, and finally develop control improvement recommendations based on the nature of the materials reviewed.

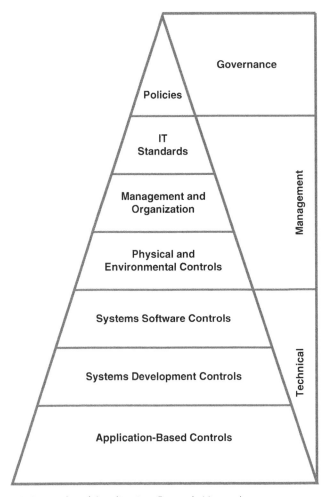

EXHIBIT 6.1 IT General and Application Controls Hierarchy

As another and perhaps more appropriate way of looking at IT general and application controls, Exhibit 6.1 describes an IT controls hierarchy. At the top of this triangle configuration are IT policies defining the overall enterprise IT organization. Some of these general control requirements are discussed in the sections that follow; others involving the enterprise audit committee are found in Chapter 15. Moving down the Exhibit 6.1 hierarchy are general controls for IT standards, organization of the IT function, and physical and environmental controls. The next level down in the hierarchy brings two categories of technical-level general controls: systems software and systems development general controls, followed by application-based controls at the base of the controls hierarchy.

Understanding and reviewing IT general controls as well as making appropriate recommendations for improvements or corrective actions are key IT audit activities. The next sections outline many of the key IT general controls areas of interest to IT auditors.

IT general controls are also discussed in other chapters. For example, Chapter 17 discusses the general controls area of compliance with IT laws and regulations, and Chapter 26 reviews auditing telecommunications networks. Strong IT general controls are important; effective applications controls are of little value sunless they are supported by strong IT general controls.

IT GOVERNANCE GENERAL CONTROLS

The concept of IT governance is relatively new. An IT auditor generally will not find any reference to IT governance in any IT management book published before the turn of this century. The concept evolved through the Committee of Sponsoring Organizations (COSO) internal control framework, as discussed in Chapter 1, where enterprise governance issues appear as the foundation of that internal controls framework as the internal controls environments component. COSO talks about a wide range of enterprise governance controls, such as the importance of an active audit committee and a senior management tone at the top, and these same high-level internal control messages apply to the IT function as well.

IT internal controls at a governance level involves ensuring that effective IT management and security principles, policies, and processes with appropriate compliance measurement tools are in place to assess and measure those controls. Effective IT governance controls require an active audit committee that goes beyond just financial reporting issues and reviews a wide range of enterprise issues, including IT matters. As discussed in Chapter 5, internal control findings and recommendations that involve IT-related issues should be reported to the audit committee in a matter that they can understand the issues.

Although Sarbanes-Oxley (SOx) rules require that every audit committee must have at least one "financial expert," there are no such requirements for a board-level IT expert. Rather, the IT audit function and the overall IT audit group should present their recommendations and issues such that board members can easily understand IT audit's concerns and issues. This is often a challenge for IT auditors not to get too technical and to present things in an easy-to-understand manner.

IT governance controls can also present concerns because sometimes top-level enterprise governance issues are not actively communicated and promoted to an enterprise's IT function. This was particularly true years ago, when many of the IT staff worked behind the locked doors of the computer room and did not have much day-to-day contact with other enterprise activities. This same isolation, however, still exists today; the IT function frequently is separated from many other enterprise activities.

Chapter 8 discusses processes for planning and performing all levels of IT general controls audits. Review steps for assessing IT infrastructure controls are included in that chapter's IT audit procedures. For example, while reviewing IT operations, an IT auditor should determine that members of the IT staff understand such matters as an enterprise's overall employee code of conduct or the existence of any enterprise-level whistleblower programs to independently report any potential problems.

IT MANAGEMENT GENERAL CONTROLS

Exhibit 6.1 shows three levels of IT controls: standards, organization and management controls, and physical and environmental general controls. Following high-level policies, these should be considered in a top-down manner. That is, IT standards should follow top-level policies, with good IT organization and management controls at the next level down. The third level of IT management general controls is the overall category of IT physical and environmental controls.

Although we are describing these as levels of internal controls, IT auditors should recognize that they are not separate internal control domains; all are related to each other on many levels. In addition, an enterprise often does not have just one IT function; it may have multiple units differing by geographic location, line of business, or IT technology. IT auditors always should look for certain minimum control requirements in each of these areas but realize some IT general controls may differ across different environments.

IT Standards

Standards exist to support the requirements of an enterprise's generally stated policies. Larger enterprises are in a position to develop their own IT standards, but many will adopt best practices or recognized professional practices as the basis for their IT standards. The ITIL set of best practices (discussed in Chapter 7) is an example of IT documents that can be established as an enterprise's IT standards.

IT auditors should look for established standards within an IT organization, covering such areas as new systems development, software acquisition, documentation, and applications control procedures, among many other issues. Evidence should be in place to demonstrate that procedures have been communicated and followed by all members of the IT organization. Examples of these IT general controls standards include:

- **E-mail communications protocols.** An enterprise can experience many e-mail abuses, such as massive and unnecessary attachments connected to messages, excessive use of "cute" graphics, or the sharing of confidential data. Similar to the auditor codes of conduct introduced in Chapter 3, an enterprise and its IT function should develop standards for e-mail use and messaging.
- **Systems development standards.** Although IT functions develop far fewer from-scratch programs and applications today and typically purchase necessary software packages, systems development standards are needed. Enterprises need to establish systems development life cycle (SDLC) process standards to develop and implement new IT applications. The SDLC process is discussed in Chapter 10.
- **IT documentation.** Standards should specify the minimum level of documentation required for each application or IT installation. These standards should include different classes of applications, processes, and physical IT facilities. Chapter 12 discusses IT documentation and records management processes.

These are just a few examples of the types of standards an IT auditor should expect to find when reviewing general controls in an IT facility. For a larger enterprise, these standards may exist at multiple levels, with general standards issued through the chief information officer (CIO) office and more detailed standards in place for development and processing centers. An IT auditor should document and understand these standards and, if appropriate, perform audit compliance procedures against these established standards.

IT Organization and Management

Effective IT organization and management processes are an important area of general controls. Whether a larger enterprise with multiple, large facility data centers or a smaller business with a server system and a limited number of attached terminals, an IT auditor should have a good understanding of overall management controls, including provisions for adequate separations of duties, financial management, and overall change management controls. If a new IT facility that has not been reviewed in the past, an IT auditor should perform a preliminary review of the IT function's organization and management controls, as described in Exhibit 6.2.

An IT audit–led preliminary survey often is not structured as a formal IT audit; it can be an informal review to better understand the internal controls processes in place. A first-time survey of the IT organizations should be documented in audit workpapers, as discussed in Chapter 5; workpapers should be updated for subsequent follow-up reviews. This is not a formal IT audit but a way to gain some background information to serve as a basis for scheduling other IT audit reviews or for determining the status of controls issues that surfaced in prior reviews.

Although a preliminary survey can cover a wide range of areas regarding IT organization and management issues, the need for adequate separations of duties is vital in many controls and is often the most major control issue. The functions of initiating, authorizing, inputting, processing, and checking data should be separated to ensure that no individual can create an error, omission, or other irregularity and then authorize it as evidence. Traditional separations of duties within an IT environment are divided between systems development and operations, where operations personnel responsible for running production systems should have little or no contact with the development process.

IT Physical and Environmental Larger System General Controls

In older, traditional IT environments, computer operations were often IT audit's prime area of internal control concerns. Computer operators had considerable power to make changes or to bypass systems controls, such as overriding data file label protections, making changes to program processing sequences, or inserting unauthorized program instructions into production applications. Although these overrides still are possible today, the complexity of large computer operating systems, the often-complex connections between systems servers, and the sheer volume of work passing through a modern IT operations center make unauthorized operator override actions much more difficult. IT audit often has greater risks to consider, and many once-common IT operations control improvement recommendations are no longer feasible. For example, older business data center computers had a terminal monitor or even a console printer attached to record operator commands; IT auditors traditionally recommended that these console logs be

1. Obtain basic information about the environment through initial exploratory discussions with information technology (IT) management.
2. Review the organizational chart and position titles to determine that appropriate separation of functions exists. Discuss any potential conflicts with IT management.
3. Obtain job descriptions of key IT personnel, and review them for adequate and appropriate qualifications, task definitions, and responsibilities. Ensure that security and control accountability are appropriately assigned to key personnel.
4. Based on discussions within management both inside and outside the IT organization, assess whether the IT organizational structure is aligned with business strategies to ensure expected IT service delivery.
5. Review documented IT policies and selected procedures for completeness and relevance with specific emphasis on security, business continuity planning, operations, and IT customer service.
6. Inquire whether responsibilities have been assigned to keep the policies and procedures current, to educate/communicate them to staff members, and to monitor compliance with them.
7. Based on discussions with senior IT management, assess whether strategic, operational, and tactical IT plans are in place to ensure alignment with the organization's overall business plans.
8. Determine the existence of an IT steering committee, and review this committee's functions through a limited review of steering committee meeting minutes.
9. Assess whether IT planning and control linkages have been established through communication or reports to the audit committee.
10. Ensure that a formal methodology is used in the development of new systems or major enhancements to systems in production. The methodology should include formal steps for definition, feasibility assessment, design, construction, testing, and implementation as well as formal approvals at every stage.
11. Determine that well-controlled processes are in place for making changes to application programs in production, including testing and documentation sign-off, and formal approvals to implement the change into production.
12. Ensure that responsibility for physical and logical security has been appropriately apportioned and that appropriate documented procedures exist.
13. Review procedures in place for operating and maintaining the physical and wireless IT network, in terms of device configuration and software parameter changes, and ensure that procedures for allocating and maintaining the network configuration are performed on a scheduled basis and under proper change management.
14. Review the business continuity and IT disaster recovery plans to ensure that detailed plans for recovery of operations have been prepared, and that the plans are documented, communicated to the appropriate personnel, and properly tested on a periodic basis.
15. Review both the IT budget and actual costs as well as performance against those measured to assess financial performance. Discuss reasons for any variances.

EXHIBIT 6.2   IT General Controls Preliminary Survey Review Steps

reviewed on a regular basis. IT operations management often ignored these log reports, but they were useful for tracing inappropriate operator activities. Today, this console activity is still recorded onto log files, but it is not even printed but recorded on server files; the sheer volume of that data makes a periodic human review of console log reports unrealistic; other tools and controls are available to help IT auditors understand operations controls. An IT auditor should gain an understanding of the IT organization, its established control procedures, and any operation's specialized duties and responsibilities.

Today, IT systems are operating in a client-server world, where powerful but very major server computers drive a wide range of terminals and storage devices. Computer operations centers are much more automated and efficient than they were not so many years ago. User terminals are protected by firewalls and are connected— through either cables or wireless connections—to complex enterprise-controlled networks or to the Internet. We have even moved to the concept of *cloud computing*, where the IT network is so vast and complex that it appears as if we are just connecting a device to a cloud in the sky to receive interconnections. There is more on cloud computing in Chapter 9. Our general controls discussion here covers in-house enterprise IT operations.

An important step in an audit review of IT operations general controls is to clearly define the planned review's objectives. All too often, management may ask IT audit to "review computer systems controls" in a data center without any clear objectives for the review. Management memories do not fade that fast and that management request for an audit may be based on IT controls as they once existed in older, legacy systems. An IT auditor should consider these questions when planning the review:

- What is the purpose of the information system operations review?
- Which specific controls and procedures are expected to be in place?
- How can evidence be gathered to determine if these general controls work?

Based on the results of this exercise, IT audit should develop a set of control objectives specifically tailored for the planned review rather than just use a standard set of internal control questions. The IT audit objectives identified always depend on the purpose of the review.

If management has requested a review of the costs and efficiency of data center operations, for example, IT audit procedures might include such areas as chargeback procedures and the job-scheduling systems. Although larger-system IT general controls reviews can have a variety of purposes, they often fit into one of four review types:

1. **Preliminary reviews of IT general controls for server-based IT operations.**
   This is type of review, to gain a general understanding or overview of the IT control environment, is outlined in Exhibit 6.2. IT auditors have performed these reviews over the years, going back to legacy mainframe systems. IT audit asks questions, observes operations, and reviews documentation, but there is typically only very limited testing, if any. For example, IT audit might inquire about the procedures for updating production program libraries and might review the documents or processes used for program library approvals. However, the auditor probably would not select a sample of the programs in the production library to determine if proper library update procedures had been followed.

   A preliminary review can help determine the need for a more detailed general controls review, an extended control risk assessment at a later date, or can gather internal controls information for a specific applications review. This type of review is limited in scope and may not cover all aspects of IT operations. Areas where this level of review would be appropriate might include a preliminary controls review of IT operations at a new acquisition or a follow-up review after a very detailed general controls review from an earlier period; the review here would emphasize changes in control procedures as well as actions taken on prior audit recommendations.

2. **Detailed general controls reviews of IT operations.** A comprehensive, detailed review of IT general controls should cover all aspects of IT operations, including systems programming, wireless and telecommunications controls, and storage management, including virtualization. A detailed general controls review, including tests of controls, often requires IT audit to spend considerable fieldwork time in both the IT operations and the development functions. The preliminary review sometimes can be performed by a less experienced auditor who is developing IT audit skills, but a detailed general controls review is best performed by more senior IT audit staff members with a good understanding of IT controls and procedures.

Based on a preliminary IT operations walk-through review, IT audit should develop an understanding of the control procedures over IT operations. The detailed audit procedures performed can be modified based on this preliminary information. Questions an IT auditor might pose could include:

- **How is work scheduled?** Some server operating system procedures do little more than initiate jobs from a production job queue file, while operations personnel sometimes have considerable authority in deciding which jobs to run. In the latter situation, IT audit might want to spend time reviewing control log reports and operator instructions. If these procedures have been automated, IT audit may want to consider a specialized review of the production control software area.

- **How is storage media managed?** Automated tools often are used here. In addition, some operations have a separate library facility where production media cartridges are mounted. Even when software has been installed, computer operators often can bypass label controls and introduce incorrect files into a production environment.

- **What types of operator procedures or instructions are used?** Server-based systems soft- and hard-copy operations documentation can take a variety of formats; IT audit should have a general understanding of these documentation formats and content to help in the design of specific audit tests.

- **How is work initiated, and how does it flow through operations?** In many client-server operations, IT production is initiated through remote job entry user terminals. In others, the production control function funnels all necessary input data to machine operations. Some functions rely on users to initiate most inputs through their network terminals. The type and nature of IT audit's tests will depend on these procedures.

The basic idea here is that IT audit should understand how the server-based operations function. The effective IT auditor should go through a set of these types of questions prior to each review. A larger systems operations function may install new procedures from time to time, changing or adding complexities to the control structure. The audit procedures to be performed in a detailed review of general controls for a legacy computer system can be extensive, depending on the size and scope of the audit. Exhibit 6.3 contains a limited set of control objectives for this type of review.

3. **Specialized or limited-scope reviews.** Because of management requests and perceived risks, IT auditors often perform limited reviews over specialized areas within

1. Determine the servers and other IT equipment is located in a secure, environmentally controlled facility.
2. Discuss physical and environmental control procedures with IT management to determine current policies and future plans.
3. Tour computer room facilities and observe physical security strengths and weaknesses, including:
   a. The existence of locking mechanisms to limit computer room access only to authorized individuals
   b. The placement of computer room perimeter walls and windows to limit access
   c. The location of power transformers, water chiller units if appropriate, and air-conditioning units to provide proper protection
   d. The general location of the computer room facilities within the overall building to minimize traffic
   e. The existence of fire detection equipment, including zone-controlled heat and smoke detectors
   f. The existence of a zone-controlled, overall fire protection system, including local extinguishers
4. Review computer room temperature, humidity, and other environmental controls, and assess their adequacy.
5. Briefly review maintenance records to ascertain that physical and environmental controls are regularly inspected and maintained.
6. Production processing should be scheduled to promote efficient use of computer equipment consistent with the requirements of systems users. Through interviews with operations management, develop an overall understanding of computer processing demands, including online and batch production work as well as any end user computing.
7. Also through interviews, describe the telecommunications network surrounding the computer system, including firewalls and connections to all servers, workstations, Internet links, and wireless connections.
8. Review procedures for scheduling regular production jobs including the use of automated job scheduling tools.
9. Match a limited number of scheduled production jobs against actual completion times to determine whether actual schedules are followed.
10. Determine that operating system job classes or priority codes are used to give proper priority to critical production jobs, and evaluate procedures for rush or rerun jobs.
11. Review documentation standards for production applications to determine that they provide operators with information regarding:
    a. Normal operations, including instructions for special forms, tape files, and report disposition
    b. Application restart and recovery procedures
12. Review procedures, automated or manual, for turning new applications or revisions over to production to determine there is a review by operations following standards.
13. Determine that policies prohibit IT operations personnel from performing programming tasks or running unauthorized jobs.
14. Determine that production source libraries cannot be accessed by operations personnel.
15. Assess IT procedures for periodically reviewing the contents of automated log files or otherwise monitoring improper operator use of server equipment.
16. Review and document procedures for changing production programs or procedure libraries when emergency situations require special handling.
17. Determine that all emergency processing activities are properly documented and are subject to subsequent management review.
18. Select several documented emergency program fixes and determine that the necessary changes were added to production processing libraries and were documented.

EXHIBIT 6.3   Larger-System General Controls Review Objectives (*Continued*)

19. Determine that an automated system is in place to log all IT systems activity, including all jobs and programs run, any reruns, abnormal terminations, or operator commands and data entered through system consoles.
20. Determine that all appropriate server activity logs are reviewed periodically, that exception situations are investigated, and that the results of investigations are documented.
21. Determine that files produced from server operating system's log monitors are retained long enough to allow investigation of unusual activities.
22. Review procedures for logging problems to determine that all abnormal software and hardware operating conditions are documented.
23. Determine that schedules exist for the submission of any critical input batch files and that procedures exist to follow up on missing data.
24. Review procedures to prohibit unauthorized input or access to production files and programs.
25. Review a limited sample of scheduled production applications to determine that appropriate systems control techniques are used.
26. Determine whether users or IT personnel are responsible for reviewing output controls, and assess whether those control reviews are being performed.

EXHIBIT 6.3 (*Continued*)

an overall IT function. These reviews can be limited to one function, such as database administration, or a specialty area, such as systems supporting a particular business unit. Often, management will request that IT audit perform such a targeted specialized review due to some identified problem, such as the identification of a fraud.

An audit of a highly specialized or technical area of IT operations often takes considerable IT auditor creativity in planning the work. Management may be concerned about the equity of the computer chargeback system and may ask the audit department to look at it. IT audit will need to gain a general understanding of the system used, spend time planning the additional procedures and tests to be performed, and then return to the actual testing.

As IT resources have grown in complexity and importance to an enterprise, auditors can expect to perform more of these specialized, limited reviews. Because the IT function is a major resource in many enterprises, it may be inappropriate to attempt to review *all* IT general controls in *all* operational areas in one single detailed review. This would be the same as if internal audit attempted to perform a review of "manufacturing" in a major plant environment. Rather than cover all manufacturing functions, internal audit might review production control one year and receiving and inspection the next, and eventually cover other significant functions. For a specialized review of a specific IT control area, such as mass storage memory management, IT audit should expand on the procedures developed for a general controls review in that area and add additional audit tests as necessary.

4. **Reviews to assess compliance with laws or regulations.** One of the major objectives of internal control, as discussed in Chapter 1, is compliance with laws and regulations. IT auditors always should be aware of objectives in this area and include appropriate tests in their reviews. Auditors working with government agencies or in enterprises that do extensive government contracting may be required to perform IT-related compliance audits often to determine if appropriate

laws and regulations are being followed. These audits will differ very much from agency to agency and from one political division to another.

A compliance-related IT review often can be combined with a preliminary or detailed general controls review, but IT auditors must be aware of the relevant procedures and regulations, such as those published by the government agency requiring the audit. Most bank examination agencies, for example, have published IT controls guidelines. When operating in this type of environment, IT auditors must be aware of the regulatory environment as well as any published procedures.

Client-Server and Smaller-Systems General IT Controls

IT auditors often face challenges in evaluating general controls in a smaller IT operation, ranging from networked client-server configurations to enterprise desktop systems. General controls evaluation problems arise because smaller systems often are installed with limited staffs in a more "user-friendly" type of environment. IT auditors, however, typically look for general IT controls in terms of the more traditional, larger mainframe IT environment discussed in the sections that follow. That is, IT auditors are looking for the strong physical security, good revision, and proper separation-of-duties controls that often do not exist or are only partially implemented in typical smaller-systems environments. This less formal approach was perhaps adequate when these small business or desktop systems were used primarily for single-office accounting or similar low–audit risk applications. The large capacity and capability of smaller systems, the growth of the Internet, and the transition to client-server computing has made these smaller systems important parts of the IT control framework. When faced with evaluating controls in these smaller computer systems settings, IT auditors sometimes revert to the traditional, almost "cookbook" types of controls recommendations. That is, they recommend that desktop systems be placed in locked rooms or that a small, two-person IT development staff is expanded to four in order to ensure proper separation of duties. There may be situations where such controls are appropriate, but often they are not applicable in a smaller business setting. IT audit can easily lose credibility if its control recommendations are not appropriate to the risks found in the smaller computer systems setting.

Enterprises today implement increasing numbers smaller client-server systems to support business units, for specific departmental computing, or provide IT for the entire enterprise. Despite their smaller size, these systems often represent significant general control concerns. IT auditors should understand the general controls surrounding smaller computer systems. Adequate general controls are necessary in order to place reliance on specific application controls.

Although some IT auditors once thought of smaller client-server systems as one generic computer system class (as opposed to larger, mainframe computers), technological changes have introduced significant differences in control procedures and IT audit concerns among them. Smaller systems can be implemented in a variety of ways, depending on the system configuration and the size of the enterprise. IT auditors should be able to recognize these differences and develop appropriate general internal control procedures to review their general controls. This section discusses these general controls in terms of smaller business Internet-connected and networked client-server systems general controls. These computer systems provide total IT support for a smaller business function or unit; they also may support unit or departmental computing functions in a larger enterprise in support of central computer systems resources. IT auditors may encounter all of these smaller computer systems in a single modern enterprise.

Client-server systems are often a combination of various types and sizes of interconnected IT systems and are found in many enterprises. The term *client-server* first appeared in IT literature in the late 1980s. It is one of those IT terms that is difficult for non–IT specialists to understand, let alone describe. As a way of thinking about this configuration, IT auditors should remember that in a local network environment each of the workstations is a *client*; a centralized processor, which contains common shared files and other resources, is called the *server*. There also may be specialized servers for such tasks as storage management or printing. Workstation users submit requests from client machines to a server, which then serves that client by doing the necessary processing.

This client-server architecture, however, goes beyond just a workstation and a server. An application that queries a centralized database can be considered the client while the database that develops the view of the database is the server to all workstations requesting database service. Similarly, an application program can request services from an operating system communications server. Exhibit 6.4 shows a client-server system sample

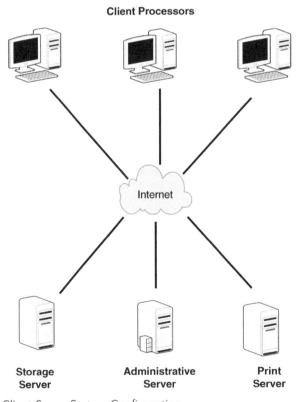

EXHIBIT 6.4 Client-Server System Configuration

configuration where a single server handles requests from multiple clients across a network. This client-server configuration, though very general, represents the typical IT system of today.

Small Business IT System Controls

If an IT system is located in a secure facility and has a relatively large IT support staff, IT auditors probably should consider it to be a "larger" computer system for purposes of IT audit planning and should review for appropriate larger system general control procedures. This definition is not particularly precise, but it would cover the typical major IT system. This same type of attribute-based description can be more difficult in the smaller-system environment. A strict computer hardware architecture definition often does not help IT audit to decide when to apply smaller-system internal control review procedures. For example, smaller desktop computers can be coupled together with attached peripheral devices to provide more computer power than many traditional mainframe machines. When reviewing controls in such an environment, IT audit should consider these linked computers to be the same as the larger systems discussed earlier in this chapter. Another problem in identifying smaller computers is that they often look like larger processors. For example, IBM first implemented a small business system in 1988 called the AS/400. Their AS/400 product line and the individual machine capacities have been expanded many times to make these systems effectively operate beyond classic mainframe systems.

Today's desktop or laptop systems have had a rapid growth curve. Starting with hobbyists building their own microcomputers using integrated circuit chips, things really got started in the late 1970s when Apple Computer Corporation was formed and produced the Apple II microcomputer. Although the machine was initially viewed as a toy by many, a spreadsheet software package, VISICALC, introduced about a year later, made the Apple II a serious tool for business decision making. Several years later, in the early 1980s, IBM introduced its personal computer and legitimized the microcomputer as a serious business processing tool. Today, many computers are still said to be "IBM compatible," even though IBM no longer manufacturers these products.

Today, personal computers, often connected into networks, are used for many business IT applications. They are often the only computer system resource for a smaller enterprise and have replaced smaller "mainframe" systems. They also may be used for specialized departmental computing, even though there may also be a larger, mainframe computer capability within an enterprise. In particular, these specialized computers are used for such applications as research laboratory or manufacturing process control rather than for pure business IT. These same machines also may be used for some business processing applications in addition to their intended specialized purposes.

Ever-increasing speed and capacity has done much to promote the use of these server systems. When the first Apple II was released, it had an internal memory of 42 k, or 42,000 memory locations. By the mid-1990s, by contrast, off-the-shelf machines typically came with 32,000,000 memory locations, or 32 mg. Today, these processors are much larger and virtually every other measure, whether processing speed, capability of running multiple tasks, or disk file memory capacity, has changed dramatically.

These smaller business unit systems can cause difficulties for IT auditors who have sometimes told their audit committee that they plan to review the general controls surrounding "all" IT systems in the enterprise. Clearly, this type of objective covers major server systems as well as any separate divisional IT systems. However, any plans to review "all" enterprise IT systems can also include specialized IT workstations in the engineering laboratory used for recording test results or systems at the end of a production distribution line that weigh packages and route them to the correct shipping dock. These definition problems will only get worse as embedded systems play a greater role in controlling business processes. Embedded systems are the computers that reside behind the dashboard of a car or on the control panel of a video recorder or kitchen microwave. As consumers, we press these flat-panel screens and generally do not think we are submitting computer system commands.

Although all of the systems just mentioned are computer systems, IT audit's reviews should emphasize the computer systems used for *business IT* purposes. To follow the previous example, the processor at the end of the distribution line probably uses a standard set of embedded software that cannot be modified by local staff. It was very possibly purchased from an outside systems vendor, and, after initial installation and testing, it simply works, with no programmer interaction. Such a machine generally has limited business or control risk implications.

IT audit often works in an environment where only smaller business systems are used, particularly when the enterprise is relatively small. An example would be a not-for-profit enterprise whose only systems needs are a server and desktop systems to support direct mailing and limited accounting-related applications. IT audit should review general controls over such a server system as if it were a classic, larger enterprise system. That is, there is still a need for systems security, integrity, and backup procedures. These types of smaller business systems generally have these common characteristics:

- **Limited IT staff.** The small-business IT system, whether a single Internet-connected desktop system or a series of units tied to a server, will have a very limited dedicated IT staff, if any. A desktop system to provide accounting reports for a small company may be maintained by a single person. A small-business or server system may have a manager/administrator and perhaps one or two systems administrators as its total IT department. Such a small IT operation creates a control risk because it is dependent on some separate small consulting firm for much of its IT support, and requirements for backing up critical files may be ignored. However, a small staff size will not in itself create internal controls concerns. IT audit should be able to look for compensating controls just as it does when reviewing a smaller accounting department where a classic separation of duties is lacking.

- **Limited programming and systems development capability.** The typical small business IT system makes extensive use of purchased software packages. The only "programming" needed may be for installing and updating purchased software, maintaining systems parameter tables, and writing simple retrieval programs. If an IT auditor finds a programming staff or extensive in-house development activity at the beginning of a review, he or she should consider some of the control procedures discussed for larger systems development functions.

- **Limited environmental controls.** Small business systems generally can be plugged into normal power systems and operate in a fairly wide range of temperatures. Because of their limited requirements, they sometimes are installed without important, easy-to-use environmental controls, such as backup drives or electrical power surge protectors. Some small business computer installations or file servers may be housed in formal, environmentally controlled computer rooms, but this is not a necessary attribute of these systems.

- **Limited physical security controls.** Because these systems have less need for environmental controls, often they are installed directly in office areas. The level of IT auditor concern regarding physical security controls depends on the type of equipment and the applications processed. IT audit sometimes may recommend that physical security be improved, particularly where critical applications are being processed. In many other instances, however, this lack of physical security controls should not present a significant internal control problem.

- **Extensive telecommunications network.** Virtually all desktop systems today are tied to the Internet. Data and applications can be uploaded or downloaded easily. In addition, materials can be downloaded easily through common USB devices. A combination of controls and policies should be established to protect the enterprise. An IT auditor should look for the effective use of installed antivirus software as well as systems firewalls; both of these are discussed in Chapter 19.

These characteristics certainly do not *define* a smaller business IT system but merely explain some common attributes. However, they should help IT audit to better decide on the control procedures to be used. When in doubt, however, IT audit should consider the system to have the internal control characteristics of a larger, more complex IT system.

Auditing General Controls for Smaller IT Systems

Some smaller IT systems may be separate operating units of a larger enterprise and provide support for the total enterprise. Such systems may have many of the attributes of a larger, mainframe computer system, including a limited but formal IT enterprise, production schedules, and a responsibility for implementing new applications. However, the smaller IT system enterprise often has no other specialized functions. IT audit will encounter a variety of computer hardware brands or product names in smaller-systems environments, but most will be open systems with a common operating system that can operate no matter what brand of hardware is used. This is different from the classic mainframe computers of an earlier era, where the manufacturer generally built the computer hardware as well as the operating system. Numerous vendors supply such small business computer systems with both improved functionality and price performance, and IT auditors will be more effective in reviewing small business IT system controls if they have an overall knowledge of some of their capabilities.

Despite the more informal nature of a typical small-business IT system, it still should have some similar general control objectives with these internal control concerns:

- **Smaller system controls over access to data and programs are often weak.** When unauthorized persons are allowed to access and modify computer files, general controls are very much weakened. IT audit should consider access to data and programs to be *the major general controls objective* when reviewing the smaller IT enterprise. This is true whether the IT department uses packaged software products or spreadsheet or database applications developed in-house.

Controls over access to data can be considered in terms of both specific applications and general controls. However, in smaller IT systems, general controls often have a greater importance than specific application data access controls because applications operating on a single small business computer system typically all operate under the same set of data access controls. In a small system, data can be improperly accessed and modified through user terminals, unauthorized use of specialized utility programs, or invalid IT requests.

▪ **Improper data access through user workstations.** Small systems—whether a series of laptops connected through a wireless system or a powerful server system—often do not have the sophisticated security controls found on the older, large, mainframe-type server systems. Rather, these smaller systems have a user logon/ password identification coupled with menu-based information security. A systems user typically enters the assigned logon code onto the terminal and receives a menu screen with the applications available to that code. Only then can the user access the applications assigned to that menu.

These menu-based security systems can provide a fairly effective control against improper access attempts but also can break down due to the informality of many smaller enterprises. Logon codes are often not changed on a regular basis, one general menu is given to virtually all employees, or terminals with more privileged IDs are left on for virtually all to use. Because users are often not aware of potential data vulnerabilities, management may give only minimal attention to such security issues. In order to review general controls in this area, IT audit should first gain an understanding of the data security system installed; it may range from a good password-based system to a highly structured set of procedures.

Because a small-business IT system may not have installed logging mechanisms to monitor invalid access attempts, IT audit should review the overall administration procedures covering the security system. These can include reviewing how often logons are changed, who has access to the system administrator's menu, and what local management's general appreciation is of IT access controls.

▪ **Unauthorized use of utility programs.** Modern small systems are often equipped with powerful utility programs, designed to be used for special problem-solving situations that can easily change any application data file. All too often, these utilities serve as substitutes for normal production update programs or are used by an IT manager for these special updates; sometimes they even are given to users. For example, an enterprise may have installed an inventory status system. Although the system normally provides proper stock-keeping records, the inventory status may become misstated from time to time for a variety of reasons. In order to help users correct their inventory status record-keeping problems, the IT administrator may have developed the practice of correcting inventory balances by using a utility program. The IT manager may be following proper management direction in the normal use of such a program, but there may be no audit trails over its use. IT audit can assess the usage of any such program through inquiry and observation.

▪ **Improper IT data and program access requests.** The informality of smaller enterprises often allows data to be accessed improperly through normal IT operations procedures. For example, someone affiliated with the IT function may initiate a special computer run, which results in an improper access to confidential data. In larger, more formal enterprises, such a request often requires special management permission, but smaller, more informal enterprises often waive such requirements. This type of access may be a greater control risk than access through use of improper programs.

IT audit should look for controls to prevent such casual IT requests through the use of a request-for-data-services type of form, approved by management. In addition, logs should be maintained listing all production IT activities as well as the name of the requester and the report recipient. Many of the control concerns over improper access to data also apply to small-system program libraries. Small-business systems typically have menu-based systems that offer some security types of controls. Without such a proper menu type of security system to limit improper access, often it is relatively easy for someone with a little knowledge to locate and potentially modify program library files.

IT audit also may find weak controls over program library updates. The one or two IT personnel in a smaller IT department who act as network administrators typically can update program libraries with little concern for documenting those changes or for obtaining any type of upper management authorization. Some of these changes may be justified in order to respond to user emergency requests, but others may not be properly authorized. It is difficult, if not impossible, to install separation-of-duties enterprise controls over small-business system program libraries. In addition, it probably will not work for IT audit to suggest that management formally review and approve all program library updates—management will neither be interested in performing nor have the technical skills to perform such reviews. The best control method here might be to install procedures that require the logging of all changes or software package updates to the production program library, with such logs subject to periodic IT auditor reviews.

This type of control takes advantage of the fact that many small-business IT systems maintain hash[1] total counts of program sizes in bytes and also can retain some form of date or version number within the program name. IT audit might then suggest this small-business computer system program library control:

▪ Establish program-naming conventions that include the date or version number included with the program name. When not available in commercially purchased software, a separate control file with this data can be established. This feature is becoming increasingly common; for example, it can be implemented within Microsoft Windows XP or Windows 7 operating systems.

▪ Have the persons authorized to make program table or parameter changes log in the version number, date, program size, and reason for the change in a manual listing subject to periodic management. If the application was developed in-house, the source code should contain comments explaining the change.

- Maintain at least one backup copy of the program library, and rotate a copy of the program library file to a secure portable disc drive in an off-site location at least once per week.
- Strengthen access controls such that nonauthorized personnel cannot easily access program library files.
- Perform an IT audit review of the library change log on a periodic basis. That review should match logged program versions, dates, and sizes with data reported on the program library file.

These steps will not provide IT audit with complete assurance that all program changes have been authorized; however, if IT audit periodically reviews logged changes and questions any discrepancies, IT personnel at that facility probably will take care to document and log any production program changes.

The message throughout this section is that there are or should be some general IT internal control concerns for all smaller systems, whether a network of laptops coupled to a server over wireless links or a free-standing office desktop system. There are many variations in the types of small-system IT configurations, but IT auditors should use some general internal control objectives to review general controls in these IT environments. Exhibit 6.5 outlines some internal control considerations for an IT audit review of a smaller-business IT system. In many instances, these review steps should be included as part of a larger, more comprehensive review in other areas of business operations.

Nonbusiness Specialized Processor IT Systems

In many enterprises today, systems can be found in areas beyond IT operations. They may be located in engineering laboratories, manufacturing control operations, marketing departments, and many other areas. These systems may be used for process control, automated design work, statistical analysis processing, or many other applications. Some are totally dedicated to specific applications while others may be used for a variety of tasks within their assigned functions. This multitude of IT machines has come about because of their relatively low cost, the familiarity of many professionals with IT techniques, and of the inability of traditional IT departments to support specialized IT needs.

Although these systems are not used for traditional business information needs, such as maintaining accounts receivable records, they often support critical applications for the enterprise. For example, an engineering department computer may support new product computer-aided design (CAD) work. Systems backup and integrity concerns in this environment may be as great as in the typical business IT center. IT audit's role in regard to specialized IT operations will vary with both management's direction and review objectives. Some internal audit organizations will have little involvement with reviews of specialized computer systems, but the internal controls reviewed here often can play an important role in support of IT audit's understanding of control procedures and in other operational audit activities.

Before attempting any review of such a specialized computer system, IT audit should obtain a rough familiarity with the functions of that operation. For example, an IT auditor who plans to review a dedicated computer-aided design and manufacturing

1. Establish and document responsibilities for the IT function. Identify persons responsible for all IT operations functions and document their authorities and responsibilities.
2. Determine if there is a complete and current inventory of systems hardware, including servers, firewalls, printers, and network controllers, as well as a complete inventory of application and systems software.
3. The network hardware inventory report should contain model and identification numbers. Review a limited sample of these items to determine whether the equipment is installed as described.
4. Trace a sample of the listed application and systems software to determine that current versions are installed, that appropriate documentation is in place, and that vendor licenses are current.
5. Review file and data backup procedures, and determine whether this data is backed up regularly to secure locations.
6. Observe computer server facilities, and verify that equipment is located in limited-access secure facilities with adequate power and environmental controls.
7. Observe key file storage backup processes to determine that media are regularly backed up to secure off-site locations.
8. Assess the adequacy of access control security procedures to determine that key systems and files are adequately protected by passwords that are regularly changed.
9. Review procedures in place for restricting, identifying, and reporting on unauthorized users of the network environment, and assess the adequacy of processes to investigate and correct security violations.
10. Assess the adequacy of systems security monitoring processes as well as new employee training practices in place to emphasize application security.
11. Determine that adequate antivirus software has been installed and is regularly updated.
12. Review the adequacy of procedures for installing new software in the systems environment, and assess that controls are in place to prevent the introduction of unauthorized software products.
13. Review a sample of key applications, and verify that they are supported by adequate continuity plans for disaster recovery purposes. Also, determine that continuity plans are tested periodically.
14. Interview persons responsible for network security to determine that adequate firewall tools have been installed and are monitored regularly.
15. Review records of systems downtime over a recent period, and determine that adequate short- and long-range measures are in place to promote continual processing improvements.
16. If available, obtain application operating schedules covering key financial and operational applications, and determine the adequate attention is given to application internal controls.
17. Interview systems manager/administrator to assess whether this person is knowledgeable and properly trained. Also, if the system is managed by outside consultants, review the adequacy of systems support efforts.
18. Interview a sample of systems users, and determine if they are satisfied with system performance, including response times and availability.

EXHIBIT 6.5 Review Objectives for Smaller-Business IT System General Controls

(CAD/CAM) computer operation needs a general understanding of the terminology, general workings, and objectives of CAD/CAM.

Reviews of these specialized IT systems are not recommended for the less experienced IT auditor. In order to find control analogies from normal business IT situations and translate them to specialized controls environments, an auditor must be fairly experienced in reviewing business IT operations. Over time, IT audit will encounter more of these specialized computer operations. The creative IT auditor can make increasing contributions to management by performing operational reviews over these computer centers on a periodic basis.

 ## IT TECHNICAL ENVIRONMENT GENERAL CONTROLS

The last three levels of IT general controls in the IT controls hierarchy diagram in Exhibit 6.1 describe more technical IT general controls: systems software, systems development, and application-based general controls. Systems software and system development general IT controls are discussed in Chapter 8. Application development general controls are discussed in Chapter 10.

This chapter has introduced the high-level process of auditing IT general controls, the pervasive controls whose effectiveness is essential for strong IT internal control environments. Whether working with a large enterprise with vast IT resources or a smaller business system, IT auditors should identify and then assess the effectiveness of their IT general controls. If IT general controls are weak, IT auditors can expect to find deficiencies in application and other internal controls throughout the organization.

Even though some IT auditors find reviews of IT technical areas, such as cybersecurity of operating systems procedures, to be more interesting from an audit perspective, enterprise IT general controls should be reviewed on a regular and ongoing basis. If an area has been reviewed in a past period, the results of those reviews should be repeated with appropriate updates and adjustments for new management policies, standards, and IT hardware and organization changes. IT auditors always should recognize that the strengths and weaknesses of many of other areas reviewed depends on these IT general controls.

 ## NOTE

1. A hash total is a summation of the numeric and alphabetic values for some computer value. It is often used as a control total.

CHAPTER SEVEN

Infrastructure Controls and ITIL Service Management Best Practices

C HAPTER 6 DISCUSSED AUDIT procedures for reviews of information technology (IT) general controls; these are the persuasive types of controls that are installed throughout an enterprise's IT systems operations and provide protection for all systems and applications. Examples of general controls might be physical locks and other security controls for a hardware server center or a common IT password security system covering all enterprise IT operations. As Chapter 6 emphasized, weak IT general controls will impact all IT applications that are part of those systems operations.

In today's world of pervasive IT processes and systems, installed throughout the enterprise and ranging from an application, to control of an accounting general ledger, to the all-pervasive Internet, IT auditors should have a strong understanding of IT internal control techniques. Although the lines of separation are sometimes difficult, we generally can think of IT controls on two broad levels: application controls that cover a specific process (such as an accounts payable application to pay invoices from purchases) and general IT controls. This latter category covers many controls that go beyond those discussed in Chapter 6; they do not relate just to specific IT applications and are important for all aspects of an enterprise's IT operations.

The concept of IT general controls goes back to the early days of centralized, mainframe computers. Today we often think of the set of processes that cover all enterprise IT operations as the IT infrastructure. This IT infrastructure is very different across enterprises, large and small, due to the relative size of their operations and the overall nature of their business. Because of the many possible variations in the types and sizes of IT systems and facilities that may be needed, there is really no one single set of control procedures here. Rather, an enterprise should implement a set of best practices that will guide it to establish its own IT general controls best practices.

An important internal control concept here often goes beyond how IT applications reports and other IT outputs are delivered to business users. Every business IT function supports a wide range of IT service management processes, which include such areas as problem management (i.e., how IT resolves issues with its business users) or configuration management (i.e., how IT keeps track of installed software and equipment versions). IT service management covers a wide range of internal control issues, and there are some well-recognized best practices that an enterprise should install.

This chapter looks at IT infrastructure general controls based on the set of worldwide recognized best practices called the Information Technology Infrastructure Library (ITIL). These ITIL-recommended service management best practices outline the type of framework an internal audit should consider when reviewing IT internal control risks and recommending effective IT general controls improvements. Because there is never a single definition for what is considered best, some refer to these as just good practices. We prefer to use the term *best practices*.

 ## ITIL SERVICE MANAGEMENT BEST PRACTICES

ITIL is an abbreviation for an actual set of technical publications, a set of best practices first developed in the 1980s by the British government's Office of Government Commerce (OGC), formerly called the Central Computer and Telecommunications Agency. It is an independent collection of best practices that was first widely recognized in IT operations first in the United Kingdom, followed by the European Union (EU), then Canada and Australia. It is now increasingly common in the United States. ITIL is a detailed framework of significant IT best practices, with comprehensive checklists, tasks, procedures, and responsibilities designed to be tailored to any IT organization. Dividing key service delivery processes between those covering IT service delivery and those for service support, ITIL has become the de facto standard for describing many fundamental processes in IT service management, such as configuration and change management.

ITIL is a formal "library" of technical publications, all published by the British OGC.[1] The publications are tightly controlled, similar to the International Standards Organization publications discussed in Chapter 18. IT auditors should be aware of ITIL and should determine if their IT functions have embraced any adopted ITIL best practices as part of their IT internal controls reviews. Our intent here is not to provide a detailed description of ITIL's service delivery components but to give internal auditors a high-level understanding of some of its components. An understanding of ITIL will allow IT auditors to better evaluate key processes and to make more effective recommendations when reviewing IT general controls.

ITIL service delivery best practices cover what is frequently called the IT infrastructure—the supporting processes that allow IT applications to function and deliver their results to systems users. All too often, IT auditors have focused their attention on the application development side of IT processes and ignored important supporting service delivery processes. An enterprise can put massive efforts, for example, in building and implementing a new budget forecasting system, but that application will be of little value unless there are good processes in place, such as problem and incident management, to allow users to report and resolve systems difficulties. Also needed are good capacity and availability processes to allow the new application to run as expected. These ITIL processes are all part of the IT infrastructure, and a well-designed and controlled application is of little value to its users without such strong service support and delivery processes in place. IT auditors should have a good understanding of these enterprise processes and then develop an appropriate test of controls. These may have been covered in an IT general controls review, but ITIL provides a good general best practices model to follow.

Although they were fairly common elsewhere in the world, ITIL best practices are now becoming widely recognized in the United States as well but have not been adequately recognized by many internal auditors. The Web site of the Information Systems Audit Control Association (ISACA) has numerous reference materials that tie ITIL best practices with the Control *Objectives* for *Information* and related *Technology* (CobiT) framework discussed in Chapter 2. Unfortunately, a search on the Institute of Internal Auditors' Web site at the time of this publication contains no references to ITIL. All internal auditors who perform reviews that touch IT infrastructure areas should understand internal control procedures following ITIL best practices.

The next sections provide an overview of some ITIL service delivery processes important for an IT auditor, including capacity or service-level management best practices. This should give an IT auditor some guidance on how IT functions, such as a help desk, should have effective processes in place in these very important areas of IT operations. ITIL does not specify standards for building and managing IT controls; it suggests new ways to implement and operate infrastructure general controls that should have already been in place.

ITIL service delivery strategies can be viewed as a continuous activity life cycle, sometimes shown as three embedded process activity rings. The outer ring defines continuous service improvement processes. That is, an ITIL-ready organization should have continuous service processes in place that encompass all other service management processes and receive inputs from outside IT customer sources. There are three independent, linked processes within the continuous service improvement ring—service design, transition, and operations best practices; each is discussed in later sections. In the center of these concentric rings is the service strategy process. This core process includes the IT organization policies and practices that were described in the COSO internal controls framework control environment element introduced in Chapter 1. Exhibit 7.1 shows this same service delivery model as a feedback flowchart process.

ITIL processes traditionally have been split between those covering service support and those for service delivery. Service support processes help make IT application operate in an efficient and customer-satisfying manner, while service delivery processes improve the efficiency and performance of IT infrastructure elements. There are five ITIL service support best practice processes, ranging from release management best practices, for placing an IT component into production, to incident management, for the orderly reporting of IT problems or events. ITIL service support processes cover good practices for any IT enterprise, whether a centralized operation using primarily

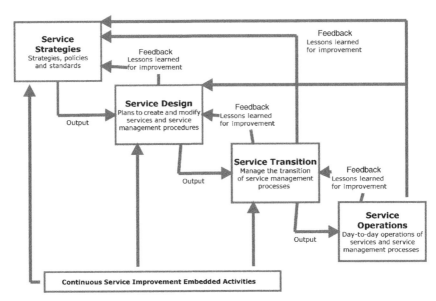

EXHIBIT 7.1 ITIL Continuous Feedback Loop

classic legacy mainframe systems as its IT central control point, to highly distributed client-server operations. Because of the many variations possible in an IT operations function, ITIL does not prescribe the details of "how" to implement service support processes, such as their configuration or change management. Rather, it suggests good practices and ways to manage inputs and relationships between these processes. There is no order or precedence among each of these best practices. They can be considered and managed separately, but all of them are somewhat linked to one another, providing a linkage between the business operations, IT technology, and infrastructure management.

Although there are many separate but interrelated elements to ITIL, we discuss only those service life cycle components that are more important for an IT auditor performing a general controls review. These ITIL best practices suggest preferred IT operations approaches to operate IT production systems in a manner that will promote efficient operations and will deliver quality services to the ultimate user or customer of these services. These best practices are particularly useful for an IT auditor performing a review and making recommendations in an IT operations area.

When IT audit is observing and reviewing IT operations internal controls, often it is useful to think of the area being reviewed in terms of the separate ITIL processes discussed in the next sections. For example, the ITIL process called incident management, or what has traditionally been called the "help desk" is a facility where systems users or customers call in to IT operations with a question or problem. Although a help desk function can be very useful, it is often a source of grousing when, for example, similar problems are called in repeatedly with no evident efforts to initiate a solution to the problem. Going beyond just a casual help desk and thinking of these activities as an overall process where matters are reported to other supporting processes will improve performance here and improve the overall quality of IT operations. When an IT auditor observes deviations from ITIL best practices, IT audit recommendations for performance improvement can become a major service to management.

ITIL'S SERVICE STRATEGIES COMPONENT

The upper left corner of Exhibit 7.1 of ITIL feedback loop processes shows a function called service strategies. This component describes the ITIL service management policies, strategies, and standards that provide input and direction to the other ITIL service design, transition, and operation processes. Those latter three components also provide inputs to service strategies to establish continuous process improvements.

As a best practice, ITIL suggests that an IT management team should first ask some hard questions about the quality of their IT service function, including:

▪ Which of our IT services or service offerings are the most distinctive?
▪ Which of our services are the most profitable?
▪ Which of our customers and stakeholders are the most satisfied?
▪ Which of our activities are most different and effective?

These are not the types of questions that IT management typically asks; they are seldom questions from management when assessing IT resources, and they are questions very seldom raised by IT auditors. Nevertheless, IT audit should consider these types of questions when performing a general IT controls review. The idea is to encourage the enterprise IT function to move from being from a resource that maintains IT processes and to one that provides valuable and cost-effective services to the overall enterprise. Exhibit 7.2 is a list of additional questions to help IT to improve its strategic capabilities and offerings.

▪ What IT services should we offer and to whom? That is, do we serve all enterprise units, a limited sample, or outside customers?
▪ How do we differentiate ourselves from competing alternatives? Outside service providers offer alternative services, but what are the unique costs or values that make this IT function a better alternative?
▪ How can we truly create value for our customers? Too often, IT handles almost redundant, required services, such as month-end financial reports that receive little attention. IT should look to see how it can better service users.
▪ How can we make a case for strategic investments? Rather than regularly just submitting budget requests for such matters as software upgrades, IT should carefully justify such requests.
▪ How should we define service quality? Through surveys and collaborative work, all interested parties should recognize how to identify quality IT services.
▪ How do we efficiently allocate our resources across our defined portfolio of offered services?
▪ How can we resolve conflicting demands for shared services?

EXHIBIT 7.2 *Questions for Developing ITIL Strategic Capabilities*

A multidisciplinary approach would be required for the questions in this exhibit because ITIL suggests that the IT organization should work with other functions, such as operations, finance, quality assurance, and internal audit, to better understand and define these key IT strategies for the enterprise. The whole idea is that an IT department or group should decide what it is in regard to the overall enterprise and what services it can offer. This type of introspective review may result in a service portfolio or catalog that defines IT's capabilities and service offerings.

ITIL service strategies introduce a best practices process that has been often ignored by both IT auditors and financial managers: financial management for IT services. Many IT auditors avoid this area, arguing that they are not accountants and do not need to worry about accounting-related issues. Classic financial internal auditors often see IT services as an issue that is too technical or of no interest. However, this is an important internal control area of potential concern and an ITIL best practice. Several other best practice areas under service strategies, such as organizational development, are not discussed here.

In its earlier days, the IT function in most enterprises was operated as a "free" support service with its expenses handled through central management and costs allocated to users with little attention given to IT-related costs. If a user department wanted some new application, it would pressure management to purchase the software package and add any additional necessary people to manage it. Over time, IT enterprises began to establish chargeback processes, but these were too often viewed as a series of "funny-money" transactions where no one paid too much attention to the actual costs of IT services.

Today, the costs and pricing of IT services are or should be a much more important consideration. The well-managed IT function should operate more as a business, where ITIL financial management is an important and key ITIL process to help manage the financial controls for that business. The objective of the service strategy financial management process is to suggest guidance for the cost-effective stewardship of assets and resources used in providing IT services. IT should be able to account fully for its spending on IT services and to attribute the costs of services delivered to the enterprise's customers. There are three separate subprocesses associated with ITIL financial management:

1. **IT budgeting** is the process of predicting and controlling the spending of money for IT resources. Budgeting consists of a periodic, usually annual, negotiation cycle to set overall budgets along with the ongoing day-to-day monitoring of current budgets. Budgeting ensures that there has been planning and funding for appropriate IT services and that IT operates within this budget. Other business functions will negotiate periodically with IT to establish expenditure plans and agreed investment programs; these ultimately set the budgets for IT.
2. **IT accounting** is the set of processes that enable IT to account fully for the way its money is spent by customer, service, and activity. IT functions often do not do a good job in this area. They have a wide variety of external costs, including software, equipment lease agreements, telecommunications costs, and others, but these costs often are not well managed or reported. They have enough data to pay the bills and evaluate some specific area costs, but IT functions often lack the level of detailed accounting that can be found in a large manufacturing enterprise, as an example.

The manufacturing cost accounting or activity based accounting model has applicability there.

3. **Charging** is the set of pricing and billing processes to charge customers for the services supplied. This requires sound IT accounting and needs to be done in a simple, fair, and well-controlled manner. The IT charging process sometime breaks down in an IT function because the billing reports of IT services are too complex or technical for many IT service customers to understand. IT needs to produce clear, understandable reports of the IT services used such that customers can verify details, understand enough to ask questions regarding service, and negotiate adjustments if necessary.

Financial management for IT supports the service strategy process through defined IT costing, pricing, and charging procedures. Although generally not operated as a profit center, the financial management process allows both IT and its customers to better think of IT service operations in business terms. The financial management process may allow IT and overall management to make decisions about what, if any, functions should be retained in-house or outsourced to an external provider.

The financial management process allows accurate cost-benefit analyses of the IT services provided and allows the IT enterprise to set and meet financial targets. It also provides timely reporting to the service-level management process, such that customers can understand the charging and pricing methods used. Of all of the ITIL service support and delivery processes, financial management is one ITIL best practice that frequently gets short shrift. IT people have a technical orientation and tend to think of financial management as an *accounting issue.* On the other side of the coin, finance and accounting professionals tend to look at these issues as too technical and beyond such transactions as equipment lease accounting or facility space charges. IT auditors should develop some financial skills as well as using their IT knowledge to review and assess financial management process internal controls. Exhibit 7.3 provides procedures for an internal audit review of the costs and pricing of IT processes. This is often not a common review area for internal audit, but given the large costs distributed to customers as well as the importance of an enterprise's IT resources, it can be an important audit area.

ITIL SERVICE DESIGN

ITIL service strategies support three other process areas, starting with the first phase in the service life cycle, service design. IT processes for service design cover areas more closely aligned with the smooth and efficient operation of the overall IT infrastructure. ITIL has identified five aspects of service design:

1. The design of each IT service offered, including their functional requirements, resource needs, and anticipated capabilities
2. The design of service management systems and tools, often presented through a formal portfolio, for the management and control of these services through their life cycles

1. Develop and document a general understanding of the cost structure for IT operations, including costs of equipment supplies and salaries.
2. Review and understand costing philosophy for IT operations: Is it an overhead function, cost recovery, or revenue generating?
3. Review processes for costing and pricing IT services:
   a. Are all IT costs covered?
   b. Based on interviews with IT users, does the costing and pricing system appear to be understandable?
   c. Is there a process in place to administer the costing process and to make adjustments if necessary?
4. Review the negotiation process with IT users to understand pricing process: Are expected costs included in service-level agreements (SLAs)?
5. Select pricing reports during a period for several processes and check to determine the prices are included in SLAs.
6. Review appropriateness of the adjustment process over a period of time to determine the corrections are investigated and applied when appropriate.
7. Review a sample of data processing services billed for one accounting period, and determine whether they cover all actual IT costs. Investigate and report on any differences.
8. Review the overall budgeting process for IT operations, and determine if it appears consistent with other enterprise budgeting procedures.
9. Assess whether management reviews actual IT costs and compares them to established budgets, taking appropriate remedial actions as required.
10. For a selected accounting period, trace IT pricing charges to appropriate accounting system entries.

EXHIBIT 7.3   Costs and Pricing IT Audit Review Steps

---

3. The design of IT architectures and management systems necessary to provide the services
4. The design of processes needed to install, operate, and improve these overall service processes
5. The design of measurement methods and metrics of the service processes and their component architectures

What this really says is that every IT function installs a lot of customer services, and these services should be managed and controlled through appropriate best practice techniques. To support efficient service delivery, ITIL has specified a series of specific processes. Some of these, such as the continuity management process, have traditionally been near and dear to the hearts of many IT auditors. Others, such as service-level agreements (SLAs) that define performance and expectations between IT and its customers should be familiar to other internal auditors who encounter similar arrangements in other areas.

Service Delivery Service Level Management

Service Level Management is the name given to the process of planning, coordinating, drafting, agreeing, monitoring, and reporting on formal agreements between both IT and the providers and recipients of IT services. This process is managed through service-level agreements (SLAs) that represent a formal agreement between IT and both providers of services to IT as well as IT end user customers. When the first ITIL service-level best practices materials were published in 1989, an SLA was an interesting but uncommon concept. Today many enterprises have introduced them—although with varying degrees of success—and IT auditors should be familiar with and understand the importance of SLAs when reviewing internal IT infrastructure controls.

As an example of an SLA, when IT contracts with an outside provider, such as for disaster recovery backups, the arrangement will be covered by a formal contract where the disaster recovery provider agrees to provide certain levels of service, following some time-response-based schedule. The governing contract here is an SLA between IT and the provider of continuity services. SLA agreements between IT and their customers are even more important, from an internal control perspective. We have used the more current term of *customer* here rather than the older and still common term *IT users*. Many groups use IT's services, and as customers, they have expectations of certain levels of service and responsiveness. These arrangements are defined through an SLA, a written agreement between the IT provider and its customers defining the key service targets and responsibilities of both parties. The emphasis should be on a mutual agreement, and SLAs should not be used as a way of holding one side or the other to ransom. A true partnership should be developed between the IT provider and the customer for mutually beneficial results; otherwise, the SLA could quickly fall into disrepute, and a culture of blame may prevent any true service quality improvements from taking place.

In an SLA, IT promises to deliver services per an agreed-on set of schedules and understands there will be penalties if service standards are not met. The goal here is to maintain and improve on service quality through a constant cycle of agreeing, monitoring, reporting, and improving the current levels of IT service. SLAs should be strategically focused on the business and on maintaining the alignment between the business and IT.

Exhibit 7.4 outlines the contents of a typical SLA. This type of document would not be found as part of a mortgage document signed at a house closing. Rather, the IT customers negotiate the IT service requirements that they are seeking, such as "average response times no more than . . ." or "financial systems close processing completed by . . ." or other factors. To temper expectations and show what could be available, an IT function usually provides a service offerings catalog. Customer IT service requirements should be negotiated and formal SLAs established. Performance against these SLAs should be monitored on an ongoing basis with performance reported regularly. Failure to meet these SLA standards could result in additional negotiations and SLA adjustments. This SLA process provides benefits for the business and IT, including:

- Because IT should be working to meet negotiated standards, IT services will tend to be of a higher quality, causing fewer interruptions. The productivity of the IT customers should improve as well.
- IT staff resources will tend to be used more efficiently when IT provides services that better meet customer expectations.
- By using SLAs, the services provided can be measured and the perception of IT operations generally will improve.

While there is no one form or format for an SLA, the following are contents that should be considered for most SLAs:

Agreement Introduction Pages
- Parties to this agreement
- Title and brief description of the agreement
- Signatories
- Dates: start, end, review
- Scope of the agreement; what is covered and what is excluded
- Responsibilities of both the service provider and the customer
- Description of the services covered

Service Hours
- Hours that each service is normally required (e.g. 24 × 7, Monday to Friday 08:00–18:00)
- Arrangements for requesting service extensions, including required notice periods (e.g., request must be made to the service desk by 12 noon for an evening extension, by 12 noon on Thursday for a weekend extension)
- Special hours allowances (e.g., public holidays)
- Service calendar

Availability
- Availability targets within agreed hours, normally expressed as percentages. The measurement period and method should be stipulated and may be expressed for the overall service, underpinning services, and critical components or all three. Since it is difficult to relate to simplistic percentage, availability can be measured in terms of the customer's inability to carry out its business activities

Reliability
- Usually expressed as the number of service breaks, or the mean time between failures (MTBF) or mean time between system incidents (MTBSI)

Support
- Support hours (where these are not the same as service hours) including arrangements for requesting support extensions
- Required notice periods (e.g., request must be made to the service desk by 12 noon for an evening extension)
- Special hours allowances (e.g., public holidays)
- Target time to respond to incidents, either physically or by other method (e.g., telephone contact, e-mail)
- Target time to resolve incidents, within each incident priority—targets vary depending on incident priorities

Throughput
- Indication of likely traffic volumes and throughput activity (e.g., number of transactions to be processed, number of concurrent users, amount of data to be transmitted over the network)

Transaction Response Times
- Target times for average or maximum workstation response times (sometimes expressed as a percentage: for example, 95% within 2 seconds)

Batch Turnaround Times
- Times for delivery of input, and the time and place for delivery of output

Changes
- Targets for approving, handling, and implementing requests for changes (RFCs), usually based on the category or urgency/priority of the change

EXHIBIT 7.4 Sample IT Service-Level Agreement Contents

IT Service Continuity and Security

■ Brief mention of IT service continuity plans and how to invoke them, and coverage of any security issues, particularly any responsibilities of the customer (e.g., backup of free-standing PCs, password changes)

■ Details of any diminished or amended service targets should a disaster situation occur (if no separate SLA exists for such a situation)

Charging

■ Details of the charging formula and periods (if charges are being made). If the SLA covers an outsourcing relationship, charges should be detailed in an annex as they are often covered by commercial in confidence provisions

Service Reporting and Reviewing

■ The content, frequency, and distribution of service reports, and the frequency of service review meetings

Performance Incentives/Penalties

■ Details of any agreement regarding financial incentives or penalties based on performance against service levels. These are more likely to be included if the services are being provided by a third-party organization. It should be noted that penalty clauses can create their own difficulties

---

EXHIBIT 7.4 (*Continued*)

■ Services provided by the third parties are more manageable when underpinning contracts are in place, and any possibilities of negative influence on the IT service provided is reduced.

■ Monitoring overall IT services under SLAs makes it possible to identify weak spots that can be improved.

The SLA process is an important component of IT operations. If an enterprise IT function does not use formal SLAs, IT auditors reviewing both IT operations general controls and business services applications should consider recommending the establishment of such formal SLA processes. SLAs can create a totally new environment within IT, where all parties will better understand their responsibilities and service obligations with the SLA as a basis for resolving many issues. IT audit can use the status of an enterprise's SLAs while assessing internal controls in a variety of areas and for making strong controls improvement recommendations.

Service Delivery Capacity Management

ITIL capacity management ensures that the capacity of the IT infrastructure is aligned to business needs to maintain the required level of service delivery at an acceptable cost through appropriate levels of capacity. Through gathering business and technical capacity data, this process should result in a capacity plan to deliver cost-justified IT capacity requirements for the enterprise. In addition to a prime objective of understanding an enterprise's IT capacity requirements and to deliver against them, capacity management is responsible for assessing the potential advantages new technologies could have for the enterprise.

The capacity management process generally is considered in terms of three subprocesses: business, service, and resource capacity management. Business capacity management is the long-term process to ensure that the future business requirements are taken into consideration and then planned and implemented as necessary. Service capacity management is responsible for ensuring that the performance of all current IT services fall within the parameters defined in existing SLAs. Finally, resource capacity management has more of a technical focus and is responsible for the management of the individual components within the IT infrastructure. The multiple inputs to these three capacity management subprocesses include:

- SLAs and SLA breaches
- Business plans and strategies
- Operational schedules as well as schedule changes
- Application development issues
- Technology constraints and acquisitions
- Incidents and problems
- Budgets and financial plans

As a result of these multiple inputs, the capacity management process—often under a single designated capacity manager—will manage IT processes, develop and maintain a formal capacity plan, and ensure certain capacity records are up to date. In addition, the capacity manager must be involved in evaluating all changes to establish their effect on capacity and performance. This capacity evaluation should happen both when changes are proposed and after they are implemented. Capacity management must pay particular attention to the cumulative effect of changes over a period of time that may cause degraded response times, file storage problems, and excess demand for processing capacity. Other capacity management process responsibilities include some duties of the network manager and the application and system manager. They are responsible for translating the business requirements into the required capacity to meet these requirements and to optimize IT performance.

Smaller enterprises and many IT facilities, of course, may not be able to justify a full- or even a part-time capacity manager. However, some resource within the IT organization should have responsibility for capacity management issues. It is an important service design issue.

The implementation of an effective capacity management process offers IT the benefits of an actual overview of the current capacity in place and the ability to plan capacity in advance. Effective capacity management should be able to estimate the impact of new applications or modifications as well as provide cost savings that are in tune with enterprise operations requirements. Proper capacity planning can significantly reduce the overall cost of ownership of an IT system. Although formal capacity planning takes time, internal and external staff resources, and software and hardware tools, the potential losses incurred without capacity planning can be significant. Lost productivity of end users in critical business functions, overpaying for network equipment or services, and the costs of upgrading systems already in production can more than justify the cost of capacity planning. This is an important ITIL process, and IT auditors should consider the capacity management processes in place when reviewing IT infrastructure general controls.

Service Delivery Availability Management

Enterprises today are increasingly dependent on their IT services being available 24 hours a day and 7 days per week (24×7). In many cases, when those IT services are unavailable, the business stops as well. It is therefore vital that an IT function manage and control the availability of its services. This can be accomplished by defining the requirements from the business regarding the availability of the IT services and then matching them with the possibilities of the IT enterprise.

Availability management depends on multiple inputs, including requirements regarding the availability of the business; information on reliability, maintainability, recoverability, and serviceability; as well as information from the other processes, incidents, problems, and achieved service levels. The objectives of the availability management process are to:

- Produce and maintain an appropriate and up-to-date availability plan that reflects the current and future needs of the enterprise.
- Provide service and guidance to all other areas of the enterprise on IT availability-related issues.
- Ensure that service availability achievements meet or exceed targets, by managing service and resource-related availability performance.
- Assist with the diagnosis and resolution of availability-related incidents and problems.
- Assess the impact of all changes on the availability plan and the performance and capacity and capacity of all services and resources.
- Ensure that proactive measures are implemented wherever those actions are cost justifiable.

Availability management activities can be described as planning, improving, and measuring actions. Planning involves determining the availability requirements to find out if and how IT can meet them. The service-level management process, discussed previously, maintains contact with the business and will be able to provide appropriate expectations to availability management. Businesses may have unrealistic expectations regarding IT systems availability when they do not understand what systems availability means in real terms. For example, business users may want 99.9% availability yet not realize that this will cost five times more than providing only 98% availability. It is the responsibility of service-level management and the availability management process to manage such expectations.

Exhibit 7.5 shows this availability and costs relationship. It does not cost very much to keep basic IT systems running, but that is all the enterprise will receive. Both management and IT auditors should keep this relationship in mind when reviewing controls and making recommendations.

An IT function can design for either "availability" or "recovery." When the business cannot afford a particular service downtime for any length of time, IT will need to build resilience into the infrastructure and ensure that preventive maintenance can be performed to keep services in operation. In many cases, building "extra availability" into the infrastructure is an expensive task that can be justified by business

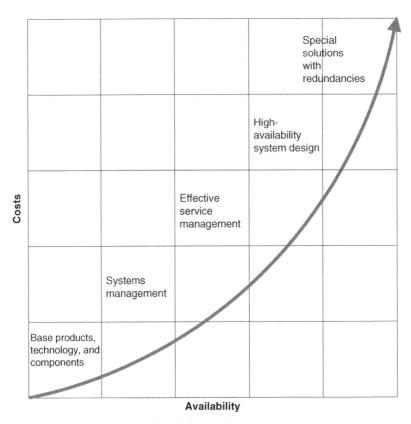

EXHIBIT 7.5   IT Availability and Cost Relationships

needs. Designing for availability is a proactive approach to avoiding downtime in IT services.

When the business can tolerate some downtime of services or when a cost justification cannot be made for building in additional resilience into the infrastructure, designing for recovery is the appropriate approach. Here, the infrastructure will be designed such that in the event of a service failure, recovery will be "as fast as possible." Designing for recovery is a more reactive management approach for availability. In any event, other processes, such as incident management, need to be in place to recover as soon as possible in case of a service interruption.

The main benefit of availability management is to have a structured process in place to deliver IT services that meet the agreed requirements of the customers. This should result in a higher availability of the IT services and increased customer satisfaction. Availability management covers an area where IT auditors often can ask some hard questions as part of their IT general controls reviews.

Service Delivery Continuity Management

As businesses are becoming ever more dependent on IT, the impact of any unavailability of IT services has increased drastically. Every time service availability or performance is reduced, IT customers cannot continue with their normal work. This trend toward a high dependency on IT support and services will continue and increasingly influence direct customers, managers, and decision makers. ITIL continuity management emphasizes that the impact of a total or even partial loss of the IT services should be estimated and continuity plans established to ensure that the business, and its supporting IT infrastructure, will always be able to continue.

ITIL calls for an appropriate strategy to be developed that contains an optimal balance of risk reduction and recovery options. ITIL also calls for some of the same business continuity and disaster recovery strategies as are discussed in Chapters 23 through 25 on IT disaster recovery and continuity management. Using the approaches outlined there, an IT organization can implement an effective set of service continuity processes. IT auditors should refer to those chapters to better understand and evaluate continuity and disaster recovery planning processes.

Service Delivery Information Systems Security Management

IT security management is another set of best practices, included in this book as part of Chapters 26 to 28. ITIL recognizes the need for information systems security within the corporate governance framework to provide a strategic direction for security activities and to ensure these activities are achieved. ITIL emphasizes that security is more than just an IT issue; it should be a management issue. The objectives of IT security are to protect the interests of those relying on IT information and the systems and communications that deliver it with the following ITIL information security objectives:

- **Availability objective.** Information is available and usable when required, and the systems that provide it can appropriately resist attacks and recover from or prevent failures.
- **Confidentiality objective.** Information is observed or disclosed to only those who have a right to know.
- **Integrity objective.** Information is complete, accurate, and protected against unauthorized modification.
- **Authenticity and nonrepudiation objective.** Business transactions as well as information exchanges between enterprises, or with partners, can be trusted.

ITIL information security management goes on to outline best practices for a complete information security management system. A very important best practice, information security management processes, are discussed in Chapter 19. An IT auditor should have the ability both to recognize the key elements of an effective information management system and to make recommendations to improve and enhance existing systems when appropriate.

 ## ITIL SERVICE TRANSITION MANAGEMENT PROCESSES

As IT auditors recognize, IT operations almost always have been subject to regular hardware or software changes, These changes may involve proper transition planning to introduce the new components, testing and validation before any release to production, and configuration management to control the inventory and relationships of the IT equipment and services. ITIL has grouped these best practices into what it calls transition management.

This area can present some significant internal control risks for IT auditors reviewing IT infrastructure operations. An IT application, for example, may be installed with solid internal controls. However, subsequent unauthorized changes to the same application or improperly configured attached equipment may introduce new control concerns.

Service Transition Change Management

The problem management process, discussed as part of service operations, often results in the need for IT changes ranging from program changes or process revisions to improve service or reduce costs. The goal of ITIL change management is to utilize standardized methods and procedures for the efficient and prompt handling of all changes, in order to minimize their impact on service quality and the day-to-day operations. ITIL change management processes include:

▪ IT hardware and system software
▪ Communications equipment and software
▪ All applications software
▪ All documentation and procedures associated with the running, support, and maintenance of live systems

The last point is of particular concern to IT auditors. All too often, IT hardware and software is changed with little concern given to changing the supporting documentation and related software. Changes to any IT components (e.g., applications software, documentation, or procedures) should be subject to a formal change management process.

IT auditors often encounter environments where the change management process is haphazard at best. Examples here are changes to applications without thinking through their implications on the overall IT infrastructure, incident management fixes that create other changes, or senior management requests for changes to solve short-term or immediate problems. A formal change management process that reviews and approves any proposed changes will almost always improve IT and enterprise internal control processes. The ITIL change management process should be tightly linked to configuration management, discussed earlier, to ensure that information regarding the possible implications of a proposed change are made available and that any possible impacts are detected and presented appropriately.

Change management processes should have high visibility and open channels of communication in order to promote smooth transitions when changes take place. To improve this process, many IT functions have instituted a formal Change Advisory Board (CAB), made up of people from IT and other IT customer functions within the enterprise, to review and approve changes. A CAB is a body that exists to approve changes and to assist in the assessment and prioritization of changes. It should be given the responsibility for ensuring that all changes are adequately assessed from both a business and a technical perspective. To achieve this mix, the CAB should consist of a team with a clear understanding of customer business needs as well as technical development and support functions. Chaired by a responsible change manager, the CAB should be composed of IT customers, applications developers, various experts/technical consultants as appropriate, and representatives of any contractor or third party if in an outsourcing situation. Although a CAB should meet regularly to review and schedule proposed changes, it should not act as an impediment to IT operations. Its goal is to provide an orderly scheduling and introduction of all types of IT infrastructure changes.

Efficient overall service management processes require a capability to change things in an orderly way, without making errors and wrong decisions. An effective change management process is indispensable for an effective IT infrastructure. When reviewing IT internal controls, internal auditors should look for an effective change management process that provides:

- Better alignment of IT services to business requirements
- Increased visibility and communication of changes to both business and service support staff
- Improved risk assessments
- Reduced adverse impact of changes on the quality of services
- Better assessments of the cost of proposed changes before they are incurred
- Fewer changes that have to be backed out, along with an increased ability to do this more easily when necessary
- Increased productivity of IT customers through fewer disruptive delays and higher-quality services
- Greater ability of IT to absorb a large volume of changes.

An effective ITIL change management process is an important component of IT infrastructure controls. The process also must align tightly with other key processes in the IT infrastructure: configuration, capacity, and release management.

Service Transition Configuration Management

Whatever their relative size, IT operations functions are complex with multiple types and versions of hardware and software components and linkages to cloud computing components (discussed in Chapter 9) that must work together in an orderly, well-managed manner. This is true for both major corporations with classic mainframe systems, farms of servers, and a multitude of storage devices and communications gear and small IT systems operation. A formal configuration management function is an important service delivery process that supports the identification, recording, and reporting of IT components, their versions, constituent components, and relationships. Items that should be under the control of configuration management include hardware, software, and associated documentation. Configuration management is not the same concept as the depreciation accounting process for asset management, although the two are related. Asset management systems maintain details on IT gear above a certain value, their business unit and location. Configuration management also maintains relationships between assets, which an asset management process usually does not. Some enterprises start with an asset management and then move on to configuration management.

A basic activity of the configuration management process is to identify various individual components in IT operations, called configuration items (CIs), and then to identify key supporting data for these CIs, including their "owners," identifying data, version numbers, and systems interrelationships. This data should be captured, organized, and recorded in what is often known as a configuration management database (CMDB). The team responsible for configuration management should select and identify these configuration structures for the entire infrastructure's CIs, including establishing relationships between each CI and connected components in the overall IT infrastructure configuration. Going beyond just a configuration status entry on the CMDB, the process should ensure that only authorized CIs have been accepted and that no CI is added, modified, replaced, or removed without an appropriate change request and an updated specification.

An IT auditor can think of the importance of the configuration management process in terms of desktop applications in the audit department. Every internal auditor today probably has a laptop computer, but unless each has consistent versions of software, these systems may have difficulty communicating with one another. This is where configuration management is important. Configuration management is really important when attempting to understand the various versions or types of software and equipment in a large IT operation.

The configuration management process also includes some control elements. A series of reviews and audits should be implemented to verify the physical existence of CIs and to check that they are correctly recorded in the configuration management system. Although we have used the word *audit* here, this is not an IT audit process but an ITIL task of the IT team responsible for the configuration management process. Configuration management should also maintain records for CI status accounting to track the status of CIs as they change from one state to another—for instance, from under development, to being tested, going live, and then being withdrawn.

The CMDB does not have to be a complex, specialized application. An enterprise can establish a very basic level of CMDB by just using spreadsheets, local databases, or even paper-based systems. In today's large and complex IT infrastructures, however, configuration management requires the use of physical and electronic libraries along with a CMDB to hold definitive copies of all software and supporting documentation. The CMDB should be based on database technology that provides flexible and powerful interrogation facilities. It should hold the relationships between all system components, including ITIL-defined incidents, problems, known errors, changes, and releases.

The existence of an effective CMDB can be a good point for IT audit to understand an enterprise's IT configuration management process and its supporting controls. If the enterprise does not have a good CMDB, IT audit can anticipate finding significant internal control problems throughout the IT infrastructure. Exhibit 7.6 outlines audit procedures for reviewing an enterprise's configuration management process.

The configuration management process interfaces directly with systems development, testing, and change and release management processes to incorporate new and

1. Review and understand existing enterprise configuration management practices as well as their interfaces to the service management processes, procurement, and development.
2. Assess the knowledge and capability of existing IT functions and its staff in terms of controls and processes for configuration, change, and release management processes.
3. Review the extent and complexity of existing configuration data, whether held in hard-copy form, in local spreadsheets, or in configuration management databases (CMDB), and develop an understanding of that database and its retrieval tools.
4. Select a production application and understand its definition on the CMDB in detail including interfaces to change management, release management, other service management processes, procurement, and development.
5. Using the installed CMDB reporting tool, define the inventory of configuration items for a selected application or system and physically trace reported CIs to actual configuration components.
6. Determine that processes are in place to link configuration management business processes and procedures with the CMDB tools.
7. Test the CMDB and other support tool(s) to determine whether key components, software, and documentation have been implemented and controlled on the CMDB.
8. Review adequacy of facilities to provide secure storage areas to manage CIs (e.g., cabinets, controlled libraries, and directories).
9. Assess adequacy of processes to communicate and train staff in the importance and use of configuration management.
10. Review problem management processes to determine the extent and appropriateness of their use of the CMDB for resolving problems.
11. Determine that appropriate access and update controls are in place to prevent unauthorized or inappropriate use of the CMDB.
12. Determine that the CMDB receives adequate backups and that it is part of the continuity plan key resources backup and recovery procedures.

EXHIBIT 7.6 ITIL Configuration Management Internal Audit Steps

updated product deliverables. Control should be passed from the project or supplier to the service provider at the scheduled time with accurate configuration records. In addition, the CMDB can be used by the service-level management process to hold details of services and to relate them to the underlying IT components. The CMDB also can be used to store inventory details of CIs, such as the supplier, cost, purchase date, and renewal date for a license. An additional bonus is the use of the CMDB to cover the legal aspects associated with the maintenance of licenses and contracts.

Service Transition Release Management

IT functions need effective processes to ensure that changes are introduced to all impacted parities in an orderly and well-controlled manner. Release management covers the transition of authorized changes to an IT service. A release typically consists of a number of problem fixes and enhancements to the service including new or changed software and hardware needed to implement the required approved changes.

Releases normally are implemented as full releases, where all of the components being changed are built, tested, distributed, and implemented together. This eliminates the danger that obsolete versions of CIs are incorrectly assumed to be unchanged and used within the release. With a full release, all elements supporting some application area or system are released as a single systems component. With all new and existing components bundled together, any problems are more likely to be detected and rectified before entry into the live environment. The disadvantage is that the amount of time, effort, and computing resources needed to build, test, distribute, and implement the full release will increase.

An alternative and common approach to release management is the use of a delta or partial release approach that includes only those CIs that changed since the last full or delta release. A delta release may be more appropriate when a full release cannot be justified due to such factors as the urgency for needed facilities or the size and related resource requirements of a delta release in comparison with a full release. There is no single correct choice, and a decision to make a delta release should be made case by case based on the CAB's recommendation. IT auditors should understand the importance of well-ordered release processes and should look for such established processes as they perform IT general controls reviews.

The previous sections have outlined ITIL service support processes at a very high level. When reviewing IT general controls, an IT auditor should think of the importance of processes such as configuration management. An IT auditor does not need to be an expert in these ITIL service support areas but should keep them in mind when reviewing IT general controls. An auditor should become familiar enough with these processes to understand controls and procedures supporting IT service support.

ITIL SERVICE OPERATION PROCESSES

The ITIL best practices described in this chapter began with the importance of setting service strategies, including basic IT policies and such higher-level areas as IT financial management. In the natural process of launching IT resources, the next set of best practices covered service design processes that handle IT capacity and availability management as well as service-level management to help users of IT services agree with users of IT services and the services that will be provided The last of these three linked ITIL processes is known as service operations, a process that allows the business customer to see the quality of the IT services offered.

Service operations cover the day-to-day service value to the overall enterprise that should be provided by IT systems and processes. The purpose of the ITIL service operation process is to help coordinate and deliver IT services to customers. This value concept often was missing in the earlier days of IT operations, but ITIL best practices bring the concept to the forefront of business and management needs.

Service Operation Event and Incident Management

ITIL service operations define separate service operation processes for event and incident management, where events are defined as any detectable occurrence that has significance for the management of the IT infrastructure or delivery of related IT services. ITIL defines many similarities between ITIL events and incidents, but our discussion here focuses on just incident management.

Incident management processes cover the activities necessary for restoring an IT service following a disruption. ITIL defines a disruption as any type of problem that prevents an IT user from receiving expected adequate services, whether it is an overall system failure, the user's inability to access an application for any of a wide variety of reasons, a password failure due to a "fat fingers" typing error, or any other problem. The reported problem is called an *incident*, which means some type of deviation from standard operations. Although many IT operations have a help desk or a customer support group, this general function is referred to here as the *service desk*. The *service desk* is usually the owner of the incident management process, although all service support groups across IT may have a role.

The objective of effective incident management processes is to restore normal operations as quickly as possible in a cost-effective manner with minimal impact on either the overall business or the user. How quickly is quickly should not be subject to interpretation, and ITIL calls for restoration time frame standards to be defined in service-level agreements. As discussed, effective SLAs are an important component of the IT infrastructure, and IT auditors should be aware of their existence. The first component of the ITIL incident management process is the detection and documentation of the incident by the service desk, as a single point of contact. These incidents can include such matters as a user calling in some specific application problem or IT operations informing the service desk of an application processing problem.

Once an incident is received, the service desk should classify it in terms of its priority, impact, and urgency. The definition of a reported incident's priority is one of the more important aspects of managing IT incidents. Every person who calls in an incident generally thinks that it is the most important. The incident management function has the difficult task of defining the relative priority of the reported incident, its importance, and its impact on the business. Exhibit 7.7 shows the typical life cycle of an incident from the initial call through resolution and closure. The point here is to help IT auditors understand service desk recommended best practices, in order for an IT auditor to ask some probing questions when reviewing IT general controls. For example, IT auditors should look for formal SLAs, as part of the service-level management process, to define the priority with which incidents need to be resolved, the effort put into their resolution, and the recovery from incidents. These SLAs should depend on:

- ▪ The *impact or criticality* of the incident on the reporting entity or overall enterprise. Incident management should assess, for example, how many users will suffer as a result of a reported technical failure of a hardware component. Similarly, a call regarding a problem with the month-end accounting close process should be assigned a higher level of criticality than a problem with an application that generates purchase orders.
- ▪ The *urgency* of the reported incident. *Urgency* refers to the speed necessary to solve an incident of a certain impact. A high-impact incident does not, by default, always have to be solved immediately. An incident call reporting some user group cannot work at all because of some service outage often should be of greater urgency than a senior manager calling to request a functionality change.
- ▪ The *size, scope, and complexity* of the incident. The incident management team should investigate the reported incident as soon as possible to determine its extent. A reported failure of some component may just mean that a device is out of service

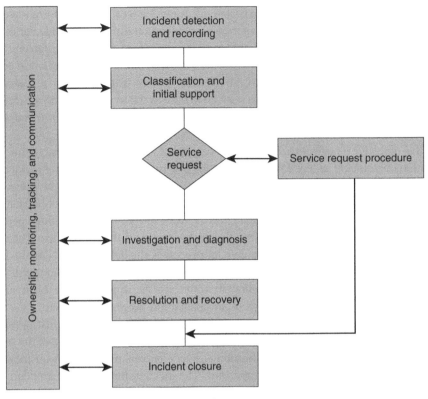

EXHIBIT 7.7 ITIL Incident Management Life Cycle

or might indicate a server is down. Those types of incidents are often not that complex and can be repaired relatively easily. A telecommunications failure that might impact multiple international units and thus might delay the monthly financial close can be much larger in size and scope.

Once an incident has been logged in, the process of investigation and diagnosis should begin. If the service desk cannot solve the incident, it should be assigned to other IT support levels for resolution. However, all parties that work on the incident should keep records of their actions by updating a common incident log file.

Some incidents can be resolved through a quick fix by the service desk, others by a more formal problem resolution, or in the case of more significant problems, by a work-around to get things back in partial operation coupled with a formal request for change (RFC) to systems, to a vendor, or to whatever parties are needed to correct such a more significant problem. In any event, efforts should be marshaled to correct the problem with the incident management function retaining ownership of the matter until resolution. Solid documentation should be maintained to track the incident until its resolution. The incident can be formally closed once matters have been fixed. If it is not easily solved, the incident should be passed to the problem management process function, as discussed in the next section.

All ITIL processes are somewhat related to one another, but in many circumstances, incident management represents the first line between users or customers of IT services and IT itself. Properly organized, incident management should be much more than just the help desks of an earlier time, when users called in with problems but frequently did not get much help beyond password resets. Incident management is a first point of contact between the customers—users—and the overall IT function. Incidents due to failures or errors within the IT infrastructure result in actual or potential variations from the planned operation of services. Sometimes the cause of these incidents may be apparent and can be addressed or fixed without further investigation. In other situations, there may be a need for a hardware or software repair, a matter that often takes some time to implement. Short-run solutions may be a work-around, a quick fix to get back in operation, or a formal RFC to the change management process to remove the error. Examples of short-term work-arounds might be instructing a customer to reboot a personal computer or resetting a communications line, without directly addressing the underlying cause of the incident.

Where the underlying cause of the incident cannot be identified, it is often appropriate to raise a problem record for the unknown error within the infrastructure. Normally a problem record is raised only if an investigation is warranted, and its actual and potential impact should be assessed. Successful processing of a problem record will result in the identification of the underlying error, and then the record can be converted into a known error once a work-around has been developed.

Service Operation Problem Management

When the incident management process encounters a deviation with an unknown cause or reason, that incident should be passed on to the ITIL problem management process for resolution. The objective here is to minimize the total impact of problems through a formal process of detection and repair as well as to take actions to prevent any recurrence. The problem management process is the next step in the criticality of some reported incident and should be considered in terms of three subprocesses: problem control, error control, and proactive problem management. ITIL defines a "problem" as an unknown underlying cause resulting from one or more incidents. A "known error" is a problem that has been diagnosed successfully and for which a work-around has been identified. The idea is not to create a second administrative function in an IT enterprise to take reported help desk incidents but to identify when and how some incidents reported to the help desk should be passed on another person or authority to better diagnose the matter and treat it as a problem. An effective problem management process can do much to improve overall IT customer service.

In addition to solving any single incident that was bumped up to the problem management process, IT should try to establish processes for better problem and error control, including maintaining data to help identify trends and suggesting improved procedures for the proactive prevention of problems. Data should be maintained on solutions and/or any available work-arounds for any resolved and closed problem records. In many instances, problem management may encounter a situation where it is necessary to go a step further and file a formal RFC, either through an IT development function or through a hardware or software vendor.

The problem management process focuses on finding patterns among incidents, problems, and known errors. A detailed review of these patterns allows an analyst to solve the problem by considering the many possibilities and narrowing things down to a solution; such a review is often called "root cause" analysis. There are many good techniques for resolving and correcting problems, which often are caused by a combination of technical and nontechnical factors. An IT auditor reviewing problem management processes should look for documented formal procedures that will support problem analysis and resolution. ITIL problem management is a good area for IT auditors to diagnose IT service delivery problems in order to better understand the overall health of IT operations. Areas where an IT auditor may ask some questions here include:

- The number of RFCs raised and their impact on the availability and reliability of the overall IT services covered
- The amount of time worked on investigations and diagnoses for various types of problems by organization unit or vendor
- The number and impact of incidents occurring before a root problem is solved or a known error is confirmed
- The plans for resolution of open problems with regard to people and other resource requirements as well as related costs and budgeted amounts

The ITIL service operation problem management process is an important area for IT auditors to consider and understand when assessing the overall health of IT infrastructure operations. An efficient incident management process is necessary to receive customer calls and take immediate corrective actions, but an effective problem management process goes a step further to analyze and solve the problem, initiating RFCs where necessary and otherwise improving IT customer satisfaction.

SERVICE DELIVERY BEST PRACTICES

The preceding paragraphs have outlined some of the ITIL service management life cycle processes that are critical for an IT audit understanding of infrastructure controls. ITIL service management outlines processes for launching, managing, and controlling all levels of IT services with an emphasis on establishing customer satisfaction. ITIL guidance goes beyond just internal controls and includes managing IT costs, establishing measurements and metrics, and other quality improvement measures.

ITIL calls for any IT function to build a program of continual service improvements to review, analyze, and make recommendations for improvements in each area of ITIL service delivery components. As a series of related processes, continuous IT improvement involves IT audit in some of these activities:

- Reviewing management information and trends to ensure that services are meeting agreed-on service levels

- Reviewing management information and trends to ensure that the output of established service management processes achieves desired results
- Periodically conducting IT audits to verify employee and process compliance
- Reviewing existing IT deliverables for relevance
- Conducting periodic customer satisfaction surveys

ITIL service management life cycle processes are increasingly being adopted by IT functions worldwide. The emphasis on service increases the importance of IT resources and supporting infrastructure to the overall enterprise and its stakeholders. IT auditors should increase their knowledge of ITIL processes and build these best practices into their ongoing internal controls reviews.

AUDITING IT INFRASTRUCTURE MANAGEMENT

The ITIL service management processes introduce an expanded and improved approach for looking at all aspects of the IT infrastructure. These processes are not independent and freestanding. Although each ITIL process can operate somewhat by itself, they all depend on the input and support from other related processes. An internal auditor reviewing controls over any of the ITIL processes must think of them in relation to other related ITIL processes. For example, Exhibit 7.8 shows the relationship of the ITIL change management process and how it is dependent on and supports other related processes.

The ITIL service management life cycle is a series of interrelated best practice processes that support the management of the IT infrastructure and of the enterprises. IT applications are in the center of this puzzle and are a key area of internal controls concerns. Our previous discussions of problem, incident, and change management ITIL

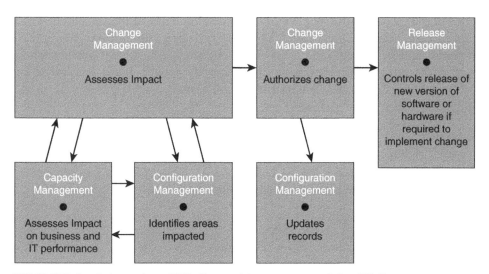

EXHIBIT 7.8 Relationship of ITIL Change Management to Other ITIL Processes
Source: Robert R. Moeller, *Brink's Modern Internal Auditing*, 7th ed. (Hoboken, NJ: John Wiley & Sons, 2009). Copyright © 2009, John Wiley & Sons. Adapted with permission of John Wiley & Sons.

processes, among others, tended to call for a very large IT function with multiple levels of staff and management resources.

An IT auditor might ask if these ITIL best practices also apply to a smaller enterprise. Our answer here is an emphatic *yes*; ITIL applies to all sizes of IT functions. In order to be ITIL compliant, an enterprise does not need multiple levels of support staff. Rather, it needs to think of the various service support and service delivery processes from an ITIL best practices perspective. A smaller IT function may not need to establish separate incident management and problem management functions, for example, but must think of each as a separate process with unique controls procedures. Even in a very small IT function, each ITIL process area should be treated as separate areas for process improvement.

IT auditors should take particular care when making recommendations regarding their IT infrastructures. The size and scope of the areas being audited and the scope of operations should always be considered. This author remembers the early days of IT controls, when many applications were developed in-house for production applications. Most audit guidance materials recommended that there be a separation of duties between people who operate the computer and those who program it. Otherwise, in those days of far simpler IT systems, there was a risk that an individual with a fraudulent intent might change an application program (e.g., write himself an unauthorized check) and then produce this personal check when operating the system. This was good control in the early days of IT but is not as relevant today. Today's IT auditors should think about the adequacy and appropriateness of IT controls in terms of how they are built into individual applications as well as the infrastructure process controls discussed in this chapter.

The IT infrastructure is an important internal control review area. All too often, IT and other internal auditors have concentrated their attention on the applications controls and the IT general controls of the past. In today's world of complex processes supporting the IT infrastructure, the ITIL processes outlined in this chapter describe some excellent areas for IT audit attention. When reviewing internal controls for any IT enterprise, whether a major enterprise-wide IT operation or the smaller function found in many of today's smaller enterprises, the effective IT auditor should concentrate on reviewing controls over key IT infrastructure processes.

 NOTE

1. ITIL publications are available from the U.K. agency called The Stationery Office (TSO) and can be found through www.tsoshop.co.uk.

CHAPTER EIGHT

Systems Software and IT Operations General Controls

VIRTUALLY EVERY COMPUTER SYSTEM has some type of master program—often called an operating system (OS)—to perform such tasks as scheduling an application program to run or saving or storing the results of an application program and outputting the results to a printer or display device. No matter what the size of the computer operations, these OS master programs and related supporting software control a computer system's operations. Chapter 6 discussed the importance of information technology (IT) general controls, the kinds of controls covering all aspects of IT operations, and Chapter 7 discussed IT infrastructure controls, processes to better manage and control IT operations. This chapter discusses the very important area of systems software and related IT operations general controls.

Whether it is a Microsoft Windows operating system on a laptop computer or Linux controlling an office server system, the OS is a key component to any computer system operation. It and the supporting systems software are essential for supporting enterprise IT operations. IT auditors need to understand the importance of the OS as well as any operations control programs in the enterprises where they are performing general controls reviews.

This chapter discusses OS concepts and surveys some of the OS types and the supporting systems software that are essential in today's typical IT operation. IT auditors should have a very general understanding of the purposes and importance of these types of IT software and should look for effective general controls when performing reviews in this important general controls area. This chapter focuses on some of the more common types of operating systems found in today's IT systems as well as the supporting software to create well-controlled IT systems operations.

IT OPERATING SYSTEM FUNDAMENTALS

An IT or computer OS is the master program that serves as the prime interface between all system hardware components and the users of that computer system— the people and sometimes other automated devices. An OS is responsible for the management and coordination of the many activities necessary to run some applications on a computer system. Many IT auditors first encounter an OS while using their laptop or desktop personal computers equipped with either Microsoft or Apple Macintosh OS programs. A version of Microsoft's Windows OS is perhaps the most familiar to many. In its multiple versions, it can be both a major help and sometimes a source of frustration.

The origins of today's OS go back to the days of mainframe computers, when the manufacturers of these devices (e.g., Burroughs, Control Data, Honeywell, IBM, Univac, etc.) each developed complex OS programs for their systems. Each was fairly unique to that computer manufacturer and its individual machine models. As an example, Univac, which is considered the founder of large-scale computer systems, had its model 1100 and 494 series of mainframe computers in the 1970s. Each Univac product line had its own OS that did not communicate with either those of other Univac machines and certainly not with those of competitors. In those early days of mainframe computers, many computer models were unique, but many of these machine OS controllers had innovative features. As example, the Univac 1100 series of computers had facilities for real-time processing in the 1970s, a feature that IBM, then the dominant computer manufacturer, did not introduce until the 1980s.

The concept of a mainframe OS really changed, however, when IBM introduced its System/360 series of computer and mainframe operating systems in the mid-1960s. The IBM System/360 was a family of mainframe computers available in widely differing capacities and price points and with a single OS, called OS/360, planned for every model. This concept of a single OS spanning an entire product line was crucial for the success of IBMs System/360. IBM's current mainframe operating systems, later called MVS and now z/OS, are distant descendants of this original system; applications written for the OS/360 can still be run on modern IBM machines.

Exhibit 8.1 illustrates how an OS interacts with both computer resources and its applications. In the center, the computer system primarily consists of its central processing unit (CPU) and random access memory (RAM) as well as the external storage devices. The CPU is the set of highly integrated circuits that define the logic of how the computer will operate. The OS gives instructions to the CPU and manages the other computer resources. The next ring out is the key software components, such as an Oracle database system. The applications are found at the outer ring. Users and IT auditors primarily deal with these outer ring applications.

Any modern OS, no matter the size of the computer system hardware, is a very complex set of software that goes beyond the skills of even the most expert systems programmers. While IT auditors regularly perform internal controls reviews of applications and review general control reviews of many aspects of the supporting control programs such as database processors, but too often the OS is taken as a given and ignored from an internal controls perspective. IT auditors should have a general

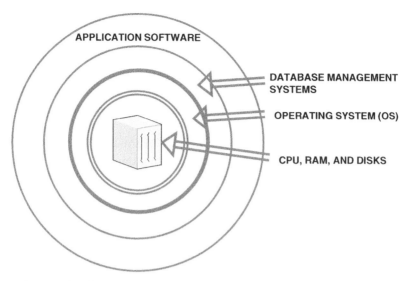

APPLICATION SOFTWARE

DATABASE MANAGEMENT SYSTEMS

OPERATING SYSTEM (OS)

CPU, RAM, AND DISKS

EXHIBIT 8.1   Role of the Computer Operating System

understanding of basic OS attributes and should consider reviewing general software and infrastructure controls surrounding an enterprise's computer systems OS resources.

Microcomputer or Personal Computer Operating Systems

The first microcomputers or personal computers (PCs) did not have the capacity or need for the elaborate operating systems that had been developed for mainframes or even what were called minicomputers; minimal operating systems were developed, often loaded from the computer's very limited read-only memory (ROM). An early disk-based operating system called Control Program for Microcomputers (CP/M) was found on many of the first early microcomputers. CP/M was popular on many of the first systems and was closely imitated by Microsoft's disk operating system (MS-DOS), which became wildly popular as the OS chosen for the IBM PC. IBM's version of that microcomputer OS was distributed by Microsoft in its early days and called IBM DOS. Microsoft began upgrading and expanding this OS through the stream of improved versions that are found on many laptop and desktop computers today, such as Windows XP or Windows 7.

Even before the IBM PC, Apple Computer Inc. (now Apple Inc.) launched a very popular microcomputer called the Apple II. A very popular machine then, the Apple II had its own primitive OS. After the introduction of the IBM PC, Apple soon launched a computer called the LISA, which had a very innovative graphical user interface (GUI) OS. LISA led to the Apple Macintosh computer with its Mac OS. Today, virtually every microcomputer OS today is based on either a Microsoft version of Windows or an Apple Mac OS.

Today's Server Operating Systems: Unix and Linux

The early mainframe computers in the 1970s were massive machines requiring complex OS supports and many environmental requirements. They were just too complex for smaller businesses or university research facilities. As the computer industry grew during that decade, several manufacturers introduced smaller, less complex computers called minicomputers. Although no longer in existence today, the prominent computer manufacturers then were Digital Equipment Corporation (DEC) and Data General (DG). Each of these had lines of computer hardware started with their own OS facilities that were far less complex than the requirements of IBM's mainframe OS.

These minicomputers were developed before the Internet, as we know it, but there was a massive professional and academic interest at that time on finding better ways to improve the use computer resources. The Unix OS was an important product of this era. Unix (or UNIX) is an OS that originated at Bell Labs in 1969 as an interactive time-sharing system, and it has evolved as a nonvendor freeware product, with many extensions and new ideas provided in a variety of versions of Unix by different companies, universities, and individuals.

Because it was not a proprietary OS owned by any computer company and because it is written in the then-standard C programming language, Unix became the first open OS that could be improved or enhanced by anyone. A wide range of Unix versions were developed and used in workstation products from Sun Microsystems, Hewlett-Packard (now HP), IBM, and other companies. The Unix environment and its client-server program model were important elements in the development of the Internet and the reshaping of computing as centered on networks rather than in individual computers.

Unix has been designed to give software developers a single set of what are called application program interfaces (APIs) to be supported by every Unix system. An API is a written contract between systems and application developers defining what the two sets of developers are to receive and responsible for providing.

Unix has continued to be an important component of many IT systems. An IT auditor usually will have no need to review the "innards" of any Unix implementation, but he or she should ask some general questions about the status of any Unix system as part of any general controls review. Exhibit 8.2 contains some Unix IT general controls review questions. An IT auditor should look for implementation of one of the standard versions of Unix. Use of a standard version will allow an enterprise to better adapt and implement new applications going forward. That is, even if an enterprise is experiencing no control problems with applications currently running under a nonstandard version of Unix, problems going forward may arise if the installed versions of Unix is not compatible.

Although Unix had its origins as a free software facility where all interested users could upload versions and modify them for their own requirements, manufacturers gained the rights to Unix and established controls that limited the ability to change versions of the OS software. IT auditors generally think of a controlled software OS, such as Unix, as a good thing, but its many users in facilities, such as university research labs, were looking for a more open version of Unix that they could improve and tweak.

As an alternative to Unix, in 1991, Linus Torvalds, a programmer based in the Helsinki, Finland, developed a new OS, called Linux. Although similar to Unix, Linux had many features that impressed computer science professionals. The Linux OS is predominantly known for its use in servers, and it can be installed on a wide variety of

1. Meet with IT personnel to develop a general understanding of type and version of the installed Unix operating system (OS).
   a. Is the OS commercial software, such as Solaris or IBM's AIX?
   b. If the OS is freeware, such as from an academic source, determine that the version installed is current.
   c. Determine whether the installed OS is supported by appropriate documentation and backup procedures.
2. Obtain auditor-level permission to access and audit UNIX procedures. If not familiar with basic commands, request IT management to supply a tutorial.
   a. Obtain a login for auditor use.
   b. Create a special directory for auditor use, and change the permissions on this directory so that only the allowed IT auditor has access to this directory and the files within it.
3. Particularly if a smaller installation system, review the server's physical security to ensure that a casual outside user cannot, at a glance, see the entire setup of the server room. Ensure that the monitor is well hidden from open viewers.
   a. Review controls to ensure that only authorized persons can access the server.
   b. Determine that the server's CPU unit has adequate security to prevent unauthorized users from resetting it or even switching it off and that there are prevention mechanisms to protect against any booting from alternate media.
   c. Determine that only appropriate personnel are allowed physical access to the room through the use of locks or swipe cards.
4. Use what are called the Unix `eeprom` parameter to ensure that the UNIX *security mode* is set to "full" and that an adequate EEPROM password is chosen to ensure that even if a malicious attacker gains physical access to the system, he or she will be unable to reboot the system without knowing the EEPROM password.
5. Obtain the hardware inventory on the system, listing all hardware devices by issuing the UNIX command `usr/platform/'uname -i'/sbin/prtdiag -v`.
6. Get a list of software installed on the system through the UNIX command `pkginfo` to gather the details of the installed software, and resolve any differences.
7. What procedure is followed when adding new users? Ensure that there exists a well-documented procedure for adding new users.
8. Assess the adequacy of procedures for adding new users to the system, and review IT and HR records for the names and designation of these personnel.
   a. Determine that users have to fill in a form or sign their acceptance of an agreement before being given a username and a password and that users are required to sign their agreement and acceptance.
   b. Determine what password restrictions, consistent with enterprise security policies, are imposed on Unix server users.

EXHIBIT 8.2   Unix General Controls Review Procedures

computer hardware, ranging from embedded devices, mobile phones, and even some watches and supercomputers. The Linux OS, installed on both desktop and laptop computers, has become increasingly popular in recent years.

The feature that makes Linux unique is that it is totally "freeware." That is, interested users can download a version of Linux at no cost, but they must agree to post any changes that they make to the software for all to see and use. All accepted changes become part of an enhanced Linux system. As an example of its growing acceptance, several years ago, even IBM installed Linux on several of its server systems.

IT auditors can expect to encounter more and more installations of Linux when reviewing IT general controls. Many users in a Linux environment find that it has more features and flexibility than even popular Windows-based applications. When an IT auditor includes a Linux OS as part of a general controls review, he or she should ask questions similar to these:

- **Linux users.** Who can perform what functions at an OS level, and do those rights seem appropriate for the person's duties?
- **Services.** What services, server functions, protocols, modules, and other functional components are installed and/or running on the system, and are they needed and authorized? Because of the open nature of Linux, a system can be filled with many unknown software components.
- **Networks and connectivity.** What protocols and devices are allowed to reach the Linux system? What other hosts are allowed to reach this system, and do they all appear appropriate?
- **File systems.** Are only approved file systems in use, and is Linux device utilization monitored?
- **Logging/Auditing.** Are all required Linux events recorded and analyzed?
- **Security configuration.** Are appropriate user access restrictions installed and system enforced, such as to password life controls and other parameters?
- **Applications.** Are only necessary and approved applications installed and running on the Linux system?

Thousands of commands can be developed through a Linux OS, and an IT auditor should meet with enterprise IT software specialists to gain a better understanding of the implemented system. An IT auditor should look for OS system configuration standards and build procedures, jointly defined by enterprise system administrators and information security groups. Although some IT auditor technical guidance may be needed, an effective audit process would then consist of a comparison of those standards to the current configuration of the Linux system. These detailed procedures are beyond the scope of this chapter, but an IT auditor can ask a systems administrator to demonstrate compliance.

IT auditors will encounter more and more Unix and Linux installations as they review general controls in larger server systems. They should take the time and effort to become familiar with these very important OS tools.

 ## FEATURES OF A COMPUTER OPERATING SYSTEM

An IT OS acts as an interface between its applications and the hardware. A key element of that hardware, particularly on a personal or microcomputer, is the circuitry to operate the computer's functions. This is known as the central processing unit (CPU), the circuit chip that controls the machine. The CPU's logic provides services for key processes, such as assigning memory and other resources, establishing task priorities for the process, loading program code into memory, and executing programs.

These programs then interacts with the user and/or other devices and performs its intended function. Although IT auditors typically do not need to understand the detailed functions of any OS, whether Windows XP, Linux or others, every OS has the same general functions:

- **Interrupts.** A central element of any OS, interrupts are a mechanism for the OS to interact with and react to its environment. Interrupts provide a computer's CPU with a way of automatically running specific code in response to events. Most CPUs and their OS support hardware interrupts that allow the programmer to specify code that can be run when that event takes place.

  When an interrupt is received, the computer's hardware automatically suspends whatever program is currently running, saves its status, and runs computer code previously associated with the interrupt; this is analogous to placing a place marker in a book in response to a phone call. Interrupts may come from either the computer's hardware or the running program.

  When a hardware device triggers an interrupt, the OS decides how to deal with the event and establishes protocols for doing so. This is similar to how a person usually responds to what may be a false smoke detector alarm in the home before just calling for help. The processing of hardware interrupts is a task that is usually delegated to software called device drivers, which may be part of the OS, part of another program, or both. A program may also trigger an interrupt to the OS. If a program wants to access hardware, for example, it may interrupt the OS, which causes control to process the request.

- **Memory Management.** An OS is responsible for managing all system memory which is currently in use by its programs. This ensures that a program does not interfere with memory already used by another program. Since programs time-share, each program must have independent access to memory. If a program fails, it may cause memory used by other programs to be affected or overwritten. Malicious programs, or viruses, may purposefully alter another program's memory or may affect the operation of the OS itself. It can take only one misbehaving program to crash a computer system. Various methods of OS memory protection exist, but all require the particular and unique features of each CPU.

- **Virtual memory.** Desktop and laptop computer CPUs generally do not have enough available random access memory (RAM) to run all of the programs that most users expect at once. Virtual memory is an operating system feature that enables a system to use RAM memory address space that is independent of other processes running in the same system, and to use a space that is larger than the actual amount of RAM present, temporarily relegating some contents from RAM to a disk, with little or no overhead. Virtual memory looks at RAM for areas that have not been used recently and copies them onto spaces in the hard disk to free up space in the RAM to load other applications. Exhibit 8.3 shows this virtual memory concept.

- **Multitasking.** The important OS concept of multitasking refers to the running of multiple independent programs on the same computer, making it seem as if the computer is performing multiple tasks at the same time. Since most computers generally can only do one thing at one time, OS time-sharing concepts are used.

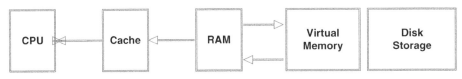

EXHIBIT 8.3 Virtual Memory Management Concepts

Each program uses a share of the computer's time to execute the program, using a piece of the OS called a scheduler, which determines how much time each program will spend executing and in which order execution control should be passed to programs. Control is passed to a process that allows programs access to the CPU and memory so that another program can use the CPU.

▪ **Disk access and file systems.** Access to data stored on disks is a central feature of all OSs. Computers store data on disks using files, which are structured in specific ways in order to allow for faster access, higher reliability and to make better use of the drive's available space. An OS defines the specific way in which files are stored on a disk and enables them to have names and attributes.

Operating systems generally support a single type of disk drive and only one kind of file system. These file systems have been limited in their capacity, speed, and the kinds of file names and directory structures they can use. These limitations often reflected limitations in the OSs they were designed for, making it very difficult for an OS to support more than one file system. However, Unix and Linux support a technology known as a virtual file system (VFS). Unix supports a wide array of storage devices, regardless of their design or file systems to be accessed through a common API. This makes it unnecessary for programs to have any knowledge about the device they are accessing. A VFS enables the OS to provide programs with unlimited access to a number of devices with an infinite variety of file systems installed on them through the use of specific device drivers and file system drivers.

▪ **Device drivers.** A device driver is a specific type of software that allows interaction with hardware devices. It is an interface for communicating through what is called a computer bus or communications subsystem, providing commands to and/or receiving data from the device and on the other end, from the requisite interfaces to the OS and software applications. It is an OS-specific hardware-dependent computer program that enables an OS, applications software package, or computer program running under the OS to interact transparently with a hardware device. It usually provides the requisite interrupt handling necessary for any necessary asynchronous time-dependent hardware interfacing needs. An OS essentially dictates how every type of device should be controlled. The function of the device driver is to translate these OS-mandated function calls into device-specific calls. In theory, a new device that is controlled in this manner should function correctly if a suitable driver is available.

▪ **Networking.** An OS supports a variety of networking protocols, hardware, and applications for using them. This means that computers running dissimilar OSs can participate in a common network for sharing resources such as files, printers, and scanners using either wired or wireless connections. Networks can essentially allow a computer's OS to access the resources of a remote computer to support the same functions as it could if those resources were connected directly to the local computer. These network connections include everything from simple communication, to using networked file systems or even sharing another computer's graphics or sound hardware.

Client-server networking involves a program on a computer somewhere that connects via a network to another computer, called a server. Servers offer various services to other network computers and users. These services usually are provided through ports or numbered access points beyond the server's network address. Each port number usually is associated with a maximum of one running program, which is responsible for handling requests to that port.

- **Security.** Computer security depends on a number of technologies working properly, but the OS provides access to a number of resources that are available to software running on the system and to external devices, such as networks. An OS is capable of distinguishing between requests that are allowed to be processed as well as others that should not be processed. An OS may distinguish between "privileged" and "nonprivileged" software transactions, and systems commonly have a form of requester *identity*, such as a username. To establish identity, there may be a process of *authentication*. Often a defined username must be entered, and each username may have an associated password as well. Other methods of authentication, such as magnetic cards or biometric data, might be used instead. Security features, discussed in Chapter 19, are a very important component of an OS.

 ## OTHER SYSTEMS SOFTWARE TOOLS

Exhibit 8.1 shows a conceptual view of a computer system, with the CPU, RAM, and disk storage devices in the center and surrounded by the OS. The next ring outside of the OS but before user applications includes systems software tools. The processes in this ring are such things as database management systems and a wide variety of software tools, including programs that are not part of the OS but also not applications. This category of software includes utility programs for such areas as utilities for file sharing, print services, e-mail, Web sites, and what are called file transfer protocols (FTPs).

Many of these utility programs have evolved because the OS for some computer systems did not have some needed services or because outside providers developed superior solutions. As an example here that dates back to the very early days of computer systems when early IBM mainframes and their COBOL program compilers did not have a very good way to sort a program's data. Other machine vendors had built efficient data sort routines into their COBOL compilers, but the major vendor at that time, IBM, had not.

To help with this weakness, a group of New York University students developed a sort program in 1968 that eventually became SyncSort (www.syncsort.com), a well-respected utility program that became almost a standard attachment for IBM mainframe applications. Although many years have now passed, a much-enhanced SyncSort is still used frequently. A large number of utility programs—by IBM and other vendors—became common in IBM mainframe systems. The IT auditor who encounters these utility programs should ask questions about the reasons for their use and assess whether they seem appropriate.

IT auditors encounter these and many other utility programs as help or service programs for their own laptop machines. Many are excellent, and often they can be downloaded at no charge or for a small license fee. In many cases for Windows- or Mac-based utility software, the actual programs today reside on the Internet, and the download only provides communication links. Perhaps the best example of such free utility software can be found with Google, with its search engine, communications software, and more. Google is a very reputable company; the software is free but includes some advertising messages.

A large body of utility programs, particularly for Windows or Mac systems as well for Unix and Linux servers, have been released by small or little-known vendors that may contain security risks or other control concerns. IT auditors should always raise questions and express concerns, when they encounter any such software. Exhibit 8.4 contains review guidelines for an auditor's search for unauthorized software. Procedures will vary by the type of OS, but an IT auditor should focus on authorization rules for installing any software as well as security rules for the software package.

Many variations of utility software may be installed on any system. In the next sections we focus on several basic software types as well as some of the risks of using unauthorized versions. The text presents only a small sample of the many software types available. In our era of freeware software, university labs or similar sources may offer many versions. Such products may be technically brilliant in design but may never advance in maintenance and upgrades. IT management and certainly IT auditors should be aware of potential risks associated with such utility software.

---

1. Review and document the software server environment, gaining an understanding of the persons or authorities responsible for authorizing and approving utility software.
2. Determine whether there is a comprehensive inventory of installed software in place, including the authorizing authority for the software and other supporting documentation.
3. Determine that the enterprise maintains a roster of approved supported software.
   a. Review documentation and controls for that supported software.
   b. Determine that appropriate cost-benefit analyses or other justifications have been developed to document the supported software.
4. Determine whether there is a process in place to regularly review software licenses and updates.
   a. On a test basis, select several installed software packages to ensure their licenses are up to date.
   b. Also on a test basis, trace several installed software packages back to their original purchase justification to determine whether supporting documentation and approval appear appropriate.
5. Identify any installed unlicensed software, and make recommendations to either remove or uninstall the software.
6. If any software has been installed as freeware, determine that it was justified and approved, that the IT organization has assessed and improved its internal controls, and that the software is still appropriate to enterprise operations.

EXHIBIT 8.4　Unauthorized Utility Software Review Guidelines

File Transfer Protocol Software

FTP is a common network utility software tool used to exchange and manipulate files over an Internet-based networks. FTP is based on client-server architecture, using separate control and data connections between the client and server applications. It is also often used as an application component to automatically transfer files for program internal functions and can be used with user-based password authentication or with anonymous user access.

This software was first developed in the very early days of dial-up IT telecommunications, and it was originally an unsecure method of transferring files because FTP had no method for data encryption. Thus, under earlier network configurations, usernames, passwords, FTP commands, and transferred files could be captured by anyone on the same network using what is called a packet sniffer detection tool.

FTP security has since been improved, and FTP processes have been built into most Web servers. There are multiple versions of this software available for transferring files. The IT auditor should attempt to assess where versions of FTP have been installed on a system, as part of a general controls review, and also should understand that this software can be used to improperly copy and capture critical data files.

Virus Protection Software

Software virus detection and other cybersecurity software tools are discussed in Chapter 20. This is a major category of utility software, no matter what computer platform or OS, because of the many threats facing all systems. There are some cybersecurity tools built into some OS versions, but an IT auditor should see effective implementation of this an important category of utility software as part of any general controls review.

Multiple vendors offer virus and IT security protection software. Because of the complexity of detecting cybersecurity problems and correcting them, a software vendor needs a strong staff to stay ahead in this ever-changing area. Some very effective freeware software products are available as well as multiple commercial packages. An enterprise must select a product that appears to suit its needs. Most versions of this software are effective, but the software must be updated almost constantly to counter new virus risks that have been identified.

We discuss these cybersecurity risks and threats in greater detail in Chapter 20. An IT audit should verify that the current version of such software covers all systems platforms, that the software is updated on a regular basis, and that there is follow-up to correct and repair any reported violations.

Automated Security Self-Evaluation Tools

A variety of tools are designed not for IT auditors but for enterprise IT management to assist in improving IT operations. One example is the Automated Security Self-Evaluation Tool (ASSET) from the U.S. National Institute of Standards and Technology (NIST). This freeware software gathers data, generates reports, and provides a centralized place for the collection of system access data, as do other self-evaluation

Network and Systems Management Software Tools*	*
Network Management Products	35
Application Management Tools	39
Software Performance Management Software	30
General Network Monitoring Software	57
Bandwidth Traffic Monitoring Tools	9
Web Usage Monitors	17
Asset Managemement/Resource Inventory Tools	21
Software License Management Tools	9
Software Compliance Tools	37
Software SQL Help Tools	33
Installation and Deployment Software Tools	
Software Distribution Products	14
Software Packaging Products	7
Drive Imaging Tools	5
Migration and Configuration Managers	15
Server Migration Aids	15
SoftwareGroup Policy Managers	22
Software Tools for Systems Administration	
Disk Degragmentation and Drive Monitoring Tools	9
Remote Troubleshooting Products	23
Network Automation and Patch Processing Tools	20
Program Scribing Tools	14
Patch Management Software Tools	19
Application Sharing Software Tools	3
Application Conflict Testing Tools	5
Software OS Security Products	
Hardware-Based Firewall Products	23
Software-Based Firewall Products	17
Security Auditing Software Tools	40
Intrusion Detection Systems	16
Intrusion Prevention Systems	24
Smart Card/Biometric Authentication Systems	13
Spam Content Filtering Tools	67
Antivirus Software Tools	21
Antispyware Tools	17
Storage and Backup Software	
Software Backup Systems	40
Storage Management Software Tools	29
Disaster Recovery Products/Services	46
Clustering and Fallover Software	13
Load-Balancing Software	17
	*Total number of Windows-related software products in each category, per *Redmond* magazine (November 2009).

EXHIBIT 8.5   Utility Software Product Categories for Windows-Based Products

tools. Our objective here is not to discuss this software but to describe it as a type of freeware.

We have presented several examples of the many types of utility programs that an IT auditor may find installed on a server system. Exhibit 8.5 is an extensive list of these general categories of software. For example, we list five different categories of installation and deployment software tools as well as vendors offering products in various categories for each. At the time of this publication, 15 different vendors offered migration and configuration management products under the category of installation and deployment software tools. Vendors will come and go over time, but there are a large number of software products out there. In addition, our list here only includes Microsoft Windows-based product and does not include other software for the Mac, Unix, Linux, and others.

Our point and warning to IT auditors is that a typical IT production system may have many of these software tools installed. Often a tool was added to a system because of a special need at one time or due to the cajoling of an overzealous salesperson. When encountering these software products as part of any IT general controls review, an IT auditor should ask:

- What is the purpose and function of the utility software, and who in the IT department is responsible for the software product?
- Is the license for the software current?
- Is the software regularly used at present?
- Are there any internal control issues or concerns associated with the software product?

There are a large number of software tools installed on any server system, and some may have served a purpose at one time but may no longer be effective. Others may have been offered by vendors that are no longer in business. An IT auditor should be aware of the types and versions of OS and OS support software installed on any system as part a general controls review. He or she can provide a genuine service to management by surveying the utility programs in place as part of a general controls review and making recommendations to update or streamline these program functions.

9

Evolving Control Issues: Wireless Networks, Cloud Computing, and Virtualization

A N INFORMATION TECHNOLOGY (IT) auditor, working in the profession for any length of time, will understand that the IT technologies and their supporting processes are changing on a continuous basis. Some of these changes—such as the move to laptop computers from desktop devices tied to a network—do not have a significant internal controls impact for IT auditors. Others do. This chapter discusses three areas where IT is changing and where IT auditors may need to take somewhat different approaches in their internal controls reviews.

Our first example is the growth of wireless networks, both public and private. IT auditors often easily access their e-mail messages or get current business news from their laptop devices and the Internet. These facilities provide a massive convenience to all systems users, but they do present some control and security threats if an enterprise's network is not properly protected through firewalls and other security controls. An IT auditor may be happy to be able to access e-mail messages or change an airline flight reservation over a wireless network, but those connections should be secure. This chapter briefly looks at some wireless network security and internal control issues.

An IT configuration called cloud computing has been evolving rapidly in recent years. Although the term sounds almost exotic to many, cloud computing has become a significant concept today with our growing dependency on Web-based applications for many business processes rather than more traditional applications downloaded to home office servers. The concept known as Web services, service-oriented architecture (SOA), or software as a service (SaaS) was first largely promoted by Microsoft several years ago but has now been embraced by many others. Today, this concept has been broadened and is known as cloud computing, a configuration where many different Internet applications supported by multiple vendors and operating on multiple servers operate together out of what looks like a large fuzzy Internet cloud. This chapter introduces some cloud computing concepts and discusses cloud-related security and controls concerns that may impact IT auditors in their assessments of IT general controls.

On a somewhat different level, storage management virtualization is another evolving IT infrastructure with general controls implications. The term *storage management virtualization* refers to the connections between a computer central processor unit (CPU) and connected or supporting mass storage drives or other devices. In past years, IT managers and auditors thought of a computer system in terms of its configuration— the disk drives and other peripheral devices that were connected to a computer's CPU. At one time, these were attached through an often complex network of hard-wired cables. However, starting around the year 2001, software tools were introduced to better manage these storage connections; this is called storage virtualization. They began as a tool for large server sites, but today virtualization concepts have been introduced on all levels of computer processors. File virtualization can introduce strong efficiencies to IT operations; however, there can also be some internal control risks if mass storage relationships are not properly managed and backed up. We will briefly introduce IT virtualization concepts important to IT auditors.

This chapter discusses these IT technical areas because they may impact IT auditors in their reviews and assessments of IT general controls. These three IT-related areas may not be familiar to many IT auditors and their managers today, but they will be control issues in many IT general controls audits going forward. Of course, the landscape is always changing, and IT auditors should always be aware of newer technology-driven internal control issues and should modify their reviews to accommodate and assess these and other new internal controls areas. IT auditors should always take a strong lead in their enterprises in understanding new technology-based processes and then translating them to reviews and assessments of internal controls.

UNDERSTANDING AND AUDITING IT WIRELESS NETWORKS

Computer system components, such as terminals or printers, traditionally have been connected to their CPUs through cables or transmission wires. In earlier days, when an employee moved from one office to another, it was often necessary for a maintenance crew to string the necessary cables to the new office location. Although they originally could not transmit electronic data, radio-based wireless communications tools began to have a significant impact on the world during World War II. Through the use of wireless networks, information could be sent overseas or behind enemy lines easily, efficiently, and more reliably. Since then, transmission standards have been developed and wireless networks have grown significantly. Using local transmission stations, wireless networks first became common for local emergency services, such as the police or fire departments, which utilized wireless networks to communicate important information quickly.

By the late 1980s, local area networks (LANs) became very common, and many computer system configurations became to be based on a network of wired computer systems. In the early 1990s, processes and standards were developed for wireless LANs, where each system was a point in a local network.

Starting with these early 1990s standards, tools were developed to implement wireless LANs. These LANs originally required communications cards between a central computer and local terminals, but they expanded to broad networks with connections to remote transmission stations and the Internet.

Wireless systems have some vulnerability risks since their data is carried as radio signals subject to snooping. Wireless LANs, however, have their own problems. Connecting network elements by radio waves instead of wires presents many challenges. From a reliability standpoint, it is difficult to predict how dependable wireless network radio coverage inside a building will be because building construction features, such as steel beams and heavily plastered walls, severely weaken radio waves. Even outside of structures, predicting coverage accurately and dependably is difficult, owing to radio transmission propagation issues. Much more troubling is the fact that wireless LANs, by their very nature, broadcast their data into space, where the data can be intercepted by anyone with the ability to listen in at the appropriate frequency. These features also facilitate internal use of wireless LANs and enable interlopers to enter such networks with the same privileges as authorized users unless appropriate security controls are in place.

Not all networks, and certainly not all wired networks, are secure. However, when a traditional LAN operates over cables within a relatively secure physical perimeter, the level of security provided by the physical construction usually is sufficient. Adding wireless transmission capabilities adds security vulnerabilities and the need for additional systems controls, such as the need to authenticate every network user. An IT auditor should look these general control and security characteristics in all wireless applications:

- **Confidentiality.** An application should contain a level of protection against interception, or eavesdropping, to provide assurance that messages sent are readable only by the intended recipients.
- **Authenticity.** Protections against spoofing or impersonation controls should be in place to ensure that messages originate from the claimed entity.
- **Integrity.** Controls should provide protection from transmission errors and/or willful modification of messages to offer assurances that a message has not changed in transmission.
- **Availability.** Assurances should be in place that application data will be available when and where it is required, as a protection against denial of service or poor reliability.

Wireless networks and wireless LANs are important areas that should be included in any IT auditor's review of general controls. The next sections discuss some key internal control characteristics of wireless networks important for IT auditors as well as considerations for reviews of IT wireless systems general controls.

Key Components of an IT Wireless System

A wireless IT system is almost a generic name, and there can be some confusion about the overall configuration of any such system. There are several basic ways to configure a wireless system. In an open system configuration, any entity that can pick up the wireless signal can potentially gain access. This is the type of wireless system, built around a wireless access point (WAP), that one encounters when accessing the Internet from a hotel room or coffee shop. For purposes of definition, a WAP is a device that allows communications connections to wireless networks using standards such as Wi-Fi, Bluetooth, or related standards. The WAP usually connects to a wired network and can relay data between the wireless devices (such as computers or printers) and wired devices on the network.

Many wireless systems in offices or homes are limited in their proximity to a WAP. Within their borders, however, they may connect to a variety of devices. Exhibit 9.1 shows such a wireless configuration with the wireless system existing inside a defined border, controlled by series of routers on the border edge. Routers are discussed in the next section; a large number of laptop computers, terminals, and other devices may be

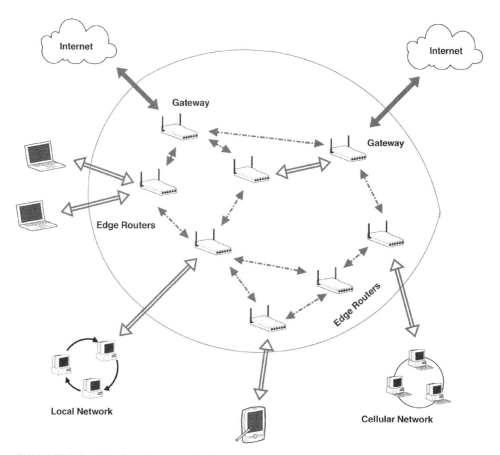

EXHIBIT 9.1 Wireless Network Architecture

attached to each router. As the exhibit shows, the wireless network is connecting to the Internet through several service providers and to some other external systems outside of the network. In addition, there are connections to local LANs, a cell phone network, and personal handheld devices. Although at a very general and high level, this exhibit illustrates the type of wireless system found in many enterprises today. From an IT auditor's perspective, two key controls in this wireless system configuration are the placement of its routers and firewalls.

Wireless System Routers

A key component of all networks, including wireless networks, a router is an electronic device used to connect two or more computers to the Internet by cable or wireless signals. A router allows several computers to communicate with each other and to the Internet at the same time. A wireless router performs the functions of a router but also acts as a wireless access point to allow access to the Internet or a computer network without the need for a cabled connection. It can function as a wired or a wireless LAN. Some routers also contain wireless antennae that allow connections from other wireless devices.

Wireless Firewalls

A firewall is a type of one-way software door where transactions and activity can exit but cannot enter. It is a system, implemented in hardware, software, or a combination of both, that is designed to prevent unauthorized access to or from a private network. Firewalls frequently are used to prevent unauthorized Internet users from accessing private networks connected to the Internet, where all messages entering or leaving an internal network, the intranet, pass through an installed firewall. This important network control examines each message and blocks those that do not meet the specified security criteria. A firewall is considered a first line of defense in protecting private information.

Wireless Network Vulnerabilities and Risks

There are a variety of control risks associated with any wireless network, including the risk of eavesdropping into system activities, illicit entry into the network enabled by a failure of user authentication, and denial of services. A major systems integrity concern here is the risk of eavesdropping. By their nature, wireless LANs intentionally radiate their radio signal network traffic into space, and once the signals are emitted, it is impossible to control who can receive them. The key control here is to encrypt all such messages. Wireless message standards allow for such encryption, but such standards are not always installed. When reviewing wireless applications, IT auditors should determine that encryption standards have been installed and that they have been applied to all critical applications.

The implementation of controls to ensure message integrity is also important for wireless systems. Network messages are transmitted in small packets of data that are then reassembled to deliver the correct message. Transmission software provides standards that should protect the integrity of all messages. Although the technical details here may be beyond many readers, an IT auditor should meet with enterprise communications software specialists responsible for their enterprise's wireless networks and discuss the implemented software default standards that emphasize message integrity and provide controls over illicit network entry.

Our discussion here emphasizes the closed wireless networks that are more common for a business enterprise. Over time, the use of open wireless network connections, that are common in some public places to provide access to the Internet and other sites, will become more prevalent. Because these wireless systems are based on radio signal messages, we may see more perpetrators trying to get around security rules and attempting to gain improper accesses.

Wireless Network Security Concerns

Security is a major issue with many enterprise wireless networks in general and wireless LANs in particular. Anyone equipped with proper tools within the geographical network range of an open, unencrypted wireless network can "sniff," or record, the network traffic, gain unauthorized access to internal network resources and to the Internet, and then possibly send spam messages or attempt other illegal actions using the wireless network's Internet addresses. Although these threats reflect issues that have long troubled many types of wired networks (e.g., individuals can plug their laptop computers into available Ethernet communication jacks within a site and get access to a local wired network), this improper access activity usually does not pose a significant problem, since many enterprises had reasonably good physical security. However, radio signals bleed or move outside of buildings and drift across property lines, making network physical security largely irrelevant.

Establishing effective wireless security procedures is a challenge to IT network administrators, enterprise management, and many IT auditors. There are strong and recognized standards to protect a wireless network, but many of those standards are defined in hardware routers—such as Cisco devices—that are wireless security options are set through controlling software with limited monitoring or controls.

Good IT processes and technology often are easily confused, and particularly so with wireless information security management issues. However, many of the same business processes that establish strong risk management practices for physical assets and wired networks also work to protect wireless resources. IT auditors can use the following cost-effective guidelines to enable enterprises to establish proper security protections as part of an overall wireless strategy. This list includes areas that represent good IT wireless internal control practices and objectives. An IT auditor can use these recommendations to better understand and evaluate enterprise wireless security processes.

- **Wireless security policy and architecture design.** Enterprise security policy, procedures, and best practices should include wireless networking as part of overall security management architecture to determine what is and is not allowed with wireless technology.
- **Treat all wireless access points as untrusted.** Access points need to be identified and evaluated on a regular basis to determine if they need to be quarantined as

untrusted devices before wireless clients can gain access to internal networks. This determination means the appropriate placement of firewalls, virtual private networks (VPNs), intrusion detection systems (IDSs), and authentication between access points or the Internet.

◼ **Access point configuration policies.** Enterprise administrators need to define their standard security settings before the wireless systems can be deployed. These settings include guidelines regarding IDs, wireless keys, and encryption.

◼ **Access point discovery.** Administrators should regularly search outward from a wired network to identify unknown access points. Such a search may identify rogue access points operating in the area—often a major concern in densely populated areas.

◼ **Access point security assessments.** An enterprise should perform regular security reviews and penetration assessments to identify poorly configured access points or defaults or easily guessed passwords.

◼ **Wireless client protection.** Wireless clients—typically user departments— should be examined regularly for good security practices. An enterprise IT function can establish good wireless procedures, but the actual users also should follow good practices.

The overall objective of this chapter is to highlight some evolving internal control areas that impact IT auditors. IT wireless systems are nothing new, but they are becoming almost standard components in many system configurations today. Chapter 26 provides more guidance on auditing IT telecommunication processes and wireless systems.

 ## UNDERSTANDING CLOUD COMPUTING

Cloud computing is a new and evolving concept that is important to many IT operations. Also closely related to the concepts of SaaS or SOA, cloud computing today is changing the way that many enterprises build and use IT applications.

A cloud symbol is often used today to refer to the Internet in this book and in other published references. The idea behind this Internet cloud is that users do not need knowledge of, expertise in, or control over the technology infrastructure "in the cloud" that supports them. This term originated in the telephone industry where, up until the 1990s, data and even early Internet circuits were hard-wired between destinations, but later long-haul telephone companies began offering wireless VPN service for data communications. The growth of these wireless networks and the Internet's World Wide Web concepts enhanced the way that we think of IT services.

Cloud computing is more than just the Internet. It is the way we think of the services that Internet-resident applications provide. Because it is impossible to determine in advance precisely the paths of Internet traffic, the cloud symbol is used to describe that which were the responsibilities of the service providers as well as the network infrastructure. The concepts of software products or services on the Internet—SOA and SaaS—soon followed.

In the early 2000s, Microsoft extended this concept of SaaS through the development of what it calls Web Services. IBM also later released what it called the Autonomic

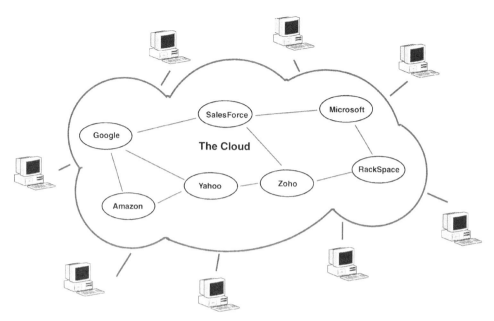

EXHIBIT 9.2   Cloud Computing Concepts

Computing Manifesto, which described automation techniques such as self-monitoring, self-healing, self-configuring, and self-optimizing in the management of complex IT systems with heterogeneous storage, servers, applications, networks, security mechanisms, and other system elements that can be virtualized across an enterprise.

Software vendors are increasingly offering their products as services on the Internet rather than as applications that are resident on individual in-house servers. A good example of this trend—and an early product type leader—is the provider of customer relationship management (CRM) software, SalesForce (www.salesforce.com/crm/products.jsp). This supplier of customer and sales tracking software tools does not sell its products as a set of programs loaded on proprietary CDs for customer use. Rather, all of the SalesForce programs and documentation is found on the Internet, and customers pay for the software only when they use the product. The SalesForce applications are used as a service to customers.

Exhibit 9.2 shows this SaaS cloud computing concept. We have highlighted several vendors that currently offer SaaS products today, including Amazon, Google, Microsoft, and SalesForce. This is only a limited example of SaaS current applications, and certainly many more will follow. Some of the benefits of SaaS applications in a cloud computing environment are:

- ▓ Reduced infrastructure costs due to centralization. With the SaaS application in the cloud, there is no need to maintain application change management and other controls.
- ▓ Increased peak load capacities. Cloud providers, such as Amazon or Google, have massive server farms with massive capacities. Their load capacities are almost infinite.

- Efficiency improvements for systems that are often underutilized.
- Consistent performance that will be monitored by the service provider.
- Application and IT services resiliency. Cloud providers have mirrored solutions that can be utilized in a disaster scenario as well as for load-balancing traffic. Whether there is a natural disaster requiring a site in a different geographic area or just heavy traffic, cloud providers should have the resiliency and capacity to ensure sustainability during an unexpected event.

IT auditors will need to take a different approach in reviewing internal controls for SaaS applications and understanding IT security in a cloud computing environment. Web and other infrastructure services today are increasingly being delivered in a cloud environment, and there is a need to rethink some audit and control considerations.

Reviewing Cloud Computing Application Controls

As any IT auditor should realize, even though an application is operating out of an SaaS environment, the need to assess and review its application internal controls does not go away. The SaaS-based application should continue to have the same audit trails, error-checking procedures, and other good practices that are found with any well-controlled IT application. An IT auditor can almost expect that a business application run under a major vendor, such as Google, has adequate internal controls.

Cloud computing represents a major change in the way applications are run and managed. Although only a limited number of vendors provide service-based software applications today, that number is expected to increase. Many vendors provide an implicit level of trust in the services they provide under the SaaS clouds, but an IT auditor should meet with their IT and business management to gain assurances that every SaaS application is well controlled.

An IT auditor should attempt to help demonstrate, to direct and indirect cloud computing users, that they can have a strong level of trust in the software services and infrastructure that make up the cloud for an enterprise. Some of the key assurance issues that should be addressed are:

- **Transparency.** Service providers must be able to demonstrate the existence of effective and robust security controls, assuring customers that their information is properly secured against unauthorized access, change, and destruction. Key questions for any service provider providing SaaS applications are:
  - What types of service provider employees have access to customer information?
  - Is a segregation of duties between provider employees maintained?
  - How are the files and data for different customers' information segregated?
  - What controls are in place to prevent, detect, and react to any security and control breaches?
- **Privacy.** Cloud computing service providers should provide assurances that privacy controls are in place that will prevent, detect, and react to breaches in a timely manner, with strong and periodically tested lines of communication.
- **Compliance.** In order to comply with various laws, regulations, and standards, there can be cloud computing concerns that the data may not be stored in one place

and may not be easily retrievable. It is critical to ensure that if authorities demand certain data, it can be provided without compromising other information. When using cloud services, there is no guarantee that an enterprise can get its information when needed or that a service provider may or may not claim a right to withhold information from authorities.

▪ **Transborder information flow.** With cloud-generated information potentially stored anywhere in the cloud, the physical location of the information can become an issue. This physical location dictates a jurisdiction and legal obligation. There are many legal issues here yet to be solved.

▪ **Certification.** Cloud computing service providers should assure their customers that they are doing the "right" things. In the future, independent third-party audits and/or service auditor reports will become a vital part of any cloud computing service provider assurance program. However, these facilities have not yet materialized.

Strong and effective standards are needed to help enterprises gain assurances regarding their cloud computing supplier's internal controls and security. At the time of this publication, there are no publicly available specific cloud computing standards.

As no defined set of standards exists, an IT auditor reviewing applications provided by a cloud computing service provider should look for strong assurances in three key areas:

1. **Events.** The service provider should regularly document and communicate changes and other factors that have affected SaaS system availability.
2. **Logs.** A service provider should provide comprehensive information about an enterprise's SaaS application and runtime environment.
3. **Monitoring.** Any such surveillance should not be intrusive and must be limited to what the cloud provider reasonably needs in order to run its facility.

Cloud computing represents a new and interesting opportunity to rework security and IT controls for a better tomorrow, and internal auditing standards should soon follow. The Information Systems Audit and Control Association (ISACA) has already provided some preliminary cloud computing audit and control guidance, and we expect to see much more in the future as SaaS applications and cloud computing grows and matures.

Cloud Computing Security and Privacy Challenges

The use of SaaS applications operating in cloud computing environment shifts a wide range of challenges and responsibilities primarily from an enterprise's IT function to an environment where some responsibilities are assumed by the cloud computing service provider while others remain the responsibility of the enterprise IT function. This is a challenge for IT auditors as well, who must understand the security and privacy components of their selected service providers.

Cloud computing and the use of SaaS applications is a new trend and an increasing number of vendors are offering suites of SaaS applications. Vendors such as Google and Amazon are building huge, multiserver cloud computer complexes, but today no established set of recognized best practices exists across these various service providers.

In some respects, the trend of enterprises shifting some their in-house IT resources to cloud service providers has some elements similar to the move to IT service bureaus in the early 1980s.

In the mid- to late 1970s, an increasing number of enterprises decided to move from their manual or unit-record punched-card processes to the new mainframe computer systems. Many had added systems development programming staffs and installed mainframe computer systems, but often with very disappointing results. A frequent problem was that these new systems did not have the capacity to process the volumes of enterprise data; when they did, often the systems experienced computer system maintenance or downtime problems.

A solution for many at that time was to convert enterprise computer systems operations to what was called a service bureau—a large centralized computer systems resource that collected input materials for many clients, processed using common systems, and delivered the output reports. These service bureaus, however, did not work well for everyone. Many firms subscribed without fully realizing what they would be getting in terms of services and integrity and internal control monitoring for the enterprise processes. Most service bureau computer operations disappeared well before the demise of the mainframe. However, some of the same things are happening today with enterprises converting some conventional applications to a cloud environment. A major problem is that enterprises do not always ask the right questions from their service providers.

When making a decision to select a service provider as part of a move to cloud computing, an enterprise should ask competing service providers some hard questions about their operations and standards. An IT auditor can take a lead in suggesting that its management should gain assurances in some of these areas when selecting a cloud computing service provider:

- **Privileged user access.** Sensitive data processed outside an enterprise and in a cloud brings with it an inherent level of risk, because outsourced services in the cloud bypass conventional physical, logical, and personnel IT controls that an IT organization would exert over its in-house systems programs. Service providers should provide thorough information about the people who manage an enterprise's data and systems in the cloud. They should supply specific information on the hiring and oversight of privileged administrators and the controls over their access.
- **Regulatory compliance.** An enterprise is ultimately responsible for the security and integrity of its own data, even when that data is held by a service provider. Cloud computing service providers should supply detailed information on their security governance policies and the results of recent external audits and security certifications. In addition, they should agree to update the enterprise on these activities on a regular basis.
- **Data location.** When an enterprise uses the cloud, it probably will not know exactly where data is hosted—not even the country. Because of data ownership laws, service providers should identify the specific jurisdictions where they will be storing and processing an enterprise's data. Service providers also should make a contractual commitment to obey local privacy requirements on behalf of their customers.

- **Data segregation.** Data in the cloud typically is stored in a shared environment alongside data from other customers. Cloud providers should provide detailed information on what is done to segregate enterprise data at rest or separate from other users and provide evidence that their security encryption schemes were designed and tested by experienced specialists. Encryption accidents can make data totally unusable and can complicate availability.
- **Recovery.** Even if an enterprise does not know the location of its cloud data, cloud providers should document what will happen to data and services in case of a disaster. They should provide evidence, including test results, that their recovery methods will replicate the data and application infrastructure across multiple sites. The services should assert whether they have the ability to do a complete restoration, and how long it will take.
- **Investigative support.** Investigating inappropriate or illegal activity may be impossible in cloud computing. Cloud services are especially difficult to investigate, because logging and data for multiple customers may be collocated and/or spread across an ever-changing set of hosts and data centers. Service providers should provide a contractual commitment to support specific forms of investigation, along with evidence that they have already successfully supported such activities.
- **Long-term viability.** An enterprise has no guarantee that cloud computing providers will never go broke or be acquired and swallowed up by a larger company. However, current providers such as Amazon, Google, IBM, and Microsoft will almost certainly continue to be around for a while. An enterprise should nevertheless gain assurances that its data will remain available even after such an event. All service providers should provide assurances that users will get their data back in a format that they can import into a replacement application.

Cloud computing and SaaS applications are new and evolving areas as this book goes to press. We can expect to see established standards and recognized best practices in future years. Companies learned enough lessons years ago when using IT service bureaus to recognize how *not* to select a cloud service provider. Cloud computing and SaaS are the wave of the future, and IT auditors should see much more of them in the years going forward.

STORAGE MANAGEMENT VIRTUALIZATION

Virtualization is the concept of pooling IT physical storage resources from multiple network storage devices into what appears to be a single storage device that is managed from a central console. Storage virtualization helps an IT storage administrator perform the tasks of backup, archiving, and recovery more easily, and in less time, by disguising the actual complexity of the overall network of IT storage devices. This author was first introduced to storage management virtualization in 2002 when he was as part of a small consulting group for EMC Corporation helping to launch an Information Technology Infrastructure Library (ITIL) consulting practice. (ITIL best practices are discussed in Chapter 7.) At that time, EMC was a leader in storage management devices, and its virtualization concepts were a major technology innovation. Virtualization has since become a widely used and important IT resource management process.

To understand IT virtualization, one should visit the earlier days of computer systems—particularly the mainframes of old. Those computers had operating systems (OSs) that controlled various attached peripheral devices, including printers, tape drives, and mass storage devices. Although earlier mainframe computer systems initially made massive use of relatively inexpensive magnetic tape drives to store data, technology quickly moved to rotating magnetic drum and then to disk drive storage devices. Although they were much more expensive in the early days of IT, disk and drum drives quickly became popular. The limitation with tape drives was that to read the 100,000th record on a tape, the drive had to pass through the first 99,999 records to find that record. Tape drives and then drum drives quickly became almost historical anecdotes, and technology moved to rotating disk drives, which were much faster and had indexing schemes that located that 100,000th record almost instantaneously.

As every IT auditor with a packed C drive on his or her laptop, full of records and other materials, can attest, there is strong need for mass storage space on all computers. Enterprises of all sizes need ways to manage and control their stored data. With enterprises creating so much information, IT operations have stored their data on multiple storage units or drives but also need to consolidate storage and get the most out of each storage unit. Schemes for managing all those devices soon become a headache. A solution has been storage virtualization, a technique to combine all storage drives into one centrally manageable resource.

Virtualization in general is the separation of a device's functions from its physical elements. With storage virtualization, a unit's physical drive is separated from its functions to store data, and multiple physical disks will appear to be a single unit. Virtualization is a very efficient method to manage and control separate physical units using specialized virtualization software. With the proper software, virtualization techniques can be used with IT hardware devices beyond storage management, network components, servers, operating systems, or even applications. In such systems, the hardware application diagrams that IT auditors had to request as part of a review of general IT controls are no longer applicable. Virtualization software assumes these unit-by-unit responsibilities.

Virtualization concepts were, in some respects, the forerunner of cloud computing. We have only mentioned virtualization here as a new concept, with little supporting detail, that IT auditors will encounter in their general controls reviews. Although IT storage management virtualization was first introduced by just one company, many hardware and storage management vendors have picked up the concept. When an IT auditor encounters an environment in which virtualization is used heavily, he or she should meet with members of the IT staff to gain an understanding of the nature of the implementation, to ensure that it has been implemented in a manner that emphasizes IT internal controls, and that IT appears to be realizing benefits from the software tools or features. Similar to cloud computing, virtualization is a software product or concept offered by many major vendors. It is a growing and still evolving concept and IT auditors should increase their understanding of it as an evolving trend in IT operations.

PART THREE

Auditing and Testing IT Application Controls

CHAPTER TEN

Selecting, Testing, and Auditing IT Applications

NFORMATION TECHNOLOGY (IT) APPLICATIONS are the tools that bring value to computer systems; they drive many if not most of today's enterprise business processes. These IT applications range from the relatively simple, such as an accounts payable system to pay vendor invoices, to the highly complex, such as an enterprise resource management (ERM) set of multiple interrelated database applications to control virtually all enterprise business processes. Many IT applications today are based on vendor-leased or purchased software, an increasing number come from Web-based services, some are developed by in-house systems and programming teams, and many others are based on spreadsheet or database desktop processes. Although the IT general control procedures discussed in Chapters 6 and 7 cover controls and best practices over all IT operations, specific control processes apply to each installed IT application. In order to perform internal controls reviews in specific areas of enterprise operations, such as accounting, distribution, or engineering, IT auditors must have the skills to understand, evaluate, and test the controls over their supporting IT applications. Reviews of specific application controls often are more critical to achieving overall audit objectives than reviews of general IT controls.

Application controls, however, are very dependent on the quality of overall IT general controls. For example, if there are inadequate controls over an IT configuration management process, as discussed in Chapter 7, it will be difficult for an IT auditor to rely on the controls built into a specific application that depends on strong configuration management processes. Even though an IT auditor, for example, may find that an IT order-entry application is properly screening sales orders for valid credit approvals, the surrounding general controls must also be considered. Without IT configuration management update controls, in this example, the order-entry system's programs could be changed, without management's authorization, perhaps to override established credit approval controls.

A typical enterprise may use a large and diverse number of production IT applications. These applications support a wide variety of functions within the enterprise, starting with accounting applications but also including such areas as manufacturing, marketing, distribution, and others, depending on business activities. These supporting applications may be implemented using a variety of IT technologies, such as centralized systems with telecommunication networks, Internet-based network systems, client-server server-based applications, and even older mainframe batch-processing systems. Some of these applications may have been developed in-house but increasingly large numbers of them are based on purchased software packages installed locally or accessed through Web-based service providers. In-house-developed applications may be written in a programming language such as C# (also called C-sharp) or Visual Basic, a database report-generator language such as SQL, or the object-oriented language Java. Application documentation may range from very complete to almost nonexistent. Despite the best efforts of IT audit to suggest improvements, the same often can be said about application controls.

Even though members of management sometimes do not have a good understanding of IT general controls issues, often they are interested in IT audit issues covering specific application controls. For example, while an IT audit report finding on general controls over IT operating systems program libraries may not generate much management interest, a finding of an incorrect discount calculation based on a foreign currency conversion problem in an accounts payable application is sure to draw attention. However, because of the relative complexity of many IT applications and because their controls often reside both within the application and in supporting user areas, audits of IT applications can be challenging.

IT auditors should survey the active applications and select the more critical and appropriate ones for review. We also discuss approaches to effectively review internal accounting controls in IT applications, using several different types of applications as examples. Finally, the chapter discusses audit approaches for evaluating and testing those application controls as well as techniques for reviewing new applications under development. We focus on the internal control characteristics of different types of applications and on how to select appropriate applications in internal controls reviews. There are many differences from one application to another; this chapter focuses on how an IT auditor should select higher-risk applications as candidates for IT audit reviews, the tools and skills needed to understand and document application internal controls, and, finally, processes to test and evaluate those applications.

 ## IT APPLICATION CONTROL ELEMENTS

People not familiar with IT sometimes think of a computer application just in terms of the system's output reports or the data displayed on terminal screens. However, every application, whether a Web-based service application, an older mainframe system, a client-server application, or an office productivity package installed on a local desktop system, has three basic components: (1) the system inputs, (2) the programs used for processing, and (3) the system outputs. Each of these has an important role in an application's internal control structure, and an IT auditor should understand these components when reviewing an IT application.

Earlier IT applications could be separated easily into these three components. As an example, the traditional computerized payroll system from long ago used time cards and a personnel paymaster file as its inputs and a set of programs to calculate pay and benefits as well as to update pay history records. The outputs from that payroll system were the printed checks, payroll register reports, and updated paymaster files. Today, that same payroll system might accept inputs from an automated plant badge reader that controls accesses and tracks attendance, a shop-floor production system that performs incentive pay calculations, various other online inputs, and a human resources database. A series of computer programs, some located at a Web-based service provider and others distributed to remote workstations, would do the processing. In many cases today, much of the payroll processing may be handled by an outside service function that does most of these activities. The modern payroll system's outputs include transactions to transmit compensation to employee bank accounts, pay vouchers mailed to employees, and input files to various tax and benefit sources, various display screens, and an updated human resources database.

Although the input, output, and computer processing system components may not be all that clear to an IT auditor performing an initial review, the same three elements exist for all applications. No matter how complex the application may appear, an IT auditor should always develop an understanding of an application by breaking down its input, output, and processing components. The next sections briefly discuss the control aspects of these application components to give an overview on selecting, auditing and testing IT applications.

Application Input Components

Every IT application needs some form of input, whether it is data manually input from transaction vouchers or supplied from some automated system. Think of a common handheld calculator: The device will generate no results unless data of some sort is input through the key panel. Although an application's programs process the data, determine the outputs, and have a major impact on controls, an IT auditor should understand the nature and sources of the input components. In traditional, batch-oriented systems, this was a fairly easy process. Application inputs often were sequential records recorded on a magnetic tape file or 80- or 90-column punched cards. Today, inputs often are generated from various automated sources, including wireless data collection devices and specialized bar code readers.

Inputs from Data Collection or Other Input Devices

Most early IT applications used punched cards as their input source. A single card carried 80 or 90 columns of alphanumeric encoded data, and users entered input transactions onto data collection sheets for keypunching onto the card formats. The original data collection sheet was the first step in the input chain, and early IT auditors were concerned that all transactions were keypunched correctly. These cards were then machine-sorted or otherwise manipulated prior to entry into a system, either read directly into a computer program or copied to magnetic tape for subsequent processing on a batch basis. That is, 500 lines of transactions may have been prepared on data collection sheets and processed as a batch. The need for all transactions to be keypunched correctly and subsequently read into the computer program made input transactions controls a key component of an application's overall internal controls.

Technology has effectively eliminated those punched-card input records today. Batch-type transactions that must be entered into an application are no longer entered by a specialized "keypunch" or data-entry department. Rather, operational departments use online terminals to enter their transactions for collection and subsequent processing. Following a processing schedule, these transactions may be input or collected and updated later in a batch mode. The data entry programs used to capture them often have some transaction-screening capabilities to eliminate any low-level errors common to earlier batch input systems. In many other situations, the entry of a transaction updates files in a real-time mode.

Transaction input data comes from many sources. A retail store captures sales inputs through a combination of sales entries entered on the point-of-sale (POS) terminal and product sales are entered through bar code readers. Similarly, data is captured on a manufacturing shop floor through various tickets and badges that are entered in readers by workers directly on the floor. Small computer chips—radio-frequency IDs (RFIDs)—embedded on the label of a component may provide inputs as to the product's identification and subsequent movement. All these input devices generate transactions for updating to some type of processing application. Input transactions are increasingly generated not from within the enterprise but from applications located in other physical locations and controlled by others. Enterprises today receive a wide variety of data transactions through the Internet, on older electronic data interchange (EDI) systems, or through wireless systems. In these cases, another enterprise may submit purchase order transactions, accounts payable remittances, or other significant business transactions. Individuals initiate sales transactions, trade securities, and perform other business through their home computers via the Internet. All of these represent input transactions to various IT applications, and each has its own unique control considerations.

An IT auditor reviewing application input controls always should look for some basic internal control elements that should be found in all IT applications. For example, there should be some means of checking that only correct data is entered. A computer program that, through its supporting validation tables, can verify that a product part or employee number is or is not valid cannot easily verify that the current quantity should have been entered as 100 as opposed to 10. The older batch systems had hash total checks to help check for these possible errors. A hash total is a nonmonetary value, such as the "sum" of all account numbers. Modern systems also need reasonableness checks built into their data collection procedures, and the programs processing the transactions need controls to prevent errors or to provide warning signals.

Application Inputs from Other Automated Systems

Today's IT applications often are highly integrated, with one application generating output data for processing by another. The transaction entered into one application may impact a variety of other interrelated applications. Thus an error or omission of an input at one point in a chain of applications may impact the processing of another connected application. In addition to understanding the sources of the transactions to an application, an IT auditor should understand the nature of other automated inputs to that same application. For example, a modern payroll system may receive inputs from a sales performance system to calculate commissions. The sales performance file that feeds the payroll system is another input. The controls there are based on the input, processing, and output controls of the sales performance system. If sales performance data represent a significant input to the payroll system, an IT auditor needs to be concerned about the controls over it as well as over any other supporting applications.

A large network of interconnected applications can present a challenge to an IT auditor attempting to review the input controls for just one application. The IT auditor may be interested in understanding application input controls for application X. However, files from applications A, B, and C may provide inputs to X while D and E provide inputs to applications A and C, respectively. An IT auditor typically does not have the time or resources to review all of these processes and must decide on the most critical ones and assume that the other less critical supporting applications are generating appropriate transactions.

Files and Database Inputs

Although usually generated by some other supporting application or updated by the application under review itself, an application's files and databases represent important inputs. In some instances, these files represent tables of data used for the validation of program data. As part of gaining an understanding of an application, an IT auditor should understand the nature and content of all supporting application files. The software that controls these files generally has various record-counting and other logical controls to determine that all transactions are correctly written onto and can be retrieved from the supporting system. Files also should have their own dating and label-checking controls to prevent them from being improperly input to a wrong processing cycle or an incorrect application. Once written as streams of sequential records on magnetic tape, today's files are input onto higher-density disk drives or USB cartridges. However, an IT auditor needs to have a general understanding not only of the type and nature of inputs to a computer application but also of the source of the file data and any controls over it. (See "Completing the IT Application Controls Audit" later in this chapter for more details.)

Databases can present particular challenges to an IT auditor. Although the term *database* often is misused to refer to almost every type of computer file, a computer system database is a method of organizing data in a format such that all important data elements point or relate to each other. In past years, many mainframe computers used what were called *hierarchical databases*, where data was organized in a grandparent-parent-child "family tree" type of structure. Using it in a manufacturing enterprise, each product might be organized as a header record that would point to each of its parts.

Those components in turn would each have a hierarchy of records comprising its individual parts. File integrity was very important here; a program error that breaks one of the connecting chains would make it difficult to retrieve the lost data.

Today, the relational database is a much more common file structure found on all types and sizes of computers. A relational database is like a multidimensional Excel spreadsheet. That is, the user can retrieve data across various database rows, columns, and pages rather than having to go to the head of each tree and search down through it to retrieve the desired data. Besides being very effective ways to organize input data to application systems, these databases allow for easy retrieval of reports for end users. Two common examples of the relational database model are Oracle Corporation's database products and IBM's DB2 database.

Application Programs

Applications are processed through a series of computer programs or sets of machine instructions. The traditional payroll application mentioned earlier would consist of computer programs to read employee's time card data, store the number of hours worked, and use the employee number on that input time card to look up the employee's rate and scheduled deductions. Based on this match, the program looks up the employee's rate of pay and multiplies this by the number of hours worked to calculate the gross pay.

A computer program is a set of instructions covering every detail of a process. A programmer writes detailed instructions for a computer system to follow. As an experiment to understand the details required to write such a larger computer program, an IT auditor who lacks programming skills should try to write down each step to follow in the morning from the time the alarm goes off until he or she arrives at the office. The next morning, the IT auditor should use these same instructions *exactly* as they are written to get up, wash and dress, and then go off to work. Following this program, most people will encounter program errors and arrive at work missing an item of clothing or worse. This is the difficulty of writing detailed computer programs. Usually it is not necessary for IT auditors to know how to write formal computer programs today beyond the simple audit retrieval applications discussed in Chapter 13, but the effective IT auditor should understand how computer programs are built and what their capabilities are in order to define appropriate control procedures.

Traditional Mainframe and Client-Server Programs

Mainframe, or what we often call legacy-type computers were used extensively for business applications since the early 1960s. These applications first were programmed in what are called first-generation actual machine languages that used binary 1s and 0s. We quickly moved to second-generation languages, what were called the assembly languages. These symbolic languages used codes to represent instructions, such as to add or store a value. Third-generation, or compiler, languages soon followed. They used actual English-like instruction statements, such as "ADD A TO B," to describe the actions to be taken. Programs called *compilers* translated these instructions into machine language. A large variety of these compiler languages were introduced in the 1960s, but COBOL[1] became the almost standard language for business data processing well into the 1980s. It is still in use today for some business applications, but specialized database and report-generator languages and object-oriented languages are now much more common.

A wide range of computer languages are used today; they include Visual Basic and Java. Many applications also are developed using English-language-like report generator languages that reside on top of a supporting computer language. Other than having the skill to write an audit retrieval request, as discussed in Chapter 13, an IT auditor today does not need to be skilled in a programming language.

Modern Computer Program Architectures

In the mainframe computer days of years past, business applications almost always were developed in-house and often were written in COBOL. Most enterprises today generally purchase or lease their software packages or access them through a Web service provider, although some IT functions still do develop their own applications. In-house development normally occurs when an enterprise has business requirements where no commercial software packages seem correct or, more significantly, when an enterprise has plans for some new strategic software-based initiative. An IT auditor today, even with a fundamental knowledge of a language such as Visual Basic, COBOL, or C, may have some initial difficulties understanding how object-oriented applications are programmed and constructed. Often these newer applications consist of many very small program code modules that pass data to one another, sometimes over remote telecommunication lines. While it is certainly not a typical IT audit need, Exhibit 10.1 describes some object-oriented high-level programming concepts. Java and C++ are two of the programming languages of today's Web-based applications.[2] An IT auditor should rely on the overall application program standards in place as well as on other programming development and maintenance controls. Rather than looking for these application programming standards in each given application reviewed, he or she should review the general systems development controls in the IT enterprise. These might be included in a general review of IT operations, as discussed in Chapter 6.

When an enterprise plans to build and launch in-house a major new or revised software application, IT audit should request the right to perform a preimplementation review of the new application development project.

Preimplementation IT audit reviews are most effective for large development efforts that cover an extended span of time and primarily components developed in-house. Exhibit 10.2 contains IT audit procedures for a review of a new application systems development controls. These control processes are closely linked with the IT general controls discussed in Chapter 6 and an IT auditor should look for them in each application selected for review. Today many new application development projects do not consist just of in-house-developed new programs. Many modern applications are constructed by building data reference tables as part of purchased software applications as well as building interfaces between these purchased applications and other existing components. Proper attention must be devoted to preserving internal controls and performing adequate testing in these situations, and the IT audit preimplementation review approach can provide service to the enterprise.

Object-oriented programming (OOP) programming languages, such as JAVA or C++, model organized around "objects" of data rather than logic-based "actions." Programs using languages, such as COBOL, were based on logical procedures that took input data, processed it, and produced output data. These older programming approaches described the processing logic but did not define the data. Object-oriented programming focuses on the data objects we want to manipulate rather than the logic required to manipulate them. Examples of objects range from human beings (described by name, address, etc.) to buildings and floors (whose properties can be described and managed) or the individual parts in a manufactured product.

The first step in OOP is to go through a data modeling exercise and identify all the objects you want to manipulate and how they relate to each other. Think of all of the furniture in the board of directors' meeting room. There will be a major table for board meetings and side tables for the support staff. The chairs in that room will be *objects* with each director, around the table, having one *class* of chair. The support staff, another class, and the CEO at the end of the table with still another. These objects are then generalized into *classes of objects*. OOP defines the logical sequences of these classes of objects. The directors' chairs are arranged around the conference table, the CEO at the end, and support staff off to the sides. OOP provides computer instructions, based on the relevant data in the class object characteristics, to allow the objects and their characteristics to communicate with each other in well-defined interfaces called *messages*. For example, the CEO's chair will be at the head or the table, and if the CEO is present, messages will be delivered to other board members.

The concepts and rules used in object-oriented programming provide these important benefits:

- The concept of a data class makes it possible to define subclasses of data objects that share some or all of the main class characteristics. Called *inheritance*, this property of OOP forces a more thorough data analysis, reduces development time, and ensures more accurate coding.
- Since a class defines only the data it needs to be concerned with, when an instance of that class (an object) is run, the OOP program will not be able to access other program data accidentally. This characteristic of *data hiding* provides greater system security and avoids unintended data corruption.
- The definition of a class is reusable both by the program for which it is initially created and also by other object-oriented programs (and, for this reason, can be more easily distributed for use in networks).
- The concept of data classes allows a programmer to create new *data types* that is not already defined in the language itself.

The OOP languages C++ and JAVA are perhaps the most popular object-oriented languages today, with JAVA frequently used in distributed applications on corporate networks and the Internet.

EXHIBIT 10.1   Object-Oriented Programming Language Concepts

Vendor-Supplied Software

Today most IT applications are based on vendor-supplied software. An outside vendor will supply the basic, often Web-based, system elements, and the enterprise's IT development function is responsible only for building custom tables, file interfaces, and output report formats around the purchased or licensed application. Often the vendor protects the actual program source code for the purchased software to prevent improper access and changes. IT auditors should be concerned that the software vendor has a reputation for quality, error-free software. Often smaller, entrepreneurial software suppliers offer very cost-effective solutions, but there can be risks in using under-capitalized software developers. If there is any doubt about the software vendor's

1. All requests for new or revised applications should follow IT standards and receive prior authorization.
2. The application development process should include sufficient requesting user interviews to develop a firm understanding of needs.
3. All new application projects should receive a detailed statement of requirements along with a formal cost benefit analysis.
4. Project plans should be prepared for all IT department development work as well as for individual application development projects.
5. Care should be given to ensuring that application development projects meet the long-range objectives of the enterprise.
6. The responsibilities for applications development work should be assigned with adequate time allowed to complete development assignments.
7. The applications development process should include sufficient user interviews to obtain a full understanding of requirements.
8. Attention must be given to internal controls, audit trails, and continuity procedures.
9. Adequate resource and capacity planning should be in place to ensure that all hardware and software is sufficient when the application is placed in production.
10. Sufficient attention, including test procedures, must be paid to backup, storage, and continuity planning for the new application.
11. Adequate controls must be installed to provide strong assurances regarding the integrity of the data processes and outputs from the application.
12. The application should be built with adequate controls for the identification and correction of processing errors.
13. All application processing data and transactions should contain strong audit trails.
14. Adequate documentation should be prepared on a technical as well as an application user level.
15. Test data should be prepared following a predetermined test plan that outlines expected results and satisfies user expectations.
16. When data is converted from an existing application, strong control procedures should be established over the conversion process.
17. If a critical application, internal audit should be given an opportunity to participate in a formal preimplementation audit.
18. There should be a formal sign-off and approval process as part of the completion of the application development process.

EXHIBIT 10.2   Internal Audit IT Application Development Review Guidelines

stability, arrangements should be made at the time of the software purchase contract to place a version of the vendor's source code in escrow in the event of its business failure. A bank or some other agency would hold a version of the protected source code for release to customers if the software vendor were to fail.

The decision to license, lease, or purchase a software package too often is based on an IT manager meeting a software salesperson at a trade show, establishing a need, and acquiring the software package without a full analysis of its costs and benefits. While lacking any form of the traditional IT preimplementation review, IT auditors can play a strong consulting-level role supporting IT management in the acquisition of a new software package. There are often many internal control issues that should be considered beyond descriptions in vendor sales brochures. Exhibit 10.3 presents an IT audit review procedure to use both when providing consulting help and when reviewing

Audit Internal Controls Review Procedure	Workpaper Reference
1. Determine that the requirements and objectives for the new application have been clearly approved and defined.	_____
2. Assess whether application requirements have been clearly defined and whether they can be satisfied by modifications of current application.	_____
3. If requirements call for a new application, determine whether an IT analysis has been performed to determine if it may be more cost-effective to develop in-house or to purchase.	_____
4. If a search for a potential purchased application must be undertaken, determine that detailed requirements have been defined through a request for proposal (RFP) approach.	_____
5. Determine that the RFP requirements for the application clearly match the existing enterprise IT environment.	_____
6. Review procedures for the distribution of RFPs to ensure that this distribution covered all appropriate vendor candidates, and raise questions if a known vendor appears missing.	_____
7. Assess whether IT enterprise documentation is in place to review all vendor proposals on a consistent basis.	_____
8. For application software vendors that appear to meet preliminary requirements, determine that the software has been effectively demonstrated through appropriate testing.	_____
9. Where multiple vendors are presenting competing software products, consistent evaluation procedures should be in place.	_____
10. Enterprise financial and legal resources should be in place to participate in software selection.	_____
11. Determine that the selected software product has adequate documentation, help facilities, and a regular update program in place.	_____
12. Determine that an implementation plan is in place to convert either data or an existing application to the new software application.	_____
13. Where appropriate, develop preliminary plans for CAATT procedures covering the new application.	_____
14. Establish internal audit workpaper records for the new, purchased software application.	_____

EXHIBIT 10.3   Purchased Software Internal Controls IT Audit Review Procedure

the decision to purchase a major new software package. An IT auditor should understand the internal controls of major purchased software applications as well as he or she understands any in-house-developed application.

Large, integrated packages, such as ERP systems, can have a major impact on all aspects of an enterprise. These database application packages may include production, purchasing, inventory, human resources, accounting, and all other business applications implemented as a linked series of databases. Data introduced to one application component, such as a revised standard cost for a manufactured part, will connect to other connected systems as necessary. For example, that revised standard cost will be reflected in inventory and financial systems, among others.

IT Application Output Components

No discussion of an application system would be complete without a description of its output components. These key application components usually consist of output screens, updated files, or even printed reports. These are important areas to survey in any application review, and IT audit should be concerned about controls contained on the output screens and control files. Older applications produced large volumes of output reports indicating the results of the processing and any control or error problems. The sheer volume and frequency of those reports often prevented users from paying adequate attention to control problems, and IT auditors frequently found control concerns that users could have identified just by reviewing their output reports.

Today's applications produce far fewer (if any) paper-based output reports; instead, results are reported on online data retrieval screens. In some cases, special online reports signal control problems and data errors; in others, users are responsible for calling up the appropriate screen to review problems. All too often, users ignore this step, and processing errors can go undetected. IT auditors always should review the scope of application output reports, screen messages and their user dispositions. Reports or screens are not the only application outputs. Transactions or updated files typically are passed to a variety of other integrated applications. Just as a modern IT application may receive inputs from a highly integrated set of input systems, it may be one link in a chain to other applications. Again and always, an IT auditor should develop a good understanding of the application reviewed as well as all of its inputs and outputs.

SELECTING APPLICATIONS FOR IT AUDIT REVIEWS

Although all significant IT operations and key applications should be subject to regular internal control reviews, IT audit typically does not have the resources or time to regularly review the controls for all enterprise IT applications. In addition, many IT applications represent a minimal level of control risk and are not essential audit candidates. As part of a specific operational review or a general IT controls review, IT audit should select only its more critical applications for review.

An IT auditor should use the risk assessment techniques discussed in Chapter 4 to identify the more critical application vulnerabilities pertaining to an enterprise's reporting, operational, and compliance requirements. Based on a high-level understanding of potential application review candidates, an effective approach is to rate all applications on a scale from 1 to 5 for each category according to these criteria:

- Does the application contain primary enterprise controls or functions?
- Based on IT audit's preliminary review, what is the design effectiveness of the application's internal controls?
- Is the application primarily based on vendor-supplied, prepackaged software, or was it developed in-house?
- Does the application support more than one critical business process?
- Has this application been changed frequently or is it stable from period to period?

- What is the complexity of making application changes (e.g., table changes versus program code changes)?
- What is the financial impact of the application controls?
- What is the overall effectiveness of the IT general controls that support the application (e.g., change management, logical security, and operational controls)?

Each application reviewed should be scored with higher numbers representing a create-audit criticality concern. For example, if application changes require updating program code, the score might be 5; changes through external tables might receive a 1 or 2. These scores, of course, are very arbitrary, but they provide a measure for each application considered.

Exhibit 10.4 shows an example of an application's control risk assessment using these scoring criteria. We have listed three example applications, A, B, and C, and have displayed them on a spreadsheet form with sample scorings. We have assigned a weighting for each of these criteria. For example, column 1 on application primary controls is given a weighting of 20 while column 6 on the complexity of changes is given a 10. Based on individual scores and their weights, a criticality score can be computed for each application. For example, for application A, this would begin as $(5 \times 20) + (1 \times 10) + (5 \times 10) + \ldots = 375$. The application that has the highest criticality scores would be the most appropriate, higher risk applications for planning an IT audit.

Although a criticality score "wins" as a candidate for application review, IT audit also must consider other factors when selecting IT applications for review. Because IT applications are often so critical to enterprise operations, IT auditors often receive specific requests from their audit committee or management to review specific application controls. Some of the factors that may further impact IT audit's decision to select one specific application over another may include:

- **Management requests.** Management often asks IT audit to review the controls in newly installed or other significant IT applications due to reported problems or their perceived strategic importance to the enterprise. Sometimes these management requests are not made for the correct reasons, however. For example, sales analysis reports may appear to be incorrect due to bad data submitted from a reporting division, but management may consider the incorrect reports to be a "computer problem" and request an IT audit application review. Initially IT audit may not be aware of such user input problems and would perform normal review procedures. When IT audit is aware of such mitigating circumstances, audit test strategies should be modified prior to starting the review.
- **Preimplementation reviews of new applications.** In many instances, IT audit should become involved in reviewing new applications before they are placed in production. This is true for in-house-developed applications and purchased software packages. Strategies for IT audit preimplementation reviews are discussed in the section titled "Application Review Case Study: Client-Server Budgeting System" later in this chapter.
- **Postimplementation application reviews.** For some critical applications that are subject to a risk analysis, IT auditors also may want to perform a detailed

	Application Selection Risk Factor Assessment								
	20	10	10	10	10	10	15	15	
Application	Application contains primary controls or functions	Design effectiveness of the application	Vendor supplied, prepackaged, or in-house developed	Supports more than one critical business process	Frequency of application changes	Complexity of application changes	Application financial impact	Effectiveness of IT general controls support	Composite score
Application A	5	1	5	5	3	3	5	2	275
Application B	1	1	2	1	1	1	4	2	170
Application C	5	2	2	1	5	5	5	2	245

EXHIBIT 10.4 Application Control Risk Assessment Example

application review sometime shortly after the actual system implementation. If an application has sufficient financial and operational controls significance, IT audit may want to schedule at least limited controls reviews on an ongoing basis.

▪ **Internal control assessment considerations.** Chapter 1 discussed the need for evaluating and testing internal controls as part of the Sarbanes-Oxley (SOx) Section 404 internal controls review process, and an application controls assessment is an important part of that evaluation. The results of understanding, documenting, and testing specific IT application controls by IT audit may provide a basis for the external auditor reviews in their SOx attestation processes.

IT audit typically is faced with requests for reviews of a large number of application candidates at any time. Auditors must take care to document why one application is select over another.

IT auditors often perform reviews of the specific applications that support an overall functional area. For example, the enterprise IT audit may schedule a combined operational and financial review of the purchasing department. This also may be the appropriate time to review the application controls for the major automated purchasing systems supporting that department. In this integrated audit approach, IT auditors can concentrate on the more technical issues surrounding the applications and on other supporting operational controls.

PERFORMING AN APPLICATION CONTROLS REVIEW: PRELIMINARY STEPS

Once an application has been selected for review, IT audit should gain a more detailed understanding of the purpose or objectives of that application, the technology approaches used, and the relationship of the application to other related processes. It may be necessary for the assigned IT auditor to do some background reading and study special technical aspects of that application. Auditors often can acquire this knowledge by reviewing past audit workpapers and applications documentation and by interviewing IT and user personnel. As an early step in this review process, IT audit should perform a walk-through of the application to better understand how it works and how its controls function. These preliminary steps will allow an IT auditor to develop specific audit tests of the application's more significant controls.

In the early days of enterprise-developed IT applications, documentation often consisted of detailed system flowcharts with supporting record layouts and little else. This documentation helped the programmer but usually was of little use to application users or IT auditors attempting to understand the application's controls. In addition, these early flowcharts were often hand-prepared and became out of date quickly. When one relatively small change was made to a complex system flowchart, designers often were reluctant to redraw their charts. Although they might have remembered the changes, other persons reviewing the documentation would not be aware of them.

Over time, application documentation evolved into a format that was oriented more toward text and functional charts. Decision tables and logic charts described the functions of individual programs while text described the overall system. Although this type of documentation was more functional and less technical, it also quickly became outdated. Programmers and system designers often did not incorporate changes into this systems documentation. Today, powerful documentation tools, such as flowchart generators, are available. A real strength of these automated documentation tools is that detailed flowcharts can be combined into summary versions with changes introduced on one chart updating all others.

IT auditors can expect to find various types and amounts of application documentation depending on the relative age and complexity of the application. Applications developed in-house sometimes have very limited documentation; in contrast, vendor-supplied applications that often have extensive documentation, including many dozens of volumes of descriptive text. Users will sometimes treat such documentation as almost encyclopedic reference materials. A review of the published documentation should be a first step to gaining an audit understanding of an application. If aspects of the documentation are missing or out of date, the IT auditor probably will have an audit report finding at the conclusion of the review. However, lack of documentation should not necessarily prevent an IT auditor from performing an application review. When performing the review, IT audit normally should look for these documentation elements:

- **Systems development methodology (SDM) initiating documents.** These documents include initial project requests, any cost/benefit justifications, and the general systems design requirements. Although many initial assumptions may have changed during the systems design and implementation process, these documents often help IT audit understand why the application was designed and controlled in the manner it is.
- **Functional design specifications.** This documentation should describe the application in some detail, including each of the program elements, database specifications, and systems controls. If major changes have been made to the application since its original implementation, the design documentation should reflect these changes. The purpose of this documentation is to allow an IT analyst to make changes or respond to user questions regarding the application.
- **Application and program change histories.** There should be some type of log or documented record listing all program changes within an application. Some IT departments keep such a log with the application documentation; others maintain it in a central file cross-referenced to the program source code. This type of documentation is an essential element to control program changes; it also provides IT audit with some feeling for the application's relative stability. A large number of ongoing change requests for a given application may mean that the application system is not achieving user objectives. Revision service support controls should follow information technology infrastructure library (ITIL) service support best practices as discussed in Chapter 7.
- **User documentation manuals.** Along with technical documentation, appropriate user documentation should be available for any application. In a modern, Web-based system, much of this user documentation may be in the form of "HELP" or "READ ME" online screens. However, this documentation should be sufficiently

comprehensive to answer a wide range of user questions. It also should be supported by evidence of a user training program, as appropriate.

IT audit should review selected application documentation to gain an understanding of the controls to be reviewed and perhaps use these materials to develop questions for later audit review interviews. Auditors also should take copies of key or representative sections for workpaper documentation. However, normally an IT auditor should not attempt to copy the entire documentation file for workpaper purposes. Many times auditors copy too much, adding considerable bulk to workpaper files but does little to accomplish audit objectives.

Conducting an Application Walk-Through Review

Once IT audit has reviewed prior workpapers, the application's documentation, and interviewed both users and IT personnel to clarify any questions raised by the documentation review, a next step is to verify the application controls and processes by a *walk-through review*. For an IT application, a walk-through review is similar to an initial review of an operational facility where the auditor tours a facility, such as a production floor. The purpose of this walk-through is to confirm IT audit's general understanding about how the IT application operates. During the walk-through, the auditor preliminarily tests application controls through sample transactions.

As an example of an application walk-through review process, assume that IT audit has been asked to review the controls over an older in-house-developed accounts payable application operating on an in-house server system. The enterprise is a manufacturing firm with other fairly sophisticated IT applications. Assume that this accounts payable application was installed several years earlier and was never reviewed when it was under development. Now management has asked IT audit to review the application's internal controls due to integrity concerns. Based on the review of application documentation, IT audit has determined that the application receives inputs from these sources:

◼ Purchase order commitments from the manufacturing material requirements planning purchasing system
◼ Notifications of goods received from the materials-receiving system
◼ Various online terminal payment transactions for indirect goods and services that are not recorded through the materials-receiving system
◼ Payment approval transactions entered through an input screen
◼ Miscellaneous payables journal transactions entered as batch data

Application data is recorded on a relational database along with tables of values for validating purchase terms, including the calculation of any purchase discounts. Based on the documentation review, application outputs include the accounts payable electronic fund transfer transactions, paper checks, transactions to the general ledger and to cost accounting applications, and various control and accounting summary screens and reports.

The prime system users here are personnel from the general accounting and purchasing departments, who set up automatic vendor payments under preagreed

---

1. Develop a general understanding of the application, its inputs and outputs, and any procedures requiring manual or other system interactions.
2. For an application with a large number of steps requiring manual processing procedures, select
   a sample of key transaction types to be processed from a normal production cycle. For
   workpaper documentation purposes, document identifying control numbers or other characteristics to trace transactions through application processes.
3. Observe or use software tools to monitor the processing of each module or workstation step,
   noting situations where the walk-through transaction has:
   a. Inputs to another application or supporting process are passed on through the node
      processing module.
   b. Transactions are held for further cycles in process or rejected as errors during the specific
      processing module.
4. Follow selected transactions through each processing module step, documenting instances
   where the documented control procedures are not being followed or where the transaction
   causes application errors or manual operator difficulties.
5. At the end of the walk-through, discuss with appropriate IT or user administrators any unusual
   or unexpected problems and document internal control status.
6. For an automated application with essentially no paper trail, follow essentially the same
   procedures but make appropriate inquiries and use software query tools to determine if
   the application is processing with appropriate controls and as expected.

EXHIBIT 10.5   Application Walk-Through IT Audit Review Steps

---

terms. The example application flowchart in Exhibit 10.5 describes general IT audit
steps for an application walk-through review, where P/O stands for purchase order and
the other key document is the purchase requisition. The steps to performing an
application walk-through for the example accounts payable application include:

1. **Briefly describe the application in the audit workpapers.** Based on its review
   of the documentation, IT audit should prepare a brief description of the application
   for later inclusion in the audit workpapers. This workpaper documentation follows
   the general format of the walk-through description except it provides greater detail,
   identifying key subsystems, input screen formats, key data file names, and output
   report formats. (For a discussion of IT audit workpapers, see Chapter 5.)
2. **Develop a block diagram description of the application.** A block diagram
   represents an abbreviated auditor-level systems or functional-level flowchart for the
   application. It should reflect the description cited in step 1 and also illustrate some
   application flow concepts. Numerous laptop system software tools are available to
   create the diagram; or a flowchart can even be a hand-drawn document to increase
   an auditor's understanding of the application reviewed. Exhibit 10.6 is an example
   of such an application process block diagram that an IT auditor can use to confirm
   his or her understanding of the application with key IT and user personnel.
3. **Select key application transactions.** Based on the previous steps, the IT auditor
   should select one or more representative transactions to trace through the
   application. This selection would be based on discussions with users and fellow
   members of the internal audit team. In this example of an accounts payable system,
   the IT auditor may select automated transactions that the receiving system should
   match against the payables purchase order records to initiate payment.

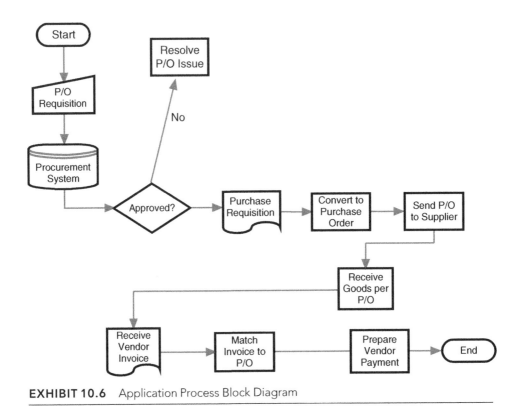

EXHIBIT 10.6 Application Process Block Diagram

4. **Walk a selected transaction through the system processes.** In the older days of manual or simpler IT applications, a walk-through amounted to just that. That is, an auditor would take an input transaction form and walk it through each of the clerical desks or steps normally used to process the transaction in order to verify the processing procedures. In a modern application, this walk-through process typically requires recording "screen shot" prints of a transaction as it is entered into a terminal and then prints that follow the transaction through subsequent steps. In our example, the walk-through transaction is a receiving report entry indicating that a valid open purchase commitment had been received. IT audit then would review the open commitments module of the system to determine whether the transaction was recorded on a transaction report or screen, then trace the transaction to a properly computed accounts payable check or to a funds-transfer transaction and then to general ledger system transactions for the correct amount.

This type of application testing is called *compliance testing*. That is, IT audit is verifying that the application is operating in compliance with preestablished control procedures. *Substantive testing* or a test of financial statement balances involves a comparison of account balances or other methods; this is used if IT audit wishes to verify that all accounts payable checks have been input to the general ledger. Tests in support of SOx Section 404 controls typically tie a single-item test to financial statement general ledger accounts.

5. **Modify the system understanding as required.** The purpose of an application walk-through is to develop a basic understanding of the application's functions and controls; thus, a walk-through review does not allow IT audit to determine whether *all* transactions are working as described. However, if IT audit discovers that the selected walk-through transactions are not working as assumed, the preliminary auditor-prepared application documentation may need to be revised. Once that documentation has been revised, IT audit may want to repeat the previous steps to determine that the auditor has a proper understanding of system transaction flows.

Walk-throughs allow IT audit to gain a preliminary understanding not only of the application and its controls, but also of its relationship with other automated systems. Limited compliance testing allows the IT auditor to confirm that the application is operating as described. Although it is not a substitute for detailed, substantive application testing, a walk-through allows an IT auditor to identify major internal control weaknesses and gain a sufficient understanding of the application to define control objectives for subsequent, detailed audit testing and evaluation procedures.

Developing Application Control Objectives

After the review of documentation and walk-through compliance testing, an IT auditor should develop detailed audit objectives and procedures for completing the application review. This definition of audit objectives depends on the type of review planned, the characteristics of the application, and the results of the preliminary review steps. A particular review might be concerned with the level of control risk and the ability of the application to support financial statements correctly. The procedures associated with these audit objectives would be tests of the financial statement balances built up from detailed application transactions.

An IT auditor also could have other objectives in reviewing an application. Management may have asked IT audit to review an application to determine if users have received sufficient training to operate it or to determine if related discount and interest calculations associated with accounts payable are performed correctly. The walk-through compliance testing may have identified significant problems, and an IT auditor may want to do little more than confirm those preliminary but troubling observations.

Specific application review audit objectives should be clearly defined. An IT auditor responsible for the detailed review might wish to summarize these objectives for appropriate members of management to review and approve. Doing this may help prevent an IT auditor from devoting resources to testing an area not considered significant. In the above-mentioned accounts payable system, an IT auditor may have established several specific objectives for this review:

▪ The accounts payable system should have adequate internal controls, such that all receipts recorded from the receiving system are correctly matched to vendor files before the preparation of disbursements.
▪ Vendor terms should be computed correctly with controls to eliminate potential duplicate payments.

- Controls should be in place to prevent or at least flag improper or unusual disbursements.
- All systems-generated disbursements should be recorded on general ledger files using correct account numbers and other descriptive codes.

Depending on management's direction, IT audit might develop other objectives for performing such a review. For example, the review could focus on database integrity or on control procedures over miscellaneous disbursements. Any review may have multiple objectives. For example, if management had asked IT audit to review the accounts payable system to ensure that no illegal or improper payments have been made, IT audit probably would also want to add a general objective to assess control risk and to determine that the system of internal controls is adequate.

Before starting any detailed application review, IT audit should document the specific objectives of the review and discuss them with those managers who had requested the review to determine if the planned approach is on target and will satisfy the audit request. This same procedure should take place even if the application review has been initiated by the internal audit department as part of a total review of an IT function. Exhibit 10.7 contains some suggested control procedures and audit objectives for an IT application

1. Develop a general understanding of the application to be reviewed: its principal business purposes, inputs, outputs, and technology environment.
2. Based on the general understanding of the application, develop a general process flowchart that identifies key decision points, inputs, outputs, and internal controls.
3. Develop an understanding of the general controls surrounding the application and its processing environment, with an emphasis on ITIL service support and service delivery general controls. (See Chapter 7.)
4. Discuss the application and its performance with key system users and IT to understand any concerns or outstanding issues.
5. Develop a testing plan for the application that emphasizes:
    a. Identification of significant transactions, accounting, and business-related controls within and surrounding the application's environment.
    b. Identify control objectives covering each of those significant controls as well as areas of concern that should satisfy the auditor that key controls are effective.
    c. Develop testing and sampling approaches for each of the key controls.
6. Gather evidence to perform tests of identified key controls, including:
    a. Copies of key files and extracts of transactions to reperform application functions.
    b. Special application transactions to test key or critical application controls.
    c. CAATT procedures or package software functions, if appropriate, to review application transactions and special functions.
    d. Manual or paper-based documentation to support the applications controls testing.
7. Schedule and perform tests of key application controls using the gathered test materials.
8. Evaluate all test results using a pass/fail approach, and communicate testing results with key systems users and IT to verify and validate the testing approach and its results.
9. Maintain copies of all testing plans and evidence, documenting the results in internal audit workpapers.
10. Develop an appropriate corrective action plan, where appropriate, to correct any problems encountered in the testing or application review.

EXHIBIT 10.7 IT Application Review Control Objectives and Audit Procedures

review. Because there are so many types and variations of IT applications, the exhibit only lists high-level audit review approaches, and an IT auditor should make other changes as appropriate.

COMPLETING THE IT APPLICATION CONTROLS AUDIT

Usually more difficult for an IT auditor to define than the objectives for an IT audit of general controls, the specific audit objectives supporting a detailed IT application audit can vary depending on whether the review covers a single application or is a module of a larger business process, such as an ERP system. The IT auditor's review strategy depends on whether (1) the application primarily uses purchased or in-house-developed software components; (2) the application is integrated with others or is a separate process; (3) it uses Web-based service providers, client-server or older, legacy computer system methods; and (4) its controls are largely automated or require extensive human intervention actions. The exact nature of an application also can vary considerably. Although the emphasis of audits once primarily was over controls in accounting-related applications, IT auditors today may review applications implemented in other areas as well such as manufacturing production planning or loan portfolio analysis. Any of these areas requires knowledge of the application's specific attributes as well as the supporting technologies. That is, an IT auditor should understand and document how the application works, then define specific audit test objectives, and finally perform a series of audit tests to verify that the application controls are in place and working as expected.

Besides the review of documentation and the walk-through, discussions with key user and responsible systems personnel can aid in the IT auditor's understanding. The amount of effort spent here depends both on the type of application reviewed and the number of users who can be of help. For example, a capital budgeting decision support application probably will have a small group of key users who have a thorough understanding of its procedures. A logistical support system, such as factory floor data collection, may be used by a large group, where it may be difficult to identify just the key system users.

The next step is to complete the documentation of the application for audit purposes. IT audit should have been making workpaper notes throughout. The documentation procedure here is largely one of summarizing where workpapers describe the understanding gained and include notes for potential follow-up review work.

Clarifying and Testing Audit Control Objectives

The previous section discussed the importance of establishing test objectives as part of an application review—the types of controls an IT auditor would expect to be in place for an application. IT audit sometimes can fail in this important next step of defining the specific objectives of the review. For example, management may expect IT audit to review an application's internal accounting controls, but an IT audit may emphasize logical security controls with minimal attention given to other established control objectives. This misunderstanding of IT audit objectives becomes especially critical when the review is not in an IT auditor's more common realm of or related accounting or related applications. For example, if management has asked IT audit to review a new manufacturing resource planning system, its objectives could include validating internal accounting controls, reviewing for materials parts flow efficiencies, checking for system compliance with applicable regulations, or a combination of these. These objectives should be summarized briefly and discussed with both audit management and application-user management.

Although the need for a clear statement of review objectives may appear an obvious early step, IT auditors too often omit this important step. Of course, the objectives of an application review may change if IT audit encounters evidence of other control problems during the course of a review. In a manufacturing resource planning review, for example, the initial objective of affirming the adequacy of the MRP application's internal controls might change to one of fraud detection if potentially invalid transactions were encountered.

Having defined these objectives, IT audit should next test the key control points within the application. Because, as part of gaining an understanding, the auditor already has done limited compliance testing and through the walk-through, these test procedures can now be expanded to make a more definitive assessment of the application's controls. In older and simpler batch-oriented systems, this task was fairly easy. IT audit looked for input data acceptance controls, for any computer-processing decision points, and for output data verification controls. Since there are only a few processes associated with such an older batch application, this identification of test procedures often could be accomplished with minimal analysis. Modern applications today with online updating, close integration with other applications, and sophisticated programming techniques all combine to make identifying test procedures difficult. Other factors include:

- Inputs to the application may have been generated by external sources, such as Web linkages, or from other applications at partner enterprises.
- Controls once performed by data input personnel are now usually built into programs.
- Modern optical scanning input devices and output documents with multi-dimensional bar codes make visual inspection difficult.
- Database files may be shared with other applications, making it difficult to determine where a change or transaction originated.
- The application may make extensive use of Web interfaces and will appear to be paperless to IT audit.

There are numerous other reasons why an IT auditor may have difficulty initially identifying IT application audit test procedures. The application's description, along with key user discussions, should help to identify some of these controls. As a rule of thumb, an IT auditor should look for points where system logic or control decisions are made within an application and then develop test procedures to verify that those decision points are correct. These points represent the key controls within an application, such as checks on the completeness of transactions or the accuracy of calculations. Exhibit 10.8 lists some typical areas of audit concern, control objectives, and test procedures for a review of a client-server application.

The following are test procedures that an IT auditor might use when assessing application internal controls. Based on the nature and objectives of the application, these may not apply to all applications, and the auditor will need to have a detailed understanding of the application and its key internal controls before developing a test plan.

Audit Concern	Control	Potential IT Audit Tests
1. File data input validation	Files for processing are available and complete.	Review validation process procedures and test operations.
2. Process functionality and calculations	Specific calculations conducted on one or more inputs and stored data elements produce appropriate data elements. Existing data tables or master file rating tables should be used to validate data.	Compare input values and output values for all scenarios by walk-throughs or reperformance tests. Review table maintenance and controls, and assess adequacy of change edits and tolerance level controls.
3. Correct functionality and calculations	Automated tracking of changes made to data, associating the change with a specific user. Automated tracking and highlighting of overrides to normal processes.	Review a sample of reports for evidence of appropriate reviews. Review access to override normal processes.
4. Data extraction, filtering, and reporting	Extract routine outputs are assessed for reasonableness and completeness. Evaluation of data used to perform estimation for financial reporting purposes.	Review design of an extract routine against data files used. Review supervisory assessment of output from extract routine for evidence of regular review and challenges. Review sample of allocations for appropriateness. Review process to assess extracted data for completeness and validity.
5. Process to process balancing	Automated checking of data received from feeder systems into or ledger systems to assure validity. Automated checking that balances on both systems match: or if not, an exception report is generated and used.	Inspect interface error reports, and search for evidence of appropriate correctibe actions. Inspect validity and completeness application parameters and settings. Review access to set and amend configurable parameters on interfaces. Inspect evidence of matching reports, checks, and error file processing to determine whether controls are operating effectively.
6. Automated functionality and aging	File extracts from supporting applications are available to provide management with data on aged transactions.	Test sample of listing transactions to validate appropriateness of aging processing.
7. Checks for duplicate transactions	Comparison of individual transactions to previously recorded transactions to match fields. Comparison of individual files to expected dates, times, sizes, and other values.	Review access to set and amend configurable parameters on duplicate transactions or files. Review processes for handling rejected files or transactions.

EXHIBIT 10.8 IT Application Review Processing Controls

This exhibit some outlines areas of IT auditor concern, potential control objectives to support those areas, and test procedures to determine if the controls are operating. These steps are oriented to an almost generic financial application that IT auditors frequently encounter. However, because there are so many different types and variations of IT applications, an IT auditor will have to custom build a review approach with consideration given to these issues:

- Tests of application inputs and outputs
- Test transaction evaluation approaches
- Other application review techniques

Tests of Application Inputs and Outputs

In the very early days of IT auditing, many audit-related tests were little more than checks to verify that all inputs to a program were accounted for correctly and that the correct number of output transactions were produced based on these inputs. An auditor's review of an automated payroll system is an example of such a set of tests of inputs and outputs. The IT auditor, of days past, would perform tests to determine that all time cards input were either accepted or rejected and that the number of output payroll checks produced could be reconciled to those system input time cards. This was a very basic test of system inputs and outputs.

Although automated applications have become much more complex, many audit test procedures today are little more than those same tests of inputs and outputs. An IT auditor should examine the outputs generated from an application, such as invoices produced by a billing system, to determine that the input data and automated computations are correct. This type of audit test is limited in nature and often will not cover all transactions or functions within an application.

The purpose of a control risk assessment or compliance test is to determine if application controls appear to be working. If all transactions or supporting data are to be reviewed, substantive testing procedures or tests of financial statement balances should be used. The extent of this testing depends on the audit objectives. For example, an IT auditor usually performs compliance tests over those aspects of an application that cover internal accounting controls related to financial statements. An IT auditor may want to perform compliance tests over other areas, such as the efficiency of administrative controls.

For older applications, tests of inputs and outputs often are quite easy to perform and are not nearly as easy for today's applications, where the auditor often does not encounter a one-to-one relationship between inputs and outputs. Test transaction approaches, discussed next, are often much easier to perform and even more meaningful. Nevertheless, tests of inputs and outputs are sometimes useful for reviews of applications. Compliance test IT audit procedures for an example automated purchasing application are outlined in Exhibit 10.9.

Test Transaction Evaluation Approaches

An IT auditor may want to ascertain that transactions entered into a system are processed correctly. For example, when reviewing a plant floor manufacturing application, an IT

1. Select a series of purchase orders generated by the application reviewed and trace them back to the requirements generated through either the procurement system or authorized manual purchase inputs, determining that all new purchase orders have been properly authorized.
2. From the sample selected in step 1, trace the purchase orders back to established records for vendor terms and prices, resolving any differences.
3. Select and trace a cycle of automated purchase orders to appropriate Web control logs to determine that all documents were transmitted without error and on a timely basis.
4. Using a sample of purchase orders received from log files, determine that vendors are documented through current, signed purchase agreements.
5. Select a sample of receiving reports, and determine that the application is working properly by matching receipts to open purchase orders and accounts payable records.
6. Select a sample of recent accounts payable vouchers and any actual checks generated for parts and materials, tracing the payments to valid receiving reports and purchase orders.
7. Using sample transactions that were either held upon receipt for noncompliance with terms or improper timing, verify that transactions are handled correctly and per established procedures.
8. Balance a full cycle sample of purchase transactions, from the input system providing inputs to the control logs and printed purchase order documents.
9. Investigate any balancing differences and verify the reported errors are valid.
10. Document all exceptions found as potential audit report items.

EXHIBIT 10.9 Automated Purchasing System Compliance Tests Example

auditor might record several shop materials transactions as they are entered on manufacturing floor terminals. After an overnight processing cycle, an IT auditor can verify that those transactions have correctly made adjustments to inventory records and that work-in-process cost reports have been properly updated. This verification can take place by reviewing special retrieval reports against data files. As part of the test transaction process, an IT auditor also can test whether error-screening controls are operating as described. The emphasis here should be on the testing of the error-verification routines within the application. IT audit can select transactions input to an application that appear to be invalid and then trace them through the application to determine that they have been properly reported on exception reports. IT audit also can consider submitting test error transactions to a system to verify that they are being properly rejected by the application.

Other Application Review Techniques

The computer-assisted audit tools and techniques (CAATTs) discussed in Chapter 13 can be useful in reviewing application controls. All too often, IT auditors use these tools to test some accounting control, such as an accounts receivable billing calculation, but do not to evaluate other application controls. Audit software can match files from different periods, identify unusual data items, perform footings and recalculations, or simulate selected functions of an application. Other useful techniques are:

▪ **Reperformance of application functions or calculations.** This type of test is applicable for both the automated and the manual aspects of application systems. For example, if a fixed-assets application performs automatic depreciation calculations, IT audit can use CAATT processes to recalculate depreciation values for selected transactions as a compliance test.

▪ **Reviews of program source code.** For applications developed in-house, IT audit can verify that a program performs a certain logic check by verifying the source code. However, this type of compliance test should be used with only the *greatest amount of caution*. Because reading and understanding program source code is complex, it is very easy to miss a program branch around the area being tested. An IT auditor should consider the specialized programs available to compare program source code with the compiled versions in production libraries.

▪ **Continuous audit monitoring approaches.** IT audit sometimes can arrange to build embedded audit procedures into production applications to allow those applications to flag control or other application exception problems. These techniques also are discussed in Chapter 13 on CAATTs and in Chapter 14 on continuous auditing techniques. This approach goes beyond just auditing an application adding procedures to make it self-auditable on a continuous basis.

▪ **Observation of procedures.** Observations may be useful when reviewing both automated and manual applications. For example, a remote workstation receiving downloaded data from a central IT system may require extensive manual procedures in order to make the proper download connection. IT audit can observe this on a test basis to determine if the manual procedures are being performed correctly.

Completing the Application Controls Review

Although compliance tests are powerful methods to test application controls, IT audit should be aware that this level of assurance is not absolute. There is a risk that an IT auditor may test an application control and find it to be working when, in fact, it does not normally work as tested. Because of the risks associated with such compliance tests, therefore, IT audit always should be careful to condition any audit reports to management with a comment or warning about the risks of incorrect results due to the limited audit tests. Sometimes the controls tested do not appear to be working correctly because IT audit does not understand some aspects of the application system. IT audit may want to review the application description and identify controls to verify that they are correct. It may be necessary to revise IT audit's understanding of the application controls and then reperform the audit risk assessment procedures.

If IT audit finds that, through compliance testing, the application controls are not working, it probably will be necessary to report these findings. The nature of this report depends very much on the severity of the control weaknesses and the nature of the review. For example, if the application is being reviewed at the request of the audit committee or senior financial management, the identified control weaknesses may prevent them from placing any reliance on the financial results produced by the application. If the control weaknesses are primarily efficiency related or operational, IT audit may want to report them just to IT management for future corrective action.

Applications can be primarily financial or operational. They can be implemented using purchased software, can be custom-developed applications located on in-house systems with extensive database and telecommunications facilities, can operate in a client-server environment, or can exist in numerous other variations. As noted, this diversity makes it difficult to provide one set of audit procedures for all applications. While IT audit can develop a general approach to reviewing most data processing applications, usually it is necessary to tailor that approach to the specific features of a given application. The next section describes how an IT auditor might perform a review of a capital budgeting application operating in a client-server environment with telecommunications links through a network linked to a larger server machine.

APPLICATION REVIEW CASE STUDY: CLIENT-SERVER BUDGETING SYSTEM

As an application review example, assume IT audit has been asked to assess the internal controls over an in-house-developed client-server architecture capital budgeting system. Assume that a financial planning department has developed the capital budgeting analysis portion of this example application using a popular desktop spreadsheet software package. Although the application has been built around a purchased software spreadsheet package, the business users have coded a series of macro instructions for running the programs. The workstation portion of this example system communicates with a server file containing mainframe budgeting system data.

Assume that IT audit has been asked by management to review general controls over both local networks and their client-server computer operations. Following the IT general controls review audit procedures discussed in Chapter 6, IT audit found that general controls in these areas were adequate. That is, users documented their desktop applications; adequate backups of files and programs were performed on server files; password procedures limited access only to authorized personnel; and other good internal control procedures were followed. Among IT audit's recommendations was to place stronger controls over telecommunications access to the local network and to install virus-scanning procedures.

Sometime after that general controls review, this example capital budgeting system was implemented on the enterprise administrative office network. Because this system provides direct input to the corporate budgeting system, management has asked IT audit to review its application controls. After discussing this review request with senior and IT management, IT audit developed these high-level review objectives:

- The spreadsheet capital budgeting system should have good internal accounting controls that are consistent with other enterprise control processes.
- The application should properly make capital budgeting decisions based on both the parameters input to the system and programmed macro formulas.
- The system should provide accurate inputs to the central or corporate budgeting system through the local file server.
- IT security and integrity controls should be secure.
- The capital budgeting system should promote efficiency within the financial planning department.

These objectives are at a very high level but represent the general format of the audit objectives that an IT auditor should formulate for this type of application review. Management typically states its objectives in words that emphasize application performance and integrity features objectives. Although these management-initiated audit objectives often are not IT technical issues, IT audit should translate them to more detailed IT control issues for the next general IT audit steps.

Review Capital Budgeting System Documentation

IT audit's first step should be to review the documentation available for this example application. Since this example is built around a commercial desktop software product, IT audit might expect to find or should ask for:

- Documentation for the capital budgeting software package, including descriptions of the spreadsheet macro procedures, and formulas
- Procedures for uploading capital budget data to the central system budgeting application through network server files as well as procedures for accepting the input data to the mainframe IT function
- Procedures to ensure the integrity of the data resident on server files

IT audit probably will not find documented procedures covering all of these elements, but there should be documentation covering the software product used, the interfaces with other applications, and the necessary manual procedures.

IT audit should review these materials to determine that they are complete enough that an auditor can gain a general understanding of the overall application. Then, after reviewing this documentation and discussing it with its financial planning users, IT audit should describe the allocation for audit workpaper documentation purposes. Since this example application is built around a spreadsheet software product, this description would primarily cover its manual interfaces. Control descriptions over file server applications and their network connections to client systems should have been covered as part of the previously mentioned general controls review. IT auditors often find it convenient to describe such an application in the form of a flowchart, although a written process description may be adequate. The purpose of this type of description is to provide IT audit with workpaper documentation of the application and to provide a basis for the identification of significant control points.

Identify Capital Budgeting Application Key Controls

Although a rather simple but compact application, this example capital budgeting application has some critical control points. For example, if the spreadsheet macro procedures are calculating capital costs correctly, present values, and such related factors, management may very well take incorrect actions regarding investment decisions. If data is incorrectly transmitted to the mainframe budgeting system, financial statement records may be incorrect. If the application is not documented properly, a change of key users in the financial planning department may make the system nearly inoperable.

1. Develop a detailed understanding of all significant automated and manual application input transactions: their nature, timing, and source.
2. Develop a strong understanding of transaction error correction procedures, both the nature of the tables or rules used for verification as well as any built-in system logic; determine that formal turnaround procedures exist to control any initial error items.
3. Using documentation or database descriptions, trace all input to output data flows with the application, showing how input elements (e.g., orders from the inventory application) will change or modify other system elements. Document this understanding in workpapers through audit data process flow diagrams.
4. Determine that controls exist for comparing the number of items input to those that have been either accepted or rejected; review error identification procedures to assess whether users can easily understand the cause and nature of any errors.
5. Review procedures for the correction and resubmission of rejected items; determine if errors are held in suspense files for analysis and corrective actions.
6. Develop a detailed understanding of all significant system output control totals, and review the nature of supporting controls for a selected single application update processing cycle and from cycle to cycle.
7. Select an input update cycle for review, and determine that the number of items input, less any rejected errors, ties to application output control totals.
8. For the selected test cycle reviewed, determine that all error items from the cycle have been corrected, resubmitted, or received proper disposition.
9. Review control totals in the subsequent processing cycle to determine that file totals have remained consistent from one cycle to the next, investigating any discrepancies.
10. Review existing error suspense files to ascertain that all error items have been investigated and corrected in a timely manner; investigate any items remaining in the error cycle to determine the reasons for any delays.
11. Review any preliminary concerns or errors with IT and responsible management to make any necessary changes to audit test procedures.
12. Document all audit review and testing activity in workpapers.

EXHIBIT 10.10   Capital Budgeting Application Input and Output IT Audit Tests

Based on IT audit's understanding of this example system, key system controls have now been defined and documented. Here, because IT audit has recently performed a general controls review, it is not necessary to reconsider those general controls during the application review. IT audit review procedures can now be developed similar to those shown in Exhibit 10.10.

Perform Application Tests of Compliance

For the final step in this application review, IT audit should perform tests of the established audit procedures. Depending on management's and IT audit's relative interest in the application, it may not be necessary to test all of the controls as listed. Many are related to one another. If no problems or weaknesses are identified in one control area, IT audit may decide to pass on the related control areas. Some of the tests of application controls might include:

▪ **Reperformance of computations.** Capital budgeting is based on some very specific and often complex computations, such as the estimation of the present value of future cash flows based on discount factors. Using another spreadsheet or other desktop system tools, IT audit could select one or several present value computations generated by the system and recalculate them to determine the reasonableness of system processes. Any major differences should be resolved.

■ **Comparison of transactions.** IT audit can select several sets of application budget schedules and trace them through the file server budget system to determine that they have been correctly transmitted.

■ **Proper approval of transactions.** Before any system-generated budget schedule is transmitted to the central budget system, it should have had proper management approvals. IT audit should select a sample of them for review.

Numerous similar compliance tests can always be performed. The imaginative IT auditor will choose which tests to perform based on the nature of the audit and management objectives. Control weaknesses should be reported to management for corrective action.

 ## AUDITING APPLICATIONS UNDER DEVELOPMENT

It is often much more efficient for an IT auditor to review an IT application for its internal controls while it is being developed and implemented rather than after it has been placed into production. The role of the IT auditor here is similar to that of a building inspector reviewing a new construction project: It is difficult to make constructive recommendations regarding the completed building. Even if some problems were found, the inspector would be under considerable pressure not to identify ones that would require significant portions of the building to be torn down and rebuilt. Rather, the building inspector identifies problems during construction and suggests how they can be corrected before completion. Similarly, the effective IT auditor should suggest corrective actions to improve system controls along the way. It is easier to implement changes during an application implementation process than after it has been completed and the system has been placed into production.

To continue with the analogy, an IT auditor must be careful not to take responsibility for *designing* the new application's controls. The building inspector points out problems but certainly does not take responsibility for fixing them. The discussion on performing effective IT audits in Chapter 5 emphasizes that it is IT audit's task to review and recommend but not to design or build the controls in any area reviewed. When reviewing new applications under development, an IT auditor should point out internal control weaknesses to the application developers but only recommend that they implement those recommendations.

Application development groups, user management, and auditors all tend to agree that, in reviewing new IT applications under development, IT audit provides another set of eyes to look at new and soon-to-be-implemented applications. This section offers approaches to reviewing new applications under development and discusses some of the pitfalls IT audit may encounter when attempting to audit them.

Objectives and Obstacles of Preimplementation Auditing

The concept of preimplementation reviews was first proposed by the then-new profession of what was called EDP auditing in the early 1970s; at that time, many traditional internal auditors were opposed to this approach. Traditionalists argued that if an auditor reviewed an application in advance of its implementation, it would be difficult to come back later and review that same application after implementation. The argument was that if an IT auditor had "blessed" the internal controls of a system under development, how could that same auditor come back later and perform a critical review? Over the years, there have been many changes to the application development process. New applications frequently are based on vendor-supplied software components, and internal auditing standards, as discussed in Chapter 3, allow an internal auditor also to act as a consultant. IT auditors have also grown to accept preimplementation reviews, acting as auditors and not consultants. IT auditors, however, face four major obstacles when reviewing new applications under development:

1. **"Them versus us" attitudes.** Although IT audit and general management both may accept the concept, IT management often expresses wariness or even resentment when IT audit announces its plan to review an application that is under development and still has many details yet to be worked out. The announcement "Hello, I'm from IT audit, and I am here to help you" may not be received favorably. Good preimplementation review procedures can establish respect for IT audit's role and add value in the development process. An IT auditor who spends many hours reviewing a complex new application with some potential control-related issues and who concludes only that "Documentation needs to be improved" will not be viewed as having added much value to the process.

2. **IT auditor role problems.** The IT auditor's role must be clearly understood by all parties and might be defined as:

   ■ **An extra member of the implementation team.** The systems design team invites the IT auditor to design review meetings. However, that IT auditor will be more of an observer than a typical member of that team. The auditor's objective is to gather data regarding key controls and processing procedures for a subsequent audit report.

   ■ **A specialized consultant.** Sometimes an IT auditor can become so involved in the systems design and development process that he or she is viewed as just another design team consultant making recommendations during the course of the implementation process. IT audit should take care to *not* be viewed in that light. Following the standards for an IT auditor as an enterprise consultant, as discussed in Chapter 3, an IT auditor should act primarily as an independent reviewer providing help to the team, not as a specialized consultant who is part of the design process.

   ■ **An internal controls expert.** In any review, IT audit always should make certain that a review of internal controls is included in the new project. However, the auditor should not be the primary designer of those controls. Otherwise, he or she may have problems reviewing the completed application and its controls at some later date.

- **An occupant of the "extra chair."** Sometimes an IT auditor does not do a proper level of preparatory work during a preimplementation review. Systems management may request an auditor to review various materials and attend design review meetings. An IT auditor who does not prepare but simply attends these meetings too frequently provides no real contributions. Nevertheless, if problems occur in the future, management may say "But IT audit was there!"
- **State-of-the-art awareness needs.** New systems applications often involve new technologies or business processes. IT auditors should be involved in their own continuous education programs to better understand state of the are issues. A general understanding of new technologies may require some additional IT auditor homework—reading vendor manuals and other documentation.
- **Many and varied preimplementation candidates.** The typical larger enterprise may have a significant number of new application projects that are potential candidates for preimplementation reviews. These projects will all have different start times, durations, and completion dates. An IT auditor needs to perform an ongoing risk assessment to select the most appropriate new review candidates.

Despite these potential obstacles, there are strong reasons for IT auditors to become actively involved in preimplementation reviews of major or critical new applications. This is particularly true in today's era of major enterprise-wide applications, such as ERPs, that require detailed planning and testing in all areas of the enterprise.

Preimplementation Review Objectives

A key objective of application preimplementation auditing is to identify and recommend control improvements such that they can be potentially installed during the application development process. However, rather than just assuming that a new IT project is a given and then reviewing its controls, IT audit also should aim to review the justification and definition of the new development project. There should be a good project management system in place that properly plans development steps and measures actual progress against those planned steps. For major projects, IT audit can evaluate the adequacy of project development controls used for the particular application. This preimplementation phase is also an excellent time for an IT auditor to gain an understanding of the new application sufficient to design future automated audit tests and to define the CAATTs as discussed in Chapter 13. Whether the implementation involves a vendor software package or an application developed in-house, IT auditors should gain overall understandings of all aspects of those application projects.

In addition, IT auditors often must comply with statutory requirements for reviewing new applications under development. Several U.S. states and other countries have legislation requiring that all new significant state agency applications be reviewed by their audit departments for IT controls prior to implementation. Auditors in many U.S. state governments can expect such legislation to appear in their own states in the future.

Preimplementation Review Problems

Preimplementation reviews often present IT audit with some very serious review and scheduling problems, including too many review candidates given limited IT audit resources. IT auditors sometimes make the mistake of announcing their intent to review *all* new applications and all major modifications prior to implementation. In a larger enterprise, dozens or even hundreds of user requests for new or major revision projects may be initiated regularly. IT audit will have no time for comprehensive preimplementation reviews and only time for little more than nominal rubber-stamp approval signatures. To overcome these difficulties, IT audit should consider these issues:

- **Select the right applications to review.** Auditors are faced with the problem of selecting only those applications of audit significance. Rather than relying on a simple value judgment or an arbitrary process, IT auditors should follow a risk-based, structured selection method for identifying those applications to review. A development group, for example, may be working on applications A, B, and C. Given the relative application risks as well as limited audit time and resources, IT audit may decide to perform preimplementation reviews only for application B. However, if significant postimplementation problems appear in C, management might later second-guess IT audit and ask why system C had not been selected for review. An IT auditor with a consistent selection approach will be able to justify the decision to review B rather than C.

- **Determine the proper IT auditor's role.** As discussed, when an application has been selected for preimplementation review, IT audit all too often can become overly involved in its systems development and implementation processes. Particularly for applications based on vendor software products, many rapidly in-house, new IT projects require extensive user and systems development team efforts, with numerous design review meetings. IT audit often is asked to participate in these design review meetings, but doing so may cause an auditor role problem. If an auditor is actively involved in the typical design review meetings where design compromises may be negotiated, he or she may find it difficult to comment on these same decisions later as audit points. However, if excluded from design meetings, IT audit may have a hard time performing the review. To be effective in reviewing new applications under development, the IT auditor's role needs to be carefully defined. IIA Standards allow an auditor to act as an internal consultant, as discussed in Chapter 3, as long as this role is carefully defined.

- **Review objectives can be difficult to define.** It is often easy to define audit review objectives at a very high level but then difficult to translate them into reality. When an auditor informs the IT department that a given application has been selected for preimplementation review and requests supporting documentation, the IT auditor may receive folders or files containing hundreds of pages of requirements studies, general design review documentation, meeting minutes, and other materials. IT audit may then be asked to review and comment on this mass of materials. An audit objectives and control procedures approach can help an auditor to choose the relevant materials to review.

Multiple implementation projects and new technologies present some major challenges to IT audit to perform effective preimplementation reviews of IT applications. However, whether for new applications developed in-house or purchased software, IT audit preimplementation reviews will usually add value to the internal controls environment in the enterprise. In addition, through preimplementation reviews, IT auditors who have been accused in an old joke as being the ones who "join the battlefield after the action is over to shoot the wounded" can now play a proactive role in the application development process.

Preimplementation Review Procedures

Many of the same audit procedures discussed in other chapters for IT internal controls reviews can also be followed for reviews of new applications under development. All too often, IT auditors argue that applications under development are somehow "different." However, as fluid and subject to ongoing developmental change as applications under development are, many of the same control objectives and procedures discussed previously for IT applications are quite appropriate for these reviews. IT auditors should tailor their preimplementation reviews along the various phases a new project's development, starting with initial project initiation, to requirements definitions definition, to development and testing, and finally to implementation. These same basic steps apply whether the application is a major in-house-developed one, a vendor service-based software package, or a user-led set of desktop applications. The only difference is on emphasis depending on the application development approach.

When IT audit has selected a given application for preimplementation review, an important first step is to review the overall planned audit program steps with IT management so that there is an understanding of what IT audit expects to find as well as the review approach. Some procedures may be tailored to fit a given application, but the next objectives should apply for most preimplementation reviews.

Application Requirements Definition Objectives

When possible, IT audit should get involved in a preimplementation review early in the development phase. Here, IT audit should review the detailed requirements study to determine the overall control status of the new application. If IT audit can identify control concerns during this phase of the application's development, it will be relatively easy for system designers to address and correct them.

Exhibit 10.11 is a set of IT audit procedures for the requirements definition phase of any project. IT audit should look for similar requirements no matter how the new application is developed. Some of these procedures, of course, may require modification if the application under review is composed of specialized technologies or will be a major modification to an existing system. However, IT audit should perform control procedures necessary to satisfy all of the control objectives listed here.

IT audit may need to decide if any special skills are required to complete the review. If the application involves the use of new or unique systems technologies, a new vendor-supplied application package, or specialized supporting software, IT audit may want to enroll in training on the software product to be used—such as through classes offered by the vendor to the development staff—or IT audit may bring in someone with specialized skills or training.

Audit Step	Workpaper Reference
1. Obtain a general understanding of the IT department's system development methodology (SDM) standards for both developing new applications and installing purchased software to assure an appropriate requirements definition study.	___
2. Obtain user-approved request documentation authorizing the detailed application development or purchase.	___
3. Review detailed project plans for the new application and ascertain, through discussions with IT and requesting users, that estimates of time and resources seem reasonable and achievable.	___
4. Determine if there was an appropriate analysis, including cost and timing considerations, to determine whether the application should be built in-house or purchased/leased.	___
5. Determine if any special skills are needed to review application internal controls, such as RFID wireless connections or an understanding of ERP databases. If appropriate, arrange for IT audit staff members to learn new skills through seminars or other training.	___
6. Identify and review significant internal controls surrounding the new application. Discuss controls with both key users and IT to develop testing procedures.	___
7. If significant portions of the application involve in-house-developed modules, assess whether appropriate consideration has been given to purchased software alternatives.	___
8. Assess whether the impact of manual aspects of the application has been given proper consideration as part of the requirements definition, such as training needs or process changes.	___
9. If the application appears to be a candidate for CAATT procedures, begin preliminary audit planning for installation.	___
10. Review the extent of user sign-offs on the requirements study; based on selected interviews, assess whether users understand the new application and any internal control or procedure ramifications.	___

EXHIBIT 10.11 Preimplementation Review Requirements Definition Checklist

For example, with some large projects that take years to develop and implement, adding a specialist to the staff to review just that project can be effective. At the completion of this phase, IT audit might write an informal audit report outlining any preliminary observations and concerns. In addition, workpapers should be started to document the new application control's procedures.

Detailed Design and Program: Development Objectives

Defining detailed design objectives is typically the longest phase of any new application's development process. IT audit may want to schedule several reviews during this phase. Each periodic review should focus on a specific area of the new application development project, but the overall purpose should be to answer some of these questions:

- Does the detailed design comply with the objectives of the general requirements definition?
- Do users understand the controls and objectives of the new application under development?

- Has proper consideration been given to application controls and security?
- Is the application being developed according to the IT department's own systems development standards?
- Is the application development process supported by a well-organized project plan, similar to IT audit planning discussed in Chapter 5?
- Have any earlier audit recommendations been incorporated into the detailed design?

During this phase, care should be taken not to become buried in detail. Some IT enterprises may attempt to use IT audit as a quality assurance function for the project. However, overall audit effectiveness will be diminished if IT audit's time is spent reviewing such things as compliance with detailed programming standards.

Reviews of this nature should be limited to periodic testing. Any control-related concerns encountered should be brought to the attention of management so that corrective action can be taken in a timely manner. If the new application is purchased software, often there are limited in-house design and programming requirements. However, the IT enterprise may have to build file conversion programs or interfaces with existing systems or table files or report generator definitions. These can represent major efforts, and IT audit still should review controls over the purchased software before it is installed and implemented.

Application Testing and Implementation Objectives

This phase includes testing of the new application and completion of documentation, user training, and conversion of data files. IT audit often is able to evaluate whether system controls appear to be working as expected and will want to test any audit modules incorporated into the application. Exhibit 10.12 is a preimplementation review application testing checklist for this preimplementation phase to help IT audit recommend whether the new application is ready for final or production implementation. Significant system control problems, coupled with management pressures to implement the application as soon as possible, can make this phase difficult. IT often promises to correct control problems in the new application during a "phase two." Auditors often find that because of other priorities, this promised phase two never seems to occur. IT audit should consider the severity of such control problems and either document them for follow-up review or inform management of the need for corrective action during the current implementation.

At the conclusion of the application testing and implementation phase, the responsible IT auditor should prepare a final report that documents the identified significant control issues and subsequently corrected by the IT development function. This report also should outline any outstanding control recommendations that have not been implemented. Reports up to this point have been informal; this final report, however, should follow normal internal audit department reporting standards.

Postimplementation Review Objectives and Reports

Although the new application is no longer in development, the postimplementation phase of a preimplementation audit often is still important. The postimplementation review should take place shortly after a new application has been implemented and has

	Audit Preimplementation Steps	Auditor Init
1.	Determine if a formal test plan exists, including an outline of key application modules detailing expected data conditions, the business rules tested, the type of test, and the expected results for each module condition tested.	___
2.	Review the results of several recent unit tests to determine if results have been mapped to the test plan, exceptions researched, and errors corrected as appropriate.	___
3.	Determine if the application being tested satisfies original application design requirements; if exceptions exist, determine that they are properly documented, reviewed, and approved by key users.	___
4.	Interview representative key users to understand their participation in the testing process; where participation appears to be lacking, discuss and document the need for user participation to ensure successful implementation.	___
5.	Review the extent of overall system testing, including key interfaces with other applications and outside service providers.	___
6.	If any original requirements have not been achieved by the completed application, assess procedures in place to determine whether to add procedures later or to otherwise allow for discrepancies.	___
7.	If appropriate, initiate a series of internal audit–developed test transactions that emphasize key controls, defined in earlier review steps; review the test results and assess application performance.	___
8.	Summarize the results of preimplementation application testing activities, and make internal audit recommendations regarding the appropriateness of the application implementation.	___

EXHIBIT 10.12   Preimplementation Review Application Testing Checklist

had time to settle down. In other words, IT audit should perform the review after the users have had an opportunity to understand the application and information systems have had time to resolve any final implementation problems or errors. Here the post-implementation review determines if application design objectives have been met and if established application controls are working. It also should look at project controls to determine if the application was completed within budget. Ideally, this review should be performed by another member of the audit staff to provide an independent assessment of the new application.

Many IT audit departments have a fairly formal procedures for issuing audit reports. Draft reports are prepared, auditees prepare their responses after some discussion and negotiation on the draft, and a final audit report is issued, with copies distributed to various levels of management. Sometimes this audit report format is inappropriate for reviews of new applications under development. An individual internal controls problem with a particular program or output report, which may be identified by an IT auditor when performing a preimplementation review, can be corrected by the application developer almost at once. There is little need to discuss such a finding in a formal audit report draft. The control concern should have been corrected long before the audit report was issued. Audit and general management, who might expect the more formal audit report with its findings and recommendations, should understand the special report format used for preimplementation reviews.

Informal, memo-type reports should be issued after each phase of the preimplementation reviews. These memo reports should discuss the scope of review activities and document any audit concerns. If some of the prior concerns have been corrected, the actions taken and current status of the control issue should be discussed. IT audit should also develop workpaper documentation covering these review activities, which will serve both to document preimplementation activities and to provide a basis for later application reviews.

At the conclusion of the preimplementation review, IT audit should issue a formal audit report following internal audit's department standards. Where appropriate, this report can discuss preimplementation audit findings and corrective actions taken. However, the main function of this final report is to highlight outstanding control issues that still need to be corrected within the new application system.

IMPORTANCE OF REVIEWING IT APPLICATION CONTROLS

An IT auditor should place a major emphasis on reviewing the supporting IT applications when performing reviews in other areas of the enterprise. Even though good general or interdependent IT control procedures may be in place, individual application controls may not all be that strong. An enterprise's applications may have been developed through a series of compromises among users or without any level of proper quality assurance. To evaluate IT application controls properly, IT audit needs a good understanding of both IT procedures and the specific control and procedural characteristics of each application area.

The effective IT auditor should spend a substantial amount of audit effort reviewing and testing controls over specific IT applications and new applications in the development process. Such reviews will provide assurance to general management that applications are operating properly and to IT management that their design and controls standards are being followed, allowing them to place greater reliance on the output results of such applications. An understanding of application control reviews is a key skill requirement for all IT auditors.

NOTES

1. Developed in the 1960s, the computer programming language COBOL stands for Common Business Oriented Language. It is still used today as a key programming language.
2. Numerous textbooks and references describe object-oriented programming. A search on the Internet will provide many references.

CHAPTER ELEVEN

Software Engineering and CMMi

THE INFORMATION TECHNOLOGY (IT) applications discussed in Chapter 10 are based on software programs, some purchased from outside vendors or downloaded from Web sources, others purchased and then customized by the enterprise's IT systems development staff, and still others built by in-house programmers and systems developers. In all instances, planning and good procedures are needed to build and implement successful IT software products. Although the process to build these applications once was called computer programming, it is increasingly known today as software engineering.

This chapter provides a high-level introduction to both software engineering and the Software Engineering Institute's Capability Maturity Model® for Integration (CMMi®), an important assessment tool for evaluating the capabilities of an IT function on many levels. CMMi has strong links to the Control Objectives for Information and related Technology (CobiT) framework, discussed in Chapter 2, and is useful for evaluating IT quality assurance as discussed in Chapter 31. It is also a measure to allow IT audit to assess how well they are doing in building and implementing the computer-assisted audit tools and techniques (CAATTs) discussed in Chapter 13. An understanding of CMMi and software engineering concepts also will help an IT auditor to better review both IT general and application controls.

SOFTWARE ENGINEERING CONCEPTS

Many IT auditors know a little about computer programming from college classes or from writing simple retrieval programs to gather audit data. While those routines are often fairly simple and easy to launch, most software development projects are much more complex. The enterprise resource planning (ERP) applications discussed in Chapter 10 on auditing IT applications are examples of very comprehensive IT systems and programs. In order to build and maintain these IT systems and programs, application developers generally need better tools to build, maintain, and operate them.

Software engineering—the application of engineering concepts to software development—is a useful tool. It is the application of systematic, disciplined, and quantifiable approaches to software development, operation, and maintenance. Software engineering is more than just designing and writing computer programs; it often involves several other IT skills and disciplines, including:

▪ **Software requirements analysis.** This is the process of systems needs analysis, the development of systems and program specifications, and validation of software requirements.
▪ **Software design.** Software often is designed with specialized modeling and development tools, such as the Unified Modeling Language (UML)[1].
▪ **Software development.** This is the construction of software through the use of programming languages.
▪ **Software testing.** Before any software is implemented, it needs to be tested in a thorough and comprehensive manner, often using specialized testing tools.
▪ **Software maintenance.** Software systems often have problems and need enhancements long after they are first completed. Tools need to be in place to install revisions in an efficient and comprehensive manner.
▪ **Software configuration management.** Since software systems often are very complex with many related components, their versions and overall configurations have to be managed in a standardized and structured way.
▪ **Software engineering management.** The management of software systems borrows heavily from project management, as discussed in Chapter 16, but software development processes often include nuances not seen in other project management disciplines.
▪ **Software development processes.** There is a wide range of formal approaches for designing and building application systems and their supporting systems; two popular process names are called agile and waterfall software development processes.
▪ **Software quality assessments.** Software engineering includes a variety of tools and approaches to improve the overall quality of all aspects of software development.

Some of the software engineering approaches summarized here are discussed briefly in other chapters. For example, Chapter 10 talks about a system development and requirements process called the systems development life cycle (SDLC), and Chapter 7 reviews the set of information technology infrastructure library (ITIL) best practices processes. However, the typical IT auditor does not need to be an expert in software engineering processes. Rather, he or she should understand these general concepts and to apply them when appropriate when reviewing IT internal control processes.

CMMI: CAPABILITY MATURITY MODEL FOR INTEGRATION

Effective IT development processes and a strong supporting IT function are necessary elements for good software engineering processes. However, over the years, often many IT software development functions were not that effective in building and delivering IT systems that met established requirements following an efficient and on-budget schedule. With frequent late deliveries, chaotic change and revision control processes, and no effective budget controls, IT systems commitments were often consistently missed. Often poor-quality deliveries of the IT systems resulted in too much rework, system functions that did not work correctly, and massive complaints from software product customers—the users—after delivery.

These IT application development problems are nothing new. As far back as the late 1960s, a series of well-publicized major U.S. software development projects failed dramatically for being massively late, not meeting specified requirements, or going way over budget. These events were known as the software crisis; a search on Google or other search engines will provide good background information on that software crisis era.

The U.S. federal government, and of course its taxpayers, were major victims of this software crisis. Over the years, the U.S. government has been a major contractor for a wide number of IT projects, and it generally purchased or arranged for this work from a variety of contractors. However, government customers frequently found that the contractors selected both missed cost or schedule estimates and delivered poor-quality software products. Faced with continuing software vendor performance frustrations over the years, the federal government entered into a contract with the Software Engineering Institute (SEI) of Carnegie Mellon University (CMU; www.seo.cmu.edu) to develop a better approach and process to measure and assess software development groups.

SEI took a design engineering approach to this software development challenge. That is, an engineering team designing a new tool, such as a military weapons system, takes a very structured approach in developing the product. The design steps are tightly controlled and documented with good procedures over such areas as revision control. The well-run design engineering organization will have its processes so well defined and managed that it can easily pick up a new assignment and deliver it in a high-quality manner.

SEI contrasted the well-ordered procedures in many design engineering functions with the almost chaotic processes often found with software development. Initially it developed a model, the Capability Maturity Model (CMM), that allows an organization to assess themselves and for others to determine where they stand in their software development maturity.

That initial CMM was a model for software development organizational improvement. CMM initially defined what is called software process maturity in terms of five distinct levels of development maturity with a series of processes operating at each of these levels. The CMM model starts with what is called Level 1, where processes are unpredictable, poorly controlled, and incomplete. IT auditors have seen this type of maturity in many enterprises where almost nothing is documented, where systems development controls are weak, and where the software development group is operating in some form of near chaos.

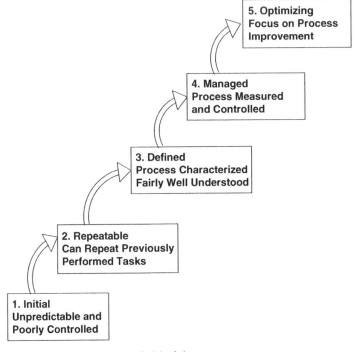

EXHIBIT 11.1 CMMi Maturity Levels Model

The initial CMM said that if a system development organization installs some better key processes, it will improve its operations to move to a next higher level of maturity. That is, an organization can move from the incomplete and unpredictable processes of Level 1 up to Level 2, where processes tend to be repeatable. These five levels of CMM processes are shown in Exhibit 11.1. The sections to come describe each process in greater detail. IT management often is interested in where it stands on these CMM evaluation scales, and internal auditors will find this a useful measure to assess.

CMM is a process model; it can be viewed as the glue that ties people and technology together. It represents a collection of best practices and a framework for organizing and prioritizing activities. Since its initial release, the CMM five-level model has been used by many companies. The SEI's official CMM guidance materials have been updated and expanded to multiple versions for such areas as IT organization services processes (CMMi-SVC) and the software acquisition process (CMMi-ACQ). Today, the model usually is referred to as CMMi to describe its role for IT integration-related processes. This chapter refers to the model as CMMi, although many references in software development literature refer to just the original CMM model.

CMMi is a technical process for improved IT software and other process development. Some IT auditors may ask why it is important. However, CMMi concepts are closely tied to the CobiT framework discussed in Chapter 2, ITIL in Chapter 7, and to other internal audit concepts throughout these chapters. On one level, CMMi is a set of software development processes although many business enterprises today do not do that much of their own IT systems development work. However, it is also a very good model to measure the overall processes in place in an IT organization. Many IT functions set their own internal goals to move their organizations up through the levels of CMMi maturity. An IT auditor working with IT organizations should develop an understanding of this very important CMMi model.

CMMi Level 1: Incomplete, Unpredictable, and Poorly Controlled Processes

An *incomplete* process is one that either is not performed or is only partially performed. One or more of the specific goals of the process area are not satisfied, and no generic goals exist for this level since there is no reason to institutionalize a partially performed process.

In the early days of IT, virtually all systems development efforts and other procedures were run on an ad hoc, seat-of-the-pants basis with very few formal IT development procedures. In those days of mainframe computing, a data processing manager might run into a key user at the water cooler and informally plan some systems change. Rather than using a formal process for requesting new IT projects, the user might ask data processing for a new system or report. Often little was documented. The data processing manager may have made a quick note regarding the request, assigned it to a programmer or analyst, and never discussed the new project until it was complete. The requested report or system may or may not have met the user's needs; it almost never met the user's completion expectations. In addition, generally there were no development standards in place.

This type of scenario was a characteristic of many early IT functions. There were often no established procedures, very little documentation, minimal revision controls, creating what was often an almost chaotic overall IT environment. This was the era of the mid-1960s going through the 1970s when IT was new with few established standard practices. Seemingly, everyone was trying to accomplish lots of things with limited resources.

Over the years, things got better. For example, IBM published a concept it called the systems development life cycle (SDLC) for building new applications. Although not widely adopted at first, this 1960s era standard procedure became the accepted way for designing and developing many new applications. The SDLC terminology and steps have varied over time, and Chapter 10 discusses this application development process from an IT audit perspective. Other procedures, such as revision control, programming standards, and quality assurance standards, were developed later and became widely accepted as the IT application development profession matured.

Unfortunately, some IT functions have not matured much. Although today's new systems are no longer requested and designed over the water cooler, standards and software revision controls often are not good in some IT organizations. These IT functions lack many, if not most, good operating procedures, and systems are developed and operated in an almost chaotic manner. Using CMMi terminology, these are described as Level 1 organizations with incomplete, unpredictable, and poorly controlled processes. The overall philosophy in this type of IT organization is to "just do it" to produce results rather than going through any level of planning or established development processes.

IT organizations today often like to brag that they are CMMi Level 2, Level 3, or higher. While no one wants to admit their IT function is operating at a CMMi Level 1 chaotic state, an IT auditor can often quickly assess when an IT function is operating at such a Level 1. The function will have few standardized procedures, and those that are documented are often not regularly followed.

CMMi Level 1 is the initial phase of the overall CMMi model. The term *incomplete* is appropriate for an IT development group to start at this initial level and improve to higher levels in the overall CMMi model. Each CMMi level is described from a systems development context in terms of (1) the activities performed by the organization, (2) the activities performed by the IT projects, and (3) the resulting process capabilities of the systems development group. These descriptions better describe an IT systems development group at each level of its relative maturity.

Level 1 Activities Performed by the Systems Development Organization

- The systems development group lacks sound management practices with decisions often made on a day-to-day basis.
- Good software engineering and development practices are undermined by ineffective planning and reaction-driven commitments to deliver requested services.

Level 1 Activities Performed in Systems Development Projects

- During any type of crisis, project leadership tends to abandon any planned procedures.
- The lack of sound systems development management practices defeats even strong software engineering development processes.

Level 1 Resulting Software Process Capabilities

- Software processes are ad hoc with unpredictable results because development processes constantly are changed or modified as the work progresses.
- There are few stable software development processes in evidence.

IT auditors of another age sometimes loved the CMMi Level 1 type of organization because their audit report findings and recommendations were so easy. It did not take much work for an IT auditor to write up a set of findings and recommendations in this environment. Often these were merely repeated from an earlier audit. The auditor knew things were chaotic, IT management knew something had to change, but the proper corrective action procedures were never implemented.

The world today is changing. With much information published about CMMi and its recommended approaches, IT managers and even non-IT senior enterprise managers often ask questions about the quality and maturity of their IT organization. Many enterprises have tried to get around this chaotic, unpredictable IT environment by ending all in-house development and relying on purchased software. This approach,

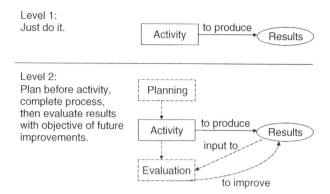

EXHIBIT 11.2 CMMi Level 1 to Level 2 Differences
Source: Robert R. Moeller, *Brink's Modern Internal Auditing,* 6th ed. (Hoboken, NJ: John Wiley & Sons, 2005). Copyright © 2005, John Wiley & Sons. Used with permission of John Wiley & Sons.

however, really does not solve the issue. Purchased software packages can eliminate some problems, but those same packages must be implemented and maintained in an orderly manner. Although many IT groups may never rise much above Level 2 or some aspects of Level 3, most organizations do strive to get above Level 1. Through recommendations and advice, internal audit can help an IT organization to make its processes controlled and predictable.

CMMi Level 2: Repeatable and Consistent Processes

A systems development function should strive to move from the chaotic, unpredictable Level 1 to Level 2. The key defining word for this level is *repeatable.* Rather than doing things in an ad hoc manner, a systems development organization should begin to establish repeatable operating practices. Exhibit 11.2 shows the differences between CMMi Level 1 and Level 2. Rather than just reacting to crises, the systems development organization should devote more attention to planning its activities and then should evaluate results with an objective of process improvement.

Systems development organizations typically do not make an immediate jump from Level 1 to 2 but essentially go through a slow process of adapting various Level 2 processes. The idea with CMMi is to improve systems development processes gradually as an organization becomes more mature. Following the three points raised previously, Level 2 can be described in this way.

Level 2 Activities Performed by the Systems Development Organization

- The systems development organization should establish effective software development policies and procedures.
- Although various specific systems development projects may differ, the systems development function should institutionalize effective project management processes to allow the repetition of successful project management practices developed in earlier projects.

Level 2 Activities Performed in Systems Development Projects

- Realistic IT project commitments should be made based on previous project results and current requirements.
- Processes should be in place to track software costs, schedules, and functionality to identify any problems meeting commitments.
- Control requirements and work products should ensure that project standards are being followed.

Level 2 Resulting Software Process Capabilities

- The software development process capability should be disciplined such that there are stable project planning and tracking processes in place and that earlier successes can be repeated.
- The project management process should be under the effective control of a project management system that follows realistic plans.

Level 2 and beyond requires the effective installation of a series of what CMMi calls key process areas (KPAs). These define the detailed processes necessary in each level and to get to Level 2 and beyond, Level 2's KPAs are:

- CMMi Level 2 KPA requirements management processes
- CMMi Level 2 KPA requirements for software project planning
- CMMi Level 2 KPA requirements for software tracking and oversight
- CMMi Level 2 KPA requirements for software quality assurance
- CMMi Level 2 KPA requirements for software configuration management
- CMMi Level 2 KPA requirements for software subcontract management

CMMi Level 2 KPA Requirements Management Processes

This software development process covers both the technical and customer requirements of software about to be developed and implemented. It is not unusual for an application development group to implement a software application without a full understanding of what the application is supposed to accomplish as well as its overall functional specifications. The CMMi requirements management process calls for IT developers to install formal processes defining the requirements of IT development efforts with these KPA objectives:

- To ensure that the requirements for software products—both new applications being developed and other software tools—are defined and understood
- To establish and maintain agreement on the requirements with all information services requestors: users, customers, and other interested parties
- To ensure that the requirements are met

Requirements should be documented and controlled to establish a basis for software development and project management use. Changes to requirements should be documented and controlled to ensure that plans, deliverables, and all related activities are consistent with these requirements. Good project management practices are discussed as part of the process description later in this chapter and in Chapter 16.

CMMi Level 2 KPA Requirements for Software Project Planning

In addition to the project management processes discussed in Chapter 16, the KPAs here call for documented estimates of the size, cost, and schedule for use in planning and tracking all software development projects. All affected groups or individuals involved in a software development effort should receive information on commitments and agreements regarding the project. In addition, the project should follow a formal management process for project planning with adequate tracking and status reporting, including measurements for the completion of milestones.

This CMMi project management KPA calls for a much higher level of detailed project planning and tracking than is used by many IT organizations. IT auditors should consider using this KPA as a standard for assessing the progress of IT development when reviewing the management of selected IT projects. Exhibit 11.3 summarizes audit procedures for an IT audit review of IT project management key processes.

CMMi Level 2 KPA Requirements for Software Tracking and Oversight

The purpose of a formal project tracking process is to monitor a project's actual progress against its plan. Monitoring is accomplished by collecting significant information about schedule, resources, costs, features, and quality and comparing this information to the

---

1. Determine that documented estimates are in place for planning and tracking all IT systems development projects.
2. Processes should be in place for documenting activities and commitments surrounding all significant project activities.
3. All affected groups involved in project development processes should provide commitment agreements regarding their projects.
4. Project planning should follow documented and approved organizational project-planning policies.
5. Management processes should be in place to track the status of all project-planning activities.
6. All project costs and activity schedules actual results should be tracked and compared with estimates in project plans.
7. Processes should be in place to initiate corrective actions when results differ significantly from project plans.
8. Project progress should be regularly tracked against the planned schedules, effort, and budgets.
9. Senior management should review project-tracking status on a regular basis.
10. Ongoing programs of corrective actions, based on lessons learned, should be in place.

EXHIBIT 11.3   KPA Status Review IT Audit Procedures
Source: Robert R. Moeller, *Brink's Modern Internal Auditing*, 6th ed. (Hoboken, NJ: John Wiley & Sons, 2005). Copyright © 2005, John Wiley & Sons. Adapted with permission of John Wiley & Sons.

original and currently approved project plan. The objectives of the CMMi software tracking and oversight KPA are:

- The process should include the information needed to conduct periodic project planning status meetings and reviews.
- Project managers and management should be provided with sufficient information to make data-based business decisions.
- The tracking process should provide information to assist future projects in their estimation and planning efforts.

In many respects, the project tracking process is a by-product of the project management review KPA process.

CMMi Level 2 KPA Requirements for Software Quality Assurance

The purpose of this KPA is to provide management with appropriate visibility into the processes used and the software products being built. This KPA involves reviewing and auditing software products and activities to ensure that they comply with applicable procedures and standards. The objectives of the software quality assurance KPA are:

- All software quality assurance activities should be planned with their plans reviewed and approved by appropriate levels of management.
- Software products and activities should adhere to applicable standards, procedures, and requirements.
- Software quality noncompliance issues that cannot be resolved with a given project should be addressed by senior management.

CMMi Level 2 KPA Requirements for Software Configuration Management

This KPA relates to establishing and maintaining the integrity of all software process products throughout their life cycle. The scope of configuration management involves identifying and controlling configuration items and units. This is similar to the ITIL configuration management process discussed in Chapter 7. In addition, the scope of this KPA includes systematically controlling all changes to active configurations as well as maintaining their integrity and traceability throughout their software life cycles. The goals of this KPA are:

- Software configuration activities should be planned.
- Changes to software work products should be formally identified and controlled.
- Configuration baselines should be established and affected groups and individuals should be informed of their status and content.

CMMi Level 2 KPA Requirements for Software Subcontract Management

The purpose of the subcontract management KPA is to select qualified subcontractors and to manage them effectively. The scope of this KPA includes processes for selecting appropriate software subcontractors, establishing commitments with those subcontractors, and tracking and reviewing subcontractor performance and results. An IT organization should have the following KPA goals and activities:

- Select only qualified software subcontractors.
- The prime contractor and the subcontractors should formally agree to their commitments and obligations to each other.
- The prime contractor should track actual results and performance against commitments.

CMMi Level 3: Defined and Predictable Processes

As we move up the systems development process improvement chain, CMMi Level 3 calls for am IT organization to use lessons learned to provide inputs to the planning and evaluation processes as well as to improve results. Called the CMMi defined level, this improved systems development level has the following characteristics.

Level 3 Activities Performed by the Systems Development Organization

- Strong documentation should be in place for the organization's standard processes for maintaining and developing software.
- Processes should be in place to integrate project management and software engineering/systems development activities to exploit effective IT system development.
- There should be ongoing support for each of the KPAs within this and other levels, including a training program to ensure skills development.

Level 3 Activities Performed in Systems Development Projects

- Projects should tailor standard software processes to develop an organization's own defined project software processes.
- Because the software process has become well defined, management should have good insights into the technical progress of all projects.

Level 3 Resulting Software Process Capabilities

- This software process capability should be standard and consistent because both software engineering and management activities are stable and repeatable.
- Costs, schedule, and functionality should be under control with the software quality tracked.

Although Level 3 here calls for IT systems development activities such as cost and schedule management, a move from Level 2 to Level 3 is often difficult. CMMi Level 3 calls for a software development organization to achieve a much higher level of organization coordination. Few organizations are able to achieve a CMMi Level 3 that contains the next SEI-defined KPAs.

CMMi Level 3 KPA Requirements for an Organizational Process Focus

This KPA calls for the organization to raise the overall importance of the software development process. All too often, IT auditors are faced with answers like "I don't know; that was an IT management decision" when asked why certain application controls are not performing with adequate control considerations. The scope of this KPA involves developing and maintaining an understanding of software development and related project processes throughout the enterprise. To operate at CMMi Level 3, there should be coordination throughout the organization to assess, develop, maintain, and improve these processes.

CMMi Level 3 KPA Requirements for an Organizational Process Definition

Very similar to the process focus of most KPAs, the purpose of this KPA is to integrate project software engineering and management activities that improve software process performance and provide a basis for cumulative, long-term benefits. The goal is to develop and maintain a standard software development processes where the data surrounding those activities are collected, reviewed, and adjusted for ongoing improvements. As a step beyond the normal software development process, attention should be devoted to ongoing improvements.

CMMi Level 3 KPA Requirements for Training Programs and Intergroup Coordination

This KPA calls for an ongoing software development training program to enhance the skills and knowledge of individuals so they can perform their roles effectively and efficiently. It also requires disciplined interaction and coordination of all project and software engineering groups within the organization. This Level 3 training KPA should be planned to support training needs of IT projects, the organization, and individuals. This intergroup coordination KPA calls for customer or end-user requirements to be recognized and agreed to by all groups. All related issues should be identified, tracked, and resolved on an intergroup basis.

CMMi Level 3 KPA Requirements for Peer Reviews

Sometimes difficult to launch, peer reviews involve the methodical and systematic examination of work products by other common or peer-level members of a software development team to identify defects and areas where changes are needed. The goal here is to establish a process that will identify defects in the software development process early and efficiently.

CMMi Level 3 KPA Requirements for Integrated Software Management

This KPA calls for aggressively integrating the organization's software engineering and management activities into coherent and defined software processes, tailored to the organization's software assets. Although defined as a separate CMMi KPA, this really says an organization should give particular attention to software development planning and coordination.

CMMi Level 3 KPA Requirements for Software Product Engineering

The software development process should consistently perform software development activities as a well-defined engineering process that integrates all software development activities in a manner to produce correct, consistent software products effectively and efficiently. Although CMMi is tailored to the consulting groups or software development type of organization that wishes to release a range of quality products to outside customers, these same concepts should exist for internal IT groups. The goal should be to develop and implement high-quality software in a consistent manner.

CMMi Level 4: Managed, Measured, and Controlled Processes

CMMi compliance becomes a very difficult challenge to a software development organization as it moves up to Levels 4 and 5. Level 4 calls for an organization to begin predicting the results needed and creating opportunities to get those results. Exhibit 11.4 describes CMMi Level 4 activities where a software development organization should attempt to predict needed and expected results and then to create opportunities to get those results.

Level 4 Activities Performed by the Systems Development Organization

- The systems development organization should set quality goals for both software products and processes.
- There should be measures of productivity and quality for all important software process activities across all projects as part of an organizational measurement program.
- The systems development organization should provide a foundation for quantitative systems development evaluations.

Level 4 Activities Performed in Systems Development Projects

- Projects should achieve control over their products and processes by narrowing the variation in their process performance to fall within acceptable boundaries.
- The risks of moving up the learning curve if a new application domain are known and carefully managed.

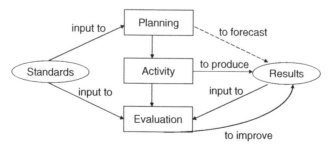

EXHIBIT 11.4   CMMi Level 4 Activities
Source: Robert R. Moeller, *Brink's Modern Internal Auditing*, 6th ed. (Hoboken, NJ: John Wiley & Sons, 2005). Copyright © 2005, John Wiley & Sons. Adapted with permission of John Wiley & Sons.

Level 4 Resulting Software Process Capabilities

- Software process capability should be predictable because the process is measured and operates within measurable limits.
- Allowances should be made for predictive trends in process and quality within quantitative bounds to allow for corrective action when any limits are exceeded.

Two specific KPA areas have been identified at this level: qualitative process management and software quality management. Their emphasis is to integrate software development activities throughout the organization.

CMMi Level 5: Optimizing Processes

Level 5 is the maximum, best practices level of CMMi. It is difficult to implement and achieve. When an enterprise has reached Level 5, it is often a case for a press release. Few enterprises have honestly achieved this level to date. Level 5 calls for an enterprise to install self-correcting mechanisms that are implemented in such a way that activities are improved constantly and continuously. The emphasis is very much on defect prevention throughout the organization and the aggressive and active management of changes.

Level 5 Activities Performed by the Systems Development Organization

- The entire organization should be focused on continuous process improvement with the goal of defect prevention.
- Data should be used for cost-benefit analysis of new technology and new process changes.
- Innovations in systems development and software engineering practices should be transferred to the entire organization.

Level 5 Activities Performed in Systems Development Projects

- Project teams should analyze defects and determine their causes.
- Project teams should evaluate processes to prevent known types of defects from recurring.

Level 5 Resulting Software Process Capabilities

- Software process capability should be improving continuously because the organization improves the range of capability and process performance of its software development projects.
- Improvements should occur both by incremental advancement of existing processes and by innovations using new technologies and methods.

CMMI BENEFITS

CMMi had its origins as a tool for improving systems development processes. This chapter has described the original IT systems development CMMi model and its levels and KPAs. Many enterprises today are not involved in heavy software development initiatives, and the other CMMi models for services or acquisition may be more appropriate. No matter what the overall enterprise objectives, however, the CMMi model provides a place to start improving processes as an enterprise moves from the unstructured Level 1 to an environment of more refined processes. It is a framework to help an enterprise develop a better shared vision, a common language, and a way to define process improvement throughout an organization.

Although CMMi got its start with government contract software developers, it has been implemented by many IT development organizations today. CMMi's roots are very much tied to the American Society for Quality quality assurance standards discussed in Chapter 31. The SEI maintains CMMi standards and publishes guidance and training materials and process-related standards.

As an example of CMMi potential benefits, this author became heavily involved with CMMi several years ago at a large U.S. insurance company where he was working on a contract basis as a project manager. The project involved a large systems implementation involving some new development work as well as extensive modification to existing systems. The company had published extensive IT procedures, but because of a very casual management approach, those procedures often were not followed. For example, this author found breakdowns in such relatively simple but important tasks as software revision control. Two programmers, for example, sometimes attempted to make changes to copies of the same program source code version. The result, of course, would be two incompatible software versions.

Although there are other ways to remedy such problems, this author suggested that the insurance company adopt CMMi processes. The effort began with some internal seminars to the IT staff on the CMMi process improvement model, explaining its benefits and outlining that the organization was in a Level 1 chaotic state of operations. With lots of training and guidance, we were able to bring the operating unit from an unstructured Level 1 to a solid Level 2 with some Level 3 KPAs completed during the author's project period.

IT AUDIT, INTERNAL CONTROL, AND CMMI

The CMMi model describes a process for improved quality software development for organizations. Although some aspects of CMMi and supporting published materials often seem tailored to the software development organization developing products for external customers, with an emphasis on major government contractors, the core CMMi model is an effective way to think about how an organization is performing and what steps it should take to improve processes. Even though a development group may not be directly focused on CMMi, an IT auditor can use this model to evaluate current performance and to recommend areas for future improvements.

What does an organization need to do to claim that it is operating at some CMMi level? The chapter describes some of the specific and important KPAs required to make any such claim. However, an organization must go through some extensive process improvement along with supporting documentation to assert that it is operating at a specific CMMi level. An organization should contract with certified registrars to review their processes and certify their CMMi level. This is particularly important if an organization needs to document its status for contract purposes.

The typical IT auditor will not have the knowledge to appraise whether the IT organization being audited is operating at CMMi Level 2 or 3, or whether it has installed and implemented the correct mix of KPAs. However, an IT auditor should have a general understanding of CMMi, as described in this chapter, and be able to ask appropriate questions if the organization reviewed is operating with CMMi processes.

Perhaps most important, when an IT auditor reviews an IT development group with very poor internal controls that are really operating at a CMMi Level 1, he or she might recommend that the IT group look at CMMi as a method to improve processes and develop better internal controls. The effective implementation of CMMi is a good way for an organization to improve its internal controls. Although most organizations will never reach CMMi Level 5, each level points to important processes for improved internal controls.

 NOTE

1. Unified Modeling Language (UML) is a standardized general-purpose modeling language in the field of software engineering. UML includes a set of graphic notation techniques to create visual models of software-intensive systems. For more information, consult www. uml-forum.com

CHAPTER TWELVE

Auditing Service-Oriented Architectures and Record Management Processes

A NY PROFESSIONAL WHO HAS been working with information technology (IT) hardware and software for more than a few years knows that IT technologies and techniques are always changing and evolving. What was a hot new concept just a few years ago sometimes disappears to be replaced by something new and different. In other cases, concepts that once seemed too advanced or even strange evolve into normal accepted practices. Client-server computer system configurations are an example of the latter. What was once a new and advanced concept in the 1990s is now a standard 1 IT process. Managing IT applications through service-oriented architecture (SOA) is another relatively new concept that will soon become part of the standard language of IT.

SOA is an IT systems approach where an application's business logic or individual functions are modularized and presented as services for consumer/client applications. A key concept is that the actual IT services provided are loosely coupled and independent of the actual application implementation. As a result, developers or system integrators can build applications by composing one or more services without knowing the underlying implementations of those services. For example, a service can be implemented in an advanced development language such as what is called dot-NET or Java, and the application consuming the service can be on a different platform or language.

This chapter introduces SOA concepts for the IT auditor and discusses internal control and IT auditor issues surrounding the development and operations of IT applications using this technology. SOA is not yet that much of an IT audit professional hot-button issue, with the Web site of the Information Systems Audit and Control Association (ISACA) only offering one other author's book on the subject but the current Web site of the Institute of Internal

Auditors (IIA) offers none, although it is a strongly evolving concept for IT applications development and implementations. IT auditors should have a general understanding of the controls and concepts surrounding SOA implementations.

The chapter also reviews the importance of effective records management systems in today's enterprises and IT environments. Today, almost all business records are created and most live their entire lives electronically. Failure to manage electronic records and physical records in accordance with established records management principles is to turn a blind eye to potential risk. This chapter also concludes with an overview of records management issues from an internal controls and IT audit perspective.

SERVICE-ORIENTED COMPUTING AND SERVICE-DRIVEN APPLICATIONS

Hardware and software vendors, as well as high-level software application developers, often use similar but slightly different terms to describe IT system concepts. We may encounter such expressions as service-oriented architectures, service-oriented design, and object-oriented design when hearing about the attributes of some new IT application. These expressions sound alike and generally reflect similar approaches to the manner in which IT applications are built and launched in our Web-oriented world today. In this chapter, we generally use the expression service-oriented architecture or SOA to describe this concept even though computer science purists may differ on some terminology details.

SOA is an IT architectural style whose goal is to achieve loose coupling among interacting software agents. It is an approach that allows interoperability between different IT systems and programming languages, providing the basis for integration between applications on different platforms through messages across network communication links. The software is built following both common and industry-specific components that are granular and modular. A service is a unit of work done by a service provider to achieve desired end results for a service consumer. Software agents play both provider and consumer roles on behalf of their owners.

The Web is filled with many often complex and sometimes differing definitions of SOA, and the definition here may be too abstract, but an IT auditor should not consider SOA as a difficult concept. Music CDs and CD players model SOA concepts. If you want to play a CD, for instance, you put your CD into a CD player, and the player broadcasts it for you. The CD player offers a CD music-playing service. When the CD ends, you can replace one music CD for another. You can also play the same music CD on a portable player or on a unit in your automobile. Both offer the same CD-playing service, but the quality of service may be different. The results of the CD music-playing service may result in a change of state for the listening consumer, perhaps a mood change from depressed to happy. We are the service client, the CD player is the service provider, and our music library of CDs acts as service broker.

Just as the CD player gives us prerecorded music, we hire someone else to provide services or do the work for us in other areas because they have the available resources and are experts. Consuming a service is usually cheaper and more effective than doing

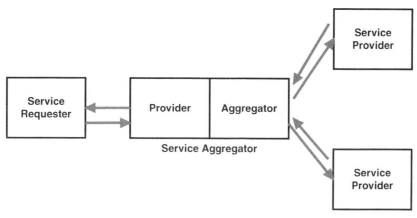

EXHIBIT 12.1 Role of the Service Aggregator

the work ourselves. Most of us realize that we are not smart enough to be experts in everything. The same rule applies to building software systems.

This concept of using the music service of a personal CD player from a library of music CDs leads to SOA concepts. The service is the basic building block of SOA; it is a way of accessing repeatable business capabilities, organized as simple software interfaces available for all providers and consumers. Exhibit 12.1 shows this basic concept of an SOA configuration with a service aggregator. The service requestor requests services from a provider who is an aggregator with a catalog of available service offerings, who will pull the request from any of multiple service providers, who return the service to the requestor and then to the provider.

If an SOA is to be effective, we need a clear understanding of the term *service*. A service is a function that is well defined, self-contained, and does not depend on the context or state of other services. Services are the building blocks of SOA and can be snapped together to make other services or assembled in sequences to make processes.

In SOA, services are usually organized in what is called a *registry*, where separate services can be snapped together to create composite applications and then fitted together into what is called an SOA blueprint. IT auditors generally encounter SOA efforts when performing an overall review of enterprise general controls, as discussed in Chapter 6, or reviewing specific application controls. While our objective is not to make an IT auditor into a computer scientist or software developer, several important SOA concepts that an IT auditor may encounter when discussing SOA processes are discussed next.

- **SOA component granularity** describes the size of the components that make up a system. An SOA implementation would try to achieve larger, or coarsely grained, components known as business services. These usually are be built out of smaller, or fine-grained, components as well as preexisting technical services. This set of components matters because chunks of larger granularity make SOA services easier for an enterprise to understand, reuse, and manage.
- **Interface versus implementation concepts** separate *what* a service does from *how* it does it. This issue matters because it simplifies the concept that the business

user's view of SOA should focus on what the service will do rather than the details of how the technology works under the hood (to use an automobile analogy).

▪ **Contracts** define the obligations between the service provider and service consumer or requestor. Obligations can include service expectations such as availability, reliability, and key performance indicators, as well as service cost and support. This definition of obligations matters because it helps business users make rational decisions about which services they can rely on. These concepts are similar to the service-level agreements (SLAs) discussed in Chapter 7.

▪ **Loose coupling** is a way of designing services that are more flexible and less dependent on each other. This method helps services to snap together or couple and recombine. An SOA environment with loose coupling matters because it is faster to assemble business solutions out of premade blocks than it is to write every new business functions from scratch.

Adopting SOA in an enterprise is not a one-application-at-a-time process but describes an overall architecture where all IT processes are organized together and connected. Services provided with Web applications where a user just double-clicks to pull up an HTML reference are an example of an SOA concept. Exhibit 12.2 illustrates a hypothetical enterprise-wide SOA configuration.

At the lower lever of the exhibit are enterprise data sources and other multiplatform systems. All elements here would be defined as services such that a custom application, for example, might be built of a combination of mainframe/legacy and Web application

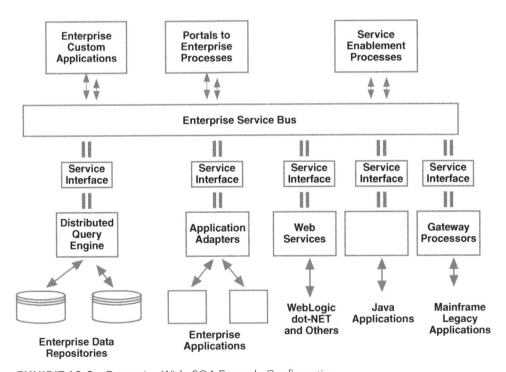

EXHIBIT 12.2 Enterprise-Wide SOA Example Configuration

components and assembled with the requests through a service bus to the proper adaptor and application. When any of those application services need an element of data—another service—a request would go up to the communication bus and back to the appropriate data source. Such an overall application would be built using some of the newer application software development tools, such as Microsoft's dot-NET[1] or Oracle's BEA WebLogic[2] and would be configured and orchestrated in clearly specified processes.

An IT auditor does not find a full SOA environment in most enterprises. Rather, an enterprise IT function, with management support, typically implements their SOA environment on a step-by-step basis following an overall blueprint to build that model. With the growing use of Web services surrounding most IT environments and software sold and delivered as individual program components rather than as full applications, IT auditors can expect to see partial and even full SOA implementations going forward.

SOA Internal Control Issues and Risks

An enterprise does not just move to an SOA IT environment by purchasing a SOA featured software package, training the IT staff, and then assuming they are off and running. SOA is more than just a new way of organizing existing IT systems. Detailed planning and new IT policies and procedures are required to move to that new environment. Even more important, such a transition requires a gradual and very structured implementation where IT processes are brought into an SOA environment in a controlled manner. In some cases, the advantages of SOA operations will be obvious to senior managers and others. For example, an enterprise that has moved a large segment of its applications to a Java or dot-NET Web-based environment often can easily justify the advantages of moving its legacy applications and other processes to an SOA environment.

IT auditors can play a strong role in reviewing processes and helping their enterprise management and IT functions transition to SOA processes. Part of doing this requires that an IT auditor understand the preimplementation review processes, as discussed in Chapter 10, be comfortable with auditing Chapter 7's IT infrastructure controls in an SOA environment, and understand good project management controls, as discussed in Chapter 16. An IT auditor needs to understand the somewhat unique characteristics of SOA and its control issues and risks. This chapter briefly discusses implementing effective SOA processes from an IT audit perspective. The next sections discuss the importance of building a planning blueprint for an SOA implementation, cleaning up existing applications and processes in advance, establishing appropriate SOA policies and procedures, and testing and implementing SOA in an effective manner.

Planning and Building an SOA Implementation Blueprint

The third letter of SOA stands for architecture, and the building of an effective architecture is an essential early step to launch SOA in an enterprise. Even if the enterprise chief information officer (CIO) has been exposed to SOA concepts or if the enterprise has implemented an SOA-like single application that gained enthusiastic comments and praise, an enterprise still needs to build an overall framework to launch any SOA process implementation.

The key to an effective SOA is to identify an existing plan or build this service set of procedures using blocks that will define the SOA similar to a series of LEGO® building blocks.[3] The blocks of these popular children's toys can be interconnected in a variety of elaborate structures and then disassembled to build a different structure. However, SOA services are more complex than LEGO blocks that are built in cubical and triangular shapes; SOA services are much broader and generally may have many different dimensions.

A key process here is to define the various service elements and the service stakeholders, including the flow of activities and decision points between the stakeholders involved in the process, in this way:

- **Business owner.** The business owner provides the application requirements for a new business capability, solution, or process to be implemented. A business owner or supporting IT staff members should develop process models to make any understanding of IT implementation service requirements easier. The business owner also needs to define nonfunctional requirements, such as expected quality of the service, for the capability, solution, or process.
- **SOA architect.** In order to launch an SOA initiative, an enterprise needs to designate a skilled SOA architect to analyze the business requirements and break them into service and process designs. The SOA architect may decide, for example, to reuse existing components rather than create new ones. When such an architect proposes a new or changed services or process implementations, this SOA architect also should deliver design specifications in terms of state diagrams, process models, and interface designs. The SOA architect formalizes the nonfunctional requirements of the component to be implemented, including its availability, security, and performance requirements.
- **Application developer.** A developer implements components based on the design specifications delivered by the SOA architect and creates test plans based on these specifications. To aid in the convergence of technology and methodology, an application developer should use parts generated by the SOA architect for implementation, including code generation or model refinements.
- **Quality manager.** A team member designated as the quality manager uses the input provided by the business owner, architect, and developer to review the correctness of the service or process that was implemented. This topic is discussed in more detail in Chapter 31. A quality manager then uses the test plans provided by the developer to execute a solution test in a staging environment and validates quality metrics, side effects, and nonfunctional characteristics.

Once a key team had been identified, the enterprise should develop an SOA blueprint that indicates a target state or a complete picture of what the SOA implementation should look like when it is completed. The SOA blueprint should outline a complete list of these necessary components:

- Business services
- Service description requirements
- Service performance metrics

Improve Business Visibility. Integrate systems and aggregate data for a consistent, accurate views of customers, including:
- Up-to-the-minute information for improved customer service
- Cross-enterprise information for targeted 1:1 activities
- Consistent, accurate, and more comprehensive information for better decision making

Achieve Business Flexibility. Create an integrated, agile software infrastructure for quickly responding to business needs:
- Provide rapid delivery of new business capabilities.
- Reduce impact of business and technology changes.
- Protect investments while creating new functionality.

Gain Business Efficiency. Streamline, automate, and enable the better tracking and visibility of enterprise business processes:
- Securely share business processes inside and outside the IT systems firewall.
- Bridge silos of data to better ensure data integrity.
- Proactively manage business decisions with key performance indicators from other sources.

EXHIBIT 12.3   Service-Oriented Architecture Key Benefits

- Interoperability standards
- Data schemas
- Policies
- Service discovery and classification requirements

Such a blueprint provides an overall outline of where enterprise and general IT management want to go with SOA. Of course, an enterprise should not begin to implement or even approve an SOA strategy unless there is a good understanding of the benefits to be achieved from the approach. Exhibit 12.3 describes some of the key benefits that an enterprise should realize from moving to an SOA environment.

Transitioning Current Applications and Processes to SOA

The transition of existing processes or applications to an SOA environment, whether older legacy systems or more recent Web-based applications, contains some of the same challenges older professionals went through when we approached the Y2K problem in the late 1990s. Although some may have now forgotten, many COBOL-based programs had system calendar date fields in a yymmdd format and many program decisions based on taking action by sorting on dates. The year 2000 caused those date-based program decisions to be recorded as 0000. The Y2K concern was that many systems would fail because of bad, out-of-sequence program dates, and at the time, many older applications were poorly documented. IT functions and IT auditors went through major efforts to get ready for Y2K, and we face some of these same concerns when reviewing and cleaning up existing processes to transition to SOA operations.

The concern with a transition to SOA is not undocumented yymmdd-format COBOL dates; rather, the typical IT function has layers of IT applications and programs, redundant and often mutually inaccessible systems, and much jumbled point-to-point integrations for its applications. These problems represent major challenges to implementing effective SOA processes. If any team implementing enterprise-wide SOA does not understand their existing IT systems, processes, and organization structures, there is a strong possibility that a poorly executed SOA implementation will fail.

SOA Policies and Procedures

The overall concept and beauty of SOA is its use of service units that can be assembled and reassembled like LEGO blocks. However, SOA will not work very well for an enterprise if one or another business decides it wants to be bit different and that its service units do not really fit with others. Using our LEGO block example, in this case some unit would want its blocks to be of a size that does not fit with any others.

There are often reasons why one or another unit needs to be different (e.g., high security issues). Nevertheless, an enterprise normally needs some type of standards-setting authority to establish policies and set the rules for its SOA services.

For many enterprises, governing bodies that create and enforce SOA policies and enterprise standards are typically called the *SOA centers of excellence* or *SOA competency centers*. These centers often consist of representatives from each business unit affected by the enterprise's SOA blueprint and plans. Almost every part of an enterprise SOA blueprint—including which services will be built, how they will be defined, and how they will interoperate—implicitly defines the SOA policies for an enterprise. Because the SOA blueprint typically contains many implicit policies, the first act of a newly constituted SOA competency center should be to ratify this blueprint as a shared goal.

Of course, it is important for each affected enterprise group to understand and agree to the implications of the SOA blueprint as it impacts their daily work activities. For that reason, ratifying an SOA blueprint should not be just a rubber-stamp activity. Everyone involved should think through how this SOA vision will affect them.

An enterprise should develop compliance procedures to monitor and assess the enforcement of its SOA policies and processes. Doing this establishes rules of the road and provides governance for SOA activities, based on the approved blueprint. Automated enforcement processes, where they can be established, are preferable to manual ones. However, not all policies can be automated, and some steps may require human judgment and intervention.

Proper SOA governance covers multiple enforcement points across the entire service life cycle. Exhibit 12.4 describes the roles and responsibilities of key persons involved in implementing SOA and being part of its life cycle. SOA policies and processes usually are divided into two categories: Design-time governance policies should ensure that SOA artifacts meet the design requirements set forth in the SOA blueprint, and runtime governance policies should ensure that SOA services meet the runtime requirements negotiated between service provider and consumer. These SOA governance processes are somewhat like the service-level agreements (SLAs) discussed in Chapter 7, where IT operations formally agrees to provide a user group input transactions according to an agreed-on schedule and IT delivers file updates and completed processes according to the contracted schedule. With SOA, we are making a series of small agreements between service providers and consumers.

The SOA life cycle describes and implements a flow of activities and decision points between the stakeholders involved in this process. It should recognize these key participants:

▪ **Business owner.** The business owner provides the requirements for a new business capability, solution, or process to be implemented. The best way to express these requirements is to define a supporting process model covering the service activity. Using process models provides an environment that makes understanding IT implementation requirements easier. The business owner also needs to define nonfunctional requirements (such as quality of service) for the capability, solution, or process.

▪ **SOA architect.** The SOA architect, often part of the IT team, analyzes the business requirements and breaks them into service and process design elements. The architect may decide to reuse an existing component rather than create a new one, in which case he or she will decide to turn the requirement into an element in the SOA life cycle to reuse the existing component. When a new or changed service or process implementation is identified, the SOA architect delivers design specifications in terms of state diagrams, process models, and interface designs. The SOA architect formalizes the nonfunctional requirements (NFRs) of the component to be implemented including availability, security, and performance.

▪ **SOA developer.** The developer implements components based on the design specifications delivered by the SOA architect and also creates test plans based on the specifications. To aid the convergence of technology and methodology, the developer uses the parts generated by the SOA architect for implementation, including code generation and model refinement tools.

▪ **SOA quality manager.** The quality manager uses the input provided by the business owner, architect, and developer to review the correctness of the service or process that was implemented. The quality manager then uses the test plans provided by the developer to execute a solution test in a staging environment and validates quality metrics, side effects, and nonfunctional characteristics.

▪ **SOA operator.** An SOA operator receives the tested and validated solutions and implements them within the standard IT processes in order for the solution to be made available to solution users and consumers. He or she uses the formalized NFR specifications to operate a virtualized solution that complies with the SLAs required by the consumers. SOA runtime governance solutions provide these kinds of capabilities by enforcing the NFRs and SLAs.

EXHIBIT 12.4 SOA Life Cycle Stakeholders

SOA Design-Time Policies

SOA design-time policies and processes are designed to ensure that services are built to meet the specifications outlined in the SOA blueprint. In particular, policies should be tailored to constrain the behavior of service designers and developers on behalf of the whole SOA effort in these broad areas:

▪ **Interoperability.** An SOA blueprint should declare a uniform method of providing interoperability among services, typically by ratifying a set of standards.

▪ **Discoverability.** Services may require specific attributes such as a business-friendly description and information regarding the location of the service within an established classification or registry catalog. These elements make it possible to discover services that can be further defined through policy.

▪ **Security.** The SOA blueprint should declare a uniform means to provide security across SOA services. The style and parameters of this security should be consistent with overall enterprise IT security practices, as discussed in Chapter 19.

■ **Uniqueness.** Services should not have the same name as preexisting services. This area often is governed by an SOA attribute or mechanism called a *namespace*. Policies can help ensure that groups do not run into this problem of duplicate names.

■ **Interface compliance.** All SOA services should be used or initiated in a uniform way. Although SOA services are more than just IT program elements, this process is similar to a Microsoft Windows RUN command. This standard form of interface should be mandated by policy.

■ **Data format compliance.** As discussed, a major objective of SOA should be the reusability of its service elements, and a way to endure reusability is to establish common data formats known as *schemas*. Doing so ensures that an address field in one service can be used properly by another service, even if differences exist in how the services store the data. Common schemas should be mandated by policy.

■ **Metrics.** Statistical information and reporting of service design issues also should be set by policy. An enterprise, and certainly IT audit, cannot measure the effectiveness of SOA operations unless some metrics have been established as both goals and minimum operating performance standards.

Design-time SOA processes should typically connect with the enterprise's system development life cycle (SDLC). The SDLC process was discussed in Chapter 10, and a similar service development life cycle can be developed here.

SOA adoption presents challenges to enterprises that are accustomed to using IT implementations to address application requirements. New structures and processes, often referred to as the *SOA life cycle*, are required that provide the basis for organizational agility and promote successful SOA adoption. SOA life cycle processes, combined with effective organizational structures, become key elements in launching effective SOA processes.

Most modern IT departments are under pressure to deliver cost-effective and timely solutions to their business. To achieve these goals, they use shared technical and organizational components and functions as well as cross-project initiatives to strengthen synergies across departments. When these solutions are combined with an enterprise mind-set to deliver services (as in a valuable service and not as in technology), an IT function can find itself on a path to effective SOA processes.

As part of this path to SOA, adoption requires that all parties—IT and management—think in terms of value chains and understand that service is something that exists to deliver consumer satisfaction. Admittedly easier said than effectively implemented, an enterprise needs to break its application-centric thinking by implementing structured processes that cross project boundaries and life cycles. When an open mind-set, methodology, people and organization, and technology are combined successfully, SOA adoption can lead to great benefits for an IT function and the overall enterprise in terms of scale, efficiency, and especially agility.

SOA Runtime Policies and Processes

Runtime governance policies will reduced political friction in an enterprise because they mostly constrain IT systems on behalf of SOA service consumers. For the most part, runtime policies exist to ensure that services behave in the ways they are supposed to, based on expectations of the service consumer. This set of policies and processes includes:

- **Service-level agreements.** SOA providers and consumers should agree on performance expectations as well as on measurements that confirm that the services are performing as expected.
- **Authentication.** Providers and consumers also should agree on how service consumers should identify themselves. Based on runtime governance standards, authentication should include such issues as the identity systems and security tokens used.
- **Authorization.** Processes should be in place to determine if a provider is allowed to invoke a service.
- **Encryption.** There should be encryption standards to keep messages coded or scrambled so they will not be read by the wrong people.
- **Signatures.** Digital signature mechanisms should be considered to ensure that messages are sent by valid providers and consumers and are not tampered with during transit. Some of the challenges of digital signatures are discussed in Chapter 17.
- **Alerts and notifications.** Conditions should be established to trigger alerts with procedures to send them to proper authorities. Alerts can signify both business and technical conditions.
- **Metrics.** Runtime key performance indicators and measurements should be established to drive decisions are set by policy.

Runtime policies typically constrain the IT operations team and IT systems on behalf of the service consumer. These processes can include support requests and responses to real-time alerts and notifications. Enabling a more responsive request to changing runtime conditions is an important value in an SOA environment.

SOA Policy Enforcement Checkpoints

Like the customs checkpoint at a border that checks passports and luggage, SOA governance sets up checkpoints to ensure that agreements between organizations are enforced. These checkpoints should include:

- **SOA registry repository.** A facility should be in place to serve as the enforcement point for SOA design-time policies and processes.
- **SOA runtime management system.** The controlling software system should have facilities to serve as the enforcement point for SOA runtime policies and processes. Virtual services are an ideal place to implement operational requirements or quality of service features, such as:
  - **Message validation.** SOA system messages should be well-formed and conform to the expectation of the service interface.
  - **Authentication and authorization.** Service messages should be organized to identify the service consumer to ensure that they are authorized to invoke the service and other important operational requirements.
  - **Message encryption and signature operational requirements.** Processes should decrypt messages, as required, and verify signatures.

▪ **Failover and load balancing.** As an important control facility that should be of particular interest to IT auditors, there should be sufficient capacity to support transaction load and service availability.

▪ **Message routing.** The managing SOA software should have strong facilities for forwarding messages to different service implementations based on the content or context of messages.

▪ **Monitoring and SLAs.** We have emphasized the importance of SLAs in several places in our discussion of SOA processes. Well-defined and monitored SLAs keep an eye on service health and performance and ensure that services are delivered as promised to consumers.

The SOA requirements mentioned here change far more frequently than just the functional logic of a service. IT auditors should realize that a core mission of SOA governance is to promote and ensure desirable behavior among its participant people and systems. IT management must clearly communicate its SOA policies and then must enforce those policies consistently throughout the SOA life cycle.

In the early days of SOA, IT architects would spend weeks or even months painstakingly documenting policies in fat books that no one read. This is similar to the early IT disaster recovery plans discussed in Chapter 23. If getting participants to be aware of these policies was not hard enough, communicating changes to policies was even harder. Manual reviews and approvals had to be put into place to force everyone to read and comply with the latest rules. Such reviews quickly became bottlenecks and encouraged people to go around policies, defeating the core mission of SOA governance.

Strong and effective SOA policy management practices are particularly important. Although it really is IT management's responsibility, IT auditors, through their reviews and audit recommendations, should help ensure that enterprise SOA policies are expressed in declarative formats that can be easily defined, changed, and removed as needed. In addition, processes should be in place to actively enforce these policies throughout the SOA life cycle. Participants here should receive immediate feedback with policy management as a critical component of these governance processes.

Effective SOA policy management removes hurdles and objections to SOA governance by providing clear guidance regarding what should be compliant with the established and approved SOA blueprint. Policy management solutions improve accountability and ensure consistent outcomes.

IT AUDITING IN SOA ENVIRONMENTS

We have discussed many aspects of SOA but only a few of its attributes and features. With its goal of breaking down software elements and functions into independent and interchangeable components that can be connected or redefined easily, more and more SOA-related functions are likely. The major database software vendors today, such as Oracle and HP, have implemented SOA principles in their enterprise resource planning database structures, and we should see a greater SOA emphasis in these products going forward.

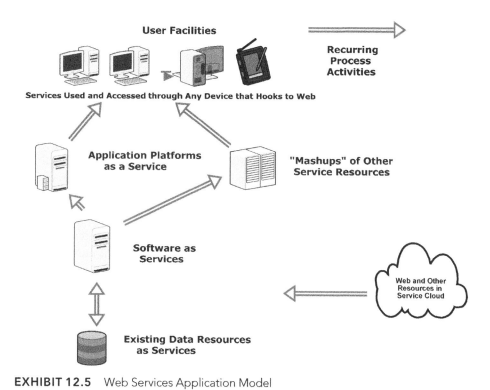

EXHIBIT 12.5   Web Services Application Model

However, the typical enterprise using SOA tools will almost certainly not begin with the full implementation shown in Exhibit 12.2. Rather, many enterprises have converted one or another key application to a Web services model. That process of converting an existing application into a Web-based and dependent environment is shown in Exhibit 12.5, describing a Web services application model. An example of this type of application can be found in one of the customer relationship management software solutions offered by SalesForce.com (www.salesforce.com/form/sem/crm), a very successful software provider that sells its software products only via the Web.

Rather than individual, separate applications, Web services are application components that communicate with other applications using open protocols within the Web and with other applications using standard communications protocols. They are self-contained, self-describing and can be used by other applications. XML, discussed in Chapter 14 on continuous auditing, and XBRL are used for Web services communications as well as for many SOA implementations.

IT auditors will encounter increasing numbers of applications based on Web services approaches in the future. Various resources will be located in what we frequently today call an IT cloud, including, storage connections to multiple files, data sources, and other resources. When considering this cloud concept, we can think of Google; a user can get multiple search results no matter the topic area requested. Web services applications may be linked to this Internet cloud as well as to their own storage resources with ongoing connections to local systems, whether local networks or wireless.

IT auditors face two review areas in such an SOA environment:

1. If an enterprise is moving to a total SOA environment, as depicted in Exhibit 12.2, the IT general controls covering the SOA environment must be audited throughout the SOA project.
2. Whether the application is an element of the enterprise SOA or a separate Web services application, IT audit may need to consider reviewing the application separately. Many of these review procedures follow our discussion of IT general controls reviews in Chapter 6 and application controls review from Chapter 10, but SOA-based systems also have some unique audit characteristics, as discussed next.

Auditing SOA Governance General Controls

An SOA environment may consist of a largely implemented total system environment or a project in development that is converting some existing or new applications to SOA. Both face some major general controls concerns, and IT auditors who have reviewed general controls following a more traditional IT systems approach will need to rethink their IT general control review approaches. Following our earlier LEGO blocks example, an IT auditor will need to review the controls and procedures for many separate components, including the controls and permissions surrounding each individual component and their interconnections.

Perhaps the major general controls issue in this SOA environment is the need for a comprehensive enterprise-level SOA blueprint covering all service elements agreed to and approved by all participating parties. These service unit considerations often go beyond just one operating division, beyond the overall enterprise, and may branch to other service providers or suppliers. A strong system of permissions as well as controls within each service element is needed. Again going back to our LEGO blocks example, each service unit should be considered as one single block, perhaps in a combination of program elements or data resources. A business unit should make the nonproprietary elements of each block available to others through clear disclosures and permissions. Some level of SOA architect function should be in place to review these service elements and establish supporting rules and procedures.

Strong infrastructure best practice procedures, as discussed in Chapter 7, are essential in an SOA environment. SOA platforms are not launched by implementing everything all at once. Rather, service and processes typically are added, modified, or deleted on an ongoing basis. The challenge is far more complex than individual program library controls, however, where the concerns focus on one program element in an application. Under SOA, these changes are to a service unit that can be part of numerous other processes, and the owner of a given service may not understand who else is using that service element. A control problem in one service may have an impact on many others. Strong testing and quality controls are necessary. SOA quality resources, as described in Exhibit 12.4 and in Chapter 31, are essential.

An IT auditor reviewing SOA general controls should expect to see some strong policy guidance, educational offerings and other materials to introduce users and other developers into these SOA processes. All parties should understand the rules and advantages of operating in an SOA environment, but they also need to understand the required supporting rules and procedures. An IT auditor should look for strong monitoring processes in place to alert users and developers when SOA rules and procedures have been violated. When appropriate, ideal monitoring processes should be self-correcting, where the user is informed and the matter is fixed.

Many of the general IT control procedures discussed in other chapters here are applicable in an SOA environment. For example, controls over systems software, discussed in Chapter 8, or the security management general controls, discussed in Chapter 19, are equally appropriate in an SOA environment. These other controls are appropriate in a variety of environments. Exhibit 12.6 outlines IT general controls in an SOA environment. The steps outline an environment where the enterprise is not 100%

---

1. Based on discussions with the chief information officer (CIO), has the enterprise developed and approved a SOA strategy for IT and business operations?
   a. If there is an approved strategy, what is its completion status at present?
   b. If there is no formal SOA strategy, what are future plans for any SOA implementations?
   c. Have any education programs been delivered to introduce the advantages of SOA to both business and IT users?
2. Has a responsible manager or coordinator been chosen to lead enterprise SOA efforts?
3. Has the enterprise obtained or is it evaluating any SOA software?
   a. Have formal evaluation criteria been established to select software?
   b. For any software product in place, has there been a formal testing and evaluation program to analyze it for full implementation?
4. Have mission-critical business applications been identified as part of the SOA strategy?
   a. For any critical applications, particularly that are not Web services based, are there plans in place to convert them to an SOA environment?
   b. Has a formal mission-critical business process layer been defined and documented for SOA applications?
   c. Is there evidence that the application services layer focuses on integration interoperability, based on database, component, and infrastructure services?
5. Has a formal service director or management team been established?
   a. Have the objectives and risks of this service director been reviewed with management?
   b. Is there evidence that enterprise SOA plans have been explained and discussed with members of the management team beyond just IT?
6. Is there evidence that SOA plans have been fully integrated with enterprise continuity plans?
7. As the enterprise moves to an SOA environment, are applications initially converted from their regular status to SOA on a test basis?
   a. As part of any test conversion to SOA, are existing application controls reviewed and assessed?
   b. Does any part of an application SOA conversion include testing the component's plug-and-play features that are the purported benefits of SOA operations?
   c. Is there evidence that the costs and benefits of any SOA conversion are formally evaluated?
8. Based on testing and evaluations, are all applications converted to SOA consistent with enterprise IT application and system security requirements?
9. On a test basis, have audit procedures been established and understood by both external and internal auditors for any SOA-converted applications?
10. Have the costs and benefits of any SOA conversions been developed and evaluated prior to any full-scale planned conversions?

EXHIBIT 12.6 IT General Controls in an SOA Environment

SOA consistent but is moving there through an ongoing implementation project that follows an approved blueprint.

Auditing Web Services Applications

Just as auditing general controls in an SOA environment is very similar to general controls IT audit reviews in many other modern IT systems, internal controls reviews of individual Web services applications have many of the same aspects as other IT application control reviews. However, an IT auditor should understand the unique internal controls characteristics of Web services applications.

For background, the Web services architecture contains three components, as shown in Exhibit 12.7: the service requester, service broker, and service provider. A service requester requests a Web service through a service broker to the service provider. The service provider then can directly request for another service to fulfill this service request from any other service provider and thereby create a chain of such additional requests. Such a provider functions as an intermediary during the process.

When applications with different access levels are invoked at runtime, they run the risk of weakening existing security levels. Unlike a portal where just minimum access rights are implemented to afford easy security management, a Web services scenario can be effective only if a certain amount of access rights have been given with an appropriate level of access rights; these rights are often negotiated dynamically.

Many of the internal controls associated with a Web services application are similar to those in any other IT application, as discussed in Chapters 10 and 11. For example, Web services application security controls for verifying users through authentication controls, having authorization controls access certain application functions, and the maintenance of user data and security policy and audit trail mechanisms are similar to normal IT applications. However, because of the organization of Web services architecture, security management controls can be an area of significant internal control vulnerabilities.

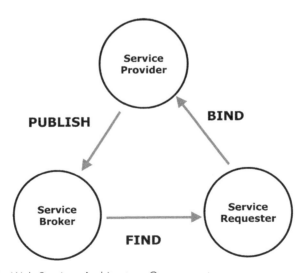

EXHIBIT 12.7 Web Services Architecture Components

Web services security management increases internal control risks because of its loosely coupled and often ambiguous service unit environment, along with a number of intermediary links, where a service function can jump across related processes. The number of elements in a Web services application can multiply rapidly; security management, therefore, becomes complex.

While reviewing the general controls in an enterprise's SOA environment is a relatively easy IT auditing task, with its emphasis on appropriate policies and strong infrastructure controls, reviews of individual Web services applications often can be complex. Any application can have multiple messages and transactions back and forth through its individual service units and other Web services components. Such an application can perform and operate with many different variations. Fully reviewing, understanding, and testing a Web services application often requires the development of continuous audit procedures, as discussed in Chapter 14. Exhibit 12.8 outlines IT audit

---

1. Develop and document a general understanding of the Web services application, not whether it is fully configured in an HTML format.
   a. Identify and document essential Web services components, including providers and Web services consumers.
   b. Develop an understanding of Web services standards, such as the use and definition of XML-based Web Services Definition Language (WSDL) to enable customers to invoke commands, and assess the use of these features by IT application developers.
2. Review the project management documentation covering the Web services application to determine if it is consistent with good control procedures.
3. Interview a selected sample of application users to assess whether they are familiar with this Web services application, including its portability features.
4. If the Web services application reviewed is one of several applications using the same vendor software, review any control weaknesses identified in other similar application reviews and determine that they have been addressed in this application review.
5. Based on discussions with IT developers, assess whether the application follows application and industry standards such that multiple partners can be added to the application's Web services.
   a. Review test results of any patching of other customer Web partners into the services framework.
   b. Determine that proper attention is given to application internal controls whenever patched into the application's Web services.
6. Review application security sign-on procedures, and determine whether they are consistent with industry and enterprise standards.
   a. Understand the security procedures in place for multiple customer Web partners.
   b. Based on discussions with the IT security functions, assess whether adequate protective measures have been installed for the Web services applications.
7. Assess the adequacy of logging tools installed for the application, including time-stamped facilities and the adequacy of audit trails for both system users and IT audit.
8. Determine that there are adequate change control procedures over the entire Web services application.
9. Assess whether Web services application development efforts are consentient with good systems development life cycle (SDLC) procedures.
10. Interview several Web services application users to determine if application performance is meeting their expectations.

EXHIBIT 12.8 Review Procedures of a Web Service Application

review procedures for an individual Web services application. These steps will help the IT auditor gain a general understanding, of internal control processes, but he or she will need to develop a more detailed understanding of the individual application in order to fully test and review it.

Eventually, the SOA environment for IT operations and Web services applications will almost certainly become or define IT standards. The concept of approaching IT services and processes as multiple building blocks that can be reused and reassembled in multiple configurations is complex but will raise questions and raise eyebrows by many in enterprise and IT management who may not initially fully understand and trust these new processes. IT auditors should build their knowledge of SOA and Web services IT processes.

ELECTRONIC RECORDS MANAGEMENT INTERNAL CONTROL ISSUES AND RISKS

Today all levels of enterprises are literally awash with electronic records—receipts for sales transactions, purchase orders and specifications for purchased materials, employee pay and personnel records, and much more. What were once paper-based records—sometimes even with carbon copies—have almost universally been replaced with IT electronic records. Although facilities usually exist to produce paper copies of electronic documents (e-documents), the IT-based versions are almost always the prime document repositories today.

All too often, enterprises do not manage their supporting e-documents consistently. Backup policies and e-document retention periods are often established on an application-by-application basis with no consistent understanding of document retention needs. In some instances, document backup records are not kept long enough to allow an enterprise to reconstruct transactions. In other instances, e-documents are retained far too long. With IT storage media very cheap today, it is easy to keep e-documents almost in perpetuity. Although it is good to have these historical records, sometimes there are good reasons to destroy records after some legally defined maximum periods.

E-documents also must be organized in a manner that they can be retrieved when necessary. We have all seen changes in IT technology where storage media formats and supporting equipment changes. As time passes, it does not make sense for an organization to retain readers or other equipment to retrieve that old stored data; even finding an outside source to retrieve the materials may be difficult.

The importance of document management can be seen in a recent American Institute of Certified Public Accountants (AICPA) top 10 technologies survey. In 2009, this list contained two items, numbers 9 and 10, very pertinent to IT document management:

> **9. Document, Forms, Content and Knowledge Management.** The "paperless" office is the process of electronically capturing, indexing, storing, protecting, searching, retrieving, managing, and controlling information using scanning, forms recognition, optical character recognition (OCR), centralized data repositories, and the management of PDFs and other document formats. Knowledge management brings structure and control to

information, allowing organizations to harness the intellectual capital contained in the underlying data.

10. Electronic Data Retention Strategies. Involve technologies that enable appropriate archiving and retrieval of key information over a given (statutory) period of time. Strategies include policies and processes to ensure destruction of information from storage and archival media in a timely and consistent manner, as well as the impact of eDiscovery rules and regulations regarding retained data.[4]

This AICPA list changes from year to year; 2008 had similar entries. The point of this is that an enterprise needs a set of e-document standards covering retention periods, record formats, and backup procedures for all of its business records. These targeted items do not tell an external auditor how to audit internal controls in these areas but highlight evolving areas that should be of concern in any review of internal controls.

Electronic records management became a major issue just prior to the enactment of the Sarbanes-Oxley Act (SOx), discussed in Chapter 1. In the late 1990s, a major motivator for the enactment of SOx was the then high-flying trading company Enron. Questions also were raised about Enron's financial soundness in the early years of this century. When the U.S. Securities and Exchange Commission announced that it was going to review Enron's financial operations, Enron's public accounting firm, Arthur Andersen, announced that all "nonessential" documentation should be destroyed, per that firm's policy. The press was then treated to a major effort by Enron's accounting firm, shredding massive amounts of documentation on a worldwide basis and in what seemed like a destruction of documentary evidence. SOx now has rules about retaining financial documentation, and those rules have been a strong motivator in encouraging enterprises to adopt e-document management processes.

IT AUDITS OF ELECTRONIC RECORDS MANAGEMENT PROCESSES

Appropriate electronic records management processes should be part of any IT application review and also should be compliant with SOx standards. Although an IT auditor should assess whether records retention controls are appropriate for any applications reviewed, it is useful to review the overall electronic records management process in an enterprise. This general controls review is both IT based, with a reliance on storage management controls, and business process based, with standards to encourage the proper identification and archiving of electronic records.

In cooperation with their financial and operational internal auditors, IT audit periodically should review an enterprise's overall electronic management processes. This process is much easier today than it was before the turn of this century. The reason is that mass storage memory devices have become so low in cost and small in size that it is not unusual for a laptop computer to be equipped with a USB device plugged into the computer capable of holding several gigabytes[5] of mass storage capacity. Of course, our needs for increased memory have grown massively. Earlier documents primarily consisted of text and numbers, while many documents today are based on drawings, elaborate graphics, and digital photographs. The IT storage requirements for even a small digital picture typically require many, many bytes or words of data storage needs when compared to a text based document.

It is relatively easy to modify IT systems such that key records are backed up and stored in an IT data retention facility. Another key aspect of electronic records retention is that some records should be converted from paper to electronic formats. While it is relatively easy to store such documents electronically, a clear process is needed to retrieve them easily. Anyone who has done a Google search and has received multiple retrieval responses, none of which is quite right, knows this problem. In addition to ease document retrieval, e- documents of all types should be part of an enterprise disaster recovery and continuity plan, as discussed in Chapter 23. It is relatively easy to back up key files and records from an IT application so that they can be retrieved as part of continuity processes; often it is more difficult to recover all types and formats of e-documents.

As part of their overall risk management processes, IT and others in the internal audit organization should perform periodic general control reviews of enterprise e-document storage and retrieval processes. Exhibit 12.9 outlines IT audit procedures for a review of e-document records management controls. If IT audit finds, through reviews of processes and tests, that the records management internal controls appear

---

1. Does the enterprise have a formal document management system in place?
   a. Does document management include both electronic and paper-based records?
   b. Is enterprise document management supported by procedures governing such matters as retention, retrieval tests, and document reference libraries?
   c. Are there appropriate, well-controlled tools in place for managing electronic documents?
2. Is there a program in place for moving existing paper-format document processes and their documents to electronic formats?
3. For all e-document conversion processes:
   a. Are logs maintained documenting conversion processes?
   b. Are databases retaining converted documents subject to strong backup and security controls?
   c. Are catalogs published describing backup contents?
   d. Are there adequate security controls over access to e-document repositories?
4. Are e-document files part of enterprise business continuity processes, and do they appear to be adequate?
5. Are software management processes in place to ensure the continued availability of stored e-documents in light of any database software or other changes?
6. On a test basis, can IT audit easily retrieve a sample of older e-documents?
7. Are there processes in place to remove or delete older shared e-documents?
   a. Are document deletion processes consistent with the document's legal requirements?
   b. Has the document retention policy been reviewed with and received approval from the audit committee?
8. Are e-document processes reviewed by IT management on a regular basis with the objective of adding continuous improvements?

EXHIBIT 12.9 Procedures for a Review of Electronic Records Document Management Controls

adequate, internal audit can rely on these processes for subsequent individual application reviews.

NOTES

1. The .NET or dot-NET framework is Microsoft's comprehensive and consistent programming model for building applications. See www.microsoft.com/net/.
2. BEA is a unit of Oracle Corporation. Information on its WebLogic application can be found at www.oracle.com/bea/index.html.
3. While this is more of a marketing site, information on LEGO blocks can be found at: http://shop.lego.com/ByTheme/Leaf.aspx?cn=392&d=104.
4. AICPA Information Technology Center, 2009 Top Technology Initiatives and Honorable Mentions//infotech.aicpa.org/Resources/Top+Technology+Initiatives/2009+Top+Technology+Initiatives+and+Honorable+Mentions.htm.
5. A gigabyte is a unit of computer memory or data storage capacity equal to 1,024 megabytes (2^{30} bytes) of storage capacity. A byte is effectively one character or number.

CHAPTER THIRTEEN

Computer-Assisted Audit Tools and Techniques

NFORMATION TECHNOLOGY (IT) AUDITORS—OFTEN working with their financial and operational internal audit counterparts—gather evidence from an enterprise's books and records to support their conclusions. This audit evidence includes any actual paper-based documents, evidence that these documents or supporting transactions were properly recorded in a timely manner, and appropriate authorizing signatures or notations. Today, most of those documents are IT based and paperless, and IT auditors have a challenge to review and understand those paperless documents and procedures to support their audit conclusions when older traditional paper-based documents have gone away. Although IT auditors test and review the internal controls surrounding those IT systems, they often need tools to better understand and evaluate the completeness and accuracy of the data stored in the files and databases of IT applications. It is almost always more efficient to use IT techniques to examine all recorded items on the supporting computer files. IT auditors can also act with greater independence by developing their own specialized file retrieval methods. There are many approaches to retrieving data through computer-assisted audit tools and techniques (CAATTs), which are independent auditor–controlled software to assist internal audit efforts.

An IT auditor must obtain evidence on the validity of accounting and operational data. However, large volumes of data or the lack of paper documents often makes this review of audit evidential materials difficult or almost impossible. This chapter describes IT audit approaches to testing, analyzing, and gathering detailed evidence from data contained on IT applications through the use of CAATTs controlled by IT auditors. These techniques allow an IT auditor to review the contents of computerized applications data in files, ranging from accounting systems on large database repositories to smaller systems residing on departmental desktop systems. Although some CAATTs require specialized data processing skills, there are many powerful audit software tools that the typical IT auditor, with no particular programming skills, can use.

There are many tools and techniques available to help make audit reviews of IT-supported systems more efficient and effective. All IT auditors should have a basic understanding of the general use of CAATTs to access and review automated data to support IT audits. If an IT auditor does not have the skills to execute a particular CAATT process, he or she should have a sufficient level of knowledge to describe it and request help from another member of the IT audit team.

 ## UNDERSTANDING COMPUTER-ASSISTED AUDIT TOOLS AND TECHNIQUES

A CAATT is a specialized computer program or process, controlled by IT or other auditors, that is used to test or otherwise analyze data on computer files. Terminologies change over time, and an IT auditor sometimes will see the term *CAAT* or *CAAP* rather than *CAATT*; the first refers to just "techniques" and the second is an abbreviation for "procedure." All of these expressions refer to similar techniques and can be used interchangeably. The American Institute of Certified Public Accountants (AICPA) uses CAATTs, the term preferred for this chapter, although the Information Systems Audit and Control Association (ISACA) and the Institute of Internal Auditors (IIA) still uses the name CAAT.

In the early years of data processing systems, auditors typically relied on printed outputs from IT systems and used conventional audit procedures to read, test, and analyze these computer-generated reports. As IT systems became more pervasive with ever larger data files, auditors needed better approaches to evaluate the documentation and records stored in large IT systems and files. In the early days, a few pioneer IT auditors developed CAATTs to read and analyze financial data. However, many auditors continued to use conventional manual techniques, relying primarily on the printed report results of IT systems.

The necessity for CAATT procedures first became evident with the Equity Funding fraud in the early 1970s. Equity Funding Corporation, a U.S. insurance company, was reporting very significant growth and earnings from the late 1960s up through the early 1970s. It was later determined, however, that Equity Funding's growth and earnings were based on a massive management fraud in which fictitious insurance policies were entered on the company's computerized records. At that time, the external auditors relied on the printed report outputs generated by the Equity Funding computer systems rather than on the data recorded on their computer files. Had the external auditors looked at the contents of those computer files, they might have detected the fraud. Equity Funding did not have a significant internal audit function, and an Equity Funding employee and then their external auditors eventually revealed the fraud. Equity Funding's external auditors then independently reviewed computer procedures to analyze the contents of computerized records. The Equity Funding fraud launched what was then called computer auditing—now IT auditing—and the use of CAATTs.

A CAATT is an auditor-controlled computer program or process that can be used to read production IT files to analyze, summarize that data, and perform other audit tests. In the days of legacy mainframe computer systems and before today's powerful desktop software tools, a CAATT often was considered to be an advanced audit technique. End users typically relied on their data processing departments to write special retrieval programs to give them various requested output reports. Later both internal and external auditors began to use what was called generalized audit software to develop their own programs independently for testing and analyzing data. This generalized software became the basis for CAATTs, a term used to define specialized IT audit systems and procedures. An example might better clarify the concept of a typical CAATT. Assume that IT audit is interested in testing the accuracy of account agings from an automated accounts receivable system; however, most calculated data for that system is stored only on computer files, with no significant paper reports describing these calculations. Financial and IT auditors are concerned that the receivables, as reported on the aged trial balance report, may not be properly aged as to the number of days due. Thus, the receivables account balances may be over- or understated. IT audit can test these agings using any of three approaches.

First, IT audit could use traditional, manual approaches where items are selected from an IT output report and then are traced back to any original source documents that may exist. IT audit can then determine if the items selected are entered properly on IT system records and if the aging calculations are correct. This method will work if paper records are available. However, because of the volume of receivable records in typical IT systems, IT audit can trace and test these items only selectively. Some exception conditions may be missed with such a manual test. In addition, IT audit might not be able to determine easily if the dates of transaction-based agings are functioning correctly.

A second approach is to perform an internal controls review over the automated accounts receivable system. The idea is that if internal controls over the application are found to be good, IT audit can rely on system output reports. IT application internal controls reviews are discussed in Chapter 10. A review of systems documentation will determine whether the system is properly aging receivables. IT audit would then test those controls by, for example, running some test transaction into the system, either through manual transactions or another CAATT. Properly performed, this review can detect significant internal control problems as well as determine whether the system is generally working in a correct, well-controlled manner. However, IT audit would be able only to estimate the total extent of the financial statement adjustments necessary due to any account aging errors. Thus, in conjunction with this test, IT audit must determine that controls over data entry and error correction are adequate.

A third and perhaps better approach is to use a CAATT application to recalculate independently all of the agings in the accounts receivable system, develop totals for the accounts receivable balance, and produce a listing of any unusual exception items. IT audit might perform this CAATT-oriented approach in five steps:

1. **Determine CAATT objectives.** IT audit should never just "use the computer" to test a system without a clear set of starting audit objectives for any CAATT. In the

previous examples, IT audit would have an objective of determining if accounts receivable agings are correctly stated.

2. **Understand the supporting IT systems.** IT audit should review IT systems documentation to determine how accounts receivable agings are calculated, where this data is stored in the system, and how items are described in system files.

3. **Develop CAATT programs.** Using generalized audit software, other retrieval packages, or a computer language processor, IT audit would write its own programs to recalculate accounts receivable agings and to generate totals from accounts receivable files.

4. **Test and process the CAATT.** After testing the programs, the IT auditor would arrange to have the CAATTs processed against production accounts receivable files.

5. **Develop audit conclusions from CAATT results.** Similar to any audit test, audit conclusions would be drawn from the results of the CAATT processing, documented in the workpapers and discussed in the audit report, as appropriate.

This is the general approach to developing and processing CAATTs. It follows the same steps IT audit would use for establishing audit objectives and performing appropriate tests on any system or process. As discussed, a CAATT is a specialized set of computer programs or procedures that are under the control of IT audit. The CAATT can be developed through generalized audit software programs run on the production computer system, specialized software run on the auditor's own laptop computer, or specialized auditor-use-only program code embedded in an otherwise normal production application. With our major reliance on IT processes in all areas of an enterprise today, CAATTs can enhance IT audit processes in some of these areas:

▪ **Increase audit coverage.** CAATTs can allow an IT auditor to review and analyze such components as massive financial databases where IT auditors do not have easy access to online screen reports and certainly not paper reports.

▪ **Focus on risk areas.** Similar to the last point and our example of testing accounts receivable agings, CAATTs often allow an IT auditor to review and investigate areas that have not received a high level of IT audit scrutiny.

▪ **Increase cost effectiveness.** Although CAATTs may require some incremental time and cost to develop, they can be very effective for analyzing large volumes of IT-resident data over multiple periods.

▪ **Improve audit credibility.** CAATTs provide IT auditors with the ability to independently look at complex databases and provide detailed analyses and recommendations; that type of analysis can very much improve IT auditor credibility.

▪ **Improve coordination of both IT and financial and operational auditors.** CAATTs often are used to analyze financial and operational processes using IT processes. They will cause both IT and other internal auditors to better talk and coordinate their audit objectives and needs.

▪ **Encourage auditor independence from IT operations.** IT auditors do not have to be heavily dependent on the IT systems and infrastructure to operate their CAATTs. Although strong coordination is essential, IT auditors can operate in a fairly independent manner.

IT auditors should have a good understanding of when CAATTs should be used to enhance the audit process, the types of software tools available to an IT auditor, and how to use a CAATT in an audit. Although some CAATTs require an IT auditor to have specialized programming knowledge, most can be implemented by any internal auditor with only a general understanding of information systems.

 ## DETERMINING THE NEED FOR CAATTS

CAATTs are powerful tools that can enhance both the audit process and auditor independence. However, these procedures sometimes can be time consuming to develop and will not always be cost effective unless properly planned and designed. IT audit needs to understand when a CAATT might increase overall audit efficiencies and when it will not. This section discusses areas where CAATTs will enhance an audit and areas to consider when developing and implementing a CAATT. Other sections discuss alternative CAATT approaches and procedures for implementing them as well as some problems with this approach.

Before developing a specific CAATT, an IT auditor should first determine if the planned approach is appropriate. All too often, a member of management or even the chief audit officer may have attended a seminar about audit efficiencies and then asks the IT audit team to "do something" to improve audit efficiency by using IT resources as part of IT audits. This was particularly true several years ago, when management expressed strong concerns about all levels of audit costs associated with Sarbanes-Oxley Act (SOx) Section 404 reviews, as discussed in Chapter 1. This type of improved audit efficiency directive often results in disappointments for all parties. Similarly, a highly technical IT auditor sometimes develops a "technically interesting" CAATT as part of an audit even though it really does not support the overall objectives of that review. The result may be interesting but will not contribute to the overall effectiveness of the IT audit's objectives. The decision to develop and implement a CAATT in support of an IT audit will depend on the nature of the data and production programs being reviewed in the audit, the CAATT tools available to IT audit, and the objectives of the audit. IT audit needs an overall understanding of CAATT procedures in order to make this decision, and should consider:

- **Audit nature or objectives.** IT audit initially should evaluate the materials to be reviewed in a planned audit and consider the size and format of any IT-based data. Audits based on values or attributes of computerized data are typically good candidates for CAATTs. For example, the above-mentioned accounts receivable audit is a good CAATT candidate because there is generally a large volume of transactions but few paper records. Many of the operational and financial audit areas discussed throughout this book are also good candidates for CAATTs.
- **Nature of the data to be reviewed.** CAATTs are most effective when both data and decision-dependent information about that data are based on automated systems. For example, a manufacturing inventory system will have most of the descriptive information about its inventory on IT system databases or files. Inventory-related data is input directly, and inventory status information is based on system

reports on output screens. Often only limited paper-based original records exist. IT audit procedures for inventory here might include an analysis of manufacturing costs, and inventory system attributes can be summarized and analyzed through a CAATT. Other computer systems are comprised of little more than log files that organize otherwise manual records. An engineering project authorization system might have summary data stored in a systems file, but most of the information about the projects may be in manual, paper-based files. CAATTs might not be very effective in these areas because IT audit also would need to review the manual data. Only audits over areas where there is heavy dependence on IT data are good potential candidates for a CAATT.

■ **Available CAATT tools and audit skills.** IT audit must develop its CAATTs using the automation tools available within the audit department or IT function. If IT audit does not have or has not budgeted for specialized CAATT software, an IT auditor cannot develop CAATTs that require such software. IT audit needs to consider the types of audit software available before embarking on any CAATT projects. That availability may be based on both audit budget constraints and product limitations.

Auditor skills also must be considered. Although training materials are available, the in-charge auditor must assess whether technical audit specialists are needed and are available for the CAATT development project. The last three points are stated in very general terms, but they are areas to be considered when planning the overall strategy for using CAATTs.

These comments point to many areas where a CAATT will be difficult or not particularly cost effective. However, IT audit should keep an open mind and always consider using CAATTs to enhance IT audit effectiveness. Given the lack of paper-based audit trails in many IT systems, an IT auditor has little choice but to use computer-assisted audit procedures. The challenge to IT audit is to identify appropriate areas for CAATTs.

Computer technology has changed extensively over the years. The batch-oriented systems of the past have been replaced by online, database-oriented systems. Large centralized computer hardware has been replaced, in many respects, by networked client-server workstations. Despite these changes, however, the auditor's basic approach for defining CAATTs has not really changed. For example, in 1979, the AICPA published an audit guide, *Computer-Assisted Audit Techniques* that provided some basic direction on the use of CAATTs. Although now long out of date and out of print, that guide contained a list of the types of audit procedures that can be performed through the use of CAATTs. Adapted for IT auditors, this set of procedures includes:

■ **Examining records based on criteria specified by IT audit.** Because the records in a manual system are visible, IT audit can scan for inconsistencies or inaccuracies without difficulty. For records in systems files, IT audit can specify audit software instructions to scan and print records that are exceptions to the criteria, so that follow-up actions can be taken. Examples of specified areas are:
   ▪ Accounts receivable balances for amounts over the credit limit
   ▪ Inventory quantities for negative and unreasonably large balances

- Payroll files for terminated employees
- Bank demand deposit files for unusually large deposits or withdrawals

▪ **Testing calculations and making computations.** IT audit can use software to perform quantitative analyses to evaluate the reasonableness of auditee representations. Such analyses might be for:
  - Extensions of inventory items
  - Depreciation amounts
  - Accuracy of sales discounts
  - Interest calculations
  - Employees' net pay computations

▪ **Comparing data on separate files.** When records on separate files should contain compatible information, software can determine if the information agrees. Comparisons could be:
  - Changes in accounts receivable balances between two dates, comparing the details of sales and cash receipts on transaction files
  - Payroll details with personnel files
  - Current and prior period inventory files to assist in reviewing for obsolete or slow-moving items

▪ **Selecting and printing audit samples.** Multiple criteria may be used for selection, such as a judgmental sample of high-dollar and old items and a random sample of all other items, which can be printed in the auditor's workpaper format or on special confirmation forms. Examples are:
  - Accounts receivables balances for confirmations
  - Inventory items for observations
  - Fixed-asset additions for vouching
  - Paid voucher records for review of expenses
  - Vendor records for accounts payable confirmations

▪ **Summarizing and resequencing data and performing analyses.** Audit software can reformat and aggregate data in a variety of ways to simulate processing or to determine the reasonableness of output results. Examples are:
  - Totaling transactions on an account file
  - Testing accounts receivables aging
  - Preparing general ledger trial balances
  - Summarizing inventory turnover statistics for obsolescence analysis
  - Resequencing inventory items by location to facilitate physical observations

▪ **Comparing data obtained through other audit procedures with IT system data files.** Audit evidence gathered manually can be converted to a machine-readable form and compared to other data files. Examples are:
  - Inventory test counts with perpetual records
  - Creditor statements with accounts payable files

Although many of these procedures originally were developed by external auditors before integrated database files existed, these techniques are generally applicable for today's IT auditors. The number and sophistication of CAATTs will increase as the individual IT auditor becomes more experienced in their use.

CAATT SOFTWARE TOOLS

In the early days of computer systems, IT users often had to submit a request to the programming department for any type of special report or analysis program. Writing computer programs was often a difficult and time-consuming process performed by IT specialists. IT auditors were often suspicious of that approach. Just as an auditor who was interested in the account balance for some population of manual records would not ask the auditee for the balance but would examine the records to calculate an auditor-developed total, auditors often preferred to use their own programs controlled by IT audit to analyze computer-based data. This led to the development of CAATT processes with several common categories or types of computer audit software:

- Generalized audit software products
- Report generator languages
- Test data techniques
- Specialized audit test and analysis software
- Expert systems and inference-based software
- Embedded audit procedures

Depending on the overall IT environment and IT audit's objectives, one or more of these CAATTs may be used in a given audit situation. Some such expert systems and inference-based software require specialized IT audit technical skills, but most can be implemented by the generalist IT auditor. In today's highly computerized environments, any effective IT audit department should use some type of audit software. With technology advances, some approaches that were common in the past are seldom used or available today.

Exhibit 13.1 contains general guidelines for developing a CAATT. The exhibit is based on ISACA guideline G3 that discusses developing CAATs, modified to make the materials more consistent with other chapters in this book. ISACA audit standards and guidelines are discussed in Chapter 3 along with references to supporting ISACA Web sites.

The next sections describe various types of CAATTs. All are IT auditor–based software routines to aid the application review and IT audit process. IT auditors should use these tools to assess internal controls in their application reviews. Often more important, an IT auditor should use CAATTs to support the objectives of the financial and operational internal auditors in an enterprise. Although we believe that all internal auditors should have the skills to develop their own CAATT applications, far too many non–IT auditors are reluctant to do so. Therefore, IT auditors should work with their financial and operational audit teams to develop effective CAATTs. The next paragraphs outline some basic CAATT procedures.

Generalized Audit Software

In the early days of IT auditing, most business applications were written in programming languages such as COBOL. Auditors at that time usually had neither the technical skills nor the time required to write their own retrieval programs to access data. When an IT auditor wanted to test or review the contents of a large data file written with a

Note: This Guideline is based heavily on the ISACA Auditing Standard Guideline G3 on the use of computer-assisted audit techniques. We have made minor editing changes, such as our preferred use of CAATT rather than CAAT; have slightly modified some sections for consistency with book materials; and have eliminated some of the text from ISACA Guideline G3 for brevity.

1. Background

1.1 Linkage to Standards and Guidelines. This ISACA standard has direct linkages to ISACA standards S5 through S14 and other standards and guidelines as discussed in Chapter 3.

1.3 Linkage to COBIT. The ISACA standard has references to CobiT as introduced in Chapter 2. For example, an IT auditor should consider CobiT DS5 *Ensure Systems Security* guidelines to ensure the achievement of IT objectives and compliance with IT-related laws and regulations by focusing on monitoring the internal control processes for IT-related activities and identifying improvement actions.

2. Planning a CAATT

2.1 Decision Factors for Using a CAATT. When planning an audit, an IT auditor should consider using an appropriate combination of manual and automated techniques. In determining whether to use the CAATT, the auditor factors to be considered include:

- Computer knowledge, expertise, and experience of the IT auditor
- Availability of suitable CAATT software tools and IT facilities
- Efficiency and effectiveness of using the CAATT over a manual technique
- IT auditor time constraints
- Integrity of the information system and IT environment
- Level of audit risk

2.2 CAATT Planning Steps. IT auditor steps for preparing for a CAATT include:

- Set the audit objectives for the planned CAATT.
- Determine the accessibility and availability of the organization's IT facilities, programs/systems, and data.
- Clearly understand the composition of data to be processed, including quantity, type, format, and layout.
- Define the procedures included in the CAATT (e.g., statistical sampling, recalculation, confirmation).
- Define output requirements.
- Determine expected CAATT resource requirements, including personnel needs and IT resource requirements,
- Obtain access to the organization's IT facilities, programs/systems, and data, including supporting documentation.
- Document the planned CAATT, including its objectives, high-level flowcharts, and run instructions.

2.3 IT Auditor Arrangements with the Auditee. Schedule review time with data owners to enhance the design of the CAATT and interpret the data. In addition, the auditee should understand the purpose, scope, timing, and goals of the CAATT. Clear expectations at the outset of the CAATT should be set and communicated. In addition, the IT auditor should arrange for:

- The retention of data files, such as detailed transaction files, covering the appropriate audit time frame
- Access to IT facilities, programs/systems, and data well in advance of the needed time period to minimize the effect on the organization's production environment, if possible

The IT auditor should assess the effect that changes to the production programs/systems may have on the use of the CAATT. In doing so, the IT auditor should consider the effect of these

EXHIBIT 13.1 Auditing Guidelines for Developing a CAATT
Source: ISACA

changes on the integrity and usefulness of the CAATT and on the programs/systems and data used by the IT auditor.

2.4 Testing the CAATT. It is critical that the IT auditor obtain reasonable assurance of the integrity, reliability, usefulness, and security of the CAATT through appropriate planning, design, testing, processing, and review of supporting documentation. This should be done before audit reliance is placed on CAATT results. The CAATT should receive sufficient review and testing to ensure it is operating as expected.

2.5 Security of Data and CAATT. Where a CAATT used to extract information for data analysis, the IT auditor should verify the integrity of the information system and IT environment from which the data are extracted.

- When a CAATT is used to extract sensitive program/system information and production data that should be kept confidential, the IT auditor should clearly understand company data classification and data-handling policies to properly safeguard the information and data with an appropriate level of confidentiality and security.
- The IT auditor should consider the level of confidentiality and security required by the organization owning the data and any relevant legislation, and should consult others, such as legal counsel and management, as necessary.
- The IT auditor should use and document the results of appropriate procedures to provide for the ongoing integrity, reliability, usefulness, and security of the CAATT. For example, the IT auditor should review program maintenance and program change controls over embedded audit software to determine that only authorized changes have been made to the CAATT.
- When the CAATT in an environment not under the control of the IT auditor, an appropriate level of control should be in effect to identify changes to them.
- When the CAATT is changed, the IT auditor should obtain assurance of its integrity, reliability, usefulness, and security through appropriate planning, design, testing, processing, and review of documentation before reliance is placed on it.

3. Performance of Audit Work

3.1 Gathering Audit Evidence. The responsible IT auditor should initiate controls on use of the CAATT to provide reasonable assurance that the audit objectives and the detailed specifications of the CAATT have been met. The IT auditor should:

- Perform a reconciliation of control totals if appropriate.
- Review output for reasonableness.
- Perform a review of the logic, parameters, or other characteristics of the CAATT.
- Review the organization's general internal security controls, such as program change controls and system access controls, which may contribute to the integrity of the CAATT. When using test data, the IT auditor should be aware that test data only point out the potential for erroneous processing; this technique does not evaluate actual production data. The IT auditor should also be aware that test data analysis can be extremely complex and time consuming, depending on the number of transactions processed, the number of programs tested, and the complexity of the programs/systems. Before using test data, the IT auditor should verify that the test data will not permanently affect the live system.

3.2 Generalized Audit Software. When using generalized audit software to access production data, the IT auditor should take appropriate steps to protect the integrity of the organization's data.

3.3 Utility Software

3.3.1 When using utility software, the IT auditor should confirm that no unplanned interventions have taken place during processing and that the utility software has been obtained from the appropriate system library. The IT auditor should also take appropriate steps to protect the integrity of the organization's system and files since these utilities can easily damage the system and its files.

EXHIBIT 13.1 (*Continued*)

3.4 Customized Software Queries or Scripts

3.4.1 Customized queries or scripts allow the IT auditor to specifically target desired information for analysis. Customized scripts are highly useful for environments where other CAATTs are not available, but usually specific technical skill sets are required to create these scripts. Therefore, the IT auditor should obtain assurance of the CAATT's integrity, reliability, usefulness, and security through appropriate planning, design and testing before placing reliance on it and should ensure that proper source data are used and that output from scripts and queries is in the proper format. Customized query and script code should be maintained in a secure location to prevent unauthorized changes from occurring.

3.5 Application Software Tracing and Mapping. When using application software tracing and mapping procedures, the IT auditor should confirm that the source code being evaluated has generated the object program currently being used in production. The internal security auditor should be aware that application software tracing and mapping only points out the potential for erroneous processing; it does not evaluate actual production data.

3.6 Continuous Monitoring and Assurance

3.7.1 Continuous assurance monitoring is an uninterrupted approach that allows IT auditors to monitor controls on a continuous basis and to gather selective audit evidence through the computer. This process is discussed in Chapter 14.

3.7.2 Continuous assurance monitoring enables IT auditors to report on subject matter within a very short time frame. In some environments, it should be possible to shorten the reporting time frame to provide almost instantaneous or truly continuous assurance.

3.7.3 By definition, continuous assurance requires a higher degree of reliance on an auditee's information system than does traditional auditing. This is a result of the need to rely on system-generated information versus externally produced information as the basis for audit testing. Hence, auditors need to make judgments on both the quality of the auditee's systems and the information produced by the system itself. Systems that are of lower quality or that produce less reliable information are often less conducive to continuous assurance than those that are of high quality and produce reliable information.

3.7.4 Environments that are of a higher quality and produce reliable information are better suited to reporting periods of a short to continuous duration. Environments that are of a lower quality or produce less reliable information should use longer reporting periods to compensate for the period of time that must pass for users to review and approve or correct information processed by the system.

4. CAATT Documentation

4.1 CAATT Workpapers. CAATT processes should be sufficiently documented to provide adequate audit evidence. The audit workpapers should contain sufficient documentation to describe the CAATT application and should include:

- CAATT objectives
- CAATT to be used
- Controls to be exercised
- Staffing and timing
- CAATT preparation and testing procedures and controls
- Details of the tests performed by the CAATT
- Details of inputs including data used, file layouts, testing periods, high-level flowcharts, and CAATT outputs, including log files and reports
- Listings of relevant parameters or source code

4.4 Audit Evidence. CAATT documentation should include:

- Outputs produced
- Description of the audit analysis work performed on the output

EXHIBIT 13.1 (*Continued*)

> ▪ Audit findings
> ▪ Audit conclusions
> ▪ Audit recommendations
>
> Data and files used should be stored in a secure location. In addition, temporary confidential data used as part of the audit should be disposed of in accordance with corporate data-handling procedures.
>
> **5. Reporting CAATT Results**
> The objectives, scope, and methodology section of the report should contain a clear description of the CAATT used. This description should not be overly detailed, but it should provide a good overview for the reader. The description of CAATT used should also be included in the body of the report, where the specific findings relating to the use of CAATTs is discussed. If the description of the CAATT used is applicable to several findings or is too detailed, it should be discussed briefly in the objectives, scope, and methodology section of the report, and the reader should be referred to an appendix with a more detailed description.

EXHIBIT 13.1 (*Continued*)

COBOL program, he or she usually had to submit a request to the data processing department to produce that report. The auditor would depend on a programmer to produce the requested report and could not fully act independently. This lack of auditor independence problem was solved in the early 1970s by the major public accounting firms, which developed simple audit retrieval programs. In addition to convenient data retrieval capabilities, this software often contained other common audit functions, such as sequence number gap detection or audit sampling procedures.

This software eventually began to be marketed as generalized audit software (GAS). It was originally based on mainframe legacy systems; several good client-server products are still on the market today. GAS offers IT auditors some of these advantages:

- **Increased independence from information systems.** GAS allows IT audit to perform tests of an application without asking the IT function to write the retrieval software, giving auditors an extra level of independence.
- **Increased audit efficiencies.** GAS software can perform such routines as confirming accounts receivable records and producing confirmation letters more efficiently than traditional audit procedures. In addition, such a CAATT should almost certainly be used over multiple years, so its development costs can be spread over time.
- **Opportunity to observe other controls.** By using an independent set of programs on the auditee's systems operations, IT audit can observe and develop a better understanding of other IT controls. For example, IT audit may observe procedural weaknesses in work schedules or tape cartridge retrievals from the data center library. While not related to the planned tests of given data files, these observations often point to areas for subsequent audit work.

Exhibit 13.2 outlines the typical work steps for planning and building a CAATT using generalized audit software. These tools were originally introduced in the

1. Define overall CAATT objectives: What do we want to test, and why?
2. Identify key applications, database files, key transactions, and cycle times that will test the audit objective.
3. Identify available audit software tools for performing the test.
4. Identify specific files and other data elements that will be tested.
5. Using audit software tools, develop procedures to perform the desired audit tests.
6. Test the CAATT against a sample set of production files, and modify the process until it is working properly.
7. Determine timings and key planned updates, and perform the actual audit CAATT test.
8. Follow up on any unusual or unexpected results, and make further corrections as necessary.
9. Report CAATT audit results.
10. Document overall audit results and the CAATT process.

EXHIBIT 13.2   Programming Steps for Developing a CAATT Application
Source: Robert R. Moeller, *Brink's Modern Internal Auditing*, 7th ed. (Hoboken, NJ: John Wiley & Sons, 2009). Copyright © 2009, John Wiley & Sons. Used with permission of John Wiley & Sons.

mainframe computer era where there were few other easy-to-use retrieval packages available. Today, IT auditors also can use other software retrieval language tools available on many computer systems.

Report Generator Languages

In days past when IT departments developed applications using compiler-based languages such as COBOL, end users relied on the IT department for all of their reports and applications. This dependency on the IT department has changed very much in today's era of powerful user-controlled tools. Today, end users with minimal training regularly produce special reports or perform complex file manipulations in addition to using conventionally programmed applications with report-generator languages. IT audit needs to understand the types of generalized retrieval languages available at any auditee location. These retrieval and report generator tools are available for most IT environments, from legacy mainframes to laptop computers and even small, handheld wireless devices. Some of these software tools, called *report generators* or *query languages*, are designed to operate only as a query language for a given database or vendor's application software package.

Others are quite general and can be used with many applications. The most general and flexible of these are computer languages require only very general instructions to produce a desired report rather than the detailed steps necessary in a complete computer program. For example, these systems produce an index-like list of all of the data items available; a programmer needs only to select items from those index lists to produce a fairly professional-looking output report. These retrieval languages take care of most other report editing and formatting functions.

Software that comes with some form of a query or report generator language can satisfy many IT audit reporting needs. For example, a fixed assets control application may have a report generator subsystem to allow customized fixed assets reports. IT auditors should consider using these same report generators for audit retrieval purposes. Many are easy to use. Vendors also provide training in the use of the software at the time it is installed. Even if IT audit plans to use its own generalized audit software, report generator products can be very helpful for audit analysis projects.

Numerous types of data retrieval products have existed since the early 1980s. Some are for the purpose of retrieving end user reports; others, such as overall application generators, are used primarily by the IT function. Many are powerful tools for CAATTs developed by IT auditors. Although there is no one definition of these auditor-friendly retrieval languages, most exhibit one or more of these characteristics:

- **Nonprocedural language.** Earlier programming languages required the programmer to follow a fixed sequence of instructions to accomplish a given task. For example, a COBOL program producing an output report must first open and read the input file, then select and sort items of interest to finally produce the report. A retrieval language does not require this same sequence of steps. The same example report could be produced with the single instruction "List data sorted by . . ." This facility makes the software easy to learn.
- **Environmental independence.** Many retrieval languages can be used on a variety of different IT systems environments. They are portable, from laptops to mainframes, operating under different types of computer hardware, operating systems, and telecommunications monitors.
- **Powerful application development facilities.** Although not necessary for IT auditors, most retrieval languages have powerful facilities to help application developers to design entire systems, including database accesses, paint procedures to program retrieval screens, and graphical output reports.

A modern retrieval language offers greater flexibility and ease of use. However, such software products may be expensive and difficult to justify if only for IT audit use. IT audit should investigate and consider using similar tools installed elsewhere in the enterprise. Typically this software is licensed to the overall enterprise, and IT audit would be one additional user.

Generalized retrieval software almost always can be used for audit retrieval purposes. Its disadvantage is that it does not have such built-in audit software functions as statistical sample selections or serial number gap detection. However, it works quite well for item selections, recalculations, file matching, and data reporting purposes. Many specialized audit functions can be coded into the retrieval language with little difficulty.

Many software products come delivered with some type of vendor-supplied retrieval package. For example, accounting software packages for general ledger accounting often come with their own report retrieval packages. Even specialized commercial software today, such as a system to control inventory in an IT document media library, comes with its own specialized retrieval software. These tools often are useful to an IT auditor for accessing and analyzing the particular data records.

A major disadvantage with the various retrieval products included in other commercial software is that an IT auditor, in a larger enterprise, may be required to learn the report generation language from multiple software products, none of which may follow a consistent syntax. There may be one or several installed on the centralized computers, plus others on divisional servers or local workstations. Even though the learning curve for writing audit retrievals with these products is typically short, IT audit may encounter both training and logistical difficulties. Laptop system audit packages, discussed in the next section, can provide a single software retrieval product for use throughout the enterprise. However, audit objectives will determine what type of audit software is best used.

Desktop and Laptop CAATTs

Desktop and laptop computers are standard IT auditor tools. Modern versions of these systems are pervasive in enterprises today, either as freestanding devices or, more typically, networked together and to central servers. Laptop or desktop computers are useful tools for developing CAATTs, and several excellent commercial audit retrieval products are available to aid IT auditors. In addition, some standard desktop software products can be used for audit retrieval purposes to access or download data and bring them to IT audit's laptop computer.

IT auditors often wish to examine and analyze the contents of data files located on various remote computer systems within the enterprise where generalized audit software or other retrieval tools may not be available for processing. For example, due to software license restrictions or system incompatibilities, IT audit's generalized audit software may be usable only on the central server systems. Data files from other locations would have to be transported to that central site using the enterprise's communications network. Even if retrieval languages were available at all locations, it might be necessary for IT audit to spend extra travel time and resources processing CAATTs at these remote locations. Desktop-based computer audit software tools can solve many of these problems.

Laptop and desktop computer audit software is a type of generalized audit software with many of the functions and features typically found on larger server systems. It is generally not designed to perform audit retrievals from other systems and to extract files from larger computer system applications. This software originally was developed for external auditors who need to access files from many different clients and IT systems. Therefore, many products have had an external auditor emphasis. Public accounting firms have developed software that they sometimes make available to their clients, and commercial vendors market others. One software product that this author has found to be quite useful in an IT audit environment is called Audit Command Language (ACL; www.acl.com).

IT audit often must extract and analyze data from very large files with millions of records. Sometimes it is more convenient for IT audit to process this data on an audit department system rather than directly on mainframe systems. Typically this larger volume of data can be processed on a much smaller audit desktop computer equipped with a very-high-capacity USB memory stick. Internal control issues regarding these USB memory devices are discussed briefly in Chapters 6 and 8. Auditor laptop systems also need a way to read files from mainframe systems, such as a network communications port to access the mainframe processors. These linkages are effective provided the mainframe files are not too large and the laptop system has a sufficient hard disk

ACL is a conversational, easy-to-use interactive command audit language that the auditor can load onto a computer system to access a fairly universal set of computer file structures. Files can be accessed through an online connection extracted from the data center.

As an example of using ACL, assume an internal auditor wanted to recalculate taxes payable account for a situation where the tax rates would be 20, 30, or 50% depending on the income level. Income less than $5,000 would result in no taxes, and the other income breaks are $10,000, $30,000, and above. An audit analysis program to recalculate those taxes would first require codes to indicate where annual income was located on the tax file. The taxes payable could then be calculated with the following ACL command statements:

TAXES_PAYABLE_COMPUTED

0				IF INCOME < 5000
		.2	*	(INCOME − 5,000)	IF (INCOME < 10,000)
1,000	+	.3	*	(INCOME − 10,000)	IF (INCOME < 30,000)
7,000	+	.5	*	(INCOME − 30,000)	

These four commands would read through the file and produce an audit total.

EXHIBIT 13.3   CAATT Programming Example Using ACL
Source: Robert R. Moeller, *Brink's Modern Internal Auditing*, 7th ed. (Hoboken, NJ: John Wiley & Sons, 2009). Copyright © 2009, John Wiley & Sons. Used with permission of John Wiley & Sons.

capacity. An alternative and often better approach is to equip the audit computer with a USB memory stick or cartridge drive. The audit computer can then process this data for the computer audit test.

The actual audit software programs used for the computer-assisted audit procedures have similar functions and capabilities as generalized audit software tools, and most types of CAATT procedures, such as testing agings or recalculating balances, can be used with audit departmental computers. The only limitation sometimes is the memory and storage capacity of smaller systems. Thus, if a large number of data files are to be compared as part of the CAATT, a laptop system will not be that efficient because only one tape drive typically is available.

Exhibit 13.3 illustrates the programming instructions necessary to develop a CAATT application using the ACL product. In this example, an IT auditor would have secured a copy or extract of the enterprise's accounts receivable master. Using the ACL, IT audit can perform this common financial audit task easily. The idea here is not to show how to write such a program but to illustrate that it is a relatively simple and easy-to-learn task.

Auditor Test Data or "Test Deck" Approaches

Test deck is an old IT audit–related term dating back to the earliest days of IT systems, when applications operated in a batch mode and used punch cards as input media. In order to test a computer application, IT auditors developed a series of test transactions that achieved known results. These transactions were originally prepared on a set of input punch cards, or a test deck. The term *test deck* is dated, but it describes a very useful CAATT approach where an IT auditor submits a series of test transactions against a live production system to determine if controls are adequate. (A better expression for this approach is *test data*, although we will continue to use the traditional name.)

For example, IT audit might use a test deck CAATT approach to test controls in a batch payroll system. IT audit would submit transactions for known employees showing standard hours of work, for others show some overtime hours, and for a third group show an excessive number of hours that should trigger an error report. A special, controlled run of the payroll system would then be arranged using these test transactions. IT audit subsequently would verify that the pay was correctly computed, the files were correctly updated, and that all expected error and transaction reports were correct. The audit test transactions then would be purged from the updated files. Through this test deck, IT audit could gain a level of assurance that the payroll system, in this example, was working correctly.

Test deck approaches fell into disuse by IT auditors as systems ceased to be batch oriented and became more complex. However, this approach—which calls for the submission of audit test transactions to a copy of a live application—is still a viable CAATT tool for testing some modern IT applications. An actual deck of test transaction cards is not necessary. Test decks—or, more properly, test data approaches—can be very useful for gathering audit evidence. Today's IT auditor will certainly not prepare a deck of test cards; rather, the approach uses a predetermined set of online transactions as the test deck. The CAATT approach allows IT audit to input a series of test transactions through an application input screen to achieve these objectives:

- A general understanding of the program logic associated with a complex system
- A determination that valid transactions are being processed correctly by the application
- A determination that invalid or incorrect transactions are being identified correctly and flagged by the application's program controls

There are limitations in this testing approach. If a given transaction type has not been prepared for the test, IT audit cannot affirm that the application works correctly in respect to that transaction. If the documentation is incomplete or incorrect, IT audit may miss a key transaction test.

Test data CAATTs also can be developed by tracing user-initiated transactions through a normal production cycle or by inputting a series of audit test transactions through a special test run of the application. There are advantages and disadvantages to each of these approaches.

Tracing and Auditing User-Initiated Transactions

An IT auditor sometimes must review and gather evidence of transaction controls for complex, online IT applications. For example, IT audit may want to verify that a manufacturing resource planning (MRP) system is operating with proper controls. Such an MRP system generally has numerous programs to:

- Control the receipt of materials into the plant.
- Place them in inventory.
- Later retrieve them from stores and assign them to manufacturing work orders.
- Add labor and other parts to complete the manufacturing process.

These numerous and various transaction types, which update or impact multiple programs, are difficult to assess through sample processing tests. When faced with a complex application, an IT auditor often is unable to identify single points in the application process to develop comprehensive CAATTs. A formal test data approach, where IT audit sets up a separate system process, is also difficult due to the overall complexity of the system.

The most reasonable approach to testing may be to trace a representative sample of normal transactions initiated through the production application. Following the example of a MRP system, an IT auditor first should identify key control points in the overall system. The next step is to observe and record transactions being entered at each of these points so that subsequently they can be traced to the appropriate online screens or reports. As part of this observation, IT audit also may want to ask users to input certain invalid transactions to ascertain that they have been correctly rejected. Exhibit 13.4 shows this user test data CAATT approach.

The tracing of user-initiated transactions is similar to the transaction walk-through approach for computer applications described in Chapter 10. The difference here, however, is that an IT auditor captures a more substantial number of normal transactions for tracing and verification. This approach is not a true CAATT but it can be combined with other CAATTs at key points to gain a better understanding of the application's processing procedures and of its controls. For example, IT audit can trace inventory transactions input through the o-line screens of a manufacturing system. Combined with a CAATT, these then could be used to compare beginning- and ending-period inventory status files to highlight the differences caused by the production online transactions.

This procedure is more like a manual testing technique than a true CAATT, emphasizing transaction input processing and the resultant outputs rather than the actual program operations. Often this method is not the best way to gain positive assurance that an application is working with all of the proper controls. However, it can be an effective way to gain some assurance that the application appears to be working with no obvious errors. Although individual programs can be tested in some detail, this may be the only way to test an entire operational application.

Application Tests Using Test Data

This CAATT approach uses auditor-prepared test data transaction or test files. If an application has only one key input point, auditor-initiated test data entered through that point for processing in a special run often can be an effective CAATT. For example, an enterprise may have an online labor hour collection system where employees input hours on a single-screen format for recording time and allocating the hours to various

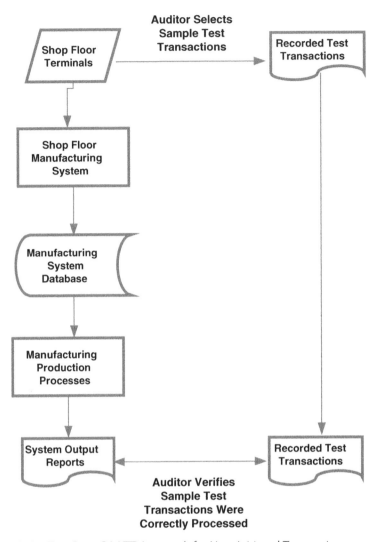

EXHIBIT 13.4 Test Data CAATT Approach for User-Initiated Transactions

projects. IT audit may be interested in verifying the integrity and correctness of the output data here.

An approach to testing this type of system is to build an audit file of representative test transactions for input to a special test run. These transactions represent differing valid and error conditions to allow IT audit to test as many conditions as possible through a special run of the application under review. Live files or copies of live files can be used for all processing. The auditor's file of test transactions is input to this test run, and IT audit subsequently verifies the results of the system processing. The test data approach can be an effective CAATT to gather evidence about smaller, self-contained IT applications. Rather than using audit software to develop retrieval reports showing file contents, this technique allows IT audit to test program logic by passing test transactions against a set of live data files and production programs to verify the correctness of application processing. The user-initiated transaction approach discussed previously has an IT auditor reviewing the results of an actual production transaction; this approach allows the auditor to develop a series of can't-happen transactions to determine how systems controls are working in these extraordinary situations. The approach also has some limitations:

- Data processing operations sometimes will object to IT audit's request to process a special run of one of their production applications for fear that the audit test data somehow will become intermingled with and corrupt the normal production data.
- Test data can effectively test only one cycle of an application. Due to the IT operations disruptions this CAATT causes, it is usually difficult to schedule multiple test cycles.
- The approach is cost effective only for more self-contained applications since it is difficult to design test data covering multiple input points.
- The preparation of a comprehensive set of test data often is more time consuming than the preparation of a conventional CAATT retrieval program.

Despite these limitations, a test data approach often is useful when IT audit reviews an application that has been implemented at multiple locations within the enterprise. By developing a standard set of test data and using it at each location, IT audit can verify, among other things, that there have been no unauthorized changes to the application programs.

Specialized Audit Test and Analysis Software

IT audit often has a need to review specialized computer files, such as those associated with the computer operating system or online transaction log files. Doing this requires a very different type of CAATT from what IT audit would develop for financial and operational application audit tests. Because computer operating systems and related files generally are very complex, generalized audit software usually will not work. Generalized audit software works best with conventional files defined in fixed record and field lengths; system software files use very specialized file format structures.

A creative and technically skilled IT auditor can use other specialized software tools to develop unique CAATTs. Many are not specifically designed for most IT auditors but for normal computer systems developers or end users. However, IT audit sometimes can make very effective use of them. Some specialized tools are listed next.

- Manufacturing production and materials scheduling software packages often contain ad hoc reporting subsystems to analyze these manufacturing files. IT audit can use them to extract a sample of production part numbers for further testing.
- Software to control the movement of computer storage media in and out of the software documentation library often has an ad hoc reporting capability. With minimal training, an IT auditor can use these report generator packages to test library operational and media management controls.

Although typically not considered CAATT software, numerous ad hoc retrieval or analysis software packages can aid IT audit in a review of IT-based data. Because this type of software is often easy to learn and use, IT audit needs only to ask if such software is available when reviewing a specialized area or application. In other instances, IT audit may need to acquire certain specialized software tools to support audit efforts.

Continuous Audit Monitor Design and Implementation

Chapter 14 provides more information on continuous monitors. They are useful, for example, when an IT auditor is working in a multibranch financial enterprise with numerous transactions among the branches. They are effective when IT audit has reviewed the significant financial applications to test internal controls and has used generalized audit software to test key elements of the financial applications. However, the IT auditor is interested in monitoring and following up on certain exception transactions that may be initiated by various branch users.

This example application has a large number of exception reports for user follow-up: IT audit is interested only in reviewing certain interbranch transactions above a specified dollar limit. Normal operational personnel also follow up on such transactions, but the IT auditor is interested in the nature of such transactions and the level of follow-up activity. A continuous audit monitor CAATT can allow IT audit to review these ongoing exception transactions.

A continuous audit monitor CAATT is special, auditor-defined software that gathers continuous evidence about transaction exceptions or potentially unauthorized items that may require auditor follow-up. This type of monitor will not allow IT audit to perform detailed tests of an application but will collect the transaction data for subsequent testing and analysis. Because it must be built into a production set of programs, a continuous audit monitor CAATT should be installed only where IT audit has a strong, ongoing review interest.

Continuing with the last example, an IT auditor gains a detailed understanding of the application and identifies where the interbranch transactions of interest can be captured in the application. The IT function then inserts program code into the application to monitor and capture all such transactions of interest. The code normally is written onto a protected log file for later audit review and analysis. Exhibit 13.5 illustrates how such a continuous audit monitor might be constructed.

Because a continuous audit monitor is an embedded set of program code, it cannot be changed easily. IT audit should design the objectives and selection criteria associated with any such monitor carefully. Properly constructed, however, it can be an effective tool to independently monitor applications where IT audit has an ongoing interest. There are some potential problems with this approach since IT audit generally is not able to implement such a procedure independently, and needs the assistance of the IT department to build the monitor into a production application.

Several of the CAATTs discussed in this chapter can be established fairly independently by IT audit. Given an understanding of file structures, IT audit can use generalized audit software to perform various tests. Similarly, many test data procedures

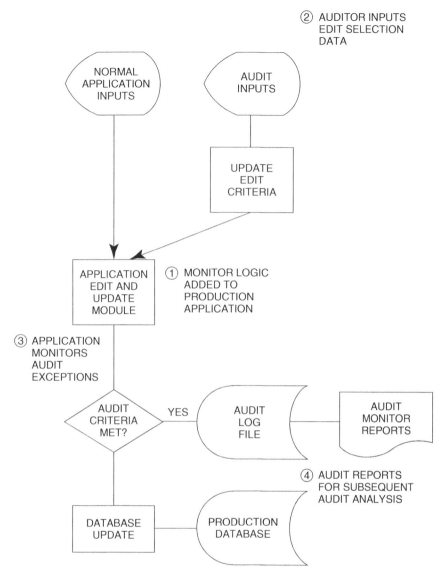

EXHIBIT 13.5 Continuous Audit Monitor CAATT

Source: Robert R. Moeller, *Brink's Modern Internal Auditing*, 7th ed. (Hoboken, NJ: John Wiley & Sons, 2009). Copyright © 2009, John Wiley & Sons. Used with permission of John Wiley & Sons.

can be established independently. However, this is not true for the continuous audit monitor, which must be embedded into a normal production application. The most efficient time to suggest the implementation of such a monitor is when an application is being developed.

If appropriate, an IT auditor can request a continuous audit monitor to be installed as part of the auditor's review of the system under development. Installing a continuous audit monitor in an application already operational is more difficult; it will require an application modification that often require changes to all associated procedures. IT audit also should recognize that because the IT function installs such a monitor, it will be aware of the program and potentially has the ability to bypass its monitoring functions. Nevertheless, a continuous audit monitor can be a powerful tool to review certain exception items associated with critical transactions. Although the example cited was for a financial application, the procedure is applicable to many other types of nonfinancial applications.

The decision of which CAATT software approach to use depends very much on overall audit objectives. IT audit should consider the appropriate type of audit software, depending on overall audit objectives, the equipment environment, auditor IT skill levels, and budget constraints. IT audit should work with financial and operational internal auditors and develop effective and repeatable CAATT procedures that should improve overall audit effectiveness.

STEPS TO BUILDING EFFECTIVE CAATTS

Exhibit 13.1 outlined some general approaches for building a CAATT. IT auditors should follow these same approaches for developing CAATTs, whether using generalized audit software, a report generator retrieval language, or downloaded data to an auditor's laptop computer. This approach is similar to the systems development approaches discussed in Chapter 10. A unique aspect of a CAATT, however, is that an IT auditor sometimes develops a CAATT for a one-time or limited-use effort rather than for an ongoing production application. For example, the CAATT may be developed to provide support for a fraud investigation; one hopes this would be a one-time but very important use of the CAATT. Because IT audit often draws conclusions and makes significant recommendations based on the results of a CAATT, it is important to use good systems practices to design and test CAATTs. A four-step approach to develop a CAATT is presented next.

1. **Determine audit objectives of the computer-assisted audit application.** All too often an internal audit manager just directs a staff IT auditor to write a CAATT for some planned audit without fully defining its objectives. The desired audit objectives should be clearly defined; this will make the subsequent identification of testing procedures a much easier task. Once IT audit has defined CAATT objectives, file layouts and systems flowcharts should be obtained to select the appropriate data sources for testing. CAATT documentation files or workpapers also should be started along with this step.
2. **Design the computer-assisted application.** The CAATT software tool used must be well understood, including its features, the overall program logic, and reporting formats. Any special codes or other data characteristics must be discussed with persons responsible for the computer application. Consideration also should be given to how IT audit will prove the results of audit tests by, for example, balancing to production application control totals. These matters should be outlined in the documentation workpapers.
3. **Program or code and then test the application.** This task usually follows step 2 very closely. Programming is performed using the generalized audit software

or some other selected software tool. Once the CAATT has been programmed, IT audit should arrange to test it on a limited population of data. The results must be verified for both correctness of program logic and the achievement of desired audit objectives. This activity also should be documented in the workpapers. Correctness of program logic means the CAATT must *work*. Sometimes an error in coding will cause the application to fail to process. The failure to achieve audit objectives is a different kind of problem. For example, in a CAATT to survey conditions in an inventory file, an auditor may make too broad of a selection, producing an output report of thousands of minor exceptions. Such CAATT logic should be revised to produce a more reasonable size selection.

4. **Process and complete the CAATT.** Making arrangements for processing a CAATT often requires coordination between IT audit and IT operations. IT audit often is interested in a specific generation of a data file, and it is necessary to arrange access to it. During the actual processing, IT audit must take steps to ensure that the files tested are the correct versions.

Depending on the nature of the CAATT, an IT auditor should prove the results and follow up on any exceptions, as required. If there are problems with the CAATT logic, IT audit should make corrections as required and repeat the steps. The CAATT application workpapers should be completed at this point, including follow-up points for improving the CAATT for future periods.

CAATTs are powerful audit aids that can be used by any internal auditor and should not be the sole responsibility of an IT audit specialist. Just as end users make increasing use of retrieval tools for their own IT needs, all members of an internal audit department should gain an understanding of available audit tools to allow them to develop their own CAATTs.

As more and more automated processes become paperless, the auditor's need to build and use CAATTs will increase. That is, the traditional paper trails that auditors once used to trace and validate transactions have been reduced or even eliminated in today's systems. Audit tools ranging from generalized audit software to continuous audit monitors will increasingly become the only options available to test and gather evidence about these paperless systems. Many operational systems have some very strong paperless elements. For example, both electronic data interchange systems and the automatic teller machines used by financial institutions have very limited paper trails, and the only way to audit such applications effectively is through the use of CAATTs. An IT auditor must be creative when designing a CAATT to gather evidence regarding these paperless applications. Many of the techniques described in this chapter apply.

 ## IMPORTANCE OF CAATTS FOR AUDIT EVIDENCE GATHERING

IT auditors sometimes do not give sufficient attention to the need to gather evidence when reviewing automated applications. Often, gaining an understanding of an automated application and evaluating its internal controls are interesting and challenging audit tasks. Some IT auditors believe that detailed confirmations of account balances or other types of evidence-gathering tests are not interesting and are too time consuming. However, these evidence-gathering procedures often provide IT audit with opportunities to implement the most creative portion of the audit project. Assume, for example, that IT audit has performed a detailed internal controls-oriented review of a large fixed-asset capital budgeting application where transactions are initiated from a variety of subsidiary systems and where the application eventually provides general ledger financial statement balances. IT audit has tested system-to-system internal controls and concludes that they are adequate; it also has manually recalculated the depreciation expenses for several selected transactions and found them to be correct.

Can an IT auditor, working with other internal auditors, conclude that the fixed assets and accumulated depreciation numbers produced by this sample system are accurate? In a large enterprise, where fixed assets may represent a substantial portion of the balance sheet, an IT auditor may decide that there is far too great of a risk in relying solely on just this internal controls review. The several transactions selected for a recalculation compliance test may not be representative of the entire population, and there may be an error in certain classes of these transactions. Although application-to-application controls may have appeared proper, some types of transactions may be assigned to incorrect account groups. Without detailed CAATT-based testing of this example fixed assets system, it is possible that these errors could go undetected.

IT auditors should have an understanding of when it is cost effective and appropriate to develop CAATTs to perform detailed tests of IT applications in order to verify the correctness of transactions or account balances. Some circumstances in which IT audit should perform this more detailed application evidence gathering and testing include:

■ There is a perception that the risk of relying just on internal controls is too high.
■ Although IT audit may have performed limited walk-through or compliance types of tests, the test results may be somewhat inconclusive and suggest a need for more detailed tests.
■ In some instances, certain internal controls may be weak or difficult to identify; and IT audit may want to develop CAATTs to perform detailed tests of the automated applications.
■ Some complex or large automated applications are involved, such as comprehensive enterprise resource planning systems.

In many instances, the decision whether to rely on just internal accounting controls and limited compliance testing or to perform detailed tests of transactions will be made by audit management. However, the use of CAATTs should be a key IT audit tool in many situations. The nature of the audit tests to be performed, the extent of data, the complexity of the application, and the tools and skills available to IT audit should all be factors in this decision. IT audit should become familiar with the various software products and techniques available for analyzing and testing IT system files. The implementation and processing of CAATTs should be part of the skill set requirement for all IT auditors.

CHAPTER FOURTEEN

Continuous Assurance Auditing, OLAP, and XBRL

CONTINUOUS ASSURANCE AUDITING (CAA) is the process of installing control-related monitors in information technology (IT) application systems such that these monitors will send signals or messages to auditors—usually IT auditors—if the automated system's processing signals a deviation with one or another installed audit limits or parameters. This concept has been around since the earliest days of IT auditing, when pioneer IT audit specialists experimented with monitoring tools known as integrated test facilities (ITFs) or system continuous audit review file (SCARF) facilities. These processes date back to the days of mainframe computers and the almost primitive technology of that era. Although these continuous audit monitor concepts sounded very interesting, they were seldom if ever successfully implemented in the era of batch processing and magnetic tape storage applications.

The concepts behind ITFs and SCARFs later evolved into CAA monitoring techniques. They remained as interesting but future-directed topics at IT audit technology–related conferences through the 1990s. Finally, technology and, to some extent the Sarbanes-Oxley Act (SOx), are making CAA a very practicable alternative for auditing automated systems. In the testimony of James Castellano before Congress regarding the fall of Enron, the chair of the American Institute of Certified Public Accountants (AICPA) emphasized the importance of using a continuous auditing approach. His February 2002 comments included:

> The transition to new reporting and auditing models is going to demand not only new audit approaches but personnel of the highest caliber. With this in mind, the profession has been working actively in the following areas:

continuous auditing or continuous assurance involves reporting on short time frames and can pertain to either reporting on the effectiveness of a system producing data or more frequent reporting on the data itself.[1] (Emphasis added.)

This chapter discusses CAA as an improved IT audit approach for reviewing today's automated systems as well as what is known as continuous monitoring (CM), business-controlled procedures that can be subject to periodic IT audits. Technology makes continuous auditing approaches much easier to implement, and SOx's evolving requirements for almost real-time financial reporting makes these concepts very attractive. These concepts lead to installed audit monitors and the ability to close an enterprise's financial reports almost in real time. CAA represents a dramatic change in the audit model and may change both auditor practices and skill requirements as it becomes more widely accepted.

Enterprises today have multiple needs to retain all forms of operating and historical information stored on their IT systems databases. When this stored data is organized in a series of large, complex, and interrelated databases, these large databases are known as data warehouses. A data warehouse environment is an almost necessary component for implementing CAA, as are the data warehouse tools of data mining and online analytical processing (OLAP). This chapter briefly discusses these concepts and their applicability to IT audit processes.

Finally, the chapter introduces XBRL, the AICPA-initiated, eXtensible Business Reporting Language. XBRL is an evolving standard for communicating business and financial information across multiple enterprises. For example, XBRL allows enterprises to code standard values on their financial reports, such as the values for total assets or accumulated depreciations, making it very easy for other users to identify these values despite different physical reporting formats. XBRL is becoming an increasingly important tool for worldwide business-related financial reporting.

IT auditors need to develop at least some general understanding of these CAA and XBRL concepts. Although CAA techniques currently are not used by many IT auditors today, an understanding of them will create audit efficiencies and improve procedures for auditing IT applications. Chapter 10 discussed processes for selecting and auditing an IT application as essentially a one-time exercise. With CAA, an IT auditor can set up automated tools to monitor such applications on a regular, continuous basis. XBRL coding is less an IT audit process but an IT coding and identification technique that is growing in importance and use. IT auditors should understand that these tools and concepts may be useful in other IT audit processes as well.

IMPLEMENTING CONTINUOUS ASSURANCE AUDITING

Going beyond just IT auditing, the more traditional process of financial auditing has gone through a series of conceptual changes over time. In its earliest days, financial auditing was primarily a process of vouching and testing, a concept that goes back to the dictionary definitions of these terms. To "vouch" means to attest, guarantee, or certify something as being true or reliable, and auditors performed tests to support that vouching process. Such often detailed types of audit procedures have been used for years. However, as processes became more highly automated, auditors began to rely primarily on reviews of internal controls to support their audit conclusions rather than the old-fashioned vouching. If the internal controls were adequate and found to be working through testing, there was less need to perform detailed transaction testing. In a phase of auditing going up through the early 1990s, auditors placed a major emphasis on reviews of internal controls as the major component of their attest work.

Over the years with an increasing number of IT applications and controls to consider plus with an ongoing emphasis on increased audit efficiency, auditors—particularly external auditors—began performing formal risk analyses over their control environments focusing only on higher-risk internal control areas. This audit risk analysis process was discussed in Chapter 4 and can be considered a third phase of auditing after, first, vouch and test and, second, internal control reviews. Many analyses of what happened after Enron, WorldCom, Tyco, HealthSouth, and a host of other corporate frauds in the early years of this century raised questions about the audit procedures used. How could these failures have happened? Why did external auditors not see internal control weaknesses and other problems? One of the concerns often cited was that financial reports were frequently unreliable. A second concern and criticism was that the supporting final audited reports often were delivered well after the official statement closing dates and contained many pro forma, or best-guess, numbers. SOx now requires that financial reports be closed and issued on a much tighter schedule, closer to the enterprise's period ending dates. That requirement points to the need for continuous close audits and auditor assurances—what may become the next phase of audit techniques.

What are Continuous Assurance Auditing and Monitoring Systems?

CAA is an audit process that produces results simultaneously with, or soon after, the occurrence of actual events. Auditor-supervised controls, for example, are installed in a major, enterprise-wide resource application that include alarm monitors and continuous analytical analysis routines to either attest results or highlight items for immediate audit analysis. A CAA is generally independent of the underlying business application with processes that test transactional data against defined control parameters. CAA processes today run automatically on a daily or weekly basis and generate exception reports or alerts for IT auditor follow-up. Similar to the traditional audit process, CAA is more detective than preventive.

Although the underlying concepts are very similar, continuous assurance auditing and continuous monitoring sometimes are confused. Their basic characteristics are listed next.

Continuous Assurance Auditing (CAA)

▪ CAAs are repetitive software audit monitors that are built into IT applications. For example, if IT audit is interested in financial transactions in some general ledger account above some specified limit, a software change can be installed to monitor any activity that meets the criterion.

- Rather than scheduling periodic IT audits to review an area, CAA records areas of potential interest for IT audit's attention. It is then IT audit's responsibility to follow up on these items.
- IT audit is generally responsible for the CAA software, often installed confidentially, and may face problems if application users make certain IT changes.

Continuous Monitoring (CM)

- In many respects, CM is very similar to CAA except that an IT function—usually at the request of management—installs CM in an application of interest.
- Rather than looking for individual exception items or unusual transactions, CM often is installed in the form of a dashboard screen—similar to the dashboard in an automobile—to monitor ongoing status.
- IT audit may review CM processes on a periodic basis, but often only to gain assurance that the overall process is working.

While the concepts between CM and CAA similar but different in their objectives, an IT auditor should have a basic understanding of CM and of the basic characteristics of CAA. In its most basic design, a CAA is an independent application that monitors another critical application while CM is a risk and control monitoring system. Exhibit 14.1 shows a CM application for an automated payments system. The CM application is a separate and parallel set of software that monitors all payment activity through periodic reviews of activity in a payments transaction file. Activity summaries are reported periodically, and any unusual items are highlighted in an exception report, probably through an e-mail notice. This type of system is very similar to the kinds of password security monitors currently in place in many enterprises. Exception activity would be reported on a regular basis, but any red-flag violations would be highlighted for immediate attention. The

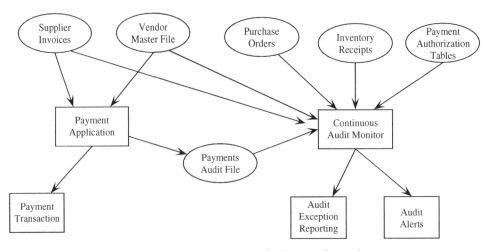

EXHIBIT 14.1   Payment System Continuous Audit Monitor Example

concepts behind CM and CAA processes are similar; we generally refer to them as just CAA or CAA/CM processes in this chapter.

Although definitions may vary across different enterprises and industries, the goal of CAA/CM processes is to provide for the timely reporting of internal control status across multiple IT applications and automated processes. Continuous auditing is the automated collection of audit evidence and indicators by an IT auditor from an entity's IT systems, processes, transactions, and controls on a frequent or continuous basis. This information enhances auditor capabilities and helps to ensure compliance with enterprise policies, procedures, and regulations. In many cases, CAA/CM can act as an early warning system to detect a control failure on a more timely basis than under traditional approaches.

In contrast, continuous monitoring is an automated feedback mechanism for management, not just the auditors, to ensure that systems and controls have been operating as designed and transactions are processed appropriately. Management can utilize this information to set business rules or tests, using analytics to identify performance gaps or unusual transactions that may suggest control failures. A CM process allows management to have greater visibility into enterprise operations–enhancing capabilities and entity-level controls while maintaining optimal performance.

CAA/CM applications imply more than just monitors that run against application transaction files, and they usually highlight exceptions. For many enterprises, IT applications are much more complex; enterprise resource planning (ERP) systems are an example. ERPs are the all-inclusive application packages, by vendors such as SAP, Oracle, or Lawson, that provide a total systems solutions, including accounting, the general ledger, human resources, and purchasing. They are complex IT applications that cover virtually all application areas in the enterprise. An average ERP implementation at a larger enterprise may cost $12 million and takes almost two years to implement. ERP implementations usually are built around a single or a closely federated set of databases. Any CAA set of monitors used must be much more complex than monitors for a single application as many transactions may be updating or depending on multiple system program tables. CAA/CM is very useful here as it allows monitoring to be installed over a complex set of processes. An ERP system is also the ideal environment to install CAA as the monitoring activity can be built around the common database structure of an ERP implementation.

Exhibit 14.2 provides a conceptual view of a CAA process. Multiple applications here are monitored for compliance with a series of predefined control conditions with all exceptions logged. At the base of the exhibit is a stream of measurable IT application processes such as might occur in a complex ERP. The audit team establishes some metrics it wishes to monitor as well as supporting standards for those metrics. As a simple example, IT audit might be interested in the sales division office ERP transactions over $10,000 because of a management-expressed concern of possible unapproved marketing activity. Metrics tools could be built into these processes to monitor all cash transfer transactions with a provision that any amount over this $10,000 limit should be flagged. The process could have multiple levels of metrics and standards with exceptions fed up to a first-level assurance process that would monitor the difference and, in some instances, send back a correcting feedback transaction to the ongoing

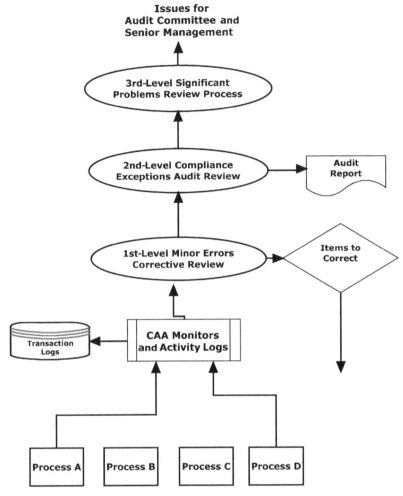

EXHIBIT 14.2 Continuous Assurance Auditing Conceptual Model

process. The first level of monitoring here might be similar to the warning notes that are sent to a corporate systems user when his or her e-mail mailbox is over 90% full.

Other discrepancies would flow up to what the exhibit shows as a second-level monitoring or auditing process. This level would produce the reports to management or emergency exception notices. Beyond reports, this level could produce more significant audit or assurance actions. In our mailbox-full example, the CAA process would initiate a transaction to prevent further accesses to the offending user. There is also a third level to CAA to monitor the auditing process. Control procedures would be built into the process to monitor ongoing CAA activity. The enterprise could use this level to report serious CAA violations to senior management and the audit committee.

The continuous audit monitoring processes just described can be performed on multiple levels. The first CAA level might be to flag and extract all transactions that pass resources between the enterprise and some entity of interest, extracting all transactions that match auditor-defined criteria for further analysis, vouching, or reporting. An example might be installing monitors to screen for all financial transactions with some group of countries or companies of interest. A second level would be a bit more sophisticated and would include some limits or logical templates in the evaluation process, such as maximums and minimums in the monitors. On a third and more analytical level, the CAA could examine the formal rules relative to the process monitored. An example here might be the use of system-generated values, such as interest rates or asset returns, and a comparison with auditor initiated reasonableness tests of those assumptions compared with historical values.

At its most basic level, CAA introduces a heightened level of monitoring to application systems. Classic auditor points of control will disappear into the processing system, changing recording and measurement tools. The cycle time for making audit-based decisions or actions will very much decrease as it is based on system measures. A CAA often is used to create an environment for 24-hour-a-day, 7-day-a-week (24/7) continuous auditing.

CAA processes already have been implemented at a variety of larger enterprises. The original AT&T ("the Telephone Company"), for example, was an early leader, and today CAA has become quite common in the insurance, stock brokerage, and medical claims processing industries. Built around an enterprise's ERP system, CAA is particularly useful for monitoring purchase and payment cycle applications with an emphasis on controls over potential vendor-related fraud. CAA is a valuable tool for any application area where cash is going out the door, including employee travel accounting, insurance claims, and money laundering controls.

Resource Requirements for Implementing CAA

Although the basic concepts of implementing a CAA in an ERP or other business applications seem relatively straightforward, the actual implementation of a CAA in an enterprise often presents challenges. In order for this monitoring process to be independent of other IT applications, the CAA should be installed with some level of independence from other IT personnel who operate in the same process area as the CAA. That is, if a CAA has an objective to monitor all marketing expense transactions over X dollars and some certain other conditions, those marketing expense system monitoring controls must be installed independently such that they cannot be easily bypassed. However, installing a CAA process in an ERP or any other complex business applications may require some IT technical skills that are beyond the capabilities of some IT auditors. Conversely, even if IT audit has the technical skills to install CAA in an enterprise's applications, IT management often may look at any such proposal skeptically. IT management often will not trust its IT auditors to install their own CAA monitoring software in production systems environment, but if IT agrees to take the CAA software module and test and modify it for production installation, the CAA's independence could be compromised.

The market is always changing, but this section introduces several vendor-supplied software solutions to install CAA. The products or approaches discussed are not the only solutions to installing CAA but represent some good starting points for the enterprise that is considering using CAA. The concepts of CAA have been described and discussed for some time at academic conferences; CAA is just beginning to be more widely recognized. For example, the July 2008 annual Institute of Internal Auditors (IIA) International Conference in San Francisco had three sessions on CAA as part of their technical program.

Good sources for more information about CAA can be found at the Rutgers University accounting Web site (http://raw.rutgers.edu/) The Rutgers site has a wealth of information on CAA approaches; the school even sponsors conferences on the effective use of CAA. Partly based on presentations from past continuous auditing presentations, we have selected several CAA implementation examples.

Microsoft's CAA Approach

Microsoft's corporate IT audit function has developed a CAA approach it calls technology-enabled continuous auditing (TECA), an internal application that serves as a bridge between CAA and CAA/CM approaches. TECA has the stated objectives of providing greater risk coverage with increased IT audit productivity, with more detailed and frequent testing, and shortened audit cycle times.

Although it is an internal and proprietary application, the Microsoft chief audit executive (CAE) gave a presentation about TECA at the 2008 IIA conference, and there are numerous Web references to it in brochures describing local IIA activities.

According to their 2008 presentation, Microsoft IT audit views its TECA application as its approach to continuous audit monitoring, allowing it to analyze transactions as they flow through Microsoft internal systems and to provide improved IT audit work flow. Linking custom applications, ERP systems, human resource applications, and others, Exhibit 14.3

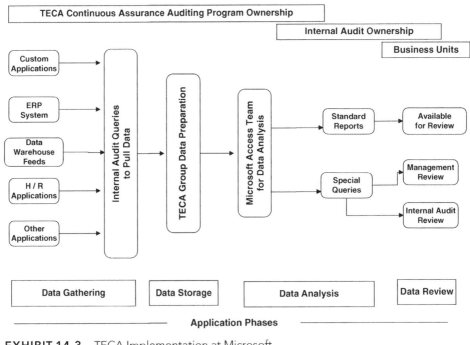

EXHIBIT 14.3 TECA Implementation at Microsoft

shows the TECA implementation at Microsoft. Space as well as our limited understanding of this application does not allow a complete description.

A major corporation with global operations, Microsoft internal audit has implemented its TECA system for monitoring travel and entertainment expense reporting, checking for duplicate reported expenses, excessive employee-reported out-of-pocket expenses, and inappropriate reported exchange rates. Other areas where their IT audit function is using TECA is for a CAA monitoring of Statement on Auditing Standards (SAS) No. 99 potential fraud activities,[2] where the application identifies potentially inappropriate journal entries posted at month-end as well as large or unusual items for internal audit follow-up.

Our description of Microsoft IT audit's TECA CAA application is based on the comments and presentation materials distributed at a public professional conference. Microsoft IT audit appears to be doing an excellent job in implementing an effective CAA process for internal audit operations.

ACL Continuous Assurance Systems

Recently many auditors have used a software product called Audit Command Language and developed by the software firm, ACL.[3] ACL is a popular software product for computer-assisted audit analysis and retrievals that was discussed in Chapter 13. That same vendor provides effective CAA tools, and the ACL approach might be described as first-generation CAA. ACL takes the approach that few organizations today have implemented fully embedded and automated CAA/CM applications. Most audit-related testing applications today are simply a series of automated data analysis tests that are manually initiated and run on a regular basis. The ACL approach goes a step further such that an IT auditor does not need to formally start and run the monitoring program. The ACL software is linked to enterprise files and applications so that it can run in the background. The software is useful for such areas as detecting unusual transaction indicators of fraud or identifying duplicate and other overpayments. ACL is not truly a continuous assurance process. The company suggests that IT auditors install and run this software based on completion of process steps and at periodic intervals. The software then takes a slice of the data, capturing all transactions since the last test process. ACL continuous assurance software is used today by all of the major public accounting firms as well as a large number of major corporations in the United States. An organization that is interested in implementing a beginning level of CAA might well consider starting with ACL's assurance product.

Dashboard Approach to Monitoring: BusinessObjects and Others

Complex information systems can be built with a wide variety of monitoring programs and displays to allow an operator to review performance and highlight any potential problems. This is similar to the driver of an automobile who faces a dashboard that monitors the car. The dashboard shows such things as the speed, progress by miles traveled, status by showing the fuel remaining, and problems by displaying warnings for such items as low oil pressure. In addition, today many drivers have installed global positioning system dashboard screens on their vehicles. This dashboard approach allows the driver to monitor overall progress while the vehicle is in operation and to take action as required. That same dashboard approach can be used with business information systems.

Today's typical online application has a continuous display for that application. In a sales order application, for example, designated users can access the progress of sales recorded, perhaps by product line or region, through an online terminal. However, that monitoring typically covers just that one sales application; another screen must be called up to review a related activities handled by other applications, such as ongoing cash collections or returns. Today's ERP applications provide a better environment for such cross-application monitoring as all of the ERP components, from receiving to general ledger processes, are under a common database structure. In addition, several good software products allow an organization to install dashboard monitors to review overall progress of business transactions and other activities to allow for prompt remedial action when necessary. Two of the better of these software tools are the offerings of BusinessObjects[4] and Cognos.[5] Each firm's products allow an organization to tie a wide variety of diverse applications to a dashboard monitor, allowing users to monitor overall activity.

The console monitors on classic mainframe computers acted as dashboards and monitored all system activity with a constant stream of messages to the operator. The same concept can be applied to today's ERP applications. This format allows an organization and IT audit to move from an environment of monitored controls to the real-time monitoring of systems operations with adjustments for continuous improvement.

 ## BENEFITS OF CONTINUOUS ASSURANCE AUDITING TOOLS

CAA allows both IT auditors and application users to deal with IT-based issues on a real-time basis. Rather than periodically scheduled IT application audits that take place only once a year or less, a CAA process provides IT audit and management with an early warning for many areas of concern and IT audit interest. CAA provides IT audit with a tool for proactive risk management. In addition, effective CAA processes should allow IT auditors to develop a better understanding of their enterprise's business environment and to support compliance and drive business performance.

Exhibit 14.4 describes some action steps for launching CAA processes in an enterprise. Although very useful for assessing internal controls or monitoring risks for some key applications, CAA processes are not applicable to all applications. Even where they are very appropriate, IT audit must make a commitment to monitor and use the tools. CAA processes sometimes are viewed only as an IT audit "technical" tools by an audit function's financial and operational internal auditors, they can provide a strong and ongoing approach to review and monitor internal controls and performance in key enterprise IT applications.

By changing traditional IT audit approaches and implementing CAA processes, IT auditors can develop a better understanding of their business environments and the risks to their enterprise to support compliance and drive improved performance. CAA processes can provide for the automation of transaction testing through the verification

- Working with senior financial managers, IT, and others, define the high-level objectives for continuous auditing within the enterprise—what types of applications or processes are expected to be monitored.
- Identify and prioritize areas to be addressed and types of continuous auditing to be performed.
- Understand the underlying business processes and application systems, and identify key information systems and data sources.
- Develop relationships with IT management and explain objective for CAA operations.
- Establish high-level objectives for enterprise CAA activities, and identify software requirements to meet those objectives.
- Review software candidates, and select appropriate tools for CAA activities.
- Install purchased CAA software, and complete IT and internal audit staff training to use the tool.
- Select a candidate application for CAA operations.
  - Identify critical control points.
  - Define control rules.
  - Develop access and analysis capabilities.
  - Define exception conditions.
  - Design technology-assisted approach to test controls and identify deficiencies.
- Perform CAA procedures for selected applications.
  - Establish exception conditions in the production application.
  - Perform systems test to ascertain monitor is working and not violating any IT production operations functions.
  - Run the tests on a regular, timely basis.
  - Identify control deficiencies or increased levels of risk.
  - Initiate appropriate audit response, and make results known to management.
  - Manage results of reported CAA audit exceptions: tracking, reporting, monitoring, and following up.
- Monitor and evaluate the effectiveness of the continuous auditing process—both the analysis (e.g., rules/indicators) and the results achieved—and vary the test parameters as required.
- Report results to senior financial management, and obtain senior management and audit committee support.

EXHIBIT 14.4   Action Steps for Launching Continuous Assurance Auditing

of transaction integrity and validity and the generation of alarms. CAA creates an environment of continuous testing where internal control failures can be detected and fixed immediately. Although there is some effort involved in implementing CAA, its approach of looking at full populations of data from areas of interest can very much increase the overall effectiveness of IT audit. Once promoted only by future-thinking speakers at technical conferences, we are now seeing IT audit functions in major enterprises, adopt CAA approaches. It is a growing future IT audit trend.

DATA WAREHOUSES, DATA MINING, AND OLAP

For many years, data storage was considered a mundane component of the IT systems infrastructure. Back in the mainframe computer days, data necessary for immediate short-term access was stored on mass storage disk or drum drives. Other less essential data was copied to magnetic tape drives. However, the process of writing and retrieving data was very slow by today's IT standards. Those old devices do not work well today as applications have grown larger and more complex and as users became eager to analyze and understand that protected data. Data storage has become a major component of the information systems enterprise with many new tools and technologies.

This section briefly introduces several important storage management practices and related internal control concepts, but space limitations as well as the breadth of the topic restrict our discussion of some types of storage management, such as virtualization. IT auditors, however, should develop an understanding of storage management practices, which are an increasingly important IT component of the IT infrastructure. Storage management control procedures are a part of IT general controls that often have been ignored.

Importance of Storage Tools

Although we have mentioned the past use of magnetic tape drives and disk or drum storage devices, computer equipment manufacturers have been experimenting and introducing new storage devices over the years. In the mainframe, legacy systems world, the emphasis was on trying to pack more data storage capacity on frequently used reliable disk drives. During the 1970s, storage techniques ranged from large rotating drum devices on some old mainframes to experiments with holographic light-based storage. Rotating disk devices and magnetic tape prevailed, and mainframe computer operations centers in the 1980s had large amounts of their floor space devoted to these storage management disk drives. During that same period, an increasing amount of storage resources resided on desktop computers with their own very reliable and increasingly high-capacity "C drive" hard disks. Systems and databases were getting larger, and there was a need for some reliable tools to handle these ever larger storage needs. Although there were other new product attempts as well, the storage world really changed when EMC Corporation[6] launched a kitchen refrigerator–size product called a Symmetrix that was really a massive array of several hundred very high speed hard disk devices controlled through a series of controllers and attached to each other and connecting server computers through extremely fast and reliable fiber channel connections. Soon other competitors launched similar storage management, capabilities increased, and storage costs dropped dramatically. Storage management as a separate technical profession was launched.

Many enterprises experimented with these new storage device offerings, trying one or another unit. This led to storage management configurations in data centers called "just bunches of disks" (JBOD) with these storage devices all connected as well as possible to servers or central computer systems. A concept called network attached storage (NAS) soon evolved where the storage devices were connected to a network to provide file-level access to the storage data. Specialized NAS servers were added to allow applications to determine the locations of stored data so that anyone on the NAS could access stored data, and additional capacity could be added easily. From NAS, we have moved to storage area networks (SANs), where all storage devices are installed in a configuration similar to the local area network of office desktop computer systems. With SANs, stored data can be spread across multiple devices with easy switching from one to another.

Technology always moves forward, and today we have content-addressed storage (CAS) that tends to move storage from being just an archive to an environment that can respond more easily to direct user and application requests in formats ranging from classic database formats to digital photos. In addition, we are increasingly using the concept of storage virtualization, where that actual physical location of the storage device is replaced by abstract logical references. Our point here is not to attempt to explain these technologies but to highlight that storage management is an increasingly important component of an enterprise's IT environment. IT auditors can provide a major service to management through reviews of storage management capabilities, including device utilization, performance, and traffic patterns. Storage management problems can limit system availability and present difficulties in meeting service-level agreements.

Data Warehouses and Data Mining

Recently, the concept of data warehousing has evolved into a unique and separate business application class. An IT auditor may ask the question, "What is a data warehouse?" A simple answer is that a data warehouse is managed data situated after and outside the operational IT facilities. The primary concept of data warehousing is that the data stored for business analysis can be accessed most effectively by separating it from the operational systems. Many of the reasons for this separation have evolved over the years. In the past, mainframe legacy systems archived data onto tapes as they became inactive, and many analysis reports ran from these tapes to minimize the performance impact on the operational systems. Advances in technology and changes in the nature of business have made many of these business analysis processes much more complex. Today data warehousing systems support the online analytical processing (OLAP) systems to be discussed.

Data warehousing systems are most successful when necessary data can be combined, like a central parts warehouse, from multiple operational systems at a place independent of the source applications. The data warehouse can combine effectively data from multiple applications, such as sales, marketing, and production systems. Many large data warehouse architectures allow for the source applications to be integrated into the data warehouse incrementally. This allows for cross-referencing and time dimension data filtering, allowing an analyst to generate queries for a given week, month, quarter, or a year or to analyze data from old and new applications.

Building a data warehouse can be a complex task for an enterprise. Data must be gathered from multiple sources, scrubbed to clean up problems, and then converted or transformed to the data warehouse databases. Exhibit 14.5 shows this general concept at a very high level, where data is extracted and transformed from supporting enterprise systems to a data warehouse for subsequent data mining analysis.

The key information elements here will be transformed to a consistent data warehouse format, existing backups will be converted, and, going forward, these systems will feed the data warehouse on a regular basis. The idea is not necessarily to move all application operations to the data warehouse repository but to convert from their separate applications for future analysis. A way to think about the data warehouse concept is to consider a department of accounting analysts where each analyst downloads some data to

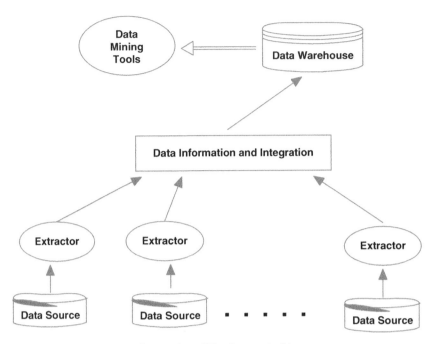

EXHIBIT 14.5 Data Mining from a Data Warehouse Architecture

his or her desktop system and produces separate analysis reports. In a warehouse type of environment, all of the separate data might be combined to one server such that all analysts can combine and share data.

An objective of a data warehouse is to make information retrieval and analysis as flexible and as open as possible. Low-end tools, such as simple query capabilities, may be adequate for users who need only to quickly reference the data warehouse; other users may require powerful multidimensional analysis tools. Data warehouse administrators should be established to identify and assign access to these query tools. There is often a progression to the higher-level tools for data warehouse users. After becoming familiar with a low-level data warehouse tool, the user may be able to justify the cost and effort involved with using a more complex tool. IT auditors should be aware of the processes in place and the controls to limit access to authorized users. Because of the massive amount of historical data contained in a data warehouse, there is a strong need for a high level of security and privacy controls and tools.

Many reports that are generated from a data warehouse facility often are canned or statistical reports of warehouse summary data. They may be produced regularly or on request. In other instances, users may perform specific queries against the data warehouse accumulated summary data. The real strength of the data warehouse is its ability to allow analysts to perform data mining. This is an evolving science where users start with summary data and drill down into detail data looking for arguments to prove or disprove a hypothesis. The tools for data mining are evolving rapidly to satisfy the need to understand the behavior of business units, such as customers and products. Even though this data mining may account for a very small percentage of the data warehouse activity, it is the key strength of the data warehouse for most enterprises. Although the reports and queries from the data warehouse summary tables are adequate to answer many "what" questions, the mining-like drill down into the detail data provides answers to "why" and "how" questions as well.

An IT auditor typically encounters a data warehouse when reviewing an IT application, where much of the data flows to or is extracted from a data warehouse, or as part of a review of IT general controls. Many of the IT audit objectives for a review of data warehouse concepts are part of regular IT audit procedures, such as IT general controls, as discussed in Chapter 6. However, Exhibit 14.6 describes some specific audit objectives for internal controls reviews in a data warehouse environment.

A. Data Warehouse Software Analysis and Acquisition
- a. Determine that a formal feasibility study was completed to define data warehousing objectives as well as projected costs and benefits.
- b. The data warehouse proposed project should be reviewed with IT and appropriate levels of senior management and should be established as an approved budget item based on these estimates.
- c. Based on the current IT resource environment, there should be a formal process to evaluate appropriate data warehousing software tools with appropriate attention given to project objectives and requirements to determine whether proposed software tools meet those requirements.
- d. Data warehouse storage devices, supporting servers, and other software tools should be installed to launch the facility.

B. Data Warehouse Project Development
- a. Formal project plans, per the project-planning requirements outlined in Chapter 16, should be established to launch data warehousing for the enterprise.
- b. There should be a risk and needs analysis to determine the applications to be included in the data warehouse process.
- c. Standards should be established such that all existing applications supplying input to the data warehouse are coded and identified on a consistent basis.
- d. Parameters should be established to review and scrub existing data for conversions to the data warehouse.

C. Software Conversion and Data Integrity Controls
- a. Audit trail controls should be established for all initial and ongoing conversions to the data warehouse, and the integrity and completeness of all conversions to the data warehouse should be reviewed and monitored.
- b. Once key applications have been converted to the data warehouse, outputs from the data warehouse should be tied to the results of existing supporting systems to ensure integrity.
- c. Any converted data potential discontinuities should be investigated and resolved when necessary.
- d. Shortly after the start of the conversion to the data warehouse, original planned project objectives should be revisited. Corrective actions should be made to ensure that planned objectives are being.

D. Data Warehouse Systems Conversion and Testing
- a. Based on a needs analysis and requirements, appropriate backup files should be converted to the data warehouse environment.
- b. Sarbanes-Oxley Section 404 documentation should be updated to reflect the conversion to a data warehouse environment.

EXHIBIT 14.6 IT Audit Objectives for a Data Warehouse Environment *(Continued)*

---

    c. Computer-assisted audit tools should be established to monitor the ongoing integrity of the data warehouse contents.

E. Uses and Integrity of Data Warehouse Contents

    a. Appropriate enterprise users, with a need to know, should receive training on the use of data warehouse retrieval tools.

    b. Conversion controls should be in place to prevent the placement of incorrect or duplicate data to the data warehouse.

    c. IT policies should be established to remove older, unnecessary data periodically.

F. Data Warehouse Security and Continuity Controls

    a. Password access controls should be established such that only authorized persons with a need to know can access the data warehouse facilities.

    b. Total data warehouse operations, including extracts from supporting systems, should be included in a comprehensive enterprise continuity plan.

    c. Partial and total continuity plan tests, including data warehouse operations, should be scheduled on a regular or surprise basis, with results analyzed and appropriate corrective actions installed.

G. Assessing Data Warehouse Costs and Benefits

    a. Procedures should be in place to monitor all specialized people and IT resource costs that are the results of the data warehouse—both due to the conversion and on an ongoing basis. Any major cost discrepancies should be reported to IT and financial management for potential corrective actions.

    b. Programs of regular application integrity and security audits should be planned and executed.

    c. The IT integrity and security results of the conversion to the data warehouse environment should be reported to management and the audit committee.

EXHIBIT 14.6   (*Continued*)

A data warehouse can be a better single and consistent source for many kinds of data than their operational systems. However, because most information will not be carried over to the data warehouse, it cannot be a source of all system interfaces. IT auditors should have a good general understanding of the concept of data warehousing. We are introducing it here in a very general manner. The IT auditor seeking more information should do a Web search for some of the many sites discussing the topic or describing data warehousing software products.

Online Analytical Processing

OLAP is a foundation process for a range of essential business applications, including sales and marketing analysis, planning, budgeting, statutory consolidation, profitability analysis, balanced scorecard, performance measurement, and data warehouse reporting. Although OLAP is neither a new nor an obscure concept, often it is not widely understood by management, IT auditors, and even many IT professionals. OLAP also can be viewed as a category of software that enables analysts, managers, and others to gain insight into data through fast, consistent, interactive access to a wide variety of possible views of information that has been transformed from raw data to reflect the real dimensions of the enterprise as understood by its users. The problem for many enterprises is the mass of data and the need to better understand any related trends. Consider a large enterprise selling multiple product lines from various facilities. Which product lines are the most profitable? In which area or markets are sales increasing or declining? Does customer return patterns represent any overall trends? Answers to these and many more are the functions of OLAP.

OLAP is the dynamic multidimensional analysis of consolidated enterprise data supporting the end user analytical and navigational data. One way of thinking about OLAP concepts is to consider the model of a very complex, very large IT spreadsheet, such as Microsoft's Excel. We normally think of spreadsheets as two-dimensional arrays of rows and columns where we can do searches, calculations, and types of analysis across these rows and columns as well as over multiple two-dimensional pages. However, sometimes the data is too complex or there is just too much of it to place in spreadsheets. OLAP software comes in here with these features:

- **Multidimensional conceptual views.** OLAP software allows calculations and modeling that can be applied across multiple dimensions, through hierarchies and/or across members. Software tools here may allow analysis across 8 to 10 dimensions.
- **Trend analysis over sequential time periods.** Beyond frequent multidimensional needs for looking at data, OLAP tools can consider any data item in terms of sequential time period trends.
- **Drill-down capabilities to deeper levels of consolidation.** Using OLAP, the user can highlight a data element and then easily drill down to examine the basic data the created that item of interest.
- **Intuitive data manipulation.** OLAP tools have the ability to allow "If A, does this imply B?" levels of data manipulation intuitive questions.
- **Rotation to new dimensional comparisons in the viewing area.** OLAP allows a user to flip a complex database on its side and examine all of the data from that different perspective.
- **Reach-through to underlying detail data.** The OLAP user can better see the data trends that supported some conclusion.

These features are some of the major attributes of an OLAP application. Enterprises typically implement OLAP in a multiuser client/server mode to offer users rapid responses to queries, regardless of database size and complexity. OLAP helps users synthesize enterprise information through comparative, personalized viewing as well as through analysis of historical and projected data in various "what-if" data model scenarios.

A variety of software products perform OLAP functions, but all of them today comply with a basic set of features first defined by software engineer E. F. Codd. Codd (1923–2003) was the inventor of the relational database model that is now used in most IT database software products, including Oracle and IBM's DB2. The general characteristics of an OLAP application are part of Codd's general model and should be part of any installed OLAP application.

OLAP is not necessary for every enterprise. Some enterprises do not have enough diverse data to make OLAP procedures cost beneficial. Many other enterprises know that they need OLAP-based solutions, but professionals tasked to select and implement them may be new to the area or may have lost track of its rapid developments. Selecting the right OLAP product is hard, but very important, if projects are to succeed. If an enterprise is considering the purchase of an OLAP product, IT audit should review the control procedures for the new software. If the enterprise is using OLAP software, IT audit should become familiar with the software product. Although we have talked about OLAP as a useful analytical tool for general business purposes, it also can be very useful for extensive audit queries over data.

XBRL: THE INTERNET-BASED EXTENSIBLE MARKUP LANGUAGE

Virtually all enterprises today are operating in an environment of Internet-supported processes. The paper-based information reports and the batch systems that once supported them have largely disappeared. Although the Internet offers a very flexible approach, it can raise questions about document integrity from recipients, management, and auditors. When IT output reports were being produced in the classic closed-shop data center, whether on paper or through online systems, there were few questions about the integrity of the reported data, providing that the supporting internal controls were adequate. As long as there were appropriate general and application controls in place, IT auditors had few questions about general data integrity and only had to perform traditional audit tests to acquire a level of assurance regarding the data. However, the free and open nature of the Internet today can raise questions about the integrity of transmitted data. How does the user know that the file of data transmitted through the Web is actually what it is represented to be?

Coding or markup languages solve some of those concerns, and XBRL, an industry standard approach for the publishing, exchange, and analysis of financial and business reports and data, offers an excellent solution. XBRL is an open-standard markup language developed by a consortium of over 200 companies and government agencies, and is strongly supported as a financial reporting tool by the AICPA in the United States. Delivering benefits to investors, accountants, regulators, executives, business and financial analysts, and information providers, XBRL is rapidly becoming a worldwide standard that provides for the publication, exchange, and analysis of complex financial information in corporate business reports in the dynamic and interactive realm of the Internet. XBRL provides a common format for critical business reporting processes, simplifying the flow of financial statements, performance reports, accounting records, and other financial information between software programs. XBRL defines a consistent format for identifying data and for business reporting to streamline the preparation and dissemination of financial data and to allow analysts, regulators, and investors to review and interpret it. As a result, XBRL can save time and money when information consumers within and outside of a company analyze complex operations and financial data. XBRL is an important tool for providing consistent business and financial reporting.

Effective XBRL processes still have not received enough IT audit, IT management, or even senior management attention. As mandates of filing financial reports in this interactive XBRL data format become a reality for enterprises throughout the world, IT auditors should have a strong role in this conversion. However, a recent IIA survey[7] of more than 200 CAEs worldwide found that more than half of them were not yet familiar with XBRL, but an overwhelming number—90%—would be interested in guidance on internal auditing's involvement in the new process of filing financial statements with XBRL.

XBRL Defined

XBRL is an Internet standard similar to HTML for Internet browsing, MP3 for digital music, or XML, the eXtensible Markup Language standard for electronic commerce. XBRL uses standard Internet XML data tags to describe financial information for public and private companies and other enterprises. Its standards and controlling group, XBRL International, is a professional affiliation of more than 200 enterprises and government jurisdictions that collaboratively produce standard specifications and taxonomies that anyone can license royalty-free for use in their applications.

XBRL can be viewed as a system of bar codes for financial statements. It allows companies to use nationally and internationally common "tags" to identify individual reporting concepts that exist in a corporate report. Information that is coded in this way can be instantly and accurately exchanged between systems. Just as we have established formats for Internet e-mail addresses or Web access links, XBRL provides both a standard description and classification system for the contents of accounting reports. Data can be taken from an accounting information system and XBRL coded to produce an electronic annual report including all financial statements, the auditors' report, and Form 10K notes. The document can then be read directly by computer programs or end users or, more likely, coupled with a style sheet to produce a printed annual report, user-friendly Web pages or an Adobe Acrobat™ file. Similarly, internal business reports and regulatory filings can be output in a variety of forms.

The Web is filled with many positive comments about it, but the statement "XBRL is . . . perhaps the most revolutionary change in financial reporting since the first general ledger"[8] says a lot. XBRL provides a method for enterprises to report their financial information in a format that can be easily read and understood by others. It allows for efficient data collection and publishing as well as serving as a tool for improved data validation and analysis. Exhibit 14.7 illustrates how XBRL can improve the transfer of data and information across systems and entities. As the exhibit shows, financial data from an enterprise's ERP, general ledger, and other financial systems can all be coded in XBRL. The US Securities and Exchange Commission (SEC) now require that financial reporting filings must be prepared in an XBRL format.

Implementing XBRL

XBRL is a new standard where visionaries have praised the concept, with established tools and standards, but to date there have been only limited early adopters beyond SEC financial reporting filings. For example, Microsoft Corporation has been filing its SEC 10K report in XBRL format since 2002, and General Electric is using it for its internal company reporting. Government regulators have seen the value of financial reports

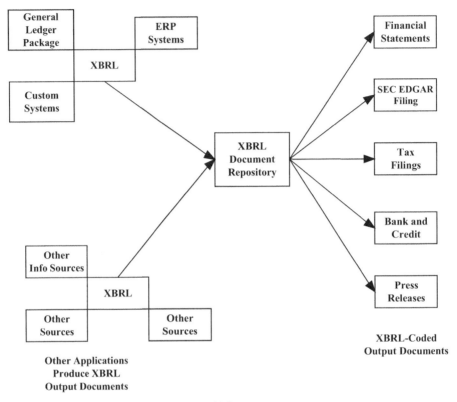

EXHIBIT 14.7 XBRL Output Document Linkages

issued in a consistent and traceable format, and the U.S. Federal Deposit Insurance Corporation now requires that federal bank status call reports be submitted in XBRL format. However, at this time, XBRL seems to be little used outside of the United States. The standard can save on costs and provide reporting flexibility by eliminating proprietary accounting system dump formats and doing away with manual copy-and-paste consolidation and reporting.

As an Internet markup language for financial data, XBRL is similar to HTML for browsers where the Internet user clicks on some tagged reference to get pointed to another site. Under XBRL, Internet financial data is tagged in a manner to be recognized and properly interpreted by others using applications based on a standardized XBRL vocabulary of terms, called a taxonomy, to map results into agreed-on categories. An example of this XBRL taxonomy are the markups or coding for well-defined concepts within the current U.S. generally accepted accounting principles (GAAP) including "accounts receivable trade" and "allowance for doubtful accounts." No matter where it is located in the report format, whether within one enterprise's reports or across multiple enterprises, a value can be recognized as the "allowance for doubtful accounts." However, GAAP may vary somewhat depending on whether an enterprise is a retailer, a minerals extraction mining company, or any of many other variations, but XBRL qualifiers set these categories. A major saving with XBRL is the reduction of the data manipulation required when the enterprise needs to reposition the output from its financial systems to meet the needs of diverse users. A quarterly Internal Revenue Service tax form is very different in format and content from the format in a quarterly SEC filing, although the information needed to file both documents typically comes from the same financial database. With XBRL, information will be entered once, and that same information can be rendered as a printed financial statement, an HTML document for a Web site, an EDGAR SEC file, a raw XML file, or a specialized reporting format, such as periodic banking and other regulatory reports.

Paperless reporting is facilitated here as well. Prior to XBRL, it was necessary to extract financial information for reports from databases such as a general ledger. That extracted information then needed to be processed multiple times, depending on user needs. For example, a typical balance sheet would need to be individually processed for SEC filings, for placement in the annual report, for examination by external auditors, and for analysis by management. Each process could require an extra handling of the information to create the desired report. With XBRL, the information is coded once and is then ready for extraction electronically into reports for all information users. With the proper tools in place, the desired output for all uses of the balance sheet information can be transmitted electronically, without the need for paper-based reports, and only one authorized version of that balance sheet with its data appears in other reports or sources where needed.

Although its use is still limited today, XBRL should soon become a worldwide standard for exchanging financial reporting information. Whether mandated by a regulatory reporting agency such as the U.S. SEC, launched by visionaries in enterprises, or just because "everyone else" will soon be using XBRL to code their financial reports, most enterprises soon will be using it as part of their financial reporting procedures. If there currently has been no action toward implementing XBRL in an enterprise, an IT auditor should have conversations with appropriate persons in the IT function as well as with senior financial management to determine their plans for XBRL implementations. As a first step, however, the IT auditor should gain some knowledge about XBLR. Since it is an XML-based, royalty-free, and open standard, much information is available through the official Web site (www.xbrl.org). That site will point interested persons to a wide variety of papers, presentation sets, and descriptions of its use.

A growing number of financial software vendors now offer tools or help facilities to code output documents with XBRL and to receive similarly coded documents. In addition to the appropriate software, the effective implementation of XBRL in an enterprise requires some management and internal control attention. Although a total XBRL implementation can be a major undertaking, Exhibit 14.8 outlines some IT audit guidelines for launching XBRL processes in an enterprise. The use of XBRL will be a senior financial and IT decision, but IT audit can act as an internal consultant in explaining its advantages and helping to ensure that it is implemented in a proper, controlled environment.

The following are steps an IT auditor should consider when acting as an internal consultant and helping to launch XBRL in an enterprise:

A. From an IT audit perspective, gain an understanding of the XBRL process, its current use within the enterprise, and any pending requirements that may mandate its use.

B. Carry out an internal survey to identify which business reporting areas might benefit from XBRL.

C. Work with IT management to assess the current installed financial application software and whether its current or planned future versions will support XBRL documents.

D. Launch a formal project and establish project plans to implement XBRL for selected financial applications within the enterprise.

E. Define a new taxonomy or extend one of the standardized XBRL taxonomy terms to meet the enterprise's needs.

F. Analyze and select tools and services necessary to analyze, transform, route, and store information to ensure a smooth transition to XBRL without affecting the current business environment.

G. Map multiple information sources into the identified XBRL taxonomy so that all of them produce data that can be used easily in a variety of applications.

H. Establish a peer-to-peer information exchange where XBRL documents are published on individual Web sites and pulled directly into desktop applications, such as spreadsheets and databases.

I. Incorporate encryption/decryption and digital signatures to XBRL data.

J. Store XBRL instances and XML documents, such as link bases and style formats, on a server.

K. Ensure that established data security and integrity processes will protect any unauthorized alteration of XBRL taxonomy data.

Launch an IT audit to assess the effectiveness and integrity of XBRL documents from several financial reporting applications.

EXHIBIT 14.8   IT Audit Guidelines for Launching XBRL Processes

Because it is still an evolving technology, there are some risks of error here. An enterprise needs to select an appropriate taxonomy and appropriately tag its data. Going back to our earlier example, there will be one taxonomy for a manufacturing and distribution business and quite another one for a petroleum refinery. Starting with the wrong taxonomy will cause multiple control problems. Once an appropriate taxonomy is selected, procedures need to be in place to ensure that the tagging of data is complete and accurate. This the same type of control concern that Internet browser users occasionally encounter when clicking on a link and getting pointed to the wrong or a nonexistent site. It is frustrating when surfing through the Web but critical when retrieving or reporting financial data. IT audit should review procedures to ensure that controls are in place for XBRL data tagging. Even though this kind of endeavor often starts as a pet project by some member of the IT group, that tagging should be documented in a controlled environment.

XBRL is rapidly becoming a "new rule" standard for Web-based financial reporting and supporting systems in the United States, but is only beginning to become more common in the European Union, and throughout the world. As John Connors, chief financial officer of Microsoft, stated in 2002 on releasing his company's financials in XBRL "We see XBRL as not only the future standard for publishing, delivery and use of financial information over the web, but also as a logical business choice."[9]

NEWER TECHNOLOGIES, THE CONTINUOUS CLOSE, AND IT AUDIT

This chapter has introduced some newer and evolving IT audit approaches and technologies that are important for IT auditors. Storage management represents a field of growing importance to the enterprise and its IT resources. CAA concepts are becoming increasingly common in the IT audit approach, and all IT auditors should have at least a good general understanding of the concept and where it might be practicable in their own enterprise.

The requirement for an enterprise to use the XBRL format is a new rule for SEC financial filings. Because it is a convenient and powerful tool, such as the use of HTML notation as opposed to plain text, for Internet communications it will soon become a standard protocol for many forms of financial reporting. This is another important concept where IT auditors should have a good understanding.

SOx rules, as discussed in Chapter 1, require all registered enterprises to close their books for periodic financial reporting following tighter and tighter schedules. External auditors performing those reviews as well as management are now requesting timely internal control assessments of those supporting systems. This fact points to the growing importance of the continuous assurance auditing techniques discussed in this chapter. As these time requirements get tighter, management will demand tools to help close accounting financial records and produce financial reports on even more quickly. The ultimate result will be the continuous close, where summary results at the end of a business day represent the overall results for the enterprise up through the end of that business day. Many enterprises are already experimenting with these approaches, and the increasing SOx regulatory requirements as well as capabilities offered by technology today will continue to point enterprises in that direction. This continuous close direction will point to new opportunities and internal controls concerns for IT auditors.

There have been data storage concerns going back to the days of punched cards, but the needs for accurate and efficient storage processes are increasing. IT auditors, whose reviews of IT controls have focused primarily on computer hardware and network general control issues, should begin to devote more attention to storage management. This chapter has also introduced several data storage concepts, such as data warehousing and OLAP, but only at a very high level. IT auditors should be aware of these trends and their internal control implications as they are installed in more and more enterprises.

NOTES

1. http://thecaq.aicpa.org/Resources/Sarbanes+Oxley/Archive++Schedule+for+Congressional+Hearings+on+Enron+Situation.htm.
2. See Chapter 21 for a description of SAS No. 99 as a standard for fraud detection and prevention.
3. ACL Services, Ltd., 1550 Alberni Street, Vancouver, British Columbia V6G 1A5, Canada, www,acl.com.

4. BusinessObjects Corporation, a division of SAP Corporation.

5. Cognos Corporation, Ottawa, Ontario, Canada.

6. EMC Corporation, Hopkinton, MA. The author of this book worked at EMC and helped to launch its Operations Management Consulting group.

7. Institute of Internal Auditors, "Survey Says Internal Auditors Need More Information about XBRL," news release, October 7, 2008.

8. *Accounting Today* (September 2000).

9. Microsoft PressPass, "Microsoft Becomes First Technology Company to Report Financials in XBRL," March 5, 2002, Microsoft.com.

PART FOUR

IV

Importance of IT Governance

CHAPTER FIFTEEN

IT Controls and the Audit Committee

NFORMATION TECHNOLOGY (IT) AUDITORS are frequently a key compo-nent in the internal audit organization of larger enterprises, which consists of financial and operational internal auditors as well as IT audit and reports to the chief audit executive (CAE). As discussed in Chapter 1 on the COSO internal controls framework and the Sarbanes-Oxley Act (SOx), an enterprise internal audit function reports to the audit committee of the board of directors. Because many audit committees focus heavily on financial reporting and SOx compliance issues, IT internal control issues sometimes are not a top priority. At the same time, often many IT audit professionals are more involved with IT-related technical internal control issues and are sometimes less involved with the CAE's audit committee reporting issues. However, because IT issues and internal controls play such an important role in modern enterprise operations, IT auditors should become more aware and involved with the activities and responsibilities of their enterprise's audit committee.

This chapter briefly reviews the role of today's audit committee and its relationships with internal audit, including its plans and budgets, as well as the reporting of significant internal control concerns. We also discuss the types of reporting that internal audit should provide to the audit committee to present the results of their work and to highlight issues that may require further action. The audit committee has the respon-sibility to set the overall direction for all internal audit activities, including IT audit. Although IT audit staff members often do not have much day-to-day contact with their audit committee, every member of the internal audit group must recognize that the audit committee is the final or ultimate repository for internal controls matters. All members of IT audit should have strong understanding of the role and responsibility of the audit committee in today's enterprise.

ROLE OF THE AUDIT COMMITTEE FOR IT AUDITORS

An audit committee is a key component of a corporate board of directors with responsibility for internal controls and financial reporting oversight. Because of this oversight responsibility and SOx requirements, audit committee members must be independent directors with no connection to enterprise management. There are no size restrictions, but a full board with 12 to 16 members often has a 5- or 6-member audit committee. An audit committee may invite members of management or others to attend committee meetings and even to join in on the committee's deliberations. However, any outside guests cannot be full voting members, per SOx rules. An enterprise's board of directors is a formal entity given the responsibility for the overall governance of that enterprise for its owners, investors or lenders. All members of the board can be held legally liable through their actions on any issue, and a board and its committees enact most formal business through resolutions, which become matters of enterprise record.

As one of the several operating committees established by the board, the audit committee has a unique role compared to other committees. It consists of only outside directors—giving it independence from management—and should be composed of a specially qualified group of outside directors who understand, monitor, coordinate, and assess the internal controls environment and related financial activities for the entire board. In order to fulfill its responsibilities to the board of directors, stockholders, and the public, an audit committee needs to launch and manage an internal audit function that should become an independent set of eyes and ears inside the enterprise, providing assessments of internal controls and other matters.

These comments are based on a corporate structure such as one with Securities and Exchange Commission (SEC) registered stock, but other nonpublic enterprises also can benefit from this audit committee structure. For example, many not-for-profit or private enterprises are large enough to have a formal board of directors and an internal audit function. Although not mandated by SOx and SEC rules, these types of organizations will also benefit from a board audit committee consisting only of independent directors.

The external auditors have a prime responsibility to an enterprise's board of directors for attesting to the accuracy and fairness of the financial statements; internal audit and its IT auditors have a large role in assessing internal controls over the reliability of financial reporting and IT processes, the effectiveness and efficiency of operations, and the enterprise's compliance with applicable laws and regulations. In particular, IT auditors assess the many IT-related security and integrity risks facing an enterprise. The audit committee has a primary responsibility for an enterprise's internal audit function. Prior to SOx, this oversight often was little more than a theoretical concept; internal audit frequently reported to the audit committee "on paper" but effectively reported to the chief financial officer or some other senior corporate officer. Today's internal audit function should have a charter-defined very active relationship with the enterprise's audit committee. These charters often are very specific regarding relationships with internal audit and typically require the audit committee to:

1. Review the resources, plans, activities, staffing, and organizational structure of IT audit as part of enterprise internal audit. These areas are summarized in Chapter 5.

2. Review the appointment, performance, and replacement of the CAE.
3. Review all audits and reports prepared by internal audit together with management's response.
4. Review with management, the CAE, and the independent accountants the adequacy of financial reporting and internal control systems. This includes the scope and results of the internal audit, program, and the cooperation afforded or limitations, if any, imposed by management on the conduct of the internal audit program.

These requirements have been part of the relationship between internal audit and its audit committee over time. The CAE should work closely with the audit committees to ensure that effective communication links are in place. The third point mentioned on audit reports is an example. Prior to SOx rules, some internal audit functions supplied their audit committees only with summaries of internal audit report findings or even submitted reports on what the CAE decided were "significant" internal audit report findings. SOx has changed the rules here. Today internal audit should not just send the audit committee reports what it *thinks* it needs to see. Rather, SOx mandates that internal audit should provide the audit committee with *all* audit reports and their supporting management responses, including sometimes fairly technical IT audit reports that internal audit management kept from audit committee reviewers.

An audit committee usually is not involved in day-to-day administrative matters regarding the internal audit function and its CAE but must ensure the ongoing quality of the internal audit function. For example, the audit committee should carefully review annual audit plans and ask appropriate questions regarding the findings and recommendations from internal audit reports. In addition, the audit committee has the ability to hire or fire the CAE, but there should be an ongoing level of cooperation here. The audit committee is not on-site on a daily basis to provide detailed internal audit supervision and must rely on management for some detailed support.

The CAE or internal auditors cannot just ignore appropriate management requests by claiming they only report to the audit committee and are not responsible to enterprise line management. Similarly, enterprise management must make certain that internal audit is part of the enterprise and not an outsider because of the audit committee relationship.

AUDIT COMMITTEE APPROVAL OF INTERNAL AUDIT PLANS AND BUDGETS

An audit committee should develop an overall understanding of the total audit needs of the enterprise. This high-level appraisal covers various special control and financial reporting issues, allowing the audit committee to determine the portion of audit or risk assessment needs to be performed by either the internal or other audit providers. As part of this role as the ultimate coordinator of the total audit effort, the audit committee is responsible for reviewing and approving higher-level plans and budgets of internal audit. Although enterprise management may have its own ideas about the total audit effort and how it should be carried out, and although the CAE has views as to what needs to be done, the approval of internal audit plans and budgets are an audit committee responsibility. The varying views of the key parties must be jointly considered and appropriately reconciled, but the audit committee has the final word here.

Audit committee reviews of all internal audit plans is essential if the policies and plans for the future are to be determined most effectively. The audit committee should assume this high-level coordination role, such that all interested parties (e.g., enterprise management, internal auditors, and external audit alike) should better understand the nature of total internal audit plans and what to expect from the suppliers of audit services. Although there are practical limitations as to how actively the audit committee can become involved in the detailed planning process, some involvement has a demonstrated high value. Typically, the chair of the audit committee is the most active person in this plan review, but even this person is subject to time limitations. Internal audit should prepare a comprehensive set of annual planning documents for the committee that give detailed plans for the upcoming year as well as longer-range plans for the future. Suggested formats for these plans are discussed in Chapter 5 on performing effective IT audits. In addition, internal audit should prepare summarized reports of past audit activities and reassessments of its coverage to give the audit committee an understanding of significant areas covered in past reviews. Although internal audit should report its activities to the audit committee on a regular basis, this summary reporting of past activity gives an overview of their areas of audit emphasis as well as highlighting any potential gaps in audit coverage.

Internal audit plans with an IT perspective sometimes can present problems for enterprise audit committee members. These very senior people often are not aware of some of the IT-related internal controls issues discussed in these chapters, such as the change and patch management issues discussed in Chapter 27. The CAE, with support of the IT audit team, should take extra steps to educate the audit committee why they feel certain more technical IT issues are important from an internal controls risk perspective.

Exhibit 15.1 is an example of a one-year audit plan for presentation to the audit committee. While such a plan would present all internal audit issues, this exhibit emphasizes IT audit concerns. The CAE would present this type of report, listing particulars for each audit, to the committee, with supporting details to answer questions and discuss supporting details. The summary report on past activities is particularly important in that it shows the areas that had been scheduled in the prior year's plan and the accomplishments against that plan.

In many enterprises, the annual audit plan is developed through both internal audit's risk analysis process and discussions with both senior management and the audit committee. Management and the audit committee may suggest areas for potential internal audit review, and internal audit should develop plans within the constraints of budget and resource limitations. If the audit committee has suggested a review of some specialized area but internal audit is unable to perform that audit due to some known constraints, the CAE should clearly communicate that deficiency to the audit committee.

Global Computer Products 20yy Summarized IT Audit Plan								
Audit	Division	Audit	Risk Rank	Est. Start	Planned Finish	Total Hours	Total Costs	Comments
E36	Electro	Inventory Planning General IT Controls	8.4					Carry-over—From 20xx
E40	Electro	Physical Inventory Observation	9.5					
E57	Electro	IT Firewall Integrity	7.4					
E71	Electro	Materials Receiving Application Review	6.2					Physical and Logical Security
E74	Electro	IT Change Controls	6.8					Operational Assessment
E80	Electro	New Marketing System	7.8					
D23	Distribution	XML Order Controls	9.1					First Audit of Process
D39	Distribution	Warehouse Physical Security	5.3					Financial Controls
D44	Distribution	IT Software Change Controls	7.2					Operational Controls
D54	Distribution	Product Incentive System	8.6					Audit Committee Request
D61	Distribution	Software Configuration Controls	8.8					
D78	Distribution	Business Continuity Planning	9.1					
D81,	Distribution	A/R Control Proceed	7.5					
AP13	Asia Pacific	G/L System Integrity	8.6					First Review of Unit
AP22	Asia Pacific	Systems Development Standards	8.2					First Review of Unit
AP31	Asia Pacific	Mfg. Control System	9.2					First Review of Unit
C67	Corporate	Wireless Systems Controls	5.3					
C68	Corporate	IT Network Management	7.3					

EXHIBIT 15.1   One-Year Audit Plan Summary for Audit Committee Review

AUDIT COMMITTEE BRIEFINGS ON IT AUDIT ISSUES

Not many years ago, IT audit concerns were unfamiliar and sometimes strange-sounding issues for senior-level managers serving on audit committees. Senior managers at this level had become familiar with a limited number of IT related internal control issues, such as the importance of effective IT disaster recovery plans or the risks of software viruses, as threats

---

Global Computer Products IT Audit Group—yyyy/mm/dd

Item AP22—Asia Pacific Region Systems Development Standards. Internal Audit Risk: 8.2
- **Background.** The Asia-Pacific region in India and China has in the past contracted with local sources to develop applications for their own office use and for corporate software tools.
- These outside contracted software development projects did not follow any consistent software development approach, and many projects ran over budget and followed poor project management techniques.
- IT Audit report ZZ–ZZ, dated 20yy/05/14, highlighted several significant systems development control weaknesses in new Asia-Pacific region application development projects and recommended:
  • The Asia-Pacific region should follow corporate IT systems development standards.
  • Greater emphasis should be given to building and testing stronger internal accounting controls prior to new application implementations.
- IT Audit is now planning to review the status of Asia-Pacific region systems development standards as part of IT Audit's planned third-quarter review IT operations in that area. The IT audit will include:
  • Compliance with corporate IT systems development standards with the Asia-Pacific group IT functions, based on a review of recently developed new applications.
  • Detailed application internal control testing for several selected new applications.

EXHIBIT 15.2   IT Audit Status Report Outline for Enterprise Audit Committee

---

to IT operations. Many business publications have talked about risks regarding some of these IT issues, but IT auditors often face challenges when trying to communicate their concerns about more technical issues to audit committee–level senior managers.

IT audit plans and risk concerns are part of overall internal audit plans, and IT auditors should have open access to their CAE. Getting messages to the audit committee, however, is sometimes a greater problem. As discussed, audit committee members are very involved with financial reporting issues, SOx compliance, and other risk issues, but typically do not regularly focus on IT audit–related issues. Using the CAE as the prime contact, IT audit needs to reach out to audit committee members to brief them on important and evolving IT-related internal control issues. For many enterprises, there may be value in scheduling a quarterly audit committee briefing on enterprise IT risks and evolving issues.

These briefings are used to educate audit committee members on the enterprise IT environment and any risk issues. This type of briefing sometimes can be done in conjunction with the enterprise's chief information officer, but often it is better for the session to be led primarily by IT audit. Although there can be many variations, Exhibit 15.2 shows a sample IT audit status report that discusses significant changes in the enterprise's IT environment and evolving risks. This briefing would also tie to the IT audit issues that were present in the IT audit plan shown in Exhibit 15.1.

AUDIT COMMITTEE REVIEW AND ACTION ON SIGNIFICANT IT AUDIT FINDINGS

An audit committee's most important responsibility is to review and take action on significant audit findings that are reported to them by their internal and external auditors, management, and others. Although the audit committee has responsibility for

---

Distribution Division Continuity Planning—Report xxx—Key IT Audit Findings

- Continuity plans, based on corporate standards, have not been completed for any IT units in the division.
- Despite the lack of formal continuity plans, corporate IT standards call for disaster recovery plan testing based on existing unit plans. The review found no evidence of any level of disaster recovery plan testing for an IT function within the division during the 12 months prior to this audit.

Corporate Wireless Network—Report yyy—Key IT Audit Findings:

- Encryption techniques are not used for any wireless transmissions, making all network transactions susceptible to spying and key document exposures.
- [Specify other key audit findings.]

EXHIBIT 15.3   IT Audit Significant Findings Audit Committee Report

---

all of these areas, our focus here is on the need for internal audit, and IT audit in particular, to report all significant findings to the audit committee on a regular and prompt basis. Part of this reporting will occur through internal audit's distribution of all audit reports to the audit committee as part of the SOx requirements outlined in Chapter 1. Although internal audit and others should certainly not filter their audit findings to tell the audit committee only what they feel is "significant," internal audit should report all audit report findings, as well as the status and disposition of those findings, but should highlight those they feel are significant audit findings. Exhibit 15.3 is an example of a significant IT-related findings report from our Global Computer Products example company. The sample report shows only IT-related items; typically a much wider range of other significant internal control findings would be included as well.

Reacting to significant audit findings requires a combination of understanding, competence, and cooperation by all of the major interested parties—internal audit, management, external auditors, and the audit committee itself. Total enterprise welfare then becomes the standard by which to judge all internal audit services, as opposed to more provincial views that the interests of management and the audit committee may conflict to some extent. Within its own area of responsibility, internal audit should act aggressively in exercising ongoing monitoring actions to assess whether appropriate corrective action items are taken.

Moving beyond the periodic IT briefings to the audit committee, as outlined in Exhibit 15.2, IT audit often has a particular responsibility to better brief the audit committee on audit findings relating to IT technical issues that non-IT specialists may not fully understand. There is a special need to clarify and explain matters here when an IT issue may appear to be too technically obscure or when some issue has been played up in the public press sufficiently to raise questions in the minds of some audit committee members. These public-type issues often arise when the news media plays up an attack by a new computer virus or worm. Depending on the size and nature of such reported incidents, IT audit should assess the attack risks in its enterprise and prepare a status report for the CAE to pass on to the audit committee.

Technical issues can cover a wide range of events. Examples of technical audit findings include an IT audit review of operating system software that found some unauthorized parameter table changes that improperly modified the pricing of data processing services between several operating divisions. Database parameter changes had been made without specific authorization, resulting in high-volume computer services resource charges incorrectly allocated across several divisions. Because these changes had been made some time previously, the computer services charges for several high-volume divisions had been incorrectly allocated.

This audit finding had implications on the expenses of several large enterprise divisions. However, when the finding was first reported on regular internal audit reports, it was difficult for many to understand the implications. To better broadcast such internal audit findings, background summaries should be prepared for senior management and the audit committee. The idea is to explain an IT audit technical issue from a business and internal accounting control perspective, which is a good way for IT audit to better communicate with the senior executives who are members of the audit committee.

IT AUDIT AND THE AUDIT COMMITTEE

IT auditors at all levels in an enterprise should be aware of the role and importance of the audit committee to their total enterprise and as the ultimate director of the internal audit function, including IT audit. As many audit committees consist of outside directors who fly in only to attend audit committee meetings, often IT auditors may not have much face-to-face exposure and contact with their audit committee members. Whenever possible, however, they should communicate enterprise IT audit concerns to audit committee members. Until the CAE and audit committee all become more IT-conversant, IT auditors should exercise care in explaining and communicating IT-related internal control concerns.

Perhaps more important, IT auditors should strive to better understand the enterprise's internal control and risk issues facing the audit committee, as key members of the board of directors. As stated, IT auditors are often one step removed from the CAE and more removed from direct audit committee contacts. However, IT audit has a responsibility to communicate IT-related internal control issues and concerns to the audit committee.

CHAPTER SIXTEEN

Val IT, Portfolio Management, and Project Management

A N INFORMATION TECHNOLOGY (IT) auditor's role is generally much more than just assessing security and reviewing IT general controls covering overall IT operations or the controls for a specific application. Although they are not the initiators of overall IT management processes, IT auditors regularly observe and review many challenges in managing overall IT investments and launching new projects to build and benefit from these many IT resources. This chapter looks at three knowledge areas that are important to IT auditors. As our first knowledge area, this chapter introduces the Val IT^{TM} enterprise value initiative of the Information Systems Audit and Control Association (ISACA) to better manage and understand IT investments, portfolio management approaches to better deal with the large number of diverse applications and IT resources in the typical enterprise, and project management good practices to better control and manage many IT activities.

Val IT is an approach developed by the ISACA-related IT Governance Institute$^{®}$ (ITGI) to help enterprises better realize value from investments in IT systems and software. Val IT is relevant to all management levels across both the business and IT functions—from the chief information officer (CIO) and senior managers directly involved and responsible for the selection, procurement, development, implementation, deployment, and benefits-realization processes. Although primarily targeted at investments involving IT, the practices included in Val IT apply to most if not all business change investments, whether they involve IT or not. These Val IT concepts are an important and useful IT governance set of principles, and IT auditors should both be aware of and use them when evaluating IT general controls. Although Val IT is supported by an extensive set of published materials, this chapter only provides an overview of concepts important to IT auditors.

One key component of Val IT, IT portfolio management is the grouping of software programs, projects, services, or assets in a manner that they can be selected, managed, and monitored to optimize their overall business value. IT portfolio management is the second topic discussed in this chapter. When managing a large number of just IT projects, the preferred term is often *IT program management*. This chapter, however, concentrates on the broader concepts of IT portfolio management, a useful linkage between enterprise strategy and the specific IT investments, initiatives, and actions undertaken to execute strategy. Effective IT portfolio management processes support the identification, evaluation, selection, execution, and monitoring of IT investments for an enterprise. It further supports the ongoing monitoring of organizational assets, including the results of investments and the resources required to create, maintain, and improve the value of those assets. Portfolio management is a key tool for maximizing business value. IT auditors will find portfolio management useful when reviewing multiple IT processes as part of general controls reviews and making some IT audit management and planning decisions.

Project management is the third and very important IT audit topic covered in this chapter. IT auditors frequently review the controls and procedures used for helping to launch new or enhanced application or systems development efforts. These projects should be organized formally, just as many IT audit efforts—short or longer term— should be organized as formal projects. This chapter conclude with an introduction to the project management standards of the Project Management Institute (PMI; www. pmi.org), an important IT audit knowledge area. Whether reviewing an existing systems development effort or launching an audit effort, the IT auditor should understand and look for good project management practices.

VAL IT: ENHANCING THE VALUE OF IT INVESTMENTS

All enterprises, large or small, exist to deliver value to their stakeholders. These enterprises face a critical challenge in ensuring that they realize value from their increasingly large-scale and complex investments in IT resources. The Val IT materials released by the ITGI, are a set of best practices to help enterprises address this challenge and to help them realize value from these IT-related investments.

Val IT attempts to address a problem faced by management at all levels as well as by its IT auditors. IT technologies and practices are always changing and adapting to new business practices. Enterprises frequently invest in new and revised systems and procedures with little additional planning or study, only to soon find that the new initiative does not work as well as promised or requires a much larger investment than anticipated. IT auditors frequently encounter this situation where, for example, an enterprise chief financial officer is frustrated by some shortcoming in the enterprise's financial systems, sees a potential better solution at a vendor-sponsored trade show, and then encourages the IT function to adopt that solution. With such pressure from senior management but little detailed investigation beyond that, enterprises often embark on new IT investments at significant cost and without really getting much value from those investments. The Val IT framework is a best practice governance

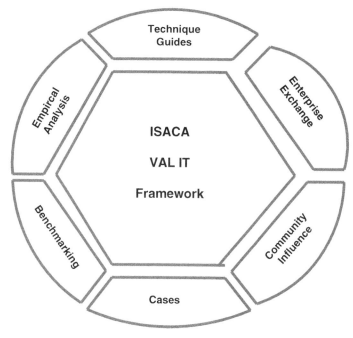

EXHIBIT 16.1 Val IT Initiative

framework that is closely aligned with the Control Objectives for Information and related Technology (CobiT) framework (discussed in Chapter 2). CobiT consists of a set of guiding principles and a number of recommended IT-related processes that conform to those principles and key management practices. Val IT encompasses a comprehensive set of research activities, publications, and auxiliary services supporting the core Val IT framework, as illustrated in Exhibit 16.1. Although CobiT sets good practices for the *means* of contributing to the process of value creation, Val IT defines good practices for the *ends*, by providing enterprises with the structure they require to measure, monitor, and optimize the realization of business value from their investments in IT.

Many enterprises today, regardless of their size, revenue, industry, region, or business activities, make large-scale investments in IT systems and related information technology resources. However, in far too many cases, this IT value simply is not realized. For example, a 2007 survey by the IT research firm Gartner found that 20% of all expenditures on IT are wasted[1]—a finding that represents, on a global basis, an annual destruction of value totaling about $600 billion. Similarly, a 2009 survey of Fortune 1000 CIOs by Goldman Sachs found that, on average, 40% of all IT spending brought no return to the enterprises.[2] The point here is that many enterprises do not measure the value of or assess their ongoing IT investments.

Designed for more than just IT auditors, the ITGI's Val IT materials[3] provide valuable guidance for assessing the value of IT investments. Creating IT-enabled values, however, is not easy. Most enterprises commonly exhibit one or more of these symptoms, which have been adapted from the published Val IT guidance materials:

▪ **Problems in delivering technical capabilities.** Many enterprises have IT functions that are not mature enough to effectively and efficiently deliver the technology capabilities needed to both support business operations and enable business change. IT auditors often encounter this environment when performing general controls reviews. This challenge highlights the need to improve IT governance and management processes either before or in conjunction with the introduction of value management practices.

▪ **Limited or no understanding of IT expenditures.** Senior enterprise managers frequently do not have a sufficiently transparent view of their IT expenditures and IT-enabled investments across all IT services, assets, and other resources. Often decision makers can only estimate how much they are investing in IT, what benefits they are gaining for the expense, and what the full business rationale for the commitment might be. Expenditures frequently are sourced from many different uncoordinated budgets, resulting in significant duplication and conflict in demand for resources. In addition and all too often, IT auditors do not focus on IT costs and pricing issues in their application and general controls reviews. This is often an important area for IT internal audit reviews.

▪ **Business abdication of decision making to the IT function.** When the roles, responsibilities, and accountabilities of an enterprise's IT function are unclear, IT functions tend to usurp the driver's seat, determining which IT-enabled business investments should be pursued, prioritizing these business investments based on the IT function's limited insights, and inappropriately relieving the business of its responsibility in defining and defending the business rationale used to justify every single IT-enabled investment decision.

▪ **Communication gaps between the IT function and the business.** Close collaboration between IT operations and other business functions is crucial to IT value creation. When such a partnership is absent, communication suffers, inefficiencies mount, synergies fail to emerge, and the work environment tends to devolve into a culture of blame. In some cases, the IT function is relegated to the role of a follower, instead of innovator, and is engaged in investment proposals too late in the decision-making process to contribute significant value. In other cases, the IT function is blamed for not delivering value from IT-enabled investments— value that only other business functions, in partnership with the IT function, can deliver.

▪ **Questioning the value of IT.** Ironically, even though enterprises continue to invest more and more in technology resources, many key executives often question whether appropriate value is actually realized from these investments. Frequently, the dominant focus is on managing IT costs rather than understanding, managing, and leveraging IT's role in the process of creating concrete business value. As IT-enabled investments increasingly involve significant organizational change, the failure to shift focus from cost to value will continue to be a major constraint to realizing value from these IT-related investments.

▪ **Major investment failures.** When IT projects stumble, the associated business costs can be enormous—and highly visible. Project cancellations can trigger unexpected and very expensive impacts across the business, and related budget overruns can starve other projects of crucial resources. All too often, these problems are ignored until it is far too late to take any corrective action.

Experienced IT auditors have encountered these symptoms in many IT organizations. All too often, IT functions have led business partners with their own requests for new priorities and services without looking at their overall value to the enterprise as a whole. The Val IT materials should encourage all parties to take a harder look at the value being received from IT investments and services. Perhaps even more important, Val IT gives IT auditors an opportunity to focus on areas for realizing greater value as part of their internal control audit report recommendations.

Launching an IT Value Management Initiative

The ITGI Val IT materials are not designed only for IT auditors but provide guidance to enterprise IT functions, the senior management funding IT resources, and all stakeholders benefiting from those IT activities. However, because this best practices guidance material is published from an ISACA-related source (and not, e.g., in a corporate board member type of publication), this material may not get sufficient necessary attention at a senior management level. However, Val IT is an excellent set of materials for IT auditors to support their internal controls reviews.

IT auditors should discuss IT value management issues with both IT and operations management and should suggest the launching of an IT value management initiative. One of the best ways to assess the enterprise's readiness to undertake a value management program is to review and evaluate the Val IT framework's principles and the extent of its commitment to implement them. These principles include:

▪ IT-enabled investments should be managed as a portfolio of investments.
▪ IT-enabled investments should include the full scope of activities required to achieve their business value.
▪ IT-enabled investments should be managed through their full economic life cycle.
▪ Value delivery practices throughout the enterprise should recognize that there are different categories of investments, which will be evaluated and managed differently.
▪ Value delivery practices will define and monitor key metrics and respond quickly to any changes or deviations.
▪ Value delivery practices will engage all stakeholders and assign appropriate accountability for the delivery of capabilities and the realization of business benefits.
▪ Value delivery practices will be monitored, evaluated, and improved continually.

IT and other senior managers involved in IT processes for an enterprise are—or should be—the ones directly involved in overseeing or carrying out value management practices. Based on the Val IT materials, an IT auditor should meet with IT and business

1. Are IT-enabled investments, such as applications or network connections, managed as a portfolio of investments?
2. Are all IT-enabled investments managed to include the full scope of activities required to achieve their business objectives for the investment?
3. Are IT-enabled investments managed through their full economic life cycle, from the costs of launching or purchasing the investment through regular operating costs and then to retirement?
4. Does IT and management recognize that there should be different categories of value delivery investments that should be evaluated and managed differently?
5. Have value delivery key metrics been defined to monitor and respond quickly to any changes or deviations?
6. Do the established value delivery practices appear to engage stakeholders and assign appropriate accountability for the delivery of capabilities and the realization of business benefits?
7. Is a continuous improvement process in place over all value delivery practices?

EXHIBIT 16.2 IT Value Management Readiness Assessment

managers to assess their readiness to move to IT value management. Although it is not suggested as a set of audit procedures, Exhibit 16.2 provides questions for an IT auditor to assess an enterprise's readiness to move to IT value management.

An IT auditor reviewing general controls processes here should consider each of the questions in the exhibit in terms of whether the enterprise and operations management team is aware of the importance of value management and has taken steps to implement this concept. Of course, all parties—IT and operations management need to be sold by the Val IT sponsor—often IT audit acting as an internal consultant—on the importance of IT value management.

The published guidance calls for an enterprise to become more involved with value management best practices. It calls for enterprises and stakeholders with initial insight into value management to develop an understanding and awareness of, and commitment to, value management principles and practices. Based on this initial assessment, a more detailed maturity analysis can be initiated based on Val IT domains of IT value governance, portfolio management, and investment management.

Getting Started in Value Management

Although not discussed in the Institute of Internal Auditors or ISACA standards (see Chapter 3) and not part of CobiT, the concepts introduced in Val IT are important for all IT auditors. We emphasize this importance because IT auditors are often involved with reviewing internal controls surrounding new IT initiatives. All too often, however, those same initiatives do not take into account IT value management considerations.

An effective way to start a value management process is to assess current readiness using the readiness assessment questions of Exhibit 16.2. These general questions will allow an IT auditor to survey the overall environment. Once the assessment has been completed, the results will provide the basis for identifying what is needed to evolve from the current to a future value management future state and for establishing the priorities for what needs to be improved.

Based on ITGI's published Val IT materials, the next five steps outline how to implement Val IT and value management in an enterprise. Differences between enterprises can be vast, and the Val IT guidance materials describe only a limited number of starting points.

Step 1. Build awareness and understanding of value management. In many enterprises, key decision makers and stakeholders do not adequately appreciate the need to create value. This concept of value does not just naturally emerge from normal business plans or activities; it has to be actively created. The problem is that, while the concepts of value management have been around for decades, the notion of value creation and preservation through business change in modern enterprises usually is treated as an implied principle, not a conscious and pervasive tenet to guide behavior.

For many enterprises, there is no shared understanding of what constitutes enterprise value, what level of effort is required to realize it, or how to measure value. As a result that impacts many enterprises, opportunities to realize value may be missed or fail in execution, and the concept of value is often eroded or destroyed.

Enterprise operational, financial, and IT managers need to establish a broad-based awareness of the need for value management and to nurture an understanding of what is needed to develop this capability, including a strong internal executive and management commitment to improving and sustaining value creation over time.

With a strong understanding of value management, organizational and individual behaviors should change to take a broader enterprise-wide view and a more disciplined, value-driven approach to decision making. This should result in an increased understanding and acceptance of the need for IT and the other business functions to work together in partnership, supported by clear roles, responsibilities, and accountabilities related to value management, leading to more value realization from IT-enabled investments.

Step 2. Implementing improved IT governance. Processes, roles, responsibilities, and accountabilities related to realizing value from IT-enabled investments need to be clearly defined and accepted. All too often, the roles, responsibilities, and accountabilities of IT and other business functions are unclear. Business decisions sometimes are made by the IT function while IT decisions are made by the business. In this environment, a culture of blame can predominate, with persisting confusion regarding accountability, responsibility, and sponsorship.

An enterprise needs to establish an IT governance framework with clearly defined roles, responsibilities, and accountabilities. This framework should be supported by strong and committed leadership, appropriate processes, organizational structures and information, and a well-aligned reward system. Under such an IT governance framework, organizational attitudes and individual behaviors should evolve toward a broader, more strategic enterprise perspective. Managers from IT and operations should take a more disciplined, value-driven approach to their decision making and accountabilities. With improved IT governance, an environment of more and efficient decision making should lead to increased trust between the IT function and the rest of the business. The result should be an increased realization of value from IT-enabled investments.

Step 3. Undertake an inventory of IT investments. For most enterprises, little, if any, visibility exists into the number, scope, and cost of current and planned IT-enabled investments or the resources either allocated or needed to support these investments. All too often, overall IT expenditures across the enterprise are not known, and often come from many different and uncoordinated budgets, often with significant duplications. In many enterprises, extensive conflicts in the demand for IT resources exists.

As a solution, an enterprise should establish portfolios of proposed and active IT investments, IT services, assets, and other resources. This concept is even greater than the Information Technology Infrastructure Library (ITIL) configuration management best practices discussed in Chapter 7. As a result of establishing these portfolios, organizational and individual attitudes and behaviors should change to take broader enterprise-wide views. Appropriate processes and practices must be in place to support this.

The benefits from such an inventory of IT investments are an increased understanding of exactly what is being spent on which IT investments, in which areas of the business, and by whom. Another benefit is the better identification of opportunities to increase value through improved allocation of funds, reductions in overall enterprise cost by eliminating redundancies, more effective use of resources, and reduction in risk from a better understanding of these IT portfolios.

Step 4. Clarifying the value of individual IT investments. For many if not most enterprises, there is no consistently applied process for determining the value of potential or current IT investments. That value could be defined as the total life cycle benefits net of total life cycle costs adjusted for risk, based on the time value of money. As a result, some stakeholders persistently question whether IT investments have generated value. Business cases for IT-enabled investments are nonexistent or poorly prepared and usually are considered merely an administrative checklist required to secure funding. Little, if any, pre-investment information exists on IT costs and there is little analytical rigor in defining these benefits or values. Few metrics exist to enable the monitoring of what, if any, value is to be or has been created. All too often, it is assumed that technology, or the IT function, will magically deliver value.

An enterprise should establish a process to develop and update comprehensive and consistently prepared business cases for its IT-enabled investments, including all of the activities required to create value. The business case should be developed through a top-down approach, starting with a clear articulation of the desired business outcomes and progressing to a description of what actions need to be accomplished by whom. These business cases should be updated and used as an operational tool throughout the complete economic life cycle of the IT investment.

As a result, organizational and individual attitudes and behaviors should change to put more effort into the planning of IT investments and the development and regular updating of business cases. A more objective assessment of IT investment business cases enables better and more objective comparisons across different types of IT investments. There are better opportunities to compare individual investments based on their relative value against other investments available and a stronger track record for selecting the best. There should also be less uncertainty and risk that the value projected will not be realized.

Step 5. Conduct IT investment evaluations, prioritizations, and selections. Currently there is no consistently applied process for objectively evaluating the relative value of all proposed and current IT-enabled investments—especially with respect to prioritizing and selecting those IT investments that appear to have the highest potential value. Today, many enterprise IT investment decisions are subjective and often highly political. Once a decision is made to proceed with an investment, it is rarely revisited unless some crisis occurs. Poorly performing IT investments are rarely remediated or canceled early enough to mitigate losses; if they are canceled, they are regarded as failures for which someone should be held accountable.

The Val IT solution is to implement portfolio management disciplines to categorize IT-enabled business investments. An enterprise should establish and rigorously apply criteria to support consistent and comparable evaluation of these IT investments throughout their full economic life cycle. As a result, organizational and individual attitudes and behaviors should change to take a broader enterprise view and embrace greater transparency.

The benefit of this five-step approach should be an increased opportunity to create value through selecting IT investments with the greatest potential to deliver value. This opportunity should be followed by the active management of those investments and early cancellation of them when it is apparent value cannot be realized. The Val IT materials provide more detail on these approaches.

The Val IT framework has assembled and integrated useful guidance and proven processes and practices for the governance, selection, and management of IT-enabled investments. Val IT describes the interrelated processes that need to be in place if enterprises are to secure optimal value from their investments. This section has merely highlighted and extracted some of the materials from the Val IT guidance materials. VAL IT is a concept that is very useful for IT auditors in assessing IT relative values in both application and general controls reviews. More important, these Val IT concepts should be communicated to IT and senior management so they can better understand their investments in IT resources.

IT SYSTEMS PORTFOLIO AND PROGRAM MANAGEMENT

Several project-related definitions are important here. The last section on Val IT emphasized the importance of portfolio management when understanding and managing a suite of IT investments. Project managers, introduced in the next section, often use the term *program* when discussing multiple projects. A program usually is a senior-level project used to manage a series of related or connected projects. For example, an enterprise may want to implement some fairly large initiative that is divided into a series of separate projects. Each of the projects can operate independently, but a program structure manages all of them together. This chapter generally uses the term *project* both for one single effort and for a program of multiple projects. A *portfolio of IT investments* usually refers to a suite or inventory of existing investments; a *program* describes a series of related in-development projects.

An IT internal audit department is responsible for a series of IT audits for their enterprise over a period of time, and the IT audit function managing these scheduled audit projects should think of them as a program or series of projects with IT audit's understanding of the relationships of each scheduled audit with other similar or related internal audit projects. Multiple and related projects usually are grouped together into programs and project portfolios. A *project management program* consists of a series of related projects managed in a coordinated way to obtain the benefits and controls that would not be available if these projects were managed individually. *Programs* generally consist of related work that may be outside the scope of the individual projects.

The need for program management generally occurs when an enterprise has some single objective that can best be achieved through a series of separate projects. For example, a plan to move a manufacturing plant facility to a new location would require a series of separate projects that all require coordination. One project here might require moving and setting up production equipment, another would move raw materials, with still another project doing IT systems conversions. Although someone should be in charge of coordinating all of these efforts, each project has separate needs and requirements. They would be managed separately but grouped together as a program.

IT audit should think of requirements for a series of related IT audit projects as a program. For example, the enterprise may be asked to review Sarbanes-Oxley (SOx) Section 404 internal controls within a series of facilities for an enterprise. Even though each of these audits would take place at different types of facilities with different geographic locations and responsible IT audit teams, each has similar high-level objectives, and a senior manager might be responsible for the overall completion of each one. These groups of projects might be organized and managed as a program, with the individual IT audit project managers all reporting to a program manager for the overall compliance effort.

Moving up to another level, *portfolio management* refers to collections of projects, programs, and other work that are grouped together to facilitate their effective management. If separate IT audit groups existed for two units of a corporation, perhaps one covering IT audits in European Union countries and the other for the United States and Canada, the IT audit activities for each could be considered as an IT audit portfolio with both classified under a higher-level portfolio at the corporate headquarters. This portfolio and program approach to project management is described in Exhibit 16.3. The idea is that reporting relationships should be established when necessary to promote efficiency and achieve overall objectives.

In addition to reviewing individual IT projects and portfolios, this guidance is also useful to IT audit where multiple but similar IT audit projects can be managed as a program or considered as a portfolio. The whole idea is that there should be a tight interaction between programs or portfolios and their individual or subordinate projects, but program management often does not totally drive or dictate individual project activity, and the separate projects will help to define the overall structure of the

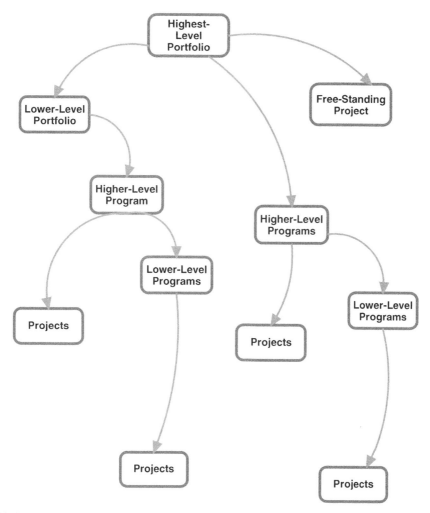

EXHIBIT 16.3 Project, Program, and Portfolio Interactions

supporting programs. The analogy between a series of individual IT audits and the overall audit function is very strong.

The next sections discuss project management in greater detail, but Exhibit 16.4 shows the relationship among project, program, and portfolio management practices in terms of such factors as their scope, change management considerations, planning, success factors, management, and monitoring. This exhibit, as well as many of the other exhibits in this chapter, has been extracted or modified from the PMI best practices materials for project, program and portfolios. Although PMI uses terms such as *project manager*, much of its guidance material is applicable to managing separate as well as either programs or portfolios of IT audits. IT auditors should develop a strong understanding of project management concepts; the PMI best practices are good tools to help manage IT audits.

	Project	Programs	Portfolios
Scope	Projects have defined objectives. Scope is progressively elaborated throughout the project life cycle.	Programs have a larger scope and provide more significant benefits.	Portfolios have a business scope that changes with the strategic goals of the enterprise.
Change	Project managers expect change and implement processes to keep change managed and controlled.	The program manager must expect change from both inside and outside the program and be prepared to manage it.	Portfolio managers continuously monitor changes in the broad environment.
Planning	Project managers require planning to evolve from high-level to detailed planning throughout the project life cycle.	Program managers develop the overall program plan and create high-level plans to guide detailed planning at the component level.	Portfolio managers create and maintain necessary process and communication relative to the aggregate portfolio.
Management	Project managers manage the project team to meet project objectives.	Program managers manage the program staff and project managers; they provide vision and overall ownership.	Portfolio managers may manage or coordinate portfolio management staff.
Success	Success is measured by product and project quality, timeliness, budget compliance, and degree of customer satisfaction.	Success is measured by the degree to which the program satisfies the needs and benefits for which it was undertaken.	Success is measured in terms of aggregate performance of portfolio components.
Monitoring	Project managers monitor and control the work of producing the products, services, or results that the project was undertaken to produce.	Program managers monitor the progress of program components to ensure that overall program goals, schedules, budget, and benefits will be met.	Portfolio managers monitor aggregate performance and value indicators.

EXHIBIT 16.4   Project, Program, and Portfolio Management Overview
Source: This exhibit is extracted or modified from Project Management Institute best practices materials for project, program, and portfolio management.

PROJECT MANAGEMENT FOR IT AUDITORS

Project management is an important skill for many enterprise professionals, whether a marketing group launching a new product, the IT team implementing a new application, or senior management organizing a business unit divestiture. Each of these and many other efforts require detailed work activities that usually are performed as individual projects by multiple resources and often under tight time constraints. No matter what their objectives and requirements, enterprise projects should follow strong project management disciplines and approaches. IT audit is often an exception and frequently does not use good project management disciplines. Although individual audits and annual audit plans all have the characteristics of formal and well-managed projects, many IT and other internal auditors fail to use formal project management approaches in planning and organizing their larger individual audits.

This section looks at project management best practices and why they should be an important tool for planning and performing all levels of IT audits. A project-based IT audit approach generally should improve IT audit's management and performance processes. We introduce the PMI's body of knowledge and discuss why its concepts are also important for IT auditors.[4] Whether at a staff level and for individual IT audits or for major audit activities, good project management techniques should improve many IT audit processes.

Project Management Process

In the past, the term *project* was often used rather loosely. IT auditors talked about their reviews as "audits" but did not think of them as projects. IT application developers or people in other areas of the enterprise were asked to organize a "project" to implement some special effort, and the organization and planning efforts for such a "project" meant different things to different people. Those efforts often involved a designated lead person calling the development group together and doing little more than saying "I want you, you, and you" to perform various project tasks. Little thought was given to project enterprise and planning. These informal efforts often failed because the project team did not understand their individual as well as overall project objectives, and both time requirements and the project scope were not defined. In many instances, there were project time and budget overruns, or the project failed for many other reasons. Often that failure was due to the lack of a consistent structured project management approach.

Project management continued to be just a poorly defined concept until mid-1990. With the exception of some U.S. government-led approaches in past years, there was no consistent approach to project management. Matters changed when the PMI was launched. Started by a small group of U.S. professionals looking for a more consistent definition of their work, by 2009 PMI was an international professional organization of about 275,000 members in 170 countries. PMI has researched, developed, and published a wide range of project management guidance materials. Its most significant publication is a standards-like document called the *Project Management Book of Knowledge (PMBOK)*,[5] a comprehensive guide to all aspects of the project management process. *PMBOK* has become the worldwide professional standard for project management practices.

Exhibit 16.5 shows *PMBOK*'s definition of a project. Although the guidance is rather lengthy and perhaps too general and comprehensive for some IT auditors, it defines the concept of a project as a temporary endeavor with a definite beginning and end date and with specific goals or objectives. Such projects operate outside of normal organization or enterprise procedures

A *project* is a temporary endeavor undertaken to create a unique product, service, or result. The temporary nature of projects indicates a definite beginning and end. The end is reached when the project's objectives have been achieved or when the project is terminated because its objectives will not or cannot be met, or when the need for the project no longer exists. *Temporary* does not necessarily mean short in duration. *Temporary* does not generally apply to the product, service, or result created by the project; most projects are undertaken to create a lasting outcome. For example, a project to build a national monument will create a result expected to last centuries. Projects can also have social, economic, and environmental impacts that far outlast the projects themselves.

Every project creates a unique product, service, or result. Although repetitive elements may be present in some project deliverables, this repetition does not change the fundamental uniqueness of the project work. For example, office buildings are constructed with the same or similar materials or by the same team, but each location is unique—with a different design, different circumstances, different contractors, and so on.

An ongoing work effort is generally a repetitive process because it follows an organization's existing procedures. In contrast, because of the unique nature of projects, there may be uncertainties about the products, services, or results that a project creates. Project tasks can be new to a project team, which necessitates more dedicated planning than other routine work. In addition, projects are undertaken at all organizational levels. A project can involve a single person, a single organizational unit, or multiple organizational units.

A project can create:

- A product that can be either a component of another item or an end item in itself.
- A capability to perform a service (e.g., a business function that supports production of distribution).
- A result, such as an outcome or document (e.g., a research project that develops knowledge that can be used to determine whether a trend is present or a new process will benefit society).

EXHIBIT 16.5 *PMBOK's Definition of a Project*

In addition to the *PMBOK* guidance covering individual projects, PMI has guidance for program and portfolio management as well as a standard for organization process management, OPM3®. *Program management* generally refers to a series of related projects; *portfolio management* covers standards for a suite of projects and programs within an enterprise. The concepts of OPM3 can be useful for organizing and managing an IT audit function. PMI also has a professional project manager certification program, where members who complete a professional examination and satisfy experience requirements are certified as a PMP (Project Management Professional). The PMI and its *PMBOK* guide are de facto standards for many project management activities in the enterprise.

Project Management Book of Knowledge

A Web search for books on the subject of project management yields thousands of titles, covering all aspects and variations of project management. The better ones, however, are based on the PMI's *PMBOK*, the de facto standard describing all aspects of project management. Here we provide an overview of the *PMBOK* project management process with an emphasis on how it can be useful for managing IT audit functions. Overall IT audit competencies should improve if auditors follow of these principles of good project management.

At present, there have been four revisions to *PMBOK*, with each new set of guidance materials building on the previous versions. The current *PMBOK*—version 4, released in 2008—defines project management as consisting of five basic process groups and nine knowledge areas that are the elements of almost all projects. Applicable to projects, programs, portfolios, and operations, these concepts have become a framework for effectively launching and executing projects. These five basic project management process groups are:

1. **Initiating.** There should be formal processes in place to launch any project effort, including a description of the project's objectives, estimated budgeting, and appropriate approvals. From an IT audit perspective, these initiating processes are discussed in Chapter 5 on performing effective IT audits.
2. **Planning.** Every project requires planning in terms of its time and resource estimates as well as for the linkages between components and other projects that require coordination. Chapter 2 on using CobiT to perform IT audits and Chapter 4 on understanding risk management will provide insights here.
3. **Executing.** This process group defines actual project activities: what needs to be done to accomplish project goals. From an IT audit perspective, these activities may range from individual application reviews or executing an ongoing program of computer-assisted audit tools and techniques to support operational internal audit activities.
4. **Controlling.** An ongoing set of processes should be in place to monitor the appropriate completion of project elements, determining that budgets and objectives are being met. This can be an important component in overall IT audit management.
5. **Closing.** The final process requires wrapping up the project effort, then both delivering the project components and summarizing and reporting the project results. For many IT audit activities, this is the production of IT audit reports, discussed in Chapter 29 on building an effective IT audit function.

PMBOK matches each of these five project management processes with nine project management knowledge areas in terms of their inputs, outputs, and tools and techniques. Project inputs include the documents, plans, and necessary resources to do the project with the outputs, and of course the completed project materials. To go from the starting project inputs to the completed end product, a wide range of tools and mechanisms is necessary. A project to build a house, for example, would need lumber, a plan, and other supplies, such as nails or roofing materials as the inputs. A hammer and a saw as well as knowledge of carpentry are the tools necessary to get started on the construction. The output in this simplified example is the completed house.

Although much more complex than requiring just lumber and a hammer and nails, the launch of an IT audit project includes a set of key components, including a plan to conduct the audit, access to documentation and other materials to gain an understanding of the areas of concern, tools such as laptop systems to perform the audit, and knowledgeable IT auditors to perform the review. In many respects, the construction of a single-residence frame house is a relatively small and simple project compared to many

IT audit efforts. Most projects launched by enterprises of any type are complex, and this complexity is what has led to PMI and its *PMBOK* best practices standards. Prior to these standards, enterprises too often launched major project efforts without adequate preparation. The results often resulted in massive cost and time overruns as well as failures even to complete the project. IT systems implementation projects of the past, as discussed in Chapter 10, were classic examples of poor project management techniques. Many other non-IT projects had the same enterprise problems. All lacked consistent and thorough project management approaches.

PMBOK has defined the project management process as taking place in a consistent and well-controlled manner. In addition to the five basic project management process groups, *PMBOK* defines nine project management knowledge areas:

1. Project Integration Management
2. Project Scope Management
3. Project Time Management
4. Project Cost Management
5. Project Quality Management
6. Project Human Resource Management
7. Project Communications Management
8. Project Risk Management
9. Project Procurement Management

PMBOK guidance describes each of these knowledge areas in terms of their inputs, tools, and outputs in considerable detail. For example, *PMBOK*'s Project Time Management knowledge area description includes input, tools, and output sections on:

- **Defining project activities.** This is the process of identifying the specific actions to be performed to produce project deliverables.
- **Sequence project activities.** The relationships between project activities should be identified and documented.
- **Estimate activity resources.** Estimates should be made for the type and quantities of people, materials, equipment, and supplies required to perform scheduled activities.
- **Estimate activity durations.** There is a need to analyze activity sequences, durations, resource requirements, and schedule restraints to create project schedules.
- **Develop project schedules.** A process is necessary to monitor the status of projects to update their progress and to manage any changes to their schedules.

These are the basic steps to manage time for any project, and they certainly are the steps an IT auditor should consider when planning the time requirements for any IT audit.

In addition to guidance on general management, *PMBOK* details the project management tools and processes needed in each of these knowledge areas. Exhibit 16.6 summarizes these *PMBOK* processes and knowledge areas. The purpose of this chapter is

Project Management Process Groups

Knowledge Area	Initiating Process Group	Planning Process Group	Executing Process Group	Monitoring and Controlling Process Group	Closing Process Group
4 Project Integration Management	4.1 Develop Project Charter	4.2 Develop Project Management Plan	4.3 Direct and Manage Project Execution	4.4 Monitor and Control Project Work 4.5 Perform Integrated Change Control	4.6 Close Project or Phase
5 Project Scope Management		5.1 Collect Requirements 5.2 Define Scope 5.3 Create Work Breakdown Structure		5.4 Verify Scope 5.5 Control Scope	
6 Project Time Management		6.1 Define Activities 6.2 Estimate Resources 6.3 Estimate Activity Resources 6.4 Estimate Durations 6.5 Develop Schedule		6.6 Control Schedule	
7 Project Cost Management		7.1 Estimate Costs 7.2 Determine Budget		7.3 Control Costs	
8 Project Quality Management		8.1 Plan Quality	8.2 Perform Quality Assurance	8.3 Perform Quality Control	
9 Project Human Resources Management		9.1 Develop Human Resources Plan	9.2 Acquire Project Team 9.3 Develop Project Team 9.4 Manage Project Team		
10 Project Communication Management		10.2 Plan Communications	10.3 Distribute Information 10.4 Manage Stakeholder Expectations	10.5 Report Performance	
11 Project Risk Management		11.1 Plan Risk Management 11.2 Identify Risks 11.3 Perform Quantitative Risk Analysis 11.4 Qualitative Risk Analysis		11.6 Monitor and Control Risks	
12 Project Procurement Management		12.1 Plan Procurements	12.2 Conduct Requirements	12.3 Administer Procurements	12.4 Close Procurements

EXHIBIT 16.6 PMBOK Process Groups and Knowledge Areas Summary

not to provide a detailed overview of all of *PMBOK*'s processes and knowledge areas but to emphasize the role of *PMBOK* for planning and implementing effective project management IT auditors.

Chapter 1 discussed how, before the Committee of Sponsoring Organizations (COSO) internal control framework was launched, there was no consistent definition of what was meant by internal control in enterprises; nor was there a regular process for defining and monitoring those internal controls. The launch of the COSO internal control framework in September 1992 as well as its adoption first in the auditing standards of the American Institute of Certified Public Accountants and subsequently in the SOx Section 404 has defined internal control standards. Just as the COSO internal controls framework ultimately defined is a now-recognized world-wide standard, *PMBOK* has become such a standard for the practice of project management. The International Standards Organization (ISO; www.iso.ch) has a draft international standard on project management, ISO 10006, that is very similar to *PMBOK* in terms of content and structure. Other ISO standards important to IT auditors are highlighted in Chapter 31, and this ISO standards approach will be the basis for effective project management standards going forward.

Developing a Project Management Plan

This chapter has not aimed to provide a detailed description of the *PMBOK* guidance material but to describe how it can be used by IT auditors to plan and execute their own IT audit projects. Knowledge of *PMBOK* will allow an IT auditor reviewing project-related areas in business operations to ask questions about how that area has used *PMBOK* principles.

To provide a better explanation of how *PMBOK* is organized and how it can become a tool to help IT auditors, we have selected one *PMBOK* element, 4.2 on developing a project plan. Although *PMBOK* is more oriented to the IT developer or manufacturing product developer, these project management concepts apply to an IT auditor as well. According to *PMBOK*, this project plan development area is "the process of documenting the actions necessary to define, prepare, integrate, and coordinate all subsidiary plans." Although the guidance here covers multiple plan areas, an IT auditor should think of this as preliminary guidance for building an IT audit plan. For example, the auditor should think of building a project plan along the lines of an enterprise that has just purchased or acquired a company that will be folded into main operations. That purchase would have taken place only after there had been some due diligence work to gain a high-level understanding of the proposed acquisition, but this example describes a situation where management may request that IT audit perform a detailed internal controls review of the new subsidiary acquisition.

Every element of *PMBOK* is described in terms of the inputs, outputs, and tool and techniques to that process area. Developing a project management plan is numbered 4.2 and is at the intersection of the Project Integration Management knowledge area and the Planning Process group, as shown in Exhibit 16.6. Again using the detailed internal controls review of the new subsidiary acquisition example, the required inputs for this process, following *PMBOK* numbering, are:

4.2.1 Project charter. *PMBOK* emphasizes the importance of a project charter similar to internal audit charters discussed in Chapter 5.

4.2.2 Outputs from Planning Process. This step would include IT audit's efforts to gather audit evidence, to document results in workpapers, and to deliver an appropriate audit report.

4.2.3 Enterprise Environment Factors. This *PMBOK* term includes such areas as supporting information systems, any facilities issues, or any applicable governmental standards. IT audit should gain knowledge of these input factors and factor them into its planning as applicable.

4.2.4 Organizational Process Assets. These include any other factors that can influence the audit plan. In this example, IT audit would use the results of the prior due diligence review as well as any IT audit work available from the prior, pre-acquisition IT auditors.

The project management plan is the single output from this process step. In our IT audit context, this would be an approved plan to initiate an IT audit. *PMBOK*'s Tools and Techniques section only calls for the need for "expert judgment." This would be the IT audit management skills necessary to tailor processes to meet the audit's needs, to allocate resources and skill levels, and to manage the audit's change management and configuration requirements.

As with all such elements, *PMBOK*'s "Develop Project Management Plan" process is not a single, free-standing process but is linked to other key *PMBOK* components. Exhibit 16.7 is a data flow diagram, adapted from the *PMBOK* guidance materials, that supports this key process and shows related linkages. This exhibit shows how various *PMBOK* processes interact to develop a project management plan. For example, the exhibit's number "4.1 Develop Project Charter" component is the major input to this 4.2 process with its steps 4.3 through 4.6 describing the processes to manage, monitor and close out the project. Just as the exhibit shows the *PMBOK* 4.2 component, there are similar data flows for 4.1 as well as for 4.3 to 4.6. Again, this process guidance should be considered in the steps necessary to manage, perform, and complete an IT audit. The activities to the right and below on the exhibit show the processes that feed this project integration management process to develop the project management plan. For example, a left-hand side process on this exhibit is labeled "8.1 Plan Quality." The related processes noted here are PMBOK's Quality Management Plan and Process Improvement plan. These are the types of IT audit quality assurance processes that are discussed in Chapter 31. *PMBOK* is even more complex than the three-dimensional COSO internal controls framework discussed in Chapter 1. The idea, however, is that many interconnected elements are necessary to build and maintain effective project management processes.

The *PMBOK* guidance materials discuss the inputs, outputs, and supporting tools for each of the numbered interrelated project management components. These are standards necessary to manage any project effectively, and IT audits should think of many of their audit activities in terms of formal *PMBOK*-type projects. Although this guidance may be too broad for smaller audits, it will serve as an excellent guide for managing many IT audits. *PMBOK* essentially provides a checklist covering essential steps for planning and performing successful individual IT audits.

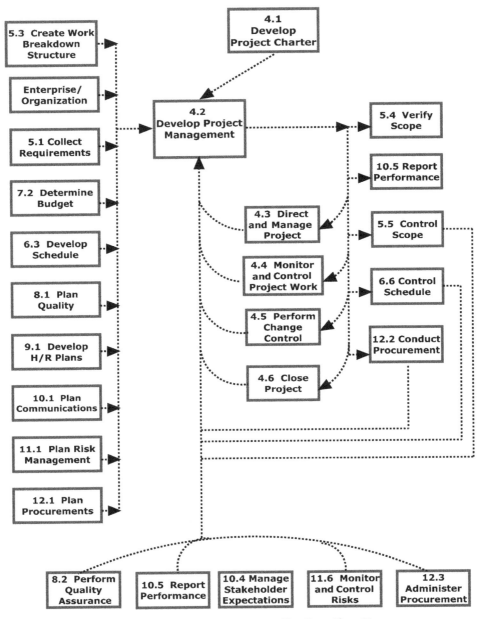

EXHIBIT 16.7 Developing a Project Management Plan Data Flow Diagram

IT auditors should develop a good understanding of project, program, and portfolio management practices. This will help them to review IT initiatives in development as well as to better review their own IT audit activities. In addition, the Val IT framework and materials presented in this chapter should receive more attention by IT functions, senior managers, and IT auditors.

NOTES

1. IT Financial Management, Gartner Consulting, www.gartner.com/it/products/consulting/GTACaseStudy.pdf.
2. IT Spending Survey 2009, Goldman Sachs, www.scribd.com/doc/7737986/Goldman-Sachs-IT-Spending-Survey.
3. John Thorp, Val IT Framework 2.0—Adding Breadth and Depth to the Value Management Road Map. *ISACA Journal* June, 2008; and IT Governance Institute, "Val IT Framework 2.0—Adding Breadth and Depth to the Value Management Road Map," *Information Systems & Control Journal* 5 (2008).
4. Project Management Institute, *Project Management Body of Knowledge (PMBOK)*, 4th ed. (Newtown Square, PA: Author, 2008).
5. Project Management Institute, *A Guide to the Project Management Book of Knowledge (PMBOK)*, 4th ed. (Newtown Square, PA: Author, 2004).

17

Compliance with IT-Related Laws and Regulations

A CONSTANT THEME THROUGHOUT these chapters has been the importance of information technology (IT) processes and applications in all aspects of enterprise operations as well as the IT auditor's important role in reviewing and assessing these IT controls and processes. IT auditors perform these reviews, following audit standards, to assess the performance of enterprise processes and applications in compliance with good operating procedures and strong internal controls. IT audit reviews also must be performed in compliance with applicable laws and legal regulations, but the number of IT-related rules is ever increasing.

Although the impact of IT-related laws is worldwide, this chapter introduces several U.S. federal acts that focus on internal controls compliance privacy protection and that should be of particularly important to U.S.-based IT auditors. While they cannot be expected to be experts on the details or legal nuances of these laws and regulations, IT auditors should have a general understanding of some of these rules. Chapter 1 discussed the Sarbanes-Oxley Act (SOx) rules that impact all internal auditors; this chapter looks at four other areas of legislation that can impact many auditors, particularly U.S.-based IT auditors. The chapter also reviews important aspects of the Computer Fraud and Abuse Act (CFAA), the Computer Security Act of 1987 (CSA), the Gramm-Leach-Bliley Act of 1999 (GLBA), and finally, the Health Insurance Portability and Accountability Act (HIPAA).

Regarding HIPAA, an IT auditor might argue: "I do IT audits for a manufacturing company; why should I worry about legislation related to health insurance?" Although HIPAA's focus is on healthcare providers, the act addresses a wide range of personal privacy records that impact all U.S. enterprises, and it has caused changes in such areas as IT security and human resource functions. Every enterprise that carries employee health insurance data in its human resource records needs to be aware of HIPAA issues, and IT auditors often can be a major aid to management in highlighting HIPAA controls and risks of violations.

The CFAA first appeared in 1984 as a response to public concern about computer crimes and was expanded in 1994 through the Computer Abuse Amendments Act. The legislation covers penalties and prohibitions for improper access to IT networks and computer systems—what the legislation calls "fraudulent trespass." IT auditors should be aware of these rules and be able, at a minimum, to point out to auditees when their activities could be in violation of CFAA rules.

The Computer Security Act of 1987 is particularly important because it is a fundamental set of U.S. federal standards for safeguarding unclassified information, implementing security and privacy policies with the federal government, and policies for cryptography. The act expands the authority of the National Institute of Standards and Technology (NIST) as a source of IT security tools and resources. This chapter explores some NIST resources in greater detail and outlines areas that are important to IT auditors.

Another legislative item important to IT auditors is the GLBA. This legislation requires financial institutions to further protect and audit their data and to take special care when sharing this data with others. Although it is directed at financial institutions, GLBA impacts many enterprises, and this chapter discusses its main components impacting IT auditors.

Beyond SOx rules from Chapter 1, GLBA rules discussed in this chapter, and industry standards such as the payment card industry data security standard (PCI-DSS) public key encryption data security standards rules discussed in Chapter 20, IT auditors worldwide encounter a wide range of industry-specific compliance rules. Many of these cover such areas as banking, securities, and electrical power generation. In other instances, internal governance rules specific to the United States or the European Union have implications that spread beyond just large governmental units. An example here are the U.S. Department of Commerce Office of Management and Budget A-123 internal control guidelines, which often have very broad impacts. The field is vast, but this chapter provides summaries of some rules that may impact IT auditors.

It is sometimes difficult to predict when legislation will have a continuing and lasting impact or when it will be just a law on the books with little ongoing compliance activity. A U.S. example here is the Foreign Corrupt Practices Act (FCPA) of the late 1970s. That legislation had some strong internal control documentation requirements that had many IT auditors thinking they would be very busy over the years keeping their enterprises in compliance with these provisions. Although the legislation remains on the books, there have been few internal controls–related enforcement actions since its enactment, and the FCPA's requirements covering internal control documentation have been all but forgotten today. However, the FCPA had some antifraud provisions that are currently very active. We do not think that GLBA or HIPAA and certainly SOx will go the same way as the FCPA, but such legislation and regulatory interests rise and fall. At the present time, IT auditors need to be aware of this privacy-related legislation and plan their review and internal control activities accordingly.

IT auditors should have a good understanding of the computer security regulations as well as GLBA and HIPAA rules discussed in this chapter. Although many of these laws and regulations focus on computer crime, federal IT security, consumer finance, and healthcare issues that will not directly impact every IT auditor, the rules have privacy provisions that are important in many other, broader areas. Of course, for an IT auditor working in an industry that is directly impacted, such as a healthcare provider for HIPAA rules, a strong knowledge of specific legislative rules is essential.

COMPUTER FRAUD AND ABUSE ACT

In the early 1980s, as IT applications and systems became more common, law enforcement agencies in the United States were faced with growing concerns about the lack of criminal laws available to fight emerging computer crimes. Although the wire and mail fraud provisions of the federal criminal code were capable of addressing some types of computer-related criminal activity, neither of those statutes provided the full range of tools needed to combat the new IT-based crimes. The response was the passage of the Comprehensive Crime Control Act of 1984, legislation that contained provisions to address the unauthorized access and use of computers and computer networks.

The original CFAA required that certain conditions had to be in place for the law and its penalties to take effect. However, technology has changed, and some of the factors in the act quickly became nonissues. For example, CFAA addressed the issue of fraudulent trespass with prohibitions against using a computer system to obtain free telephone service, an issue common in the earlier days of expensive telephone service charges but not so important today.

As technology changes and new IT-related threats have surfaced, the CFAA has been amended or supported by other U.S. legislation. For example, the Computer Abuse Amendments Act of 1994 addressed such issues as "unauthorized entry onto an online system, exceeding authorized access [rights] and exchanging information on gaining unauthorized access." The law was also enhanced to cover foreign computers as part of the Patriot Act early in this century. The criminal offenses under the CFAA include:

- Knowingly accessing a computer without authorization in order to obtain national security data
- Intentionally accessing a computer without authorization to obtain:
  - Information contained in a financial record of a financial institution, or contained in a file of a consumer reporting agency on a consumer
  - Information from any department or agency of the United States
  - Information from any protected computer if the conduct involves an interstate or foreign communication
- Intentionally accessing without authorization a government computer and affecting the use of the government's operation of the computer
- Knowingly accessing a protected computer with the intent to defraud and thereby obtaining anything of value
- Knowingly causing the transmission of a program, information, code, or command that causes damage or intentionally accessing a computer without authorization, and as a result of such conduct, causes damage that results in:
  - Loss to one or more persons during any one-year period aggregating at least $5,000 in value

OFFENSE	Section	Sentence*
Obtaining National Security Information	(a)(1)	10 (20) years
Compromising the Confidentiality of a Computer	(a)(2)	1 or 5
Trespassing in a Government Computer	(a)(3)	1 (10)
Accessing a Computer to Defraud and Obtain Value	(a)(4)	5(10)
Knowing Transmission and Intentional Damage	(a)(5)(A)(i)	10 (20 or life)
Intentional Access and Reckless Damage	(a)(5)(A)(ii)	5(20)
Intentional Access and Damage	(a)(5)(A)(iii)	1 (10)
Trafficking in Passwords	(a)(6)	1 (10)
Extortion Involving Threats to Damage Computer	(a)(7)	5(10)
*The maximum prison sentences for second convictions are noted in parentheses.		

EXHIBIT 17.1   Summary of CFAA Provisions

- The modification of the medical examination, diagnosis, treatment, or care of one or more individuals
- Physical injury to any person
- A threat to public health or safety
- Damage affecting a government computer system
- Knowingly and with the intent to defraud trafficking in a password or similar information through which a computer may be accessed without authorization

The CFAA specifically covers what are called "protected computers"—systems exclusively for the use of a financial institution or the United States Government or, in the case of a computer not exclusively for such use, used by or for a financial institution or IT systems used in or affecting interstate or foreign commerce or communication, including a computer located outside the United States that is used in a manner that affects interstate or foreign commerce. This jurisdiction statement, which is paraphrased from the legislation, shows how such laws can have a broad coverage.

Exhibit 17.1 summarizes the major provisions of CFAA and its penalties for violations. Our intent is not to describe the details of these provisions or to discuss the differences between specific types of violation. Rather, our point is that there can be serious penalties for improperly tampering with a protected computer system. IT auditors should be aware of these issues when reviewing controls over IT applications and processes. IT auditors will not normally be looking for CFAA violators but should be aware of the rules and tailor other reviews with these types of IT fraud and abuse penalties in mind.

COMPUTER SECURITY ACT OF 1987

As IT systems and processes became more and more prevalent beginning in the early 1980s, congressional-level concerns were expressed in the United States about the poor controls of IT classified information as well as a lack of many general IT standards. We tend to forget today that many IT processes were much different in those earlier days. In that era, there was a major reliance on mainframe systems. Most systems and software operating systems were distributed by one vendor, IBM; many other manufacturers of that era manufactured what were called minicomputers. Some businesses viewed the microcomputers that came to be known as personal computers almost as toys, and the World Wide Web concepts for powering the Internet were just getting started. Much critical classified U.S. government data was also being placed on computer systems, but government agencies established their own rules with no overlapping rules or responsibilities for computer security among federal agencies.

To remedy these conflicts, the CSA was enacted as the first major U.S. government effort to legislate protection and defense for unclassified information in government-related computer systems. The act mandated that the National Bureau of Standards develop and implement procedures to improve the security and privacy of sensitive material and create a means for establishing minimum acceptable security practices.

The CSA arose out of particular concerns about IT database vulnerabilities and that unclassified information could be pieced together to create a national security threat. The CSA legislation was designed to assess the vulnerability of government computers, develop technical and management strategies against access to sensitive information, and establish mandatory training for employees in computer and communication security.

The act defines "sensitive information" to include any unclassified information that, if lost, misused, or accessed or modified without authorization, could adversely affect the national interest, conduct of federal programs, or individual privacy. The CSA requires federal agencies to identify their computer systems that contain sensitive information, establish training programs to increase security awareness and knowledge of security practices, and establish a plan for the security and privacy of each computer system with sensitive information. However, the CSA has had little effect on keeping secure personal and private information held by the federal government. Security flaws in government computer systems are exposed routinely, and security lapses remain a major threat to the privacy of personal information in government databases.

For IT auditors, the most important element of the CSA was the creation of the National Institute of Science and Technology (NIST), an agency that grew out of the Bureau of Standards and that publishes some excellent IT systems standards and guidance. NIST develops standards in a wide range of areas—from fire protection research to nanotechnology; IT auditors will find the materials released by NIST's Information Technology Security and Networking (ITSN) Division a useful information source. The ITSN is the focal point for addressing NIST-wide IT security issues. Functions of the ITSN include establishing, implementing, and testing information security policies, procedures, and technologies for NIST's administrative and scientific environments. The ITSN also investigates computer security breaches by a NIST user or through a NIST system. NIST also publishes the Federal Information Processing Standards, which are requirements for all U.S. federal government computer systems. Most readers of this book are not working in a U.S. government environment, but many NIST standards in such areas as IT security still are useful reference sources.

Exhibit 17.2 is a list of selected current NIST IT-related documents. Many are more oriented to the federal government; others are far more technical than most IT auditors need; and some are old and out of date. Nevertheless, these materials are useful references for IT auditors wishing more information in a specialized area, such as encryption procedures.

This list of NIST documents, current as of 2009, relates to review and examination of records and activities in order to assess the adequacy of system controls, to ensure compliance with established policies and operational procedures, and to provide the supporting requirement for actions of an entity to be traced uniquely to that entity. The full documents can be found at http://csrc.nist.gov/publications/PubsFIPS.html.

FIPS 200	Security Controls for Federal Information Systems
FIPS 199	Standards for Security Categorization of Federal Information and Information Systems
FIPS 191	Guideline for the Analysis of Local Area Network Security
FIPS 140-2	Security Requirements for Cryptographic Modules
SP 800-92	Guide to Computer Security Log Management
SP 800-55	Security Metrics Guide for Information Technology Systems
SP 800-53	A Guide for Assessing the Security Controls in Federal Information Systems
SP 800-53	Security Controls for Federal Information Systems
SP 800-50	Building an Information Technology Security Awareness and Training Program
SP 800-42	Guideline on Network Security Testing
SP 800-41	Guidelines on Firewalls and Firewall Policy
SP 800-37	Guidelines for the Security Certification and Accreditation of Federal Information Technology Systems
SP 800-30	Risk Management Guide for Information Technology Systems
SP 800-26	Security Self-Assessment Guide for Information Technology Systems
SP 800-18	Guide for Developing Security Plans for Information Technology Systems
SP 800-16	Information Technology Security Training Requirements: A Role- and Performance-Based Model
NISTIR 7316	Assessment of Access Control Systems
NISTIR 7284	Personal Identity Verification Card Management Report
NISTIR 6981	Policy Expression and Enforcement for Handheld Devices
March 2006	Minimum Security Requirements for Federal Information and Information Systems: Federal Information Processing Standard (FIPS) 200 Approved by the Secretary of Commerce
January 2006	Testing and Validation of Personal Identity Verification (PIV) Components and Subsystems for Conformance to Federal Information Processing Standard 201
August 2005	Implementation of FIPS 201, Personal Identity Verification (PIV) of Federal Employees and Contractors
May 2005	Recommended Security Controls for Federal Information Systems: Guidance for Selecting Cost-Effective Controls Using a Risk-Based Process
November 2004	Understanding the New NIST Standards and Guidelines Required by FISMA: How Three Mandated Documents Are Changing the Dynamic of Information Security for the Federal Government
March 2004	Federal Information Processing Standard (FIPS) 199, Standards for Security Categorization of Federal Information and Information Systems
August 2003	IT Security Metrics
June 2003	ASSET: Security Assessment Tool for Federal Agencies
January 2002	Guidelines on Firewalls and Firewall Policy
September 2001	Security Self-Assessment Guide for Information Technology Systems
February 2000	Guideline for Implementing Cryptography in the Federal Government

EXHIBIT 17.2   NIST Audit and Accountability Published Documents

GRAMM-LEACH-BLILEY ACT

Officially known as the Financial Modernization Act of 1999, the GLBA is a privacy-related set of requirements with an objective to protect U.S. consumers' personal financial information held by financial institutions. The legislation has three principal parts: (1) the Financial Privacy Rule, (2) the Safeguards Rule, and (3) what is called its "pretexting provisions." Most professionals have not heard of what GLBA calls "pretexting": a concept and part of GLBA discussed in the sections to come. GLBA gives authority to eight different U.S. federal agencies and individual U.S. states to administer and enforce a new set of privacy-release rules that apply to what are generally called "financial institutions." These institutions include not only traditional banks, securities firms, and insurance companies but also enterprises providing many other types of financial products and services to consumers. Among these are the lending, brokering, or servicing any type of consumer loans, transferring or safeguarding money, preparing individual tax returns, providing financial advice or credit counseling, residential real estate settlement services, collecting consumer debts, and an array of other activities. With GLBA, these nontraditional "financial institutions" are regulated by the Federal Trade Commission (FTC) either directly or through other federal and state agencies.

IT auditors working for a bank or insurance company today probably have been involved with the 1999 GLBA and its privacy-related provisions, but the act impacts many other enterprises due to its expanded definition of "financial institutions." GLBA rules also are being applied to many state-regulated financial institutions. As an example, insurance companies in the United States have been regulated on a state-by-state basis with the National Association of Insurance Commissioners (NAIC) acting as a central coordinating and standards-setting group. The NAIC has imposed the federally mandated GLBA rules on its individual state-regulated insurance companies. This is an example of how U.S. federal regulations sometimes move from a U.S. authority like the Securities and Exchange Commission, for SOx matters, to rules covering state laws and international rules. We often forget that, in the United States, some corporate regulations and many other legislative rules are effective on a state-by-state basis. For example, motor vehicle driver licenses are issued by each of the states. Similarly, although the certified public accountant (CPA) examination is administered by the American Institute of Certified Public Accountants, CPAs are licensed on an individual state basis through individual boards of accountancy. Through the authority of the NAIC, a state rule-coordinating body, GLBA rules are being adopted by most to the states in the United States.

GLBA Financial Privacy Rules

U.S. consumers frequently encounter the GLBA and its Financial Privacy Rule today when they receive a note from a credit card provider discussing privacy rules for that credit card. The GLBA Financial Privacy Rule requires financial institutions to give their customers these privacy notices that explain the institution's information collection and sharing practices. This privacy notice must be a clear, conspicuous, and accurate statement of the company's privacy practices; it should include what information the company collects about its consumers and customers, with whom it shares this consumer credit information, and how it protects or safeguards the information. The notice applies to the "nonpublic personal information" the company gathers and discloses about its consumers and customers; in practice, that may be most or all of the information a company has about its customers. For example, nonpublic personal information could include information: that a consumer or customer puts on a credit or sales contract application; about the individual from another source, such as a credit bureau; or about transactions between the individual and the company such as an account balance. Indeed, even the fact that an individual is listed as a consumer or customer of a particular financial institution is classified under GLBA as nonpublic personal information. Matters that the company has reason to believe are lawfully public—such as mortgage loan information in a jurisdiction where that information is publicly recorded—are not restricted by GLBA.

GLBA-mandated privacy notices must contain the following information elements:

- Types of nonpublic personal information an enterprise collects regarding its customer
- Types of nonpublic personal information the enterprise will disclose to others about the customer
- The parties to whom the enterprise discloses this information, other than under an exception to the prohibition on nondisclosure
- The customer or client's right to "opt out" of the disclosure along with simple rules for this opting out process
- Enterprise policies with respect to sharing information on a person who is no longer a customer or client
- Enterprise practices for protecting the confidentiality and security the customer's or client's nonpublic personal information

Many consumers today pay little attention to these notices, even though they may state that the company may share their account data with others. GLBA gives the customer the right to opt out of or say no to having his or her private information shared with certain third parties. The privacy notice must explain how—and offer a reasonable way—consumers can opt out. For example, providing a toll-free telephone number or a detachable form with a preprinted address is a reasonable way for customers to opt out; but requiring someone to write a letter as the only way to opt out is not. The privacy notice also must explain that consumers have a right to say no to the sharing of certain information, such as credit report or application information, with the financial institution's separate divisions or affiliates.

GLBA puts some limits on how anyone who receives nonpublic personal information from a financial institution can use or redisclose the information. If a lender discloses customer information to a service provider responsible for mailing account statements, where the consumer has no right to opt out, that service provider may use the information only for limited purposes—such as for mailing account statements—and may not sell the information or use it for marketing.

This GLBA Federal Privacy Rule gets more complex in its details. Our intention here is merely to explain these privacy rules in general. An IT auditor, when performing appropriate application reviews, should recognize that all personal financial information is very private and cannot be arbitrarily sold or otherwise distributed. Consumers have rights to opt out and say no, and the enterprise must keep appropriate records of these actions and respect consumer privacy rights. IT auditors working with any financial institutions or applications should be aware of how GLBA privacy applies to their enterprise. The same is true for any enterprise that has a consumer-related credit granting and billing facility. A risk for an enterprise is that it may take the GLBA privacy rules as an almost trivial matter, perhaps fail to honor an opt-out request or improperly sell a mailing list, and then find itself facing class action litigation for damages due to the failure to comply.

GLBA Safeguards Rule

The act's Safeguards Rule requires financial institutions to have a security plan in place to protect the confidentiality and integrity of personal consumer information. When consumers open an account or purchase some product, they often disclose some elements of their personal information (e.g., an address, telephone number, or a credit card number) as part of the transaction process. An enterprise must have a security plan in place to protect the confidentiality and integrity of that consumer-supplied personal data. It should cover more than just the business continuity risks discussed in Chapter 25 and include controls to prevent hackers from accessing data files, disgruntled employees accessing customer information, or just simple carelessness. The GLBA Safeguards Rule requires that every financial institution, regardless of size, must create and implement a written information security plan for the protection of customer data. The scope and complexity of this security plan may be scaled to the size of the institution and the sensitivity of the information it maintains. The plan should be based on a risk analysis that identifies all foreseeable threats to the security, confidentiality, and integrity of customer information. Based on that risk analysis, financial institutions must document and implement security measures that include: administrative measures such as employee training; technical protections including passwords, encryption controls, and firewalls; and physical safeguards such as locks on doors and computers. Financial institutions must designate one or more of their employees to coordinate these safeguards and must conduct periodic reviews to determine whether their security programs require updating in light of changed circumstances.

IT auditors should be aware of how an enterprise can demonstrate compliance with the GLBA Safeguards Rule in five ways:

1. **Environmental risk analysis.** The enterprise should formally identify the internal and external risks to the security, confidentiality, and integrity of all customer personal information. Risk analysis approaches were discussed in Chapter 4. This process should cover the risks or loss or disclosure for all sources of personal information, whether on automated systems or manual records.

2. **Designing and implementing safeguards.** These safeguards are essentially the internal control procedures discussed in Chapter 1 and elsewhere as part of the internal controls framework of the Committee of Sponsoring Organizations (COSO).

3. **Monitoring and auditing.** Continuous audit assurance monitoring processes, such as discussed in Chapter 14, should be in place. IT audit can play an important monitoring and auditing role here by regularly scheduling reviews of the adequacy of the security plan and performing appropriate compliance tests.

4. **Constant improvements program.** As a result of any weaknesses found in audits or other tests, the enterprise should have a program in place to constantly improve its security plan. That program should be well documented to describe the plan's progress.

5. **Overseeing security providers and partners.** Many partners and other enterprises may have access to the same personal information or may have access to systems network connections where that personal privacy can be violated. Adequate policies, controls, and audit procedures need to be in place here as well.

The GLBA Safeguards Rule applies to a wide range of providers of financial products and services, including mortgage brokers, nonbank lenders, appraisers, credit reporting agencies, professional tax preparers, and retailers that issue their own credit cards. Banks are not subject to the Safeguards Rule but must comply with similar regulations that have been issued by federal banking agencies. Failure to comply with the Safeguards Rule may result in fines or other enforcement action by the FTC.

GLBA Pretexting Provisions

Using an expression that will set off the spell-checkers in most word processing programs, GLBA prohibits "pretexting," the use of false pretenses, including fraudulent statements and impersonation, to obtain consumers' personal financial information, such as bank balances. Pretexters use a variety of tactics to get personal information. For example, a pretexter may call, claim she is from a survey firm, ask a few questions to perhaps get the name of one's bank, and then use the information gathered to call the target person's financial institution, pretending to be that person or someone with authorized access to that account. She might claim that she has forgotten her checkbook and needs information about her account. In this way, the pretexter may be able to obtain personal information about the target victim, such as a social security number, bank and credit card account numbers, information in someone's credit report, and the existence and size of personal savings and investment portfolios.

Under GLBA's Pretexting Provisions, it is illegal for anyone to:

- Use false, fictitious, or fraudulent statements or documents to get customer information from a financial institution or directly from a customer of a financial institution.
- Use forged, counterfeit, lost, or stolen documents to get customer information from a financial institution or directly from a customer of a financial institution.

■ Ask another person to get someone else's customer information using false, fictitious, or fraudulent statements or using false, fictitious, or fraudulent documents or forged, counterfeit, lost, or stolen documents.

Pretexting leads to security and privacy risks or exposure to identity theft. This occurs when someone hijacks your personal identifying information to open new charge accounts, order merchandise, or borrow money. Consumers targeted by identity thieves usually do not know they have been victimized until the hijackers fail to pay the bills or repay the loans, and collection agencies begin dunning the targeted consumers for payment of accounts they did not even know they had. According to the FTC, the most common forms of identity theft are:

■ **Credit card fraud.** A credit card account is opened in a consumer's name or an existing credit card account is taken over.
■ **Communications services fraud.** The identity thief opens telephone, cellular, or other utility service in the consumer's name.
■ **Bank fraud.** A checking or savings account is opened in the consumer's name, and/or fraudulent checks are written.
■ **Fraudulent loans.** The identity thief gets a loan, such as a car loan, in the consumer's name.

A separate U.S. federal law related to GLBA, the Identity Theft and Assumption Deterrence Act, makes it a federal crime when someone "knowingly transfers or uses, without lawful authority, a means of identification of another person with the intent to commit, or to aid or abet, any unlawful activity that constitutes a violation of federal law, or that constitutes a felony under any applicable state or local law." Here, a name or social security number is considered a "means of identification," as is a credit card number, cellular telephone electronic serial number, or any other piece of information that may be used alone or in conjunction with other information to identify a specific individual.

GLBA rules can impact many IT auditors, particularly those working in financial institution IT systems and applications. Although many aspects of GLBA are designed primarily to protect consumer financial information, what is considered "consumer financial information" has become so broad that GLBA impacts a wide range of enterprises, IT application processes, and IT auditors in the United States.

IT auditors working with financial and credit-granting enterprises should become aware of these GLBA rules as well as the general privacy rules that are applicable for many other enterprises. The Web is the most appropriate source to obtain additional more detailed and current information on the act and its provisions. Two good sources are:

1. **Federal Trade Commission.** This U.S. government source provides an overview view of GLBA as well as its most current rules at: www.ftc.gov/privacy/privacyi-nitiatives/glbact.html.
2. **National Association of Insurance Commissioners.** This state-by-state regulatory enterprise has extensive GLBA information at www.techdata.com/content/tdenterprise/glba_resources.asp.

Internal audit should meet with financial management and the corporate counsel to assess whether the enterprise can be defined as a financial institution under the terms of the Gramm-Leach-Bliley Act (GLBA). If impacted, internal audit procedures should:

1. Determine the enterprise regularly sends out financial privacy notices, and assess follow-up procedures in place to correct returned letters or to provide answers to customers regarding these notices.
2. Assess record-keeping and other controls as well as supporting IT systems regarding the privacy notice opt-out rules. Select a sample of customers who have requested to opt out and determine whether these privacy procedures are operating.
3. Review general record privacy and security procedures over all GLBA-impacted materials. Good practices here will include strong IT application password controls and office procedures covering paper-oriented records.
4. Determine whether the enterprise has a formal security plan in place to protect the integrity and confidentiality of personal consumer information. This assessment should include both paper and IT systems.
5. Determine whether an environmental risk analysis is in place to formally identify all internal and external risks to the security, confidentiality, and integrity of all customer personal information.
6. Review continuous monitoring processes in place surrounding controls over customer personal information databases, and assess their adequacy.
7. Review the adequacy of continual improvements programs surrounding GLBA security controls, and comment on their adequacy.
8. Assess the adequacy of information programs within the enterprise to inform all employees of the requirements of GLBA and their need to protect customer personal information.
9. Based on the results of supporting IT application reviews, determine whether adequate controls are in place to prevent violations of GLBA pretexting provisions.
10. Determine whether the enterprise has taken adequate steps to inform other related organizations of its GLBA provisions.

EXHIBIT 17.3   Procedures for Auditing Gramm-Leach-Bliley Act Compliance

Exhibit 17.3 outlines IT audit steps for reviewing compliance with GLBA controls and procedures. These audit procedures must be expanded for some enterprises; the objective of this exhibit is to provide some general audit steps to consider for an operational review of financial institutions to demonstrate GLBA compliance.

IT auditors should have a general understanding of GLBA rules and whether their own enterprise qualifies as a "financial institution" under these rules. When the rules apply, application reviews should emphasize compliance with GLBA privacy rules and procedures for effective opt-out controls. Violations of these rules can become a minefield for enterprises.

HIPAA: HEALTHCARE AND MUCH MORE

A U.S.-based IT auditor today who is visiting a doctor for an annual physical or some other procedure will be asked to sign what looks like an innocuous disclosure permission agreement when checking in at the front desk. The permission document asks the patient to agree to allow his or her medical records to be shared or disclosed as part of that visit. If the auditor-patient asks why, the response usually will be that this is a "legal requirement of HIPAA." The medical patient's typical reaction is to sign the document and move on, not fully understanding why the signature was requested. Although HIPAA is a healthcare-related set of rules, it contains a set of privacy-related legislative rules that go beyond healthcare and impacts many enterprises and their IT auditors.

Whether working for a U.S. manufacturing company, a financial services enterprise, or many others, all internal auditors need to have at least a general understanding of some HIPAA rules. Enacted in 1999 with the final rules released over subsequent years, HIPAA has had a major impact on the privacy and security of personal medical records and many other personal records. Individuals encounter HIPAA when visiting a doctor's office or for many other medical-related matters. Human resource functions in enterprises also are seeing the impact of HIPAA requirements today in their administration of employee healthcare plans and medical treatment records. Of course, HIPAA has had a large and growing impact on the entire healthcare industry and all affiliated delivery providers. Even more significantly, HIPAA rules cover a wide range of business processes based on electronic commerce. HIPAA has four primary objectives:

1. **Ensure health portability by eliminating preexisting condition job locks.** This was the original motivation that led to the passage of HIPAA. People were diagnosed with some condition and then were unable to acquire new health coverage when changing employers because information about that individual's health condition was shared with others.
2. **Reduce healthcare fraud and abuse.** These words are from the congressional hearings leading to the legislation when some examples of alleged fraud and abuse were cited such as what is called patient dumping, when hospitals' emergency departments fail to provide emergency medical screening and stabilizing treatment to individuals needing emergency care.
3. **Enforce standards for health information.** This is covered by the HIPAA privacy and security rules to be outlined.
4. **Guarantee security and privacy of health information.**

This section provides a brief overview of HIPAA objectives and rules covering privacy and security. It is not an exhaustive introduction to all aspects of HIPAA. We have introduced the act as a legislatively driven set of rules that continue to impact many IT auditors. The progress of the HIPAA legislation also illustrates how the government-sponsored rule-making process often works. HIPAA rules initially were issued in draft form in 1999 following an early published schedule. The drafts resulted in numerous comments, revised rules drafts were issued with still more comments, and the final rules were issued in 2006, much later than originally planned.

HIPAA Patient Record Privacy Rules

Ongoing concerns regarding medical patient privacy were the motivating reason for the U.S. Congress originally passing HIPAA. We visit a medical care provider, discuss some concern or problem, and then expect treatment in a confidential manner. We do not want the results of that visit to be communicated back to our employer's human resource department, to some insurance company that has no need to know, or to be left on a desk in the medical care provider's office for anyone to pick up. Even worse, we do not want any personal, confidential matters to be shared in a manner that may limit our future employment options. This personal information privacy concern is the basis for much of HIPAA. However, many parties need to have some information about our healthcare condition to provide adequate coverage or reimbursement, and virtually all healthcare operations require detailed and complex supporting systems. HIPAA privacy rules cover five general areas as are briefly outlined next. These comments do not provide exhaustive coverage of and are not intended to be a reference source for HIPAA rules; they are intended to provide the nonmedical professional—an IT auditor—with an overview of the HIPAA rules.

1. **Medical records uses and disclosures.** An enterprise that is subject to HIPAA rules must take steps to limit the use and disclosure of personal medical information to "the minimum necessary to accomplish the intended purpose of the use, disclosure, or request" for non–treatment-related matters. We start this overview of HIPAA rules by directly quoting some of the rules' actual words. Using expressions such as "the minimum necessary," the act contains many such guidelines that are subject to enterprise-specific practices, validated through other rulings or litigation over time.

   This section of HIPAA rules specifies that individual health information loses its HIPAA protection if the individual covered is "de-identified" in a manner that this health information will not contain any of 18 specific identifiers regarding the individual and relatives, employers, or household members. This requirement says a lot about HIPAA. In order to make a health-related information system HIPAA compliant, the legislation identifies these 18 specific factors that a specialist in database retrieval might use to identify an individual. That is, an individual's medical information that is placed in some type of file or IT system is generally protected from general disclosure to others, but that information can be shared if it meets certain specific conditions.

2. **Authorization requirements.** This is the section of HIPAA that many users of healthcare services first encounter. Healthcare providers must obtain written approval to disclose healthcare information on everything with the exception of emergency situations. An individual has the right to refuse such a disclosure, and healthcare providers must have a strong record retention requirement to keep track of all of these disclosures. These are the documents, as previously discussed, that an individual is asked to sign when visiting a physician's office.

3. **Privacy practice communications.** Healthcare providers must have published privacy practices that they provide to healthcare users. Individuals then have the right to formally request restrictions in this policy, and providers must accommodate reasonable requests.

4. **Medical record access and amendment rights.** Individuals have the right to inspect and copy all or a portion of their personal health information. In addition, individuals have the right to request amendments to those healthcare records. Finally, the healthcare provider must keep a record of all other parties that

requested access to these personal healthcare records in the six-month period prior to any request.

5. **HIPAA privacy administration.** Going beyond the records access and disclosure rules, HIPAA has an extensive set of privacy administrative requirements that apply to what are called "covered entities"—medical offices, laboratories, hospitals, and all others involved with personal healthcare. These privacy administration rules include:

- The provider must designate a "Privacy Official" who is responsible for the development and implementation of these HIPAA policies and procedures.
- The provider must train members of its workforce on these HIPAA privacy-related policies and procedures and must maintain documentation to demonstrate that the training has been provided.
- A healthcare provider must have in place administrative, technical, and physical safeguards to protect the privacy of personal health information.
- The healthcare provider must apply "appropriate sanctions" against employees who fail to comply with these privacy policies and procedures.
- The provider must develop and implement policies and procedures that are designed to comply with the elements of the HIPAA regulations, and this documentation must be maintained in written or electronic form for six years.

These HIPAA rules primarily cover access to personal healthcare information, but they also outline other areas that define good IT systems and other operating practices that should be implemented elsewhere in the enterprise. An example would be the requirement that healthcare providers maintain documentation covering their training programs. These types of rules have existed for Federal Drug Administration medical or drug programs, are now part of HIPAA, and are a good idea for many corporate training programs. Enterprises sometimes spend resources training their employees but often do not bother to document that activity.

HIPAA rules are particularly important for an IT auditor working in a healthcare-related enterprise, such as a hospital or medical claims insurance company. However, the rules extend to other areas, such as medical insurance claims processing in an enterprise's human resources department or factory floor safety and industrial accident reporting. Healthcare-related enterprises should have strong HIPAA compliance rules and procedures, but it is beyond the scope of this book to provide a detailed description of these rules. However, IT auditors will encounter areas where HIPAA compliance is required in many other environments. Exhibit 17.4 describes some HIPAA healthcare procedures that should be in place in any enterprise. Although an IT auditor will typically not be installing these procedures, knowledge of them is useful for performing related application reviews.

HIPAA Cryptography and Security Requirements

In addition to its medical records authorization and release privacy rules, HIPAA contains some very specific and, for smaller enterprises, difficult-to-implement IT security requirements. It pushes to the edges of IT security practices and requires such things as secure electronic signatures, even though currently there exist limited

1. Is the enterprise defined as a healthcare-related enterprise and subject to HIPAA rules? (If not, there is no need to complete these steps.)
2. Has an enterprise-wide information security officer been appointed for HIPAA compliance and has a general implementation plan been developed?
3. Have policies and procedures to protect patient health information been developed and implemented?
4. Is there a process for the ongoing support and monitoring of HIPAA rules and regulations?
5. Are processes in place to develop comprehensive privacy and security policies, procedures, controls, and technologies, and are those processes consistent with existing IT systems rules?
6. The enterprise should have a formal contingency plan in place that includes:
   - Application and data criticality analysis
   - Data backup planning
   - Disaster recovery plans
   - Emergency mode operations plan
   - Periodic testing and revisions to the plan
7. Are there formal information access control processes, including access authorization, access establishment rules, and access modification procedures?
8. Controls over access to information systems media should include processes for:
   - Accountability
   - Data backup
   - Data storage
   - Disposal of data
9. Personnel security policy/procedures should:
   - Ensure the supervision of maintenance personnel by an authorized, knowledgeable person.
   - Maintain a complete record of access authorizations.
   - Ensure that operating and maintenance personnel have proper access authorization.
   - Have a personnel clearance procedure.
10. Formal termination procedures should be in place, including the changing of appropriate combination locks and the removal from access lists.
11. Physical access controls throughout the facility should include:
    - Emergency mode operation plans
    - Equipment control into and out of facility
    - Facility security plans
    - Procedures for verifying access authorizations prior to physical access
    - Maintenance records
    - Need-to-know procedures for personnel access
    - Sign-in for visitors and escort, if appropriate
    - Testing and revisions to the physical access plan.
12. All networks and communications should be protected through:
    - Automatic logoff
    - Unique user identification
    - Passwords and PINs
    - Telephone callbacks

EXHIBIT 17.4   Internal Audit HIPAA Requirements Procedures

technically mature techniques to provide such security on open networks such as the Internet. We are still at a point where a skilled computer hacker can intercept a cell phone call; such a call covering healthcare-related matters could create a violation of HIPAA security requirements. Technology will change, control procedures will improve, hackers will get ever smarter, and violations will be settled in the courts.

The basic reason behind these security rules was that the typical pre-HIPAA security of the healthcare administrative system was often inadequate. Enterprises can improve systems security not just by purchasing and installing new software but first by improving human-driven policies. The HIPAA Security Standards rules were not finalized and put into effect until April 2003, and compliance with these rules did not take effect until 2006. Among other areas, these rules cover what HIPAA calls "covered entities" and include:

- Doctors and other healthcare providers who process healthcare claims electronically
- Health plans, including enterprises that "self-insure"
- Healthcare clearinghouses—billing services and others that provide data formatting services for electronic claims submission

Thus, HIPAA security rules apply to all enterprises, whether a single doctor's office, a major hospital, and a small professional office that handles its own healthcare claims processing through self-insurance.

Security is a key HIPAA element of keeping personal health information private, and these rules cover good security practices for much more than just medical records, such as requirements for strong disaster recovery standards. The published rules consist of both "required" and what HIPAA calls "addressable" rules. The latter are rules that an enterprise is not required to implement due to its small size and limited resources. The "required" HIPAA rules represent many good information security practices that are appropriate to any enterprise. Other HIPAA security areas are beyond the scope of this book, such as requirements for public key infrastructure (PKI) environments that include digital signatures.

HIPAA Security Administrative Procedures

HIPAA requires administrative procedures to be in place to guard data integrity, confidentiality, and availability. These procedures must be carefully documented per HIPAA rules, and Exhibit 17.5 lists some of these "required" administrative procedures. We have listed the implementation rules here in a very general manner; published HIPAA rules tend to be very detailed. Many of these requirements, such as a documented and tested contingency plan or formal policies for information access controls, are similar to the types of control procedures IT auditors have been recommending over the years. Some represent good practices that should be in place in many enterprises. Rule 3 refers to the need for what is called a Sanctions Policy—a formal set of rules for people who violate security policy. This is a good idea for most enterprises. Now, as an administrative rule, a HIPAA-impacted healthcare provider will face a penalty if its established rules and procedures are found inadequate.

HIPAA security requirements also include some physical safeguard rules that are similar to the physical access controls that have existed over IT data centers for years. Here, however, HIPAA goes beyond the classic IT operations center and calls for strong

These provisions apply to what are called "covered" entities or enterprises under HIPAA rules and must be part of an enterprise's HIPAA security and compliance plan.

1. **Risk analysis.** Enterprises must conduct a thorough assessment of the potential risks of information confidentiality, integrity, and availability.
2. **Risk management.** Covered enterprises must implement reasonable and appropriate security measures to reduce overall risks to an acceptable level.
3. **Sanctions policy.** Sanctions or related penalties must be applied to workforce members who violate the enterprise's security policy. This might translate into some type of three-strikes-and-you're-out policy.
4. **Information systems security activity reporting.** Security logs, incident reports, and related security activity reports should be filed and reviewed on a regular basis.
5. **Incident response.** Processes should be in place to identify, investigate, mitigate, and document security incidents.
6. **Backup procedures.** Appropriate procedures must be in place to recover any loss of data.
7. **Disaster recovery.** Every covered enterprise must establish procedures to cover any loss of data.
8. **Emergency mode of operations.** Processes must be in place to ensure the security of patient information when operating in an emergency mode.
9. **Related business contracts.** An enterprise must include language in contracts with suppliers of related services that require the supplier to adopt adequate security measures to report security incidents to the enterprise, to ensure that these subcontractors implement appropriate security measures, and to provide for the termination of the contract in case of a security breach.
10. **Disposal of patient information.** Policies and procedures should be in place to address the final disposition of such patient information as recycled disk devices.
11. **Media reuse.** Processes must be in place to ensure the removal of sensitive information from electronic media, such as disk drives, before reuse.
12. **Unique user identification.** Unique identifiers must be assigned to all systems users in order to prevent shared accounts and to track system behavior.
13. **Emergency access procedures.** Procedures must be established to allow for the accessing of electronic information during an emergency.
14. **Documentation.** Procedures must be established to guarantee information security, maintain the documentation for a period of six years, and review it periodically.

EXHIBIT 17.5   HIPAA Required Implementation Specifications

---

guidelines and documentation over workstation use and location. Although IT auditors typically have not raised many internal control concerns regarding physical controls for networked terminals in a business environment, the HIPAA-regulated healthcare environment introduces new issues. A medical environment workstation that may be used by doctors, nurses, or other staff members requires strong logical and physical controls to protect the personal privacy of the patient records that may pass through those workstations.

Technical Security Services and Mechanisms

HIPAA rules require that processes be put in place to guard the integrity, confidentiality, and availability of medical records data and to prevent unauthorized access to any data that is transmitted over communication networks. The rules here require information systems security controls that are often stronger than those found in many larger enterprises today and include:

- **Access control.** Strong control mechanisms based on the context of the data or the role/position of authorized users must be established. In addition, control processes always must be in place to allow emergency access from data center operations if required.
- **Audit controls.** Here and throughout all of the HIPAA rules are requirements for strong audit controls, including such things as documentation revision processes and traditional audit trails.
- **Data authentication.** Strong systems controls over data integrity are required here. These are the same types of applications controls discussed in Chapter 10.
- **Entity authentication.** Controls must be in place such that when one work-station attempts to access another, it should be authenticated. This process may include passwords, telephone callbacks, or even biometric controls. This require-ment goes beyond many enterprise practices in place today where information is often freely shared through an e-mail note with attachments.
- **Communications and network controls.** A wide range of controls is suggested here, including alarms, encryption, event reporting, message authentication, and others. The HIPAA-impacted enterprise must implement a very secure network.

HIPAA requires that electronic signature controls be established that will provide the same legal weight to electronic data signatures as is associated with a traditional signature on a paper document. HIPAA prescribes network message integrity, no repudiation, and user authentication for any message with an electronic signature. For many, this can be a challenge. Digital signature processes are available today, but they are somewhat cumbersome. This is a classic case of the U.S. government establishing ideal or desired rules even when there currently exist no practical solutions. Legislators sometimes think that if they set a high standard, industry and other groups will charge ahead to make things happen. This sometimes does work, but if not, rules will need to be revised.

Going Forward: HIPAA and E-Commerce

Although designed to protect and authenticate medical information, HIPAA rules outline some strong guidelines for all electronic commerce processes. A major require-ment here will be improved standards and processes for electronic signatures. There is still more to be accomplished before these processes become common and commercially available, and NIST, discussed earlier in this chapter, is taking a leadership role in the development of a federal PKI rule that supports digital signatures and other public key–enabled security services. NIST is coordinating with industry and technical groups that are developing technology to foster the interoperability of PKI products and projects.

HIPAA rules have pushed progress in many areas of IT security and integrity. IT auditors should stay aware of these ongoing rules and required standards even if they do not work directly for a healthcare enterprise. The chapter has provided a very limited introduction to these complex and important rules. Beyond just healthcare enterprises, the rules apply whenever health-related records are maintained by a human resources function. An IT auditor can find more HIPAA information on the Web at:

1. **U.S. Department of Health and Human Services.** Copies of HIPAA rules and other supporting reference materials are available from: http://hhs.gov/ocr/privacy.
2. **HIPAA Advisories.** A site maintained by Phoenix Health Systems as a public service is a good source for HIPAA information: www.phoenixhealth.com/hipaadvisory.

HIPAA compliance is a U.S. legal requirement. While government compliance auditors are not going to be visiting hospitals, large healthcare facilities, and certainly not commercial enterprise human resources departments, an individual who feels there has been a violation can file a complaint with the U.S. Department of Justice (DOJ). That could certainly occur if some key information from an employee's medical insurance claim records became public knowledge due to a records security breakdown. The DOJ has a complaint-driven/voluntary compliance approach.

If the DOJ decides to take action regarding some complaint, it currently has a one-free-violation policy where it first emphasizes working with the noncompliant enterprise and then, if corrective action is not taken, will consider the imposition of civil monetary penalties.

IT auditors should be aware of HIPAA rules, at least on a high level. They are a major reason for an IT auditor to recommend strong security and confidentiality controls over any area that might impact an employee's medical health records.

OTHER PERSONAL PRIVACY AND SECURITY LEGISLATIVE REQUIREMENTS

GLBA and HIPAA are two important U.S. privacy and security legislative initiatives that should remain on IT auditors' radar screens. These are in addition to the due care standards of the PCI-DSS discussed in Chapter 20. There are also other recent privacy-related U.S. federal initiatives, such as the Children's Online Privacy Protection Act, which regulates the collection of children's personal information. In addition, some 35 (and counting) U.S. states have introduced their own data protection acts. Because these rules are not always consistent on a state-by-state basis, compliance can become a major enterprise challenge. An enterprise's legal counsel should be the authority most aware of these issues, and IT audit should closely coordinate activities with its legal counsel to ensure that IT audit reviews recognize and support these legal compliance rules.

Other related regulatory drivers exist on a worldwide basis and include the European Union Data Protection standard, the Canadian Personal Information Protection and Electronic Documents Act, and a related Japanese data protection law. Each of these has data security requirements that are common but not identical to HIPAA data security rules. Another international privacy and security standard is described in the International Standards Enterprise (ISO) standard 15408, a framework to evaluate IT security. ISO standards are introduced in Chapter 18, although a combination of space limitations and their relevance to the practice of IT auditing limited complete descriptions of these laws and regulations. A common thread for these initiatives is the personal privacy protection for much of the information about an individual that is kept in IT systems records.

The HIPAA and GLBA legislation discussed in this chapter may very well point to other legislative initiatives in areas beyond healthcare and personal financial privacy protections. As this book goes to press, an extensive health care act was just passed (often called "Obamacare") with many rules yet to be published. There will be many opportunities for IT auditors in current and future enterprises, and all IT auditors should have a high-level awareness of these rules. When an IT auditor is working in a healthcare or financial enterprise that is directly impacted by HIPAA or GLBA rules, a strong understanding of these rules and how they impact IT audit activities is essential.

 ## IT-RELATED LAWS, REGULATIONS, AND AUDIT STANDARDS

IT auditors, in the course of their reviews, are expected to assess compliance with all applicable laws and regulations. This chapter has highlighted several rules that are applicable to today's IT-related environments, along with other rules, such as SOx, that are better known and very much apply to IT auditors. Chapter 3 discussed IIA and ISACA auditing standards and ISACA standard S9, *Irregularities and Illegal Acts*, is applicable here. Exhibit 17.6 is an extract of that standard showing areas of an IT auditor's responsibility.

Note: This exhibit is only an *extract* of those elements of ISACA Auditing Standard S9 showing an IS auditor's responsibility for reviewing irregularities and illegal acts.

Introduction
01   ISACA standards contain basic principles and essential procedures, which are mandatory, together with related guidance.
02   The purpose of this ISACA Standard is to establish and provide guidance on irregularities and illegal acts that the IS auditor should consider during the audit process.

Standard
03   In planning and performing the audit to reduce audit risk to a low level, the IS auditor should consider the risk of irregularities and illegal acts.
04   The IS auditor should maintain an attitude of professional skepticism during the audit, recognizing the possibility that material misstatements due to irregularities and illegal acts could exist, irrespective of his/her evaluation of the risk of irregularities and illegal acts.
05   The IS auditor should obtain an understanding of the organization and its environment, including internal controls.

EXHIBIT 17.6   ISACA Standard S9 Irregularities and Illegal Acts Extract
Source: IT Standards, Guidelines, and Tools and Techniques for Audit Assurance and Control Professionals. © 2005 ISACA. All rights reserved. Used by permission.

06   The IT auditor should obtain sufficient and appropriate audit evidence to determine whether management or others within the organization have knowledge of any actual, suspected, or alleged irregularities and illegal acts.

07   When performing audit procedures to obtain an understanding of the organization and its environment, the IS auditor should consider unusual or unexpected relationships that may indicate a risk of material misstatements due to irregularities and illegal acts.

08   The IT auditor should design and perform procedures to test the appropriateness of internal control and the risk of management override of controls.

09   When the IT auditor identifies a misstatement, the auditor should assess whether such a misstatement may be indicative of an irregularity or illegal act. If there is such an indication, the IT auditor should consider the implications in relation to other aspects of the audit and in particular the representations of management.

10   The IT auditor should obtain written representations from management at least annually or more often depending on the audit engagement. It should:
- Acknowledge its responsibility for the design and implementation of internal controls to prevent and detect irregularities or illegal acts.
- Disclose to the IT auditor the results of the risk assessment that a material misstatement may exist as a result of an irregularity or illegal act.
- Disclose to the IT auditor its knowledge of irregularities or illegal acts affecting the organization in relation to:
  - Management
  - Employees who have significant roles in internal control
- Disclose to the IT auditor its knowledge of any allegations of irregularities or illegal acts, or suspected irregularities or illegal acts affecting the organization as communicated by employees, former employees, regulators, and others.

11   If the IT auditor has identified a material irregularity or illegal act, or obtains information that a material irregularity or illegal act may exist, the IS [information security] auditor should communicate these matters to the appropriate level of management in a timely manner.

12   If the IT auditor has identified a material irregularity or illegal act involving management or employees who have significant roles in internal control, the IT auditor should communicate these matters in a timely manner to those charged with governance.

13   The IT auditor should advise the appropriate level of management and those charged with governance of material weaknesses in the design and implementation of internal control to prevent and detect irregularities and illegal acts that may have come to the IT auditor's attention during the audit.

14   If the IT auditor encounters exceptional circumstances that affect the auditor's ability to continue performing the audit because of a material misstatement or illegal act, the IS auditor should consider the legal and professional responsibilities applicable in the circumstances, including whether there is a requirement for the IS auditor to report to those who entered into the engagement or in some cases those charged with governance or regulatory authorities or consider withdrawing from the engagement.

15   The IT auditor should document all communications, planning, results, evaluations, and conclusions relating to material irregularities and illegal acts that have been reported to management, those charged with governance, regulators, and others.

Commentary

16   The IT auditor should refer to ISACA Auditing Guideline G19, Irregularities and Illegal Acts, for a definition of what constitutes an irregularity and illegal act.

17   The IT auditor should obtain reasonable assurance that there are no material misstatements due to irregularities and illegal acts. An IT auditor cannot obtain absolute assurance because of factors such as the use of judgement, the extent of testing, and the inherent limitations of

EXHIBIT 17.6   (*Continued*)

internal controls. Audit evidence available to the IS auditor during an audit should be persuasive in nature rather than conclusive.

18 The risk of not detecting a material misstatement resulting from an illegal act is higher than the risk of not detecting a material misstatement resulting from an irregularity or error, because illegal acts may involve complex schemes designed to conceal or hide events or intentional misrepresentations to the IS auditor.

19 The IT auditor's previous experience and knowledge of the organization should assist the IS auditor during the audit. When making inquiries and performing audit procedures, the IS auditor should not be expected to fully disregard past experience, but should be expected to maintain a level of professional skepticism. The IT auditor should not be satisfied with less than persuasive audit evidence based on a belief that management and those charged with governance are honest and have integrity. The IT auditor and the engagement team should discuss the organization's susceptibility to irregularities and illegal acts as part of the planning process and throughout the duration of the audit.

20 To evaluate the risk of material irregularities and illegal acts existence, the IT auditor should consider the use of:
- His/her previous knowledge and experience with the organization (including his/her experience about the honesty and integrity of management and those charged with governance)
- Information obtained making inquiries of management
- Management representations and internal control sign-offs
- Other reliable information obtained during the course of the audit
- Management's assessment of the risk of irregularities and illegal acts, and its process for identifying and responding to these risks

EXHIBIT 17.6   (*Continued*)

We live in a world where IT process, such as the Internet, and supporting systems are ever more critical. We can expect to see more and more laws and regulations, on a worldwide basis, covering these IT-related issues. IT auditors should be aware of them and look for appropriate levels of compliance in their ongoing audit activities.

CHAPTER EIGHTEEN

Understanding and Reviewing Compliance with ISO Standards

I N THE YEARS FOLLOWING World War II, the United States emerged as the worldwide economic and political leader. Due to this dominance, many in the United States all but ignored many commercial best practice standards developed and used elsewhere in our globally connected economy. These international best practice standards are collaborative efforts that take into account a wide range of national needs and requirements. The source of many of these standards is the International Standards Organization (ISO; www.iso.org), an international body based in Geneva, Switzerland, that has issued well-recognized standards covering a wide range of areas, such as specifications for fastener screw threads in an automobile engine, the thickness of a personal credit card, and information technology (IT) quality standards. These standards have been expanded over the years to cover many areas that are important for enterprise governance and quality.

IT auditors should have an understanding of the role of any ISO standards that are appropriate in their enterprises. The implementation of most ISO standards often brings an IT auditor out of the internal audit office and to enterprise production areas. Enterprise quality auditors, as described in Chapter 31, are usually the audit professionals most involved with ISO standards. Quality auditors often have quite different objectives and approaches from those of Institute of Internal Auditors (IIA) or Information Systems Audit and Control Association (ISACA) internal audit teams. Chapter 31 discusses the role of quality auditors following American Society for Quality (ASQ) standards, but several of ISO standards are important for all IT auditors.

The proper implementation of and compliance with relevant ISO standards are important to enterprises and to IT auditors. An enterprise may embrace many different published standards; an IT auditor should be aware of the IT-critical standards and consider them as part of internal controls reviews.

This chapter provides an overview and introduction to several of the many ISO standards that are particularly important for IT auditors, with a focus on ISO 9001 quality standards and ISO 27001 computer security standards. The chapter also introduces several other ISO standards, including those for IT management systems, for risk management, and for quality management. Compliance with appropriate ISO standards is important worldwide today, as enterprises establish worldwide compliance benchmarks. That is, if an enterprise follows some ISO standard and if its compliance to the standard is accredited by a recognized outside reviewer, the enterprise's compliance to the standards will be recognized worldwide.

BACKGROUND AND IMPORTANCE OF ISO STANDARDS IN A WORLD OF GLOBAL COMMERCE

The ISO is responsible for developing and publishing a wide range of international standards in many business and process areas. Some of these standards are very broad, such as ISO 14001, covering effective environmental control systems, while others are very detailed and precise, such as a standard covering the size and thickness of a plastic credit card. The broad ISO standards are important because they allow all worldwide enterprises to be talking in the same language when they can claim that they have, for example, an effective ISO 14001 environmental control system. Many of the more detailed standards are also very critical in order to allow, for example, an ATM (automated teller machine) anywhere in the world to expect to receive the same size and thickness of a credit card.

ISO standards are developed through the collaborative efforts of many national standards-setting organizations, such as the American National Standards Institute or other groups throughout the world. The standards-setting process begins with a generally recognized need for a standard in some area. An example would be ISO 27001, which outlines the high-level requirements for an effective information security management system. This standard was developed through the efforts of international technical committees sponsored by the ISO in cooperation with the International Electrotechnical Commission (IEC) international standards-setting groups. The standard is not specific in its detailed requirements but contains many high-level statements along the lines of "The organization shall." In some respects, this type of guidance is built into IT audit programs discussed in many of these chapters.

Because of the numerous international governmental authorities, professional groups, and individual experts involved in the ISO standards-setting process, the building and approval of any ISO document typically is long and slow. An expert committee develops an initial draft standard covering some area; the draft then is sent out for a review and comments with a review response due date; and the ISO committee finally reviews draft comments before either issuing the new standard or sending a revised draft out for yet another round of reviews and suggested changes. Typically, after many drafts and comment periods, the ISO standard is published. Enterprises then can take the necessary steps to comply with the standard. To certify their compliance, they must contract with a certified outside ISO auditor, with skills in that standard, to attest to their compliance.

Many U.S. enterprises first got involved with these international standards through the launch of ISO 9000 quality management system standards in the 1980s. Companies were faced with the high-quality design standards found in many non-U.S. products at that time, such as Japanese automobiles. Japanese enterprises had designed many high-quality products by following what became ISO 9000, and U.S. manufacturers began to modify their own processes to comply with these higher standards of product quality. Compliance with the ISO 9000 standard allowed worldwide enterprises to design their operations in accordance with a single, consistent standard and then to assert that they have a quality management system in place in accordance with the international standard.

ISO standards are much more specific and controlled than the Information Technology Infrastructure Library (ITIL) best practices guidelines discussed in Chapter 7. The standards are published and controlled by the ISO organization in Geneva following strict copyright rules. The materials cannot downloaded through a casual Web search; they must be purchased. Many of the actual ISO standards are very detailed outlines of practices to be followed. While certainly out of context, Exhibit 18.1 is an extract from a small section of the ISO 27001 information security management systems standard on the control of documents for an information security management system (ISMS). The guidance is clear and unambiguous and often points to other sections of this standard for follow-up. For example, line 5.b states that management should define the roles and responsibilities for information security. This is a prompt for appropriate levels of action. The guidance also is like a checklist of questions for IT auditor reviews. It says that the IT auditor should encourage

---

5 Management Responsibility
Management Commitment
Management shall provide evidence of its commitment to the establishment, implementation, operation, monitoring, review, maintenance and improvement of the ISMS by:
a) establishing an ISMS policy;
b) establishing roles and responsibilities for information security;
c) ensuring roles and responsibilities for information security;
d) communicating to the organization the importance of meeting information security objectives and conforming to the information security policy, its responsibilities under the law and the need for continual improvement;
e) providing sufficient resources to establish, implement, operate, monitor, review, maintain and improve the ISMA (see 5.2.1);
f) deciding the criteria for accepting risks and the acceptable levels of risk;
g) enduring that internal ISMS audit are conducted (see 6); and
h) conducting management reviews of the ISMS (see 7).

EXHIBIT 18.1   ISO Standards Example: 27001 on Management Commitment
Source: These terms and definitions, taken from ISO/IEC 27001:2005 Information Technology Security Techniques—Information security management systems—Requirements clause 5.1 a through h, are reproduced with permission of the International Organization for Standardization. This Technical Report can be obtained from any ISO member and from the Web site of the ISO Central Secretariat at the following address: www.iso.org. Copyright remains with ISO.

managers to define their information security roles and responsibilities in order to remain in compliance with an ISO standard.

An enterprise can follow and rely on ISO standards similar to the ITIL best practices discussed in Chapter 7, but ISO standards are much more than ITIL's recommended best practices. They represent performance measures for an enterprise and its peers. By adhering to these worldwide standards, an enterprise can verify that it is operating in accordance with a consistent international standard. ISO 13485 on quality management regulatory requirements for medical devices provides an example. This standard defines the quality requirements covering human healthcare devices. The standard calls for an enterprise manufacturing such devices to establish appropriate calibration controls. Because of the diversity of calibration approaches, the standard cannot specify just one approach; it does, however, require that enterprises have appropriate mechanisms in place.

It is one thing for an enterprise to read an ISO standard and change its processes to follow it; it is another thing to demonstrate to others that it is following the standard. This ISO certification is a process similar to an external audit of financial records performed by certified public accountants (CPAs). Financial statement audits require a licensed CPA external auditor to assess whether an enterprise's financial reports are "fairly stated" following good internal controls and recognized accounting standards. These are high-level words, but such a signed external audit report along with the final reported results provides a level of assurance that the financial reports are fairly stated and are based on good internal control procedures.

The ISO certification process is also similar to a CPA-led financial audit that is based on compliance with generally accepted auditing standards (GAAS) performed by a major public accounting firm. No "Big 4" set of major ISO auditing firms exists, but national standards-setting organizations qualify outside reviewers to perform external audits of various ISO standards. There is no ISO GAAS, however, but a wide degree of diversity in audit objectives since a reviewer for ISO 27001 on IT security management systems will be looking for different control procedures than would an ISO auditor for 13485 medical device quality management systems. In all cases, however, the qualified ISO outside auditor may identify areas for corrective actions and publish a report to management similar to an internal audit process. Once the ISO auditor's recommendations are corrected, the outside reviewer will certify that the enterprise is in compliance with that standard.

Once certified, the enterprise can advertise to the outside world that it has a process in place that meets that specific ISO standard. For example, a customer for the medical diagnostic device would want to know if a potential supplier is in compliance with ISO 13485. That same medical device manufacturer would also want to gain assurance that its prime component suppliers are ISO qualified.

ISO STANDARDS OVERVIEW

Compliance with appropriate ISO standards is not the same type of a requirement for an enterprise as the types of appropriate internal controls that must be implemented in order to certify for an audited financial statement. Because of SEC financial reporting rules, the lack of an audited financial report or a report with an unfavorable auditor's opinion can be very damaging for a publicly traded enterprise. Virtually all publicly traded enterprises are expected to have audited financial statements, but the rules are not the same regarding compliance with ISO standards. In most instances, compliance with an ISO standard is voluntary only but still often essential. We have cited the ISO standard covering the thickness and size of a personal credit card as an example. An enterprise that manufactured cards or card readers that were not in compliance with such a standard would soon fail in the marketplace.

ISO standards covering quality management systems are a bit different. An enterprise can all but ignore a standard such as ISO 9000 calling for a quality management process and still succeed within a national marketplace. For example, in the United States, some senior managers historically looked at this standard as "too much paperwork" and made only minimal efforts to achieve compliance. However, as we move to a more worldwide business-trading environment, many enterprises request such certifications today from their suppliers. What was once just nice to have has become almost mandatory in the United States for manufacturing and many other enterprises.

IT auditors should attempt to learn more about the status of ISO standards compliance within their enterprises. Some ISO standards, such as the thread pattern on a bolt or the thickness of a credit card, would have to become mandatory, or the internal auditor's enterprise would not be in business manufacturing non-compliant products. Quality standards, such as our one-paragraph Exhibit 18.1 extract, require that improved processes be established and monitored. If an enterprise has a separate quality audit function, as described in Chapter 31, IT audit should develop an understanding of levels of activity and compliance with appropriate ISO quality standards. Although there are a wide range of ISO standards, the next sections discuss several that are important for IT auditors in today's world of heightened internal controls and governance.

ISO 9001 Quality Management Systems

ISO 9000 has a heritage dating back to World War II, when both sides of the conflict required strong product uniformity while operating at extremely high levels of production volume. Even if the products produced were bullets and bombs, they still had to work correctly, and there was a need for strict product quality control. On the western Allies' side, some strong quality assurance standard procedures and the professions of industrial engineers and production quality control specialists arose. After the war, ISO was established as part of the General Agreement on Trade and Tariffs, one of the international agreements to bring the world to more of a peacetime environment. ISO 9000 on quality management systems was one of these earlier ISO standards. It first received most attention in the newly recovering European countries.

Japan was another rebuilding and recovering postwar country that strongly embraced quality management systems. In the 1950s and 1960s, the Japanese invited a series of U.S.-based quality systems experts, such as W. Edwards Deming and others, to help at many of their plants. While these quality systems experts had been all but ignored in the United States, their philosophies and techniques were heavily embraced by Japanese industry, and by the mid-1970s, Japanese electronic and automobile manufacturers began to make deep inroads into U.S. markets due to the quality and value of their products. Many in the United States began to recognize that these Japanese-manufactured products were superior in many respects to their own. ISO 9000 quality standards became an increasingly important factor to measure and assess the quality of products worldwide.

ISO 9000 is a family of standards for quality management systems. Maintained by ISO, these standards include requirements for such matters as:

- Monitoring processes to ensure they are effective
- Keeping adequate records
- Checking output for defects, with appropriate corrective action where necessary
- Regularly reviewing individual processes and the quality system for effectiveness
- Facilitating continual improvement

Each of these items refers to processes, not specific actions. However, for an enterprise to assert that it is in compliance with ISO 9000 (actually 9001), for example—that it is monitoring key processes to be effective—often it must make significant changes to management procedures and supporting documentation. Compliance with an ISO standard also creates a required level of expectations. Any enterprise, on a worldwide scope, that holds to such standards is stating that it has effective quality systems in place. An enterprise that has been independently audited and certified to be in conformance with ISO 9001, for example, may publicly state that it is "ISO 9001 certified" or "ISO 9001 registered." Certification to an ISO 9000 standard does not guarantee the compliance (and therefore the quality) of end products and services; rather, it certifies that consistent business and production processes are being applied.

The actual certification is achieved through a review by a registered ISO auditor certified for the particular ISO standard. As discussed, this process is similar to the CPA's review and certified audit of an enterprise's financial statements. Regulated by their national standards organizations, ISO auditors are authorized to register an enterprise's compliance with unique ISO standards.

ISO 9000 and other ISO standards impose heavy documentation requirements on an enterprise. It is not sufficient for an enterprise just to claim some process has been once documented. There must be an ongoing process to keep that documentation current over time. In past years, many enterprises went through one-time efforts to create documentation and failed to keep it current. Many IT auditors have faced this kind of situation where they frequently ask if some system or process they are reviewing is documented. If the documentation is out of date or nonexistent, this lack of documentation often would become an audit report finding but would result in little definitive corrective action. ISO 9000 compliance raises documentation requirements for quality processes to a whole new level. An outside reviewer must certify that the enterprise is in compliance in order for the enterprise to advertise to the outside world that it is in compliance with the ISO standard.

As a clarification, what is commonly referred to as just ISO 9000 is not one standard but really a series of "certifiable" standards and guidelines:

ISO 9001. Certifiable standard dealing with design
ISO 9002. Certifiable standard dealing with manufacturing
ISO 9003. Certifiable standard dealing with manufacturing and assembly
ISO 9004. Guideline defining a quality system

These standards are updated periodically with the current year appended to the standard number. To add to the complexity, an enterprise can claim compliance only with an earlier version, such as ISO 9000:1994. A QS 9000 series of standards is similar but pertains just to the automotive industry. A *certifiable standard* is subject to review by an outside auditor, as discussed. The current version of the ISO quality standard 9001 is ISO 9001:2008, although it includes only a few new definitions from the more recognized ISO 9001:2000. For purposes of this discussion, we just use the more generic term of ISO 9000 to refer to all of these quality management system standards.

ISO 9000 is a set of standards for a continual improvement-driven quality system, no matter whether a manufactured component or a service process. Exhibit 18.2 shows such a quality management system process that is driven by internal procedures for continual improvements as well as customer requests. In this continual process, existing processes should be monitored, actions planned for improvements, and the action items implemented for subsequent monitoring and further improvements. For many, the

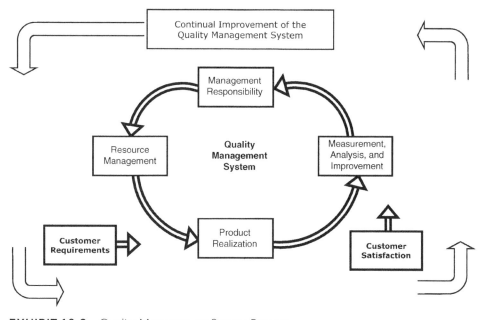

EXHIBIT 18.2 Quality Management System Process

continual improvement quality process is nothing new. IT auditors and systems development professionals have used essentially the same set of general processes since the early days of IT systems development, in what was called the systems development life cycle (SDLC), a process to develop new IT systems discussed in Chapter 10. However, many SDLC-developed applications called for a great deal of documentation, which often was not prepared. Many of today's IT applications are developed through more informal and iterative rapid application development processes.

Solid and accurate documentation is extremely important for an enterprise seeking to claim ISO registration, ISO registration a global requirement. When ISO 9001:2000 Section 4.2.3 states, among other provisions, that "[a] documented procedure should be established to define the controls needed" along with such subsections as "a) to approve documents for adequacy of issue," an enterprise or process documentation control system is needed to demonstrate compliance with that standard. ISO best practices call for a hierarchy of documentation in any area starting with top-level manuals to explain the whys and then down to instructions describing the hows of the practice. Exhibit 18.3 shows this documentation hierarchy with Documentation and Forms on the bottom part of triangle providing proof. This documentation is essential to support a quality management system and certainly is required by ISO external certification auditors.

This section has provided a very high-level description of the ISO 9000 quality management process. Compliance with these ISO 9000 processes are important for all types of enterprises to assert to their own internal management and to the outside world that the enterprise is focused on quality. In 1995, the American Institute of Certified Public Accountants became the first major worldwide professional organization to become ISO 9001 certified.[1] Neither ISACA nor the IIA has been certified. Organizations of all levels should consider adopting ISO 9000 processes.

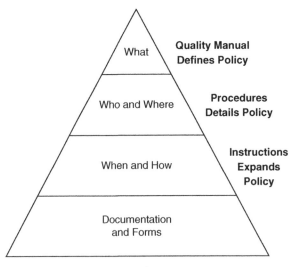

EXHIBIT 18.3 ISO Documentation Hierarchy

ISO IT Security Standards: ISO 27001 and 27002

There two ISMS standards, ISO 127001 and ISO 27002. ISO 27002 represents an important IT-related security standard designed to help any enterprise that needs to establish a comprehensive information security management program or improve its current information security practices.

ISO 27002 is a standard concerning both a wide range of information sources and information security in a general sense. Because such information can exist in many forms, the standard takes a very broad approach and includes a wide range of standards covering security regarding:

- Data and software electronic files
- All formats of paper documents, including printed materials, handwritten notes, and photographs
- Video and audio recordings
- Telephone conversations as well as e-mail, fax, video, and other forms of messages

The idea here is that all forms of information, not just IT, have value and need to be protected, just like any other corporate asset. Many enterprises today do not even consider security standards in these broad areas, but the ISO standard suggests they should be covered when appropriate. In addition, the infrastructure that supports this information, including networks, systems, and functions, also must be protected from a wide range of threats, including everything from human error and equipment failure to theft, fraud, vandalism, sabotage, fire, flood, and even terrorism.

Similar to all other ISO standards, this published standard does not really prescribe *what* is specifically required but outlines areas where security-related standards are required. Exhibit 18.4 outlines some ISO 27002 topics. The standard does not contain detailed requirements for each of these areas—a thorough and consistent international standard would require a huge, extensive text that would not be all inclusive and would soon be out of date. Rather, as an example, line 4.2 calls for security standards covering third-party access policies. ISO calls for the enterprise to have a documented and approved processes covering third-party access policies. An enterprise should develop its own more detailed standards and procedures in this area. Their type and extent can depend on many factors, but an ISO 27002–compliant enterprise should address this issue along with the other topic areas in the standard.

As a first step to implementing ISO 27002, an enterprise should identify its own information security needs and requirements. Doing this requires performing an information security risk assessment along the lines of the Committee of Sponsoring Organizations enterprise risk management (COSO ERM) processes discussed in Chapter 4. Such an assessment should focus on the identification of major security threats and vulnerabilities as well as an assessment of how likely it is that each will cause a security incident. This process should help to pinpoint an enterprise's unique information security needs and requirements.

As part of getting ready for the ISO 27002 information security standards-setting process, an enterprise should identify and understand all of the legal, statutory,

1. Scope: A high level description of the application of this standard
2. Terms and definitions: Consistent with other ISO standards, all major terms are defined (e.g. Definition of what is meant by "Confidentiality")
3. The standards or need for a high level information security policy
4. Requirements for an enterprise security organization:
   4.1 Information security infrastructure
   4.2 Security and third party access policies
   4.3 Outsourcing considerations
5. Asset classification and control standards:
   5.1 Accountability for assets
   5.2 Information classifications
6. Personnel security
   6.1 Security considerations in job definitions and resources
   6.2 User training for personnel security
   6.3 Standards for responding to security incidents and malfunctions
7. Physical and environmental security including requirements for:
   7.1 Secure areas
   7.2 Equipment security
   7.3 General controls
8. Communications and operations management
   8.1 Operational procedures and responsibility
   8.2 System planning and acceptance
   8.3 Protections against malicious software
   8.4 Housekeeping
   8.5 Network management requirements
   8.6 Media handling and security
   8.7 Exchanges of information and software
9. Access control
   9.1 Business requirements for access control
   9.2 User access management
   9.3 User responsibilities for security standards
   9.4 Network access control
   9.5 Operating system access control
   9.6 Application access management
   9.7 Monitoring standards for systems access and use
   9.8 Mobile computing and related networking
10. System development and maintenance standards
    10.1 Security requirements hardware and software systems
    10.2 Application systems security
    10.3 Cryptographic controls
    10.4 Security of system files
    10.5 Security in development and support processes
11. Business continuity management standards
12. Security standards covering compliance issues
    12.1 Compliance with legal requirements
    12.2 Reviews of security policy and technical compliance
    12.3 Systems audit considerations

EXHIBIT 18.4   ISO 27002 Standards Topics Areas

regulatory, and contractual requirements that it, its trading partners, contractors, and its service providers must meet. Doing this requires an understanding and identification of an enterprise's unique legal information security needs and requirements.

ISO 27002 is the first of a series of international standards meant for any enterprise that uses internal or external computer systems, possesses confidential data, depends on IT to carry out its business activities, or simply wishes to adopt a higher level of security by complying with a standard. The standard is relatively new and not in common application in the United States. Just as ISO 9000 has become a guarantee of quality, compliance with ISO 27002 enables partners to be confident in an enterprise's overall security. Compliance should promote an increased level of mutual confidence between partners, where each can attest that it has established security in compliance with a recognized set of standards. In addition, as ISO 27002 compliance becomes more common, it may result in lower premiums for computer risk insurance but certainly will yield better protection of confidential data and improved privacy practices and compliance with privacy laws. ISO 27002 is a structured and internationally recognized methodology that should help an enterprise to develop better management of information security on a continuing basis. The standard also supports the ISMS requirements of the related security standard, ISO 27001.

IT Security Technique Requirements: ISO 27001

ISO 27002 is a high-level code of practice covering security controls. ISO 27001 is what ISO defines as the "specification" for an ISMS. That is, this standard is designed to measure, monitor, and control security management from a top-down perspective. The standard essentially explains how to apply ISO 27002, and it defines the implementation of this standard as a six-part process:

1. **Define a security policy.** A fundamental component of any standard is the need for a formal policy statement approved by senior management. All other compliance aspects of the standard will be measured against this policy statement.
2. **Define the scope of the ISMS.** ISO 27002 defines security in rather broad terms that may not be appropriate or needed for all enterprises. Having defined a high-level security policy, an enterprise needs to define the scope of its ISMS that will be implemented. For example, ISO 27002 defines an element of security requirements as video and audio recordings. This may not be necessary for a given organization; in that case, it would be specifically excluded for its ISMS scope.
3. **Undertake a risk assessment.** The enterprise should identify a risk assessment methodology that is suited to its ISMS environment and then both develop criteria for accepting risks and define what constitutes acceptable levels of risk.
4. **Manage the risk.** This is a major process that includes formal risk identification, risk analysis, and options for the treatment of those risks. The latter can include applying appropriate risk avoidance controls, accepting risks, taking other steps to avoid them, or transferring the risks to other parties such as insurers or suppliers.
5. **Select control objectives and controls to be implemented.** This is the same IT audit and control process discussed in Chapter 5 on planning and performing

effective IT audits. For each defined control objective, the enterprise should define an appropriate controls procedure.

6. **Prepare a statement of applicability.** This is the formal documentation that is necessary to wrap up the ISMS documentation process. Such documentation matches up control objectives with procedures to manage and implement the ISMS.

As can be seen from these six steps, risk analysis and security policies are fundamental to this standard. Setting up these practices is not an internal audit attest function, but IT audit can provide strong help to management by offering to serve as an internal consultant and to help in performing adequate risk assessment procedures.

Because of strict ISO copyright rules, we have not included extracts of ISO 27001 in this chapter. The actual ISO standards are presented in tight and unambiguous text. Little specific detail is provided, but there is enough to allow an enterprise to implement its ISMS. Each formal standard concludes with an appendix section listing control procedures for each of the objective details in the standard. However, ISO 27001 should not be considered as a comprehensive set of control procedures that will change as technology changes; rather, it is an outline for the framework of an ISMS that should be continually implemented, monitored, and maintained.

ISO 27002 and ISO 27001 are already global standards, with established compliance, and certification schemes in place, particularly in the United Kingdom and the European Union. Both standards will continue to evolve, to track technology, and will expand with even wider changes. Although these standards have only been discussion topics in ISACA publications at present, we can expect the Control Objectives for Information related Technology (CobiT) framework, discussed in Chapter 2, to tie in much more closely with ISO 27002 standards in future years. There can be little doubt that these ISO standards will continue to grow in influence and that adoption will continue to expand.

IT auditors should monitor the status of this standard that calls for appropriate ISMS within their IT function. Such an enterprise IT department can delay fully implementing ISO 27002 and an ISMS, but a vendor or other major stakeholder may demand evidence of compliance. IT auditors can be of help with such matters.

Service Quality Management: ISO 20000

Many professionals will agree that we live in a world with too many standards—many of which are similar to others with objectives that are not closely connected to each other. ISO 2000 on service quality management introduces some of this much-needed standards convergence. This is an international standard for IT Service management, and it introduces many of the ITIL service management best practices that were discussed in Chapter 7. ISO 2000 consists of a Part 1 on implementing service management and a following Part 2 section describing best practices for service management. The Part 1 standard specifies the need for a series of service management documented processes, such as defining requirements for implementing such a management system, new or changed service requirements, and documented relationship, control, resolution, and release processes. Quite correctly, the standard takes the best practices approach of ITIL and calls for formal documented processes to support them.

ISO 2000 calls for an enterprise to adopt and be certified that it has adopted the ITIL best practices discussed in Chapter 7. Formally, this standard "promotes the adoption of an integrated process approach to effectively deliver managed services to meet the business and customer requirements." ISO 2000 is the first global standard for IT service management, and is fully compatible and supportive of the ITIL framework. It will undoubtedly have a significant impact on the use and acceptance of ITIL best practices and the whole IT Service Management landscape.

In future years, IT auditors should see an increasing level of recognition on the importance of ISO service related standards. In our increasingly global economy, no matter what national restrictions may be imposed across borders from time to time, internal standards are needed to define common practices and to better facilitate communication. When an enterprise or service organization—anywhere in the world—has achieved ISO 9000 quality management certification, customers and users can expect a certain minimum level of documentation and process standards. The ISO 27001 IT security standards should soon reach a similar level of importance and recognition. With our comments on ISO 2000 on ITIL and ISO 9000's similarities with the Sarbanes-Oxley Act (SOx), we should see increasing convergence trends between ISO and standards in other areas. Internal and IT auditors at all levels should understand and embrace these important ISO standards.

ISO 19011 QUALITY MANAGEMENT SYSTEMS AUDITING

Every ISO standard discussed here contains references on the need to audit that particular quality system. The published standard offers resources for an enterprise to "save time, effort and money" in its management systems auditing processes. ISO 19011 very much relates to the ASQ quality audit standards discussed in Chapter 31, and it outlines four critical decision/support resources for the efficient planning, conduct, and evaluation of quality and/or environmental audits:

1. The need for a clear explanation of the principles of management systems auditing
2. Guidance on the management of audit programs
3. Guidance on the conduct of internal or external audits
4. Advice on the competence and evaluation of auditors

These are topics discussed in other chapters of this book. The reader may wonder about the need for an ISO international standard here, but it is directed at quality auditors worldwide, including many who have not had exposure to IT auditing or the IIA and ISACA auditing standards discussed in Chapters 3.

This ISO standard also outlines five principles of auditing that are very similar to other principles that we have discussed for other IT auditing topics:

1. **Ethical conduct.** Auditors performing ISO 19011 audits should be honest and do the right thing.
2. **Fair presentation.** Auditors should be evenhanded when reporting results.

3. **Exercise due professional care.** Auditors should do what is reasonable and normally expected.
4. **Independence.** Auditors should avoid conflicts of interest to ensure their integrity.
5. **Evidence-based approaches.** Investigate first and then report the facts.

The ISO 19011 standard contains a detailed set of the principles of auditing from an ISO, quality audit perspective. Exhibit 18.5 is a high-level outline of topic areas in this standard. There are some duplicate titles in the subheadings, as the standard places some topics, such as the Audit Report, under multiple audit principles. This is a very comprehensive overview of internal auditing from a quality audit perspective. While space does not allow a detailed summary of this standard, virtually all of those related to internal auditing principles are described in other chapters in this book.

IT audit professionals will soon see a greater recognition of ISO standards, with an emphasis on ISO 19011 describing auditing standards. As an example, the IIA sent out a survey in August 2008 over its GAIN network, mentioned in Chapter 3, to assess IIA internal auditor involvement with ISO 19011. About 1,500 queries were sent out but only about 150 replies were received. Questions were along the lines of "Does your

---

Ethical Conduct
- Audit Team
- Audit Plan
- Work Documents
- Opening Meeting
- Audit Report
- Report Distribution
- Personal Attributes

Fair Presentation
- Findings
- Audit Report
- Personal Attributes
- Outcomes

Due Professional Care
- Audit Report
- Auditor Judgment
- Findings
- Conclusions

Independence
- Selecting Auditors
- Assigning Work
- Follow-Up Activities

Evidence-Based Approach
- Collecting Evidence
- Findings
- Conclusion
- Audit Report

EXHIBIT 18.5 ISO 19011 IT Audit Standards Outline

internal audit activity have any input or review role related to the annual quality management system (QMS) audit program?" The results generally showed that IIA internal auditors have little involvement with the quality auditors (described in Chapter 31) who would be responsible for implementing this ISO standard.[2] Based on survey results, generally 70% of the responses showed no involvement with ISO 19011 in their enterprises.

ISO STANDARDS AND IT AUDITORS

As we become more and more of a global commerce world with many interconnections and relationships, the ISO standards become more important for all enterprises. Although standards describing component dimensions—such as the tread pattern and size of a bolt—are essential for commerce, the "softer" quality system standards, such as ISO 9000, are equally important. Enterprises in one location will refuse to do business with enterprises elsewhere unless they can certify their compliance to some ISO standard.

Although many IT auditors have not been familiar with ISO standards in the past, we expect this to change. CobiT will almost certainly become more closely aligned with ISO 27002, and the IIA's GAIN survey regarding the level internal auditor involvement with ISO 19011 shows that the IIA is at least thinking about this new international standard. When appropriate, IT auditors should try to incorporate appropriate IS standards in their IT internal controls audits.

NOTES

1. www.qualitydigest.com/june99/html/body_iso_9000.html.
2. The Institute of Internal Auditors GAIN Network, "International Organization for Standardization (ISO) 9001:2000 Quality Management System Type: Executive Summary Report," April 10, 2008.

CHAPTER NINETEEN

Controls to Establish an Effective IT Security Environment

C ONCERNS REGARDING INFORMATION TECHNOLOGY (IT) security are perhaps the most major issue impacting IT auditors. Other chapters have talked about the importance of establishing effective internal controls, following Sarbanes-Oxley (SOx) rules, or using the Control objectives for information Technology (CobiT) framework, but IT security risks and incidents are the topics that create news headlines. This IT security risk is a greater concern in today's world of vast Internet connections and increasing reliance on cloud computing strategies. An enterprise's audit committee and senior management are often the parties that read about IT security breaches elsewhere and often question the chief audit executive (CAE) and IT auditors about enterprise IT security.

To gain this assurance about having effective IT security, an enterprise needs to establish and build an effective IT security environment. This task is the responsibility of IT operations and enterprise management at all levels. IT auditors can assist in this process by using their knowledge of effective internal controls to both review existing IT security controls and to act as internal consultants to help improve them. They can assist an enterprise in establishing an effective security environment.

This chapter will focus on building an effective IT security environment from three perspectives. We will introduce the generally accepted systems security principles (GASSP) that have been promoted by the Information Systems Audit and Control Association (ISACA) and others. They can be a major aid in establishing an effective IT security environment. As a second topic, we will explore ways to build effective IT perimeter security. While the locked computer operations center from the mainframe days is less of a risk today, security risks are much greater in today's Internet-based e-commerce environments where network controls define the security perimeter. The chapter will discuss some IT perimeter security controls that IT auditors should consider when reviewing internal controls in these areas.

As a third topic for this chapter, we will discuss the importance of establishing an effective, enterprise-wide security strategy. Just as an employee code of conduct sets some high level rules for all enterprise stakeholders, an effective IT security strategy establishes some IT security-related rules. A well designed and well implemented IT security strategy can improve many aspects of enterprise operations. IT auditors should be aware of effective best or good practices in these areas and should use these to make effective IT security recommendations in their audit reviews.

GENERALLY ACCEPTED SECURITY STANDARDS

Either through their own work, contacts with fellow financial internal auditors or their external auditors, many IT auditors are aware of what are called generally accepted accounting principles and auditing standards (GAAP and GAAS, respectively). While GAAP is being replaced with international accounting standards today, these are the informal rules that external auditors use to assess enterprise accounting practices and then to perform audits of financial statements. They are not point-by-point specific rules but sets of general good practices that external auditors have used over the years.

With an approach similar to GAAP and GAAS, IT auditors and enterprise IT management have GSSP as a set of best practices for developing effective IT security practices and standards. GASSP is a consensus set of IT security-related principles, standards, conventions, and mechanisms that IT security practitioners should employ, that information processing products should provide, and that information owners should acknowledge to ensure the security of their information and IT systems. GASSP relates to physical, technical, and administrative information security and encompasses pervasive, broad functional, and detailed security principles. Its nomenclature defines a series rules, procedures, and practices that relate to the implementation of effective IT security practices in an enterprise. With ongoing rapid changes in IT technology, GASSP is expected to evolve accordingly.

GASSPs origins go back to 1990 when the U.S. National Research Council published *Computers at Risk* (CAR),[1] in what became a landmark book that emphasized the urgent need for the United States to better focus attention on information security. The GASSP document is a direct result of a key recommendation from that CAR report calling for the development of a comprehensive set of Generally Accepted System Security Principles that would provide a clear definition of IT security's essential features, assurances, and practices. The CAR report proposed using GAAP as a model for GASSP and also cited building codes and standards by the Underwriter's Laboratory[2] as examples of GASSP in other fields.

The International Information Security Foundation (I^2SF), a unit of the International Information Systems Security Certification Consortium (ISC)[2] that also sponsors the CISSP certification discussed in Chapter 30, launched a professional committee to develop GASSP. They along with ISACA published the description of GASSP, with its current version 2.0 released in 1999.[3] As its name implies, these principles are generally accepted, that is, they represent concepts commonly being used at the present time to secure IT resources. The principles in that GASSP study are not new to the security profession. They are based on the premise that (almost) everyone should apply them when developing or maintaining an IT security system.

GASSP Principles

GASSP is based on eight high-level principles that management, IT security specialists, and IT auditors can use as an anchor on which to build and their IT security programs. These principles are intended to be a security guide when creating new systems, practices, or policies. They are not designed to produce specific answers, and should be applied as a whole, pragmatically and reasonably. Each of these eight principles is expressed as a one-line section heading and explained in the following list:

1. **IT security supports the mission of the enterprise.** The purpose of IT security is to protect an enterprise's valuable resources, such as information, hardware, and software. Through the selection and application of appropriate safeguards, security helps the enterprise's mission by protecting its physical and financial resources, reputation, legal position, employees, and other tangible and intangible assets. Unfortunately, security is sometimes viewed as thwarting the mission of the enterprise by imposing poorly selected, bothersome rules and procedures on users, managers, and systems. As a result, IT auditors should be aware that well-chosen security rules and procedures do not exist for their own sake—they are put in place to protect important assets and support the overall organizational mission.

   Security, therefore, is a means to an end and not an end in itself. For example, an enterprise's security good practices are usually secondary to their need to make a profit. Security, then, *ought to* increase the firm's ability to make a profit. In a public-sector agency, security is usually secondary to that agency's providing services to citizens. Security, then, *ought to* help improve these public services. Thus, managers and security specialists need to understand both their overall enterprise mission and how each IT system supports that mission. After these system roles have been defined, these security requirements can then be explicitly stated in terms of the enterprise's mission.

2. **IT Security is an integral element of sound management.** IT systems are often critical assets that support the mission of an enterprise. Protecting these assets can be as important as protecting other resources, such as cash, physical assets, or employees. However, including security considerations in the management of information and IT systems do not completely eliminate the possibility that these assets will be harmed. Ultimately, management must decide what level of risk they are willing to accept, taking into account the cost of security controls.

   As with other resources, the management of information and IT systems may transcend organizational boundaries. When an enterprise's information and IT systems are linked with external systems, management's responsibilities extend beyond the enterprise and both management and IT audit should know what general levels or types of security are employed on those external systems and should seek assurances that the external system provides adequate security for their enterprise's needs.

3. **IT security should be cost-effective.** The costs and benefits of security should be carefully examined *in both monetary and nonmonetary terms* to ensure that the cost of controls does not exceed expected benefits. Security should be appropriate and proportionate to the value of and degree of reliance on the IT systems and to the severity, probability, and extent of potential harm. Requirements for security vary, depending on the particular IT system.

In general, IT security is a smart business practice, and by appropriately investing in security measures, an enterprise can reduce the frequency and severity of IT security-related losses. For example, an enterprise may estimate that it is experiencing significant losses per year in inventory through the fraudulent manipulation of its IT inventory control system. Security measures, such as an improved access control system, may significantly reduce this loss. Moreover, a sound security program can thwart hackers and reduce the frequency of viruses.

Security benefits have both direct and indirect costs. Direct costs include purchasing, installing, and administering security measures, such as access control software or fire suppression systems. Additionally, security measures can sometimes affect system performance, employee morale, or even retraining requirements. All of these should be considered in addition to the basic cost of an IT security control itself. In many cases, such as in the costs of administering an access control package, these additional costs may well exceed the initial cost of the control. Solutions to security problems should not be chosen if they cost more, in monetary or non monetary terms, directly or indirectly, rather than simply tolerating the problem.

4. **Systems owners have security responsibilities outside of their own organization.** If a system has external users, its owners have a responsibility to share appropriate knowledge about the existence and general extent of security measures so that other users can be *confident* that their system is adequately secure. This does not imply that all systems must meet any minimum level of security, but does imply that system owners should inform their clients or users about the nature of the security.

The difference between responsibility and accountability for IT security is not always clear. In general, *responsibility* is a broader term, defining obligations and expected behaviors. The term implies a proactive stance on the part of the responsible party and a causal relationship between the responsible party and a given outcome. The term *accountability* generally refers to the *ability to hold* people responsible for their actions. Therefore, people could be responsible for their actions but may not be held accountable. For example, an anonymous user on a system is responsible for behaving according to accepted norms but cannot be held accountable if a compromise occurs since the action cannot be traced to an individual.

This principle implicitly states that people and organizations have a shared responsibility and accountability for their IT systems which may be shared. In addition to sharing information about security, enterprise managers should act in a timely, coordinated manner to prevent and to respond to breaches of security to help prevent damage to others. However, taking such action should *not* jeopardize the security of systems.

5. **IT security responsibilities and accountabilities should be made explicit.** The security-related responsibility and accountability of owners, providers, and users of IT systems and other parties concerned with IT systems security should be explicit. These responsibilities may be internal to an enterprise or may extend across enterprise boundaries. Even a smaller enterprise should prepare documentation that state an enterprise's security policies and explicit IT security responsibilities. However, this element does *not* mean that individual accountabilities must be provided for on all systems. For example, many information dissemination systems do not require user identification or use other technical means of user identification and, therefore, cannot hold users accountable.

6. **IT security requires a comprehensive and integrated approach.** Providing effective IT security requires a comprehensive approach that considers a variety of areas both within and outside of the IT security field and extending throughout the entire information life cycle. To work effectively, security controls often depend on the proper functioning of other controls. Many such interdependencies exist. If appropriately chosen, managerial, operational, and technical controls can work together synergistically. However, without a firm understanding of the interdependencies of security controls, they can actually undermine one another. For example, without proper training on how and when to use a virus-detection package, users may apply the package incorrectly and, therefore, ineffectively. As a result, users may mistakenly believe that if their system has been checked once, it will always be virus-free and may inadvertently spread a virus. In reality, these interdependencies are usually more complicated and difficult to ascertain.

   The effectiveness of security controls also depends on such factors as system management, legal issues, quality assurance, and internal and management controls. IT security also needs to work with traditional security disciplines including physical and personnel security. Many other important interdependencies exist that are often unique to the enterprise or system environment. Managers should recognize how IT security relates to other areas of systems and enterprise management.

7. **IT security should be periodically reassessed.** IT systems and the environments in which they operate are dynamic. System technology and users, data and information in the systems, risks associated with the system, and security requirements are ever-changing. Many types of changes affect system security including: technological developments, changes in the value or use of information; or the emergence of a new threat. In addition, security is untested and *never* perfect when a new system is implemented, and system users and operators discover new ways to intentionally or unintentionally bypass or subvert security. Changes in an IT system or its environment can create new vulnerabilities. Strict adherence to security procedures is rare, and procedures become outdated over time making it necessary to periodically reassess IT systems security.

8. **IT security is constrained by societal factors.** The ability of security to support the mission of an enterprise may be limited by such factors, as social issues where security and workplace privacy can be in conflict. For example, security is often

implemented on an IT system by identifying users and tracking their actions. However, expectations of privacy vary and can be violated by some security measures. In addition, security controls may be mandated by law in some cases. Although privacy is an extremely important societal issue, it is not the only one. The flow of information, especially between a government and its citizens, is another situation where security may need to be modified to support a societal goal. In addition, some authentication measures may be considered invasive in some environments and cultures.

Security measures should be selected and implemented with a recognition of the rights and legitimate interests of others. This may involve balancing the security needs of information owners and users with societal goals. However, rules and expectations change with regard to the appropriate use of security controls. These changes may either increase or decrease security. The relationship between security and societal norms is not necessarily antagonistic. Security can enhance the access and flow of data and information by providing more accurate and reliable information and greater availability of systems. Security can also increase the privacy afforded to an individual or help achieve other goals set by society.

As an IT auditor can observe, these eight GASSP principles are not definitive but outline a general framework that should be the basis for many aspects of good IT security. An IT auditor cannot use them to make an audit point saying that an auditee, for example, is in violation of "GASSP Principle 3." Rather, these eight principles should be used to form a basis to assess the strengths and weaknesses of any IT security system or environment being reviewed.

GASSP is strongly promoted through ISACA materials and referenced as an outside resource through the Institute of Internal Auditors' Web site. IT auditors may see a greater use and acceptance of GASSP in future years. These principles should help an IT auditor to better assess security in many environments. GASSP can provide the basis for an effective IT security environment in an enterprise.

Role of GASSP in the IT Organization

Moving beyond the previous eight GASSP principles, an enterprise, its IT security function, and certainly IT audit will have to rethink and reorganize some practices in order to embrace GASSP. Exhibit 19.1 shows the high-level role of GASSP in an enterprise, with consideration given to its installed technology products and other factors. While there are many ways to implement GASSP, the IT auditor should not lose track that GASSP is based on some broad and strong IT security principles. These pervasive principles address the properties of IT security information confidentiality, integrity, and availability. They provide general guidance to establish and maintain the security of information.

We will go around the points in this exhibit to briefly describe some to the key elements of GASSP and how they relate to one another and to an overall IT security environment. Each of these areas may differ, based on the enterprise, its size, and domicile. We start at the center of this exhibit with the security standards and other

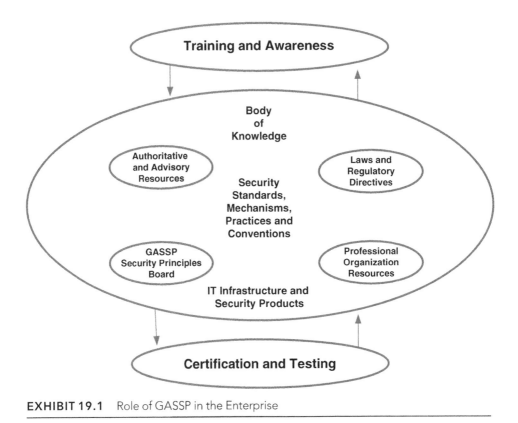

EXHIBIT 19.1   Role of GASSP in the Enterprise

mechanisms, move up to the body of knowledge, and then clockwise around to the other factors necessary to form an effective security environment using GASSP.

- **Security Standards, Mechanisms, Practices, and Conventions.** The core of any effective security environment is a set of strong enterprise-specific security standards, mechanisms, practices, and conventions. These are the types of issues that an IT auditor should have reviewed and hopefully found effective in an IT general controls review.
- **Body of Knowledge.** We have summarized GASSPs principles here, but a wide variety of persons in an enterprise should understand these broad principles and have expressed a commitment to understand and implement them on a regular basis. The idea is that if there is a question about some IT security practice, the enterprise should go back to these broad principles to interpret and resolve any issues.
- **Laws and Regulatory Directives.** Every enterprise is subject to a variety and often differing set of laws and regulations. A good example here can be found in personal privacy laws that differ greatly from one country to another. GASSP must always be interpreted based on these different and sometimes often changing rules.
- **Professional Organization Resources.** Professional organizations such as ISACA or the IIA regularly issue guidelines and standards that add new requirements to IT security approaches or change approaches. An enterprise must be aware of these matters and make changes to its IT security environment accordingly.

- **IT Infrastructure and Security Products.** There are a wide variety of IT application and infrastructure products that may help direct or modify approaches to IT security. While an enterprise should not install products that are deficient in these security principles, it is always necessary to be aware of any unique characteristics of any such installed produce and to make appropriate adjustment to other IT security practices.
- **GASSP Security Principles Board.** When an enterprise embraces GASSP, it needs to install some authoritative persons in an enterprise to properly interpret its applications of GASSP. Someone from the IT security function, the quality assurance group, or a representative from IT audit may be an appropriate resource here. While no one in the enterprise may be an "expert" on GASSP, the idea is to appoint a reasonable person who understands GASSP principles, can interpret them based on any questions raised, and can be an umpire or referee when needed.
- **Authoritative and Advisory Resources.** Although they do not typically sell consulting services, an enterprise should be closely tied with ISACA or (ISC)^2 publications and resources for any updates and other interpretive materials about GASSP.
- **Training and Awareness.** GASSP is of little value to an enterprise unless key stakeholders are trained on its principles. System developers, in particular, should be aware of the GASSP principles and use it when launching secure, effective applications for the enterprise. Similarly, IT auditors should learn and use the GASSP framework in their internal controls.
- **Certification and Testing.** There are no GASSP certifications or testing programs in place at present, but such efforts will be updated if there are any significant updates or changes to GASSP in the future.

GASSP principles have been released for some years but they still have not received a wide level of acceptance by enterprises in the United States to date. However, with our ever-changing and technologically advancing world today as well as ever-growing IT security concerns, GASSP provides an effective basis or framework for looking at and assessing IT security.

 ## EFFECTIVE IT PERIMETER SECURITY

IT perimeter security once referred to little more than locks on the computer room door and a building entrance guard back in the days of mainframe centralized computer systems. The walls and door to that mainframe computer center of old represented the perimeter or an enterprise's IT operations. Today, that perimeter boundary has really changed with such things as connections to wireless virtual local area networks (LANs), the Internet and worldwide telecommunications networks, and connections to cloud computing services using Software as a Service (SaaS) processing strategies. The concept of a security perimeter surrounding an enterprise's IT resources has certainly changed, but there is still a need—even a greater need—for effective IT perimeter in today's environments.

IT auditors should understand and focus both their general and applications controls reviews on this concept of IT perimeter security.

ESTABLISHING AN EFFECTIVE, ENTERPRISE-WIDE SECURITY STRATEGY

Perimeter security in today's IT-centric and wireless communications world involves complex architectures and continually emerging and evolving technologies. To ensure an enterprise has a secure external IT systems perimeter, all appropriate technologies must be evaluated. By following the basic fundamental design concepts, such as using a top-down security model to identify and evaluate security assets, applying the connection trust model to external connections and implementing a multiple trust zone architecture appropriate to the organization, a sound perimeter architecture should result. A top-down security approach is where more senior management understands the seriousness and initiates a process, such as IT security, which is then systematically percolated down to through the ranks and to the lower level operations staff. This differs from a bottom-up approach, in which the less-senior operational staff initiates the process and then propagates their findings upward to management as proposed policy recommendations. As management has no information on what associated threat is and its implications—ideas on resource allocations, possible returns, and methods to implement security—this approach has at times almost sparked a fiasco. IT audit can often take the lead in initiating such a top-down approach by securing an initial buy-in from the audit committee through their audit recommendations.

Perimeter security requires implementing an architecture that utilizes existing IT components, based on a defense-in-depth approach to the security of the external network perimeter, to help ensure the perimeter security of any network will be well protected. Before undertaking the design or implementation of an enterprise network and its components, a comprehensive security architecture should be developed.

The reality, however, is that many enterprises, while recognizing the need for security, often neglect or reduce significant IT perimeter security concerns. An enterprise should design and implement a top-down security infrastructure strategy and approach to support an enterprise's communication needs and allow it to transact business securely in today's electronic world. Exhibit 19.2 shows this top-down security

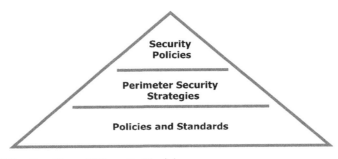

EXHIBIT 19.2   Top-Down IT Security Model

model, and the paragraphs following will discuss its elements in greater detail. The security infrastructure should apply equally to pre-existing connections and to new initiative connections, and an organization's network should be protected based on the risk it represents to the enterprise.

The top level of the Exhibit 19.2 model calls for effective security policies. Although it sometimes seems almost too obvious, an IT auditor reviewing controls in an IT security environment should initially develop an understanding of existing IT security policies for the enterprise. Although usually only at a high level, any such set of policies should cover all aspects of IT security. It may be sufficient to state that the enterprise's IT security polices will be based on the principles of ISO27002, as discussed in Chapter 18, as well as CobiT from Chapter 2.

These strategies should be supported by detailed security standards that cover performing system monitoring, configuring a system as an application or web server, or configuring a firewall to segregate systems into designated zones. The standards should be application- and operating-system-specific, and detailed enough to enable a knowledgeable user to perform the activities highlighted in a standard or configure the system or application. Finally, the standards should specify the steps to be taken, such as sign-offs, if a breach of these standards is required.

IT security operations and an IT auditor should think of perimeter security in terms of a series of trust zones. That is, IT operations should identify and classify all current connections and systems into logical security-related zones. A key element of this security classification is access to the Internet and other network connections such as vendor support systems. The following are four potential classifications for interconnected systems:

1. **Trusted Systems and Processes.** These are systems are directly under the control of the IT organization. Trusted users and systems potentially require full access to internal systems.
2. **Semi Trusted Systems and Processes.** These are often vendor support and some business partner systems that require authenticated access to protect exposed systems that are not publicly accessible.
3. **Untrusted Systems and Processes.** Customer-related systems and processes often require authenticated access rights to specific information resources on exposed systems that are publicly accessible. However, these systems are not fully secure and untrusted.
4. **Hostile Systems and Process Threats.** Very restricted access should be allowed for these types of systems, and unauthorized access attempts should be detectable in real time.

Following these classifications, connections such as support vendors, customers, subsidiaries, and business partners, should be reviewed and allocated to a level of trust based on the level of control that can be maintained. However, identifying each connection in a large organization can be difficult at best. An effective method to launch such a classification is to conduct a workshop with a broad range of knowledgeable staff members who understand the associated concepts and who are familiar with other projects within the enterprise and its IT operations. Although it is unlikely that a single workshop will identify all connections, this type of exercise may help to identify the majority of connections and other staff members within an enterprise that may be responsible for identifying these and other connections.

These connections and their network connections protocols should be documented and used to develop detailed controls to allow accesses to and from appropriate destinations. As a result, the enterprise should segregate different parts of its network into multiple trust zones.

The segregation and classification of systems and processes provides for the separation of systems based on the defined trust categories. An enterprise's internal IT network always should have its own network segment, including web, mail, domain name, and other servers, that should be classified into appropriate trust zones and partitioned or segmented appropriately. This may result in each of these services being segmented on separate zones or may result in a number of these services being implemented into a single zone. The final design of a perimeter security architecture will be dependent on the classification of systems and services, but the design of these security zones and classifications is a critical component of IT perimeter security.

 BEST PRACTICES FOR IT AUDIT AND SECURITY

To summarize our comments about the importance of an effective IT perimeter security strategy, as well as comments in related chapters, we were impressed by the benchmark study findings of the IT Policy Governance Group,[4] an IT study group with a membership including the IIA, ISACA, companies such as Oracle and many others. This study benchmarked more than 100 practices for information security and IT audit in such areas as managing the IT architecture; managing information and data; managing IT operations; ensuring systems security; monitoring and evaluating; managing quality; managing risks and governance. Some of the key findings from this benchmarking study were:

- About 1 in 10 of the organizations surveyed (12%) experience the best outcomes for information security and IT audit with the lowest levels of data loss or theft, least business disruption, and fewest problems with audit. This says that IT audit has been viewed as effective for a minority of enterprises today, and there is much need for improvements.
- A majority of organizations reviewed, nearly 7 in 10 (69%) are experiencing higher rates of data loss or theft, higher levels of business disruptions from IT failures, and more difficulty with passing regulatory audits in IT. This says that enterprises continue to experience data loses and other security risks and have trouble complying with regulatory audits.
- Almost 2 in 10 organizations (19%) experience the worst outcomes with the highest rates of data loss or theft, the highest levels of business downtime, and the most difficulties passing audits in IT.

This really says that many enterprises continue to experience IT security threats but have problems with their current IT audit processes.

The study goes on to emphasize the importance of using CobiT, as discussed in Chapter 2, ITIL from Chapter 7, and ISO security standards, as introduced in Chapters 18 and 25. Based on a recent benchmarking study across a wide range of enterprises and conducted by a series of well-known IT professional organizations and vendors, this IT policy study has information supportive of many themes in this book, with an emphasis in particular on IT security. The interested IT auditor may consider these issues further by exploring the IT Policy Institute at www.itpolicycompliance.com.

NOTES

1. Marjory Blumenthal, *Computers at Risk: Safe Computing in the Information Age*, National Research Council, System Security Study Committee, DEC, 1990.
2. www.ul.com/global/eng/pages/.
3. Generally Accepted System Security Principles (GASSP), Version 2.0, June 1999, www .isaca.org.
4. Guidance for Best Practices in Information Security and IT Audit, 2009, www .itpolicycompliance.com.

CHAPTER TWENTY

Cybersecurity and Privacy Controls

I N TODAY'S WORLD OF Web-dominated systems and communications as well as networked and wireless communications, security and privacy controls over data and information are increasingly important. Although we cannot forget any remaining paper-based manual processes, most of today's security and privacy concerns are focused on information technology (IT) systems and processes. We are calling this broad area cybersecurity, an expression based on an early name for highly automated processes: cybernetics. Security and privacy controls over these IT processes are a very important area of IT audit control concerns.

This chapter discusses IT audit cybersecurity and privacy control activities from two focus areas. First, we focus on some of the many cybersecurity and privacy concerns that auditors should consider in their reviews of IT-based systems and processes. We have limited our focus to only some of these process areas because the field of IT security controls is vast and sometimes very technical. Nevertheless, IT auditors should have a general understanding of internal controls procedures here and their associated risks.

Our second cybersecurity and privacy controls focus area includes IT audit internal procedures. Following the old saying about the shoemaker's children having no shoes, IT audit functions sometimes fail to implement appropriate security and privacy protection controls over their own IT audit processes, such as audit evidence materials, IT audit workpapers, auditor laptop computer resources, and many others. Although every audit department is different, the chapter suggests best practices for an IT audit function.

The chapter concludes with a discussion on the payment card industry data security standard data security standards (PCI-DSS), a guideline that has been developed by major credit card companies, such as Visa and American Express, to help enterprises that process card payments prevent credit card fraud and to provide some protection from various credit security vulnerabilities and threats. Because credit cards are so pervasive, an enterprise that processes, stores, or transmits payment card data must be PCI-DSS compliant or risk losing the ability to process credit card payments. IT auditors should understand the high-level key elements of this standard and incorporate it in their reviews where appropriate.

Cybersecurity practices can be very complex, and IT auditors may not be technical experts in all of these areas. However, all IT auditors should have a high-level understanding of cybersecurity risks, high-level controls, and preventive mechanisms. Also, IT auditors should understand when they need to seek the help and advice of seasoned security experts when performing IT audits.

IT NETWORK SECURITY FUNDAMENTALS

We do not hear too much about major bank robberies today. In past times, when banks carried large amounts of cash in vaults that were locked at night but open and protected by guards during the day, it was not uncommon for thieves to arrive, overpower staff and guards, and depart carrying the cash from the vault. Today, the environment is very different. A bank may control a huge amount of assets, but those assets are only records on computer files; would-be thieves cannot easily run off with a bag full of those assets. In addition, although the bank does have some cash potentially subject to theft, extremely strong cash controls are in place, including video cameras, the ability to trace currency serial numbers, and others.

IT auditors should recognize that IT security procedures today are not the same as those past days of bank vault robberies. Sometimes it is easy for a perpetrator to gain access to valuable data records without detection or at least any active surveillance. The thief sometimes can directly download this valuable data without an immediate trace in order to use it for criminal purposes. The IT asset thief also may be taking assets more valuable than cash, such as credit card authorization numbers that will allow massive purchases elsewhere, passwords to gain access to other even more valuable systems, or even the "identities" of people to use for further fraudulent transactions.

Lacking proper internal control procedures, an enterprise's IT systems hardware, software, and data face may face any or all four basic classes of threats:

1. **Interruptions.** A system asset can become lost, unavailable, or unusable through the malicious destruction of a program, theft of a hardware component, or improper use of network resources.
2. **Interceptions.** An outside party, such as a person, program, or another computer system, can gain access to an IT asset. An example of this type of threat may be wiretapping to obtain data or the illicit use of program resources. Interceptions often leave few traces and are difficult to detect.
3. **Modification.** Here, an unauthorized intruder not only accesses but makes changes to data, programs, or even hardware components. Even though modifications often can be quickly detected, in some cases they can go on almost unnoticed.
4. **Fabrication.** This threat occurs when an unauthorized person introduces counterfeit objects into an IT environment. These might include spurious transactions to a new work communications system or inserting records in an established database.

These threats were serious even in the early days of IT systems with large legacy systems, batch transactions, data stored on mass storage disk and tape drives, and limited telecommunications connections. Security threats have risen exponentially in our current environment of the Internet, wireless communications, enterprise resource planning (ERP) databases, and computing devices ranging from sophisticated server systems to small handheld devices. IT auditors reviewing internal controls in this environment should be aware of these new vulnerabilities.

Just as IT systems have become more sophisticated and better controlled, threats against them have increased. We regularly see press accounts of some computer security breach and the theft or destruction of sensitive data. As a single example and certainly not a unique one, just after the end of the holiday shopping season in 2007, the U.S. clothing store retailer TJX Companies announced that someone had hacked into its IT systems and made copies of customer debit and credit card account numbers, addresses, and other identifying data from customers of their some 2,000 discount clothing stores.[1] Just as bank robbers in the old days ran off with the stolen cash—sometimes in bags of cash in small bills—never to be found again, perpetrators who have thousands and thousands of credit card numbers and other personal information can use them in ways that are difficult to trace.

This TJX theft took place over the weeks before and after the holiday shopping season. The data was stolen through the daily transfers of sales data from many of the company's stores. TJX did not detect this breach initially because the daily sales transmittals from stores over a communications network seemed to have no problems. The perpetrators just made duplicate copies of the data for their own use.

Many such computer security breaches occur worldwide regularly. They frequently involve highly technical exploitations of what might appear to be good internal technical controls. IT auditors sometimes will not have all the technical skills to assess many of these IT environments and to make appropriate technical recommendations, but they should develop a basic understanding of computer security concepts for use in a wide range of IT audit reviews.

Security of Data

Whether it is customer account data located in a major ERP system database or internal audit project data collected on a staff member's laptop, enterprise data needs to be protected. Although there can be multiple variations and configurations, Exhibit 20.1 illustrates basic security of data concepts and shows four ways IT data should be protected. Each of these modes is not necessary for all data, but IT auditors may find it useful to think of data security along these concepts.

In some instances, data may require some basic confidentiality protection, as shown on the upper left corner of the exhibit. The control emphasis here is not from threats to the outside protective walls, but internal controls allowing programs and data to be protected and self-contained. An example here is the building cornerstone of earlier times in which some key records were sealed, never to be seen again while the building was standing. Those foundation cornerstones were essentially time capsules of data at the time construction and not used to retain critical data. Storing key data in this

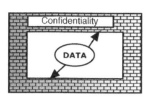
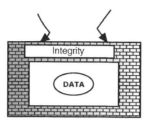
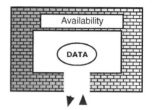

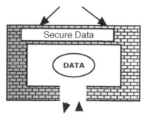

EXHIBIT 20.1   Security of Data Concepts

manner generally does little good in most situations, and data must be treated in a protected, confidential manner where it can be accessed if necessary. However, although there can always be threats, data should be protected from any unexpected spillage or seepage.

Moving clockwise around the exhibit, data integrity is a greater concern. For any data repository, there may be outsiders who try to breach that data protection wall to gain access. In our TJX example, a perpetrator gained access to company data and destroyed its integrity by making unauthorized copies.

Although the wall of confidentiality is important, data generally must become available to others. Data availability is a two-way portal, and the programs and processes controlling the data should make it available only to proper, authorized sources. Password-type controls are very important here and are discussed in the next section.

The last illustration on this exhibit combines the other three strategies into the concept of a secure data environment. Two other data security concepts are very important here: firewalls and protections against viruses. Both of these are discussed further in sections to come. IT auditors should think of computer security in terms of these three concepts of confidentiality, integrity, and availability.

Importance of IT Passwords

Passwords are a basic IT control in which a user of a system or data must enter some personal code known only to the user to gain access to the IT resource. Although there can be other more complex configurations, Exhibit 20.2 shows a basic IT password logon exchange. A user enters a password to gain application acceptance, but if the password is incorrect, system access is denied.

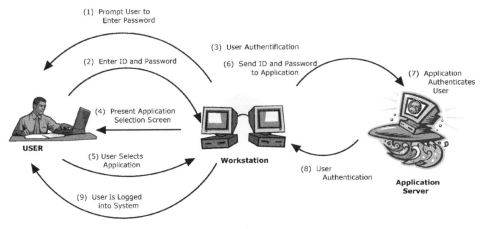

EXHIBIT 20.2 Basic IT Password Logon Exchange

When reviewing an IT application area, an IT auditor should always look for the effective use of passwords. The IT security literature is filled with extensive guidance on the use of passwords. Some best practices include:

■ Passwords are a user's responsibility to establish, but administrative rules should be established to make them hard for others to guess. For example, controls and guidance should be in place to prevent the use of easy to guess passwords such as birthdates or nicknames.
■ Passwords should be structured such that they are difficult for outsiders to guess easily. For example, IT security can set rules requiring a mix of letters and numerals in a password.
■ Processes should be in place to require frequent password changes. Some computer operating systems administer this control; otherwise, procedures should be in place requiring regular password changes.
■ Processes should be in place to monitor passwords, deny access if perhaps three invalid password attempts are made, and allow passwords to be reset through an administrative procedure. These processes should allow a user to receive a duplicate password if a password has been forgotten.
■ Strong enterprise people-oriented procedures should be in place regarding the use of passwords. That is, guidance should prohibit the sharing of passwords or posting them in easy-to-see places.

The effective use of passwords is an important IT security authentication control. There are other authentication systems, such as fingerprint scanners or even eye pupil scanners for some highly sensitive applications, but effective password systems are perhaps the best for regular business application. IT auditors should be aware of the requirements for good password controls and look for effective password systems as part of their many reviews of IT general controls and applications.

Viruses and Malicious Program Code

A computer virus is typically a very small program routine that can copy itself and infect another computer without permission or knowledge of the user. The term *virus* is used because it is the kind of program that can attach itself to another system and then spread like a disease to others as they come in contact with that same set of virus code. A virus can spread from one computer to another only when the virus code is taken to some other uninfected computer—for instance, by a user sending it over a network or the Internet, or by carrying it on a removable medium such as a compact disc or USB drive repository. Viruses also can spread to other computers by infecting files on a network file system that is accessed by another computer.

Computer viruses first came into the world in the days of the ARPANET, the early 1970s forerunner of the Internet. Someone—and the author is subject to speculation—introduced a program on an early ARPANET network that displayed the message "I'M THE CREEPER: CATCH ME IF YOU CAN" on many system programs.

In the early 1980s days of Apple II and IBM PC computers, viruses reappeared on the floppy disks that were used to share programs and data from computer to computer. Also, although the Creeper message was perhaps "cute," virus programs began to become malicious. For example, some early viruses just inhabited and took over the memory space of someone's computer, and then copied themselves on a floppy disk inserted into that computer. When a user took that floppy disk and inserted it into another computer, the virus reappeared on that other computer. We often forget that these were the days when a popular system, such as the Apple II, had only 32k of memory, and blocking that memory disabled the system.

As time passed, viruses became even more destructive and today are often called malware. One type of malware was called a Trojan horse, name from Greek mythology, that attaches to someone's computer and then sits silently until some date or event occurs. An example of a Trojan horse routine—and this has happened—is a programmer who inserts code to maliciously delete key data if his or her employee number no longer appears on the payroll systems register file. Another type of Trojan horse program is called a logic bomb, an unknown program that triggers only when some other event occurs. As an example, a programmer worried about being fired could insert such a logic bomb routine into the employer's payroll system to delete all systems files if that programmer's ID was ever deleted from payroll records.

Exhibit 20.3 lists some of the more common types of malicious code programs. There are many other examples of and stories about malware, but the objective of this chapter is not to describe all such conditions. The software industry has responded to malware threats with a variety of commercial products that constantly monitor for bad software, and, when encountered, either block or repair the bad program code. Many people around the world are trying to build a more complex and difficult-to-detect malware routines, and the virus prevention software vendors are working just as fast to patch their program code and prevent introductions. This author, for example, has virus protection software loaded on his desktop machine that flashes an Internet-led message that the antivirus software has been updated sometimes once or twice daily.

Code Type	Characteristics
Virus	Attaches itself to programs and propagates copies of itself to other programs
Trojan horse	Contains unexpected functionality that later performs a disguised function
Logic bomb	Program that triggers only when some other specified event occurs
Time bomb	Program that triggers only when some other specified time period is met
Trapdoor	Undocumented software entry point that circumvents system protections
Worm	Propagates copies of itself through a network
Rabbit	Software code that replicates itself without limit to exhaust the resource

EXHIBIT 20.3   Types of Malicious Program Code

IT auditors should recognize that software viruses and other malware are constant threats and look for the effective implementation of antivirus software for every computer system reviewed, whether a corporate-level central IT system or a business laptop. An IT auditor should determine that a current version of the software protection software is installed, that it is regularly updated, and that action is taken when viruses are detected. Policies and software controls should be in place to restrict unauthorized software from being introduced into IT systems operations, whether they are attempts to download unauthorized programs from the Internet or USB devices or CDs that employees want to load on their home laptops.

Phishing and Other Identity Threats

Our massive dependence on the Internet as well as the growth of online shopping and banking has caused increasingly widespread cybersecurity risks. Financial motivations have led to an explosion of tactics designed to trick users into divulging their usernames, passwords, and other confidential information, which can then be used to commit a wide range of crimes based on identity fraud. A typical cybersecurity crime has been for a malware program to clean out the victim's bank account. The information also often is used to help perpetrators commit further fraud and gain unauthorized access to networks. New cybersecurity threats appear regularly, and this section looks at a few of them.

■ **Phishing.** The fraud activity known as phishing, a hackers' term, comes from the scam's parallels with fishing, where fake e-mails and Web sites are used as bait to capture a victim's confidential information. (The victim who is being netted is the "phish.") In phishing attacks, scammers send out authentic-looking e-mails that claim to come from well-known, legitimate institutions. The recipient is encouraged to click on a Web site link in the e-mail. In doing so, a victim is taken to a bogus (or "spoofed") site that is virtually indistinguishable from the real thing.

Even though only a small percentage of people fall prey to the trick, phishers can make a significant amount of money while the bogus site is up and running— the average length of time for a phishing site to remain online is just four days, according to the Anti-Phishing Workgroup (APWG; www.antiphishing.org), a workgroup committed to wiping out Internet scams and frauds. With the relatively low cost of setting up a Web site and sending out thousands of e-mails, only a relatively few victims are needed to turn phishing into a profitable scheme. There have been many reported phishing attacks. APWG's reports revealed ongoing worldwide increases in phishing attacks over recent years. This is a cybersecurity risk.

- **Phaxing.** In a related authentication threat called phaxing, criminals send faxes to an enterprise's customers, asking them to log on to the Internet and then send back their fax numbers or URL Internet addresses.

Criminals frequently are looking for social engineering ways to dupe users and steal their identity. Effective controls are not necessarily that complex. For example, users should beware of faxes with a URL[2] address in them asking the recipient to contact the sender via the Internet. A very simple control is always to call the supposed sender, using a number from the phone book, to confirm they sent the fax before responding via the Internet. If one fails to respond in that manner, there is a chance of having one's identity and authentication information stolen or bank account rifled.

Identify theft schemes are a growing risk. It is an enterprise's responsibility to educate its user community and warn people to avoid such frauds, but IT auditors should be aware of these schemes and provide appropriate warnings when asked.

IT System Firewalls

A firewall is a process that filters traffic between a protected, or "inside," and a less protected, or untrusted "outside," environment. It is a specialized type of software that either allows or prevents certain types of transactions. Exhibit 20.4 illustrates a very simple firewall configuration. An enterprise has many needs to install firewalls both between the enterprise systems network and the outside world through the Internet or

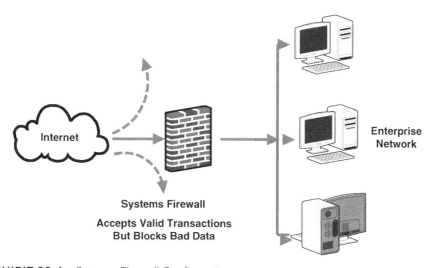

Internet

Systems Firewall

Accepts Valid Transactions But Blocks Bad Data

Enterprise Network

EXHIBIT 20.4 Systems Firewall Configuration

other resources. Firewalls monitor traffic, route some to designated network locations, and block others.

Basically, a firewall is a barrier to keep destructive data away from an enterprise's network and systems. Its function is similar to a physical firewall that keeps a fire in a building from spreading from one area, such as stairwell, to the next. A firewall often is set up as a screening router, a proxy gateway, or a guard. From an IT audit perspective, however, rather than understanding the technical details of the configurations, firewalls can be used for some of these applications:

- Screening router configuration firewalls can be used in situations where, for example, an enterprise may have three local area networks (LANs), one for its corporate offices, one for U.S. operations, and a third for EU facilities. Corporate is allowed to send and receive messages to both facility LANs, but perhaps the United States and European Union are allowed to send certain specified things to corporate and are not allowed full access across the two facility LANs.
- A proxy gateway firewall is used when an enterprise wants to set up online price lists and product offerings for outsiders, but the firewall prevents outsiders from modifying this price and product information or accessing supporting files connected with the product offerings.
- A guard firewall is used when an enterprise allows its employees to access most areas of the Web but prohibits access to such things as sports scores or online gambling sites.

Besides just screening or monitoring network and Web addresses, firewalls also can monitor the specific content in a message or Web page. They can audit this activity and even report on improper access attempts. Firewalls must be configured correctly, but the configuration must be updated regularly for the internal and external environments. Firewalls protect an environment, however, only if they control all access to a network perimeter. For example, if a firewall was set up to control all access to a LAN but if one device on that LAN has a dial-up modem connection, security can be breached. Firewalls are strong security controls but are often the targets for penetrators.

When performing a data security review, an IT auditor should understand the location and nature of installed firewalls. It is important that the firewall configuration provides adequate protection and is updated regularly. In addition, an IT auditor should look for appropriate review and follow-up activity regarding firewall violation reports.

Other Computer Security Issues

Our discussion of malicious code, passwords, and firewalls lists only a few of the many security issues that IT networks face today. Others include elaborate access controls, the need to use encryption when transmitting data, multilevel security in database administration, and many more. From an IT audit perspective, perhaps some of the most important computer security issues focus on the need to establish strong management support for the IT security programs in place and for overall stakeholder education programs to impress everyone about IT network security threats and vulnerabilities.

Whether an active program to monitor for malware, the placement of firewalls, and other issues, IT auditors should include network and cybersecurity control procedures in their ongoing IT internal control reviews. In many respects, as these issues become more technically complex, risks increase. As IT auditors may not be strong IT security specialists, they should always be able to request help from the IT security specialists with the enterprise.

IT SYSTEMS PRIVACY CONCERNS

Privacy is the expectation that confidential personal information disclosed in a private place will not be disclosed to third parties, when that disclosure would cause either embarrassment or emotional distress to a person of reasonable sensitivities. Privacy *information* should be interpreted broadly to include facts, images (e.g., photographs, videotapes, and sound recordings), and disparaging opinions. It certainly covers all aspects of IT systems and networks.

In our complex networks of Internet-connected systems and ever-advancing technologies, privacy issues on many levels are growing concerns. There are many issues here about how much personal data and information individuals should allow to be given to interested enterprises, government authorities, and even other individuals. Similarly, from a privacy and security perspective, an enterprise wants adequate levels of protection. Chapter 17, for example, talks about two U.S.-based laws, the Health Insurance Portability and Accountability Act and the Gramm-Leach-Bliley Act, that established some privacy rules that should be in an IT auditor's general areas of interest. Other IT-related privacy issues should be on an IT auditor's radar screen. In some instances, these are evolving issues, but IT auditors should be aware of them as they perform internal controls reviews, particularly in areas related to IT networks. Although they do not discuss only internal control audit issues, the next sections describe some evolving privacy issues in today's world of network cybersecurity concerns.

Data Profiling Privacy Issues

As part of everyday life, data is collected from individuals and enterprises, frequently without our consent and often without our realization. For individuals, data is collected and stored in a computer system in these and many more instances:

- Bills paid with credit cards create a data trail consisting of the purchase amount, type, date, and time.
- The use of supermarket preferred customer cards creates a comprehensive customer repository of all purchases.
- A car, equipped with a radio transponder, passes through an electronic toll booth, and the owner's account is debited, and a record is created of the location, date, time, and account identification.
- We surf the Internet and visit Web sites, recording activities known as cookies. These are software monitors that vendors build into their products to monitor customer usage.

▪ When we subscribe to a magazine, sign up for an investment advisory service, join a professional association, fill out a warranty card, give money to charities, donate to a political candidate, tithe to a religious organization, invest in mutual funds, make a telephone call, and interact with a government agency, we are initiating transactions that leave a data trail stored in an IT system.

Although we are not yet to the point where the content of all of these databases are combined, we are close. In the aftermath of the 9/11 terrorist attacks, U.S. government and law enforcement authorities proposed the development of an airline traveler screening program that would compile data from many consumer data files. That proposal was highly controversial and was not implemented, but a limited version may be developed in future years.

The legal protections for privacy in the United States are weak, and the unfettered collection of data from numerous sources, in an environment where there are few legal restrictions on how the data can be used and merged, can violate privacy and trample on civil liberties. There are few restrictions in the United States on how data can be collected and merged, although laws exist in EU countries, Canada, New Zealand, and Australia. IT auditors should have a general understanding of these issues as part of their audit activities.

Online Privacy and E-Commerce Issues

As discussed in previous sections, Internet privacy threats are commonplace. We must recognize that the Internet originally was originally designed as an inherently *insecure* communications vehicle. Hackers often demonstrate they can easily penetrate the most secure facilities such as in military and financial institutions. In addition, enterprises have designed numerous ways to track Web users as they travel and shop throughout Internet sites using a common cyber-snooping tool called a cookie. As discussed previously with our TJX example, identity thieves are able to shop online anonymously using the credit identities of others, and Web-based information brokers can sell sensitive personal data, including social security numbers, relatively cheaply.

There has been extensive media coverage of these issues with a growing public awareness of online privacy issues. Some form of a U.S. Internet privacy law is expected to be passed in the coming years that will provide strong consumer protections in this area. Although our comments are speculative, such legislation could mandate that every commercial Web site provide a privacy policy, clearly explain its data collection practices, and provide meaningful ways for visitors to prevent their personal data from being captured and sold to other enterprises.

IT auditors should be aware of any evolving issues here. Knowledgeable individuals can take steps to prevent their Web-surfing practices from being captured by the Web sites they visit. But, realistically, few people have the requisite knowledge or patience to take advantage of such privacy-enhancing strategies.

Radio Frequency Identification

When a consumer waves his keychain in front of the gasoline pump's meter to automatically pay for the fuel just pumped, he is likely to be using radio frequency identification (RFID) technology. This technology often is used in building-access cards—ID cards that enable individuals to gain entry into a building or into an office within a building. Yet another application is employee identification cards. RFIDs often are called contactless ID cards because users need only wave the card within a few inches of the reader in order to gain access.

In the applications described here—paying for fuel or gaining entry into a secure building—the individual is well aware of each and every use in which the RFID tag is accessed. But RFID tags also are tiny and can be embedded in items in ways that are virtually invisible. Reading devices also can be invisible. In the future, RFID readers could be embedded in streetlight poles, and an RFID tag associated with an individual— perhaps embedded in a driver's license—used to record the transactions that person engages in, such as buying a newspaper at the corner vending machine, entering a supermarket and purchasing groceries, using public transit, entering a workplace, and so on. If RFID tags were embedded in driver's licenses, which most people carry with them at all times, we could live in a society where location privacy and anonymity are a thing of the past.

Could such a scenario actually happen? Many people find it hard to imagine that we would allow such uses of RFID to occur. However, IT auditors might confront this type of evolving concern. The challenge for many IT auditors is that auditee management and staff may expect an IT auditor to have extensive knowledge in these areas. The Internet is a good source for more information about the privacy issues discussed here.

Lack of U.S. Federal Privacy Protection Laws

Citizens of nearly all developed countries throughout the world enjoy rights to privacy through laws that are called data protection acts. In most such nations, comprehensive, or omnibus, data protection laws govern how personal information can be used by government agencies and commercial entities. The use of personal information is usually an "opt in" under such laws. In other words, an individual's personal information cannot be used, say, for marketing unless that person gives affirmative consent.

The United States has no such general law but does have laws covering specific sectors, such as the Telephone Consumer Protection Act (telemarketing), the Fair Credit Reporting Act (credit reports and employment background checks), and the previously discussed HIPAA (medical records privacy). Gaps here leave many uses of personal information unprotected. For example, the "junk" mail one often receives when subscribing to magazines is not covered by a specific law.

The privacy approach taken in the United States is referred to as "opt out." For example, a consumer's personal information is used to send unsolicited ads unless the consumer opts out of receiving this stuff and signs up for the direct marketing industry's Mail Preference Service (MPS; www.dmachoice.org/MPS/proto1.php), a service to prohibit unwanted consumer mail. And even that does not guarantee that your mailbox will be "junk" free. The MPS is a voluntary standard. Although members of the Direct Marketing Association must subscribe to it as a condition of membership, not all companies that market to individuals are members. Most IT auditors need only to witness the spam in their e-mail inboxes.

PCI-DSS FUNDAMENTALS

Launched in September 2007 by the Payment Card Industry (PCI) council—a world-wide industry group led by American Express, Discover, Master Card, Visa, and others—their PCI-DSS data security standard must be used by anyone wanting to accept credit cards as a form of payment. Because credit cards are so pervasive in enterprise commerce and because the failure to comply with this standard can result in a variety of fines and, potentially, the loss of the right of an enterprise to accept credit cards at all, we are providing an overview of this important new cybersecurity standard.[3]

PCI-DSS is a new worldwide standard that has been established to comply with a huge number of local and national rules and guidelines for the major credit card companies. The standard contains configuration and audit guidelines that cover *any* IT device that accepts credit cards as payment. The term *any* is quite broad; beyond standard computer systems, it applies to the point-of-sale devices found in retail stores, any site accepting e-mail payments, and a wide range of others.

Exhibit 20.5 shows the 12 basic requirements for a PCI-DSS implementation. Although they are very high level and oriented to the credit card industry, many are just good general network security practices.

	PCI-DSS Requirements	Category
1	Install and maintain a firewall configuration to protect cardholder data.	Build and maintain a secure network.
2	Do not use vendor-supplied defaults for system passwords and other security parameters.	Build and maintain a secure network.
3	Protect stored data, and do not store card and transaction data unnecessarily.	Protect cardholder data.
4	Encrypt transmission of cardholder data and sensitive information across public networks.	Protect cardholder data.
5	Use and regularly update antivirus software.	Maintain a vulnerability management program.
6	Develop and maintain secure systems and applications.	Maintain a vulnerability management program.
7	Restrict access to data by business need to know.	Implement strong access control measures.
8	Assign a unique ID to each person with computer access.	Implement strong access control measures.
9	Restrict physical access to cardholder data.	Implement strong access control measures.
10	Track and monitor all access to network resources and cardholder data.	Regularly monitor and test networks.
11	Regularly test security systems and processes.	Regularly monitor and test networks.
12	Establish and maintain high-level security principles and procedures.	Maintain an information security policy.

EXHIBIT 20.5   PCI-DSS Requirements

Effective use of these requirements means going a little further in understanding cybersecurity control needs. For example, requirement 11 is the need to regularly test security systems and processes. This might require an enterprise to:

- Test security controls annually.
- Run internal and external data scans quarterly.
- Perform annual penetration tests on systems and applications.
- Use tools for network and host intrusion detection.
- Implement file integrity monitoring procedures.

At the present time, many enterprises worldwide are working to achieve PCI-DSS compliance. It is a hybrid and best practices standard where participating enterprises are required to demonstrate compliance. It is also a good example of the growing importance of cybersecurity issues.

IT auditors whose enterprises are involved with credit card payment transactions may be familiar with PCI-DSS compliance efforts here; if they are not, they should discuss this status with their legal counsel. Although these standards have been led by the credit card industry, we can expect to see other industry similar standards going forward.

 ## AUDITING IT SECURITY AND PRIVACY

IT audit should consider performing reviews of IT or cybersecurity controls and verifying compliance with established privacy procedures. As we have discussed, though, this overall area of network security can be very complex and technical. We recommend that an IT auditor with strong, specialized technical training, initiate a detailed, technical review of cybersecurity practices in his or her enterprise.

IT auditors need strong technical skills to perform a credible "deep-dive" technical review in these areas. Still, many of the areas discussed cover strong risks and internal control issues that an IT auditor with only general knowledge of the area and a good understanding of the associated risks can assess.

The use and implementation of IT firewalls is a good example of an effective IT audit review area. We have discussed, for example, the configurations of IT firewalls that can be implemented. In many instances, an IT auditor does not need to know the technical attributes of a proxy firewall. Rather, the IT auditor can ask some general but very control-specific questions that will enable him or her to gain a high-level understanding of the status in preparation for a cybersecurity review in this area.

As an example, assume that an IT auditor is reviewing cybersecurity controls covering the LAN at a small operating division. The IT auditor might ask some questions along the lines of:

- Can you give me a diagram of the network showing all internal and external connections within the network?
- Have you installed firewalls for the network, and do they protect all access points?

- Is there any way that devices on the network can communicate to other devices—such as a dial-up line through a modem—and bypass the firewall barrier?
- What types of actions or transactions does the firewall screen for?
- Are firewall parameters regularly updated, and when was the last update?
- What types of improper access attempts are monitored through the firewall?
- What types of corrective action procedures are in place for attempted firewall violations?
- Can I review some of your recent firewall violation actions documentation?

None of these questions requires an auditor to have a strong level of technical knowledge. Rather, the IT auditor is recognizing here that firewalls are an effective security control and is asking, in a general manner, how they have been installed for a LAN. Of course, an IT auditor always faces the risk of receiving a techno-babble type of answer from an IT person who either really wants to impress you or resents the IT audit process. In that case, the best solution is to write down the response and follow up later with some IT auditor-friendly technical resource. However, the general responses to these questions might indicate some control strengths and weaknesses.

Exhibit 20.6 contains some cybersecurity internal control audit procedures covering the areas discussed here. Although these procedures do not provide complete coverage of all cybersecurity issues facing an enterprise and do not cover some evolving privacy issues, IT auditors should develop a high-level understanding of the risks and controls in this important area. As we become a more highly networked and interconnected world, enterprises need to build and establish strong and effective controls. Even though an IT auditor may not be a technical guru, a general understanding of risks and control issues in these broad areas will help make him or her a more effective aid to enterprise management.

SECURITY AND PRIVACY IN THE INTERNAL AUDIT DEPARTMENT

Internal auditors—both as an operating department in the enterprise and as operational and financial internal auditors—need to establish their own security and privacy procedures and best practices. IT auditors regularly visit a site and capture information and data, either in hard- or soft-copy format. Depending on the nature of a review, that captured audit evidence material must be maintained in a secure and confidential manner.

Most, if not all, IT audit functions today have moved from the days of pencil-and-paper workpaper records and voluminous manual supporting records to auditor laptop computers and extensive automated processes. In years past, IT auditors and traditional internal auditors kept their work in thick binders. After an individual audit was completed, the approved workpapers were filed in a fairly secure audit department library. There was always a risk that a workpaper binder could become lost, but in today's laptop era, there may be greater IT audit privacy and security risks.

1. Network configuration security controls
   a. Review network configuration diagrams to determine that connections to other networks and computer systems are minimized.
   b. Determine that connections to the Internet are limited and used only when necessary.
   c. Assess the extent of wireless and determine that they are appropriately secured.
   d. Review the extent of dial-up connections in place, and determine that they are secured with usage monitored.
2. Network system access controls
   a. Assess the adequacy of physical security controls surrounding prime or main data centers.
   b. Review any remote facilities, such as research lab sites, and determine that they are following approved central IT processes.
   c. Review configuration to determine that there are no unattended, unsecure workstations attached to the network.
   d. Assess whether suitable physical protections—including hardware, telecommunications equipment, cables, and wiring—are in place for all data centers.
   e. Review the adequacy of backup provisions for electrical power, communication, and storage.
3. Review the extent and currency of written cybersecurity procedures covering:
   a. Personnel screening for new hires
   b. Information protection and key document controls
   c. Password and system access procedures
   d. Utilizations of facilities for business use and restrictions on personal use of system resources
   e. Disposal of sensitive information.
4. Security prevention countermeasure controls
   a. Review overall password policies to determine that there procedures in place to monitor password violations, to require regular password changes, and to monitor violations.
   b. Determine that an effective password reset policy is in place where appropriate measures are taken to indentify the true owner before granting new passwords.
   c. Review the location and purpose of all installed firewalls and assess their appropriateness.
   d. Determine that firewall activity is audited and that corrective actions are taken when required.
   e. Review the adequacy of protection procedures in place to prevent sniffing and spoofing.
   f. Assess policies in place for using encryption, and determine whether encryptions procedures are adequate.
5. Security incident monitoring and investigation techniques
   a. Determine whether there are formal incident reporting and investigation procedures in place.
   b. Determine that appropriate investigation and action plans are implemented in the event of security breaches.
   c. On a test basis, review actions taken on any reported suspicious events to determine that applicable corrective actions were taken.
   d. Review the skills, training, and documented actions of the established incident response team to assess effectiveness.
   e. Determine whether there has been adequate coordination with law enforcement agencies to, at a minimum, support cybersecurity issues.
6. Cybersecurity training
   a. Determine that all affected staff members are trained in cybersecurity risks and issues, as appropriate.
   b. Look for a program of enterprise-wide security training to raise awareness and highlight potential risks.

EXHIBIT 20.6   Cybersecurity Internal Controls Audit Procedures

Auditor Computer Security and Control

IT auditor use of notebook, laptop or desktop computers is essentially a standard procedure today. Based on Microsoft or Apple operating system software, these machines are used to write audit narratives and audit report findings with word-processing software, to prepare analyses and other schedules with spreadsheet software, to communicate with others on the audit team as well as the Web through e-mail and the Internet, and for many other tasks.

IT auditors carry their laptops with them, work on them while on flights to audit assignments, and take them to auditee sites. An auditor's laptop may carry critical files and information, and the machine also has some intrinsic value. Carried through airport lounges or tossed into the backseat of rental cars, these machines can be a security risk, subject to theft. Aside from the cost of the laptop itself, the major cost of any loss is the IT audit data contained in the system's files. Some important techniques for protecting auditor laptops are presented next.

- **Auditor personal responsibility for auditor laptops.** Through training, audit department standards, and just good guidance, all IT auditors with an assigned notebook or laptop should be reminded that they have a strong responsibility for its security. This can include such simple guidance as to keep it in the trunk of their automobile rather than the backseat, not to leave it sitting unattended, and not to allow a family member to use it such that files could be erased or corrupted.
- **File backup procedures.** Whether using a backup site at the headquarters internal audit office or a special USB, device, auditor laptop computers should be backed up regularly. Storage devices have become very cheap, and software tools for backups are readily available. Procedures should be established for IT auditors to perform a 100% daily backup of their systems. There is no need to keep multiple versions here, but the current backup copy can replace the current day's version.
- **Physical locks and mechanisms.** Laptops can be connected to a desk or some other difficult-to-move object using a variety of small, relatively inexpensive devices that are similar to a cable bicycle lock. An internal audit function should purchase such locks for IT auditor use.
- **Antivirus and other tools.** This chapter has discussed computer malware and the need for antivirus protection. The same types of software tools should be installed in all auditor laptops.

An IT auditor's laptop computer is often a repository for auditor narratives, copies of documents, and other key items of audit evidence. Good security procedures should be established to protect these important IT audit resources. Even when an IT audit function does not use laptops and relies on desktop machines, similar auditor security practices should be installed.

Workpaper Security

Workpapers are the key documents that carry auditor evidence and the results of the IT audit assignment work. Good workpaper documentation procedures and audit department security over those workpapers are very important. Sarbanes-Oxley rules discussed in Chapter 1 require that, as audit evidence, workpaper files should be retained for a seven-year period. Also, in a litigation situation, IT audit workpapers can become legal evidence in civil or even criminal court proceedings.

In today's environment, workpaper documentation can be a combination of soft-copy computer files and hard-copy documents. IT audit needs strong procedures to catalog, store, and secure its workpapers. Just as a book in a public library has a catalog number to allow its easy retrieval, an IT audit function should develop some kind of numbering scheme to catalog its workpapers. There is no one best approach here, but in launching such a program, IT audit should realize that seven years is a long time, and there can be many changes in the enterprise and its operating units.

Just as a major purpose of the library book numbering process is to allow people to check out a book for their use, audit workpapers should be organized in such a manner that a workpaper binder can be checked out for use. This use should be limited to other members of the IT audit staff and external auditors on request. Tracking records should be maintained to identify the location of any checked-out workpapers at any time.

Workpaper security is a concern, and whether the files are in hard- or soft-copy format, procedures should be installed to back up and protect them. Hard-copy documents should be kept in a secure, locked facility with limited access. Because a seven-year accumulation can create a large volume of materials, older workpapers should be stored with one of the secure document repository services that are common in today's business environments. Soft-copy workpaper materials should be backed up as well. The concern here is that such things as file formats can change. As this book goes to press in 2010, consider the IT formats of perhaps 5 to 10 years earlier: floppy disk files and earlier versions of word-processing software. A backup storage of those older devices would present problems today if enterprises needed to read or review them today. We cannot predict the future here, but technology changes will almost certainly make old soft-copy versions hard to use or read, arrangements should be made to convert them before it becomes too late.

Exhibit 20.7 contains some IT audit workpaper security best practices. Workpapers are important documentation describing IT audit activities, and access security over these materials is important. Although other members of the audit team must have access to older workpapers for a variety of reasons, extreme attention should be given to preventing any alteration of workpapers once the audit assignment has been completed and the documentation has been approved. There is always the danger that a rogue member of the IT audit team will make after-the-fact changes to the audit workpapers. This can be prevented through read-only controls installed on soft-copy versions, but protection for hard-copy versions is difficult to ensure.

Audit Reports and Privacy

Internal audit reports, described in Chapter 5, are documents that describe IT audit's activities for a planned audit project, the procedures performed, findings and recommendations, and auditee management's responses to those findings along with plans for corrective action. By their nature, audit reports are not documents for mass distribution. They should be shared only with auditee management, enterprise senior management,

- Establish general internal audit department workpaper standards defining best practices for such areas as capturing audit evidence, recording volume bulk evidence materials, and others.
- Develop general procedures for preparing workpapers in either hard-copy, paper-based formats as well as office systems–based soft copies and establish guidelines for when either should be used.
- Establish a general indexing or numbering system for all workpapers that identifies the unit, type of audit, and year of audit as well as general workpaper cross-referencing guidance.
- For laptop or desktop computer soft-copy workpapers:
  - Develop consistent file and file folder naming conventions that identify originators and dates of last changes.
  - Establish read and data update security controls.
  - Back up files to a secure server or other facility at least daily.
  - Establish workpaper update procedures such that when a printed version of a workpaper is updated, the automated version is updated as well.
  - Copy workpapers of completed audits to a secure repository so that data can be later accessed, given seven-year minimum retention requirements.
- For hard-copy, paper-based workpapers:
  - Establish consistent content naming conventions with descriptive names, dates, and auditor initials included on all workpaper sheets.
  - Establish security rules for paper-based workpapers during the audit process to prevent unauthorized persons from accessing workpaper files left on auditor desks and the like.
  - Develop consistent procedures for transporting and shipping workpaper files.
  - Because subsequent content alterations sometimes are difficult to trace, establish strong audit staff standards and guidelines on the improper alteration of workpapers.
  - Place all current workpapers in a secure facility with strong check-in and check-out rules.
  - Make arrangement for all older workpapers to be retained in a bulk storage repository.
- Build a comprehensive database to link all workpapers to the audit, completed report, and significant findings.
- Whether hard or soft copy, establish consistent workpaper review practices to identify the timing of supervisory reviews and nature of any changes.
- On a limited and test basis, perform quality reviews of older audit workpaper files to determine their ongoing accessibility.

EXHIBIT 20.7   IT Audit Workpaper Security Best Practices

external audit, and the audit committee. Of course, they can also be subject to court ordered disclosures as well. Disclaimers should be added to report documents stating that they are not to be copied or shared, and the chief audit executive (CAE) and members of the audit team should regularly emphasize the confidentiality needs for these documents.

Our comments here on workpapers have emphasized related security issues. Published audit reports raise a privacy issue as well. Comments in the findings section of an audit report can damage the professional credibility of portions of the enterprise and members of management. Audit reports should be secured from and protected from access by unauthorized persons.

IT Audit Security and Privacy Standards and Training

IT audit security and privacy procedures represent some best practices that should be considered by IT audit functions, no matter their size, industry, or geographic location.

However, it is one matter for the CAE to agree and install such procedures; it is another for all members of IT audit to be aware of and to follow these practices on an ongoing basis.

IT audit should establish departmental standards for workpaper security and privacy. Arrangements for a formal library repository should be established within the enterprise. This typically would be located in close proximity to the CAE, other members of internal audit, and enterprise headquarters. However, for a large, multi-unit enterprise and larger IT audit function, off-site or multiple workpaper library repositories could be established. The locations should be secure with overall administrative control assigned to an administrative staff member. With ongoing seven-year retention requirements, the hard- and soft-copy workpaper repositories and libraries should be organized such that later retrieval will be comparatively easy.

Security and privacy standards should be included in audit department procedures and training. In particular, as discussed, every member of the audit team should recognize and acknowledge the privacy and protection needs of assigned audit computers. Although IT auditors make security and privacy-related recommendations in many audit areas, they always should remember that these rules are extremely important for internal audit itself as well.

IT Audit's Privacy and Cybersecurity Roles

IT auditors should be aware of the growing and evolving cybersecurity and privacy issues, both in their enterprises and worldwide. As discussed, many of the issues here can become quite technical, but all IT auditors should acquire a general understanding of many of the areas discussed in this chapter. For example, most if not all laptop computer users are at least aware of the risks of computer viruses. An IT auditor should go a step further and understand the kinds of controls that can be applied to eliminate such risks and then take actions to prevent them.

The cybersecurity and privacy risks and issues discussed in this chapter are constantly changing and evolving. Software vendors, for example, develop a new protection technique for some type of malware virus only to have someone beat or get around the protection almost as soon as it is released. Although many IT auditors will not become experts on many of these often highly technical issues, all IT auditors should have a good understanding of cybersecurity and related IT privacy risks.

 NOTES

1. Numerous Web accounts have been published of this breach, such as: http://www .associatedcontent.com/article/128326/tj_maxx_and_marshalls_customers_data .html.
2. URL is an abbreviation for Uniform Resource Locator, the global address of documents, and other resources on the Internet.
3. More information on the standard can be found in PCI's Web site: www.pcisecurity standards.org.

21

IT Fraud Detection and Prevention

B USINESSES IN THE UNITED States and worldwide regularly go through rounds of failures that often are based on questionable business activities and sometimes fraud. The worldwide recession starting in 2009 was highlighted by a massive $50 billion Ponzi scheme fraud in the United States by Bernard Madoff.[1] (A Ponzi scheme is a fraudulent investment operation that pays returns to separate investors from their own money or money paid by subsequent investors rather than from any actual profit earned.)

The Madoff fraud was extraordinary because of its size, but almost like clockwork, other fraudulent business activities are discovered in the United States and elsewhere. The Madoff Ponzi scheme was a "rob Peter to pay Paul" type of fraud and did not directly involve any level of improper business transactions or the manipulation of information technology (IT) transactions. More typically, an IT auditor will read about or encounter a fraudulent activity based on questionable, improper business practices. For example, the corporate financial scandals that led to the enactment of the Sarbanes-Oxley Act (SOx) at the beginning of this century are examples of financial fraud by senior corporate officers. Fraudulent activity can occur at all levels of the enterprise, but in mid-2002 just before and after the enactment of SOx, corporate officers in Enron appeared to be the principal troublemakers in a slew of financial frauds. However, despite the publicity surrounding senior corporate officers as the troublemakers, fraud can take place at all levels. Just as a chief executive officer (CEO), in cooperation with the chief financial officer (CFO), may fraudulently manipulate earnings to boost reported profits and their individual bonus compensation, a midlevel manager or even a staff-level employee may be tempted to initiate some fraudulent action for personal gain or just to get even with someone because of job frustration. Unfortunately, the publicity surrounding Enron and other incidents of fraud has created an almost everybody-does-it attitude in recent years. Ernst & Young in its 2008 tenth annual Global Fraud Survey[2] reported that about 85% of the worst business-related frauds were caused by insider employees on the payroll and that over half of those frauds were initiated by members of management.

An effective IT auditor needs to recognize potential fraudulent business practices as part of any IT application or general controls review and then should recommend controls and procedures to limit exposure to the fraudulent activity. This chapter outlines some of the red flags—common conditions that an IT auditor might encounter when faced with a potential fraud. The chapter then discusses steps to identify, test, and properly process fraudulent activities. We also discuss fraud-related auditing standards both from the perspective of the Institute of Internal Auditors (IIA) and Information Systems Audit and Control Association (ISACA) Standards as well as U.S. external auditing fraud investigation standards. In addition, the chapter will introduce the standards and activities of the Association of Certified Fraud Examiners (ACFE). Fraud investigation can be a very detailed and specialized activity, but all IT auditors should have a high-level understanding of how to "smell" potential fraud conditions, how to audit for potentially fraudulent activities, and some processes for investigating and reporting fraud. Fraudulent activities represent a breakdown in a wide range of good practices and procedures, and IT auditors must recognize that fraudulent activities can always exist.

UNDERSTANDING AND RECOGNIZING FRAUD IN AN IT ENVIRONMENT

Fraud is one of those terms that many people use even though they do not fully understand what they are talking about. To better understand fraud, an IT auditor might first look at the dictionary or legal definition of the word.[3] The common-law definition of *fraud* is the obtaining of money or property by means of false token, symbol, or device. In other words, someone improperly authorizes a document that causes an improper transfer of money or some other thing of value. Whether it affects an individual or an overall enterprise, fraud can be costly, and effective internal controls are an enterprise's first line of defense against fraud. A comprehensive, fully implemented, and regularly monitored system of internal controls is essential for the prevention and detection of losses that arise from fraud. IT auditors—in their application and IT security reviews—sometimes find themselves very involved in fraud-related issues. When a fraud is discovered in the enterprise, IT or other internal auditors are often one of the first resources called to conduct an investigation to determine the extent of the fraud. In other situations, IT or other internal auditors discover a fraud during a scheduled audit and then investigate and report the matter to their corporate consul or legal authorities. However, historically neither internal nor external auditors have looked for fraud regularly as part of their scheduled audits. This has changed in recent years.

Auditors today, both internal and external, are taking on a more important role in the detection and prevention of fraud. This chapter discusses controls to prevent and detect fraud including the American Institute of Certified Public Accountants (AICPA) auditing standard on fraud, Statement on Auditing Standards (SAS) No. 99, *Consideration of Fraud in a Financial Statement Audit.* The SAS series of large corporation financial reporting auditing standards has essentially gone away with the enactment of SOx and its Public Corporation Auditing Oversight Board (PCAOB), but SAS No. 99 was a last but very important auditing standard. This chapter also discusses IT and internal audit initiatives here as well as procedures to detect and prevent IT systems fraud. Fraud has been with us from time immemorial, but auditors in the past have claimed that detecting fraud was beyond their responsibilities. Today, all auditors are finding themselves with an increasing responsibility to detect fraud in the course of their review activities as well as to recommend appropriate controls to prevent future frauds. This chapter also highlights the impact of fraud in internal auditing based on recently published guidance released by a task force from the IIA, the AICPA, and the ACFE, "Managing the Business Risk of Fraud."[4] Although it is more oriented to financial and operational fraud issues, it highlights the importance of fraud considerations for IT auditors as well.

 ## RED FLAGS: FRAUD DETECTION SIGNS FOR IT AND OTHER INTERNAL AUDITORS

Fraudulent activities are easiest to identify after the fraud has been uncovered. However, that does not do us much good as we are suffering the loss from that fraud. An employee who has been embezzling money over an extended period eventually will be caught through some slip-up that reveals the fraud. After such a fraud is discovered, often it is easy to look at the situation after the fact and say such things as "But she was such a good employee—she didn't miss a day of work for nearly two years! How could she have done this?" or "Now that I think about it, I wondered how he could afford all of those long weekend trips to expensive places!" It is easy to analyze the facts after a fraud has been discovered as a lesson learned, but auditors and management should look for indicators of possible fraudulent activities in advance with a skeptical eye. They should look for what are called red flags."

For example, the SOx legislation, discussed in Chapter 1, has criminal penalties for fraudulent activities. The first corporation and CFO to be indicted for accounting fraud under the then new SOx rules was a healthcare provider called HealthSouth Corporation. Then the largest U.S. provider of outpatient surgery and diagnostic and rehabilitative services, HealthSouth operated in approximately 1,900 locations in 50 states as well as some international facilities. It reported in excess of $1.4 billion of fictitious earnings over a six-year period in order to meet analyst estimates and to keep the stock price high. Several of its financial and other officers pleaded guilty, claiming and testifying against the CEO who demanded they report the fraudulent earnings. This accounting fraud had been happening for at least 10 years, and numerous red-flag signs of possible fraud seemingly were ignored by its external auditors and others:

▪ HealthSouth's year 2000 pretax earnings more than doubled to $559 million, although its sales grew only 3%. Pretax earnings for 2001 were nearly twice 1999 levels, although sales rose just 8%. There is nothing wrong with fantastic earnings growth, but analysts and certainly auditors might have asked some hard questions.

▪ In late 2002, HealthSouth's internal auditors were denied access to key corporate financial records. Internal audit reported this to their outside auditors and to their audit committee; neither party took any action on these overall internal audit concerns.

▪ The HealthSouth CEO spent a considerable amount of time and attention on sports and popular music performers, flying his management staff off to events and bringing sports stars in to work with the company.

These are just a few examples of the activities that were occurring around the company that, while not improper in themselves, suggest possible fraud. Fantastic reported earnings gains does not automatically mean fraud but can raise questions. Similarly, elaborate corporate-sponsored social events may raise questions about how the enterprise is managing its resources rather than pointing to fraud. However, these kinds of activities and others can raise questions. At HealthSouth, an ex-employee even sent an e-mail to the external auditors suggesting they look in three specific accounts for potential fraudulent activity. This is more than a red flag; it is an attempt to blow the whistle. Based on this tip, a high-level investigation was launched by HealthSouth's external auditors, but nothing was found. There were many red flags raised here, but internal management pressure on a normally dominant CEO to back off from some fictitious financial reports eventually started a chain of events that soon exposed the fraud.

What we call a red flag is a warning signal to the noninvolved observer that something does not look right. A huge increase in reported profits with not that much of an increase in unit sales may sound wonderful and be totally plausible. However, that is the type of red-flag indicator that should cause an auditor or fraud examiner to say: "This seems unusual—how can this so?"

Red flags are normally the first indications of a potential fraud. Someone sees something that does not look right and then often begins a low-level investigation. Internal auditors are often the very first people to become involved. Exhibit 21.1 lists some typical red-flag signs in financial or internal controls areas that could point to potential financial fraud activities. None of these is an absolute indicator of fraud, but internal auditors should always be skeptical in their reviews and be aware of such warning signals. Although an IT auditor may not see some of these warnings as part of IT applications or general controls reviews, he or she should be aware of these matters. When an IT auditor sees evidence of one or more red flags, it may be time to dig a little deeper. For example, if some primarily financial matter does not look right as part of an IT application review, the financial side of the internal audit group should be consulted. Unfortunately, IT and other internal auditors often fail to detect frauds for one of these reasons:

▪ **Unwillingness to look for fraud.** Based on their training and past experience, IT as well as financial and operational internal auditors historically have not actively looked for fraud. Prior to more recent changes in audit standards, often they tended

---

This list represents red flags that may be warning signals for evidence of financial fraud.

- Lack of written corporate policies and standard operating procedures or an environment where published policies and procedures are badly out of date
- Separate operating units frequently set their own rules in many areas and lack compliance with organization internal control policies.
- Weak internal control policies, especially covering the division of duties
- Disorganized operations in such areas as purchasing, receiving, warehousing, or regional offices
- Audit findings that have found unrecorded transactions or missing records
- Counterfeit copies or evidence of alterations to documents
- Photocopied or questionable handwriting on documents
- Sales records with excessive voids or credits
- Bank accounts not reconciled on a timely basis, or stale items on bank reconciliations
- Continuous out-of-balance conditions on subsidiary ledgers
- Unusual financial statement relationships
- Continuous unexplained differences between physical inventory counts and perpetual inventory records
- Bank checks written to cash in large amounts
- Handwritten checks prepared outside of the automated accounts payable system
- Continuous or unusual fund transfers among company bank accounts
- Fund transfers to offshore banks
- Transactions not consistent with the entity's business
- Poor screening procedures for new employees, including a lack of background or reference checks
- Based on past incidents, a reluctance by management to report criminal wrongdoing
- Unusual transfers of personal assets
- Evidence of officers or employees with lifestyles apparently beyond their means
- Officers or employees with ongoing unused vacation time balances
- Frequent or unusual related-party transactions
- Employees in close association with suppliers
- Employees in close relationship with one another in areas where separation of duties could be circumvented
- Expense-account abuse such as managers not following established rules
- Business assets dissipating without explanation

EXHIBIT 21.1   Red Flags Indicating Risk of Potential Financial Fraud
Source: Adapted from the AICPA Web site, www.aicpa.org.

---

to view fraud investigations as police types of activities, not their primary internal audit responsibilities.

- **Too much trust is placed on auditees.** All internal auditors usually try to maintain a friendly, cordial attitude toward auditees in their enterprise. Because they encounter these same people in the cafeteria or at an annual company picnic, there is usually a level of trust here. IT auditors quite correctly often try to give their auditees the benefit of the doubt.
- **Not enough emphasis is placed on potential fraud issues in audit findings.** Internal audit report findings often point to some of the same red flags mentioned in Exhibit 21.1. They are included as audit report findings pointing out such matters as missing records, ignored application error reports, or accounts that

were not reconciled. However, internal auditors often do not consider potential fraud in these audit findings. Unless it is a glaringly large issue, IT auditors do not even consider fraud issues when developing such an audit report finding.

▪ **Fraud concerns often receive inadequate support from management.** The hint of possible fraud requires auditors to extend their procedures and often dig a lot deeper. However, general management may be reluctant to give an individual auditor extra time to do so. Unless there are strong suspicions to the contrary, management often wants the audit team to move on and stop spending time in what management often feels is an extremely low risk area.

▪ **Internal auditors sometimes fail to focus on high-risk fraud areas.** Fraud can occur in many areas, ranging from employee travel expense reporting to treasury function relations with offshore banks. Often there is a much greater risk in the latter type of fraud, but auditors may tend to focus on the former. It may be comparatively easy to find problems in employee travel expenses; internal audits often do not include such high-risk areas as treasury function relations with offshore banks.

Fraud is a word that can have many meanings, but we are referring to it in terms of fraud as a criminal act. There are over 300 references to fraud in U.S. federal criminal statutes, and the term appears throughout the SOx legislation. Most of those federal references are based on federal general fraud statute definition:

> Whoever, in any manner within the jurisdiction of any department or agency of the United States, knowingly and willfully falsifies, conceals, or covers up by any trick, scheme, or device a material fact, or makes any false, fictitious, or fraudulent writing or document knowingly the same to contain any false, fictitious, or fraudulent statement or entry, shall be fined not more than . . . or imprisoned not more than . . . or both.[5]

Although this definition is stated in U.S. legalese, it is a strong statement. The external auditor's reference to the word *material*—meaning something minor that can be ignored—is not included here, and anything false, fictitious, or fraudulent could be considered a violation. There are multiple state statutes generally modeled after these federal rules, and IT auditors should be aware of their own state rules.

To help detect fraud, auditors should have a general understanding of why people commit fraud. An enterprise can have the red-flag environment, but it will not necessarily be subject to fraudulent activities unless one or more employees decide to engage in fraud. Exhibit 21.2 lists some typical excuses for committing a fraud. These are all reasons where strong internal controls are in place and the fraud is committed by only one person. Fraud detection is much harder when there is collusion between multiple persons. In the HealthSouth fraud, a very aggressive CEO assembled a top management team he called "the company" to prepare the fraudulent financial reports. Members of "the company" were highly compensated and received many incentives. The fraud did not become public until a member of "the company" began to have concerns about this growing accounting fraud. Whenever multiple people are in the same fraud together, there is always a possibility that someone will break ranks.

- **Employee has desperate need for money.** This probably is the major motivator and the type of fraud that is most difficult to detect. Whether due to a nasty divorce or a drug problem, the need for money can cause employees to resort to criminal actions.
- **Job frustrations.** Employees can become frustrated, feel their company "doesn't give a damn" about them, and feel free to act inappropriately. Job layoffs or pay grade freezes can foster such feelings.
- **Everybody-does-it attitudes.** This type of situation is common in smaller, retail-type environment where an employee thinks that everyone else is stealing as well. This attitude also can come up when senior managers seem to be living extravagantly at the same time the company is incurring losses.
- **Challenges to beat the system.** This is a particular problem with would-be hackers in IT systems environments. However, in many cases, an employee, for example, tries to set up a fictitious account to see if he or she can bill the company and receive cash in return.
- **Lax internal controls making fraud easy.** This is a basic motivation that encourages many frauds. Poor internal controls often encourage potential perpetrators to assume that the fraud will not be detected.
- **Low probability of detection.** Similar to the weak internal controls point, if an employee knows that chances of getting caught are nil, the temptation to commit fraud is greater.
- **Low probability of prosecution.** When an enterprise seemingly never brings criminal charges against someone, the word gets out, and people may view getting caught as an acceptable risk with little worry about prosecution.
- **Top management that does not seem to care.** Employees often collectively determine when another employee seems to get away after breaking some rule or when very appropriate behavior is not rewarded.
- **Low organizational loyalty or feelings of ownership.** In today's complex world, we often have situations where the owners of some business operation are an ocean and many organizational layers away. It is easy to have attitudes where no one really seems to care on a day-by-day basis.
- **Unreasonable budget expectations or other financial targets.** Organizations sometimes establish expectations that are all but impossible to meet. This can create an environment where people will bend the rules to meet those targets.
- **Less-than-competitive compensation and poor promotion opportunities.** If people cannot receive what they feel are appropriate rewards through normal compensation, they may bend the rules to benefit themselves.

EXHIBIT 21.2   Excuses and Reasons for Committing Fraud

Major frauds involving senior management participation are difficult to detect; frauds that occur at lower levels in the enterprise often are easier to detect with a proper level of auditor investigation. For example, a payroll process can present a wide range of opportunities for fraud through the use of such mechanisms as inflating the actual hours worked for an employee, hacking into the application to initiate improper payment transfers, generating payment vouchers for fictitious or terminated employees, or issuing duplicate vouchers for an employee. These are the classic issues that are part of many internal and IT audit procedures. However, rather than just an internal control violation, an auditor should think of these items in terms of potential areas for employee fraud. Auditors have performed these basic internal control review procedures over the years but sometimes forget that there could be a fraud issue as well. In the HealthSouth fraud, it was later discovered that the external auditors did not even do a classic bank balance confirmation with HealthSouth's banks. This is a standard test where the auditor asks the bank to independently confirm the audit client's bank balance as of a certain date. In their promotion of audit efficiency over the years, auditors—particularly external auditors—have dropped many of these traditional procedures. It may be time to revisit some.

PUBLIC ACCOUNTING'S ROLE IN FRAUD DETECTION

The external auditor's responsibility for the detection of fraud in financial statements has been an ongoing but contentious issue over the years. The very first AICPA Statement on Auditing Standards (SAS No. 1) was released in 1939 in response to an early accounting fraud that became known as the McKesson & Robbins case, a fictitious inventory fraud where the external auditors failed to observe the inventory counting. However, the external auditors were given no responsibility then to attempt to detect such frauds. For many years, AICPA auditing standards stated: "The auditor has no responsibility to plan and perform the audit to obtain reasonable assurance that misstatements, whether caused by errors or fraud, that are not material to the financial statements are detected." In other words, external auditors then were responsible only to determine if the financial statements were fairly stated; they had no responsibility to detect errors or fraudulent activity. The public accounting profession stood by this position for many years. Even up to the mid-1980s, leading up to the internal controls framework of the Committee of Sponsoring Organizations discussed in Chapter 1, AICPA audit standards still did not call for external auditors to assume any responsibility for the detection of fraud

Despite continuing pressure, AICPA audit standards regarding the external auditor's responsibility for fraud did not change until 1997, when this responsibility for fraud was reintroduced in SAS No. 82: "the auditor has a responsibility to plan and perform the audit to obtain reasonable assurance about whether the financial statements are free of material misstatement, whether caused by error or fraud." This revised but tighter standard was issued after much professional discussion, and it was released at about the peak of what was known as the dot-com bubble, when the investing public was concerned about their investments surging forward and not that much with fraud.

Moving to early in this century with the failures of Enron and a host of others, concerns about fraudulent financial reporting changed. After the establishment of SOx and the new PCAOB, the AICPA released SAS No. 99 in December 2002 on the auditor's responsibility for detecting fraudulent financial reporting. With this auditing standard, an external auditor is now responsible for providing reasonable assurance that audited financial statements are free of material misstatement, whether caused by error or fraud. SAS No. 99 was a major change in external auditor responsibilities.

SAS No. 99 requires external financial statement auditors to take on an attitude of professional skepticism regarding possible fraud. Putting aside any prior beliefs as to management's honesty, the standard calls for the external audit team to exchange ideas or brainstorm on how frauds could occur in the enterprise they are about to audit. These discussions should identify fraud risks and always should keep in mind the characteristics that are present when frauds occur: incentives, opportunities, and ability to rationalize. Throughout the audit, the engagement team should think about and explore this question: "If someone wanted to perpetrate a fraud here, how would it be done?" From these discussions, the external audit team should be in a better position to design audit tests that are responsive to the risks of fraud. The guidance here is that the external audit team always should go into an audit engagement anticipating that there may be some level of fraudulent activity.

The external auditor engagement team now is expected to ask management and others in the enterprise about their perceptions of the risk of fraud and whether they are aware of any ongoing fraud investigations or open issues. The external auditors should make a point of talking to all levels of employees, both managers and others, giving them an opportunity to blow the whistle and encouraging someone to step forward. It might also help deter others from committing fraud if they are concerned that a coworker may turn them in during a subsequent audit. During an audit, the external audit engagement team should test areas, locations, and accounts that otherwise might not be tested. The team should design tests that would be unpredictable and unexpected by the client. This represents a major change in external auditing standards.

SAS No. 99 also recognizes that management is often in a position to override controls in order to commit financial statement fraud. The auditing standard calls for procedures to test for management override of controls on every financial audit. SAS No. 99 requires a major external audit emphasis in detecting fraud, including procedures that external auditors are expected to perform in every audit engagement. This was a major change from the laissez-faire approach that was common in many past external audit engagements.

In addition to imposing a very tough fraud detection auditing standard on its members, the AICPA has taken strong steps to bring external auditors up to speed regarding situations that encourage fraud by providing both educational materials and case studies. Its Web pages are filed with case studies, publications, continuing professional education courses, and other references on management fraud issues. You do not have to be an AICPA member to access the site, and there are member and nonmember prices for purchasing these reference materials. For many years the AICPA avoided getting involved in fraud prevention and detection work; its SAS No. 99 standards and published antifraud guidance materials very much raises the bar for all certified public accountants. The IIA, the AICPA, and the ACFE also released "Managing the Business Risk of Fraud." Some concepts from it are included in our IT auditor guidance in the next sections.

IIA STANDARDS AND ISACA MATERIALS FOR DETECTING AND INVESTIGATING FRAUD

Internal auditors are often in a better position to detect fraud than external auditors who limit most of their client visits to around the quarterly and annual financial statement dates, while internal auditors are by definition internal to the enterprise and at enterprise sites sometimes daily. Just through observation, an internal auditor may be in a much better position to see a red flag that an external auditor could easily miss, despite the AICPA's fraud standard. The shipping supervisor who shows up at the annual holiday party in an expensive Italian suit and sporting a brand-name gold wristwatch might raise a small blip on the radar screen of another company party participant, an internal auditor. There are many very valid reasons to justify expensive clothes, but such a show of wealth could be something for an internal auditor to remember going forward with an audit scheduled in that area.

All internal auditors—financial, operational, or IT specialists—run into many such concerns and potential fraud issues in the course of their scheduled reviews. They also typically get involved in much more detailed, transaction-level reviews than their external audit counterparts and see questionable documents or transactions more frequently. If management feels there may be a potential fraud in the enterprise, the first step is almost always to contact internal audit, which will communicate with the corporate legal department. Internal auditors can discuss any potential concerns and get a quick opinion whether some concern requires more attention. If there are strong signs of an active fraud, corporate legal almost always will be ready to jump in to the matter and help.

Fraud matters are handled differently in the IIA and ISACA auditing standards summarized in Chapter 3. There is a specific IIA standard on fraud, 1210.A2:

> Internal auditors must have sufficient knowledge to evaluate the risk of fraud and the manner in which it is managed by the organization, but are not expected to have the expertise of a person whose primary responsibility is detecting and investigating fraud.

This says that an internal auditor should be able to evaluate the risks of a fraud and how the auditor's organization management deals with fraud issues, but an internal auditor is not expected to be an expert in detecting and investigating fraud.

IIA internal audit standards are supported by what are called Practice Advisories, guidance that provides more support for certain IIA standards. Interestingly, until the IIA standards were revised and updated in 2009, two such IIA Practice Advisories, 1210.A2-1 and 2, on the identification and investigation of fraud provided an internal auditor with some guidance in detecting and investigating fraud. Beyond their current guidance, those Practice Advisories are no longer part of the current IIA standards.

The IIA has not taken the strong position on detecting fraud that the AICPA has. A mid-2010 search on the IIA Web site using the key word "fraud" just does not give the wealth of material as is now found on the AICPA site. There are references to articles on fraud in older issues of the IIA publication, *The Internal Auditor*, but not much more. Other fraud-related articles, such as those included in Practice Advisories, are listed but available only to IIA members. The IIA also has special conferences on the topic, but the AICPA is taking a much stronger professional lead in providing guidance to auditors.

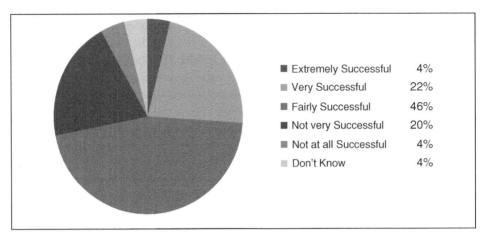

■ Extremely Successful	4%
■ Very Successful	22%
■ Fairly Successful	46%
■ Not very Successful	20%
■ Not at all Successful	4%
■ Don't Know	4%

EXHIBIT 21.3 Success of Internal Auditors in Detecting Bribery or Corrupt Practices
Source: IIA @ theiia.org

ISACA auditing standards impact all IT auditors more directly. Its IT Audit Standards have no guidance on detecting or preventing IT fraud. A search on the ISACA Web site (www.isaca.org) for "fraud" returns nothing. ISACA evidently believes that an IT auditor's responsibility for detecting fraud in this area is in recommending adequate controls to limit or prevent such "computer crimes" as identity thefts, as discussed in Chapter 22.

Although not directly related just to fraud as we defined the term, the Ernst & Young Tenth Global Fraud Survey contains a chart, based on its survey results, on the success of internal auditors on detecting bribery or corrupt practices. The results are shown in Exhibit 21.3. With only 26% saying internal auditors were extremely or very successful in the fraud-related investigations and another 24% responding that their internal auditors were either not very or not at all successful in detecting fraud, all internal auditors have room for improvements here.

IT AUDIT FRAUD RISK ASSESSMENTS

IT auditors typically do not begin their IT general controls or applications controls reviews by looking for the possibility of fraud. Rather, giving matters the benefit of the doubt, an IT auditor generally will assume that the IT internal controls in the areas reviewed are appropriate. However, while high-level favorable impressions are always appropriate, an IT auditor should tailor any review to assess the risk for the possibility of fraud activities in the area reviewed.

Regulators, professional standard setters, and law enforcement authorities have emphasized the crucial role risk assessment plays in developing and maintaining effective fraud risk management programs and in assessing internal controls. When reviewing an entity for potential IT risks, an internal auditor should identify and assess fraud risks in conjunction with a total IT-resources enterprise risk assessment or on a stand-alone basis tailored to meet individual needs, complexities, and goals.

The foundation of an effective fraud risk management program should be seen as a component of a larger enterprise-wide risk management effort that identifies where fraud may occur and who the perpetrators might be. To this end, control activities always should consider both the fraud scheme and the individuals within and outside the organization who could perpetrate each scheme. Fraud, by definition, entails intentional misconduct that is designed to evade detection. As such, the IT auditors forming the fraud risk assessment team should attempt to anticipate the behavior of a potential fraud perpetrator, asking questions such as:

- How might a fraud perpetrator exploit weaknesses in the system of IT controls?
- How could a perpetrator override or circumvent controls?
- What could a perpetrator do to conceal the fraud?

With this in mind, an IT systems fraud risk assessment generally should include three key elements:

1. **Identify inherent IT-related fraud risk.** IT audit should gather information about the population of overall enterprise IT fraud risks that could apply to the enterprise as a whole and to its individual IT organizational units. Much easier to say than to execute, this process should consider all types of IT fraud schemes and scenarios; incentives, pressures, and opportunities to commit fraud; and other IT fraud risks specific to the enterprise.
2. **Assess likelihood and significance of inherent IT fraud risk.** IT audit should assess the relative likelihood and potential significance of identified IT fraud risks based on historical information, known fraud schemes, and interviews with staff, including business process owners.
3. **Respond to reasonably likely and significant inherent and residual IT fraud risks.** IT audit should decide on potential responses to address identified risks and then should perform a cost-benefit analysis of fraud risks over which the enterprise wants to implement controls or specific fraud detection procedures.

The process is complex, but IT audit should document its IT fraud risks through a fraud risk assessment document. The idea is to document all of the identified potential IT fraud risks and then classify each risk by its likelihood, significance, existing antifraud controls, effectiveness of those controls, residual risks, and potential fraud risk responses. Exhibit 21.4 is an example of such a fraud risk assessment framework schedule, based on a financial reporting fraud example from the IIA, AICPA, ACFE document mentioned earlier. Although this is only a limited document with a few entries, fraud risks should be considered under these classifications:

- **Type of fraud.** The schedules should be organized by the major fraud risk area. In this example, several potential financial reported frauds have been identified.

Type of Fraud	Fraud Risk	Likelihood	Significance	People of Business Area	Existing Anti-Fraud Controls	Controls Effectiveness	Residual Risks	Fraud Risk Responses
Financial Reporting	Revenue Backdating Agreements	Reasonably Possible	Material	Sales Personnel	Strong Contract Administrative Systems	Tested by Internal Audit	N/A	Periodic Testing
Financial Reporting	Holding Books Open	Reasonably Possible	Material	Accounting	Reconciliation of Invoice Ledger to G/L	Tested by Management		Cut-Off Testing
Financial Reporting	Holding Books Open	Reasonably Possible	Material	Accounting	Standard Monthly Close Process	Tested by Internal Audit	Risk of Management Override	Testing of Late J/A's
Financial Reporting	Holding Books Open	Reasonably Possible	Material	Accounting	Strong Procedures for Shipping and Receiving	Tested by Internal Audit		
Financial Reporting	Holding Books Open	Reasonably Possible	Material	Accounting	Established Consolidation Processes	Tested by Internal Audit		
Financial Reporting	Late Shipments	Reasonably Possible	Significant	Shipping Dept.	Daily Reconciliation of Shipping Logs to Sales	Tested by Management	Risk of Management Override	Disaggregated Sales Analysis
Financial Reporting	Side Letter Agreements	Probable	Material	Sales Personnel	Annual Training of Sales and Finance Personnel	Tested by Management	Risk of Management Override	
Financial Reporting	Inappropriate Journal Entries	Reasonably Possible	Material	Accounting	G/L System Access Controls	Tested by IT Audit	N/A	
Financial Reporting	Early Delivery of Products	Reasonably Possible	Significant	Sales and Shipping	Systematic Matching of Sales Orders to Shipping Documents	Tested by Management	Mitigated by Controls	

EXHIBIT 21.4   Fraud Risk Assessment Framework Example

- **Fraud risk.** Potential fraud schemes have been identified.
- **Likelihood.** Audit and management should do a best guess here.
- **Significance to the enterprise.** Quantitative and qualitative factors should be considered here.
- **People or department subject to fraud risk.** An assessment of which people or departments inside or outside are subject to the risk.
- **Existing antifraud controls.** All significant controls covering the area of concern should be mapped.
- **Effectiveness of controls.** This is an assessment by management as to whether the antifraud controls are operating effectively.
- **Residual risks.** An assessment of whether fraud risks are mitigated adequately by established controls.
- **Fraud risk responses.** This should be an assessment of the need to implement additional controls, establishing proactive fraud auditing procedures, or reducing risk by exiting the activity.

This type of schedule will be a challenging document for IT audit as well as management teams to prepare for the first time, given the amount of review and discussion and approval necessary to complete it. However, once developed and reviewed by appropriate persons, the schedule should be updated at least quarterly and used to develop fraud prevention strategies.

IT AUDIT FRAUD INVESTIGATIONS

In addition to helping to build and review controls to prevent and detect IT systems–related fraud, IT auditors sometimes may become involved in fraud investigations in conjunction with the overall internal audit function and through the chief audit officer. Although appropriate legal authorities should be used here for many fraud investigations, IT audit often can play a key role in other, less important matters in conjunction with financial and operational internal auditors. IT auditors generally should not aspire to be detectives here but can help to gather information for fact-finding discoveries or provide supporting materials for larger matters. IT audit often gets involved in potential fraud-related matters because of some troubling information encountered during a systems software or IT application audit or an anonymous tip.

When faced with such potential fraud information, IT audit's first step always should be to consult with the enterprise's corporate counsel. Because of the nature of the allegation as well as the extent of initial information, the matter may be turned over to legal authorities, such as the federal district attorney's office or state prosecutors. Legal counsel may suggest that other authorities get involved in the matter at once. In smaller, seemingly less important but very IT-technical matters, IT audit often is asked to take responsibility for the investigation. Often these investigations involve just detailed reviews of key files, transaction registers, or documents. The evidence gathered from those reviews becomes the basis for any further action to be taken.

Fraud-related investigations require an IT auditor to operate rather differently. In any fraud-related review, an auditor should have three major objectives:

1. **Prove the loss.** Fraud-related reviews usually start out with the finding that someone stole something—perhaps a set of proprietary software code. The investigative review led by IT audit should assemble as much relevant material as necessary to determine overall size and scope of the loss.
2. **Establish responsibility and intent.** This is the "Who did it?" step. As much as possible, the audit team should attempt to identify everyone responsible for the matter and if there was any special or different intent associated with the fraud action.
3. **Prove the audit investigative methods used.** The investigative team needs to be able to prove that its fraud-related conclusions were based on a detailed, step-by-step investigative process, not just an uncoordinated witch hunt. The review should be documented using the best IT audit review processes. Of particular importance here, all documents used need to be secured.

Many other procedures are associated with a fraud-related examination of IT systems and software materials. The objective of this book is not to describe the overall process of IT-related fraud examinations but to discuss the increased emphasis on fraud detection and prevention as outlined by newer standards, particularly the AICPA SAS No. 99 and the AICPA, IIA, ACFE fraud management publications. IT auditors interested in learning more about fraud investigations should explore the publications of the ACFE at www.acfe .com. This professional organization has a variety of educational and guidance material and also has an examination-based professional certification.

IT FRAUD PREVENTION PROCESSES

Going beyond improper access attempts or denial of service malicious software, discussed in Chapters 9 and 26, IT-related fraud covers a wide range of issues and concerns. In today's business environment, information systems are virtually always a key component of any modern financial or accounting-related fraud. Because IT systems and processes support so many areas and cross so many lines in an enterprise, we can think of IT-related fraud in multiple dimensions, ranging from minor to significant fraudulent activities:

- **Internet access issues.** Enterprises often establish both guidelines and controls to restrict employee non-business Internet use, but the Web is so pervasive that it is difficult to separate personal from business use. Again, such rules are frequently ignored by employees and sometimes bypassed by software that will allow them to get around firewall barriers. There is always the risk of access violations abuse here, but the enterprise should potentially monitor employee Internet usage through software monitoring tools. Many may wink at such matters, but an enterprise associate should not be spending substantial amounts of workday time browsing the Internet or completing home shopping transactions. A concern here is that an employee can launch a fraudulent business operation using company resources and the Internet.

▪ **Improper personal use of IT resources.** An enterprise should establish rules stating that there should be no personal files or programs on work-supplied systems. Such rules frequently are ignored by employees, who may use word-processing or spreadsheet resources to perform some personal work as part of their business-related work they may take home evenings. An enterprise should emphasize to employees that they should not be doing personal business while at the workplace. In addition to introducing viruses or other harmful software to enterprise systems, perhaps even greater than the risk of fraud here is the possibility of an employee selling key proprietary software code to a competitor or someone who could benefit from that code.

▪ **Illegal use of software.** Employees sometimes attempt to steal/download copies of company software or install their own software on enterprise computer resources. In doing so, they are violating enterprise rules and often putting their employers in violation of software license agreements. In addition, they may be introducing viruses into enterprise systems. Although an enterprise should have systems firewalls installed to protect it from such improper software, there is always the risk of such malignant software slipping through.

▪ **Computer security and confidentiality fraud matters.** Employees can violate password protections and gain improper access to computer systems and files. Even if they are only trying to "see if it works," they are performing a fraudulent act by violating computer security rules.

▪ **Information theft through USB[6] devices or other data abuse computer fraud.** Today, storage devices about the size of an auto ignition key can be plugged into a computer system and used to download multiple gigabytes of recorded information. These simple storage management devices can present an enterprise with a significant risk of theft or loss of data, such as customer records. It is one thing to improperly access a computer system by violating password controls and another to improperly view, modify, or copy data or files. These matters can be a significant cause of IT-related fraudulent activities and computer crime.

▪ **Embezzlement or unauthorized electronic fund transfers.** Stealing money or other resources through improper or unauthorized transactions is the most significant cause of IT systems and network fraud. Whether a perpetrator initiates a transaction to send an accounts payable check to the home address or facilitates a major bank transfer, this can be a major area for computer crime.

These examples run the gamut from what might be considered fairly minor to significant IT fraud-related abuses. We mention the minor items to point out the range of items that can be considered computer fraud. If an employee is given a laptop computer for work and told it is only for business use, and then that employee uses that same laptop to write a book report as part of his or her child's homework, does this activity represent computer crime or fraud? The answer here is really yes, per the established rules. If the enterprise had set up rules, they were done for good reason and employees should not violate them. However, should IT audit launch a review to discover violations in this area? Probably not; there are more important high-risk areas on which to spend limited time and resources. A strong code of conduct and ethics program should be the predominant control procedure here.

This example illustrates that there are many possibilities for computer fraud and abuse. It is a very complex area where strong technical skills are needed to understand tools and methods. This is an area where the rules are changing continually. Individuals with fraudulent intent are finding new ways to violate established automated controls, and skilled professionals are finding ways to detect and prevent this fraudulent activity. Chapters 19 and 20 also discuss IT security and privacy controls in networked environments.

A related computer systems fraud detection area is computer forensics, the detailed examination of computers and their peripheral devices, using computer investigation and analysis techniques to find potential legal evidence in a fraud situation. The idea here is that essentially anything written on a computer file can be recovered, even though it may have been erased or deleted through an operating system command. The evidence required to be found covers a wide range of subjects, such as theft of trade secrets, theft or destruction of intellectual property, fraud, and other civil cases involving wrongful dismissals, breaches of contracts, and discrimination issues.

Recovered computer data often is a gold mine in a fraud investigation. Perpetrators may feel that they have covered their tracks by deleting files, but computer forensics tools often allow full recovery. Forensic examinations involve the examination of computer media, such as CD-ROMs, hard disk drives, backup tapes, and any other media used to store data. The forensic specialist uses specialized software to discover data that resides in a computer system, or can recover deleted/erased, encrypted, or damaged file information and recover passwords, so that documents can be read.

We have used this example of computer forensics as one approach to aid computer fraud investigations. This is an area that requires specialized tools and training; many IT auditors probably will not have the skills to perform such an analysis without obtaining help. As an indicator of interest in this area, the AICPA has just launched a new credential, Certified in Financial Forensics (CFF), that will combine specialized forensic accounting expertise with the core knowledge and skills that make CPAs trusted business advisors. The CFF is a newer CPA specialty certification. In addition, the ISACA Web site contains numerous papers on IT forensics, a good source for more information on the topic.

Other than direct testimony by an eyewitness, documentary materials are usually the most compelling form of evidence, and paper trails traditionally have been a gold mine for IT fraud investigators. In past years, documentary evidence was often limited to paper-based documents where investigators preferred original documents as the best form of evidence. However, documents today are produced on personal computers. Many of these documents are no longer printed and are e-mailed to the recipient directly from the computer. Because of the change in the way information is distributed and/or the way people communicate, copies of computer files are now as good as the original electronic document.

We have used computer forensics here as an example of a technology-based technique for fraud detection. Firewall software to protect a system or user from entering transactions or accessing systems beyond a fixed region is another example.

Virus protection software is a third. A full discussion of the computer fraud aspects of these and other areas is beyond the scope of this book. The IT auditor must realize that computer fraud is a large and complex area.

 ## FRAUD DETECTION AND THE IT AUDITOR

Fraud always has been with us, no matter how well we build strong standards for honesty, through codes of conduct and the like, and build ever stronger controls to prevent fraud. Badly burned by the accounting scandals that led to SOx, the AICPA and external auditors have taken on a major task to better detect fraudulent activities in their financial statement audits. Time will tell how effective the SAS No. 99 rules are, but they call for a new way of thinking when planning and conducting financial statement audits.

IT auditors need to give greater consideration to fraud in their audit work. They always have been involved in some level of fraud investigation work when called on by management, but fraud detection and prevention considerations needs to become a more significant component of every internal audit. Perhaps IT auditors should enter a new technology-based internal audit engagement by asking themselves some questions about where a new auditee might commit a fraudulent act. Similar to the SAS No. 99 guidance, IT auditors should retain a level of skepticism about the potential for fraud in their ongoing work assignments around IT applications and systems.

IT auditors should have a general level of understanding of both the red flags that indicate a possibility of general and IT-related fraud and general IT audit review procedures, which include an investigation for fraud in the course all IT audits. An IT auditor should not begin a new IT audit with the expectation that the auditee is somehow fraudulent or dishonest. Rather, the auditor should understand that fraud can exist at many levels. Where suspicion arises in the course of a review, the IT auditor should report the matter to proper authorities and assist in any fraud investigation, as requested.

 ## NOTES

1. Robert Lenzner, "Bernie Madoff's $50 Billion Ponzi Scheme," *Forbes* magazine, December 12, 2008, www.forbes.com/2008/12/12/madoff-ponzi-hedge-pf-ii-in_rl_1212croesus_inl.html.
2. Ernst & Young, "Corruption of Compliance—10th Global Fraud Survey," 2008, www.ey.com.
3. A Web search will show many definitions for fraud.
4. IIA, AICPA, and ACFE, "Managing the Business Risk of Fraud: A Practical Guide," 2008; downloadable from: http://fvs.aicpa.org/NR/rdonlyres/98BD10EC-CC12-4D14-848D-E5BDB181F4EE/0/managing_business_risk_fraud.pdf.
5. There are numerous Web references to the fraud statute. Wikipedia at http://en.wikipedia.org/wiki/Federal_crime is a good reference.
6. USB is the common abbreviation for Universal Serial Bus, an external bus standard that supports data transfer rates of 12 megabytes per second. A USB port can be used to connect peripheral devices, such as mice, modems, and keyboards.

CHAPTER TWENTY-TWO

Identity and Access Management

IDENTITY AND ACCESS MANAGEMENT are information technology (IT)–related processes for managing who has access to systems-related information over time. This cross-functional activity involves the creation of distinct identities for individuals and systems as well as the association of system- and application-level accounts to these identities. Some define this concept of identity and access management as little more than establishing controls over IT-access accounts or even controls covering user data storage and retrieval database directories. Each of these definitions is a critical component of any identity management system, but the managing of digital identities is a key concern.

Identity and access management processes are used to initiate, capture, record, and manage user identities and related access permissions to an enterprise's largely IT-based proprietary information. Access management includes a wide range of stakeholders, including financial and operational management, vendors, customers, shop floor machines, and even generic administrative accounts and controllers for electronic badge access. Effective identity and access management processes allow an enterprise to facilitate the administration of its IT user accounts and to implement proper data security controls.

Although some may view identity and access management as just an IT function, this process includes many business units throughout today's IT-centric enterprises. For example, senior management needs to feel comfortable that processes exist for managing access to their enterprise IT resources and that significant risks inherent in the process have been addressed. Similarly, business units need to understand identity and access management control concerns and how to manage them effectively. IT functions also need to understand how strong identity and access management controls can support business processes without exposing the enterprise to undue risks.

From an IT audit perspective, addressing these needs requires a solid understanding of fundamental identity and access management concepts. In addition, IT auditors must be able to obtain information from business and IT management to understand the current state of their enterprise-wide identity and access management processes. Access management strategies can then be developed based on how closely existing processes align with an enterprise's business objectives, risk appetite, and needs.

Because identity and access management touches every part of an enterprise, from accessing facility front doors to retrieving corporate-level banking and financial information, IT auditors and all of internal audit up through the chief audit executive should have be concerned with how their enterprise can control IT identity and access management more effectively and should gain an understanding of the magnitude of identity and access management concerns in their enterprise. Poor or loosely controlled identity and access management processes may lead to regulatory noncompliance issues and an inability to determine whether enterprise data is being misused.

IT audit should understand its enterprise's identity and access management strategies and how those strategies can increase the effectiveness of enterprise access controls. Internal control issues here go beyond just IT operations, and IT audit often can be an effective resource in helping to bridge gaps between IT and user issues and concerns. This chapter introduces identity and access management issues and recommends effective internal controls in today's business and IT environments. Many of the comments in this chapter are similar to professional guidance released by the Institute of Internal Auditors on identity and access management.[1]

 ## IMPORTANCE OF IDENTITY AND ACCESS MANAGEMENT

A major element of the identity management process is the password verification step common when signing on to a business network IT system or logging on to many Web sites. Someone may have signed on to a Web site a long time ago and continues to use that same password going forward. This is a weak identity management link because the original password owner can pass it on to someone else. Doing this represents a particular vulnerability if the password allows access to a wide range of systems and data.

Identity management is more effective when the server operating system deletes passwords perhaps every 30 or 60 days and requires established, regular users to acquire a new password before accessing systems resources again. Since the request to establish a new password is sent only to the originally identified user, this identity management control prevents unauthorized persons from regularly accessing systems resources using a stolen or borrowed password.

Each of these classic access control processes can be breached easily by unauthorized persons. Although that may not be of great concern when an improper access is a Web subscription to an online newspaper (where the only the risk is unauthorized persons reading the publication), there is a much greater risk with improper access to other IT resources. For years, enterprises have faced the complex problem of managing identities and credentials for their technology resources. What was once a simple issue that was confined within the walls of the IT data server center has become a growing and complex problem.

Many larger enterprises face a challenge in effectively managing the identity and access permissions granted to their users in today's Web-based and distributed IT environments. Over recent years, IT departments have built system administration groups, as discussed in Chapters 7 and 8, to manage the multitude of servers, databases, and desktop systems in today's IT enterprises. However, even with strong system infrastructure processes and controls in place, managing access to the enterprise's resources remains a challenge.

IT auditors need to recognize that effective identity and access management controls are important enterprise processes and somewhat beyond the security risks and threats discussed in Chapters 19 through 21. IT auditors should have a good understanding of these issues and apply them in many IT general and application control reviews.

IDENTITY MANAGEMENT PROCESSES

Exhibit 22.1 shows the steps in identity and access management processes, starting with some entity submitting a request to approving and then granting access. Although these steps are performed through a series of separate and even manual procedures, they will operate most effectively as a system of linked automated processes. The idea here is that the entity requesting access rights may be an individual system user, a group or category of users, or another automated system.

The details may vary depending on the enterprise and its IT operations, but effective identify and access management processes should be in place to initiate, modify, track, record, and terminate the specific identifiers associated with each IT access account, whether human or nonhuman. An enterprise, then, should use its identity and access management processes to manage these identifiers and their respective association with user accounts. IT auditors should look for effective processes here to balance IT security and control objectives with application account user account access needs.

Identity and Access Management Key Concepts

As every IT auditor knows, the world of IT systems and processes is filled with new terminology, some of which is not always clear and understood by many business professionals. The concepts of identity and access management fall in that category. They are IT security terms that go beyond basic systems and programs and cover both business operations and IT security issues.

To start this discussion, the concept of *identity* refers to the element or combination of elements that are used to uniquely describe a person or machine. An identity can be a unique identifier tied to its originator, such as a password or a personal identification (ID) number, or it can be something that is the personal possession of an individual, such as an ID card, security badge, or software token. Identity also can be defined through a fingerprint or retinal pattern. Any or a combination of these elements can define an owner's identity.

Persons use their identity marker to gain access to some entity or IT resource, depending on the rights that the identity was granted. These information access rights

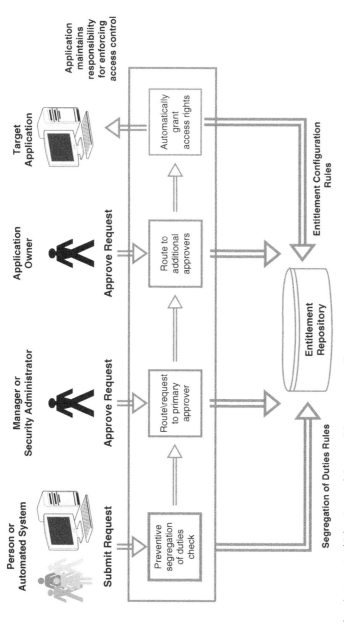

EXHIBIT 22.1 Automated Identity and Access Management Processes

can be granted to allow individuals or systems users to access data or to perform various levels of transactional functions. Transactional functions may include the rights to copy, transfer, add, change, delete, review, approve, or cancel some data element, and access controls set these rules. As a related concept, the term *entitlements* refers to the collection of access rights to perform transactional and other access functions.

Although we typically think of identities in terms of human users, this same concept can be applied to other managed elements, such as service accounts, machine identities, and other nonhuman identifiers. Failure to control any of these identities and the access they have can be detrimental to an enterprise's overall internal control framework.

Two other concepts are important for effective identity management. *Provisioning* refers to the process of an identity's creation, change, termination, validation, approval, propagation, and communication stages. The provisioning process varies in breadth and length of time to complete identity activities based on the specific needs or requirements of the enterprise. This identity management provisioning process should be governed by enterprise-specific policies documented and approved by both the IT functions and appropriate business units.

Identity management processes should be a part of ongoing enterprise-wide activities and should be supported by enterprise-wide identity and access management procedures. These may include the establishment of identity and password parameters, the management of manual or automated identity and access management systems, and the periodic monitoring, auditing, reconciliation, and reporting of identity and access management systems.

The other important identity management concept is enforcement. *Enforcement* refers to the authentication, authorization, and logging of identities as they are used within the enterprise's IT systems. The enforcement of access rights occurs primarily through automated processes or mechanisms.

Identity Management Processes

An IT identity management process should have features to initiate, modify, track, record, and terminate the specific identifiers associated with each IT resources account, whether human or machine automated. This type of process should manage all systems identifiers and their respective associations with user accounts. An identity management process should incorporate user account applications needs and have tools to validate, approve, propagate, and communicate access requests.

Identities take many forms within an enterprise and may include, among other options, any of these:

- Employees who are users of IT resources
- Vendors and subcontractor consultants
- Hardware devices that perform systems functions similar to a user, such as fixed and mobile applications
- Software vendor application service accounts to perform such functions as automatic updates

- IT hardware devices that perform functions within and across IT environments or applications
- Functional or batch accounts processes, such as overnight report backup downloads

Identity management is more than just a user inputting a password to review or update an account. It applies to a wide range of both human and device access connections. As a key element of effective identity management, specific and universally applied identifiers should be associated with each established identity type. That is, different rules should be established for both management and review procedures associated with different types of accounts. For example, a user batch account may be subject to older, manually documented policies and may require a different type of review from today's more typical user online account. Once the need for an identity has been determined, however, the identity rules or definitions have to be created in the IT environment. *Onboarding* is another term associated with identity management. It refers to the manual or automated process used to create these types of identity, which involves the creation of an identity's profile—whether an individual or a machine—and the necessary information required to describe that identity.

A key component of an IT identity management process should be an entitlement repository database as shown in the center bottom of Exhibit 22.1. This is often a log-file mechanism designed to initiate, modify, track, record, and terminate the entitlements or access permissions assigned to user accounts. The idea here is to use software log-file tools to group user accounts by functions, such as workgroups, roles, or profiles and then to manage entitlements for each user. The concept of an entitlement repository database is similar to the configuration management and other databases discussed as part of IT infrastructure management processes in Chapter 7.

When reviewing IT access management processes, IT auditors should look for some form of entitlement management database or repository. In addition, there should be evidence that IT security management conducts periodic reviews of access rights to detect situations where users accumulate entitlements as they move within the enterprise or where users are assigned improper entitlements. To assess the adequacy of these access rights controls, an IT auditor should request reports of IT access rights and discuss potential needed changes with IT department security management.

 ## SEPARATION OF DUTIES IDENTIFY MANAGEMENT CONTROLS

Other chapters have referred to the importance of internal controls over the separation of duties. This classic type of control says, for example, that the person who writes checks should not be same person who approves those checks. This separation-of-duties internal control is also appropriate for identity and access management controls.

During the provisioning process of granting access rights to individual or system requestors, the access request approval process should evaluate whether the request will cause a segregation-of-duties conflict. For example, because of a requestor's job status, that individual should not have the right to update or even read certain files. When establishing or changing a user's identity, the IT security may note a potential segregation-of-duties conflict. In this case, the IT security group should notify the business owner or approver of the potential problem. When possible, this segregation-of-duties analysis can be automated and used as a preventive control through rights tables located in an entitlement repository database.

As part of its access management monitoring process, an enterprise should establish a top-down review process to periodically review the access rights granted to all identities residing in its IT environment. This review should be facilitated by the IT security function but should be conducted primarily by the organization with approvals received from each responsible business owner. IT security can review matters according to rules, but business unit management will have the best knowledge to understand any separation-of-duties issues that may have been granted access rights. In addition, privileged and IT account identities should be reviewed by an appropriate manager or system owner. IT audit can play a major role in facilitating this review process through its IT-security related general controls reviews.

ACCESS MANAGEMENT PROVISIONING

A term not familiar to most IT auditors or operations professionals, *provisioning* refers to the access management process to identify, validate, approve, propagate, and approve IT access requests. Depending on the nature of the access request and the persons being granted access, provisioning requests for the creation, deletion, or changes of system access elements to an identity may be initiated through manual paper-based forms, system or electronic requests, or even calls to a help desk. This process should be formally documented in a procedure that details how requests are to be made for the different types of identities, where the requests need to be routed, and both specific time frames and fulfillment expectations for making requests.

An identity request normally should be part of a multistep approval process, with the initial request approval granted by the requestor's supervisor and approved prior to when the request is submitted to the IT department. Once the first level of approval is granted, a second approval level may be necessary, depending on the nature or criticality of access request, and it should be granted from the application owner. After the appropriate approvals have been secured, the request should be routed to the IT network security function for fulfillment. Once creation of the identity is approved in a manner consistent with enterprise and IT policies, the identity should be set up in the appropriate automated application or process.

The identity and access management process should be somewhat more formal than the common user ID and password request arrangements for employees in many enterprises today. All too often, we assign access rights to employees, in particular, without fully thinking about the nature of the access resources we are giving to the employee. More consideration should be given to the requestor's function within the organization and how the identity will be used. The access granted to the identity owner should be based on roles, rules, or user-specific requestor needs.

The creation of the identity requires an understanding of how it will be used, the software applications it will use, and any schedule restrictions the identity may be subject to or need relief from. The identity also should be created with a corresponding password containing restrictions that are specific to the application and in compliance with enterprise policies.

When granting an identity to a person, many IT departments assign a temporary password that the user must change during the initial login attempt. During an identity management process, the entitlements or access rights assigned to the identity should be evaluated in conjunction with the identity's functional role in the enterprise to determine whether there are conflict-of-interest issues regarding segregation of duties.

Based on a formal policy statement, an enterprise should define how to communicate the creation, deletion, and changes of user identities. Often these identities are best established in a centralized security function, separate from IT, to initiate access management identity communications. In addition, that IT security function should establish a mechanism to receive and send communications related to identity change activities. When communicating about an identity's creation or changes through electronic or even paper records, the IT function should be aware of any data classification restrictions and requirements over identity configuration information. Also, any communications that contain restricted access information need to be handled in a secure manner, such as the use of sealed interoffice mail envelopes or encrypted e-mail messages.

As discussed, an entitlement repository is a system or database that tracks the privileges granted to users over time and records access requests, approvals, start and end dates, and details related to the specific access being granted. IT auditors can request access to such a repository system when reviewing access activities, performing user entitlement reviews, and determining whether access activities were approved. This logging-generated entitlement data should be maintained with the retention period based on the nature of the access being logged, any regulatory and audit requirements, corporate policies, and data storage constraints.

AUTHENTICATION AND AUTHORIZATION

Effective access management requires a strong enforcement of identities with their corresponding access rights occurs during the user's login to an application or process. During this login, the target application should perform a check to validate or authenticate the user's identity. This authentication process can require several different forms. Systems can require authentication by using something the user knows, such as a password; something the user has, such as a smart card or badge; or a specific user characteristic, such as a fingerprint.

Once the identity is recognized and validated, the target application should authorize the user to perform functions in the application based on the access rights associated with the user's identity. Authorization of the user identity should be based on the access rights granted during the provisioning process. Sometimes the authentication of a user's identity may not correlate with the access rights that were intended to be granted to the user during the provisioning process. As a result, monitoring and verification of access rights are important parts of the identity and access management process. Exhibit 22.2 illustrates this authentication and authorization process.

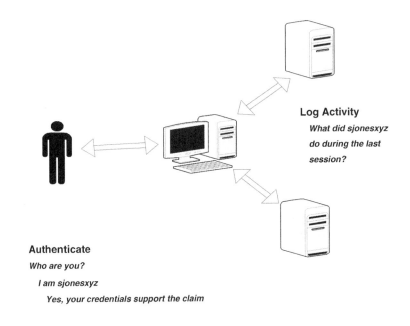

Log Activity

What did sjonesxyz
do during the last
session?

Authenticate

Who are you?

I am sjonesxyz

Yes, your credentials support the claim

Authorize

What can sjonesxyz
do on this system?
Sjonesxyz is authorized
to perform the following
system functions . . .

EXHIBIT 22.2 Access Management Authentication and Authorization Process

Logging user identities, their access rights, and the functions they perform is an important part of identity and access management. These user identities provide a means to examine whether user access rights are in compliance with the rights approved for the user identity. Also, logging controls help to identify situations where user identities and their access rights are misaligned with the access rights necessary for a user identity to perform its functional responsibilities and situations where user identities are not performing all of the functions granted to them through the provisioning process.

As part of any identity and access management review, IT auditors should look for an active IT security program of the review and analysis of enterprise entitlement repository logging files. It is not enough just to log activities, with follow-up only to correct problems; the tools must be used to analyze and improve access management processes. Among other matters, this type of logging activity review should include user identities accessing or attempting to access applications outside normal business hours or making what appears to be too-frequent password change requests, or multiple unauthorized attempts to perform certain functions by registered users.

There may be nothing wrong with some of these logged activities, and some may be due to unique user needs. However, an effective identity and access management program ensures that tools are in place to monitor these activities and provides evidence of follow-up to resolve any issues.

 ## AUDITING IDENTITY AND ACCESS MANAGEMENT PROCESSES

IT auditors normally examine elements of many identity and access management processes, such as password controls, as part of their regular reviews of IT general and specific application internal controls. This chapter has outlined identity and access management as a unique and important IT process. However, although those reviews focus on elements of this process, they often do not do not evaluate the entire process. However, IT auditors should look for the presence of and consider examining the IT identity and access management processes that exist within their IT function and overall enterprise.

Before developing an identity management audit approach or assisting with the creation of identity management processes, IT audit should review any existing identity management policies and procedures for adequacy. Following the high-level process flow of Exhibit 22.1, IT audit should look for both IT and business operations processes to identify identities and to check for the adequacy of access management segregation-of-duties controls and other matters. All too often, IT audit finds little more than basic software system function password controls. However, once existing identity and access processes are identified, IT audit can assist management by conducting a risk assessment exercise that looks at existing processes, identifies security access vulnerabilities, and enables the enterprise to develop more effective processes. IT auditors can be valuable internal consultants in developing an effective program here because of their visibility into all levels of the enterprise and their understanding of what areas need to have a better identity management focus.

As part of this review process, IT auditors need to clearly identify and understand the different user identities that can exist within an enterprise. Within each category of users, and in particular across complex enterprise organization structures, several identity groups may have subgroups in a hierarchy that follows functional organization charts. Those units most likely to have multiple subgroups include vendors and machine-based batch accounts with complex or dotted-line responsibility connections.

IT audit also should work with appropriate members of IT security and general management to identify access management life cycle components, including provisioning, administration, and enforcement. To define these components, IT auditors need to understand and assess the established process controls and supporting documentation that relate to access management provisioning process. For example, if some processes are manual, there should be evidence that adequate staff-level administrative access management training is delivered regularly. When processes are automated, feedback generated should identify whether each process is working.

As with any process, it is critical to identify the controls that affect it. Within the identity life cycle process, several key control areas exist that need to be reviewed. Controls can include approval processes for creating identities, access revocation processes, entitlement reviews, and access logging. Before an identity is created, evidence should be in place to demonstrate that someone in the enterprise with proper authority has approved it. For instance, a hiring manager is likely to approve a new employee's access rights, but this same hiring manager also should work with human resources to help establish the person's identity in the system. This process typically includes collecting various pieces of personal information, determining whether the person has worked for the company previously, and eventually creating computer accounts for the person. Each step in this process needs to be reviewed to determine that there are appropriate controls throughout this identity life cycle, since the creation of identities must be controlled to prevent the introduction of unknown users into the environment.

In addition, audit evidence should be in place to demonstrate that when an enterprise needs to deactivate or remove user identities, they are deactivated and are no longer needed. IT auditors should look for procedures and actual evidence that clearly identify what needs to happen when people leave the enterprise. Reviews also need to be conducted to confirm that the appropriate actions took place.

Evaluating Document Entitlement Management

IT audits of access entitlement management processes should start with an assessment of the entitlements documentation that has been granted to users of platforms and applications, and the user's roles within these applications. Auditors should determine how entitlements are grouped together and what permissions users, IT devices, service accounts, machine accounts, and batch accounts have been established. There should be approved, documented procedures in place for this entitlement creation, assignment, and removal.

An IT auditor should recognize that larger identity management programs may have processes for creating new entitlements, grouping them together, and assigning them to either people or roles within the enterprise; smaller enterprises may use little more than paper forms or spreadsheets to request and track access. Regardless of the method used, someone in the enterprise needs to be responsible for approving access and making sure that accesses are granted on the systems or applications. Access approval is a key entitlement management control, and this process needs to be considered carefully, based on the nature of the enterprise.

For example, granting access rights in smaller companies is frequently a straightforward decision, and an auditor can easily understand and assess the control processes. In larger enterprises, however, the same granting of access rights often can be difficult to assess without clear control paths defining the process. Due to the complex reporting and management structure of many enterprises, it may be hard for a designated approver to know the kind of access a person requires to perform a particular job function. An IT auditor should assess whether controls are in place here and that systems are configured only after an appropriate approval is received.

IT auditors also should be aware that entitlement repositories have enforcement mechanisms that need appropriate configurations. That is, many applications are capable of independently managing entitlements, including authentication performance and authorization functions. For example, applications may be connected to a central authentication mechanism, such as a directory, or a central authorization process, such as a portal or Web access management technology. Many business processes depend on these applications and use multiple mechanisms for authentication and authorization enforcement. Regardless of which entitlement mechanism is used, an IT auditor should identify where the entitlement information is stored and how the entitlement information is managed.

An important aspect of reviewing controls for entitlement repositories is whether the audited system contains the appropriate entitlements. An IT auditor should assess whether the contents and organization of the repository accurately reflects the entitlements that are already in place. Often there are discrepancies between what is and what should be; determining where the weaknesses occur may require an IT auditor investigation and discussion with both the IT security function and management. Similar to our discussion regarding identity repository information, all standard systems, databases, and application security standards should be reviewed in IT audit reviews of configuration management databases as discussed in Chapter 7.

The primary function of access management entitlement repository reconciliation is to verify that actual access aligns with approved access, as described. IT auditors should look for documented evidence of processes for this access review and reconciliation. A key issue here is that processes should be in place for repeatable and reliable reconciliations.

Simply reviewing the logical access and stating that it is appropriate is often not enough. Auditors should be aware of the dangers of rubber-stamp reviews, where the person responsible for performing the review initials an approval on the entitlement report with little further analysis. Any review process here should be thought of as a form of identification validation, and the person performing the review should have some knowledge of the person for whom he or she is vouching. This can be accomplished through lower-level managers conducting reviews of their direct reports rather than having more senior individuals review those with whom they rarely interact.

Due to their general knowledge of IT internal controls and enterprise operations, IT auditors can be an important aid to management in reviewing enterprise identity and access management processes. Much of an IT auditor's efforts may involve acting as an internal consultant in assessing and offering advice to help improve this important security area.

Identity and Access Management General Controls Review

The previous sections discussed IT identity and access management processes, an important element of IT security and an overall enterprise internal control. This overall process goes beyond just the password controls over an individual application and calls for strong organization procedures that allow multiple persons and devices to request access to IT resources with facilities to review and approve those requests and then to grant access. Many of the control procedures here can be considered part of overall general controls reviews over IT operations or as specific review steps as part of an applications control review. Based on their risk assessment audit planning, IT audit may want to schedule a specific review over the identity and access management processes.

Exhibit 22.3 contains IT audit procedures for an identity and access management operations and internal controls review. In many respects, such a review should be a combined effort with the enterprise's IT, operational, and financial internal auditors.

1. Review procedures to determine that specific procedures are in place for IT access management activities.
   a. Determine that the access management processes include all significant applications and other IT process areas.
   b. Determine whether access management policies and procedures have been communicated to the appropriate individuals in the enterprise.
   c. When applicable, determine that IT devices are also included in access management processes.
   d. Education and other processes should be in place to communicate access management rules to enterprise staff members.
2. Review and document, for audit purposes, the IT access management process.
   a. Is there a consistent access management process covering all major elements in the enterprise?
   b. Does the enterprise have a documented access management strategy?
   c. Is there a documented identity management process?
   d. Based on a limited review with non-IT personnel, does there appear to be a general understanding of the enterprise access management process?
3. Have the individual elements of the enterprise's access management process been subject to risk analysis, and have all issues from that risk exercise been addressed?
4. When any improper access violations cover regulatory issues, are those regulatory issues being addressed by IT and management?
5. Based on a limited review of systems users, does the access management process for issues related to segregation of duties and do these processes appear to be documented and understood?
   a. Define how segregation-of-duty conflicts identified within access management processes are resolved.
   b. Are there mechanisms in place to capture or identify segregation-of-duties conflicts before access is granted?
6. Based on a review of processes and discussions with IT security management, can access management processes demonstrate that only appropriate people have access to protected IT information?
   a. How often does the enterprise review the accesses granted to its users?
   b. When access reviews are performed, how is inappropriate access identified, logged, and addressed?
7. Are there appropriate controls in place to prevent people from adding access to systems and applications outside the approved process?
   a. Assess the appropriateness of any "super-user" rights that may have been granted to permit the ability to add, modify, or delete users from applications in the environment.
   b. Determine whether a periodic review of users traces their access permissions to access request forms.
8. Determine where there are strong controls over the authentication and authorization process and whether the means of authentication presents opportunities for users to circumvent it.
9. Determine whether the IT leadership has a uniform approach, across its applications, to enforce access.
   a. Are passwords synchronized among the applications used in the organization?
   b. How are synchronization mechanisms managed, if they are used at all?
   c. Without synchronization, what mechanisms are in place to prevent users from accessing applications to which they are not granted access?
10. Determine whether there is an appropriate entitlement repository facility in place, and define what types of events are logged, where they are captured, and how frequently they are reviewed.
    a. For the event logs used, determine when and how they are reviewed.
    b. When logs are reviewed and discrepancies are discovered, how are these items resolved?

EXHIBIT 22.3   IT Audit Program for Review of Identity and Access Management Processes

Many aspects of these reviews go beyond IT application rights and control procedures in operational areas, and include segregation-of-duties issues and cover requestor identity management and access entitlement processes.

As we move to applications based more on Internet services and ever-widening nets of Internet connectivity, IT auditors should be aware of the importance of good identity and access management internal control procedures. This area does not include some of the more technical IT security issues discussed in Chapters 19 and 20, but it is important to overall enterprise internal controls.

NOTE

1. Institute of Internal Auditors, *Identity and Access Management*, Global Technology Audit Guide (GTAG) series, www.theiia.org/technology.

CHAPTER TWENTY-THREE

Establishing Effective IT Disaster Recovery Processes

V IRTUALLY NO ENTERPRISES TODAY would be able to function without full access to their information technology (IT) systems and the supporting communication networks, data repositories, and overall IT infrastructure. However, those same IT systems could be subject to any of a wide range of failures, and the enterprise needs to have facilities and resources in place to recover and restore IT operations in a prompt and orderly manner. Going back to IT's earlier days, these recovery procedures were known as IT disaster recovery planning, processes to support the recovery of computer systems, applications, and data files.

Over time, IT auditors and other business professionals have come to realize that an enterprise will need to do more than just restore its computer systems operations when faced with some disaster-related event, such as a fire or flood in a main operations facility. There is always a need to restore and get all business operations restored and functioning; this is generally known as business continuity planning and will be discussed in Chapter 25. This chapter emphasizes the IT aspects of recovery planning, what IT auditors call IT disaster recovery planning.

With a focus on computer servers, storage devices, and other IT resources, enterprises should have effective IT disaster recovery procedures in place for keeping backup versions of older files in secure locations along with processes for restoring those backup data files. While earlier backup processes were often based on fairly simple systems configurations, today's larger-scale integrated systems have made backup and recovery much more complex. In years past, IT audit often reviewed these procedures and found them weak and lacking adequate testing. However, despite frequent comments in IT audit reports, this issue often does not receive sufficient high level management and audit committee attention.

September 11, 2001, frequently referred to as 9/11 in the U.S., was a major disaster event that has changed much of our thinking on IT disaster recovery concepts. Two terrorist-led airliners crashed into the two 100+ story New York World Trade Center towers, among other targets, causing those buildings to collapse. In addition to a massive loss of life and property, these events triggered the activation of a series of enterprise IT disaster recovery plans. The World Trade Center was populated with a large number of IT systems-based financial institutions, most with what were thought to have adequate IT disaster recovery plans in place, but many of those disaster recovery plans were later found to be wanting. In the immediate aftermath of the 9/11 terrorist event, telephone lines were clogged, bridges to get out of Manhattan were closed, and airlines were shut down. Many of the individual IT disaster recovery plans in place just did not work and only a limited number of enterprises had disaster recovery plans that were effective.

This chapter introduces some best practices for effective IT business disaster recovery planning for IT auditors to use when reviewing internal controls in this enterprise-critical area. In past years, IT audit was often one of the few voices in an enterprise raising disaster recovery concerns, and this IT audit role continues an important internal control concern today. In addition, management at all levels generally recognizes the need for effective IT disaster recovery provisions. Along with other groups such as legal and IT security, IT auditors continue to have a key role in reviewing, testing, and evaluating their enterprise's IT disaster recovery and business continuity planning.

This chapter briefly introduces some of the technical tools that improve IT disaster recovery procedures today. While not a deep technical discussion, we will review some tools in place today where an IT auditor should, at least, have a general understanding. For example, this chapter will introduce data mirroring techniques—a process where duplicates of IT application transactions are routed to another site. IT auditors certainly do not need to understand the technical configurations here, but should have enough knowledge to ask some high-level questions about what plans and procedures have been considered.

 ## IT DISASTER AND BUSINESS CONTINUITY PLANNING TODAY

IT audit reports over the years have raised issues on the risks of an enterprise losing a substantial element of its IT resources due to some disaster event. Many of these IT audit concerns go back to earlier days when IT resources were often based on centralized data centers, and when raising IT audit risks by IT audit was often a "hard sell." This author recalls leading an IT audit of disaster recovery planning for a then-major U.S. corporation in the early 1990s where one of its major data centers was located close to a high-traffic airport—with the risk of an airline incident—and where there was no effective recovery plan in place. When IT audit concerns about the lack of an effective IT recovery plan were first raised, the chief information officer (CIO) shrugged it off saying such a disaster could "never happen." In the end, IT audit and this author had to raise these concerns in a meeting with the audit committee to get the corporation to launch such a disaster planning effort.

During the 1980s and early 1990s, a common IT disaster recovery solution was to make arrangements with a remote disaster recovery data processing facility to handle any emergency processing. Key backup files and programs were stored at off-site locations, with plans calling for the IT staff to shift to that alternate facility in the event of a disaster event. Professionals thought of IT disasters primarily in terms of fires, floods, or some other bad weather situation. In those earlier legacy mainframe systems days, enterprises sometimes even took what today sound like rather bizarre actions for developing their IT disaster recovery plans. These included signing "reciprocal agreements" with nearby locations having similar IT resources so that each could move to that other location for processing in the event of an emergency at either. Reciprocal agreements between two CIOs then sounded good in theory, but they have never really worked beyond low-level almost humanitarian help. That nearby reciprocal agreement site might be out of service for the same weather-related disaster or probably would not be interested in someone else running their systems in off-shift time periods. As a final impediment, corporate legal consul would have a dozen reasons to say no to such a reciprocal agreement.

Others established raised floor vacant space at one of their facilities and secured an agreement with their computer system hardware and network providers to quickly move in a replacement system in the event of an emergency. Computer hardware vendors today will still agree to replace equipment in the event of an emergency. In fact, this is easier today as most computer hardware is usually off-the-shelf rather than being largely custom manufactured as was common in the past

Those disaster recovery plans of the 1980s and early 1990s were often not that sound, but a series of specialized disaster recovery vendors soon appeared with fully equipped computer systems sites operating at idle or what are called "hot sites" to serve as an emergency backup facility. In those days of centralized IT facilities, enterprises contracted to use those sites as their disaster recovery facility, ran periodic tests and kept key backup files there. Even though technology changes have caused some challenges to these disaster recovery operations, a limited number of specialized "hot site" backup vendors still provide the primary IT backup solution for some enterprises moving into this twenty-first century.

With our era today of client-server storage virtualization and Web-based applications, as discussed in Chapter 9, an enterprise today faces a new set of risks around its IT assets. There typically is not one major or central computer facility for handling major automated applications but a wide range desktop of devices, servers, and other hardware connected through often very complex communications, storage management networks, and links to the Internet. Enterprises do not have all of their IT resources tied around one or several central data centers, and management is more interested in keeping its IT up and running rather than worry about the risk of losing a central computer systems facility. The concept of IT disaster recovery planning, going back to the 1970s, was based on having processes in place to resume operations if some single disaster made the computer center inoperable. That is not true today, but an enterprise needs to establish business process business continuity when faced with unexpected events.

The language and strategic approaches to IT business continuity and disaster recovery planning has changed today. While we certainly cannot deny that the events of 9/11 represented a major disaster, professionals today more typically think in terms of the importance of a business continuity plan (BCP), the procedures and processes necessary to restore overall business operations as discussed in Chapter 25. While that chapter discusses the need for a BCP, this chapter focuses on a subset of the BCP, the Disaster Recovery Plan (DRP). The user of an on-line order processing system cares less about whether the server is operating but if a customer order, submitted through an Internet site, can be processed properly and efficiently. The application should be restored and operating as quickly and efficiently as possible but the key objective is to support and restore the business processes.

BUILDING AND AUDITING AN IT DISASTER RECOVERY PLAN

While some critical business processes can be recovered without IT, systems resources are needed to support the recovery of most of these processes. Both IT and other senior enterprise management should determine the maximum allowable downtime of its major IT systems that can occur before it becomes an issue that could jeopardize the entire organization, whether it be hours, days, weeks, or more. This allowance estimate is a key component of disaster recovery planning, a key component of IT recovery.

Some enterprises use different terms to include the recovery of IT systems, data, information management systems and processes, and other related systems, but an enterprise should develop a detailed DRP that documents its IT and information management systems recovery strategies. The DRP should cover detailed recovery instructions that may include references to procedures, vendor preferences, system diagrams, and other related recovery materials. These detailed recovery procedures, of course, must be updated when system and business processes change. Examples of the components that may be recovered as part of a DRP include:

- Detailed descriptions of IT systems components, including both IT servers, storage resources and other network connections:
    - A summary of applications and key supporting data needed by the organization
    - Detailed descriptions of the servers and other hardware
    - The communications network, such as telephone, radio, wireless and Internet linkages
    - External, third-party connections
- IT infrastructure components, including logon services, software distribution, and remote access services
- All supporting information management systems, including file rooms and both electric and manual document management systems

The whole idea here is that an enterprise needs to effectively inventory all of its IT components and then develop an understanding of what it needs to accomplish to recover them in the event of an extended emergency outage. For many IT organizations, the existence of a configuration management database (CMDB), as discussed in Chapter 7, will become a good starting point for any IT DRP. The whole idea is that an enterprise needs to have a record of what components they have and what they need to get back in operations in the light of an extended outage.

Whether an IT audit review of general controls over an office server system, a major IT operation, or a desktop spreadsheet application used for office records, IT auditors should always look for the existence of a current and tested DRP. With the strong awareness for some levels of processes in place, IT auditors generally will not be breaking "new ground" when they look for the existence of DRP procedures. However, they may often find them out of date, not tested, or too-often just ineffective.

The following sections describe procedures for IT audit DRP reviews from the perspectives of a centralized IT operation serving multiple units in an enterprise, a single but smaller server level system serving a business unit, and related procedures from several different perspectives. The objective of each of these environments to assure that business continuity processes are in place. Although there is room for that type of assistance, the IT auditor's role in each of these descriptions should be to assess the adequacy of DRP procedures and to make effective recommendations.

No matter the size of the IT environment and the business areas covered, an IT auditor develops a good understanding of the relative risks associated with any potential losses or unexpected interruption in services, the technologies used and employed, and the technical and business nature of the environment. While there is really no "one size fits all" here, an IT auditor should strive to understand the DRP environment and the nature of ongoing testing and evaluation requirements in order to make appropriate IT audit recommendations.

IT Auditor Centralized Data Center Disaster Recovery Plan Reviews

A DRP is an outline of the steps necessary to help an enterprise recover from major service disruptions, whether a fire or serious weather emergency, a computer equipment or network equipment failure, or any other form of major disruption. The goal of a DRP is to help an enterprise reduce the impact of a disaster outage or extended service interruption to an acceptable level and to bring business operations back. The prime emphasis of a DRP is to get all impacted computer systems and data processing operations working while the business continuity plans discussed in Chapter 25 emphasize the needs for continuous operation of a business unit, beyond just its IT resources.

As discussed, while IT operations functions have had DRPs in place for some time, those older approaches were often not that effective in actually getting key business processes operating again. Just as there are key separate steps necessary for planning and for conducting an IT audit, there are some key steps necessary for an effective DRP.

IT auditors will generally find that their enterprise and its IT operations have some kind of DRP in place today. The need for some form of DRP has been built into organization cultures over the years, with strong recommendations for such a plan by their external and internal auditors. Sometimes, those older DRPs are not that strong or current at any future point in time. With their strong understandings of DRP requirements and knowledge of IT resources, IT auditors should review the status of enterprise DRPs as part of their ongoing reviews of IT general controls.

1. Review the existing DRP with the responsible manager.
   1.1. Does the plan appear to be current and up to date?
   1.2. Does the DRP cover all areas of IT operations?
   1.3. Are there open DRP issues to be resolved?
   1.4. Has the DRP been reviewed with key members of management?
   1.5. Has the plan been reviewed with external auditors?
2. Examine the contents and format of the DRP.
   2.1. Based on an understanding of organization operations and IT facilities, does the DRP appear to cover key business processes?
   2.2. Are there adequate levels of business impact analysis and risk assessments as part of the DRP documentation?
   2.3. Does the plan appear to cover appropriate procedures for backups and off-site storage?
   2.4. Does the DRP carry step-by-step outlined procedures for executing it in the event of an emergency?
   2.5. Are call list chains included in the DRP?
   2.6. Does the DRP include key vendor and emergency supply contacts?
   2.7. Does the DRP document contacts for fire, police, and external media?
   2.8. Is there a process in place to provide for regular and automatic updates of the DRP?
3. Review the overall training and understanding of the DRP.
   3.1. Discuss the DRP with several members of the team designated execute the plan to determine their understanding.
   3.2. Do members in IT operations and systems appear to understand their DRP roles and responsibilities?
   3.3. Based on discussions with key persons in critical business process areas, do they appear to have a general understanding of their business recovery roles?
   3.4. Based on an interview with the CFO or designee, assess whether there is adequate understanding of the DRP and how it will operate.
   3.5. Review DRP training records to determine if the training appears to be adequate, timely, and regularly scheduled.
4. Review the results of recent DRP tests.
   4.1. Is there a formal program of testing critical DRP elements?
   4.2. Are testing results documented in a lessons-learned format?
   4.3. Does DRP testing cover both business recovery as well as IT functions?
5. Review of DRP backup procedures.
   5.1. If a remote hot-site vendor is used, review the contract and related documentation for currency.
   5.2. Review the documented results of hot-site tests.
   5.3. Review the adequacy of other backup vendor or location procedures.
6. Prepare IT internal audit documentation assessing the overall adequacy of the organization's DRP.

EXHIBIT 23.1   Internal Audit Disaster Recovery Plan Review Points

As a first step to reviewing DRP procedures, IT audit should gain a detailed understanding of any related existing procedures. Exhibit 23.1 describes some initial IT audit steps to gain an understanding of an enterprise's DRP. The plan should appear to be current, tested on a regular basis, and understood by both IT and general management. Of course, if the enterprise has not established a DRP or if their existing plan seems well out of date or never tested, IT audit will have an audit committee concerns issue.

An effective DRP is critical for an enterprise, and management is responsible for the survivability and sustainability of total operations to serve customers and service recipients. Many companies and most government enterprises are required by law to develop these IT disaster recovery and business continuity plans. In other instances, other legislation effectively requires a DRP. The Sarbanes-Oxley Act (SOx), for example, requires registered enterprises to be able to report their financial results in a timely manner. A systems failure to report results is not an excuse, and an effective DRP will help to support the enterprise here.

DRP Project Management, Risk Analysis, and Business Impact Analysis

We have combined the first three elements of Exhibit 23.1 to one IT audit step. When reviewing the DRP in place for an IT unit, IT auditors will normally not be involved in the very important project management processes to build such a plan. Unless IT audit is involved in a DRP build preimplementation process, similar to approaches used for auditing applications under development and highlighted in Chapter 10, IT audit will generally not be involved in the project management processes for building the DRP, but only to review the completed DRP documentation. An enterprise IT function, often in cooperation with key application owners, will often be involved with launching a project for developing a DRP.

When reviewing an IT DRP, particularly a newly launched one, an IT auditor should ask to see the project plans that were created to build the multiple application DRPs covering major applications. More important, an IT auditor should look for evidence of a risk assessment to determine those applications that will receive full recovery treatment in the DRP.

To clarify things here, the entire configuration of hardware and software should be set up for full recovery in a DRP program. Once restored, all of the IT hardware and software should be operating again in a production manner. However, it may not be necessary to restore all application transactions or processes for some lower risk applications. Business continuity procedures should attempt to capture any active transactions that were in process during a system outage. In an airline reservations system, for example, DRP procedures should be designed to capture all transactions in process throughout the processing cycle. Streaming technologies that allow this are discussed in the section on data mirroring procedures later in this chapter. However, other files and processes may be fairly static and may not recover that immediate of a DRP restoration level. An account validation file that contains valid general ledger (G/L) codes would be an example here. Such files are generally only updated periodically, and if a system failed at 3:00 on Tuesday, it would generally be sufficient to restore the G/L code file from a past update.

Exhibit 23.2 contains a DRP review of IT audit procedures for an IT audit review of a major or centralized data server center review. While there are few common hardware and software configurations today, an IT auditor should look for evidence that IT management has considered business continuity risks on a major application-by-application basis and has built a series of DRPs that cover those key applications. A major sub-set of a centralized facility should be an emergency response plan. These are processes in an almost building "fire drill" mode that allows the IT facility to react

1. Has a BRP been developed, approved, and tested for central or headquarters IT facilities?
2. Develop and document an understanding, from an internal audit perspective, of the enterprise's IT environment, including the identification of application, Web, and database servers as well as networks and Internet connections.
3. Based on an internal audit review, does the existing central DRP cover all supporting server systems and networked facilities?
4. Is the environment multitiered with, for example, an application server linking to another nested operating environment? If so, determine that the existing DRP covers these extended resources.
5. Since a client-server environment typically depends on networked connections provided by communications vendors, has the DRP allowed for the failure of any of those elements?
6. Are virtualization techniques used for storage management facilities? Are clear documentation and procedures in place to readily restore virtualization links in the event of a major disruption?
7. Does the client-server link appropriately with any older legacy applications, and does the existing DRP cover that overall environment?
8. Where elements in the enterprise and the client-server environment are not included in the overall DRP, have provisions been made to include them?
9. Has a risk analysis been performed to identify the most critical applications, data repositories, and business functions?
10. Have interdependencies in the network been identified? For example, what would be the implications of the failure of a remote server in the operating environment?
11. Are backup processes in place for all key elements of the operating environment, and have efforts been established to coordinate those backups?
12. Is there a comprehensive DRP testing program in place covering all critical elements of the systems environment?
13. Does the DRP contain provisions for the potential loss of system elements, such as key server systems, and the ongoing recovery of the IT environment?
14. Does the DRP testing cover business operations as well as IT resources, and has internal audit been involved with observing critical portions of that testing?
15. On a test basis, determine that emergency response plans are in place and have been tested for critical elements of the network.
16. Is there an ongoing, enterprise-wide training program in place to inform all enterprise stakeholders of their DRP risks and responsibilities?

EXHIBIT 23.2 IT Audit Steps for a DRP Client-Server Readiness Review

in the event of an unexpected emergency. Emergency response plans do not promote business continuity. They are last ditch efforts to "abandon ship" in the event of an emergency. Backup files and other procedures should be in place, but an immediate priority should be to preserve the health and safety of the IT personnel located at the centralized IT facility.

Emergency Response Plan Operations

As part of any continuity planning review, IT auditors should attempt to gain assurance that appropriate emergency procedures are in place to respond to and stabilize the situation following an incident or event. In the older days of IT, disaster recovery plans were often published in thick books and located on the desks of a few key enterprise managers. The idea was that in the event of some emergency event, people would pull out their disaster recovery manuals to look up such data as the telephone number of the designated backup site to report the emergency or instructions for other emergency procedures. The material in these books might have worked in theory if the manuals were always kept up to date and the nature of the crisis event allowed time to review the manual first and then react. Many real life events are much more crisis oriented with little time to dig out the disaster recovery manual and read its documented information. When the building is on fire, for example, human nature says that one should get out of the building as soon as possible, not spend time studying the published evacuation instructions. Enterprises need to think through these various possible situations in advance, and IT auditors should review existing published materials with some skepticism.

Enterprises should establish Emergency Response Plans with an emphasis on two significant types of emergency incidents. The first is a fire-in-the-building type of incident where the supporting emergency response plan would include posted fire exits and frequent fire drills. This type of emergency response plan should cover all enterprise operations, including IT resources, and should be regularly tested. A second level of emergency response plan should cover specific individual incidents that may or may not turn out to be significant, but must be corrected at once followed by an investigation and a plan of corrective action to prevent further incidents. These are called emergency *incidents,* and often include such matters as security breaches or the theft of hardware or software. A good emergency incident response plan should be acted on quickly to minimize the effects of any further breaches. It should also be formulated to reduce any negative publicity and to focus attention on quick reaction time. The emergency incident response plan can be separated into four sections:

1. **Immediate Response Activities.** Whether a security breach, a theft of assets, or physical intrusion, resources should be in place to investigate the matter and take immediate corrective action.
2. **Incident Investigation.** All reported matters should be fully investigated to determine the situation that caused the emergency and possible future corrective actions going forward.
3. **Correction or Restoration.** Resources should be available to correct or restore things as necessary. Since emergency incidents can cover a wide variety of areas, these resources may include information systems security specialists, building security managers, or others.
4. **Emergency Incident Reporting.** The entire emergency incident and the actions subsequently taken should be documented along with an analysis of lessons-learned and any further plans for corrective actions.

Emergency incident responses must be decisive and executed quickly. IT auditors should assess established plans, recognizing the need to first act quickly and then only later to build short-term strategies. Quick actions are needed with little room for error. By staging fire-drill like practices and measuring response times, response time speed and accuracy can be improved. Reacting quickly may minimize the impact of resource unavailability and the potential damage caused by any future systems or facility compromises. An enterprise faces many potential emergency incidents or threats beyond a massive 9/11 type of emergency causing the overall failure of IT resources.

While the focus should always be on more major business continuity planning issues, an enterprise needs to have mechanisms in place to respond to every level of unexpected emergency event.

IT auditors should look for appropriate emergency response plans as a component of many IT audit reviews. These plans will exist at a total facility level, such as a fire escape plan, or at an individual level, such as a plan to respond to a security breach. In many areas of the enterprise, auditors should ask if appropriate emergency response plans are in place, are they regularly updated and current, and have been tested.

Client-Server Continuity Planning IT Audit Procedures

A client-server IT environment may contain multiple server systems covering applications, databases, and Web operations. It is characteristic of most enterprises today where there is limited enterprise IT support but where IT systems are critical for ongoing business operations. These are the types of IT applications that support activities such as distribution and billing for a smaller enterprise with an in-house IT staff. These types of critical applications are often installed by an outside provider who gets the key applications with an admonition to establish a DRP. However, all too often, such DRP efforts are never launched or, if they once were published, quickly become out of date and ignored.

The small to medium-sized enterprise that does not have an effective DRP for its IT operations faces a substantial risk. The Web is filled with quotes from various sources that generally predict that a major IT failure at a smaller enterprise that does not have an effective DRP can easily force the enterprise to fail. The IT audit resources in such an enterprise can often serve as major voices in alerting enterprise management to the risk of a key application failure and the need for effective DRP procedures.

The basic steps to build an effective DRP for a small to medium-sized enterprise are essentially the same as building such a plan for a larger enterprise. A key activity is to backup, backup, and backup key files and applications, and IT audit can be a key resource to review existed DRP processes and to make appropriate IT audit recommendations. The small to medium-sized enterprise will often not have arrangements for a formal "hot site" for its emergency backup processing, reasoning that the supporting hardware and software vendors can install replacement facilities in a short span of time.

There are often fewer IT audit resources in smaller system client-server environments. However, as part of their general controls reviews of IT operations or reviews of internal controls surrounding other operations, IT audit should be sensitive to the needs for an effective DRP. Although there are many variations here in terms of the size and business of the enterprise, Exhibit 23.2 is an IT audit readiness checklist for a client-server environment DRP. The idea here is that IT audit should survey and assess DRP readiness and make recommendations for improvements as appropriate.

Continuity Planning for Desktop and Laptop Applications

Technology is constantly increasing the power and capabilities of desktop and laptop applications and systems. USB devices, about the size of the pencil erasers common in an earlier generation, can plug into a laptop computer to provide 8 to 16[1] or more of memory.

Although such devices are very cheap today, their size and capacity was almost unheard of not that many years ago. Similarly, while desktop and laptop devices once had to be connected to larger systems through bulky cable arrangements, the devices today can be connected through wireless arrangements.

Because of this power and flexibility, key managers in many enterprises have built critical files and other information repositories on their personal laptop and desktop devices. While these systems typically do not contain enterprise-level customer business transactions, they are often repositories for other key enterprise documents, such as capital budgeting analyses, new product plans, and key product engineering data. An effective DRP is just as if not more important for these data files than the supporting databases for business applications. These personal systems, particularly the laptop devices that can easily slip into an airline bag and with control often limited to the owner of the system, can raise DRP concerns, and certainly cause potential security risks.

Many IT auditors should be aware of the DRP risks surrounding laptop devices in particular. IT auditors themselves are using laptop audit computers to record the results, store test results, and carry many other audit report-related data. While the IT audit function should have strong procedures regularly requiring IT auditors to back up their work to a centralized location, an incident such as a stolen or damaged audit computer—with appropriate backup resources—can impact IT audit progress and even represent a security breach. Just as an IT audit function should have strong procedures for the backup and retention of work on single desktop and laptop devices, an enterprise should have some strong enterprise-wide backup and DRP procedures for all stakeholders using laptops and other portable devices. Exhibit 23.3 outlines some best practices for effective DRP processes and backup procedures for what were once called desktop and laptop personal computer systems.

---

1. Does the enterprise restrict business data and applications to company-controlled devices?
2. Are inventory records maintained regarding the number of desktop and laptop systems in use, their owners, and the application activities?
3. Are enterprise policies in place restricting or limiting the use of desktop or laptop devices for sensitive data?
4. Has the enterprise-wide DRP considered organization IT risks and resources located on desktop or laptop devices?
5. Are there enterprise-wide procedures in place that require employees to download key files and programs to remote storage devices?
6. Where such backup procedures are in place, are associates following these system download and backup rules? Assess this functionality by reviewing procedures on a test basis.
7. Are there active training programs in place to inform desktop and laptop system users of the risks of data loss?
8. On a test basis, determine whether business operations can be restored from the backup storage files system to replacement systems for continued business operations.
9. Along with desktop and laptop system DRP processes, has proper attention been given to systems security and integrity concerns?
10. Are there processes in place to integrate and coordinate desktop and laptop processes with normal enterprise process resources?

EXHIBIT 23.3 Desktop and Laptop Systems DRP Processes

BUILDING THE IT DISASTER RECOVERY PLAN

Before the days of the Internet and during the era of legacy mainframe computers, IT disaster recovery plans were often out of date almost as soon as they were published and distributed, and focused on just recovering IT-hardware based resources from a disaster event but not on recovering the business and its key operations. Many enterprises today have established some form of disaster recovery plan for good business and internal control reasons, but enterprises that established disaster recovery plans following those old rules probably do not have an effective DRP in place today.

This section outlines steps to build an effective IT DRP for an enterprise. IT auditors can often play a key role in this process with their knowledge of business systems, and the internal control requirements of the Committee of Sponsoring Organizations (COSO) or Control Objectives for Information and related Technology (CobIT) frameworks, as outlined in Chapters 1 and 2. Although the words disaster recovery or DRP are not found specifically in the SOx legislation, the astute audit committee or chief financial officer (CFO) should realize that an enterprise must have an effective DRP in place and working both in order to attest the internal controls are effective as required in SOx Section 404 and to release its financial results in a timely manner.

If an enterprise already has an existing DRP for part or all of its business activities, this DRP may need to be reviewed to determine whether that existing plan can effectively meet projected recovery and business continuity needs—and we have emphasized the business recovery aspect of the plan here. All too often, some enterprises have taken their old style disaster recovery plans and just renamed them with minimal thought to today's business continuity requirements. DRP should be current or have been regularly updated. It should have a detailed section on incident and risk assessment covering all key business activities and include a strategy for recovery of all significant business processes including applications, communications resources, and other IT assets. There should be assignments for Disaster and Business Teams as discussed below. The DRP should contain detailed instructions for the business recovery process including the overall enterprise. Once any existing DRP has been reviewed and an assessment made of its adequacy, the DRP should be enhanced and updated as required.

If no DRP exists or the current version is very much in need of help, a project should be launched to create a new DRP with a designated project manager appointed to lead the effort. This individual should have good leadership qualities, an understanding of business processes, skills with IT security management, and strong project management capabilities. An ideal condidate should perhaps have Project Manager Professional (PMP) credentials,[2] and for some enterprises, the information security officer may possibly be an ideal candidate for this role. In other cases, IT auditors may be requested to act as consultants here. The objectives and deliverables for such a DRP project need to be clearly defined to enable the assigned overall DRP project team to ensure that their work is consistent with original project expectations.

A DRP project's principle objective should be for the development and testing of a well structured and coherent plan that will enable the enterprise to recover normal business operations as quickly and effectively as possible from any unforeseen disaster or emergency which interrupts normal IT services. There should also be sub-objectives to ensure that all employees fully understand their duties in implementing the DRP, that information security policies are adhered to within all planned activities, and that the proposed business continuity arrangements are cost effective. The DRP deliverables should consist of:

- Business risk and impact analysis
- Documented activities necessary to prepare the enterprise for various possible emergencies
- Detailed activities for initially dealing with a disaster event
- Procedures for managing the business recovery processes, including testing plans
- Plans for DRP training at multiple levels in the enterprise
- Procedures for keeping the DRP up to date

Each of these major DRP components is discussed in the following sections. A major objective here is to allow the enterprise to restore business operations as quickly and effectively as possible in light of a disaster event. This is an activity that requires active participation on many levels, and one where IT auditors should understand these processes and should make appropriate recommendations for improving the effectiveness of an enterprise's DRP.

Risks, Business Impact Analysis, and the Impact of Potential Emergencies

The identification and analysis of risks, as part of IT audit planning and discussed in Chapter 4, is an important DRP analysis component. Risk or business impact analysis is a particularly important process for determining what applications and processes to include in the overall DRP. The thinking here is different from the past when recovery analysts and sometimes IT auditors focused too much on the subjective probabilities of some event occurring. That is, there were extensive discussions covering the potential probability of a tornado, an earthquake, or some other catastrophic event at a centralized data center location. Those analyses focused on the loss of an older technology centralized data center but not on the continuity and recovery of today's Internet-based and often wireless applications.

Today's DRP should include a descriptive list of the enterprise's key business areas, typically ranked in order of importance to the business, as well as a brief description of the business process and its main dependencies on systems, communications, personnel, and data. If the enterprise has already prepared an assessment of its key business processes, this can be an excellent time for the DRP team to update that documentation and to evaluate the relative importance of each. It should be emphasized that this is an inventory of *business processes*, not critical application systems. While the two are often one and the same, it is important that they be considered as the key processes necessary to keep the business operating.

A next step here is to look at those key business processes in terms of potential business process outage failure impacts. Exhibit 23.4 shows this type of analysis in an

	Customer Service Failures	Loss of Customers	Loss of Revenue	Penalty Clause Exposures	Possible Litigation	Loss of Key Information
Business Process	<2 hr	< 2 hr	< 2 hr	< 2 hr	< 2 hr	< 2 hr
	2–24 hr	2–24 hr	2–24 hr	2–24 hr	2–24 hr	2–24 hr
	24–48 hr	24–48 hr	24–48 hr	24–48 hr	24–48 hr	24–48 hr
	2–5 days	2–5 days	2 - 5 days	2–5 days	2–5 days	2–5 days
	> 6 days	> 6 days	> 6 days	> 6 days	> 6 days	> 6 days

EXHIBIT 23.4   Business Criticality Risk Analysis Schedule
Note: This schedule is used to analyze risks by key business processes of the impact of various types of failures. For example, what is the relative risk of loss of customers if the process is out less than 2 hours, 2 to 24, etc.?

Excel worksheet. Each separate key business process would be listed in the column on the left with risk of failure factors considered for each key business process such factors as the Customer Service Failures, Loss of Customers, and the like. Within each of these risk factors, the impact or criticality of various levels of outages should be considered. Factors such as a specified application failure of less than two hours that will impact customer services but will cause a minimal Loss of Customers and essentially no risk of exposure to Possible Litigation, could be described on the chart. While monetary values can be added to such a worksheet, this can be equally effective as just a worksheet to highlight key time-based exposures. The concept behind these results in an outages analysis table and the steps necessary to get back in operation are components of what is usually called a Business Impact Analysis (BIA). A newer term in the world of disaster recovery and business continuity planning, BIA is the process of defining the key business process risks that will impact business operations as a result of a loss of services.

The concept behind this type of schedule is to look at all significant enterprise applications or processes and assess their time based failure impacts. For example, under the Financial Liability columns, each key application would be assessed when there might be a financial liability to the enterprise if a given application were down less the two hours or more.

Based on the outage risks, the DRP team should study and document its recovery requirements for their key business processes. This includes business process procedures, automated systems, and hardware plus software requirements. In addition, any existing backup and recovery procedures should be reevaluated. In larger enterprises, DRP-like arrangements are sometimes made by individual business units that may not be consistent with overall enterprise-wide DRP arrangements. Again, the emphasis here should be on recovering business operations, not just on getting the automated systems reloaded and operating again.

Preparing for Possible Contingencies

Once the DRP project team has reviewed key IT systems to support key business processes and assessed related business risks, the next steps should be to minimize the effects of potential emergencies. An objective here is to identify ways of preventing an emergency situation from turning into an even more severe disaster for the enterprise

	Customer Service Impact	Loss of Customers	Additional Recovery due to Outage	Penalty Clause Exposures	Possible Litigation	Loss of Key Information
Business Process	< 2 hr 2–24 hr 24–48 hr 2–5 days > 6 days	< 2 hr 2–24 hr 24–48 hr 2–5 days > 6 days	< 2 hr 2–24 hr 24–48 hr 2–5 days > 6 days	< 2 hr 2–24 hr 24–48 hr 2–5 days > 6 days	< 2 hr 2–24 hr 24–48 hr 2–5 days > 6 days	< 2 hr 2–24 hr 24–48 hr 2–5 days > 6 days

EXHIBIT 23.5   Disaster Recovery Business Failure Impact Analysis Worksheet
For each business process, estimate the impacts of systems failures on various external factors. For example, how long will a particular process be out of service before the enterprise experiences a loss of customers?

due to the lack of preparedness. The DRP project team should focus on activities that are essential to the continued viability of the business and should develop appropriate backup and recovery procedures for the identified critical applications. The complexity and related cost of these backup business continuity procedures will depend on the identified business process restoration needs as outlined in the Exhibit 23.5 BCP business failure impact analysis worksheet.

Enterprises have a variety of options for establishing a disaster recovery backup strategy. Larger enterprises often have the resources to do much of this on their own although many rely on outside vendors to provide backup processing services. An enterprise should generally commit to one or more of the following strategies:

- **Fully Mirrored Recovery Operations.** This approach requires building what is called a fully mirrored duplicate site with linkages between the live site and the back-up, mirrored alternate facility. This requires specialized storage management hardware and software and is almost always the most expensive option. Fully mirrored strategies will provide the greatest level of recovery assurance.
- **Switchable Hot Site Facility.** Here arrangements are made with a vendor who will guarantee to maintain an identical site with communications to enable the transfer of all data processing operations to this hot recovery site within an agreed time period, usually less than one to two hours. Because of the need to keep the equivalent of an exact duplicate site in waiting, the costs here can be almost as high as a fully mirrored arrangement.
- **Traditional Hot Site.** With this strategy, the enterprise will contract with a disaster recovery vendor with a compatible site to enable the switching of IT operations to that site within an agreed time period, usually less than eight hours after notification. This is a very common recovery approach that was very much challenged after 9/11. There were just too many enterprises in distress contacting the same hot site vendors that did not expect so many to have a disaster event simultaneously.
- **Cold Site Facility.** This was a more common approach when disaster recovery sites were viewed as being very expensive and enterprise IT management wanted a better cost-effective solution. This strategy involves establishing emergency site space to allow the enterprise to begin processing as well as a standby arrangement with vendors to deliver minimum hardware configuration. This strategy also goes

back to the days of classic mainframe computers that required air conditioning and water cooling operations that were located under raised floor computer room sites. In theory, those cold sites could be operational within two to three days.

- ▪ **Relocate and Restore.** This is the weakest level of backup strategy. It involves the identification of a suitable location, hardware, and peripherals, and the reinstallation of systems and backed up software and data *after* an emergency has occurred. Some managers have been guilty of advocating this approach where they have just backed up their software and data with no firm plans beyond just making arrangements if something happens. This strategy is inadequate for today's business processes.

- ▪ **No Strategy.** Almost unheard of today, there are still some enterprises that have no backup and restore strategy for their IT operations. This is often an, "I'll get to building my DRP later, I'm too busy right now!" type of approach. This approach carries the highest risk of all, and in the event of a disaster, this strategy usually ends up with the enterprise going out of business. The IT auditor that encounters this situation should emphasize this as a strong business risk warning to the audit committee.

An enterprise DRP must contain appropriate strategy for the backup and recovery of an enterprise's IT and for business continuity. These DRP procedures, especially for key business processes, should be designed to get business operations back in operation per management requirements. While in some instances, a decision to use a hot site strategy will be the major direction for almost all applications, some highly critical process may require full mirroring capabilities. Such a mixed mode of backup strategies can be appropriate if the enterprise decides that full mirroring is only justified for that one highly critical process while the others will rely on an adequate but appropriate hot site strategy.

An enterprise may have a mixed set of backup strategies with some being stronger than others. However, all key processes in an enterprise should have some level of backup and restoration policy that allows the overall business to remain in operation. While not all processes may require full mirroring, for example, all should be part of a consistent, comprehensive approach that will allow the overall business to get back in operation in the event of a serious disruption. The cost of recovery can be a major factor here, and the DRP team should outline cost options and get the application owners to buy-in to an option through appropriate agreements. IT audit, in its periodic reviews of DRP procedures throughout the enterprise, should highlight any discrepancies encountered here.

The DRP should have a high priority objective to provide an adequate level of service to all customers throughout an emergency. Critical customer service activities should be included in the DRP, ordered in a priority sequence with restoration steps outlined in some level of detail. There are business managers who understand customer needs, but they may not necessarily be part of the recovery site DRP team, particularly if it would be operating at a remote hot site. Documentation describing key customers and customer service activities should be essential components of the DRP. The emphasis should be on getting the enterprise back in operation!

No matter what backup strategy is used, key files and documents should always be stored in secure off-site locations. Disaster recovery and business recovery teams should be designated and trained, with periodic tests to assure their ongoing familiarity with processes.

Disaster Recovery: Handling the Emergency

Building a DRP would appear to be a relatively easy process when a team sits in a closed room, brainstorms, talks through, and plots a disaster recovery strategy. It suddenly becomes more difficult when alarm bells ring signifying that an emergency event has occurred. One of the first tasks is to determine to what level the emergency situation requires activation of the full DRP and notification of the emergency response team. This notification should normally be communicated in a pre-agreed call list driven format with members of the disaster recovery team instructed to assemble at a designated off-site location. In addition, management and key employees should be kept informed of developments affecting the DRP activation and its impact on their areas of responsibility. The DRP project team leader would be responsible for this notification activity.

The objective of this DRP phase is to get the enterprise back in operation. This almost always involves contacting the designated alternate processing site, activating communications lines, making arrangements to get the team to that site, and otherwise taking steps to restore operations. Assuming the team is using a hot site vendor, the disaster recovery team should arrive at a backup site, get operating systems versions and key databases loaded, and begin production operations. These steps are often far easier said than done, and it is sometimes a challenge to get communications lines connected and up and running in the new environment. This is processing that must be handled in a tight time frame with the objective of having as many as possible critical business processes restored and operating quickly.

For the DRP and its resultant recovery to be effective, the recovery team must carefully consider and plan for the potentially complex series of activities needed to recover from a serious emergency. A planned approach is likely to result in a more coherent and structured recovery. It is likely that a serious disruptive event will produce unexpected results which may differ in some ways from the predicted outcomes contained within this plan. The recovery team should review any predefined procedures or strategies in the light of the actual situation arising following the emergency event and modify these procedures as appropriate.

Business Continuity Plan Enterprise Training

Extensive DRP processes and published documents are of little value unless the people responsible for executing those DRP processes are regularly trained in their use. While many traditional disaster recovery plans were published in thick books full of data with the idea that team members would look up critical references, e-mail addresses, telephone numbers, and the like after a disaster event, this approach was not very practical in a 9/11 type of disaster where the entire building has suddenly collapsed into dust. Secure, on-line plans will provide some help here, but what is needed is a DRP team familiar with the Emergency Response Plans discussed earlier and trained in the general processes necessary in the event of an extreme emergency. Certain DRP team members must know enough about the plan so they will react almost instinctively in the event of a severe emergency situation.

In order to act without having to flip through a published plan to decide the next step, the DRP project team needs to launch a business continuity planning training program for members of the enterprise on many need-to-know levels with four suggested levels of DRP training:

Level 1 Training: General Management Overview. Training here should be given to a wide range of people, starting even with the audit committee, to outline the overall strategy for recovery in the event of an emergency event and to describe expectations of how the enterprise would operate in a business continuity environment.

Level 2 Training: Key Application Systems Users. Training here should be focused on recovery procedures for critical applications. In many instances, critical applications should function in a business as usual sense except that processing will take place at the alternate hot site. However, some normal resources, such as user help desks, will often not work in the same manner. The training here should be oriented to designated critical applications and how they are planned to operate and should operate in a case analysis mode where users can review DRP processes for their applications and hopefully ask detailed questions or point out areas where corrective action may be needed.

Level 3 Training: IT Operations and Systems Staffs. The IT staff, both in infrastructure operations and systems support, are the persons who usually will be most impacted by a business continuity that requires operations in a recovery mode. Training here should emphasize and reemphasize key elements of the DRP; it should take the format of regular and periodic fire drills. In some instances, this training can be based on actual DRP tests while game-type simulation may be effective in others.

Level 4 Training: DRP Team Members. The team who built and launched the DRP should have the greatest familiarity with established DRP procedures. Nevertheless, their knowledge needs to be refreshed and updated on an ongoing basis.

An effective training program is a final step to building an effective DRP. While IT auditors, as part of their normal assurance level activities, will typically not be leading an enterprise project to build and launch an enterprise DRP, they will often be very involved in its development and practices. In addition, they should include the status of continuity planning in the regular audits of both IT operations and other business areas.

 ## DISASTER RECOVERY PLANNING AND SERVICE LEVEL AGREEMENTS

An enterprise and its IT function cannot just arbitrarily publish and release a DRP for its business processes and application areas. There must be a strong buy-in from the users and application owners as well as their joint assurances of expectations and service delivery. If a senior executive in a specific user department feels that some of his or her business processes must *always* be operational with a full backup capability for significant transactions, that department should negotiate with IT to provide that level of business continuity service and also must recognize the necessary costs of additional hardware and software to provide that capability. In the long ago past days of downloaded tape copies periodically shipped to a remote location, anything close to an immediate backup was only a theoretical concept. A transaction had to be written first in the main system and its database and then copied to a backup facility. There was always a delay, ranging from weekly or daily backup files to almost immediate real-time systems approaches. Newer storage management approaches today, called mirroring, can provide immediate backups. These techniques are described in the following sections. They are very effective but certainly more expensive.

In order to make a DRP work effectively between IT and business units, the DRP team should negotiate their recovery expectations through formal service level agreements (SLAs). An SLA is a contract between the business process owner and the provider of IT services for specified service objectives. SLAs are discussed as part of the ITIL (Information Technology Infrastructure Library) service delivery best practices in Chapter 7 and are fundamental to business continuity activities. IT auditors should be aware of the importance of SLAs and should look for effective SLA implementations. An SLA is an agreement between IT and business operations to define minimum levels of expected computer systems backup and recovery. They are effectively a contract between IT and key user areas to support both normal day-to-day operations as well as the actions to be taken in the event of a serious service disruption. SLAs describe expected and promised levels of business continuity services and are basic building blocks for establishing effective business continuity plans.

While all IT enterprises should establish internal SLAs, they are encountered most frequently with contracts for the services of outside IT providers. For example, an IT services vendor may agree to handle the processing of some application at a rate of x cents per transaction and will also agree to process these transactions within a specified turnaround time. The enterprise pays for these services based on the transaction rate and recognizes adjustments if expected turnaround time standards are missed. Similar SLA arrangements between users of services and information systems should be made within the enterprise, but the internal costs are normally based on internal budget amounts. For a DRP-related SLA, the befitting user business function will specify its backup needs and will accept a periodic budget charge for those information systems and related services. If promised SLA targets are missed, a budget credit would be issued. Even though these SLA debit and credit amounts often are based on internal "funny money" transactions, they can become an important measure of management performance.

Business recovery SLAs are frequently structured to cover most if not all departments or functions in the enterprise. As part of these charges, they are also receiving an information systems function commitment or promise to provide an agreed on level of business continuity services. When a business area has specific needs, special or unique SLAs should be created. IT auditors should be aware of the importance of SLAs when reviewing business continuity planning and the enterprise's DRP. As referenced, Chapter 7 has more information on building and launching SLAs. This is the type of contract that sets appropriate rules and expectations.

NEWER DISASTER RECOVERY PLAN TECHNOLOGIES: DATA MIRRORING TECHNIQUES

IT auditors regularly inquire whether key files are backed up on a regular basis when reviewing general systems or applications controls. However, many system backup procedures to download copies of critical transactions are not effective in today's world of constant streams of real-time transactions. Full file or database backups taken every week, every day, or even every hour along with captured streams of interim transactions are just not effective in our world of constantly updated applications. When a system shuts down because of some emergency, it is necessary to go back to the most recent database backup as a benchmark or starting point and then reprocess all of the transactions that had been submitted after the last backup to the present. However, when the business process is very active, such as for high volume trading or ordering, it is almost impossible to get caught up reprocessing past transactions without shutting down the actual application. An airline ticketing and scheduling system is an example. In order for the enterprise to survive, the system must be operational virtually at all times around the clock and at a high-level availability rate. For an enterprise to state that it is operating and available nearly 100% or 99.99% of available time, it can only be out of operation less than one hour per year. Exhibit 23.6 outlines these high availability percentages, and many modern enterprises seek to assure themselves and their stakeholders that they are nearly 100% available.

Legal and regulatory mandates for business continuity often now make this high availability a top priority, and an enterprise needs to move and copy its data in order to rapidly recover critical business operations in the event of data loss, data corruption, or disaster. There have been many new technology advancements over recent years that allow rapid and frequent backups. A technology known as RAID (Rapid Array of Independent Disks), for example, is often used where data is simultaneously copied to multiple locations on one or more disk files to create redundancy. We encounter RAID at a very basic level on a desktop computer using Microsoft's XP operating systems today where, if there is a power failure or the like, a restored version of disk files is retained. While not much help in a total disk "crash," this technology provides perhaps the most efficient level of backup and recovery for desktop computer systems.

Perhaps the most efficient backup strategy today is through what is called mirroring. Mirroring is just what the name implies. If we set two glass mirrors on the table in front of

Availability	Number of Decimal 9s	Estimated Downtime
99%	Two 9s	87 hours a year
99.9%	Three 9s	8 hours a year
99.99%	Four 9s	52 minutes a year
99.999%	Five 9s	5 minutes a year
99.9999%	Six 9s	Less than 1 minute a year

EXHIBIT 23.6 *High Availability Percentages*

us at 45 degree angles, when looking at them, we will see two images of ourselves at once. Mirroring data achieve the same results. Pressing the enter key for a computer transaction immediately writes it to two more mirrored storage devices. This process involves establishing a "shadow" disk that is updated in parallel with the primary disk, providing a real-time or near real-time copy of the primary disk. Local mirroring provides the first level of data protection with a mirror disk attached to another system at another site, often through an internet connection. In the event of data loss on the primary disk, the data can be retrieved seamlessly from the mirror disk. The process of mirroring distinguished itself during the 9/11 World Trade Center terrorist attack. Systems where mirroring was installed essentially lost no computer systems data when those two buildings were destroyed. Businesses picked up on operations at remote sites as soon as they were able to get to those sites, with essentially no loss of data.

Mirroring is an evolving method for data backup retrieval today, and IT auditors certainly do not need to become "experts" on the application or use of these methods. More important, an IT auditor should be generally aware that such instant are available and can be installed to promote business continuity.

AUDITING BUSINESS CONTINUITY PLANS

IT auditors can and should play an important role in an enterprise's DRP development as well as its testing processes. IT audit might offer its resources to observe and comment on the results of DRP tests, to suggest testing scenarios, or to offer consultative advice on the progress of the DRP development. While IT audit can be part of these DRP processes, they should periodically step back, assert their independence, and schedule periodic audits regarding the adequacy of DRP processes and business recovery procedures in general. Audits should be planned and scheduled as part of IT audit's regular risk assessment and audit planning process.

While IT audit may play the role of observer in the DRP testing process, formal IT audits should be scheduled to periodically assess all aspects of DRP readiness and the adequacy processes in place. IT audit must be careful of the fine line between acting as an internal consultant to the DRP team and auditing their processes, where the audit committee may be the party interested in the overall adequacy of the DRP process for the continuance of the corporation. IT audit's review of enterprise DRP processes should be based on such matters as the adequacy and currency of its DRP documentation, the results of scheduled tests, and a host of other issues. Exhibit 23.7 outlines review points for an IT audit review of enterprise DRP processes. While every enterprise is different, the exhibit points out some general areas that should be considered in an IT audit review of enterprise DRP procedures. These focus on an audit of one self-contained set of resources and processes but can be expanded for a larger, multi-location enterprise.

The establishment of adequate business continuity processes is an important component of an enterprise's internal control as was discussed in Chapters 1 and 2 on COSO, SOx Section 404 internal controls, and the CobiT framework. IT audit should communicate the results of its reviews here with senior enterprise management as well as the audit committee. The results of the DRP audit should be included in the

1. Plan and schedule this review following IT and internal audit's planning risk assessment approaches.
   1.1. Review the results of any past IT audit DRP review, noting audit findings and corrective action plans.
   1.2. Determine the scope of this DRP review: specific business units or enterprise wide.
   1.3. Schedule staff to initiate the internal audit.
2. Review the existing DRP processes with IT, security, and other responsible managers.
   2.1. Does the DRP appear to be current and up to date?
   2.2. Does the DRP cover all areas of the enterprise, including business processes, or just primarily IT operations?
   2.3. If multiple DRPs exist for various business units, do they appear to be consistent in their approach and depth?
   2.4. Are there open DRP issues to be resolved?
   2.5. Has the DRP been reviewed with key members of management, and do they appear to understand their responsibilities under the DRP?
   2.6. Has internal audit's DRP review plan been reviewed with the audit committee?
3. Examine the contents and format of the major DRPs.
   3.1. Based on internal audit's understanding of enterprise operations, does the DRP appear to cover key business processes and their supporting IT tools?
   3.2. Does the DRP documentation contain adequate levels of business impact analyses and risk assessments?
   3.3. Does the plan appear to cover appropriate procedures for backups—such as the use of mirroring—and off-site storage?
   3.4. Does the DRP carry step-by-step outlined procedures for executing it in the event of an emergency?
   3.5. Are call list chains included in the DRP?
   3.6. Does the DRP include key vendor and emergency supply contacts?
   3.7. Does the DRP document contacts for fire, police, and external media?
   3.8. Is there a process in place to provide for regular and automatic updates of the DRP?
4. Review the business and IT service-level agreements (SLAs) covering DRP activities.
   4.1. Determine that the enterprise has established appropriate SLAs covering the DRP.
   4.2. Interview several interested parties to assess that they understand their DRP roles and responsibilities.
5. Review the overall training and understanding of the DRP.
   5.1. Discuss the DRP with several members of the team designated to execute the plan to determine their understanding.
   5.2. Do members in IT operations and systems appear to understand their roles and responsibilities?
   5.3. Based on discussions with key persons in critical business process areas, do they appear to have a general understanding of their business recovery roles?
   5.4. Based on an interview with the CFO or designee, assess whether there is adequate understanding of the DRP and how it will operate.
   5.5. Review DRP training records to determine if the training appears to be adequate, timely, and regularly scheduled.
6. Review the results of recent DRP tests.
   6.1. Is there a formal program of testing critical DRP elements?
   6.2. Are testing results documented in a lessons-learned format?
   6.3. Does DRP testing cover both business recovery as well as IT functions?
7. Review DRP backup procedures.
   7.1. If a remote hot-site vendor is used, review the contract and related documentation for currency.
   7.2. Review the documented results of hot-site tests.
   7.3. Review the adequacy of other backup vendor or location procedures.
8. Prepare internal audit documentation assessing the overall adequacy of the enterprise's DRP.

EXHIBIT 23.7   IT Audit Program for a Disaster Plan Review

internal materials that would be part of the enterprise's SOx Section 404 assessment of internal controls.

DISASTER RECOVERY AND BUSINESS CONTINUITY PLANNING GOING FORWARD

As enterprises become ever more dependent on their automated business systems, procedures to keep those processes in operation in light of some emergency or other disaster have become increasingly important. The enterprise's staff can no longer get by with pulling out their No. 2 pencils and completing old paper forms as backup processes. Our automated systems are tied to complex in-house and Internet cloud-based databases where those old procedures are no longer applicable. Going forward, the 9/11 World Trade Center terrorist event proved that many older business continuity procedures were just not applicable. The mirroring processes discussed in this chapter point to a direction for business continuity planning.

The old "disaster recovery" rules have changed as well. It is no longer sufficient for IT operations to move to a hot site backup location to begin processing and assume the enterprise will soon be back in operations. Processes must focus on restoring business operations in light of an extended interruption in IT services. Business requires the ability to get all of its processes back in operation with minimal delay. IT auditors have an important role here in helping management to implement effective DRP processes and regularly assess their operations and controls. Although there can be many variations and approaches to an effective implementation, all IT auditors should have at least a general knowledge of DRP requirements and how to assess such a process. In today's highly automated world, an understanding of DRP requirements and best practices should be part of an IT auditor's skill set. They are also a key component of the business continuity plans discussed in Chapter 25.

NOTES

1. GB refers to a gigabyte of memory, a unit of computer storage meaning either exactly 1 billion character unit bytes (1000^3, or 10^9) or approximately 1.07 billion bytes (1024^3, or 2^{30}).
2. PMP or Project Management Professional is an examination- and experience-based qualification administered by the Project Management Institute (www.pmi.org).

CHAPTER TWENTY-FOUR

Electronic Archiving and Data Retention

S INCE THE EARLIEST DAYS of information technology (IT) systems and applications, IT auditors have regularly emphasized the importance of saving backup copies of systems and data files to allow for their recovery in the event of an unexpected error or disaster. Although these earlier IT systems often were 100% backed up, IT and businesses faced a challenge in retrieving specific records. Often major or master files were backed up, but there were no copies of supporting transaction or other interface files. System reconstruction was a challenge. However, as a last resort, paper-based records often were available to support specific transactions, allowing enabled laborious data reconstructions.

Today, many enterprises have moved to an almost paperless environment where no paper-based records support specific IT records and transactions. IT systems and business transactions are often initiated by an IT system generating a network and Internet-based transaction to an IT application or a user initiating a transaction through a network terminal or wireless handheld device. However, in order to establish an audit trail of these records, systems should be designed to allow for an easy and efficient retrieval of all transactions, including their electronic records. This information retrieval need is particularly important for IT systems today because, in addition to the need to provide strong transaction audit trails, enterprises often face legal requirements to provide backup archival records.

This chapter discusses the importance of establishing effective records management, electronic data records management, and data retention systems. IT operations and business management is responsible for establishing these systems, but IT auditors should be aware of some best practices for effective records management and electronic data archival controls. IT auditors should perform reviews of these procedures as part of both their general and application controls reviews.

The topics discussed in this chapter are closely related to establishing effective IT disaster recovery and continuity plans, as discussed in Chapter 23, and the business continuity processes outlined in Chapter 25. Whether it is to support and recover from a systems failure or a legal requirement, an enterprise needs to have effective electronic document controls and procedures in place. These controls include strong enterprise-wide document management policies, document classification standards, and effective electronic archiving processes. Because the days of paper-based backup records have all but disappeared, IT auditors should recognize the importance of effective IT electronic records management procedures and should both review and test procedures to help ensure strong document management internal controls.

ELEMENTS OF A SUCCESSFUL ELECTRONIC RECORDS MANAGEMENT PROCESS

Every enterprise function and department uses some kind of documents. Documentation is the virtual infrastructure that supports an organization's processes and management. We use documents for instruction, communication, notification, authorization, and guidance. Within them are defined the requirements for design, manufacture, process control, implementation plans, and regulatory compliance. In the older days of paper-based business documents, many if not most enterprises had procedures, sometime good and often limited, for archiving their key documents. In days past, backup tapes of downloaded IT files and paper records were filed almost haphazardly. Today, there is a need for effective electronic document management processes.

Every enterprise today has a need for good electronic document management practices, but individual enterprises may face some specific requirements. In some cases, legal rules mandate good records management practices; in other situations, good records management will protect an enterprise from litigation risks. For example, a medical services enterprise in the United States faces some very specific records management rules due to the requirements of the U.S. Health Insurance Portability and Accountability Act (HIPPA) as discussed in Chapter 17. A manufacturer of any sort needs to keep detailed records of the components used in its products, testing records, sales details, and a wide variety of other supporting details.

Although a large number of procedural details are necessary, Exhibit 24.1 shows the major elements and activities in an electronic records management process. An enterprise needs start with a set of policies and defined goals for its electronic document management process. This flows into steps to define or create documents consistently and to classify them in a manner that restricts access to those who have an authorized need to know or use them. The next steps in the process are procedures to secure these electronic documents and allow their retrieval when needed. Steps should be in place to preserve electronic documents but to dispose of them periodically due to time or space considerations.

Our electronic records management processes end with procedures for audits of the process, ranging from IT steps to assess its security and integrity to operational audit steps to review it. Electronic document management is more than just an IT process, but IT auditors should be aware of these important processes when reviewing IT general and application controls. The next sections discuss this process in greater detail.

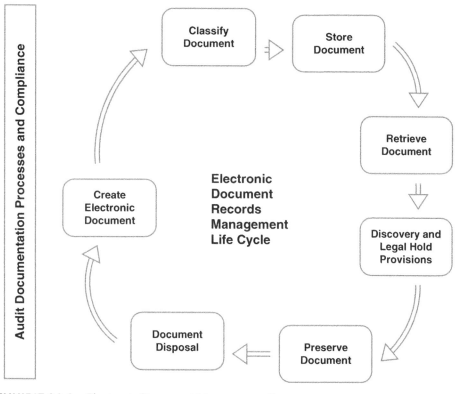

EXHIBIT 24.1 Electronic Document Management Process

Establishing Common Goals, Roles, and Responsibilities

An enterprise today contains multiple electronic documents covering its business activities, whether product-planning documents, sales and other accounting records, or e-mail notes prepared on staff laptops. Records of many of these documents are essential for recording ongoing business activities, such as the contract terms for a vendor supply purchase. Other documents may not be that essential. An example might be a staff sign-up e-mail notice for the annual summer picnic or an individual's friendly note, over the enterprise e-mail system, inviting a fellow employee for lunch.

Technology and the low cost of storage today make retention of many such electronic documents easy. A complete record of all such documents can provide a level of protection in the event of some litigation actions but also can be a smoking gun if the record is subjected to a court-ordered document search.

Business records—both electronic and paper based—were a big issue leading to the passage of the Sarbanes-Oxley Act (SOx), as outlined in Chapter 1. The bankruptcy of the large trading firm, Enron, and its external auditors, Arthur Andersen, in essence launched the events that led to SOx. Business document control was a major issue there. Andersen had had a firm-wide policy to destroy all nonessential records after completing a financial audit. This concept of "nonessential" was not very well defined, and Andersen's auditors at Enron generally retained many documents to support their audit work. However, when the Securities and Exchange Commission indicated it wanted to visit Enron, Andersen's legal counsel issued a hurried directive for its auditors to comply with policy and destroy all such "nonessential" documents.

Just as Enron was slipping into bankruptcy, reporters and observers worldwide were treated to a spectacle of a massive destruction of Andersen's documents supporting its Enron audit work. It was difficult to not suspect criminal evidence destruction as both Enron and then Andersen subsequently failed. Andersen at Enron had had a vague document control policy that evidently no one followed strongly until it was invoked with the pending Enron failure crisis.

Every enterprise needs to establish a strong document—and particularly electronic document—control policy that all stakeholders know and understand. That policy should include:

- Aspects of electronic documents that need to be controlled, including their content, medium, and interrelationship with other electronic and paper-based documents
- Ownership responsibilities for the authorization, protection, and document access rights
- Document ownership responsibilities

Exhibit 24.2 is an example of an electronic document policy for a smaller to midsize example company, Global Computer Products. An enterprise should launch this type of policy for its electronic documents control process. The procedure should be followed with a program of education and training such that all staff members understand their responsibilities here.

An IT auditor should look for similar policies and guidance materials when reviewing overall electronic document management controls. Strong procedures here will guide an IT auditor's review of these very important processes. Although policies can cover a wide variety of areas, they should include document classification procedures, retention storage, and electronic document archive preservation issues. Process procedures should include: aspects of documents that are needed for controls, including their content, medium, and interrelation with other documents; the relationships between electronic documents and business records; and effective processes handling document revisions and deviations.

Data Archival Policies and Document Classification Procedures

Document classification is a practice that should cover all areas of business activity, and it directly affects how an enterprise understands business processes at a very elementary level. It should be fundamental to asset management, risk assessment, and the strategic use of security controls within the IT infrastructure of any enterprise. Without the understanding of different classes of documents and data according to their assessed risk and value, it is very difficult to allocate and maximize resources to ensure continuity of business operations.

For years, military systems worldwide have been using variations of a five-level (unclassified, sensitive but unclassified, confidential, secret, and top secret) classification scheme. This structure often is found in enterprise environments, using classifications such as private, sensitive, critical, and confidential, among others. However, because these words often are not well defined or understood, misinterpretation and confusion can arise.

Electronic Document Security

Global Computer Products

All Global Computer Products Associates are responsible for the security and integrity of all electronic documents that they use or create as part of normal business activities. This policy applies to documents that are the output products of Corporate systems and transmitted to an Associate, electronic documents received from another Corporate partner, and enterprise-related documents prepared on an Associate's personal computer system.

- The same guidelines that have been in place for paper-based documents, such as Restricted Viewing, also apply to all electronic documents.
- Associates are responsible for maintaining the security and integrity of all electronic documents in their possession.
- Electronic documents, either as attachments or copies, should not be shared with others unless an Associate has a strong understanding that they are authorized to review the document.
- Associates are responsible for backing up all of the business-related electronic documents on a regular basis.
- Depending on the nature and criticality of documents, Associates should work with Information Security to ensure that appropriate electronic documents are included in the organization disaster recovery plan.
- Also, depending on their nature and criticality, Associates should establish change management records for all critical documents.
- When electronic document access is restricted to employees only, to managers or above, Associates should report any observed access violations to appropriate members of management or Internal Audit.
- Associates are responsible for deleting or disposing of an obsolete or otherwise older electronic document version in a responsible manner.

EXHIBIT 24.2   Electronic Document Policy Example

To be effective, an enterprise's electronic document classification scheme should clearly describe the association between the data and supporting business processes. This scheme should be used and understood by stakeholders at all levels. Exhibit 24.3 is an example of document classification categories for an enterprise. For example, if an electronic document has been assigned a level of Enterprise Management Restricted, meaning that only senior managers can gain read access to it and members of the originator's department can update it, there should be strict rules prohibiting others from either accessing or updating the document.

Enterprises and IT auditors should look for strong relationships between document owners and effective records management processes. Whenever a new IT application is launched, whether from purchased software or in-house developed, every electronic document that is part of that application should be identified and classified. Some of these identified documents, of course, may be just interim control logs with little need for retention, but many others should have strong classification rules associated with them.

The Control Objectives for Information and related Technology (CobiT) framework discussed in Chapter 2 recommends, in section DS5.8, that "[m]anagement should

Governments have long classified their electronic and paper documents as unclassified (open access to all), restricted, confidential, secret, and top secret. Enterprises need to establish similar schemes based on these guidelines.

- **Enterprise Public.** Documents that are for public consumption. People assume a document without a label is public.
- **Enterprise Nondisclosure Confidential.** Documents that can be viewed only by primarily corporate recipients who have signed a nondisclosure agreement. This classification should be closely linked with IT security controls.
- **Enterprise Employee Confidential.** Documents that should be viewed only by recipients who are full- or part-time employees. Some companies may create separate tags for full-time and part-time staff as well as contractors and other designated stakeholders. This classification should be closely linked with IT security controls.
- **Enterprise Key Employee or Insider Restricted.** For publicly held companies, this category would apply to sensitive information that cannot be disclosed externally or to the general employee community.
- **Enterprise Management Restricted.** Documents that should be viewed only by the senior management of an organization and not the general employee community. There can be multiple levels of restriction here.
- **Enterprise Board Restricted.** For publicly held companies, with electronic board books, this classification designates the board of director community.
- **Enterprise Individual Private.** Documents that include health, financial, or any other personal private information that could identify an individual.
- **Enterprise "Project."** Documents related to strategic alliances or mergers and acquisitions; additional classifications should be created specific to that project. These would be highly secured documents.

EXHIBIT 24.3   Enterprise Document Classification Categories

implement procedures to ensure that all data are classified in terms of sensitivity by a formal and explicit decision by the data owner according to the data classification scheme." Although an IT function usually is not responsible for maintaining different business applications, in many enterprises, it is not clear just who owns the business information system and its electronic records. CobiT control objective DS5.8 goes on to state: "Owners should determine disposition and sharing of data, as well as whether and when programs and files are to be maintained, archived or deleted. Evidence of owner approval and data disposition should be maintained."

Other CobiT control objectives define electronic document controls that should be applied following assessed data sensitivity and criticality levels. Once business data have been properly classified and requirements have been documented, standards and procedures should be built around these requirements and enforced by the use of internal controls. Exhibit 24.4 describes such a data and document classification process. The result here should be the gradual evolution of IT processes toward regulatory compliance and alignment with business strategies.

IT auditors should develop a strong understanding of an enterprise's document classification policies and look for compliance with these policies as part of IT application and general controls reviews. IT auditors should understand the effectiveness of policies in place both for electronic documents and for the entire IT security environment.

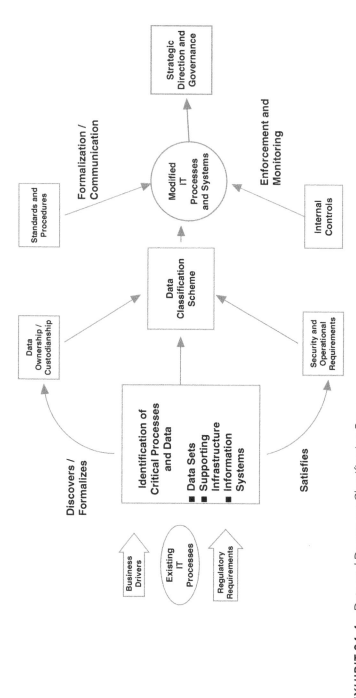

EXHIBIT 24.4 Data and Document Classification Process

Where weaknesses or deficiencies have been identified, formal change request processes should be in place to make necessary corrections.

Electronic Records Documentation Retention, Storage, and Disposition

Some types of archived documents need to be kept for long periods, if not in perpetuity; many other electronic documents have a limited life and do not need to be kept in storage forever. The previously discussed Arthur Andersen destruction of Enron documents resulted in some U.S. SOx rules for documentation retention. Although it had been part of federal tax rules for years, a seven-year document retention requirement became a requirement for SOx-related documents. However, many other electronic documents need to be retained for either shorter or longer periods. An enterprise needs to have a defined electronic document retention and disposition policy as well as secure facilities for document storage.

A document disposition process should be something like the attic or garage spring cleaning process that many homeowners undertake. However, any such exercise should be more than the fetch-and-pitch type of exercise that sometimes occurs. An enterprise should periodically go through a formal document disposition process, covering both electronic and paper documents. When documents are deleted, there should be a clear documentation trail describing the date and reasons for disposal as well as a record of the approving authority for the dispositions.

Back in the days of primarily paper-based documents, records storage was an ongoing issue. Records often occupied valuable office space, incurring space and insurance costs, and were subject to security breaches. Document storage is less of a problem in today's environment of electronic documents and increasingly low-cost storage devices. Key documents should be stored in secure IT system facilities and, most important, should be part of the enterprise's disaster recovery process, as discussed in Chapter 23.

 ## ELECTRONIC DOCUMENTATION STANDARDS

Although many of the electronic documentation discussed in the previous section just call for good common-sense documentation procedures, there also are some formal standards for electronic documentation, both for the United States and worldwide. Just as Chapter 18 discussed the importance of International Standards Organization (ISO) standards for IT security and quality management, there are also standards from the ISO and National Bureau of Standards covering electronic documentation. In the United States, the key professional organization that issues and supports these standards is the Association for Information and Image Management (AIIM, www.aiim.org), which publishes electronic document standards.

As an example, the 2007 AIIM standards development policies and procedures for documents approved by the American National Standards Institute that define document standards for many specialized electronic documents, such as electronic image managing, document photographic images, and optical scanning. Another standard provides guidelines for the design and creation of printed paper forms to be filled out and returned by users and scanned for processing by electronic image management systems.

These document standards promote the interchangeability and quality control of electronic document products, with an objective of eliminating misunderstandings or confusion between manufacturers and users with respect to products for which the standards are adopted.

These are technical standards that an enterprise needs to adopt when doing business in a multi-industry scale. For example, an electronic bill of materials for some specialized product should follow AIIM standards to support the ease of communications. Conversely, the standards can be almost too much for a smaller business with only a limited marketplace and business activities. An IT auditor typically does not have to know the characteristics or details of any of these standards but should realize that such standards exist and that enterprise management should implement them where appropriate.

 ## IMPLEMENTING ELECTRONIC IT DATA ARCHIVING

Electronic records are a means of recording information about some business transaction or decision. They should consist of one or more documents, and associated contextual information, in a form that allows the document information to be used as evidence that will stand up in a court of law. The principal role of electronic document archiving is to store records, potentially even indefinitely, and make them available to those entitled to access them.

There are other important functions necessary to support this role, including defining document disposal schedules, advising the enterprise on record keeping, and establishing consistent polices for the necessary destruction of records. When electronic records are stored in an archive, there are always challenges that these records should be understandable and readable indefinitely, even though the system that created the document that forms part of the record has long since disappeared. A goal of electronic records archiving is to provide a means of finding records pertinent to those who wish to find them and to ensure that the record maintains its evidentiary status (i.e., it can be retrieved in a format that can be understood).

Technology changes rapidly, and it does not take long for electronic document formats to all but disappear technologically. Consider the magnetic tapes that were common storage devices for many years. From the 1970s through the early 1990s, they were in a fairly standard format of a 3/4-inch-wide tape of 12 data tracks. An enterprise that needs to access records stored on such tapes can find services available to read and process data from them. However, some earlier tape drives were based on 1-inch wide tapes or as narrow as 1/2-inch tapes with only 9 tracks. Retrieving data archived in these old formats is almost impossible today. To address these electronic records archiving issues, an enterprise must ensure that the document description language used in its documents is not tied to a particular product or system.

Document Metadata

A useful concept in data archiving, *metadata* is the structured information that describes, explains, locates, or otherwise makes it easier to retrieve, use, or manage an information resource. Metadata refers to data about data—information about information. Metadata often is used in reference to an IT system—or its machine-understandable information. For example, in a library environment, metadata refers to any formal scheme of resource description. It applies to any type of object, digital or nondigital. Traditional library cataloging numbering schemes are a form of metadata.

Various types of textual and nontextual objects are metadata, including published books, electronic documents, archival retrieval tools, art objects, educational and training materials, and scientific data sets. The term can be used to describe a resource for document discovery and identification purposes, such as a document's title, abstract, author, and keywords. It is also a scheme to describe how compound objects are put together, such as pages that are ordered to form chapters. It also provides information to help manage a resource, such as when and how it was created, file type and other technical information, and who can access it.

For many business professionals and IT auditors, metadata can be a difficult and elusive concept. For example, a Google search today for a "metadata definition" returns some 15 different variations. The important concept is that metadata refers to data about data; descriptive tools or notations to better define some sets of data.

Metadata can be embedded in a digital object or stored separately. It is often embedded in the hypertext markup language (HTML), which forms the basis of many Internet documents. Metadata can help organize electronic resources, facilitate interoperability and legacy resource integration, and provide digital identifications, and support archiving and preservation. Although the description is very abstract, Exhibit 24.5 shows the relationship of metadata for individual file records and overall data files. Its shows two separate documents on a data record with metadata defining each document as well as

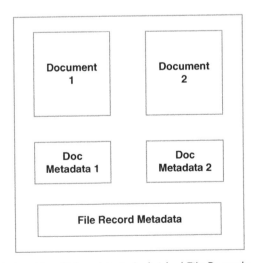

EXHIBIT 24.5 Relationship of Metadata to Individual File Records

metadata for the overall record. Every record in a similar file would have this identifying metadata.

Document Archiving, Metadata, and the IT Auditor

As discussed, *metadata* is one of those abstract terms that sounds impressive but is not well understood. From an IT auditor's perspective, it is important that all archived electronic records are stored along with some form of descriptive references or metadata. Whether it is because of litigation threats, process improvement needs, or just historical interests, there is almost always a need to capture archived data along with some form of attached metadata. The challenge is that data formats and their metadata definitions will often change over time, making retrieval difficult without supporting definitions.

Whether it is current file data records or archives stored on older equipment, IT auditors should always be aware of the importance of records metadata to translate stored information into a form that is understandable in the present. An IT auditor should be skeptical when a business or IT function advises that certain data will be kept in archives in almost perpetuity unless that IT function has retained the metadata and has a plan to continually access the data. Technologies change, and what may be a standard data definition or description today can soon go away. The typical IT auditor has seen many such changes over not too many years.

Whenever an IT auditor reviewing an application is told that certain records are archived for historical purposes, he or she should ask if that information is really needed for such an extended period and then about the types of metadata being retained along with the basic archived records. An IT auditor should understand the concept of metadata and why it is important the electronic document retrievals.

AUDITING ELECTRONIC DOCUMENT RETENTION AND ARCHIVAL PROCESSES

IT auditors should understand their enterprise's established internal control and processing procedures for electronic document archiving and retrieval. Many of the IT audit internal control issues discussed in this chapter should be part of both IT general controls reviews as well reviews of specific applications, and many internal audit steps here are included in audit procedures covered in other chapters. However, Exhibit 24.6 outlines IT audit steps for a general controls review of an enterprise's electronic document records management processes. These steps can form a separate, special review or be embedded in other IT systems reviews.

In our increasingly paperless environment, we need to remember that traditional paper documentation is rapidly going away. That will make many procedures much easier but will introduce some new levels of internal controls risk. Document management here has gone away from the old days of file clerks and today represents some very important internal controls processes for many enterprises.

1. Review existing document classification procedures and determine that appropriate procedures are in place to limit access for both electronic and paper documents, ranging from open access, associates, and up to senior manager–restricted levels.
   a. Determine that document classification procedures are closely linked with IT security processes.
   b. Document that classification rules should be included in both associate training programs and in IT systems development procedures.
2. Select a sample of enterprise-wide and departmental business electronic documents, and determine that they have been properly classified per enterprise procedures and that those classifications appear appropriate.
   a. Determine that a library or some other method exists to catalog and classify electronic documents.
   b. Trace the existing document catalog with electronic documents used in some selected workgroup, such as a departmental marketing function, to determine whether the catalog is current.
3. Review processes in place for creating new electronic documents, and assess whether adequate consideration is given to key components, such as document criticality.
4. Assess whether processes are in place and are being followed for archiving certain key documents.
   a. Determine whether some form of metadata notation is used to attach document format description to critical documents.
   b. Review document archiving rules, and assess whether they appear reasonable, given business operations.
   c. Discuss electronic document-archiving policies with financial management and legal counsel to assess whether procedures appear reasonable.
5. Determine whether critical documents are included as part of the enterprise disaster recovery program.
6. Review electronic document disposition procedures, and assess whether a regular procedure is in place to review and remove excess and obsolete documents.
7. Review procures for placing documents in legal hold, when required, and review the overall security and integrity of those procedures.
8. Based on discussions with legal counsel and senior management, assess whether electronic documentation retention and control procedures appear to keep the enterprise in compliance with document management laws and good operating procedures.
9. Beyond this internal audit review, determine whether procedures exist to review electronic document management compliance on an ongoing basis.
10. Determine whether electronic document management procedures are well documented and appear to be well understood by associates at all levels.

EXHIBIT 24.6   Audit Steps for a Review of Electronic Document Management Processes

CHAPTER TWENTY-FIVE

Business Continuity Management, BS 25999, and ISO 27001

VIRTUALLY ALL ENTERPRISES TODAY have information technology (IT) systems and supporting communication networks, data repositories, and overall IT infrastructure components to maintain their continuing operations. Those same IT resources could be subject to any of a wide range of failures, and the enterprise needs to have facilities and resources in place to recover and restore its operations and IT facilities in a prompt and orderly manner. In IT's earlier days, there was a major emphasis on disaster recovery planning—the recovery of IT computer hardware systems, applications, and data files—but little attention was given to recovering basic business processes. IT disaster recovery continues to be important, and Chapter 23 outlined procedures for establishing effective IT disaster recovery plans. However, effective IT recovery procedures often are of limited value unless an enterprise has strong overall business continuity management (BCM) practices in place.

For many professionals, terminology often presents some ambiguities here. A Web search for either "IT disaster recovery" or "continuity planning" brings up various references for both concepts, ignoring what we feel are significant differences between these two areas. Most of these references focus on IT disaster recovery planning rather than more general BCM processes. As an example of this ambiguity, a professional organization once called the Disaster Recovery Institute is now known as DRII, or officially the Institute for Contingency Management (www.drii.org).

This chapter goes beyond just IT disaster recovery and focuses on BCM best practices for IT auditors when they are first establishing and then reviewing internal controls in this enterprise-critical area. Enterprises of all levels and sizes should establish effective business continuity plans (BCPs) for more than just their IT operations. Enterprise management should recognize the need for effective and tested BCM good practices. In the United States, many federal regulations now contain requirements for effective IT business continuity programs. Along with other groups such as legal and IT security, IT auditors have a key role in reviewing, testing, and evaluating their BCM programs and business continuity planning processes.

A major emphasis of this chapter is an introduction to BS 25999, a British Standards Institute (BSI; www.bsigroup.com) framework for business continuity management that has received worldwide recognition. Although BS 25999 is not yet a full, ISO worldwide standard, it is an important guideline linked to the international standard, ISO27001. Some IT-related International Standards Organization (ISO) international standards are discussed in Chapter 18 and the Information Technology Infrastructure Library (ITIL) best practices introduced in Chapter 7. Going beyond just IT processes, BS 25999 outlines an approach for embedding BCM into an overall enterprise culture with standards to develop a BCM strategy, to implement response procedures, and then to exercise, maintain, and review these BCM processes.

No matter the size of operations or the criticality of its IT resources, every enterprise should have effective BCM plans in place. With its emphasis on people, physical facilities, and other resources, an effective BCM plan requires the participation of a broad spectrum of enterprise managers and others. However, because IT resources are a key BCM component, IT auditors should understand and play a key role in embedding BCM in an enterprise.

IT BUSINESS CONTINUITY MANAGEMENT PLANNING NEEDS TODAY

As highlighted in the Chapter 23 discussion on IT disaster recovery planning, internal audit reports often have raised issues on the risks of an enterprise losing a substantial amount of its IT resources due to some disaster event and the need for IT disaster recovery plans. Many of these internal audit concerns go back to earlier days, when IT systems were based on centralized data centers and there were few connected network resources, such as are found in today's Internet-based environments. In addition, those earlier applications were often operated on a batch basis with data collected on reels of magnetic tapes and even paper-based input transaction documents. For example, an earlier accounts payable application might operate with an accounting staff preparing invoice approval transactions—either as paper documents or as online transactions. This application would then be run perhaps once per week to process payment checks and update accounting transactions.

Effective recovery procedures for such earlier applications required saving periodic backup files and transaction records. If there was a system failure, the IT function would call up files from the last update, and users might be asked to resubmit any missed transactions to reprocess the application. In the days of mainframe computer systems and centralized systems, this IT recovery process was relatively simple. Business continuity attention was focused just on getting computer system resources restarted and key transaction files restored.

Business processes have grown much more complex today with, for example, our use of worldwide Internet-based transaction processing systems, the introduction of cloud computing configurations, and complex enterprise resource planning (ERP) database systems, among others. Although we can restore many IT resources through disaster recovery procedures outlined in Chapter 23 and can capture many lost data transactions through techniques such as data mirroring discussed in Chapter 24, often the restoration of overall business processes has been ignored.

In addition to concerns about restoring operations after a disaster or business continuity event, enterprises today recognize that any form of IT systems downtime can be very costly and are also concerned about the continued and high availability of their IT resources. The Web is filled with estimates of the business cost of IT downtime to an enterprise. For example, in January 2001, the DRI estimated that the average impact of an hour of systems downtime is $89,500 for an airline reservations system or $2.6 million for a credit card authorization provider, among others.[1] eBay's Internet auction site went down for 22 hours in August 1999 causing $4 million in lost fees and a $5 billion drop in eBay's market value.[2] A systems failure interrupts normal business processing, but a disaster that causes the loss of key records can be even more severe. The message here is high systems availability and business continuity are very important to an enterprise, and internal auditors should continually look for areas where they can suggest business continuity planning and IT availability improvements. In a more recent event, Google's e-mail service, used by millions worldwide, crashed and was out of service for two hours in late 2009, causing major disturbances worldwide.[3]

Business continuity planning and effective BCM processes, however, extend beyond IT and involve the recovery, resumption, and maintenance of the entire business operations. The restoration of IT systems and electronic data is important, but recovery of these systems and data is not always enough to restore business operations. There are many aspects to business continuity, but the discussion in this chapter covers business operations with extensive supporting IT operations.

BCM involves the prioritization of business objectives and the critical operations that are essential for recovery. The processes should be structured as an enterprise-wide framework that considers how every critical process, business unit, department, and system will respond to disruptions and which recovery solutions should be implemented. This framework should include a plan for short- and long-term recovery operations. Without enterprise-wide BCM processes that consider all critical elements of the business, an enterprise may not be able to resume customer service and other operations at an acceptable level. Although complete BCM procedures are often lacking in many enterprises today, management also should prioritize business objectives and critical operations that are essential for survival, given that restoration of all business units may not be feasible because of cost, logistics, and other unforeseen circumstances.

An effective BCM should include regular plan updates based on changes in business processes, audit recommendations, and lessons learned from testing. The BS 25999 BCM good practice guidelines explains how to implement such a plan. Changes in business processes include technological advances that allow faster and more efficient processing, thereby reducing acceptable business process recovery periods. In response to competitive and customer demands, many enterprises today are moving toward shorter recovery periods and designing technology recovery solutions into business processes. These technological advances underscore the importance of maintaining a current, enterprise-wide BCM processes.

The next sections describe the BS 25999 BCM good practice guidelines and outlines suggested internal audit activities and procedures in this very key area. Although the implementation of an effective BCM process is an overall management responsibility, auditors should have an important role in helping to implement and test BCM procedures. Their activities on helping to develop IT disaster recovery plans often give management a good perspective on developing effective BCM procedures.

 ## BS 25999 GOOD PRACTICE GUIDELINES

There is an important difference between a business standard and a guideline. When an IT auditor finds that an organization unit is in violation of a published recognized standard, this certainly is a discrepancy to report to the audit committee and management as well as an area where an IT auditor, acting as an internal consultant, can help management make the necessary adjustments to achieve compliance with that standard. Guidelines are different. Recommended best practices cover areas that an enterprise should *try* to achieve, but their management is not required to follow them to the letter. In our IT audit environments, the ITIL best practices discussed in Chapter 7 are an example of best practice guidelines.

Because there can be so many variations in business operations and what any enterprise needs to do to achieve continuity in the event of some unexpected event or catastrophe, it is difficult to prescribe any BCM standards in detail. A set of recognized best practices is usually the most helpful. It points to areas that enterprise management should consider, and if a best practice rule is not adhered to, there should be documented reasons why those they were ignored.

Business continuity guidelines have been developed by various professional organizations, such as the U.S. National Fire Protection Association, by computer vendors, such as HP, and by several national standards organizations. The perhaps best and most recognized business continuity best practice materials have been released by the British Standards Institute and its related Business Continuity Institute, which publishes good practice guidelines tied closely to BS 25999. Exhibit 25.1 is an overview of BS 25999 and the BCM process. It describes BCM as a five-stage life cycle that aims to embed BCM into an enterprise. This chapter will discuss this BCM process in greater detail.

BCM Policy and Program Management

Exhibit 25.1 shows BCM as a circular, continuous life cycle process with its core called BCM Program Management. A first step for launching an effective BCM program is that someone or some function in the enterprise is made responsible for defining and managing the BCM program. Historically, enterprises looked to their IT function and assumed that it would manage these BCM operations because of its responsibility for the IT disaster recovery plan, file backups, and periodic tests of that plan.

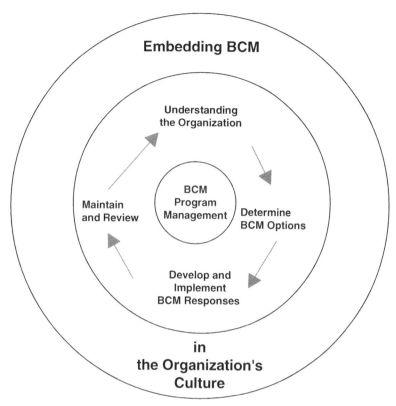

EXHIBIT 25.1 Business Continuity Management Life Cycle

However, often other continuity concern operations and functions go beyond just IT, and other parties in the enterprise may take responsibility for an enterprise-wide BCM program.

For enterprises with an established risk management function, the chief risk officer is often the appropriate person to take the BCM program responsibility. In other situations, the chief information officer can assume overall responsibility here, or the task can be given to the enterprise's quality assurance function. Of course, in smaller enterprises, internal audit working as internal consultants also can take this responsibility. In all cases, the audit committee should review and approve this BCM strategy.

In order to establish an effective BCM process, an enterprise needs to establish a high-level policy to define the scope and objectives of its BCM plans. It is easy for a senior manager to state that an enterprise's BCM plans will cover "everything," but high-level scope restrictions are needed. Even though such broad statements may sound impressive, there may be certain products or services that do not need to be included in any top tier of the BCM plans.

Under the leadership of the person or function given responsibility for BCM, a team should be established to develop a business continuity policy for the enterprise. This business continuity policy development process can include the following steps:

- Review any existing enterprise continuity planning materials, such as IT disaster recovery plans or weather emergency plans to determine the appropriateness of the enterprise's BCM procedures.
- Identify any good practice guidelines, regulations, or legislation that must be included in any BCM plan.
- Perform a high-level BCM risk assessment. That is, identify all key systems, product lines, business units, or other functions that require the highest BCM priorities.
- Develop the BCM policy in draft form, and discuss its assumptions to obtain approval from senior management and the audit committee.
- Publish the approved BCM policy as a high-level guide to launch the overall enterprise BCM program.

The approved BCM should then become a basis for enterprise continuity planning activities. This is a core concept that will allow the enterprise to embed continuity planning into the overall enterprise culture. The BS25999 guidance materials use this approach as beginning steps to launch an effective set of BCM processes. As discussed, this template is very close to the ISO 27001 standard business continuity processes, as well as the Committee of Sponsoring Organizations internal controls framework, discussed in Chapter 1.

Business Organization Understanding, Impact Analysis, and Risk Assessments

The BCM life cycle process, as illustrated in Exhibit 25.1, is circular and continuous. A good first step in this process is for the BCM implementation team to redefine key enterprise processes. This exercise goes beyond just looking at the organization chart and understanding how business units and its components report to one another; there is a need to recognize and understand three key enterprise-specific BCM components:

- **Business impact analysis.** This very important exercise requires the evaluation, over time, of the impact of continuity disruptions to the enterprise's ability to operate.
- **Continuity recovery requirements analysis.** There is a need to estimate the resources, facilities, and external resources that each activity will require to establish a resumption of operations.
- **BCM-related risk assessments.** Looking at the overall picture of enterprise activities, there is a need to estimate the likelihood and impact on specific functions from known threats.

These three activities are not one-time events. Every enterprise is dynamic, and the BCM team needs constantly to monitor and update these important BCM components. Business impact analysis (BIA) is a key starting point here.

An enterprise BIA should be a first step in performing an effective set of BCM processes. An enterprise must thoroughly review and understand its general business operations and drivers and the impact on the business if one or more of these drivers are affected. That is, a management team should step back and look at overall the overall business operations and identify key concerns or events that would impact business operations.

Examples of these BIA drivers to be examined include:

- **Finances.** What are the enterprise's costs if business interruptions occur? A BIA analysis team should consider all scenarios. If critical systems fail, the enterprise will incur costs that, historically, often are underestimated. The BIA team should, as accurately as possible, determine costs for unavailable critical assets such as data, people, and buildings. There are several ways to calculate these downtime costs, and the U.S. government's Federal Emergency Management Agency Web site (www.fema.gov) is a good reference.
- **Contractual obligations.** In the past, when an enterprise's system failed, it could just recover the system and continue. Today, enterprises have business relationships that require partners to communicate electronically, and these partners depend on each other's systems. Because these systems interact as intranet or extranet services, a great deal of exposure results. In many cases, if one system fails, orders will not be processed and contracts will not be fulfilled. The BIA response and recovery analysis should consider this and ensure all involved that the enterprise and its partners are protected from supply chain interruption.
- **Regulatory issues.** Many enterprises are governed or audited by regulatory agencies and/or policies. In the U.S. banking industry, for example, state and federal laws prescribe redundancy behaviors to protect customers. Rules mandate that banks, savings and loans, and others can survive outages and interruptions.[4] They must have adequate backup strategies along with documented and tested procedures that protect data from loss. Of course, the Sarbanes-Oxley Act (SOx) discussed in Chapter 1 calls for continuity management as an important internal control.

These are examples of some issues that should be considered in a BIA. The idea is to go beyond just considering what happens if a basic process fails and to look at the wider implications surrounding any such failure. An effective BIA process should identify the costs linked to failures, such as loss of cash flow, replacement of equipment, salaries paid to catch up with a backlog of work, loss of profits, and so on. A BIA should quantify the importance of business components and suggest appropriate fund allocations for measures to protect them. The possibilities of failures are likely to be assessed in terms of their impacts on safety, finances, marketing, legal compliance, and quality assurance. Where possible, impacts should be expressed monetarily for purposes of comparison. For example, an enterprise may incur a substantial marketing expense in the wake of a disaster to rebuild customer confidence.

Performing an Effective Business Impact Analysis

In order to conduct a BIA, an enterprise team needs to determine and document the impact of all identified disruptions to activities that support key products and services. Exhibit 25.2 shows levels of impact criteria, ranked from 0 to 5, based on financial and reputation significance. These classifications are examples; many other measures can be

Level	Impact	Financial Criteria	Reputation
5	Catastrophic	Over $10 Million	National media coverage or major product withdrawal
4	Intolerable	$5 to $10 Million	Local media coverage and reduced professional reputation
3	Major	$1 to $5 Million	Media coverage in trade publications and customer complaints
2	Significant	$50,000 to $1 Million	Limited coverage in media and some customer complaints
1	Minor	Less than $50,000	Negligible impact on reputation
0	No Impact		

EXHIBIT 25.2   Impact Analysis Criteria

used as well. For each identified area, a designated team should take a hard look at their enterprise activities, involve appropriate people in operations and other functions for analyses, and implement the following six steps to conduct a successful BIA:

1. Identify gross revenue and net profit estimated for each significant business activity. This data will set the upper bound for business losses related to business operations. It will not, however, set the limits for reputation, regulatory, or legal losses that can rise above yearly revenue.
2. Define the critical enterprise business systems, and then link the revenue data from step 1 to these critical systems.
3. Classify each system as business critical, important, or noncritical with an assessment of what would happen if a particular system was not available for periods of over an hour, a day, or a week.
4. Estimate the time-based financial and reputation impacts to recover operations associated with each system using the criteria shown in Exhibit 25.2. Other criteria could be used as well, but the exhibit provides an example of the process.
5. Determine maximum tolerable periods of disruption (MTPDs) for each identified activity. These are management estimates of how much time is required for an interruption to become fully intolerable.
6. Identify the maximum acceptable outage for each system and the time from the detection of the outage to the restoration of operations. For example, if an online bookseller's Web site is down for over a week, it may lose all customers to its competition. However, an overnight outage may result in only a few lost orders. Some real-time financial industry systems may have very low maximum acceptable outage values, where more elongated global supply-chain processes with built-in delays may have outage values that exceed a month.

The result of these data assessments should be collected on a system spreadsheet to form a BIA assessment. A sample spreadsheet is shown in Exhibit 25.3. The first data line in the schedule shows that the finance department has established a two-day MTPD estimate for its accounts receivable functions with no impact if it is out of operation for

Activity Classification			Timeline						
Department	Activity	MTPD	< 1 D	1 Day	2 D	1 Wk	2 Wl	1 Mnth	> 1 Mnth
Finance	Accounts Receivable	2 D	0	1	1	2	4	4	4
Production	Production Scheduling	2 D	1	1	2	2	2	4	4
Finance	Accounts Payable	3 Mnth	0	0	0	0	0	1	1
Finance	Payroll	2 Wk	0	0	0	2	2	3	3
Production	Tooling Line 1	2 D	1	1	2	2	2	3	4
Production	Tooling Line 2	4 D	0	1	1	1	1	2	2
Production	Materials Receiving	4 D	0	0	1	1	2	2	3
Sales	Order Processing	1 D	0	1	1	2	2	3	3
Sales	Credit Controls	2 D	0	1	2	2	3	3	3

EXHIBIT 25.3   Business Impact Analysis Threshold Measurements

less than one day and minor impacts over one or two days. The failure becomes significant for a week and intolerable for all periods greater than one week.

Such a BIA report can be used to request and prioritize resources and incident response activity. If done properly, such a BIA schedule should be in a format that an enterprise chief financial officer and finance department management can understand and include in building overall BCM processes.

Estimating Continuity Requirements

At the same time that the BIA data is being gathered and analyzed, the enterprise should gather and collect continuity requirements. It is often assumed that for a limited period of time, the required resources after a disruption will be a fraction of the numbers used during normal operations. However, in some cases, the requirements in the early stages of a recovery often are higher than with normal operations due to untested backlog resources. Thus, the enterprise should estimate the resources that each activity will require after any resumption to normal operations. These may include:

- Staff resources, including the skills and knowledge requirements of people to resume operations.
- Premises facility requirements.
- Supporting technology and plant equipment needs. This includes IT equipment, manufacturing tools, and other assets necessary to reestablish operations.
- Necessary supporting backup information. Many IT operations today do an excellent job in backing up all data files, but often many paper-based documents or others do not receive this level of backup attention.
- External services and supplies requirements.

Following the continuous BCM approach pictured in Exhibit 25.1, an enterprise needs to regularly review and update this requirements assessment. It should always take into account any extra activity that will be necessary because of the interruption and the need to clear any process backlogs. This continuity requirement analysis and the development of a BIA are the major components in an effective BCM process.

Evaluating Threats through Risk Assessments

The third element in this first component of business continuity management best practice guidelines is the need to evaluate threats through a formal risk assessment. In the context of a BCM process, risk assessment looks at the probability and impact of a variety of specific threats that can cause a business interruption. An enterprise should prioritize these risks to better implement measures to reduce the likelihood or mitigate their impact.

Understanding and implementing effective overall risk management practices are important audit, control, and security areas of concern. Chapter 4 looked at risk management from the overall perspective of the Committee of Sponsoring Organizations (COSO) enterprise risk management (ERM) guidelines, and these concepts are important for implementing effective BCM processes. Chapter 4 also discussed how the enterprise should understand its overall appetite for risks and then should take risk-based actions based on that high-level philosophy. Here the enterprise should focus on its systems and process risks in much more detail. For example, a sales-driven enterprise should perform a BIA to focus on the risks of its sales order entry processes failing. Risk analysis here focuses on the risks of the failure of system or process, such as the order entry systems failing.

As Chapter 4 emphasized, it is often difficult to scope risk analysis activities across the entire enterprise. By focusing on the resources required to operate the enterprise's most critical activities, as defined in the BIA analysis, the goal of risk management can be reduced to a more manageable scope. Nevertheless, even a good, well-organized risk analysis process often has some serious limitations because:

- It is impossible to identify all threats.
- Estimates of the probability of a risk occurring are often of limited value; too often they are based only on guesswork or inaccurate information.
- Although we usually identify risk impacts as high, medium, or low, these assessments usually change over time and at different rates.
- It is often too easy to overemphasize the risk impact of minor events; we should understand the wide spectrum of risks but devote most attention to the major risks.

After completing its BIA analysis and estimating the related continuity requirements, an enterprise should perform a formal risk assessment that identifies the internal and external threats that could cause a disruption in operations. This process requires an assessment of threat probabilities of potential impacts, prioritized according to an agreed formula.

All realistic threats should be identified, but emphasis should be given to those that are easier to control. Staff or facility issues can be prioritized, for example, but it is difficult to make risk estimates where an enterprise is less susceptible, such as bad weather or even earthquakes. This process then requires establishing numerical scales

1. Establish a scoring system for impacts and probabilities.
2. List threats to urgent processes that were determined by the BIA.
3. Estimate the impact the impact on the enterprise to BIA threats using the scoring system.
4. Determine the likelihood or probability of each BIA threat and weigh them per established scoring system.
5. Calculate a relative risk for each identified BIA item and weigh them according to a numerical scoring system.
6. Calculate relative risks for each item by combining the scores for impact and probability for each threat using an agreed formula.
7. Prioritize calculated risk using an approach that includes measures to control these threats.
8. Obtain management approval for these risk priorities.
9. Review any earlier risk management control strategies with an objective to bring all assessments in concurrence with current risk management approaches for the threats.
10. Consider the use of other appropriate risk management strategies, such as:
    a. Transferring risks through increased insurance.
    b. Formally accepting risks where impacts or probabilities are low.
    c. Reducing risks through introduction of other controls.
    d. Avoiding risks through such tactics as removing source or cause of threat.
11. Ensure that planned risk measures do not increase other risks, such as outsourcing an activity that may decrease some risks but increase others.
12. Obtain senior management and audit committee approval for these proposed risk management controls.

EXHIBIT 25.4   Risk Assessment Process Steps

(1, 2, 3, or more detailed) for all events to identify each risk category. Exhibit 25.4 outlines the key steps in the risk assessment process.

As a result of its BIA and these risk assessment rankings, the enterprise should develop loss mitigation approaches that reduce the likelihood and shorten the time of any disruptions. There are a variety of common approaches for assessing probabilities, evaluating solutions, and assessing threats with several of these approaches discussed in Chapter 4. These approaches will not prevent identified risks from occurring but will allow enterprise management to gain a better understanding of the various types of risks it faces.

Determining Continuity Management Choices

The BIA and supporting risk assessment exercises provide an enterprise with a variety of choices for actions going forward. A good next step is to make some item-by-item risk mitigation choices. An enterprise will find many different types of risks here, and one risk management strategy is not appropriate for all. Most of the identified risks can be covered, however, by following one of four basic strategies:

1. **Business continuity.** This risk-by-risk strategy seeks to improve an enterprise's reliance on differing disruptions by ensuring that critical activities continue at some level of service while normal operations are restored. The IT disaster recovery strategies discussed in Chapter 23 are examples of this type of strategy. An enterprise can establish or contract for a hot-site backup facility for its IT operations.

In the event of a failure of principal facilities, it can move key processes to that backup facility.

2. **Acceptance of the risk.** There are always some risks that might be acceptable or for which costs to establish preventive controls might be so high that risk prevention measures cannot be established. A manufacturing facility in another country may face the risk of nationalization due to unstable government polices there. Such a nationalization action may never occur. A best strategy here might be for management just to hope that such an action will never happen and continue business as usual. Of course, in this type of atmosphere, management always should realize that such risks exist and use prudence in ongoing operations in the area.

3. **Risk transfers.** For some risks, the best response may be to transfer them. This might be done through conventional insurance, contractual arrangements, or arranging for a third party to take the risk in another way. In many situations, however, risks cannot be fully transferred. Fire insurance, for example, will largely cover the loss of a plant and its production equipment but will not cover lost business from that plant. Some risk transfers, such as the loss of reputation or of stakeholder value, or a reduction in market share, often are beyond enterprise management's control and are not subjects for risk transfers.

4. **Change, suspension, or terminations.** In some situations, it might be appropriate to change, suspend, or terminate some service, product, activity, function, or process. This option should be considered only when there are no conflicts with the enterprise's compliance rules, high-level objectives, or stakeholder expectations. If the enterprise has been on record for supporting some risk-based initiative, it should not just terminate the initiative without proper explanation.

An important factor in this analysis is the series of MTPD estimates, such as were shown in Exhibit 25.3. Management has determined that it can live without a resumption of services based on these estimates. Internal auditors, in particular, should review these estimates and, where appropriate, ask some hard questions to best determine if management really can live with those estimated tolerable periods of outage.

Risk assessment decisions here complete the first phase of the BS 25999 business continuity good practice guidelines. An enterprise should think of its risks not just as single issues but as part of a broad spectrum of various business and operational risks, first identified in a BIA evaluation, then identified as a critical activity, and then evaluated through specific activity risk assessments. Of course, following the BCM model description in Exhibit 25.1, this is one element of a continuous process that may be subject to refinement and revisions as the enterprise defines and improves its BCM processes.

Developing Effective BCM Strategies

This element of the BCM life cycle model describes processes for understanding the business organization. As result of its BIA and other processes completed in that BCM phase, an enterprise should be in a position to choose appropriate continuity strategies to enable it to meet its BCM objectives. The enterprise should launch a suite of alternative operating processes to use after an interruption to maintain or resume business activities in each key area. Based on assessed risks, these strategies should depend on a range of factors, such as the maximum tolerable period of disruption or MTPD for some critical activity, the cost of implementing a strategy, or the consequences of any inaction.

A significant difference between following the BCM model and older, more traditional approaches is that planners should not think of just one continuity strategy for the enterprise but rather a stream of different activity-level approaches. The complex interdependencies on services, business processes, data, and technologies need to be analyzed with appropriate tactics chosen to address the needs of:

- **People in the enterprise.** An enterprise needs to identify appropriate strategies for maintaining the core skills and knowledge of its people. Many of the needs here cover such areas as documented job descriptions, succession planning, and other practices that should be promoted by a good human resources function. However, BCM strategies always should recognize that key people may not be available to resume an activity at a key point in time, and people-based continuity processes always should be in place.
- **Premises or work site needs.** The enterprise should devise a strategy for reducing the impact of the unavailability of normal work sites. In most cases, doing this involves identifying alternative locations for continuing operations or even a work-from-home strategy for some activities. If some enterprise facilities are involved in heavy manufacturing or chemical processing, however, an alternate site might not be readily available. Other activity-level strategies may include withdrawing from operations in the short term.
- **Supporting technologies.** Enterprises are dependent on their IT facilities, telecommunications network processors, product-testing resources, and a wide range of other devices, based on the product or industry. Although many enterprises have developed strong IT disaster recovery plans, as discussed in Chapter 23, they need to gain a good understanding of their other technology-based activities to develop appropriate BCM strategies.
- **Physical and virtual information.** In addition to IT resources and other technology-based tools, an enterprise has a wide range of information-related activities that are represented in physical or hard-copy as well as virtual or soft-copy formats. Any information required to deliver critical activities should have appropriate confidentiality, integrity, availability, and currency controls.
- **Equipment and supplies.** The enterprise should identify and maintain an inventory of the core supplies and equipment that support critical activities. Activity-based strategies may include the storage of supplies at alternative locations, arrangements with third parties for delivery of supplies, holding certain materials in separate warehouses, or the identification of alternative supply sources. Where critical activities are dependent on specialist supplies, alternative suppliers should be identified or contractual arrangements should be made with existing key suppliers.
- **Stakeholders, partners, and contractors.** The enterprise should develop appropriate strategies to manage relationships with key stakeholders, business or service partners, and contractors. The BCM strategy should consider and protect the interests of these key stakeholders.

> ■ Fires at major facilities
> ■ Major weather disturbances
> ■ Electrical power, telecommunications, or other utility failures
> ■ Computer systems failure
> ■ Business records loss or corruption
> ■ Major frauds
> ■ Terrorist attacks
> ■ Major strikes or civil disturbances
> ■ Legal or unfavorable government actions
> ■ Pandemic health crises

EXHIBIT 25.5   Major Disaster Recovery Threats
Note: This list does not include such very major threats as war, government nationalizations, or major earthquakes.

Developing a business continuity strategy can be a major effort covering all enterprise activities. A good approach is to focus planning on the major types of threats that may impact any unit of an enterprise. Although such a list can be more detailed, Exhibit 25.5 lists some major disaster recovery threats that can impact an enterprise. The overall BCM should consider these threats in relation to the linkages and interconnections among all major enterprise activities. Because of the many interconnections that exist, often there are few freestanding, totally independent activities.

The product of this BCM step will be a set of continuity plans for each activity as well as comprehensive strategy for the enterprise. Such a strategic plan should be detailed and comprehensive. The plan should outline the types of factors and components needed to develop and implement a BCM response plan for a business unit.

This type of a continuity strategy document should normally not be a one-time plan developed by a staff-level team with no input from others. Rather, initial drafts should be circulated to key members of the enterprise with requests for input. Operating personnel looking at such a plan document from their personal perspectives will almost certainly ask some questions and provide useful responses. This strategy plan will be a continuous document, updated and modified as needs dictate. Of course, the general or overall plan should receive senior management and audit committee approval.

Developing and Implementing BCM Response Strategies

This second element of the BCM life cycle covers the development and implementation of appropriate plans and arrangements to ensure the continuity of critical activities and the effective management of any continuity-related incidents. Prior to developing and implementing effective response strategies, an enterprise should identify its critical activities, evaluate threats to those activities, and choose appropriate strategies to reduce the likelihood and impacts of incidents. These first two components of the BCM life cycle should be ready and in place before response strategies are developed.

The aim of the various plans in this component of a BCM process is to identify, in advance, the actions and the resources needed to enable the enterprise to manage interruptions, whatever their cause. The range of threats to be planned for should fall within the enterprise's risk appetite. A concept discussed in Chapter 4, *risk appetite* refers to the amount of risk an enterprise is willing to accept in various situations. If an enterprise is evaluating the risks of property threats to a plant facility, if it has a high appetite for risk and assumes that no one will try to break in, it may simply lock a gate and put up a no trespassing sign. The enterprise is willing to accept the risk that someone could break in. A low appetite says an enterprise is concerned about the risk of break-ins, and it might only install an on-duty guard to protect the perimeter.

Incident Response Structures

There is a need to define an incident response structure that will enable effective responses and recovery from disruptions. Although an enterprise may face a wide variety and range of potential incidents, a team should be in place to respond to any such events. Certainly one group of professionals should not be expected to respond to all incidents. A weather-related event at a distribution facility, the failure of a major telecommunications facility, or an unexpected government regulatory action are all incidents, and appropriate teams should be in place to respond to each.

Although the type and nature of incidents will vary, the designated recovery teams should follow an incident timeline structure as shown in Exhibit 25.6. Within minutes to hours of some incident, a designated team should be prepared to assess damages and invoke an established BCP plan for that area. Once the plan goes into action, the objective should be to recover and resume operations back to a "normal" state as quickly as possible.

Incident Management Plans

For each major activity area, the enterprise should develop a series of incident response plans covering major anticipated events in that area. The idea is not to develop *specific* emergency response plans but to classify the major types of incidents that may impact various areas of operations. These plans should focus on people-related activities, stakeholder management, and media communications.

People-related activities are particularly important here. Incident management plans should satisfy the interests of those whose welfare might be at risk as a result of an incident. Too often, IT auditors and other disaster recovery planners think primarily in terms of restoring systems and give little thought to the welfare of people. Incidents such as major weather disturbances or facility fires have major people-related concerns that should be considered.

Business Continuity Plans

The purpose of a BCP is to enable an enterprise unit or activity to recover or maintain its activities in the event of a disruption of normal operations. BCPs really are the culmination of the BCM process. An enterprise should have multiple plans based on its major critical activities, and each plan should focus on the time scales in which these activities are to be recovered, the recovery levels needed for each critical activity, and designated situations when each plan can be utilized.

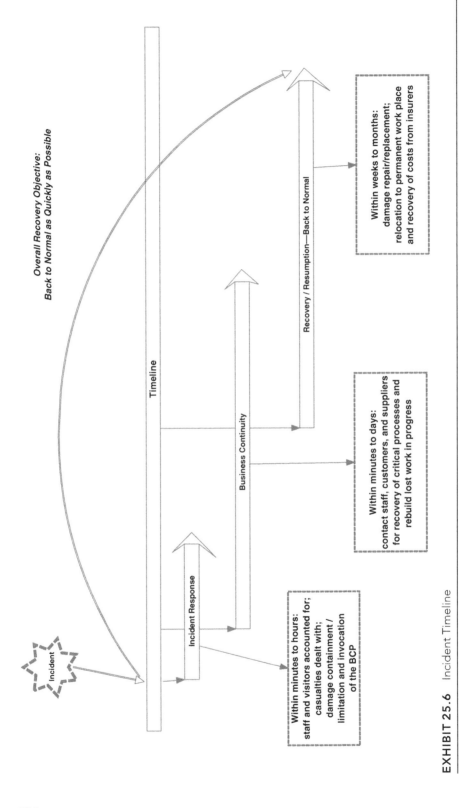

Overall Recovery Objective:
Back to Normal as Quickly as Possible

Timeline

Incident

Incident Response

Business Continuity

Recovery / Resumption—Back to Normal

Within minutes to hours:
staff and visitors accounted for;
casualties dealt with;
damage containment /
limitation and invocation
of the BCP

Within minutes to days:
contact staff, customers, and suppliers
for recovery of critical processes and
rebuild lost work in progress

Within weeks to months:
damage repair/replacement;
relocation to permanent work place
and recovery of costs from insurers

EXHIBIT 25.6 Incident Timeline

Developing a series of BCPs for even a medium-size enterprise can be a major task. Exhibit 25.5 lists 10 major types of threats that can impact an enterprise and its units. The nature of BCPs for each threat will differ and each may be very different for business units or activities. For example, an enterprise with one manufacturing facility in the United States and another in India may face similar threats of a major facility fire. However, the nature of responding to that threat in each facility location, beyond just extinguishing the blaze, will vary. Because considerations surrounding business recovery will depend so much on local conditions, BCPs for individual business units—such as the manufacturing facilities in the United States and in India—should be developed locally following corporate-level guidelines.

Business Unit BCM Planning

Following a standard set of mutually agreed threats, as described in Exhibit 25.5, enterprise management should charge each of its major business units with the responsibility to develop its own individual activity BCPs following an enterprise-wide BCM guideline, and Exhibit 25.7 outlines business unit BCP general requirements. This type of BCP should be developed by individual critical resources in the enterprise, subject to advice and then review by the responsible BCM management team. Based on the nature of the threat, different specialists in the overall enterprise and in the specific business units should assist in the BCP development. Thus, facility security resources would help to develop local BCPs covering fire or severe weather threats while risk management and legal resources would be involved with developing terrorism threat BCPs.

Building a series of consistent BCPs across the enterprise can be a daunting task. However, each significant business unit should be charged with developing a plan that is consistent with others but meets local standards. The BCM management team, or internal audit acting as enterprise consultants, should be responsible for approving these plans and coordinating activities across business units where needed.

---

1. Plan Purpose and Scope
   a. Critical activities to be recovered
   b. Time scales and recovery periods needed for each critical activity
2. Criteria or conditions for activating the plan
3. Persons responsible for plan activities
   a. Communications strategy for contacting plan participants
   b. Senior management, government, legal, and other plan contacts
4. Backup resources—IT, paper records, or other—needed to restart operations
5. Facilities for restarting operations
6. Transportation requirements
7. Supplies and logistical requirements
8. Linkages or connections with other operating processes
   a. IT network linkages
   b. Parts or product needs
9. Communications with other stakeholders
10. Preliminary testing to determine whether systems are operating

---

EXHIBIT 25.7   Business Continuity Plan Requirements

Assuring BCM Plan Effectiveness

The BCM life cycle is a continuous process where its elements must be validated regularly by exercises and reviews to ensure they are up to date. This is really a major change from older techniques where disaster recovery plans were often developed, published in thick books, but never really tested or updated. When IT auditors in the past asked about such plans, an auditee manager would point to the book and the auditor would often note that the plan was in compliance. We should do better today with regular testing and maintenance of BCM processes.

Internal audit should take a strong role in this BCM process through reviewing these plans as part of special and regular audits and assisting in BCP testing processes. All involved parties should remember that the objective of a strong, functional BCM is not massive files of documentation but processes that will allow an enterprise to quickly resume normal operations in the event of some unexpected incident or threat.

Exercising the BCM Plan

Regular tests or exercises of established plans should be part of the BCM process. We have used the term *exercise* here in addition to the more traditional approach of performing just tests of plans. An exercise should be designed to allow the enterprise to recover from an incident and verify that the BCP covers all critical activities, their dependencies and priorities. The scale and complexity of these test exercises can vary from a simple desk check to a complex full-scope test as described in Exhibit 25.8.

The level and frequency of these exercises will depend on the overall perceived risks confronting an enterprise as well as the criticality of the activity or unit being tested. Because BCPs are based on a number of business units and the multiple types of threats the enterprise may face, not every BCP can be tested every year. However, individual business units should develop their own BCPs following enterprise level standards and should at least desk-check test their plans annually. IT and internal audit should build tests of specific BCPs as part of their periodic operational and financial internal controls operational reviews. When internal audit arrives at a business unit for a scheduled operational review, a medium-level test of that unit's BCP—perhaps a walk-through review—should be part of the audit procedures. With the status and currency of their plans subject to periodic internal audit reviews, business units will be encouraged both to self-test and to keep their BCPs up to date.

BCM Plan Maintenance

A clearly defined and documented BCM maintenance program should be established to ensure that any changes in activities are reflected in overall and individual BCPs. For example, new products, services, or changes in business reporting arrangements should be reflected in updated BCM materials. This level of update review is easy to say but often difficult to implement. The team responsible for enterprise-wide BCM activities should take a lead in this update process as an annual program exercise and also when needed.

As part of a BCM maintenance program, all components of the process should be reviewed with their assumptions challenged. Updates to the plan should be communicated

Test Complexity	Type of Test	Testing Process	Testing Frequency	Testing Objectives
Simple	Desk check	Review and challenge content of published BCPs	At least annually	Audit or validate published BCPs
Medium	Walk-through of BCP	Challenge content of published process	Annually	Validate roles of all systems and plan participants
	BCP simulation	Create a test situation to validate that the BCP contains both necessary and sufficient information to enable successful recovery	Annually or part of regular internal audit reviews	Validate that the BCP contains both necessary and sufficient information to enable a successful recovery
	Critical Activities exercise	Activate the BCP or a significant portion of it in a controlled environment that does not jeopardize regular operations or overall business functions	Less than annually assuming other medium tests cause no concerns	Validate full recovery processes in a controlled and limited manner
Complex	Exercise full BCP including indent management and all other plan characteristics	Test all functions even including a temporary shut-down of normal operations in a controlled and well-monitored manner	Less frequently than annually. This can be a very expensive and risky test	Test all elements of the BCP

EXHIBIT 25.8   BCM Test Exercise Types and Scopes

to enterprise personnel and organizational units as appropriate. Keeping BCM documentation up to date is always a challenge and is a key task. Just as personnel records are updated due to organizational changes or as a general ledger system is updated to add a new account as a result of some business activity change, an enterprise must update its BCM. Keeping the enterprise BCM and its supporting BCPs current should be a major and regular enterprise activity.

Embedding BCM in the Enterprise Culture

Although it is important to build BCM procedures and individual BCPs within an enterprise, it is more important to embed these BCM principles within the overall enterprise culture, ranging from senior management down to staff-level functions. The successful establishment of an enterprise-wide BCM program requires a strong level of enthusiasm and readiness. The BCM management team can lead this effort, but everyone should recognize the importance of the BCM program.

The launch of an overall BCM program and individual business activity-level BCPs is a major enterprise-wide effort. However, it is often easy for teams to build these materials but then forget about updating and testing them once the effort has been completed. In order for the effort to be successful over time, it must be built into the enterprise's overall culture.

Enterprise-wide training programs should be launched to make all team members aware of the existence of the BCM and its importance to overall business continuity in the event of any threats. Although a BCM covers many threats, the training should emphasize how to raise alarms, how to respond to threats and evacuate work sites, and what to do once they have evacuated from the sites. Most important here, the enterprise staff should have a basic knowledge of recovery plans. No matter the nature of the threat, the basic objectives of a BCM program should be to evacuate and clear the danger area and then to resume business operations.

AUDITING BCM PROCESSES

BCM processes generally are launched and managed by a special function in the enterprise, such as risk management, and often work closely with IT due to the important nature of computer systems disaster recovery in the overall process. IT and internal audit should have a major role in this BCM process, acting as an internal consultant in helping to launch the BCM process, starting with BIA reviews and moving through the process to help build effective BCPs. Internal audit's most important role here, however, should be in reviewing and assessing the overall readiness and fitness of BCM procedures. This role is particularly important as it is internal audit that reports the results of BCM reviews and actions taken on recommendations for improvements to the audit committee.

The nature of threats facing an enterprise—including building or facility fires, weather situations, terrorism actions, or major IT failures—makes the audit process somewhat difficult. A larger enterprise may have multiple major activities and business units around the globe, and their recovery plans will range from severe weather response plans to IT systems recoveries. Internal and IT audit should review BCM processes as part of their normal reviews in other areas. This process should go beyond just IT audits and cover continuity planning for all audits and areas of an enterprise.

The BCM process for an enterprise is both a large, comprehensive program covering continuity management for all enterprise business units and activities as well as detailed and specific BCPs covering exact threats and supporting all business activities and functional locations. Internal audit periodically should review both areas: the overall BCM process to assess the effectiveness of the program and specific BCP assessments performed as part of other internal audits.

Internal Audit BCM Self-Assessment Reviews

Because of the multiple threat types impacting an enterprise activity and the many different units or activities that are part of most enterprises, an internal and IT audit review of a single BCP type covering all enterprise business units is often just not practical. Because of differences in local conditions—such as establishing contacts with fire departments in different locations—the local business units are the best resources to build their own BCPs. As a first-level BCP test, those local units should -assess and then update their own BCM procedures.

Internal audit should build procedures to assess the status of local business unit BCP readiness as part of all of their regular financial, operational, or scheduled IT audits. Exhibit 25.9 outlines internal audit steps for reviewing the status of local business unit BCP readiness as part of regular internal audits. The idea is that internal audit should assess the status of local BCPs based on established standards, determine if those business units have self-assessed their BCPs, and perform more detailed reviews as necessary.

Internal audit should perform a local self-assessment review as part of every scheduled audit. Each review does not have to consist of complete BCM audits. For example, assume an enterprise has installed a customer service call center located at an offshore location to help solve customer product problems. Such a center does not produce products, has limited in-house IT systems, but very much supports overall enterprise business operations. The greatest continuity threat to such a facility may be a severe weather condition at the location and concerns regarding both the welfare of the local staff and the transfer of call center operations to an alternate site. That local facility should have a specific BCP covering plant facility risks, following overall enterprise BCM guidance.

Internal auditors should review the adequacy of local unit BCPs as part of other reviews that they perform at local facilities. For example, as part of a regularly scheduled SOx internal controls review at that same call center facility, internal audit should determine if the facility has established a BCP plan covering facility emergencies, such as weather or fires. Internal audit also should check to determine that details supporting the BCP are current, such as correct contact links with local fire and weather emergency authorities as well as evidence that the facility has tested at least portions of this BCP periodically.

These are very simple, elementary steps where internal audit should regularly assess whether the local unit has processes in place to restore operations in the event of an emergency. If the local unit BCP is missing or has no evidence of even desk-check testing, internal audit should make an audit finding point as part of its current internal audit review and also should pass this information on to the team responsible for overall enterprise BCM processes.

Auditing the Enterprise BCM Process

In addition to internal audit reviews of BCP readiness as part of other audits, IT audit may want to consider the overall status of the enterprise's BCM processes. Such a review, as described in Exhibit 25.9, assumes that the enterprise has launched an overall enterprise BCM and has developed guidance for maintaining and testing those processes. Internal and IT audit's role here would be to assess the overall status of that plan and determine whether there are processes in place to ensure the continuance of operations in any of the affected risk areas.

1. Has the enterprise taken a strong position or commitment for business continuity management (BCM) beyond just restoring IT resources?
   a. Has the audit committee formally endorsed this commitment?
   b. Has a dedicated group, such as risk management, been given BCM responsibilities?
   c. Does the BCM program follow BS 25999 best practices or some other recognized review process?
2. Has the enterprise established high-level business continuity policies that include strong commitments for resuming activities in the event of interruptions?
3. Has the enterprise performed a business impact analysis (BIA) over its key facilities and functions?
   a. Based on organization charts and other materials, are all significant operations covered in the BIA?
   b. Has the BCM management team communicated BIA process instructions to all significant enterprise activities?
   c. Were adequate project or program management techniques employed to monitor critical BIA activities?
   d. Are there documented processes in place defining criteria for critical activities?
      i. Have maximum tolerable periods of disruption been established for each critical activity?
      ii. Does the review of BIA activities give adequate consideration to related inter-dependent activities?
   e. Was an adequate risk analysis performed for all identified critical activities?
   f. For each identified critical business activity, were appropriate business continuity decisions performed to accept, transfer, or change the risk?
4. As part of enterprise unit BIA reviews, have adequate continuity arrangements been made and documented to communicate with insurance carriers?
5. Have adequate business continuity strategies, covering key people, premises, and technology, been identified for all key activities?
6. For each identified key activity, have appropriate incident response plans been established?
   a. For each incident response plan reviewed, are adequate procedures in place to invoke the plan?
   b. Have personnel roles and responsibilities been defined to manage BCM programs?
7. Have business continuity plans (BCPs) been established for all key activities following standard formats or enterprise guidance?
   a. Do BCPs contain detailed action plans and personnel task lists?
   b. Based on a test review of selected BCPs, are recovery resource requirements adequately identified?
8. Are programs in place to test key BCPs adequately?
   a. Do BCP tests include the full recovery and continuity of operations?
   b. Where any shortcomings are involved in a BCP test, are there adequate procedures to perform corrective actions?
9. Are there adequate training programs in place to emphasize the importance of BCM processes to all levels of personnel?
10. Have senior management and the audit committee reviewed and approved enterprise BCM plans and processes?

EXHIBIT 25.9   Review Steps for an Internal Audit Review of Enterprise BCM Processes

If an enterprise has launched an overall BCM process, internal audit may want to review its overall status as a single one-time audit with later follow-up reviews on the status of any recommended corrective actions. These reviews will allow internal audit to advise the audit committee about whether the enterprise appears to be ready to respond to any of several threats and to resume operations in the most effective manner possible.

If internal audit finds shortcomings in local unit BCP self-assessment reviews, it may be necessary to repeat a review of the overall BCM process. For example, there may have been insufficient local unit training in building local BCPs or update processes may be lacking. Internal and IT audit can play an ongoing and key role in reviewing BCM processes here. Although this book focuses primarily on IT internal control issues, effective BCM procedures cover all enterprise operations, including IT.

Our review procedures assume that the enterprise has adopted the BS 25999 good practice guidelines or is following ISO 27001 procedures. The idea here is that an enterprise's key facilities and operations should have comprehensive programs in place to recover operations in the event of severe disruption.

 ## LINKING THE BCM WITH OTHER STANDARDS AND PROCESSES

Business continuity management is an important and very critical set of processes that go beyond just IT procedures. Every enterprise can face many different threats across its units and activities. Thus, processes must be in place to restore operations as effectively and efficiently as possible. This chapter has emphasized the BS 25999 good practice guidelines, although the newer ISO 27001 standards will become more common in the years going forward.

Business continuity is much more than the IT disaster recovery processes discussed in Chapter 23 and should be much more than just an IT audit-related matter. Nevertheless, IT auditors should have the skills and knowledge to help all units of the enterprise achieve adequate business continuity plans and BCM processes. IT audit can perform a major service to management by using its disaster recovery skills to install effective business continuity programs throughout the enterprise.

 ## NOTES

1. "The Business Case for Disaster Recovery Planning: Calculating the Cost of Downtime," Iron Mountain Corporation, January 2001, www.ironmountaincorp.com.
2. "Technology on the Web," *Forbes*, March 29, 2004.
3. "Google E-mail Crash Hits Millions," *Financial Times*, February 29, 2009.
4. In the United States, the Federal Deposit Insurance Corporation (FDIC) is responsible for many of these consumer-banking rules. See www.fdic.gov.

CHAPTER TWENTY-SIX

Auditing Telecommunications and IT Communications Networks

ALTHOUGH AN INFORMATION TECHNOLOGY (IT) auditor's internal controls review emphasis over the years has been on the general controls surrounding system's operations, often consisting of servers, storage devices and other components, or controls over individual application, IT telecommunications and their related internal controls are sometimes ignored or bypassed. However, this is also is a major area of IT internal control risks and vulnerabilities. While IT systems have been connected to local and external telecommunications devices since the earliest days of IT systems, technologies today are rapidly changing as we move to paperless, Internet-based systems. While the term telecommunications historically has referred to IT networked connections using classic telephone systems connected together with wires and cables, today technologies have expanded to a wide range of networked technologies, virtual private networks, and wireless systems.

This rapid adoption of global enterprise telecommunications systems in recent years has transformed the concepts of enterprise physical and logical IT security boundaries. Although some industries, such as financial services, have been using private telecommunications networks for many decades to connect their trading partners electronically, the current use of Internet-based systems has now resulted in the major usage of intercompany networks across many industries to electronically integrate trading partners as well as the emergence of public networks, including the Internet, for intercompany connectivity.

This use of telecommunications networking to integrate enterprises electronically brings such benefits as a rapid access to all levels of information, improved communications, reduced costs, increased collaboration with business partners, improved customer service, and an unprecedented ability to conduct effective electronic commerce. However, it also presents enterprises with a new set of IT internal control and security concerns.

With today's integration of networks between enterprises to facilitate electronic commerce, simple solutions to IT telecommunications security are no longer appropriate or possible. This chapter identifies some key security risks, internal controls and best practice countermeasures for controlling the connection of proprietary enterprise networks to one or more external parties over private or public wired and wireless networks.

The concepts covered in this chapter are broad and a more detailed discussion would require a full reference book of guidance materials for a more thorough internal control and security-based description and discussion. Many of the concepts discussed in this chapter also support or expand the Chapter 9 discussion on evolving internal controls issues that include wireless networks. This chapter provides a high level introduction to IT telecommunications systems and networks with an emphasis on such areas as virtual private networks (VPNs), intrusion detection systems, related security and their internal controls. This chapter's objective is not to make an IT auditor a telecommunications expert, but to provide a general IT auditor-related background information on some important telecommunications and IT network components.

 ## NETWORK SECURITY CONCEPTS

While IT auditors are not responsible for designing the telecommunications networks, as installed at their enterprises, they should have a good understanding of these network components. An IT auditor should have an objective of evaluating an enterprise's IT telecommunications security strengths and weaknesses as well as the internal controls in place. While IT auditors will normally encounter telecommunications systems as mechanisms to manage and transmit data, these common concepts and terminologies apply to voice, data, video and other systems network technologies. Exhibit 26.1 describes a simple telecommunications circuit between a transmitter across a network

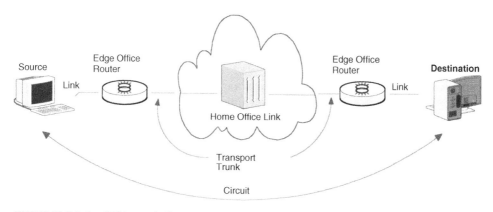

EXHIBIT 26.1 IT Network Components

involving multiple links and switches. Some of the terminology concepts supporting an IT telecommunications network include:

- **Transmitter.** Sometimes known as the send or source, this is the network component that originates a network information transfer. It might consist of a data terminal, voice telephone, host computer system, or video camera.
- **Receiver.** Sometimes known as the sink, target or destination device, a network receiver accepts the transferred information. Similar to transmitters, receivers can operate in different forms of media.
- **Circuit.** This is the logical, and often physical, connection between two or more elements in a network. Network circuits may be used for either access from an outside customer or customer premises to the edge of the network or for transport within it.
- **Link.** A two-point segment of an end-to-end circuit, such as from a terminal to a switch. The same term is used for telephone networks, but we will think of it here as a connection to IT equipment.
- **Trunk.** A telecommunications circuit used for sharing among multiple users and with any usage contention managed by network switching devices. For example, in an office telephone system a central office trunk connects the central office "switchboard" to the telephone company central office.
- **Channel.** A one-way connection between a telecommunications transmitter and receiver. A channel is a logical connection over a physical circuit to support a network communication.
- **Switch.** A network device that establishes, maintains, and changes logical connections over physical network circuits. A common example of a switch is a Private Branch Exchange (PBX) to establish telephone and telecommunication connections within an enterprise office.
- **Network.** The fabric of elements that work together to support the transfer of information. A telecommunications network can include everything from the transmitters to the switches. When a network extends beyond an office—such as with its local PBX—to other components, we often think of it as a wide area network (WAN).

The terminology and equipment supporting IT telecommunications networks has its origins in classic voice telephone networks. Although there have been many technology changes over time, many of these concepts have not changed all that much.

Data networks are generally configured as dedicated, switched, or virtual circuits. Dedicated circuits are used for a single user, although the source devices may be connected through a single office local area network such as a LAN, WAN, or other connections. They offer their users the advantage of a high degree of availability and specified levels of capacity, quality, and security. Traditionally, dedicated IT networks have been connected to large IT data centers that communicate intensively; similarly, many large enterprises with multiple locations have used dedicated circuit networks to tie together multiple locations.

Switched circuits are connected through an IT network through one or more intermediate switching devices. This configuration was traditionally established in the form of telephone central office PBX exchanges, where circuits are shared on demand

and as available. This configuration often results in significant operating efficiencies, and most data and voice calls today are carried over switched circuits, although the trend is to virtual circuits. The following sections outline some other key IT tele-communications concepts that are important for IT auditors.

Network Routers

Routers are physical or hardware devices that join multiple wired or wireless networks together. Whether on a wired or wireless network, a router connects networks and ensures that information does not go where it is not needed. This is crucial for keeping large volumes of data from clogging connections and making sure that information does make it to the intended destination. Routers are extremely important and useful in dealing with separate computer networks, joining them and passing information from one to the other and, in some cases, performing translations of various IT language protocols between the networks. A router also protects networks from one another, preventing the traffic on one from unnecessarily spilling over to the other.

As the number of networks attached to one another grows, the configuration controls for handling traffic among them grows almost exponentially, and the process-ing power of the router is increased. Regardless of how many networks are attached, though, the basic operation and function of the router remains the same. Since the Internet is one huge network made up of tens of thousands of smaller networks, its use of routers is an absolute necessity.

Although they are necessary, routers can introduce some security risks because they can present a potential abuse as a detectable launching point for incursions into IT networks. However, a router can also buttress the network it services against even sophisticated attacks, or at worst, it can offer a vulnerable target from which to reach invalid or private devices that otherwise would be unreachable.

An enterprise's IT functions and its network administration is responsible for installing and configuring router devices. This involves establishing and maintaining some detailed security tables to manage the device. The network administrator who seeks to secure a network must consider the role played by the external routers in enforcing the security of the local networks. However, much of this security role is performed by router hardware vendors, often with security functionality that contains a high level of sophistication.

An IT auditor often does not need to know the technical details of how an enterprise's routers are managed and configured. Rather, the auditor should look for documentation and best practices supporting good IT security environment controls in the IT systems configuration. These basic concepts were discussed in Chapter 19. An IT auditor performing an IT general controls review should meet with the IT network administration function and assess the router related internal controls environment by asking questions and gathering information in the following areas:

- Are the routers installed currently up to date on their system versions and revisions?
- Are router tables actively managed and updated when required?
- Is there management and coordination between network and other connected routers within the enterprise?

■ Have controls been implemented to limit access to the services by which a router can be managed?

■ Have software filters been installed in routers to prevent such functions as the Denial of Service (DOS) transactions or obviously spoofed traffic?

■ Do the installed routers deny all incoming traffic to critical hosts, such as firewalls or the firewall management console or deny all outgoing traffic, except that with a source address internal to the network? This outgoing filter is essential to prevent the protected network from becoming an unwitting amplifier in a network attack.

Routers are key elements in the IT network security environment. If installed at a high level, an IT auditor should recognize their role and function in establishing a secure and well controlled IT network environment.

Firewalls

Besides basic physical security for an IT site, firewalls are the next most important aspect in controlling digital access into and out of the enterprise's IT network. They are a means of controlling the points of connectivity to the outside world, typically through the Internet. Firewalls were introduced in Chapter 20 and illustrated there in Exhibit 20.4, and we discuss them here from the perspective of IT telecommunications security.

The basic function of a firewall is to establish a protected boundary between outside information sources such as the Internet and internal IT resources. Sometimes this inside is referred to as the "trusted" side and the external Internet as the "un-trusted" side. As a generality this is all right. However, there are security risks and this rule of thumb is often not specific enough.

A firewall is a controlled barrier mechanism to control network traffic into and out of an enterprise intranet. Firewalls are basically application specific routers. They run on dedicated embedded systems such as an internet appliance or they can be software programs running on a general server platform. In most cases these systems will have two network interfaces, one for the external network such as the Internet and one for the internal intranet side. The firewall process can tightly control what is allowed to traverse from one side to the other. Firewalls can range from being fairly simple to very complex.

When installing firewalls, the enterprise IT security function should develop a comprehensive understanding of the system network and application architecture prior to their implementation. Knowledge of what must be permitted into and out of the network is an essential prerequisite to have an understanding of what must be excluded from the network. When this step is omitted, firewalls may be configured to ensure continued systems connectivity but also face the risk of improper network intrusions. The root cause of any knowledge gap here is often organizational schisms between applications, the system and the network administrators. It is often best to overcome these issues by involving all these parties in discussions to establish the required network traffic.

As with most aspects of IT security, deciding what type of firewall to use will depend on factors such as traffic levels, services needing protection and the complexity of rules required. The greater the number of services that must be able to traverse the firewall the more complex the requirement becomes. The difficulty for firewalls is distinguishing between legitimate and illegitimate traffic. An IT auditor should look for a requirements study in any evaluation process here.

The most basic protection a firewall provides is the ability to block network traffic to certain destinations, but an enterprise and its IT auditors should understand what firewalls do protect against and what protection do they not provide. If configured correctly, firewalls can provide a reasonable form of protection from external threats including some denial of service (DOS)[1] attacks. If not configured correctly they can be major security holes in an organization.

Similar to our discussions regarding routers, an IT auditor will typically not be an expert on the configuration and technical details surrounding installed enterprise firewalls. However, the auditor should look for some thoughtful study and analysis in installing enterprise systems firewalls as well as ongoing vulnerability analysis. Firewalls are important but are not the major panacea to IT network security. IT auditors should avoid the common misconception: *"I have a firewall—I'm safe."* Firewall vulnerabilities exist, and if a firewall is the only layer of defense, the enterprise can be as vulnerable to a knowledgeable attack as if it did not have one. An IT auditor should always look for multiple layers of network security controls when reviewing IT tele-communications networks.

EFFECTIVE IT NETWORK SECURITY CONTROLS

As a first step to undertaking the design or implementation of an enterprise IT network, an IT auditor should understand the enterprise's network security configuration and its internal control architecture. As part of this understanding, there is a need to understand the key concepts that should be considered when designing and implementing a security infrastructure to support an enterprise's communication needs and allow it to transact business securely in today's IT environments. The IT network security infrastructure should apply equally to pre-existing connections and to new initiative connections. As always, the network should be protected based on the risk it represents to the enterprise.

The network perimeter configuration is shown in Exhibit 26.1 as the cloud-shaped area surrounding the home office links and the internal trunk connections. It is often a first point where some form of security and traffic filtering should be implemented. This is often the first system that is accessed by external parties, and IT network controls depends on the enterprise, the type of connection and the sort of data or information that is being transmitted over the IT network. As a result, there should be many combinations of countermeasures and connections at this perimeter border to enhance IT internal controls and network security.

A common driver of security within enterprises is their IT security policy, and this policy should conform to relevant standards, such as ISO 27001 discussed in Chapter 18. The policy should define the IT network and security responsibilities within an enterprise and the key information assets that are required to be protected. A formal and well-understood policy here should guide the guiding security principles to be adhered to within the enterprise.

A key concept of any enterprise security program or facility is its depth. That is, there should be multiple layers of defense mechanisms that have to be circumvented to gain access to internal information assets and resources. Perimeter security, while important, must be supported by a strong internal security foundation. A single thin layer of perimeter security generally does not protect an enterprise adequately. Once a way is found through or around that thin layer of security, the security system can become ineffective.

The best source of examples for this multiple-level security concept can often be found in controls outside of just the technology-based areas. An IT auditor can think in terms along the lines of how does a traditional bank or any enterprise protect its assets? While the bank may be located in a sturdy building with bars on the windows and guards by the doors, a typical bank has any other additional levels of controls such as alarm systems, closed-circuit television, account reconciliations and, of course, a vault. Such a security system has been designed to ensure that if one layer is bypassed, there are several more layers either to trap the intruders or to make it easier to identify and subsequently apprehend them. In summary, the controls should make the risk of being caught higher than the reward for penetrating the security network.

Using our same bank analogy, any enterprise should protect its information assets as well. It should set limits on who can access enterprise applications and how they are allowed to update or use them. There should be security configured in multiple layers of defense for these, such as filtering routers, firewalls, what are called demilitarized zones and intrusion detection mechanisms. All these controls should work together to ensure that if one layer of security is breached, there will be another layer with different characteristics that either will protect the enterprise's assets or assist in detecting the intrusion.

This concept of a perimeter security defense applies to all enterprises. Many network security controls have been discussed in Chapters 19 through 22 on IT security risks and threats. In some environments, this can be a very major but often highly technical issue for some IT auditors and certainly for many members of general management. With regular and periodic reports of IT network intrusions and other improper activities, we are constantly reminded of the threats here. However, enterprise professionals often ignore these security risks and regularly move more and more of their activities to Internet-based and other IT network systems. While there are many different security systems and controls here, we will focus and briefly discuss the importance of effective intrusion detection systems and virtual private networks, both areas that IT auditors frequently encounter in their IT general and applications controls reviews.

Intrusion Detection Systems

Whether a neighborhood jewelry shop, a used car parts lot filled with rusting old cars, or a branch bank, virtually every type of enterprise needs some type of burglar alarm or intrusion detection system (IDS). The jewelry shop may have a burglar alarm bell that rings on an outside pedestrian street, the car parts lot may have the proverbial junkyard dogs to scare off intruders, and the bank may have sophisticated alarm mechanisms. We install these systems because there is always someone who may want to improperly take something from the facility or to break into protected boundaries. IT networks face similar risks of improper intruders and have the need for some type of IDS.

An IDS is a specialized software tool or hardware device that monitors an IT network and system activities for malicious activities or policy violations. These types of systems monitor transaction traffic and other events occurring in an IT system or network and analyze them for signs of possible incidents, including IT security policy violations or imminent threats of violation, acceptable use policies, or standard security practices.

IDSs operate as either network-based or host-based IT systems. The latter were discussed in Chapter 20. In a network-based IDS, sensors are located at network borders or choke points in the network to be monitored. The sensor captures all network traffic and analyzes the content of individual packets for malicious traffic. It operates as an independent platform that identifies intrusions by examining network traffic and monitors multiple hosts. Because of all of the variations in traffic, network monitoring requires more than just an easy "Here's a problem – Let's fix it!" approach. Exhibit 26.2 describes some of the IDS control procedure issues and approaches that an IT auditor should understand.

Terms are used by IT network security specialists to describe IT network security concepts and controls.

Alert/Alarm
An effective system will have mechanisms to provide signals suggesting that it has been or is being attacked.

True Positive
Alarms that highlight or produce a legitimate intrusion detection system attack.

False Positive
An event that signals an intrusion detection system to produce an alarm when no attack has taken place.

False Negative
A failure of an intrusion detection system to detect an actual attack. This is perhaps the most serious concern in an intrusion detection system as an attack is taking place but alarms are not signaled.

True Negative
When no attack has taken place and no alarm is raised. An IT security function should be satisfied with this level of messages.

Noise
Data or interference that can trigger a false positive. Careful tuning of any intrusion detection system should have an objective of eliminating such noise.

Site Policy
The guidelines within an enterprise and its IT function that control the rules and configurations of an intrusion detection system.

Site Policy Awareness
The need for an enterprise intrusion detection system administrator to dynamically change system rules and configurations in response to changing environmental and intrusion threat activity.

Confidence Value
A value an enterprise places on its intrusion detection system, based on past performance and analysis, to help determine its ability to identify an attack effectively.

Alarm Filtering
The process of categorizing attack alerts produced from an intrusion detection system in order to distinguish false positives from actual attacks.

EXHIBIT 26.2 Intrusion Detection Terminology

An IDS will be configured as either a passive or reactive system. In a passive system, an IDS sensor detects a potential security breach, logs the information and signals an alert on a console and for the owner. When these types of passive systems are installed, IT auditors often have internal control concerns. Enterprise IT security often fails to actively review such monitor reports for potential problems, and even worse, take corrective action in a timely manner. A reactive system can also cause problems. Here, the IDS responds to the suspicious activity by resetting the connection or by reprogramming the firewall to block network traffic from the suspected malicious source. This can happen automatically or at the command of an operator.

Though they both relate to network security, an IDS differs from a firewall, discussed previously, in that a firewall looks outwardly for intrusions in order to stop them from happening. Firewalls limit access between networks to prevent intrusion and do not signal an attack from inside the network. An IDS evaluates a suspected intrusion once it has taken place, watches for attacks that originate from within a system and then signals an alarm.

On the other side of the coin on such network security systems, intrusion *prevention* is the process of performing intrusion detection first and then attempting to stop detected possible incidents. Combined intrusion detection and prevention systems are primarily focused on identifying possible incidents, logging information about them, attempting to stop them, and reporting them to security administrators. In addition, an enterprise may use such a system for other purposes, such as identifying problems with security policies, documenting existing threats, and deterring individuals from violating security policies. IDSs, particularly with strong prevention tools, have become a necessary addition to the security infrastructure of nearly any enterprise.

Intrusion detection and prevention systems are important elements of any IT network security architecture. An IT auditor should gain an initial understanding of the types and nature intrusion detection and prevention controls installed in an enterprise's IT network. Exhibit 26.3 outlines some IT audit control procedures as part of a general controls review of IT network security processes. In general, an IT auditor should seek determine if effective processes and tools have been installed and are used effectively. As transactions volumes increase and network threats continue an IT auditor should look for effective preventive and detective controls here.

Virtual Private Networks

Today many enterprises have remote offices and employees working from their home offices, both of which must gain access to their corporate network on a regular basis to perform their daily business. In the past, the traditional solution here was to use dedicated or leased lines for communicating with remote locations or branches, all relatively high cost solutions. VPNs usually offer significant cost savings over long-distance communication costs.

Instead of requiring the enterprise's offsite workers or business partners to install long-haul dedicated links or dial-in long distance to the corporate modem bank, a VPN enables remote users to connect to the enterprise's network, simply by placing a local call to their Internet service provider (ISP) or by using existing broadband connections.

1. Meet with the IT security function to understand the nature and status of any IT intrusion detection systems (IDS) installed.
   a. If IDS products are in place, gather documentation to understand their status and features.
   b. If there is no IDS capability, discuss reasons—from a risk perspective—why such tools have not been implemented.
2. Use IT network diagrams to identify and document locations of the IDS components.
   a. Do IDS components appear to be located at key IT network choke points?
   b. Has the same IDS technology been installed on servers and other host systems?
   c. Does the IDS appear to cover all areas of potential IT transaction activity, including business process systems and personal IT networks?
3. Based on discussions with IT security management, is the installed IDS a passive or reactive system?
4. Review and understand the nature of established intrusion prohibition rules, and assess whether they appear consistent with other systems and business operations.
5. If a passive type of IDS, review a sample of monitor logs to assess the nature of any reported intrusion violations.
   a. Meet with people and review systems responsible for monitoring intrusions, and determine whether they are following consistent and comprehensive procedures.
   b. Select several reported intrusion violations—systems or people—and assess the appropriateness of correction and remediation procedures.
   c. Determine that intrusion violation rules are reviewed and updated on a regular basis.
6. If the IDS operates as a reactive system, develop an understanding of the system rules and actions.
   a. Select a sample of IDS-based corrective actions and determine if the actions appear correct.
   b. Review processes in place to review and update components of the reactive IDS.
7. Review IDS procedures for handling such matters as false positives, and assess whether handling appears appropriate.
8. Review supporting software or consulting contracts for managing and maintaining the IDS, and assess whether it is actively managed and regularly updated.
9. Determine that appropriate processes and procedures are in place to change IDS sensors or system components due to enterprise network or system changes.
10. Meet with appropriate members of management to assess whether they appear to understand the risks and nature of the installed IDS.

EXHIBIT 26.3   Intrusion Detection and Prevention IT Audit Control Procedures

In either case, the remote users then can connect to the corporate network via the ISP and the Internet.

The main reason why an enterprise would consider implementation of a VPN over the Internet is the potential to realize significant cost savings over time. While the initial installation costs of a traditional solution such as dedicated or leased lines for communicating with remote locations or branches would be roughly the same as a VPN solution, a VPN will quickly yield cost savings. In addition, there can be significant cost savings by carrying other traffic, such as voice messages, over the Internet as well.

There is a strong need for the protection of information in transit for these remote access locations, and effective IT telecommunications security over these branch network connections or internal networks is essential. Enterprises that have remote

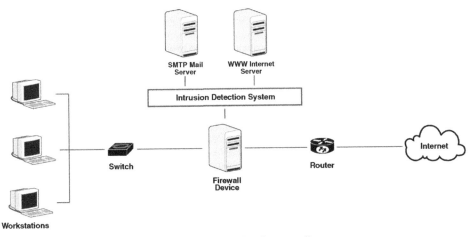

SMTP Mail Server   WWW Internet Server

Intrusion Detection System

Switch   Firewall Device   Router   Internet

Workstations

EXHIBIT 26.4   VPN Configuration Integrated with Firewall

users had historically requested that their employees use their personal telephones in dial-up connections to access the corporate network. However, there are weaknesses and significant security vulnerabilities in the use of dial-up connections. While dial-up telephone access connections usually represent the lowest cost and simplest solution, VPN connections are becoming increasingly popular. Their aim is to provide the remote user with a simple means of becoming part of the corporate network. Once connected, the remote user can use network resources as if physically in the office and connected to the corporate network.

VPNs allow remote users to connect through the Internet with a dial-up modem or a high-speed solution, such as cable or asymmetric digital subscriber line (DSL). Many users today use DSL lines or wireless connections to connect their home computers to the Internet, and a VPN allows them to link with their enterprise network. As with any network connection, a VPN solution can be a security risk if not properly configured and maintained, although it has many advantages over the traditional dial-up connection.

Although there are multiple ways to configure and implement a VPN, Exhibit 26.4 shows a VPN configured with a firewall. Remote users may use the home computer DSL lines or other connections to enter the Internet. A transaction addressed and directed to the enterprise router then passes the activity to an installed firewall. The network activity would then have to pass through an intrusion detection barrier before reaching enterprise systems and servers. This is a simple system diagram with only one firewall access gate, a potential single point of failure; many other configurations are common as well.

VPN Risks

A VPN should normally be configured as a secure, private communication link or tunnel between two or more devices across the Internet. The VPN system can be either a computer running VPN software or a VPN enabled router special device. It allows a home computer to be connected to an office network or can allow two home computers in different locations to connect to each over the Internet. A VPN is a very good IT telecommunications approach, but it comes with some risks from an internal controls perspective.

Properly configured, VPN data travels across a public network like the Internet in a secure encrypted manner. If anyone "listens" to the VPN communications, they will be blocked because VPN data should be encrypted. However, any VPN faces a major security risk if that encryption software has not been properly installed, tested, and monitored. An IT auditor when reviewing a VPN's internal controls should look for evidence of an adequate enterprise IT security function assessment of their security and legal risks arising out of using VPNs, and a strong implementation of controls to protect data while they are entering the VPN as well as at the point on leaving the VPN. The failure to secure information while unencrypted over a given network path could result in confidentiality, integrity, non-repudiation, and/or availability issues.

Most small- to medium-sized enterprises will usually contract with a third-party vendor to help them install, configure, and even sometimes manage their VPN. However, reliance on third-party service providers could result in risks such as the choice of an inappropriate provider, lacking strong VPN-based governance and management processes. Based on our Chapter 7 discussion on IT infrastructure controls, there should be active measuring and monitoring of service level agreements (SLA) and metrics supporting the VPN.

Any VPN can cause some major risks to the enterprise if there has been an inadequate backup and redundancy strategy when implementing it. The Exhibit 26.4 VPN illustration is an example. Although many VPNs have been implemented following that type of configuration, there can be risks associated with a failure to provide redundancy or back up and both a lack of reliability, inadequate capacity, and the lack of confidentiality on operation parameters or data. An IT auditor should meet with IT management and its security functions and assess whether adequate attention has been given to assessing VPN risks and well as adequate risk protection procedures.

AUDITING A VPN INSTALLATION

Although this chapter has discussed a variety of IT telecommunication issues, VPNs are relatively new and represent an important area for an IT audit internal controls review. Before launching any VPN review, an IT auditor should obtain some technical and configuration knowledge of the VPN installation to be reviewed as well as an understanding of such technical areas as the encryption technologies used, network security architecture, and security technologies. On a high-level, much of this information can be found in other chapters in this book, and a Web search can yield even more. As part of the audit-planning process, an IT auditor should initially perform a high-level risk assessment, gathering requirements for the VPN configuration.

As discussed in all IT audit reviews, the responsible IT auditor should clearly define the scope and objective of the VPN review. In addition, all affected stakeholders should be explicitly identified as part of the planned audit's scope. Any key concerns of the stakeholders should also be included, as appropriate, in the scope and objectives of the

1. Meet with IT management to understand responsibilities for managing VPN operations. If a third-party vendor is used, establish or obtain right-to-audit privileges.
   a. Document and understand proposed VPN technology, such as VPN model, VPN architecture, VPN configuration/topology and planned VPN usage.
   b. Assess whether expected VPN benefits are being achieved.
2. If the VPN has been implemented within the last year or is still being developed, review project status reports, management approval, budget documents, project plans, and other status reports to determine whether the VPN is being launched in a well-controlled manner.
   a. Evaluate the actual implementation of the technologies against the plans, and identify any deviations.
   b. Discuss the VPN with members of operating management, and assess whether their expectations are being met.
3. Review the actual VPN development contracts, SLA and metrics measures that were agreed on, and assess whether well-controlled procedures are being followed.
4. Evaluate the actual security architecture and encryption technology implemented for conformance with the approved VPN design.
5. Document the current or planned VPN, and determine that it meets approved project plans.
   a. Confirm whether the solution is certified to conform to one of the PPTP, L2TP, or IPSec protocols.
   b. If the VPN is primarily developed in-house, identify the persons responsible for VPN operations, and assess whether training appears adequate.
6. Evaluate the VPN redundancy and backups established, and determine whether they are consistent with enterprise disaster recovery plans and good operating practices.
   a. Through a review of VPN operations, determine that their redundancy and backup facilities are functioning appropriately.
   b. Determine that appropriate security tools and processes are in place for such things as virus checking and intrusion detection.
7. Evaluate the adequacy of the VPN testing and migration processes to assess whether they address all kinds of users and cover such things as capacity, bandwidth, access control, and encryption in an appropriate manner.
8. Determine that the implemented VPN and its technology are being used as intended.
9. Evaluate the progress of the VPN implementation with reference to its appropriateness and adequacy to mitigate the risks—security risk, third-party risk, business risk, implementation risk, and operating risk.
10. Determine that the VPN and its usage are in conformance with enterprise and other good security policies and procedures including strong data classifications.
11. Determine whether third parties accessing the VPN via extranets have signed the relevant security and confidentiality agreements and are complying with the same.
12. Ensure that SLAs and metrics, including quality of service assessments, are measured, monitored, and escalated on a regular basis for timely actions.

EXHIBIT 26.5   IT Audit Steps for a Review of VPN Internal Controls

review. Also, in case the VPN review scope includes third-party providers, the IT auditor must assure a right to audit clause was included in their contracts. The audit should then be scoped and launched consistent with the objectives of the review.

The responsible IT auditor should gather and study the available VPN documentation, such as business systems documentation, contracts, service level agreements and log reports. Discussions with stakeholders and service providers as well as observations can be used in gathering, analyzing, and interpreting the collected VPN data. Where appropriate, the IT auditor should test significant processes and functions in the VPN environment to verify that they are performing as intended.

Particularly if this is a relatively new VPN installation, other information gathering items that should be included in the review are:

- Requirements for the proposed VPN solution, including any cost-benefit analyses, as well as evidence of business and IT approvals
- The proposed VPN technology, such as hardware models, VPN architecture, and the network configuration and topology
- The VPN security architecture and features, including its encryption technologies
- VPN redundancy, disaster recovery and backup facilities
- Documentation supporting the selection process for the choice of the service provider as well as supporting project management materials and monitoring mechanisms
- The VPN service provider contract, supporting SLAs and metrics
- Statutory requirements, if any, that needs to be fulfilled for this VPN

Based on these gathered materials, an IT auditor should launch a review of the enterprise VPN. Exhibit 26.5 outlines IT audit steps for a review of an enterprise's VPN system. In performing this review, the inferences and recommendations should be based on an objective analysis and interpretation of the data. The results of this review should include audit report findings and recommendations for corrective actions.

NOTE

1. Denial of Service (DOS) Attack. A malicious attempt to make a computer resource unavailable to its intended users. Although the means to carry out, motives for, and targets of a DOS attack may vary, it generally consists of the concerted efforts of a person or people to prevent an Internetsite or service from functioning efficiently or at all, temporarily or indefinitely.

CHAPTER TWENTY-SEVEN

Change and Patch Management Controls

NFORMATION TECHNOLOGY (IT) CHANGE and patch management control processes are executed within an enterprise's IT department to manage the enhancements, updates, incremental fixes, or patches to production systems, including:

- Application program code revisions
- System upgrades to operating systems, databases, support software, and applications
- IT infrastructure changes as discussed in Chapter 7, such as servers, cabling, routers, and firewalls
- Systems software and application program patches supplied by the vendor to fix small problems or introduce other revisions

Collectively, the more comprehensive fixes are called IT changes; the smaller or quick-fix types of changes are usually called patches. Enterprises have to deal effectively with these IT changes because virtually every business decision requires one or more changes to its IT-related assets. When IT changes fail or are poorly controlled, the impact on the business can range from minor inconveniences to events that hinder the achievement of business objectives or the ability to comply with laws and regulations.

This chapter provides guidance for IT auditors to assess an IT organization's change management capabilities and supporting internal controls processes by asking the right questions and performing application reviews. When reviewing IT change and patch management processes, IT auditors face the risks of unauthorized or unacceptable changes, low change success rates, too many emergency changes, or delayed project change-related implementations. IT auditors should have a working knowledge of their

IT change management processes and be able to distinguish quickly ineffective processes as well as to recognize any red-flag indicators that point to IT environment change management control issues.

Change management is often difficult for an enterprise to master because so many stakeholders are involved, including business managers, application system developers, IT operations staff, and external auditors. However, this is not a reason for an enterprise to be complacent about inadequate controls or low change management performance. A stable and well-managed IT production environment requires that implemented changes are predictable and repeatable, following controlled processes that are defined, monitored, and enforced. The necessary IT controls to achieve these changes should be similar to the controls used in financial processes to reduce the risk of fraud and errors.

This chapter defines IT change and patch management processes from an IT audit perspective and explains why enterprise IT management should care about managing those processes. The chapter presents an IT audit change and patch management audit program and discusses some of the change and patch management tools available to support IT auditors. An objective of this chapter, however, is not to identify specific software tools but to help IT auditors ask the right questions to help them assess an enterprise's IT change and patch management processes.

IT CHANGE MANAGEMENT PROCESSES

IT operations and their supporting processes require ongoing changes, whether updating new tax rules at the end of the year, installing new versions of program software, or making changes to the local network to facilitate a new business facility. Many of these changes are fairly significant in their impact to the enterprise and should be initiated through formal IT processes, such as the application selection process discussed in Chapter 10. Other changes, although small in their size and required implementation resources, are often critical to the enterprise.

An example of these smaller changes might be the discovery of a parameter table error late in a financial close process in a program to produce necessary status results. Often it is necessary to make a late-night emergency change to update such a table to get the system running again and to produce the financial reports. This is an example of a patch change. The necessary and often quick fix can be installed to get processes operating with the changes formally documented the next day.

This type of emergency IT systems change is the type of quick-fix patch necessary in many IT operations. In this example, the IT operations staff will encounter the error, contact the responsible person for resolution or make any necessary quick fix per established documentation, and then install the patch. These types of emergencies happen, but they should be exceptions, not regular occurrences. Matters can get out of hand quickly if patch-related changes are installed on a frequent and regular basis without formal authorizations.

The IT change creates risks, and any system patches must be treated as normal IT general and application control changes. There is a tight relationship between IT change and risk when IT assets seem to be in a state of constant change. Effective IT change management enables an enterprise to move safely from one known and defined state to another, regardless of the reason for making a change.

IT auditors should be aware of and understand the internal control processes supporting the IT patch and change management processes in their enterprises. These changes can be separated into changes to individual applications and infrastructure-type IT patches. Many of these changes may be emergency responses, but well-controlled processes should be in place to support them. The next sections discuss IT patch management internal controls for applications and for the IT infrastructure.

IT Application Patch Management Processes

Effective IT change management processes must provide enterprise management with visibility into the what, why, and when nature of IT application changes, how efficiently and effectively changes are being implemented, and what problems are caused by these changes. IT and management should understand the patch-related changes costs and the benefits the changes provide.

Virtually every business decision requires some level of changes in their IT applications based on these factors:

- External environment matters due to competitive market issues or stakeholder demands
- Regulatory environment changes or new requirements
- Enterprise changes in business objectives, goals, strategies, requirements, processes, or shifts in priorities
- Vendor-related changes including new products, upgrades, patches, and marketing initiatives
- Partner- and supplier-induced changes
- Changes as a result of operational problems, performance, or capacity requirements

Some of these changes may result in major system systems initiatives, but many others are less significant. Nevertheless, all changes should be managed, monitored, and controlled. IT auditors will not be involved in reviewing all changes, but they should have a good understanding of the IT application change management process and how it is implemented in their enterprise. Exhibit 27.1 outlines requirements for this IT change management process. Some of these elements may not be fully or strongly in place for emergency patch changes, but an IT auditor should look for elements of these steps for all IT changes.

A key requirement for effective IT application management is that an IT function should have comprehensive, well-defined preventive, detective, and corrective controls in place for all of its operations as well as clear definitions of responsibility for the IT staff with a defined separation of duties. Change management controls enable an IT function to address new IT application requirements without having to increase other resources. Effective IT application change management mitigates risk, lowers cost, and provides resources for additional services.

Whether dealing with a more significant, major change or an emergency short-term fix, an IT application change management process should be in place that typically includes these eight activities:

1. Identify and document the need for the change. Whether an emergency patch or a major application change, all such activities should be documented.
2. Prepare for the change.
   a. Document in detail the change request.
   b. Document the change test plan. Even if it is an emergency patch, there should be some documented approach either to test the change or to otherwise determine that it was correct.
   c. Document a change rollback plan, in case of change failure. This step is essential for all IT application changes.
   d. Write a step-by-step procedure that incorporates the change, the test plan, and the rollback plan.
   e. Submit the change procedure to appropriate levels of IT management in the form of a change request following enterprise SDLC procedures.
3. Develop the business justification for the planned change and obtain approvals. Emergency fixes may be after the fact, but all should have documented evidence of management approvals.
   a. Assess the impact, cost, and benefits associated with the change request.
   b. Review and assess the risks and impacts of the change request, including any legal or regulatory impacts.
4. Authorize the change request.
   a. Authorize, reject, or request additional information on the change request.
   b. Prioritize the change request with respect to any others that are pending.
   c. Even if the change was in the nature of an emergency patch, the change activity should be communicated to receive after-the-fact approval.
5. Schedule, coordinate, and implement the change.
   a. Schedule and assign staff members responsible for implementing and testing the change.
   b. Whenever practicable, test the change in a preproduction environment.
   c. Communicate the change to stakeholders likely to be affected.
   d. Approve the change for implementation.
   e. Implement the change as requested.
6. Verify and review the implemented change with consideration given to these points:
   a. Was the change successful?
   b. Was the change process followed?
   c. What was the variance between the planned and implemented change?
   d. Were internal control, operations, and regulatory compliance requirements maintained?
   e. If there were any problems or concerns with the changes, what lessons were learned to improve the change management process?
7. Following step 2c, roll back the change if unsuccessful.
8. Close the change request and communicate with the affected parties, making any necessary adjustments to the change management process.

EXHIBIT 27.1   IT Application Change Management Processes

Although effective IT application change management mitigates some risks, the process itself is often fraught with a high level of risk for an IT function. The change management process should be as effective and efficient as possible, but in deploying emergency changes, it is extremely difficult to prevent errors, irregularities, and unintended disruptions. Strong IT application change management processes will also assist an enterprise in maintaining ongoing compliance with regulatory issues as well as supporting Sarbanes-Oxley (SOx) compliance. Outlined in Chapter 1, SOx Section 404 requires management to validate and assess controls over financial reporting processes, including IT controls. Uncontrolled changes in an IT production environment can lead to errors that, if pervasive or critical, could be considered significant deficiencies that must be reported to the audit committee.

The Committee of Sponsoring Organizations Enterprise Risk Management (COSO ERM) model, discussed in Chapter 4, provides an effective way to look at IT application change management in an enterprise. The COSO ERM model depicted in Exhibit 4.6 shows eight elements to consider, starting with the internal environment, then objective setting and event identification, and moving up to the element of monitoring. The Institute of Internal Auditors (IIA), through its Global Technology Audit Guide (GTAG) publications, has described the use of COSO ERM as a model for risk management.[1] Exhibit 27.2 describes using COSO ERM as a model for change management; this slightly modified extract from the IIA GTAG guide uses only one dimension of the model to describe key IT change management activities in an enterprise.

COSO ERM Risk Monitoring
- Enterprise IT should develop monthly performance metrics and monitor IT application change activities for review and analysis by IT management.
- IT audit should perform regular reviews of change management process internal controls and performance.
- Conduct annual control self-assessments (CSAs) by business units and the IT department.
- IT should develop periodic reports on change management performance for review provided by the board to senior management.

ERM Information and Communications
- Senior management should recognize and emphasize the importance of strong IT application change control processes and procedures.
- Change controls-related service desk issues should be communicated for resolution and trend analysis. (See Chapter 7 for ITIL service desk information.)
- IT application change policies, as well as any revisions, should be communicated to all affected personnel.

Risk Management Control Activities
- Common IT change controls processes should be in place and documented.
- An IT management committee or board should be in place to establish an effective change control committee structure.
- Change control logs should be used for all changes, whether major updates or smaller patches.
- There should be a segregation of duties between developers and technical staff responsible for installing changes.
- Automated revision and version controls should be in place to enforce the process of promoting changes into production.
- Automated processes should be employed to return production environments to a prechange state.
- Clear delegations of change authority should be documented.
- Approvals for all changes should be documented.
- Automated systems and data backups should be in place, providing the ability to restore from prior-state approved environments.

EXHIBIT 27.2   IT Change Management Requirements following COSO ERM

Change Control Risk Assessments
- Thorough risk assessments of all proposed IT changes should be performed.
- Risks due to changes should be well understood by IT personnel.
- Business continuity planning should be in place.
- Business insurance needs assessments should be performed for major change activities.
- Risk factors should be used to assess and determine classifications of each change and the level of testing and approval.

Objective Setting and Change Event Identification
- Management should establish business objectives and strategies for the IT application change management process, whether major changes or smaller patches.
- IT management should establish objectives for change processes, identifying events that could prevent the successful achievement of business objectives and adherence to change process.

IT Change Management Internal Environment Considerations
- Senior and IT management should clearly demonstrate that IT application change management is important.
- The presence of an effective culture of change management is important.
- There should be no tolerance for out-of-process changes or unauthorized changes; while emergency patch changes may be necessary, they should be documented and followed up for approval.
- Change-related documentation should exist for IT change-related procedures for managing changes in applications, databases, operating systems, and all other IT assets.
- IT change process training should be provided for all affected personnel.
- Defined roles and responsibilities should be enforced.
- Service-level agreements (SLAs) and contracts with vendors should be in place that define process and performance standards.
- Enterprise-level standards and guidelines for IT change processes should be in place.

EXHIBIT 27.2 (*Continued*)

Application change management processes for an enterprise will be at risk if the factors described in COSO ERM have not been considered and implemented. These elements should be implemented in any IT function. Often they are emphasized in larger, better-organized IT systems, but many times they are ignored for the numerous quick fixes that sometimes plague many IT operations. In such a poorly managed IT function, programmers and systems specialists can make program changes to make things run smoothly, but they often fail to consider the need for change logs, revision documentation, and other good IT change management practices.

Unauthorized, untracked IT application changes create potential exposures for fraud when IT management and others are not aware of what is being done to their IT systems. Even without fraudulent intent, improper and undocumented patch changes often are poorly or inadequately implemented, causing IT application business requirements to be misinterpreted with respect to required IT changes.

Too many of these program and systems patch changes can cause large disruptions in IT operations due to failed changes, resulting outages, service impairments, rework, or unplanned work. Since these quick-fix changes often are not evaluated with respect to one another, it is difficult to forecast the impact of a change on existing business processes; the result may be IT resources working on the wrong things or on tasks that are less important. The change activities may also be done out of their intended sequence, resulting in rework and duplications of effort.

IT auditors, in their general and application control reviews, often see numerous patch changes piled on other changes, which are often called systems thrashing. Here an IT function may have no ability to control its operational environment, with many systems resources being spent on correcting unauthorized application changes and project activities. In this environment, IT resources are regularly diverted to rework in order to address the unintended consequences of unmanaged changes. In addition, there may be high turnover in the IT technical staff and evidence of burnout in key staff members.

IT auditors often can develop an understanding of the effectiveness of IT application change and patch management processes by gathering and reviewing some metrics about the extent of IT application patch and change activities for given applications and across all systems. IT functions should be keeping such metrics to monitor their own performance, but when they are not available, IT audit should dig back to IT operations production records to understand performance here. The next section has more guidance on developing these metrics.

IT application change management processes should be predictable, repeatable, managed, and measurable; that is, every application change—even emergency patches—should be planned and managed in a predictable manner. Although an IT function can certainly not plan for emergency application failures, requiring program, table quick-fix, or patch changes, general backup plans should be in place to correct matters. The process here is very similar to the emergency response plans for IT disaster recovery, discussed in Chapter 23.

Appropriate stakeholders as well as IT systems and management resources should be involved in assessing risks associated with proposed changes and prioritizing their implementations. This process really requires strong two-way communications. All too often, IT may want to install some application change because of a regular software upgrade, and application users are hesitant because of their comfort with the existing application. In other situations, users may want to install some system change even though IT is reluctant. There must be strong, two-way discussions, and IT audit should assess the adequacy of these processes.

Participants in the IT application change process should understand the relevant categories and priorities of changes and the levels of formality and rigor required to implement each one, ranging from vendor software application upgrades, to IT function–developed changes, to late-night emergency fixes. Effective IT application change management processes require understanding, awareness, visible sponsorship, and appropriate actions by all involved parties, balancing the risks and costs of changes with opportunities.

IT professionals responsible for IT application changes, and particularly the patch management process, should understand their enterprise's risk tolerance regarding installing changes and patches and help to identify and distribute them in an enterprise. The concept of risk appetite was discussed in Chapter 4 and is often an important measure. IT should attempt to forecast the impact of an application change on the business. Determining the risk appetite is often the most difficult step in implementing an application change and patch management strategy. To better understand this process,

Network Changes	IT Hardware Changes	Application Changes	Infrastructure Changes
Install cabling	Add new production server	Add new version of application	Expand/build data or call center
Upgrade switch and router software	Add patches to operating software	Install new application	Upgrade heating or cooling facilities
Install firewalls	Add new peripheral device	Upgrade to new database system	Install new backup power facility
Change Internet addresses	Install monitoring software	Increase number of software license "seats"	Install new version of staff laptop computers

EXHIBIT 27.3 Categories of IT Application Changes and Patches

Exhibit 27.3 outlines some of the major categories of IT application changes and patches along with examples of each. Of course, such a list will be much more extensive given all of the hardware, software, and infrastructure components that are subject to change management activities.

An effective IT application change and patch management process is evidenced by strong process standards, rigorous discipline and enforcement of violations of those standards, a centralized and consistent standards-setting authority, and cross-departmental communication and collaboration. Everyone in the IT organization should be following the same change management procedures, similar to IT procedures discussed for other general controls, as discussed in Chapter 6.

IT application change management controls, embedded in well-defined IT operational processes, will help to ensure the consistency and predictability necessary to achieve business goals that rely on these processes. A culture of effective IT application change and patch management will be perpetuated by a combination of senior management tone at the top messages and preventive, detective, and corrective controls, which serve to deter future unauthorized changes. Effective IT application change and process management processes are a general control area, as discussed in Chapter 6, and are used throughout an IT organization. They also can be viewed as an application control, as discussed in Chapter 10 on auditing IT application controls. However, because an effective change process is so important to so many aspects of IT operations and business processes, we also discuss them here as a special area for IT auditor attention. Exhibit 27.4 describes IT application change and patch management controls. Exhibit 27.5 outlines IT application preventive, detective, and protective change management controls.

Infrastructure Emergency Change and Patch Management

The last section addressed application patch management processes for specific IT applications, whether residing on a central enterprise database server or residing on a laptop with network connections to other enterprise resources. Strong change and patch control procedures are important here because an incorrect or unauthorized change could impact enterprise production systems. Change management controls are equally important over infrastructure controls.

---

1. Create a change and patch and vulnerability group. This group reviews proposed new changes and schedules change activities based on its recommendations.
2. Continuously monitor proposed changes and patches for vulnerabilities, remediations, and threats.
3. Prioritize application and infrastructure changes and patches, establishing phased deployments as appropriate.
4. Establish standards and procedures to test all changes and patches prior to deployment.
5. Deploy enterprise-wide automated patching solutions for responses to vendor software updates.
6. Coordinate all change management processes with established ITIL change management best practices.
7. Create an inventory of all information technology assets as part of the configuration management database. (See Chapter 7.)
8. Use standardized change configurations for IT resources as much as possible.
9. Verify that vulnerabilities have been remediated.
10. Consistently measure the effectiveness of the enterprise's change, patch, and vulnerability management program, and apply corrective actions as necessary.
11. Train applicable staff on vulnerability monitoring and remediation techniques.
12. Periodically test the effectiveness of the organization's change, patch, and vulnerability management programs.

EXHIBIT 27.4   IT Application Change and Patch Management Controls

---

Change Management Preventive Controls
■ IT change authorizations
  • Current documentation should be in place describing IT change management processes, including participant roles and responsibilities.
  • Responsibilities, with assigned levels of authorizations, should be formally assigned to persons responsible for the change management process.
■ Separation of duties and responsibilities controls
  • Organization charts and other documentation should show clear assignments and responsibilities for persons responsible for change management, including change authorizations, scheduling, process implementation, and approval responsibilities.
  • Clear policies should describe the categories and tiers of changes, approval levels, and responsibilities for moving changes and the levels of formality, approval, from initiation to the implementation stage.
  • The responsibility for initiating changes in production systems and operations should be strictly limited to those responsible for implementing system changes and not others, such as application programmers.
  • IT and user training and awareness programs should be in place to promote a culture of change management.
■ Change management supervision and monitoring
  • Documentation, including published lists of authorized changes and other artifacts, should be in place to show that the change process is effectively monitored, supervised, and enforced.
  • Change management supervisory minutes should be available to show a clear record of change management activities.

EXHIBIT 27.5   IT Preventive, Detective, and Corrective Change Management Controls

---

Change Management Detective Controls

▪ Supervision and monitoring
  - Production equipment changes should be tracked through audit logs, work tickets, and change orders. These should identify the date, time, implementer, and system along with details of the changes made.
  - Change activities should be reviewed to ensure that all change objective and plans have been met. Any variances should be reported and explained.
  - There should be documented evidence regarding implemented changes, indicating the successful implementation, acceptance by a change manager, and closure of the change order.

▪ Sampling procedures should be used to audit the accuracy of reconciliations between production changes and authorized changes.
  - Walk-throughs of the change management process should be performed to ensure that the changes were implemented within scope.
  - Using a sample of detective controls changes, ensure that changes are mapped to authorized work.

Corrective and Recovery Change Controls

▪ All changes made outside of the change management process should be identified, with documentation describing rationale and corrective actions taken.

▪ Postimplementation change controls reviews should be performed, based on the degree of change, importance of the business activities undergoing change, and significance of the potential risks to the enterprise.

▪ For any changes that have failed during the period reviewed, problem managers should rule out the scheduled changes and review production changes on the affected infrastructure.

EXHIBIT 27.5   (*Continued*)

The IT infrastructure, described in Chapter 7, includes all of the systems and services in an IT operation beyond specific applications. These may include the computer hardware environment including database servers, the telecommunications network, other attached components, and people-based functions such as systems software specialists and the help desk. IT operations often have fairly structured change management controls, with software update processes and the like, but infrastructure change and patch control procedures often present significant risks to an IT organization.

There are numerous types of infrastructure changes. Some examples of changes in a typical IT organization include:

▪ Operating system changes where a software vendor delivers a new version or corrective patch with no consideration given to the implications of that patch on other production applications

▪ New versions of system software that are delivered by vendors and installed with little consideration to their impact on other production applications

▪ Patch changes by an enterprise systems software specialist to "improve efficiency" in systems operations, with little consideration given to their impact on other production operations

▪ Changes to the production network environment by adding a new device or otherwise changing the network configuration

▪ IT personnel changes, such as changing the shift hours of a help desk function from 24/7 to 24/5

The nature and extent of IT infrastructure changes can be massive and very extensive. However, often such infrastructures changes are not subjected to the same change controls typically found in IT production applications. Patch-related IT infrastructure changes are even more critical. For example, a network engineer might add a new device to the telecommunications network simply by plugging the unit into an available bus bar slot or plug, in the interest of improved efficiency and without testing or otherwise reviewing the implications of that change. This level of undocumented change to an application system could very much violate IT procedures, but many times such infrastructure patch changes can go unnoticed.

An enterprise IT function should establish change and patch monitoring standards for infrastructure changes as well as for its applications, following the general procedures outlined in Exhibit 27.2. Although we are not introducing changes to specific applications, the standards for infrastructure changes should be the same or even stronger. An unauthorized and improper infrastructure change can easily impact the overall IT operation.

As discussed in Chapter 31 on quality assurance and in other chapters, the establishment of activity metrics is a very important technique for an IT auditor to assess an operation or activity over time. The idea is to establish some standard, such as the number of system changes in a week, and then to assess the number that were not formally authorized before the change activity. In this example, an IT organization would measure and report on the success of its change activities. The IT organization would then establish a measure for assessing the change management performance.

Exhibit 27.6 is an example of this type of metric measure. For each group or area monitored, we are counting the number of production changes in a period—perhaps a month—and then the number of known unauthorized changes during that period as well as the mean time to repair or correct the system or process in this area. The product of these three numbers is a measure of the percent of time spent on unplanned work. This type of metric might be useful to IT management to assess its change management processes. It is just one example of a metric; management and IT audit can establish any of a series of such measures to assess how they are performing in an area.

An IT function can use a number of infrastructure-related change management metrics to assess its change and patch management practices. These are areas that IT audit should look for when assessing internal controls over IT change and patch management internal controls. Although not every IT function will develop metrics and measure performance on all of these areas, some to consider include:

- **Number of changes authorized per week, as measured by the change management log of authorized changes.** In general, more changes indicate more change productivity, as long as the change success rate remains high. A large IT function will be faced with a large number of infrastructure changes, in particular,

Number of Production Changes for Period		Number of Known Unauthorized Changes		Mean Time to Correct or Repair Problem		Percent of Time on Unplanned Work
	X		X		=	

EXHIBIT 27.6 Change Management Metric Measures

and recognition of this ongoing change activity is a good change management metric.

▪ **Number of unauthorized changes.** These changes, often not discovered until after the fact, circumvent established, formal change processes. This metric can be developed by taking the number of actual changes made and subtracting the number of authorized changes. A large number of unauthorized changes indicates that the real way to make changes is to recommend improvements to this management process.

▪ **Numbers of emergency changes and patches.** This metric can be developed by counting the number of changes that required an urgent approval during a period using the change review board process or emergency changes that were implemented and documented after the fact. A lower number typically is better. Too often many emergency changes indicate that the real way to make changes is to use the emergency change process for either convenience or speed.

▪ **Percentage of patches deployed in planned software releases.** When patches are deployed in planned software releases, they should not cause production disruptions and typically have much higher change success rates. A higher-value metric typically is better.

▪ **Percentage of time spent on unplanned work.** Planned work is the time spent on authorized projects and tasks. Unplanned work includes break/fix cycles, rework, and emergency changes. For this metric, a lower measure of unplanned work is better.

The preceding list shows some types of metrics that can be developed to assess IT change management operations. IT auditors should review any existing change management activities in place and assess whether the metrics appear to assess the established IT the change process and whether the key change management metrics being used monitor IT process effectiveness and drive business value.

Importance of IT Patch Management Controls

Although we often discuss IT change and patch management in the same context, patch management does have some unique characteristics. Patch management is an area of IT systems management that involves acquiring, testing, and installing multiple code changes, or patches, to an active computer system or application. System software and application software vendors supply these patches, which sometimes are required and other times are optional, for an IT function. Patch management tasks include:

▪ Maintaining current knowledge of available patches
▪ Deciding what patches are appropriate for particular systems
▪ Ensuring that patches are installed properly
▪ Testing systems after installation
▪ Documenting all associated procedures
▪ Determining if any configuration changes have been installed

Patch management is part of change management, but it is often viewed as a "make-do" fix rather than an elegant solution. Sometimes patches are ineffective and can even cause more problems than they fix. An IT function should have an effective patch management program that promotes a consistently configured environment that is secure against known vulnerabilities in operating system and application software. Unfortunately, managing enterprise IT patch updates for all the applications and operating system versions is fairly complicated, and the situation only becomes more complex when additional platforms, availability requirements, and remote offices and workers are factored in.

Although many internal control aspects of IT applications change and patch management are similar, IT auditors should be aware of some unique characteristics and requirements of IT patch management. Just as an enterprise may have its own unique technology needs, successful patch management programs will vary in design and implementation. However, there are some basic requirements that should be addressed and included in all patch management efforts, as outlined in the next sections.

Security and Patch Information Requirements

Security issues are a key component of patch management. Before installing a patch recommended by a software vendor, IT should understand any security issues and software updates relevant to that patch and to the enterprise's environment. An IT function needs a point person or team responsible for keeping up to date on newly released patches and security issues that affect the systems and applications deployed in its environment. This team also can take the lead in alerting administrators and users of security issues or updates to the applications and systems that they support and use. A comprehensive and accurate configuration management system, as discussed in Chapter 7, can help determine whether all existing systems are accounted for when researching and processing information on patches and updates. These are tasks for the IT systems software function.

Patch Prioritization and Scheduling

Scheduling guidelines and plans should exist in patch management programs, including the normal application of patches and updates to systems. Security or other critical updates should receive immediate priority; other patches should be installed through a program of standard patch releases and updates. Such a patch management schedule can be time or event based or may be driven by the release of software vendor service packs or maintenance releases. In either instance, modifications and customizations can and should be made based on availability requirements, system criticality, and available resources.

A patch management scheduling plan should emphasize necessary critical security and functionality patches and updates. Such a plan should help an enterprise IT function deal with the prioritization and scheduling of updates that, by their nature, must be deployed rapidly. A number of factors are routinely considered when determining patch priority and scheduling urgency. Vendor-reported high, medium, or low criticality is a key input for calculating a patch's significance and priority, as is the existence of a known malicious code risk. Another factor that should be taken into account is the relative importance of an application and its data in the support of the overall business.

Patch Testing

Ideally, the breadth and detail of patch testing should relate directly to the criticality of systems, the data handled, and the complexity of the environment, such as the number of supported platforms, applications, or remote offices. The patch testing process begins with the acquisition of the software updates and continues through acceptance testing after production deployment. The first component of patch testing should be the verification of the patch's source and integrity.

The actual mechanics of testing a patch vary widely. This testing could range from simply installing a patch and making sure the system reboots, to a procedure that could involve the execution of a battery of detailed and elaborate test scripts to validate continued system and application functionality. In the end, a suitable approach toward detailed patch testing is dictated by system criticality and requirements, available resources, and patch severity.

Change Management

Effective change management is vital to every stage of the patch management process. Patches and updates should be performed and tracked through a formal change management system. It is highly unlikely that an enterprise-wide patch management program can be successful without proper integration with the overall change management system of the enterprise.

Like any environmental changes, patch application plans submitted through change management must have associated contingency and back-out plans that include recovery plans if something goes wrong during or as a result of the application of a patch or update. Also, information on risk mitigation should be included in the change management solution. For example, how are desktop patches going to be phased and scheduled to prevent mass outages and support desk overload? Monitoring and acceptance plans also should be included in the change management process. How will updates be certified as successful? There should be specific milestones and acceptance criteria to guide the verification of the patch' success and to allow for the closure of the update in the change management system.

Patch Installation and Deployment

Installation and deployment is where the actual work of applying patches and updates to production systems occurs. This stage is the most visible to the enterprise as a whole, and the effort expended throughout the entire patch management process is what dictates the overall success of a given deployment and the patch management program. When applying patches, and especially security updates, it is critical that these updates must be made in a controlled and predictable fashion. Without an organized and controlled patch application process, the system's overall status may tend to drift and compliance with mandated patch and update levels may diminish.

Patch management automatic processes, such as Windows updates, are appropriate for smaller enterprises, but users and administrators generally should not be permitted to apply patches arbitrarily. This restriction should be addressed at a policy level with technical controls to limit when and by whom patches can be applied. The type of controls enforced will vary but should include items such as restricted user permissions to update the system and network-based access controls.

Audit and Assessment

IT systems management should perform regular assessments to gauge the success and extent of patch management efforts. This assessment should try to determine what systems need to be patched for any given vulnerability or bug and if the systems that are supposed to be updated actually have been patched. The major requirement for such an assessment is the ability to accurately track deployed hardware and software throughout the enterprise, including remote users and office locations.

System discovery and auditing are also components of this patch management assessment process. Asset and host management systems can help to administer and report on known systems, but often systems have been either unknowingly or intentionally excluded from inventory databases and management infrastructures. System discovery tools can help uncover these systems and assist in bringing them under the umbrella of formal system management and patch compliance. Organizations typically use either their own discovery and assessment mechanisms or one of the various managed vulnerability assessment tools. Regardless of the tools used, the goal is to discover unknown systems and assess their compliance with enterprise IT update and configuration guidelines. We have used the term *auditing* here as it is used in patch management professional literature, not in relation to IT auditing.

Consistency and Compliance

The audit and assessment element of a patch management program will help identify systems that are out of compliance with established guidelines, but additional work is required to reduce noncompliance. To supplement postimplementation assessments, controls should be in place to ensure that newly deployed and rebuilt systems are current with regard to their patch levels.

System build tools, discussed in the next section, and guidelines are the primary means of ensuring compliance with patch requirements at installation. As new patches are approved and deployed, build images and scripts should be updated so that all newly built systems are appropriately patched, and associated build documentation should be updated to reflect these changes. In addition to updates to build tools and documentation, operational procedures must exist to facilitate ongoing compliance of newly built systems.

Effective patch management processes is an area that is often all but ignored by many IT auditors in their reviews of general controls and change management processes. The importance of strong patch management change controls has been emphasized by the U.S. National Institute of Science and Technology, which has released several publications on effective patch management.[2]

Although technology is the core issue of patch management, focusing only on technology to solve problems or to improve internal controls is not the answer. IT auditors should work with IT software management to install patch management software or vulnerability assessment tools to support patch management oversight.

Patch management, ignored too often in the change management process, is an important area that should be included in many IT audit internal control reviews.

 ## AUDITING IT CHANGE AND PATCH MANAGEMENT CONTROLS

Effective IT change controls, at both an individual application and an overall infrastructure level, are important, higher-risk areas in an enterprise's overall control structure. IT auditors should understand the basic components of IT change and patch management. While the term *change management*, as used here, does not include the entire systems development life cycle process, such as application development or configuration management, it is an important area for IT audit attention.

IT audits of the change and patch management process assess the internal controls and management of changes to production hardware, network devices, operating systems, and application software. An enterprise's management uses this IT change management process to ensure that all authorized changes meet the enterprise's needs, creating business value. Exhibit 27.7 outlines some change management procedures audit steps for both application and infrastructure changes. Many of these points, such as the need for appropriate change reporting documentation and the need for change performance logs, cover all types of application, infrastructure, and patch-level change activities. However, patch management activities often introduce some unique audit considerations. Because patch management is a special area in the change management process that sometimes is ignored by IT auditors, Exhibit 27.8 describes a set of IT audit patch management procedures. IT patch management is also an area that often does not receive appropriate attention from management, and IT audit should consider at least scheduling an initial review focused on just patch management. That review possibly can later be combined with an overall review of application and infrastructure change management. Preliminary steps that should be accomplished during the launch of these change and patch management audit procedures include:

■ IT change management policies, standards, and procedures
■ Work flow diagrams depicting the IT change management process
■ IT personnel and departmental organization charts highlighting participants in change management with an emphasis on managers and supervisors responsible for developing and implementing those changes
■ Information regarding third-party service providers involved in the process, including relevant service-level agreements and contracts
■ Descriptions and diagrams showing the IT hardware, including descriptions of network devices, servers, libraries, and databases
■ IT operations metrics, standards, and service-level commitments directly relating to change and problem management
■ Sample reports showing how metrics, standards, and service-level commitments are reported to management
■ Selected service desk problem reports, lists of authorized changes over a selected recent test period, and supporting change control logs

1. Determine that IT change management policies, standards, and procedures apply broadly enough to ensure management control of the production environment. Ensure that they provide for:
   1a. Business case documentation to guide prioritization of change efforts
   1b. Risk and impact assessments considering impacts on a sample of operational system and application changes
   1c. Procedures for the categorization and prioritization of changes as well as the specific handling of emergency changes
   1d. Procedures for the testing of installed changes, including unit, regression, system, integration, and user acceptance testing as appropriate
   1e. Communication to change requesters regarding their change request status
   1f. Requirements definitions for major changes
   1g. Appropriate change-related related documentation, including adequate communication of pending changes
   1h. Appropriate segregation of the development, test, and production environments
   1i. Evidence of adequate consideration of change-related business continuity impacts
   1j. An incident resolution process for investigating change management failures
   1k. Evidence the controls have been defined throughout the process of change

2. Review IT operations metrics, standards, service-level agreements (SLAs), and related reports, and determine that they provide management with independent, timely, accurate, concise, and relevant information on the effects of changes and any problem impacts on IT operations and its business goals. Using a one-week or month sample period, measures should include:
   2a. Number of application and infrastructure changes authorized per week
   2b. Number of actual changes made per week and their actual lag times since authorization
   2c. Number of unauthorized changes during the same period, based on change control logs and other evidence
   2d. Application and infrastructure change success rate—the number of changes successfully implemented without causing an outage or other evidence of failure
   2e. Number of emergency changes required and documented during sample period

3. Review policies, standards, and procedures to determine that changes require business users' and IT operations management approval, and those approvals are required at appropriate points in the change process.

4. Based on the review of IT change management standards and procedures, select a completed sample to ensure that they have received adequate testing and met appropriate approval, requirements before their transfer to a production environment.

5. Based on a sample of components implemented into production, determine that they are the same as the components developed, tested, and approved.

6. Through interviews and reviews of documentation, determine that a postimplementation review has been performed for each significant change to assess its effectiveness, as measured by the business case applied in initiating the change.

7. Based on a sample of recent changes, ensure that these changes and software controls are updated properly and integrated into the enterprise configuration management database.

8. Review IT change management policies, standards, and procedures to ensure that changes are thoroughly documented, including what was changed, when, and by whom. Each change should carry an accurate description of its disposition, including whether it is in development, implemented, backed out, or canceled.

9. Based on problem management standards and procedures, determine that each problem record explicitly records any change found to have caused or contributed to the problem.

10. Review emergency change procedures, and based on the changes reviewed, make sure that emergency changes can be implemented quickly, effectively, and in a way that preserves accountability, traceability, and independent review.

EXHIBIT 27.7 IT Change Management Procedures Audit Steps

1. Determine that IT patch management procedures have been established that are consistent with application and infrastructure change management standards and procedures but also that they reflect the unique requirements of patch management controls. Ensure that patch management processes provide for:

   1a. Business case documentation to guide prioritization of change efforts
   1b. Risk and impact assessments considering impacts on a sample of operational system and application changes
   1c. Procedures for the categorization and prioritization of changes as well as the specific handling of emergency changes
   1.d Procedures for the testing of installed changes, including unit, regression, system, integration, and user acceptance testing as appropriate
   1.e Communication to change requesters regarding their change request status
   1f. Requirements definitions for major changes
   1g. Appropriate change-related related documentation, including adequate communication of pending changes
   1h. Appropriate segregation of the development, test, and production environments
   1i. Evidence of adequate consideration of change-related business continuity impacts
   1j. An incident resolution process for investigating change management failures
   1k. Evidence that the controls have been defined throughout the process of change

EXHIBIT 27.8 IT Patch Management Audit Procedures

IT auditors should realize that many applications, infrastructure, and patch changes operate in a dynamic process manner. A production application, for example, may have been supplied by a software vendor that produces periodic revision releases that go through formal review and training processes before they are released. However, from time to time there may be late-night or emergency problems in running the application, where a fix must be installed quickly to get the application back up and running. The IT function should pay particular attention to providing some level of testing and documenting those emergency changes before they are installed.

As discussed, infrastructure change and patch management often presents significant audit and internal control concerns. The issue is that there are so many different types of infrastructure changes in a larger IT function, as discussed, ranging from hardware to software and even to people-related changes. Change management standards and procedures should be established in all of these infrastructure areas. An enterprise education process is needed here, advising members of the IT staff on the impacts of infrastructure as well as the need to test them and seek approval when appropriate. The systems engineer called in to fix a downed server system late at night may not think she is making a change by just fixing the immediate problem at hand. However, the nature of the fix often results in a small but subtle infrastructure change that alters the configuration environment.

System patches are an even greater area of concern. Any personal user of Microsoft Windows who subscribes to automatic updates may receive a notice that a patch to fix a security risk has been downloaded to that system. As individuals, we tend to think that this is good and give the matter little further thought. However, many operating system patches can be large and potentially impact more systems resources. IT auditors should recognize the importance and internal control significance of these patches and assess whether documentation and controls are adequate.

Change and patch management controls are an important area that should be part of the IT auditor's internal control review procedures. They are becoming particularly significant as our systems are moving away from the traditional IT systems and programming shop with specialized in-house software and application programming groups to make the changes to our service-based Web environments of today.

 NOTES

1. *Change and Patch Management Controls: Critical for Organizational Success*, The Institute of Internal Auditors Global Technology Audit Guide Series, (Altamonte Springs, FL: IIA).
2. National Institute of Standards and Technology, "Creating a Patch and Vulnerability Management Program," Special Publication 800-40 Version 2.0 (November 2005), http://csrc.nist.gov/publications/nistpubs/800-40-Ver2/SP800-40v2.pdf.

CHAPTER TWENTY-EIGHT

Six Sigma and Lean Technologies

ENTERPRISE INFORMATION TECHNOLOGY (IT) auditors should often go beyond just their scheduled IT audits and, acting as internal consultants, look for ways to improve operations in such areas as shop-floor production processes or for office administrative procedures. Because of their overall emphasis on IT operations, IT auditors often can have a major role here through their internal controls reviews and the corrective actions recommended in audit reports; IT auditors also can have a strong role in process improvements by serving as internal consultants to their enterprise. There is no single solution or method for implementing best practices to improve operations; many different approaches have been tried over the years. Some of these are still active while others are forgotten footnotes in business history.

An overall quality improvement approach called six sigma was based on Japanese quality assurance techniques and now has been used successfully in the United States and elsewhere in the world to reduce errors and improve efficiencies in all aspects of enterprise operations. Six sigma has its roots in statistical quality control procedures but is viewed as much more of a process improvement approach. However, because of its roots in Japanese quality manufacturing processes, knowledgeable six sigma practitioners are designated as green belt certified (using Japanese jujitsu terminology) and experts are certified as black belts. When an enterprise adopts a six sigma approach, it can become an almost all-consuming exercise for many in operations.

Chapter 31 discusses quality assurance auditing processes and the role of the American Society for Quality (ASQ) quality auditors. Although those quality auditors normally have some understanding of six sigma concepts, IT auditors should have a basic understanding of six sigma concepts and how they are applied to IT audit concerns and in many areas of an enterprise.

This chapter provides a high-level introduction to six sigma concepts and how they can be used in many aspects of enterprise IT operations. An overview of six sigma is provided here as well as some what are called lean approaches to implementing six sigma. *Lean* is an term that is used increasingly in business procedures today. It is an approach that takes a comprehensive but very document-oriented process and its steps down to just the essential bare minimums. The lean techniques are valuable for implementing many aspects of six sigma operations.

Even though an IT audit function may not be using six sigma concepts as part of its overall audit procedures and operations, IT auditors should have a basic understanding of this important quality improvement concept. An IT auditor also will encounter auditees in all levels of operations who may talk about their six sigma achievements and activities. An effective IT auditor should have at least sufficient background information to understand these concepts and to ask important review questions.

 ## SIX SIGMA BACKGROUND AND CONCEPTS

Most IT auditors will recognize "sigma" as one of the letters of the Greek alphabet. As an uppercase letter, sigma appears as Σ in print and in mathematics, and this symbol normally refers to the sum of a series of numbers following it. In its lowercase form, sigma appears as σ and it is used to express the variability from some process.

These Σ-based summation and variability measures have been used by professionals at all levels to describe formulas that measure product or process quality. For example, quality assurance professionals have traditionally defined their quality measures in terms of three or four statistically defined sigma levels as a norm. That is, they would define their error or problem levels based on the statistical-based or Σ-defined levels 6,200 and 67,000 problems per million opportunities. We can think of these measures in terms of some part rolling off a highly automated production line. Whether in the United States or elsewhere, enterprises would accept that level of problems with these high-volume production parts, assuming they could fix or repair things later. We only mention statistical concepts here; an IT auditor should consult one of the many available references to learn more.[1]

Six sigma and quality concepts got started in the 1970s when a Japanese company took over production processing for what had been a Motorola plant producing Quasar brand television sets. The Japanese company installed its own production and quality procedures and was soon producing products with only 1/20th of the defects that had been tolerated by Motorola production management. The Japanese company was operating at what became known as six sigma.

Motorola enthusiastically implemented these same six sigma quality standards throughout its production and other operations. It quickly became a recognized leader in quality operations, and the company received the U.S. government's Malcolm Baldridge National Quality Award in 1988. Many other major companies, such as General Electric and Allied Signal, subsequently embraced six sigma concepts to improve customer service and productivity. Six sigma remains an important process improvement process today.

Although six sigma had its origins as a statistical quality assurance measure, its real importance is as a concept to improve overall process quality, whether in manufactured products or service-related processes. It is not the kind of concept where the chief executive officer (CEO) announces at a major meeting that the enterprise is going to improve its overall service and quality with little action beyond those broad statements. Rather, an effective six sigma initiative is implemented through the efforts of small teams using what is called a Design-Measure-Analyze-Improve-Control (DMAIC) model with the steps:

- **Define** the goals for the improvement activity.
- **Measure** the activity covering the existing system.
- **Analyze** to identify ways to eliminate gaps between the current performance of the system and the desired goal.
- **Improve** the system initiatives.
- **Control** the new or revised system.

These DMAIC steps outline the overall philosophy behind the six sigma process. Although it got started as a precise—with many decimal points—quality and process improvement process, six sigma today is much more about the steps necessary to improve existing enterprise processes by observing all types and levels of them, then developing a hypothesis to improve the observed operation, followed by making predictions to improve the area of concern. Six sigma once was oriented to primarily manufacturing processes, but it is very applicable to many business processes today, including IT operations. A designated six sigma team then installs the suggested changes, tests the results of those changes, and repeats these steps as necessary to make effective improvements.

IT auditors should recognize some very strong differences between a six sigma–led team operating in an area of enterprise operations and the more typical auditee environments. IT auditors review applications and IT operations and make recommendations for improvement through their published audit reports. An IT auditor's recommendations are based on compliance with standards and best practices as well as suggested approaches that may be developed through discussions before the release of the published audit report. These are not flexible or best-guess recommendations, and IT audit often may not return for an extended period to see if those internal audit recommendations have been implemented.

Six sigma process improvements do not come from outsiders such as a consultant visiting an operation and making suggestions to improve processes. Rather, a team of specialists from within an area of operations will review its own processes and implement improvements in familiar areas of operations. There are opportunities here for IT auditors on three levels. First, when IT audit discovers a six sigma process in place when reviewing some general controls area, it might expand its procedures and consider a review of the effectiveness of that existing six sigma program as well as other internal control processes. As a second area of opportunity, IT auditors may want to consider recommending six sigma processes as part of their reviews of internal controls in some IT operational area. As a third point, IT auditors also should consider the use of six sigma processes to improve their own internal audit operations.

All of these opportunities, of course, require that an IT audit team have some understanding of six sigma processes. Although quality auditors (discussed in Chapter 31) are typically very well aware of six sigma processes, the typical Information Systems Audit and Control Association (ISACA)–or Institute of Internal Auditors (IIA)–heritage IT auditor has not been exposed to these important concepts. The ISACA Web site does reference multiple articles linking six sigma with Control Objectives for Information and related Technology (CobiT) and the Information Technology Infrastructure Library. A search on the IIA Web site home page for "six sigma" returns a limited number of references. For example, the IIA's online newsletter contained an article on six sigma and risk analysis[2] by an internal auditor from Textron Corporation, an early user of six sigma. The next sections provide a high-level overview of six sigma for IT auditors, who should develop a general understanding of these processes.

IMPLEMENTING SIX SIGMA

The concept behind six sigma calls for an enterprise to implement processes that will deliver no more than 3.4 defects per million opportunities (DPMO) for a defective production product or process step. Although we are using the term *six sigma* throughout this chapter, often it is now referenced in publications as 6 σ, a term understood by quality specialists but not many others. At first glance, 3.4 defects per million sounds like a very tough standard to meet. However, a Web search will provide information on thousands of companies that have implemented successful six sigma programs. In many cases, the effort was been launched by a fairly senior manager who heard about the success of other enterprises and acted as a catalyst for improving service quality. The whole idea is less about statistical-led quality management and more about the process of establishing a new initiative throughout the enterprise. For many enterprises, six sigma is launched along the lines of a family moving to a new religion. One family member may have been exposed to the new religious philosophy, took some additional training, and then brought in missionaries from the new religion to teach and convert other family members. They will subscribe to the new philosophy, establish goals, and continue to actively follow and work under that new religion.

This analogy is admittedly weak because the newly converted family will view their new religion as an approach to better spiritual values and other intangible future benefits. Six sigma calls for an enterprise to establish some very definite goals that will begin to provide benefits once deployed. Exhibit 28.1 outlines the types of deployment and process goals an enterprise might attempt to achieve by adopting a six sigma program. Although many of these goals are general and apply primarily to production process operations, others are very applicable to IT operations, such as the process-level goals to

- Improve cycle times.
- Reduce process resource requirements.
- Improve process yield through reduction in defects.
- Reduce all levels of variability and improve process capability.

We can think of each of these goals from the perspective of IT operations, and an IT auditor may consider these areas when performing an IT general controls review, as discussed in Chapter 6.

Six Sigma Enterprise Deployment Goals

- ▪ Goals to Enhance Business Needs
  - Increase shareholder value.
  - Increase revenues, returns on investment (ROI), and profitability.
  - Improve market share.
- ▪ Operations-Level Goals
  - Reduce material and labor costs.
  - Eliminate production rework at all levels.
  - Improve production and process throughput.
- ▪ Process-Level Goals
  - Improve cycle times.
  - Reduce process resource requirements.
  - Improve process yield through reduction in defects.
  - Reduce all levels of variability and improve process capability.
- ▪ Identify Operations Value Streams Deployment Goals
  - Define the processes that are critical to enterprise performance.
  - Analyze how key processes bring value to customers.
- ▪ Determine Metrics and Current Performance Levels
  - Develop techniques to measure key value streams.
  - Identify processes that are stable and subject to statistical control.
  - Establish process measures, such as cycle times, costs, and quality opportunities.
  - Define process "should-be" objectives where appropriate.
  - Define benchmark or best-in-class performance measures.
- ▪ Establish Breakthrough Strategies for New Performance Levels
  - Identify the variables that make the most differences to process performance and establish settings or goals for them.
  - Identify areas where processes can be designed to become more robust.
  - Define areas where process redesign will yield production of quality improvements.
- ▪ Standardize New Production or Process Approaches
  - Develop and release operational procedures covering new approaches.
  - Train people, as necessary, to use new approaches.
  - When necessary, implement statistical measures to control process variation.
  - Modify inventory, accounting, and other business systems to ensure that the improved process performance is reflected in overall operations.

EXHIBIT 28.1   Six Sigma Deployment and Process Goals

Six Sigma Leadership Roles and Responsibilities

An effective implementation of six sigma in an enterprise requires designated leadership and a strong, trained team of employees who are launching six sigma projects in addition to their own normal job responsibilities. Six sigma introduces a series of new professional certifications, each of which has special training responsibilities. An enterprise leadership team launching and managing six sigma should include:

- ▪ **Six sigma executive council.** A top-level group of senior managers across the enterprise should be formed to manage the six sigma initiative. This group suggests and approves high-impact six sigma projects, tracks progress, reviews program effectiveness, and generally communicates the message throughout the enterprise.

Although the analogy is not complete, the six sigma executive council takes sort of an audit committee role on a six sigma initiative.

▪ **Six sigma director.** This person directs and manages all six sigma efforts for an enterprise. The director is the six sigma program manager for multiple six sigma projects and leads overall deployment efforts, such as shown in Exhibit 28.1. The director leads and evaluates the overall initiative and communicates progress to customers, suppliers, and the enterprise.

▪ **Master black belt.** This is the one full-time agent directly committed to leading a six sigma initiative. Certified six sigma black belts (CSSBBs) have displayed proven knowledge and expertise in implementing six sigma. This involves both "textbook" knowledge of the subject matter (methodologies, tools, principles, and related topics such as leadership and change management) and real-world, successful application of the methodology and tools with experience in more than one other six sigma project.

An individual can become a certified CSSBB in a variety of ways: from a professional organization, such as the ASQ; from some consulting companies; or from a six sigma active company (e.g., General Electric, Motorola, etc.). No one way is necessarily better than another; however, it is widely accepted that private companies with mature six sigma programs serve as the best vehicles for certification. An IT auditor wishing to learn more should do a Web search for "certified CSSBB." that will provided many references to six sima books, training courses and other information.

▪ **Six sigma black belts.** These are the six sigma experts in an enterprise. Black belts lead overall process improvement efforts and take direct responsibility for specific key six sigma projects. A black belt should have a demonstrated understanding of the black belt body of knowledge, as shown in Exhibit 28.2,[3] and a proficiency in achieving the results of six sigma approaches. Black belts frequently serve their organizations for assignments of one or two years, returning to their regular job duties thereafter.

▪ **Green belts.** These professionals have a basic understanding of six sigma processes and serve as part-time assistants to their enterprises while maintaining normal job responsibilities. They work on six sigma projects but at a more junior-level than black belts.

▪ **Six sigma improvement teams.** Following the leadership of black and green belts, many other persons may be assigned to a six sigma project on a part-time basis. Depending on the nature of a project, there may be a need for detailed data gathering, process testing, or preparation of documentation to achieve six sigma results.

Beyond these designated six sigma leaders, usually many others in an enterprise are assigned to this type of project to analyze and achieve results. The concept here is that a team of designated six sigma "belts" should study operational areas to identify areas in which to eliminate errors or waste to bring operations down to the six sigma standard of less than 3.4 DPMO. IT auditors who are accustomed to reviewing documents for internal control violations but who sometimes give small violations a "pass" may find six sigma rules quite tight. There is almost no tolerance for any errors or exceptions under six sigma

High-Level Six Sigma Understandings

- [ ] Overview of Six Sigma and Its Language
- [ ] DMAIC Methodology Overview
- [ ] Financial Benefits of Six Sigma
- [ ] Understanding the Impact of Six Sigma to the Enterprise

Define Six Sigma Elements

- [ ] Project Management
- [ ] Project Definition
- [ ] Project Charter
- [ ] Developing a Business Case
- [ ] Chartering a Six Sigma Team
- [ ] Defining Roles and Responsibilities
- [ ] Gathering Voice of the Customer and Support for a Project
- [ ] Translating Customer Needs into Specific Requirements
- [ ] Define Phase Review Elements

Measure

- [ ] Process Mapping (As-Is Process)
- [ ] Understanding Data Attributes (Continuous Versus Discrete)
- [ ] Defining Metrics
- [ ] Measurement System Analysis
- [ ] Gauge Repeatability and Reproducibility
- [ ] Data Collection Techniques
- [ ] Calculating Sample Size
- [ ] Data Collection Plan
- [ ] Understanding Variation
- [ ] Measuring Process Capability
- [ ] Calculating Process Sigma Level
- [ ] Rolled Throughput Yield
- [ ] Visually Displaying Baseline Performance
- [ ] Statistical Software Training
- [ ] Measurement Phase Review

Analyze

- [ ] Visually Displaying Data (Histogram, Run Chart, Pareto Chart, Scatter Diagram)
- [ ] Detailed (Lower-Level) Process Mapping of Critical Areas
- [ ] Value-Added Analysis
- [ ] Cause-and-Effect Analysis (aka Fishbone, Ishikawa)
- [ ] Affinity Diagram
- [ ] Data Segmentation and Stratification
- [ ] Correlation and Regression (Linear, Multiple)
- [ ] Process Performance (Cp, CpK, Pp, PpK, CpM)
- [ ] Short-Term versus Long-Term Capability
- [ ] Nonnormal Data Distribution Transformations
- [ ] Central Limit Theorem
- [ ] Goodness of Fit Testing
- [ ] Hypothesis Testing
- [ ] Analysis of Variance (ANOVA), Two Sample T-Tests, Chi Squared Test

EXHIBIT 28.2 Black Belt Body of Knowledge

Source: Robert R. Moeller, *Brink's Modern Internal Auditing*, 7th ed. (Hoboken, NJ: John Wiley & Sons, 2009). Copyright © 2009, John Wiley & Sons. Used with permission of John Wiley & Sons.

☐ Design of Experiments (DOE): Full, Fractional Factorials
☐ Verification of Root Causes
☐ Determining Opportunity (Defects and Financial) for Improvement
☐ Project Charter Review and Revision
☐ Statistical Software Training
☐ Analyze Phase Review

Improve

☐ Brainstorming
☐ Multivoting
☐ Process Simulation
☐ Quality Function Deployment (House of Quality)
☐ Selecting a Solution
☐ Failure Modes and Effects Analysis (FMEA)
☐ Poka Yoke (Mistake-Proofing Your New Process)
☐ Piloting Your Solution
☐ Implementation Planning
☐ Statistical Software Training
☐ Culture Modification Planning for Your Organization
☐ Improve Phase Review

Control

☐ Assessing the Results of Process Improvement
☐ Statistical Process Control (SPC)
☐ Rational Subgroupings
☐ Establishing Process Standards for Inputs, Process, and Outputs
☐ Developing a Process Control Plan
☐ Documenting the Process
☐ Statistical Software Training
☐ Control Phase Review

EXHIBIT 28.2 (*Continued*)

rules. Even when an enterprise has not formally adopted an overall six sigma program, IT auditors should consider user using six sigma rules as part of their internal audit activities.

Launching the Six Sigma Project

A successful six sigma initiative in an enterprise does not require the implementation of just one large project but many smaller efforts to initiate improvements. Similar to IT auditors performing reviews to improve internal controls, a six sigma team will look at virtually all processes and attempt to find opportunities for improvements. A critical difference is that IT auditors generally start with a high-level approach, such as a plan to review internal controls in some operating unit. The six sigma team typically will develop detailed flowcharts covering both large and small operations and then ask these questions to better understand a process:

■ For which stakeholder does a process primarily exist?
■ What value does the process create or what outputs are produced?

- Who is the owner of the process?
- Who or what supporting area provides the inputs to the process?
- What are the inputs to the process?
- What resources—people, IT, or other—does this process use?
- Are there any subprocesses with their own discrete start and end points?
- What steps in the process create value?

Based on this preliminary information, the six sigma team should then establish some process improvement objectives. These can cover a wide variety of areas, and each process should be given a high-level objective, such as to "help customers better find the replacement parts needed for a product," to "improve product delivery times," or to "reduce office staff voice message telephone tag communications." The six sigma process can then look at all operations in the enterprise, ranging from major to most mundane.

The six sigma team then creates high-level process maps for each area reviewed. However, because six sigma improvements often emphasize activities outside of the enterprise, such as customers and suppliers, the analysis should cover their needs and requirements. Using six sigma terminology, a series of what are called Supplier-Inputs-Process-Outputs-Customer (SIPOC) charts can be created to describe the overall process. Exhibit 28.3 is an example of such a SIPOC chart that describes customer service process for car repair process example operations.

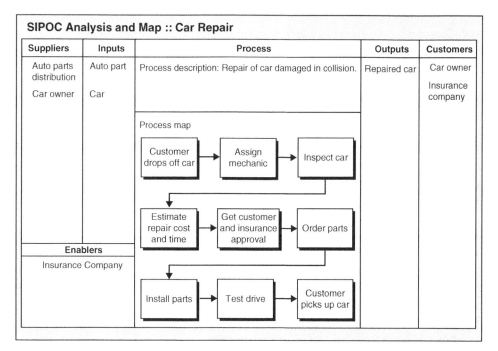

EXHIBIT 28.3 Six Sigma SIPOC Chart Example
Source: U.S. Army Business Transformations, www.army.mil/ArmyBTKC/focus/cpi/tools3_il.htm#img

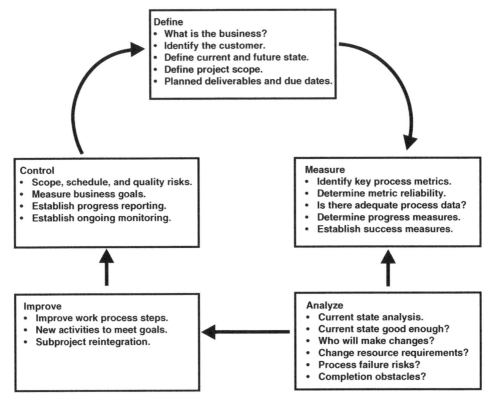

EXHIBIT 28.4 DMAIC Procedures for a Six Sigma Project
Source: Robert R. Moeller, *Brink's Modern Internal Auditing*, 7th ed. (Hoboken, NJ: John Wiley & Sons, 2009). Copyright © 2009, John Wiley & Sons. Used with permission of John Wiley & Sons.

Based on this SIPOC analysis, the black belts who performed the work should design and propose a six sigma process improvement project. Based on the data gathered, the team should document opportunities to improve, estimate the potential cost savings, and then identify a sponsor from the business area reviewed. Usually a senior manager from some area of operations will recognize potential savings and will take responsibility for the expected process improvements. The proposed project will then be reviewed and approved as an active six sigma project. The overall management of any six sigma project is similar to the project management processes discussed in Chapter 16.

Six sigma projects follow the DMAIC steps discussed previously, and Exhibit 28.4 describes the use of these procedures for a project. This should be a repetitive process based on an objective of constant improvement. The first steps of defining the project are particularly important. Project goals, potential rates of investment returns, and such expectations as customer or employee satisfaction levels should be defined. The activities of measuring, analyzing, and taking steps to improve the process then would follow. The final control activities call for the project team to implement and institutionalize the recommended and installed process improvements.

We have described six sigma here only at a very high level. Actually analyzing and reengineering processes often requires a very detailed mathematical and quantitative analysis. Six sigma procedures, as discussed, really got started in the United States through Motorola's improved processes for the manufacture of handheld cellular telephones. These are small but very technical devices where quality is very important, but achieving six sigma quality is a challenge.

Six sigma is a growing trend in enterprises, and IT auditors may encounter these initiatives frequently. IT auditors should work with the enterprise's quality and six sigma teams to learn more about how the concept is being applied in the IT auditor's organization. Often there are some strong benefits for an IT auditor to work with or observe black and green belt team activities in their six sigma process improvement activities.

LEAN SIX SIGMA

At about the same time as the launching of six sigma processes, another initiative began to be used in the United States called lean manufacturing. Its efforts began with U.S. auto manufacturers who were attempting to replicate techniques used by Japanese manufacturers, such as Toyota. The main difference between these two concepts is that six sigma emphasizes quality while lean manufacturing emphasizes speed of production. Over time, these two ideas have somewhat merged together into what is called lean six sigma. This combined concept is based on the recognition by many industry leaders that you cannot do "just quality" or "just speed"; a balanced process is needed to help an enterprise focus on improving service quality, as defined by the customer, within a set time limit.

Lean six sigma is a service management concept that is increasingly used by major enterprises. To cite one small example, *Fortune* magazine contained an interview with Gary Reiner, chief information officer of General Electric.[4] One of the questions was: "What does Jeff Immelt [the CEO] want from you?" Reiner responded: "Three things. My responsibility for IT, Lean Six Sigma, and sourcing." The interview then contains some further reference to General Electric's use of the lean six sigma technique.

The origins of lean manufacturing date back well before the twentieth century, even though it was not called lean then. The word *lean* later arose from studies on the differences between some very successful Japanese car makers and the traditional North American car makers. The key thought processes within lean are the identifying of "waste" or "non-value-added activities" from the customer's perspective and then determining how to eliminate them effectively. Waste is defined as the activity or activities that a customer would not want to pay for and/or that add no value to the product or service from the customer's perspective.

The determination of value is a key concept behind lean production and manu-facturing. *Value* is defined as an item or feature for which a customer is willing to pay. All other aspects of the process are deemed waste. The lean framework has been used as a tool to focus resources and energies on producing the value-added features while identifying and eliminating non-value-added activities. Lean production brought an emphasis on improved quality assurance, manpower reductions, a focus on customer value, and the concept of just-in-time manufacturing. This latter concept says that production materials do not need to be placed in stockrooms but should be introduced to the production process only when needed.

For some time in the 1990s, both lean and six sigma had their own separate adherents, each arguing that one was better than the other. Eventually, specialists began to realize the lean techniques alone cannot bring a process under the statistical controls that are so important in reducing exceptions. However, six sigma alone cannot dramatically improve process speeds or reduce the need for invested capital. Thus, lean six sigma was launched.

Lean six sigma uses many of the tools and procedures discussed for six sigma. For example, a key component of any analysis here is the same basic DMAIC cycle approach shown in Exhibit 28.4. Today there is much more emphasis on analyzing non-value-added components in a process and measuring process cycle efficiencies. The same black and green belts still identify and develop process improvement projects. The overall objective of lean six sigma is to reduce statistical error rates to six sigma levels and to establish dramatic improvements in process efficiency and to eliminate waste in all level of operations.

Although efficiency improvements sometimes are hard to define with the strong set of statistical measures that form the backbone of six sigma, lean six sigma also emphasizes improvements in the overall process value stream and the elimination of waste. Exhibit 28.5 contains some examples of process waste, some of the areas that

Type of Waste	Process Improvement Waste Examples
Complexity	Unnecessary IT application production steps, excessive or difficult-to-understand documentation, or difficult-to-interpret error messages
Labor	Excessive headcount, ineffective operations, poorly trained personnel in data centers and other areas of IT operations
Overproduction	Producing more than customer demands or production in advance of customer needs
Facility Space	Too much space allocated for IT equipment and resources, such as special forms that are seldom used or earlier revisions of equipment that have not been disposed
Energy Resources	Wasted power requirements or demands for excessive human energy
Process Defects	Repair, rework; multiple steps to resolve IT service desk problems
Materials	Scrap; ordering more than is needed, ranging from printer supplies to office equipment
Idle Materials	Software tools and documentation that are no longer used or were never installed
Time	All human, machine, and IT processes that waste time
Transportation	Movements of any sort that add no value
Safety Hazards	Unsafe or accident-prone environments

EXHIBIT 28.5   Lean Six Sigma IT Process Waste Example
Source: Robert R. Moeller, Brink's Modern Internal Auditing, 7th ed. (Hoboken, NJ: John Wiley & Sons, 2009). Copyright © 2009, John Wiley & Sons. Used with permission of John Wiley & Sons.

lean six sigma techniques attempt to reduce and that many IT auditors will see as potential areas for improvement.

An IT auditor learning about basic six sigma techniques may wonder what the differences between it and lean are, and why should one care? In many respects, people do not really understand the fine differences between the two approaches and refer to everything as six sigma, whether lean or not. Pure six sigma is much more statistically process oriented; the lean approach focuses on process improvements and the elimination of waste. When an IT auditor visits an auditee who claims the enterprise is implementing six sigma, often it is sufficient to understand these differences in approach.

When an IT auditor encounters a lean or six sigma program in an enterprise, an internal controls assessment of that program may be appropriate. Exhibit 28.6 contains IT audit procedures for a review of a six sigma program. As with all internal audit projects, an IT auditor does not have to be a black belt expert to assess the six sigma process in place; all the auditor needs to do is ask some appropriate questions about how the programs in place are documented, whether benefits have been analyzed, and if project objectives have been met. As in many other areas, IT audit here reviews an overall process from a third-party objective perspective and assesses how it is doing.

1. Plan and schedule the audit.
   1.1. Establish high-level objectives for the review.
   1.2. Confirm planned review with audit committee, senior management, and persons responsible for six sigma activities.
   1.3. Arrange for six sigma training for audit staff members performing the review.
   1.4. Schedule audit per normal internal audit planning cycle.
2. Review and understand six sigma organization.
   2.1. Understand six sigma organization, and meet with director to understand recent achievements and current projects.
   2.2. Understand the number and responsibilities of master, black, and green belts assigned to six sigma projects.
       2.2.1. Determine that adequate procedures are in place for belt certifications.
       2.2.2. Review adequacy of six sigma team operating procedures for such areas as documentation of reviews, testing procedures, and documentation requirements.
   2.3. Review and assesses adequacy of six sigma budgeting processes in place, and assess reasons for any significant variances.
   2.4. Review overall effectiveness of six sigma deployment, including supporting systems, communications processes, and recognition systems.
3. Review and assess six sigma project management processes.
   3.1. Review procedures for developing, planning, and managing six sigma projects to determine that they are consistent with good project management procedures. (See Chapter 14.)
   3.2. Determine that appropriate objectives, such as cost per unit measures, have been established and are monitored in six sigma projects.
   3.3. On a sample basis, review project documentation for completed six sigma projects to determine adequacy and completeness of processes.
   3.4. Determine that adequate procedures are in place for reporting progress and results of six sigma projects to the overall enterprise.

EXHIBIT 28.6 Internal Audit Procedures for a Review of a Six Sigma Program
Source: Robert R. Moeller, *Brink's Modern Internal Auditing*, 7th ed. (Hoboken, NJ: John Wiley & Sons, 2009). Copyright © 2009, John Wiley & Sons. Used with permission of John Wiley & Sons.

4. Select one or more completed six sigma projects and assess whether adequate attention was given to DMAIC steps for each project.
    4.1. Define steps. Clearly define the objectives of each project, along with an analysis of the current state, planned future state, due dates, and deliverables.
    4.2. Measure steps. Establish key metrics along with processes to use those metrics to achieve project success.
    4.3. Analyze steps. Use evidence to determine that current-state benchmarks were established as well as measurement results that will point to measurable process improvements.
    4.4. Improvement steps: Establish processes, including measurement tools, to implement suggested improvements or approaches.
    4.5. Control steps for new processes. Establish measurement steps to demonstrate that the new process is working as predicted or, if not, to revise for next round of improvements.
5. Assess adequacy and completeness of six sigma deployment.
    5.1. Where appropriate, review adequacy of selected completed six sigma projects for their emphasis on:
        5.1.1. Asset utilization improvements.
        5.1.2. Profit and revenue improvements.
        5.1.3. Service and customer relationship improvements.
        5.1.4. Product introduction and process improvements.
    5.2. Determine that adequate processes are in place to analyze results and initiate corrective actions.
    5.3. On a sample basis, select several six sigma projects that have been recently implemented and assess if objectives have been adequately met.
6. Determine that adequate communication tools are in place to report results of six sigma work to all constituents.

EXHIBIT 28.6   (*Continued*)

Six sigma and its related lean techniques are newer areas that are increasing in use and acceptance. IT auditors should develop a better understanding of these processes and assess the achievements and controls surrounding any such enterprise initiatives. A way to better understand these concepts may be to apply them to overall internal audit processes. Admittedly, IT audit accomplishments should not be based on speed of delivery but certainly they can emphasize an operating style that accepts zero defects. IT auditors should learn more about lean six sigma procedures.

 NOTES

1. A very basic reference is Craig Gygi and Neil DeCarlo, *Six Sigma for Dummies* (Hoboken, NJ: John Wiley & Sons, 2005).
2. *Risk Assessments Six Sigma Style*, Internal Auditor Online Edition (December 2009), www.theiia.org
3. This exhibit contains references to some quality assurance terminology, such as fishbone and Ishikawa techniques that are not included in this book or chapter. A Web search of the terms will provide more background information.
4. "Information Worth Billions," *Fortune*, July 21, 2008, p. 73.

CHAPTER TWENTY-NINE

Building an Effective IT Internal Audit Function

P REVIOUS CHAPTERS HAVE DISCUSSED an enterprise's information technology (IT) audit function. For most enterprises today, IT audit is not a single, unique function within an enterprise but a separate unit or component of the internal audit group, led by a chief audit executive (CAE) reporting to the audit committee of the board of directors. Although a very important component of the internal audit function, IT audit generally follows the overall procedures and practices for the overall internal audit function.

This chapter covers the essential activities of both an internal audit and an IT audit department. It introduces some practices necessary to build an effective internal audit function, starting with an authorizing charter, as well as the basic processes of building, staffing, and managing an effective IT audit department. As a foundation point here, there is a need to establish a formal internal audit charter as a basic authorizing document that has common elements no matter whether internal audit is serving a large corporate structure or a smaller not-for-profit entity. This important audit committee–approved document outlines internal audit's authority and responsibility to operate within an enterprise.

This chapter discusses steps to building an effective IT audit function within a corporate internal audit group, including typical IT audit position descriptions and organizational structures. We also introduce the first steps in planning IT audit activities: defining and understanding what is called the audit universe, which is made up of potential auditable entities in the enterprise and those that are important to IT audit. No matter what industry, geographic location, or size of the enterprise, all IT audit functions need to follow some similar good practice procedures.

Some enterprises today do not have a separate IT audit group but have a team of what were once just operational and financial internal auditors who also have the skills necessary to review and understand all levels of IT controls. To support such an IT-audit enhanced function, this chapter also reviews important IT audit policies and procedures as well as the first steps to review enterprise-auditable IT entities.

IT audit once was a separate and sometimes almost troublesome function in many internal audit groups. The pervasiveness of IT resources today has made it an essential component of any internal audit function. IT auditors need to understand the rules and procedures that will form an effective IT audit function for their enterprise.

 ## ESTABLISHING AN IT INTERNAL AUDIT FUNCTION

There is no one optimal way to organize an IT audit function as part of the financial and operational internal audit group in an enterprise today. There can be many differences in type of business, geographic span, and enterprise structure, with differing IT audit needs for each. The core internal audit function for each, however, must follow the Institute of Internal Auditors (IIA) Standards for the Professional Practice of Internal Auditing, as discussed in Chapter 3, and must have the support and recognition of enterprise management.

With IT functions so important to most enterprises today, there is almost always a need to have a specialized IT audit function or to have regular financial or operational internal audit groups with strong IT-related technical skills. Every internal audit function should have at least one person on staff with strong skills in understanding and evaluating IT controls. The next paragraphs review some elements required to build and manage an effective IT audit function as part of an enterprise internal audit group.

A key requirement for any effective enterprise is a strong leader; and for internal audit, that leader is a CAE who understands the needs of the overall enterprise and its potential control risks as well as the contributions that internal audit can make. This person must have the support of both the audit committee and senior management. Most large enterprises today have multiple units spread across the world. Even if geographically positioned in one location, the larger enterprise will almost always have multiple specialty functions with control risks that may require separate IT audit emphasis. The effective IT audit department must be organized in a manner that serves senior management and the audit committee by providing the best, most cost-effective audit services to the entire enterprise.

Any effective CAE today also must have a strong understanding of IT internal controls issues and why they are important to the enterprise. There is always a need to build a strong internal audit function that has an effective IT audit component. The effective CAE should have a good understanding of IT controls issues in order to communicate the results of IT audit's findings to the audit committee.

There is no single or optimal way to organize an IT audit function in an enterprise today. Because it will be a component of the overall internal audit function, IT audit resources should be organized in the same manner as other elements of that internal audit function or department. A CAE who has been tasked with establishing a new IT audit function or reengineering an existing one has a variety of options, depending on the enterprise's overall business, its geographic and logistical structures, the various control risks it faces, and its overall culture.

INTERNAL AUDIT CHARTER: AN IMPORTANT IT AUDIT AUTHORIZATION

An internal audit charter is a formal document, approved by the audit committee, to describe the mission, independence, objectivity, scope, responsibilities, authority, accountability, and standards of the enterprise internal audit function. In an enterprise, internal audit has free rein to look at records and to ask questions at all levels. Internal auditors have a lot of authority here, and some type of authorizing authority is needed. Because the internal function reports to the board's audit committee in a corporate structure, that audit committee normally should authorize the rights and responsibilities through a formal authorizing document or resolution—usually called an internal audit charter.

There are no fixed requirements for such an authorizing document, but an internal audit charter should affirm internal and IT audit's:

- ▪ Independence and objectivity
- ▪ Scope of responsibility
- ▪ Authority and accountability

This charter, then, is the authorizing document that an internal auditor can use when a manager in a separate and sometimes remote organization business unit questions why the internal auditor is asking to see certain IT systems documents or to gain access to some enterprise IT server facility. The charter should say that senior management—the board of director's audit committee—has authorized internal audit to access enterprise systems and records. More important, the charter provides a high level of authorization for the enterprise's IT audit function.

There is also no fixed format for the contents of a charter. The IIA's internal audit standards, discussed in Chapter 3, refer to the need for an IT audit charter, but the IIA's Web site (theiia.org) does not provide much specific guidance. A general Web search for internal audit charters will provide a variety of posted examples, but most of these are primarily from government and academic institutions. Exhibit 29.1 is an example IT audit charter for our example company, Global Computer Products. It clearly outlines internal audit's authority and responsibilities, such as developing a risk-based audit plan, assessing IT resources, and issuing timely audit reports.

An internal audit charter will be little more than a nice-sounding document unless there is a strong internal audit function in place to launch and perform these key enterprise governance activities. These activities include understanding the areas in any enterprise that should be candidates for internal audit reviews, building an effective IT audit function, and establishing support procedures to allow those IT audits. Although an internal audit charter is an essential authorization for an internal audit function, the charter of many such functions was developed and approved in the past. The CAE

Global Computer Products

Internal Audit's Mission

The mission of Global Computer Products Internal Audit is to ensure that company operations follow high standards both by providing an independent, objective assurance function and by advising on best practice. By using a systematic and disciplined approach, Internal Audit helps Global Computer Products accomplish its objectives by evaluating and improving the effectiveness of risk management, internal control, and governance processes.

Independence and Objectivity

To ensure independence, Internal Audit reports directly to the Board of Directors Audit Committee, and to maintain objectivity, Internal Audit is not involved in day-to-day company operations or internal control procedures.

Scope and Responsibilities

The scope of Internal Audit's work includes the review of risk management procedures, internal control, computer-based information systems, and governance processes. This work also involves periodic testing of transactions, best practice reviews, special investigations, appraisals of legal and regulatory requirements, and measures to help prevent and detect fraud.

To fulfill its responsibilities, Internal Audit shall:

- ☐ Identify and assess potential risks to Global Computer Products' operations.
- ☐ Review the adequacy of controls established to ensure compliance with policies, plans, procedures, and business objectives.
- ☐ Assess the reliability and security of financial and management information and supporting systems and operations that produce this information.
- ☐ Assess the means of safeguarding assets.
- ☐ Review established processes and propose improvements.
- ☐ Appraise the use of resources with regard to economy, efficiency, and effectiveness.
- ☐ Follow up on recommendations to make sure that effective remedial action is taken.
- ☐ Carry out ad hoc appraisals, investigations, or reviews requested by the Audit Committee and Management.

Internal Audit's Authority

In order to promote effective controls at reasonable cost, Internal Audit is authorized, in the course of its activities, to:

- ☐ Enter all areas of Global Computer Products operations, including its computer system facilities, and have access to any documents and records considered necessary for the performance of its functions.
- ☐ Require all members of staff and management to supply requested information and explanations within a reasonable period of time.

EXHIBIT 29.1 Sample Internal Audit Charter

Accountability

Internal Audit shall prepare, in liaison with Management and the Audit Committee, an annual audit plan that is based on business risks, the results of other internal audits, and input from Management. The plan shall be presented to Senior Management, including the General Counsel, for approval by the Audit Committee. Any needed adjustments to the plan should be communicated to and approved by the Audit Committee.

Internal Audit is responsible for planning, conducting, reporting, and following up on audit projects included in the audit plan and deciding on the scope and timing of these audits. The results of each internal audit will be reported through a detailed audit report that summarizes the objectives and scope of the audit as well as observations and recommendations. In all cases, follow-up work will be undertaken to ensure adequate response to internal audit recommendations. Internal Audit also will submit an annual report to Senior Management and to the Audit Committee on the results of the audit work, including significant risk exposures and control issues.

Standards

Internal Audit adheres to the standards and professional practices published by the Institute of Internal Auditors as well as the Information Technology Governance Institute.

EXHIBIT 29.1 (*Continued*)

---

should review the existing charter periodically and present it to the audit committee to reaffirm his or her understanding of the role and responsibilities of internal audit.

ROLE OF THE CHIEF AUDIT EXECUTIVE

As discussed, the CAE is the person responsible for all of internal audit, including the IT audit function. The title *internal audit director* was more common in years past; today's IIA standards support the title *CAE*, the most senior internal audit officer in the enterprise with ultimate responsibility for the entire audit function. No matter whether the company is a Fortune 50–size major corporation or a relatively small private or not-for-profit enterprise, the CAE is the person to lead and direct all of internal audit including IT audit. A CAE should have knowledge and an understanding of these areas:

- **Enterprise operations and risk issues.** In addition to managing the internal audit function, the CAE should have knowledge regarding all aspects of the enterprise's operations, including financial, IT, and operational matters.
- **Human resources and internal audit administration.** Responsible for the audit staff, the CAE must build an effective organization and both recruit and lead an effective internal audit team, including IT audit.
- **Relationships with the audit committee and management.** The CAE is the internal audit spokesperson for the audit committee and all levels of enterprise management.
- **Corporate governance, accounting, and regulatory issues.** Whether it is Sarbanes-Oxley, accounting and finance issues, or other regulatory matters

impacting the enterprise, the CAE should have at least general understanding and knowledge. Some CAEs, however, may not have strong IT audit technical skills and must rely on their IT audit staff for technical support.

■ **Internal audit team building and administration.** No matter what size the internal audit function is, the CAE is responsible for building an effective function that receives admiration and respect from the recipients of audit services.

■ **Technology.** The CAE should have a general understanding of how technology is used within his or her enterprise as well as how it can be applied to promote IT audit services.

■ **Risk-based audit planning and process excellence.** The CAE should understand risk assessment processes as they are applied to enterprise operations and also should be able to think of enterprise operations in terms of key processes.

■ **Negotiating skills and relationship management.** The CAE often is in the middle between issues raised by the IT audit team and a sometimes hostile management who may take exception to IT audit's findings and recommendations; the CAE often is called on to negotiate an appropriate resolution to these issues as part of building an effective internal audit team.

■ **Internal audit's assurance and consulting roles.** Although these roles sometimes can become blurred, the CAE always should emphasize to both the IT audit team and management the separate roles of providing IT audit assurance services and providing consulting services.

■ **Standards for the Professional Practice of Internal Auditing.** The CAE should be an "expert" on these IIA standards and should help apply them to all aspects of IT audit activities.

The CAE has an important job in both leading an effective IT audit department and delivering overall internal audit services to the enterprise. Although many members of the audit team may have stronger or more specialized knowledge in some areas, the CAE is really the key person who represents internal audit to the enterprise. IT auditors should be very aware of the roles and responsibilities of their CAE in leading their internal audit function.

 ## IT AUDIT SPECIALISTS

Virtually every internal audit function will have staff- and supervisor-level internal auditors with financial and operational internal audit skills. In addition, most internal audit functions should have some level of IT audit specialists. However, the aim of this chapter is not to describe the roles of financial and operational internal auditors but to focus on the very important role of IT auditors in an internal audit function.

Since the mainframe computer system days of the early 1970s, the role of IT audit specialists—IT auditors—has been growing. Many staff internal auditors can be successful in an enterprise with only a general knowledge and can learn much more through training, but IT auditors need special training and skills. Most if not all internal audit functions need at least one specialist on staff with strong IT-related internal control skills covering such areas as systems security, IT application internal controls, and computer systems infrastructure management. Many of these IT audit knowledge needs have been discussed in other chapters. This type of IT auditor skill requirement goes beyond entry-level positions where a person has a bachelor's degree in computer science but with little more than an understanding of Internet manipulation and accessing spreadsheets.

The skill requirements for the IT audit specialists in an internal audit group will very much depend on the technical maturity of the enterprise's IT functions. An enterprise that has its applications based on an enterprise resource planning set of linked applications tied to complex databases will require a different set of information systems audit specialist skills than would an enterprise where most of its IT resources are based on Web-based software as a service (SaaS) applications, as discussed in Chapter 9. Due to the span and breadth of ever-changing IT technologies, information systems auditors face with a wide range of knowledge requirements. Exhibit 29.2 outlines the basic knowledge requirements that would be expected from an experienced or seasoned IT audit specialist.

Finding and recruiting an IT auditor with information systems skills and knowledge sometimes is a challenge. It is often difficult to find professionals with the appropriate technical skills and then to screen and identify the better candidates. Internal audit hiring managers or CAEs who have come from a Certified Public Accountant (CPA) finance and

---

Information technologies are pervasive in business and span a wide range of options and technologies. However, an IT internal auditor should be expected to have at least a high-level working knowledge of these areas:

- **Business application systems,** whether for accounting, business or other purposes, and the basic balancing and integrity controls surrounding all automated systems
- **Data management processes**—whether a formal database or spreadsheet tabled data—and the importance of validating and maintaining that data
- **Systems development life cycle (SLDC) processes** to implement and build business application systems
- **Storage management and the importance of backup and recovery processes**
- **Computer operating systems basic functions**—whether on a laptop or larger system—and the potential risks and vulnerabilities if such operating systems are not updated or maintained
- **Computer systems architectures,** with an emphasis on use of the Web, client-server configurations, and telecommunications
- **IT service operations processes,** with an emphasis on problem management, access controls, and general application management
- **IT service design processes,** with an emphasis on continuity, capacity, and information security management processes
- **Governance and service strategy processes,** including essential IT financial management processes
- **Programming or coding techniques** sufficient to construct and implement computer-assisted audit procedures appropriate to the enterprise environment
- **Ongoing interest and curiosity to understand and explore newer and evolving technology concepts,** such as storage management virtualization

EXHIBIT 29.2   IT Auditor Basic Knowledge Requirements

accounting background sometimes have difficulty in identifying appropriate audit specialist candidates. Of course, if the IT audit function has already established an information systems audit function, peer-level interviews for the recruitment process often are of great help. An enterprise may seek candidates who have achieved Certified Information Systems Auditor (CISA) credentials. The CISA and other IT auditor professional credentials are discussed in Chapter 30.

In addition to the IT auditor internal controls requirements outlined in Exhibit 29.2, every member of an internal audit function—from the CAE to junior staff auditors— should have some minimal level of knowledge covering IT control procedures. With the almost pervasive use of automated Web-based tools today, all internal audit staff members should have some familiarity with an enterprise's IT systems and applications.

 ## IT AUDIT MANAGERS AND SUPERVISORS

Depending on the overall enterprise size, supervisors or managers may work together to create an effective IT audit function through their close planning, monitoring, and supervising of the audit staff members who actually perform IT audits. The CAE normally is an internal audit generalist with a good knowledge of enterprise internal controls issues but often with limited IT audit practices understanding. Internal audit functions that have multiple IT auditors on the team generally will need a manager with responsibilities for IT activities. Exhibit 29.3 is a sample position description for an IT audit manager. Such an IT audit manager often is expected to have a CISA certification in addition to being a Certified Internal Auditor (CIA) in order to better communicate IT internal controls issues with both enterprise management and the IT audit staff.

We have outlined the requirements for an IT audit manager, who would be actively supervising and leading a team of IT auditors. However, many internal audit functions are not large enough to justify more than two or three IT auditors. In those cases, often there is no need to have a separate IT audit management function. One member of the IT audit team should be designated as the in-charge IT auditor, and all members of the IT audit group should be working IT auditors, reporting to the CAE or one of the other internal audit team managers.

We perhaps too often insist that a professional certification—such as a CPA, CIA, or CISA—is a *requirement* for certain types of IT audit positions. Although these certifications certainly are a measure of demonstrated skills, a CAE building an effective IT audit organization should always consider the skills and aptitudes of candidates rather than just the initials after their names. For example, an IT audit staff member may have joined an enterprise IT audit group with a bachelor's degree in economics. If that same new professional joined the IT audit department, acquired a CIA, and performed well in accounting and financial internal control audits, the lack of a CISA should not necessarily prevent him or her from being a candidate for an IT audit manager performing financial reviews.

Enterprise human resource functions may impose requirements here, but the CAE should play a lead in insisting that there are appropriate position descriptions in place for all members of the IT audit management team. They should be structured in such a

Job Responsibilities

The Manager, Information Technology or IT Internal Audit, has responsibility for assisting the Chief Audit Executive (the "Director") in providing guidance and supervision for the IT audit specialists in the Internal Audit Department. Additionally, the IT Audit Manager is responsible for:

1. Executing the IT application and general controls reviews portion of the Internal Audit Annual Audit Plan
2. Assisting other members of the audit team in developing and launching automated IT audit procedures
3. Providing advice and counsel on new systems, initiatives, and IT services under development from an internal controls perspective
4. Assisting the Director in the coordination of IT audit activities, including Sarbanes-Oxley Section 404 internal controls assessments, with the independent registered public accountants
5. Effectively and efficiently managing IT-specialist internal audit function resources
6. Hiring, training, and professionally developing the IT audit team
7. Overseeing the quality of work performed by the IT internal audit team, ensuring compliance with applicable standards

IT Audit Manager Key Competencies

- In-depth knowledge of both IT audit and internal audit practices and principles, including ISACA and IIA Standards
- Strong knowledge of the CobiT and COSO internal controls frameworks
- Strong knowledge and understanding of the current IT technical environment, including database systems, telecommunications, and IT change controls
- Solid knowledge and experience with regulatory rules and requirements affecting the internal auditing and IT management practices (e.g., Sarbanes-Oxley Act)
- Broad-based experience and understanding of computer-assisted audit tools and techniques
- Detail oriented with strong analytical and problem-solving abilities
- Solid leadership, management, and administrative skills
- Strong interpersonal, communication, and presentation skills

Required Skills

The Manager, IT Audit should have a **Bachelor of Science degree** in Computer Science or Business Administration with a major in information systems development; a minimum of **seven years** of progressive IT audit and/or public accounting experience; and both a **Certified Information System Auditor (CISA)** and **Certified Internal Auditor (CIA)** designation.

EXHIBIT 29.3   IT Audit Manager Position Description

manner that all members of the IT audit staff can recognize the requirements to move from one level on up to the next. For example, an IT audit field supervisor should clearly understand the additional requirements to move up to an IT auditor manager level if such a position becomes available and open.

INTERNAL AND IT AUDIT POLICIES AND PROCEDURES

A regular step in many IT and other internal audits is to request to see a copy of the approved policies and procedures for the area to be reviewed. These policies set the rules for some area of operations and provide the basis for internal audit's assessment of controls in that area. However, like the shoemaker's children who have no shoes,

IT audit functions often do not take the time and effort to implement their own policies and procedures.

Every IT audit function should develop a set of policies and procedures that govern its operations and serve both as guidance to the overall internal audit staff and as background to users of IT audit services. The internal audit charter is a good starting point. It should be broadly communicated and posted within internal audit facility offices. In addition to general enterprise policies, internal audit procedures should be issued in an internal audit procedure manual covering such areas as IT audit travel policies or the rules for auditor continuing education. The size and content of any IT audit procedures manual will vary depending on the size of the function and the overall enterprise, but it should contain the these elements:

- **Internal audit charter and other basic IT audit authorizing documents.** This material was discussed earlier in the chapter.
- **Enterprise ethics and code of conduct rules.** These enterprise-wide rules, which particularly impact all internal as well as IT auditors, are discussed in Chapter 3 on professional practice standards.
- **Internal audit department rules and procedures.** These are the rules that cover everything from vacation policy to decorum while on the job.
- **IT auditing standards.** These are the guidelines for performing all IT audits. Some key points include requirements for testing evidence, documenting audit results, and preparing IT audit reports.

Much of the background material on how to perform IT audits can be found in reference materials, such as this book. An IT audit function should document this material in a manner easily understood by all members of the IT audit department. Although the examples here are in a paper format, normally we would expect to find this material in a soft-copy format as read-only files located on IT auditor laptop computers.

As an example of an IT audit procedure, Exhibit 29.4 is a procedure page for preparing an audit program, taken from the Global Computer Products example company. Audit procedures will vary depending on the philosophy and technical expertise of the audit department systems. However, to achieve effective coverage, the audit procedures should be consistent with the complexity of the activities reviewed.

In addition, IT audit should establish standards for their audit workpapers, related communications, and retention policies. As much as practicable, these should be consistent with procedures established for the financial and operational internal audit groups. Auditors should ensure that workpapers are well organized, clearly written, and address all areas in the scope of the audit. They should contain sufficient evidence of the tasks performed and support the conclusions reached. Formal procedures should ensure that management and the audit committee receive summarized audit findings that effectively communicate the results of the audit. Full audit reports should be available for review by the audit committee. Policies should establish appropriate workpaper retention periods. Of course, all IT audit department standards should be based on the IIA's International Standards for the Professional Practice of Internal Auditing as discussed in Chapter 3.

Internal Audit Standards—Preparing Audit Programs
Standard X-YYY yyyy/mm/dd

Global Computer Products

The in-charge auditor for any assigned review should gather supporting documentation and meet with appropriate managers to complete and document the following:

- **A risk assessment process to describe and analyze the risks inherent in the selected line of business.** Auditors should update the risk assessment at least annually, or more frequently if necessary, to reflect changes to internal control or work processes and to incorporate new lines of business. The level of risk should be one of the most significant factors considered when determining the frequency of audits.
- **An audit plan,** based on the Audit Committee's approved annual plan, detailing Internal Audit's budgeting and planning processes. The plan should describe audit goals, schedules, staffing needs, and reporting. This audit plan should be defined by combining the results of the risk assessment and the resources required to yield the timing and frequency of the planned internal audits. The internal auditors should report the status of planned versus actual audits, and any changes to the annual audit plan, to the Audit Committee for its approval on a periodic basis.
- **An audit cycle that identifies the frequency of audits.** Auditors usually determine the frequency by performing a risk assessment, as noted, of areas to be audited. While staff and time availability may influence the audit cycle, they should not be overriding factors in reducing the frequency of audits for high-risk areas.
- **Development of approved audit work programs that set out for each audit area the required scope and resources,** including the selection of audit procedures, the extent of testing, and the basis for conclusions. Well-planned, properly structured audit programs are essential to strong risk management and to the development of comprehensive internal control systems.

EXHIBIT 29.4 *Audit Program Preparation Procedure Sample Page*

ORGANIZING AN EFFECTIVE IT AUDIT FUNCTION

Organizing an effective and efficient IT audit function, normally structured as part of an enterprise's internal audit group, presents a number challenges. Often an IT audit function was launched in the "old days" before our massive use of the Internet and SaaS applications and before IT applications and processes were as pervasive as in today's business operations. IT audit was set up as a specialized function within internal audit along with financial and operational internal auditors. However, as time passes, management and the audit committee may believe that IT audit is not always meeting its expected goals.

Periodically, it is a good idea for the CAE, with audit committee approval, to review the current IT audit function to determine that it is effective and meeting expectations. Although there may be many minor variations, IT audit functions are commonly organized as (1) a separate group that plans and performs its own reviews separate from the other members of the operational and financial internal audit function, (2) a group that is fully integrated with other internal audit functions, or (3) a group acting as special or technical project consultants to other internal auditors or to management. There are strengths and weaknesses to each approach, and decisions here will depend more on the CAE's methods than on the wishes of its IT auditors.

IT Audit as a Separate Internal Audit Specialty

IT audit really first got started as a specialty function within conventional internal audit groups. Back in the days of large mainframe computers, many internal audit functions were composed of auditors who were oriented primarily to financial controls and had little knowledge of IT systems controls. Internal audit functions began to add specialists to their staffs to review IT controls—the first IT auditors. Many enterprises today continue to retain their IT auditors as a separate group within the internal audit function.

Often internal audit is organized by the types of audits to be performed. An audit department might be divided into three groups of specialists: information systems or IT auditors, financial audit specialists, and purely operational auditors. This approach rests on the logic that individual internal auditors may be most effective if given responsibility for an area in which they have expertise and experience, recognizing that efficiency often is achieved through specialization. The problems and control risks pertaining to a particular audit area often can best be handled through the assignment of internal auditors who have the necessary special expertise. This situation is particularly true for IT auditors where there is a need for specialists to review, understand, and evaluate controls in areas such as cybersecurity, wireless telecommunications networks, or software change controls.

At the same time, there can be disadvantages to this type of audit approach. All too often, internal audit projects may not be well coordinated, such as situations where operational auditors reviewed some area and published their audit report, and IT audit comes back shortly thereafter to do an applications review covering the same general area. Also, where several types of audits exist at a given field location, it may be necessary for each specialist auditor to travel there. This extra cost in time and money should be clearly offset by the added efficiency gained from the specialist internal auditors. Exhibit 29.5 is an organization chart from this type of IT audit organization. It shows that specialized groups have been established for operational, information systems, and financial auditing as well as teams for special and IT audit projects. A risk with this approach is that specialist IT auditors may spend too much time on their own areas and in the process miss the big picture. This sometimes occurs in technical, IT-audit areas, where auditors may spend too much time on technical control issues and miss significant control concern risks in the process. Often it is very difficult for the CAE to create a team of integrated auditors when specialized groups have been established.

Although tight, specific definitions of audit tasks can promote efficiency and allow for more effective, specialized audits, a variety of assignments keeps an IT auditor from getting in a rut and performing audit reviews in too mechanical a fashion. Here, the audit staff is alert, well motivated and can bring a fresh approach to old problems—something that frequently pays good dividends. Mixed assignments for individual IT auditors lend themselves best to growth and professional development and help to create

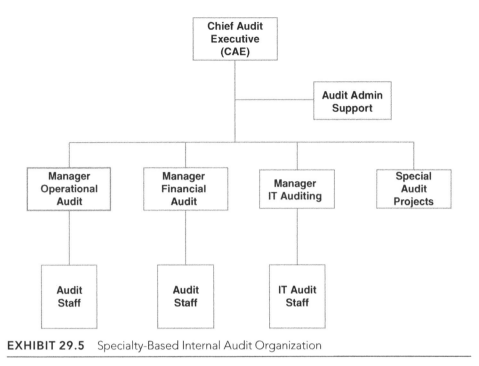

EXHIBIT 29.5 Specialty-Based Internal Audit Organization

the *integrated auditor*. This integrated audit approach promotes adequate education and training opportunities to all members of the audit staff.

On balance, any gains through audit specialization may be more than offset by the factors just discussed. Internal audit management faces the danger that these gains will appear to be more substantial than they actually are. The specialist approach should be used cautiously and only when the enterprise has strong needs for auditors with unique abilities. In many instances, this type of IT audit organizational structure can be at odds with the objectives of achieving maximum quality of the audit effort, especially as IT audit focus moves from reviewing lower-level procedures and toward broader managerial issues.

Fully Integrated or Combined IT Audit Function

The *integrated auditor*—an internal auditor with combined financial, operational, and IT skills—has been an objective of many internal audit professionals for some time. The idea is to build an internal audit staff where team members all generally have a combination of these skills. There would be no reason for just performing a specialized IT audits here, and the audit staff would be trained and charged to handle reviews in any and all of these areas. This idea of having a staff of internal auditors each with a variety of skills was a very popular idea until the late 1980s.

This idea, however, has broken down over time. Areas such as cybersecurity internal controls vulnerability issues, for example, require some very specialized knowledge areas; the typical internal auditor with those skills cannot necessarily be expected to have a complete understanding of Sarbanes-Oxley issues as well.

A better approach here is to build an internal audit staff where all team members are expected to have some knowledge of internal control issues in a wide variety of areas. However, each member of the team may have recognized skills in one or another specific area. With a larger internal audit staff, this approach can be very efficient, but scheduling is often a challenge.

In other words, all internal auditors should have a mix of skills. This author has championed this concept, referred to as the internal auditors' common body of knowledge[1] (CBOK), elsewhere. All internal auditors should have a mix of some of these skills. Even though an internal auditor has strong IT internal controls skills, he or she should be able to understand basic financial systems internal controls issues and the like. An internal audit department would not have a special group or function for just IT audit issues, but all would operate as a team sharing ideas and performing work on similar audit projects.

IT Auditors as Specialists or Technical Consultants

Perhaps the best approach to organizing an effective IT audit function that serves the overall enterprise but also has some strong technical skills is to establish a small team of highly technical IT auditors to work on special projects. All members of the internal audit team would be expected to have some general IT controls-related skills, but the technical team would be pulled in for more difficult control concern issues.

With this concept, a small team of internal auditors would be available to assist or even act as internal consultants in some areas where there was a need. Of course, this approach will work only for larger enterprises, but it can be an effective way to provide skilled technical support in some special areas while the remainder of the audit team operates at a generally high level.

 ## IMPORTANCE OF A STRONG IT AUDIT FUNCTION

This chapter has explored some of the essential beginning steps to build and maintain an effective IT audit function. Starting with an authorizing charter approved by the audit committee, the designated CAE, internal auditors, and IT audit specialists should work to build an effective internal IT audit organization that serves all aspects of the enterprise. Internal audit also needs to be an effective resource for the overall enterprise with its own defined operating practices, position descriptions, and appropriate policies and procedures. However, IT audit is not an outside consulting practice with any day-to-day connections; it always will be a key function on the internal department and, thus, must be part of that enterprise in terms of operating style and adherence to enterprise rules, such as work hours or even business attire. Nevertheless, although IT audit is part of an enterprise, we must never forget that an effective IT audit department is unique.

A major component in an audit function is a strong and effective overall operational and financial internal audit group as well as a strong IT audit resource, all led by an effective CAE and an interested and involved audit committee. With the constant evolution of new technologies and related internal control issues, IT audit is often a leader in assessing and evaluating the overall enterprise internal audit function and should work closely with other internal auditors, emphasizing internal controls risks and improved IT-based internal audit approaches.

Internal audit and its IT audit function is unique and special because, with the exception of the chief executive officer and sometimes the general counsel, it is perhaps the only unit that reports directly to the audit committee. Yet, every employee, no matter how many levels removed down the ladder on an enterprise chart, theoretically has a reporting relationship to to that same board, but IT audit has direct access. Internal audit has a unique position in any enterprise as it has the right—and even obligation—to assess risks, schedule reviews in any venue of operations, and then both report the results of those reviews and request corrective actions when appropriate. This important role should provide a strong level of professional attention and respect for all members of internal audit and its IT audit specialists

 NOTE

1. For more information on these internal audit knowledge needs, see Robert R. Moeller, *Brink's Modern Internal Auditing: A Common Body of Knowledge*, 7th ed. (Hoboken, NJ: John Wiley & Sons, 2009).

CHAPTER THIRTY

Professional Certifications: CISA, CIA, and More

W E LIVE IN A world filled with various and sometimes too many professional certification designations. For example, a civil engineer designing highway bridges will seek a very important and well-recognized professional engineer (PE) certification and a household interior designer may take an examination to become a not nearly so well recognized Certified Kitchen Designer (CKD). These certifications may be viewed very positively by an employer or customer looking for a candidate to fill a position requiring appropriate job skills. A PE is essential for a civil engineer, and a CKD may give a candidate some additional points in a job selection process.

Many professional certifications are worthwhile, and others are often almost too specialized to be of much value to some professionals. With its major software products, Microsoft had some 17 professional certifications, at last count, for its many and important software tools.[1] These include such designations as Microsoft Certified Desktop Support Technician (MCDST), Microsoft Certified Solution Developer (MCSD), and Microsoft Certified Application Specialist (MCAS). Each certification, and others, demonstrates professional knowledge and skills in a specialized area. However, a business card with MCDST after the person's name may not get a professional that much recognition because the credential is not well known or understood.

Individual professional certifications should be based on some generally recognized strong standards. Many will recognize the importance of the previously referenced PE certification, but the CKD may not receive the same credit. Also, a professional designation should cover a fairly broad professional area. The MCAS designation may be valuable, but enterprises need application developers with skills in more than just Microsoft products.

Information technology (IT) and other internal auditors also have a need for strong and well-recognized professional certifications. Many have joined the profession with no specific certification requirements beyond their undergraduate college degrees. Others attained accounting degrees and prepared for the Certified Public Accountant (CPA) examination. Hiring managers once assumed that potential internal auditor candidates must have a CPA to become qualified as an internal auditor, but, over time, many realized that the internal audit profession and particularly IT audit required people with more qualifications than just a CPA. Things changed through an initiative by the Institute of Internal Auditors (IIA) to design a program and qualifying test to create the Certified Internal Auditor® (CIA) certification. Today, beyond or separate from the CIA, an internal auditor can become a Certified Information Systems Auditor (CISA), a Certified Fraud Examiner (CFE), or any of a number of other certifications. Some may be very valuable for a typical IT auditor; others may not be acknowledged as that important. This chapter discusses the professional designations that are most important for today's IT internal auditor. In particular, this chapter looks at the CISA and CIA certifications, including their qualification and examination requirements.

The chapter does not discuss the CPA examination. Although certainly more oriented to external auditors, the CPA is still the best and most recognized accounting, auditing, and internal control examination for all U.S.-based financial professionals, including internal auditors. It should be an objective for any internal auditor with a financial background who has not already attained CPA certification. The other professional examinations discussed in this chapter, such as the CIA, should also be considered a strong objective for many IT internal auditors.

CERTIFIED INFORMATION SYSTEMS AUDITOR CREDENTIALS

Previous chapters have mentioned the rivalry between the Institute of Internal Auditors and what was once the EDP Auditors Association (now the Information Systems Audit and Control Association [ISACA]). As mentioned, the professional organization that is now ISACA was founded by internal auditors who felt the IIA was not paying enough attention to technology and information systems or IT issues. Over the years, these two professional groups have been operating somewhat in parallel, and ISACA is responsible for the CISA certification examination and professional designation. The CISA is the prime professional credential for IT auditors. It is similar to the IIA's CIA, to be discussed, but the CISA designation is more focused on IT audit focused than the IIA's CIA. The CISA examination is open to all individuals who have an interest and skills in information systems audit, control, and security. The examination is four hours in duration and consists of 200 multiple-choice questions. The test is offered each year in June and December at numerous worldwide locations.

In addition to passing the CISA examination, a candidate must have a minimum of five years of professional information systems auditing, internal control, or security-related work experience. A maximum of one year of information systems experience *or* one year of financial or operational auditing experience can be substituted for one of those five years of information systems auditing, control, or security experience. In addition,

1. **The IS Audit Process (10%).** Provide IS audit services in accordance with IS audit standards, guidelines, and best practices to assist the enterprise in ensuring that its information technology and business systems are protected and controlled.
2. **IT Governance (15%).** Provide assurance that the organization has the structure, policies, accountability, mechanisms, and monitoring practices in place to achieve the requirements of corporate governance of IT.
3. **Systems and Infrastructure Life Cycle (16%).** Provide assurance that the IT service management practices for the development/acquisition, testing, implementation, maintenance and disposal of systems, and infrastructure will meet the enterprise's objectives.
4. **IT Service Delivery and Support (14%).** Provide assurance that the IT service management practices will ensure delivery of the level of services required to meet the enterprise's objectives.
5. **Protection of Information Assets (31%).** Provide assurance that the security architecture (policies, standards, procedures and controls) ensures the confidentiality integrity, and availability of information assets.
6. **Business Continuity and Disaster Recovery (14%).** Provide assurance that, in the event of a disruption, the business continuity and disaster recovery processes will ensure the timely resumption of IT services, while minimizing the business impact.

EXHIBIT 30.1 CISA Examination Content Area

60 to 120 completed college semester credit hours (the equivalent of an associate's or bachelor's degree) can be substituted for one or two years, respectively, of information systems auditing, control, or security experience. Two years as a full-time university instructor in a related field (e.g., computer science, accounting, information systems auditing) can be substituted for one year of information systems auditing, control, or security experience.

This experience must have been gained within the ten-year period preceding the application date for certification or within five years from the date of initially passing the examination. Retaking and passing the examination will be required if the application for certification is not submitted within five years from the passing date of the examination. All experience is verified independently with employers.

Per ISACA guidelines, the tasks and knowledge required of information systems audit professional now and in the future serve as the blueprint for the CISA examination. Exhibit 30.1 shows the six broad subject areas included in the examination. More information about the requirements in each of these knowledge areas can be found at the ISACA Web site (www.isaca.org) or in a variety of reference materials listed there. That same Web site also sample questions.

The CISA examination has education, experience, and continuing education requirements similar to the CIA examination to be discussed. The CISA is a fairly detailed examination of IT audit and technical knowledge in an extensive set of areas. The CISA designation has been a globally accepted standard of achievement in the information systems (IS) audit, control, and security field since 1978 and has been recognized by many government agencies and major business groups around the world. More than 60,000 people have attained the CISA certification since its inception.

With the breadth of the areas tested, its experience and education requirements, and the need for ongoing continuing education, the CISA is the core qualifying certification for most IT auditors. An IT auditor working closely with an internal audit group should consider attaining a CISA as well as a CIA and may want to gain one of the other IT audit certificates discussed in this chapter. However, the CISA is the key certification today that identifies an IT auditor as a professional in the field.

 CERTIFIED INFORMATION SECURITY MANAGER CREDENTIALS

The ISACA-sponsored Certified Information Security Manager® (CISM®) certification, which focuses on IT audit management, has been earned by over 10,000 professionals since its introduction in 2003. Unlike other security certifications with a greater technical orientation, such as the Certified Information Systems Security Professional (CISSP) discussed in a later section, the CISM is a qualifying certification for the individual who manages, designs, oversees, and assesses an enterprise's information security program. CISM defines core competencies and international performance standards that those who have information security management responsibilities should master.

The CISM certification program goes beyond just IT audit knowledge areas. It was developed specifically for experienced IT security managers and those who have information security management responsibilities. The CISM certification promotes international practices and provides executive management with assurance that those who earn the designation have the required experience and knowledge to provide effective security management and consulting services.

To earn the CISM designation, candidates are required to get a passing score on the CISM exam, which is offered twice a year in over 260 locations worldwide. This 200-question multiple-choice examination currently is offered in four languages—English, Japanese, Korean, and Spanish—with questions designed to test practical knowledge and experience. CISM examination candidates must submit evidence of a minimum of five years of work experience in professional information security management. Waivers for this experience requirement are similar to those for CISAs. For example, a maximum of one year of information systems, operating, or programming experience, or one year of information security experience can be substituted for one year of information systems security management experience. In addition to passing the CISM examination, the candidate must agree to abide by the ISACA code of conduct (introduced in Chapter 3).

The CISM exam covers five information security management areas, representing the work performed by many information security managers. Each area represents a current market perspective of what is performed and what should be known by information security managers. Exhibit 30.2 is a summary of the topics found in the CISM examination.

We present only a few of the examination requirements in this exhibit. The requirements cover a wide range of areas that will be a challenge to any enterprise establishing an effective information security environment. IT auditors who seek to expand their career objectives might well move to greater IT security responsibilities and acquire CISM certification.

1. **Information Security Governance (23%)**
   - Develop an information security strategy aligned with business goals and objectives, and align that information security strategy with corporate governance, consistent with applicable laws and regulations.
   - Develop business cases justifying investment in information security.
   - Identify current and potential legal and regulatory requirements affecting information security.
   - Identify technology, business environment, risk tolerance, and other drivers affecting the enterprise and their impact on information security.
   - Obtain senior management commitment to information security.
   - Define roles and responsibilities for information security throughout the organization.
   - Establish internal and external reporting and communication channels that support information security.

2. **Information Risk Management (22%)**
   - Identify and manage information security risks to achieve business objectives, and establish a process for information asset classification and ownership.
   - Implement a systematic and structured information risk assessment process.
   - Ensure that business impact assessments are conducted periodically.
   - Ensure that threat and vulnerability evaluations are performed on an ongoing basis.
   - Identify and periodically evaluate information security controls and countermeasures to mitigate risk to acceptable levels.
   - Integrate risk, threat, and vulnerability identification and management into life cycle processes (e.g., development, procurement, and employment life cycles).
   - Report significant changes in information risk to appropriate levels of management for acceptance on both a periodic and an event-driven basis.

3. **Information Security Program Development (17%)**
   - Create and maintain a program to implement the information security strategy.
   - Specify the activities to be performed within the information security program.
   - Ensure alignment between the information security program and other assurance functions.
   - Identify the internal and external resources required to execute the information security program.
   - Establish, communicate, and maintain information security policies that support the security strategy.
   - Design and develop a program for information security awareness, training, and education.
   - Ensure the development, communication, and maintenance of standards, procedures, and other documentation that support information security policies.
   - Integrate information security requirements into the organization's processes and life cycle activities.
   - Develop a process to integrate information security controls into contracts.
   - Establish metrics to evaluate the effectiveness of the information security program.

4. **Information Security Program Management (24%)**
   - Oversee and direct information security activities to execute the information security program.
   - Manage internal and external resources required to execute the information security program.
   - Ensure that processes and procedures are performed in compliance with the organization's information security policies and standards; ensure that the information security controls agreed to in contracts with business partners, customers, third parties, and others are performed; ensure that information security is an integral part of the systems development

EXHIBIT 30.2   CISM Examination Content Areas

Source: www.isaca.org.

process; ensure that information security is maintained throughout the organization's processes and systems life cycle activities; provide information security advice and guidance, including risk analysis and control selection, to the enterprise; provide information security awareness, training and education to stakeholders; and monitor, measure, test and report on the effectiveness and efficiency of information security controls and compliance with information security policies.

- Ensure that noncompliance issues and other variances are resolved in a timely manner.

5. **Incident Management and Response (14%)**
- Plan, develop, and manage the capability to detect, respond to, and recover from information security incidents.
- Develop and implement processes for detecting, identifying, analyzing, and responding to information security incidents.
- Establish escalation and communication processes and lines of authority.
- Develop plans to respond to and document information security incidents.
- Establish the capability to investigate information security incidents.
- Develop a process to communicate with internal parties and external organizations, including media, law enforcement, and customers.
- Integrate information security incident response plans with the enterprise's disaster recovery (DR) and business continuity plan (BCP).
- Organize, train, and equip teams to respond to information security incidents.
- Periodically test and refine information security incident response plans.
- Manage the response to information security incidents.
- Conduct reviews to identify causes of information security incidents, develop corrective actions, and reassess risk.

EXHIBIT 30.2   *(Continued)*

CERTIFICATE IN THE GOVERNANCE OF ENTERPRISE IT

The concept of increased and more effective corporate governance became a major issue after the enactment of the Sarbanes-Oxley Act (SOx) early in this century. A similar emphasis on the need for better IT governance followed. To support this governance need, ISACA sponsors the Certificate in the Governance of Enterprise IT (CGEIT). This certification covers the knowledge and application of IT governance principles and practices. The CGEIT is designed for professionals who have management, advisory, or assurance responsibilities that require tasks and knowledge related to IT governance. Earning this designation will enable professionals to respond to the growing business demand for a comprehensive IT governance program that defines responsibility and accountability across the entire enterprise.

The concept behind the CGEIT examination and certification is that IT has become increasingly important to the achievement of enterprise goals and delivery of benefits, and increasing realization that this governance must be extended to IT. As an integral part of enterprise governance, IT governance consists of the leadership, organizational structures and processes that ensure the enterprise's IT function sustains its overall strategies and objectives.

CGEIT certification has an objective of benefiting individuals, through the recognition of their IT governance–related professional knowledge, competencies, skill sets, abilities, and experiences. It will also add value to the enterprises they support by demonstrating visible commitment to excellence in IT governance practices.

The CGEIT examination is a half-day, 120-question examination that is offered once a year in a wide range of international locations. The certification examination has been developed for professionals who have a significant management, advisory, or assurance role relating to the governance of IT. The certification examination covers six domain areas, with the percentages of concentration as indicated:

1. IT governance framework (25%)
2. Strategic alignment (15%)
3. Value delivery (15%)
4. Risk management (20%)
5. Resource management (13%)
6. Performance measurement (12%)

The overall requirements for CGEIT certification are similar to the CISA and CISM, as discussed. Although a relatively new certification and not as well recognized as the CISA or the CISM, acquiring CGEIT certification may be a good career path for IT auditors moving from audit assurance work to the often larger IT corporate governance issues.

 ## CERTIFIED INTERNAL AUDITOR RESPONSIBILITIES AND REQUIREMENTS

Sponsored by the IIA, the CIA designation is the only globally accepted certification for all internal auditors and is the major standard by which individuals can demonstrate their competency and professionalism in internal auditing. The CIA examination was first offered in August 1974 to 654 candidates; there are over 75,000 CIAs to date. Administered by the IIA Board of Regents, the CIA is an 11-hour examination that is offered worldwide through computer-based testing services. It consists of four separate examination sections:

Part I: The Internal Audit Activity's Role in Governance, Risk, and Control
Part II: Conducting the Internal Audit Engagement
Part III: Business Analysis and Information Technology
Part IV: Business Management Skills

By applying to become a CIA candidate, an individual agrees to accept the conditions of the program including eligibility requirements, exam confidentiality, acceptance of the CIA's code of ethics, continuing professional education (CPE), and any other conditions enacted by the Board of Regents or its Certification Department.

To take the CIA examination, candidates must hold a bachelor's degree or its equivalent from an accredited college-level institution; a copy of the candidate's diploma, transcripts, or other written proof of completion of a degree program must accompany the application. With the exception of full-time undergraduate degree students in their senior year, candidates will not be allowed to sit for the exam until the educational requirement is met.

Applicants who do not possess a bachelor's degree or who are unsure whether their educational achievements or professional designations qualify as equivalents can apply for a waiver through a formal request to the Board of Regents, who are the final judges of the acceptability of professional or educational attainment in lieu of a bachelor's degree and of equivalents. Information submitted should be sufficiently detailed to enable the Board of Regents to determine equivalency.

CIA candidates must exhibit high moral and professional character and must submit a character reference completed by another CIA, the candidate's supervisor, manager, or an appropriate educator. In addition, CIA candidates are required to have completed 24 months of internal auditing or equivalent experience in audit/assessment disciplines, external auditing, quality assurance, compliance, or internal control–related work. Either a master's degree or work experience in related business professions (such as accounting, law, or finance) can be substituted for one year of experience. Work experience must be verified by a CIA or the candidate's supervisor. Candidates may sit for the CIA exam prior to satisfying their experience requirement, but they will not be certified until the experience requirement has been met.

Candidates with other appropriate professional certifications can apply for a waiver from Part IV examination requirements. For example, in the United States, candidates with a CISA (discussed earlier) or a CPA do not have to take the Part IV section of the CIA examination. There are similar approved waivers for other professional certifications in countries around the world, such as a Chartered Accountant (CA) in the United Kingdom or Canada.

The CIA exam is "nondisclosed." Candidates must agree to keep the exam contents confidential and should not discuss the specific exam content with anyone except the IIA's Certification Department. Unauthorized disclosure of exam material will be considered a breach of the code of ethics and could result in a candidate's disqualification or other censure.

CIA Examination

Exhibit 30.3 contains an overview of the possible contents of the CIA examination's four parts. These are general topic areas and may change at any time. As shown in the exhibit, candidates may be tested for their **p**roficiency (P) or **a**wareness (A) in any given subject area. Awareness means that the candidate must be aware of general issues in a topic area; proficiency indicates that the candidate has a strong understanding and knowledge of how to apply that subject area. Two subject points from Exhibit 30.3 might better explain these differences:

1. Section A on Business Processes from Exhibit 30.3, Part III, on Business Analysis and Information Technology contains 10 subject areas, some labeled A and others P. Subject area 4, for example, calls for the CIA candidate to have a proficient knowledge of project management techniques. This IT audit knowledge requirement is outlined in Chapter 16 on IT audit portfolio and project management.
2. Section B on Financial Accounting and Finance in Part III on Business Analysis and Information Technology also has 10 subject areas, some labeled A and others P.

The following sections outline the concentration requirements for the Certified Internal Auditor (CIA) examination. Knowledge requirements are labeled **A** or **P** where:

P = Candidates must exhibit proficiency (thorough understanding and ability to apply concepts) in these topic areas.

A = Candidates must exhibit awareness (knowledge of terminology and fundamentals) in these topic areas.

Part I: The Internal Audit Activity's Role in Governance, Risk, and Control

100 Multiple-Choice Questions   *2 hours and 45 minutes*

A. Comply with the IIA'S Attribute Standards (15–25%)   Level P

1. Define purpose, authority, and responsibility of the internal audit activity.
    a. Determine if the purpose, authority, and responsibility of internal audit activity are clearly documented and approved.
    b. Determine if the purpose, authority, and responsibility of internal audit activity are communicated to the engagement clients.
    c. Demonstrate an understanding of the purpose, authority, and responsibility of the internal audit activity.
2. Maintain independence and objectivity.
3. a. Foster independence.
       1) Understand organizational independence.
       2) Recognize the importance of organizational independence.
       3) Determine if the internal audit activity is properly aligned to achieve organizational independence.
    b. Foster objectivity.
       1) Establish policies to promote objectivity.
       2) Assess individual objectivity.
       3) Maintain individual objectivity.
       4) Recognize and mitigate impairments to independence and objectivity.
4. Determine if the required knowledge, skills, and competencies are available.
    a. Understand the knowledge, skills, and competencies that an internal auditor needs to possess.
    b. Identify the knowledge, skills, and competencies required to fulfill the responsibilities of the internal audit activity.
5. Develop and/or procure necessary knowledge, skills and competencies collectively required by internal audit activity.
6. Exercise due professional care.
7. Promote continuing professional development.
    a. Develop and implement a plan for continuing professional development for internal audit staff.
    b. Enhance individual competency through continuing professional development.
8. Promote quality assurance and improvement of the internal audit activity.
    a. Establish and maintain a quality assurance and improvement program.
    b. Monitor the effectiveness of the quality assurance and improvement program.
    c. Report the results of the quality assurance and improvement program to the board or other governing body.
    d. Conduct quality assurance procedures and recommend improvements to the performance of the internal audit activity.
9. Abide by and promote compliance with The IIA Code of Ethics.

EXHIBIT 30.3   CIA Examination Summary

Source: Printed with permission of the Institute of Internal Auditors, 247 Maitland Avenue, Altamonte Springs, FL 32701-4201 USA.

B. Establish a Risk-Based Plan to Determine the Priorities of the Internal Audit Activity (15–25%)   Level P

1. Establish a framework for assessing risk.
2. Use the framework to:
   a. Identify sources of potential engagements (e.g., audit universe, management request, regulatory mandate).
   b. Assess organization-wide risk.
   c. Solicit potential engagement topics from various sources.
   d. Collect and analyze data on proposed engagements.
   e. Rank and validate risk priorities.
3. Identify internal audit resource requirements.
4. Coordinate the internal audit activity's efforts with:
   a. External auditor
   b. Regulatory oversight bodies
   c. Other internal assurance functions (e.g., health and safety department)
5. Select engagements.
   a. Participate in the engagement selection process.
   b. Select engagements.
   c. Communicate and obtain approval of the engagement plan from board.

C. Understand the Internal Audit Activity's Role in Organizational Governance (10–20%)   Level P

1. Obtain board's approval of audit charter.
2. Communicate plan of engagements.
3. Report significant audit issues.
4. Communicate key performance indicators to board on a regular basis.
5. Discuss areas of significant risk.
6. Support board in enterprise-wide risk assessment.
7. Review positioning of the internal audit function within the risk management framework within the organization.
8. Monitor compliance with the corporate code of conduct/business practices.
9. Report on the effectiveness of the control framework.
10. Assist board in assessing the independence of the external auditor.
11. Assess ethical climate of the board.
12. Assess ethical climate of the organization.
13. Assess compliance with policies in specific areas (e.g., derivatives).
14. Assess organization's reporting mechanism to the board.
15. Conduct follow-up and report on management response to regulatory body reviews.
16. Conduct follow-up and report on management response to external audit.
17. Assess the adequacy of the performance measurement system, achievement of corporate objective.
18. Support a culture of fraud awareness and encourage the reporting of improprieties.

D. Perform Other Internal Audit Roles and Responsibilities (0–10%)   Level P

1. Ethics/Compliance
   a. Investigate and recommend resolution for ethics/compliance complaints.
   b. Determine disposition of ethics violations.
   c. Foster healthy ethical climate.
   d. Maintain and administer business conduct policy (e.g., conflict of interest).
   e. Report on compliance.

EXHIBIT 30.3   *(Continued)*

2. Risk Management
   a. Develop and implement an organization-wide risk and control framework.
   b. Coordinate enterprise-wide risk assessment.
   c. Report corporate risk assessment to board.
   d. Review business continuity planning process.
3. Privacy
   a. Determine privacy vulnerabilities.
   b. Report on compliance.
4. Information or physical security
   a. Determine security vulnerabilities.
   b. Determine disposition of security violations.
   c. Report on compliance.

E. Governance, Risk, and Control Knowledge Elements (15–25%)	**Levels**
1. Corporate governance principles	A
2. Alternative control frameworks	A
3. Risk vocabulary and concepts	P
4. Risk management techniques	P
5. Risk/control implications of different organizational structures	P
6. Risk/control implications of different leadership styles	A
7. Change management	A
8. Conflict management	A
9. Management control techniques	P
10. Types of control (preventive, detective, input, output)	P

F. Plan Engagements (15–25%)	**Level P**

1. Initiate preliminary communication with engagement client.
2. Conduct a preliminary survey of the area of engagement.
   a. Obtain input from engagement client.
   b. Perform analytical reviews.
   c. Perform benchmarking.
   d. Conduct interviews.
   e. Review prior audit reports and other relevant documentation.
   f. Map processes.
   g. Develop checklists.
3. Complete a detailed risk assessment of the area (prioritize or evaluate risk/control factors).
4. Coordinate audit engagement efforts with
   a. External auditor
   b. Regulatory oversight bodies
5. Establish/refine engagement objectives and identify/finalize the scope of engagement.
6. Identify or develop criteria for assurance engagements (criteria against which to audit).
7. Consider the potential for fraud when planning an engagement.
   a. Be knowledgeable of the risk factors and red flags of fraud.
   b. Identify common types of fraud associated with the engagement area.
   c. Determine if risk of fraud requires special consideration when conducting an engagement.

EXHIBIT 30.3   (*Continued*)

8. Determine engagement procedures.
9. Determine the level of staff and resources needed for the engagement.
10. Establish adequate planning and supervision of the engagement.
11. Prepare engagement work program.

Part II: Conducting the Internal Audit Engagement

100 Multiple-Choice Questions   *2 hours and 45 minutes*

A. Conduct Engagements (25–35%)   Level P

1. Research and apply appropriate standards:
   a. IIA Professional Practices Framework (Code of Ethics, Standards, Practice Advisories)
   b. Other professional, legal, and regulatory standards
2. Maintain an awareness of the potential for fraud when conducting an engagement.
   a. Notice indicators or symptoms of fraud.
   b. Design appropriate engagement steps to address significant risk of fraud.
   c. Employ audit tests to detect fraud.
   d. Determine if any suspected fraud merits investigation.
3. Collect data.
4. Evaluate the relevance, sufficiency, and competence of evidence.
5. Analyze and interpret data.
6. Develop work papers.
7. Review work papers.
8. Communicate interim progress.
9. Draw conclusions.
10. Develop recommendations when appropriate.
11. Report engagement results.
    a. Conduct exit conference.
    b. Prepare report or other communication.
    c. Approve engagement report.
    d. Determine distribution of report.
    e. Obtain management response to report.
12. Conduct client satisfaction survey.
13. Complete performance appraisals of engagement staff.

B. Conduct Specific Engagements (25–35%)   Level P

1. Conduct assurance engagements.
   a. Fraud investigation
      1) Determine appropriate parties to be involved with investigation.
      2) Establish facts and extent of fraud (e.g., interviews, interrogations and data analysis).
      1) Report outcomes to appropriate parties.
      2) Complete a process review to improve controls to prevent fraud and recommend changes.
   b. Risk and control self-assessment
      1) Facilitated approach
         (a) Client-facilitated
         (b) Audit-facilitated
      1) Questionnaire approach
      2) Self-certification approach

EXHIBIT 30.3   (*Continued*)

c. Audits of third parties and contract auditing
d. Quality audit engagements
e. Due diligence audit engagements
f. Security audit engagements
g. Privacy audit engagements
h. Performance (key performance indicators) audit engagements
i. Operational (efficiency and effectiveness) audit engagements
j. Financial audit engagements
k. Information technology (IT) audit engagements
   1) Operating systems
      (a) Mainframe
      (b) Workstations
      (c) Server
   2) Application development
      (a) Application authentication
      (b) Systems development methodology
      (c) Change control
      (d) End user computing
   3) Data and network communications/connections (e.g., LAN, VAN, and WAN)
   4) Voice communications
   5) System security (e.g., firewalls, access control)
   6) Contingency planning
   7) Databases
   8) Functional areas of IT operations (e.g., data center operations)
   9) Web infrastructure
   10) Software licensing
   11) Electronic funds transfer (EFT) and electronic data interchange (EDI)
   12) e-Commerce
   13) Information protection (e.g., viruses, privacy)
   14) Encryption
   15) Enterprise-wide resource planning (ERP) software (e.g., SAP R/3)
l. Compliance audit engagements
2. Conduct consulting engagements
   a. Internal control training
   b. Business process review
   c. Benchmarking
   d. Information technology (IT) and systems development
   e. Design of performance measurement systems

C. Monitor Engagement Outcomes (5–15%)   Level P

1. Determine appropriate follow-up activity by the internal audit activity.
2. Identify appropriate method to monitor engagement outcomes.
3. Conduct follow-up activity.
4. Communicate monitoring plan and results.

D. Fraud Knowledge Elements (5–15%)

1. Discovery sampling - *Level A*
2. Interrogation techniques - *Level A*
3. Forensic auditing - *Level A*
4. Use of computers in analyzing data - *Level P*

EXHIBIT 30.3   (*Continued*)

5. Red flag - *Level P*
6. Types of fraud - *Level P*

E. Engagement Tools (15–25%)

1. Sampling - *Level A*
   a. Non-statistical (judgmental)
   b. Statistical
2. Statistical analyses (process control techniques) - *Level A*
3. Data gathering tools - *Level P*
   a. Interviewing
   b. Questionnaires
   c. Checklists
4. Analytical review techniques - *Level P*
   a. Ratio estimation
   b. Variance analysis (e.g., budget vs. actual)
   c. Other reasonableness tests
5. Observation - *Level P*
6. Problem solving - *Level P*
7. Risk and control self-assessment (CSA) - *Level A*
8. Computerized audit tools and techniques - *Level P*
   a. Embedded audit modules
   b. Data extraction techniques
   c. Generalized audit software (e.g., ACL, IDEA)
   d. Spreadsheet analysis
   e. Automated work papers (e.g., Lotus Notes, Auditor Assistant)
9. Process mapping including flowcharting - *Level P*

Part III: Business Analysis and Information Technology

100 Multiple-Choice Questions   *2 hours and 45 minutes*

A. Business Processes (15–25%)

1. Quality management (e.g., TQM) - *Level A*
2. The International Organization for Standardization (ISO) framework - *Level A*
3. Forecasting - *Level A*
4. Project management techniques - *Level P*
5. Business process analysis (e.g., workflow analysis and bottleneck management, theory of constraints) - *Level P*
6. Inventory management techniques and concepts - *Level P*
7. Marketing - pricing objectives and policies - *Level A*
8. Marketing - supply chain management - *Level A*
9. Human Resources (individual performance management and measurement; supervision; environmental factors that affect performance; facilitation techniques; personnel sourcing/staffing; training and development; safety) - *Level P*
10. Balanced scorecard - *Level A*

B. Financial Accounting and Finance (15–25%)

1. Basic concepts and underlying principles of financial accounting (e.g., statements, terminology, relationships) - *Level P*

EXHIBIT 30.3   *(Continued)*

2. Intermediate concepts of financial accounting (e.g., bonds, leases, pensions, intangible assets, R&D) - *Level A*
3. Advanced concepts of financial accounting (e.g., consolidation, partnerships, foreign currency transactions) - *Level A*
4. Financial statement analysis - *Level P*
5. Cost of capital evaluation - *Level A*
6. Types of debt and equity - *Level A*
7. Financial instruments (e.g., derivatives) - *Level A*
8. Cash management (treasury functions) - *Level A*
9. Valuation models - *Level A*
    a. Inventory valuation
    b. Business valuation
10. Business development life cycles - *Level A*

C. Managerial Accounting (10–20%)

1. Cost concepts (e.g., absorption, variable, fixed) - *Level P*
2. Capital budgeting - *Level A*
3. Operating budget - *Level P*
4. Transfer pricing - *Level A*
5. Cost-volume-profit analysis - *Level A*
6. Relevant cost - *Level A*
7. Costing systems (e.g., activity-based, standard) - *Level A*
8. Responsibility accounting - *Level A*

D. Regulatory, Legal, and Economics (5–15%)   Level A

1. Impact of government legislation and regulation on business
2. Trade legislation and regulations
3. Taxation schemes
4. Contracts
5. Nature and rules of legal evidence
6. Key economic indicators

E. Information Technology - IT (30–40%)   Level A

1. Control frameworks (e.g., eSAC, CobiT)
2. Data and network communications/connections (e.g., LAN, VAN, and WAN)
3. Electronic funds transfer (EFT)
4. e-Commerce
5. Electronic data interchange (EDI)
6. Functional areas of IT operations (e.g., data center operations)
7. Encryption
8. Information protection (e.g. viruses, privacy)
9. Evaluate investment in IT (cost of ownership)
10. Enterprise-wide resource planning (ERP) software (e.g., SAP R/3)
11. Operating systems
12. Application development
13. Voice communications
14. Contingency planning
15. Systems security (e.g. firewalls, access control)
16. Databases
17. Software licensing
18. Web infrastructure

EXHIBIT 30.3 *(Continued)*

Part IV: Business Management Skills

100 Multiple-Choice Questions   *2 hours and 45 minutes*

A. Strategic Management (20–30%)   Level A

1. Global analytical techniques
   a. Structural analysis of industries
   b. Competitive strategies (e.g., Porter's model)
   c. Competitive analysis
   d. Market signals
   e. Industry evolution
2. Industry environments
   a. Competitive strategies related to:
      1) Fragmented industries
      2) Emerging industries
      3) Declining industries
   b. Competition in global industries
      1) Sources/impediments
      2) Evolution of global markets
      3) Strategic alternatives
      4) Trends affecting competition
3. Strategic decisions
   a. Analysis of integration strategies
   b. Capacity expansion
   c. Entry into new businesses
4. Portfolio techniques of competitive analysis
5. Product life cycles

B. Global Business Environments (15–25%)   Level A

1. Cultural/legal/political environments
   a. Balancing global requirements and local imperatives
   b. Global mindsets (personal characteristics/competencies)
   c. Sources and methods for managing complexities and contradictions
   d. Managing multicultural teams
2. Economic/financial environments
   a. Global, multinational, international, and multilocal compared and contrasted
   b. Requirements for entering the global market place
   c. Creating organizational adaptability
   d. Managing training and development.

C. Organizational Behavior (20–30%)   Level A

1. Motivation
   a. Relevance and implication of various theories
   b. Impact of job design, rewards, work schedules, etc.
2. Communication
   a. The process
   b. Organizational dynamics
   c. Impact of computerization
3. Performance
   a. Productivity
   b. Effectiveness

EXHIBIT 30.3   (*Continued*)

4. Structure
   a. Centralized/decentralized
   b. Departmentalization
   c. New configurations (e.g., hourglass, cluster, network)

D. Management Skills (20–30%)   Level A

1. Group dynamics
   a. Traits (e.g., cohesiveness, roles, norms, groupthink)
   b. Stages of group development
   c. Organizational politics
   d. Criteria and determinants of effectiveness
2. Team building
   a. Methods used in team building
   b. Assessing team performance
3. Leadership skills
   a. Theories compared and contrasted
   b. Leadership grid (topology of leadership styles)
   c. Mentoring
4. Personal time management

E. Negotiating (5-15%)   Level A

1. Conflict resolution
   a. Competitive/cooperative
   b. Compromise, forcing, smoothing, etc.
2. Added-value negotiating
   a. Description
   b. Specific steps

EXHIBIT 30.3   *(Continued)*

Subject area 7 calls for the CIA candidate to have an awareness of financial instruments such as derivatives. However, a typical CIA internal auditor often has little more than a very high-level general understanding of financial derivative concepts.

The CIA examination covers a wide range of topics that are significant to many IT auditors, and each of the A or P topic areas in Exhibit 30.3 possibly may be covered in any particular examination. The examination is updated periodically and reflects current topics of interest to IT internal auditors. Some topic areas in the CIA examination may cause challenges for many IT and financial-oriented internal auditors. For example, Part III, section B, point 4 calls for the CIA candidate to be proficient in financial statement analysis. Beyond a general understanding of simple financial ratio analysis, this CIA knowledge requirement may be asking internal auditor candidates too much. Conversely, section E, point 1 of Part III calls for IT and internal auditors only to be aware of the Control Objectives for Information and Related Technology (CobiT) framework. As discussed in Chapter 2, an understanding of the CobiT framework should be a requirement for all IT auditors.

Professionals can quibble about the extent of proficiency or awareness required for an internal auditor to become a CIA, but the topics outlined in Exhibit 30.3 represent a comprehensive knowledge requirement for all IT internal auditors. Many of these subject areas have been discussed in other chapters of this book, and IT auditors should consider taking the CIA examination to demonstrate their overall internal audit knowledge.

Maintaining Your CIA Certification

An internal auditor does not have to be a member of the IIA to take the CIA examination, although the IIA strongly encourages membership. All CIAs—IIA members and non-members—must be familiar with and agree to abide by the IIA's *International Standards for the Professional Practice of Internal Auditing* as well as the IIA's code of ethics. These two, outlined in Chapter 3, set the standards of practice and conduct for all internal auditors and are very consistent with the ISACA standards also discussed in Chapter 3. The IIA standards are particularly important; they were revised in 2008 from internal auditor best practices where the guidance said that an internal auditor "should" to an important new internal audit standards requirement specifying that an internal auditor "must."

Upon certification, CIAs are required to maintain their knowledge and skills and to stay abreast of improvements and developments in internal auditing standards, procedures, and techniques. Practicing CIAs must complete and report 80 CPE hours of credits every two years. CIAs must report their CPE activities to the IIA per published deadlines; any who fail to meet these requirements by the reporting deadline will be placed on inactive status and may not use their designation.

Similar to the CISA, the CIA is a worldwide certification; in contrast, the CPA is a U.S. certification and the CA is a certification in the United Kingdom and separately in Canada. The CIA is the only internationally recognized designation for internal auditors. The examination is currently offered in English, French, Spanish, Mandarin Chinese, Czech, German, Hebrew, Italian, Japanese, and Portuguese as well as an ever-growing list of other languages. The examination once was a challenge for many because candidates had to present themselves at testing sites for proctored sit-down examinations; today it is offered through a worldwide chain of computer-based testing sites. A candidate must meet registration requirements, receive a testing site "ticket," and then arrange to visit an authorized testing site. (For more information on the CIA, see the IIA Web site, www. theiia.org.)

BEYOND THE CIA: OTHER IIA CERTIFICATIONS

The IIA's Board of Regents offers several other professional certification examinations and certificates: the Certification in Control Self-Assessment® (CCSA), the Certified Government Auditing Professional® (CGAP), and the Certified Financial Services Auditor® (CFSA). These separate examinations, each consisting of 125 multiple-choice questions and lasting 3 hours and 15 minutes, can be taken as substitutes for Part IV of the regular CIA examination. Each is also offered through the same computer-based testing facilities as the CIA examination.

CCSA Examination and Requirements

The IIA has promoted a control self-assessment (CSA) process and a supporting examinations, the Certified Control Self-Assessment® (CCSA) examination. Control self-assessment is an exercise where business participants, usually following their internal auditor's leadership, formally assess their internal controls and processes. These types of processes are discussed in Chapter 14 on establishing continuous improvement programs for enterprises and IT audit functions. ISACA does not have the same type of program for IT auditors, but many will find value in the IIA's CSA methodology. Because the IIA views CSAs as an important and unique process, it has established a certification examination in this area.

The CCSA exam tests a candidate's understanding of important CSA fundamentals, processes, and related topics such as risk, controls, and business objectives. In contrast to the experience requirements and overall rigor of the CIA examination, the CCSA is a single 3-hour, 125-question examination that tests candidates for their knowledge of CSA processes in six broad domains:

1. CSA Fundamentals (5–10%)
2. CSA Program Integration (15–25%)
3. Elements of the CSA Process (15–25%)
4. Business Objectives/Enterprise Performance (10–15%)
5. Risk Identification and Assessment (15–20%)
6. Control Theory and Application (20–25%)

Each of these areas requires the CCSA candidate to demonstrate CSA process knowledge in the discipline. The examination is based on the same topic proficiency and awareness approaches found in the CIA examination. Based on information published on the IIA Web site (www.theiia.org), Exhibit 30.4 shows the examination's knowledge requirements for just the CCSA Domain 3 area. This sample question provides an overview of the CSA process. The topics tested on the CCSA exam are framed in the context of a variety of industry situations. Candidates are not expected to be familiar with industry-specific internal controls but should be able to relate to risks and controls that generally apply to business processes in various industries. The IIA Web site also contains some sample CCSA examination questions. After completion of the CCSA examination, the successful candidate should be able to serve as an experienced CSA session facilitator.

Candidates for the CCSA are not required to have CIA credentials or even to be internal auditors. The experience requirements for the CCSA are that a candidate must have had a strong level of experience in the control self-assessment field. Other requirements, however, such as accepting the IIA's code of ethics and continuing education requirements, are similar to the CIA. The CCSA alone will give a practitioner a level of expertise in this area, but it should be combined with another certification, such as the CIA. Completion of the CCSA examination also can serve as a substitute for Part IV of the CIA examination.

CGAP Requirements

IT and other internal auditors working in government positions have some special task and skill requirements. Whether working for one of the many branches of the U.S. government or at a state or local level, an internal auditor is faced with a different set of

---

CCSA Examination Sample Domain Topic Outline

NOTE: Domain 3 is one of the six domain or topic areas in the CCSA examination. This section covers about 20% of the test's overall content. In these domain content areas, a candidate will be expected to either have a **P** (proficiency) or **A** (awareness) of the subject area.

Domain 3—Elements of the CSA Process
A. Management's priorities and concerns (P)
B. Project and logistics management (P)
C. Business objectives, processes, challenges, and threats for the area under review (P)
D. Resource identification and allocation (A)
    1. Participants
    2. CSA team
E. Culture of area under review (P)
F. Question development techniques (P)
G. Technology supporting the CSA process (P)
H. Facilitation techniques and tools (P)
I. Group dynamics (P)
J. Fraud awareness (A)
    1. Red flags/symptoms of fraud
    2. Communication and investigation channels
    3. Responding to evidence
K. Evaluation/analytical tools and techniques (trend analysis, data synthesis, scenarios) (A)
L. Formulating recommendations or actions plans (practical, feasible, cost effective) (P)
M. Nature of evidence (sufficiency, relevance, adequacy) (A)
N. Reporting techniques and considerations (types, audience, sensitive issues, access to information) (P)
O. Motivational techniques (creating support and commitment for recommendations) (A)
P. Monitoring, tracking, and follow-up techniques (A)
Q. Awareness of legal, regulatory, and ethical considerations (A)
R. Measuring CSA program effectiveness (A)

EXHIBIT 30.4 CCSA Examination Domain 3 Topics
Source: www.theiia.org/certification/specialty-certifications/cfsa/cfsa-exam-content/

---

knowledge and skill requirements than the typical internal auditor working the private sector. Attainment of the CGAP allows a candidate to demonstrate these government auditing skills.

CGAP is a specialty certification designed specifically for and by government auditing practitioners. This examination is available only in the United States at this time. It tests a candidate's comprehension of government auditing practices, methodologies, and environment as well as related standards and control/risk models.

The requirements for the CGAP are similar to the IIA's CIA and CCSA just described. Candidates for this 3-hour and 15-minute examination must have had two years of auditing experience in a government environment (federal, state/provincial, local, quasi-governmental areas, or authority/crown corporation). Work experience must be verified by a CGAP, CIA, CCSA, CFSA, or the candidate's supervisor. The CGAP examination and approximate concentration of questions covers these four domains:

1. Standards and Control/Risk Models (5–10%)
2. Government Auditing Practice (35–45%)

3. Government Auditing Methodologies and Skills (20–25%)
4. Government Auditing Environment (25–35%)

This book does not cover the specialized field of government internal auditing. Government auditors have some very specialized knowledge requirements. The IIA's CGAP is a vehicle for U.S.-based internal auditors working in any of many levels of government to demonstrate their internal audit skills.

CFSA Examination and Requirements

The CFSA is another of the IIA's specialty certifications and is tailored to demonstrate an individual internal auditor's competence and professionalism in banking, insurance, and securities financial services areas. Candidates may choose any one of these disciplines when taking the exam, regardless of their current occupational field. This exam is available in the United States and Canada only at this time. The examination covers four domains:

1. Financial Services Auditing
2. Banking
3. Insurance
4. Securities

Each of these financial domains can be very different. For example, the specialized knowledge requirements for banking are often very different from those for the field of insurance. Exhibit 30.5 shows the CFSA application topic outline for the insurance industry—a broad range of topics. Because of very specialized country-by-country rules and practices, the CFSA examination is limited to the United States and Canada. Some of the topics in Exhibit 30.5 illustrate why questions must be very oriented to specific country rules and practices.

A. Applications/Processes
  1. Marketing, Sales, and Distribution
  2. Underwriting
  3. Reinsurance
  4. Actuarial
  5. Claims
  6. Financial Reporting
  7. Compliance
  8. Investment Operations
  9. Risk Management
 10. Premium Audit
 11. Administration

B. Laws and Regulations
  1. The McCarran Ferguson Act
  2. State Insurance Commissions

EXHIBIT 30.5 CFSA Insurance Industry Examination Topics
Source: www.theiia.org/certification/specialty-certifications/cfsa/cfsa-exam-content/

3. The NAIC
4. The Securities and Exchange Commission
5. ERISA
6. State Model Laws

C. Products
1. Life, Pension, and Annuity
   a. Individual Insurance
      i) Whole Life
      ii) Term Life
      iii) Universal Life
      iv) Endowments
   b. Group Insurance
      i) Life
      ii) Accident and Health
      iii) Accidental Death and Dismemberment
      iv) Disability
      v) Dental
      vi) HMOs
      vii) Managed Care
      viii) Utilization Management
      ix) Preferred Provider Organizations
      x) Administrative Service Only
   c. Pensions
      i) Qualified Plans
      ii) Tax Favored Individual Retirement Plans
      iii) Qualification Rules
      iv) Plan Discrimination
      v) Savings Plans
      vi) Vesting
      vii) Fiduciaries
      viii) Prohibited Transactions
      ix) Annuity
      x) Fixed Annuities
      xi) Variable Annuities
   d. Reinsurance
2. Property and Casualty Products
   a. Workers Compensation
   b. General Liability
   c. Automobile
   d. Homeowners
   e. Umbrella Coverage
   f. Financial Guarantees
   g. Other

EXHIBIT 30.5 *(Continued)*

Importance of the CIA Specialty Certification Examinations

This chapter began with some rather cynical comments about the plethora of professional certifications, using Certified Kitchen Designers (CKDs) as perhaps an extreme example. The CIA examination and its professional designation are important for internal auditors as professionals and for managers reviewing credentials, we question the need for many of the additional IIA professional certifications as special, separate designations. Because they are new and do not have a wide sphere of recognition, an internal auditor claiming he or she is just a CFSA may not impress too many people at this time.

Nevertheless, any of these special certifications may be very important for an internal auditor working in a specialized area and who desires to complete Part IV of a CIA examination by taking these specialty examinations. For an internal auditor working in a government environment at any level, for example, a CIA and a CGAP are very important. The overall CIA examination is an important test for all internal auditors, and all IT auditors should consider earning both the CIA and the CISA.

CISSP INFORMATION SYSTEMS SECURITY PROFESSIONAL CERTIFICATION

A professional organization known as the International Information Systems Security Certification Consortium or (ISC)^2 is responsible for one of the more challenging and better-recognized internal audit–related professional certifications and examinations, the Certified Information System Security Professional (CISSP). This examination and designation are well recognized but difficult to achieve. This certification is aimed at more technically oriented information systems security professionals, not ordinary internal auditors. It is also in contrast to the CISM, discussed above, that the CISM focuses on information security *managers* while the CISSP is a qualification for technical IT security specialists.

With the possible exception of the CISM examination, the CISSP examination is on a much higher, much more technical level than other internal auditor certification examinations discussed in this chapter. The examinations are closely proctored, training materials are reviewed and approved by (ISC)^2, and the overall quality of the examination is high. Someone with CISSP certification almost certainly will have a high knowledge of information systems security.

CERTIFIED FRAUD EXAMINER CERTIFICATION

Concerns regarding fraud and fraud investigations are becoming increasingly important to all auditors. Chapter 21 discussed IT fraud detection and prevention and how external and internal auditors in the past believed that it was not their responsibility to investigate and detect fraud. However, in today's post-SOx era, internal and external auditors now have a strong responsibility to investigate for fraud and to take appropriate actions when it is identified.

The Association of Certified Fraud Examiners (ACFE) is a professional enterprise very involved with fraud-related issues for the internal auditor. The ACFE has its own professional examination and certification, the Certified Fraud Examiner (CFE). Obtaining a CFE designation is regarded as an indicator of excellence in the antifraud profession. CFE members have experienced growth in enterprise fraud and fraud examination techniques. As CFEs, they can position themselves as leaders in the antifraud community.

The CFE examination is based on four broad areas:

1. Criminology and Ethics
2. Financial Transactions
3. Legal Elements of Fraud
4. Fraud Examination and Investigation

These topic areas are beyond the experience and training of many IT auditors. The ACFE, of course, has its own publications, conferences, and local chapters to provide an IT internal auditor with a greater level of information about fraud and fraud investigations.

Although it is a relatively new professional organization, the ACFE has gained prominence in our post-SOx era. It has its own Web site (www.acfe.com), and much of the fraud material published on AICPA Web pages on fraud and discussed in Chapter 21 are based on ACFE materials. In addition, the ACFE Web site contains a sample examination to allow an internal auditor to determine if he or she is ready to take the CFE test. The candidate registers for this online exam and takes it over a machine-timed interval.

ASQ INTERNAL AUDIT CERTIFICATIONS

Chapter 31 discusses the American Society for Quality (ASQ) and its quality auditor certifications. The ASQ sponsors a wide range of examinations and certifications for all aspects of its operations, including the Certified Quality Auditor (CQA) examination and certification. A CQA is a professional who understands the standards and principles of quality management auditing and the techniques of examining, questioning, evaluating, and reporting to determine a quality system's adequacy and deficiencies. The CQA analyzes all elements of a quality system and judges its degree of adherence to the criteria of industrial management and quality evaluation and control systems. The difference between a regular internal auditor and a CQA is that the latter often works in a quality assurance group and spends more time on process-oriented reviews than the IIA internal auditor's financial and operational reviews. CQA auditors typically work in production areas and often perform more hands-on reviews as compared to CISA IT auditors or CIA-level internal auditors.

Chapter 31 also discusses the differences and similarities between the IIA-heritage internal auditors and ASQ quality auditors. Although many ASQ auditors are also IIA members, they often seek their own professional CQA certification. To achieve quality auditor certification, the candidate is required to pass a five-hour, multiple-choice examination that measures comprehension of the quality audit profession. As the minimum professional expectations, a CQA quality auditor must:

■ Possess the knowledge to effectively conduct different types of objective, ethically based audits using and interpreting applicable standards/requirements.

- Be able to develop and communicate an audit plan within a defined scope that identifies applicable standards, necessary personnel, required documents and tools, and an audit agenda.
- Be able to effectively execute an audit plan, including the opening meeting, performing the audit, and the closing meeting, using generally accepted auditing techniques and verifying, documenting, and communicating findings as appropriate for the audit.
- Be able to objectively present verified nonconformance to the audited standard and evaluate the effectiveness of the resulting follow-up/corrective action activities in an ethical and timely manner.
- Know and be able to apply basic auditing tools and techniques, such as flowcharting, the concept of variation, observation techniques, and physical examination techniques. A CQA must also demonstrate a general knowledge of quality control tools, descriptive statistics, and applicable sampling theories.

The requirements listed here are similar to those of the IIA-oriented internal auditor, but the CQA uses different approaches and terminologies. For example, the last list mentions "verified nonconformance to the audited standard" and "the concept of variation." These are specialized ASQ terms, although many other concepts go back to standard IIA internal audit processes. The CQA examination is based on the ASQ's Body of Knowledge, a comprehensive set of key knowledge areas and practices for the CQA.

A CQA-certified auditor has professional and continuing education requirements similar to those of a CIA. If nothing else, the ASQ is perhaps more stringent than ISACA or the IIA and requires recertification every three years for all CSQs. Professionals who have not completed required continuing educational requirements must retake the CQA examination to regain their certification.

The ASQ has two other specialized quality auditor certifications, one for biomedical quality audits and the other for hazard analysis and critical control point systems. The ASQ is very responsive to member requests to build separate certifications when there is a special demand. These ASQ special certification are a different area of quality auditing.

OTHER INTERNAL AUDITOR CERTIFICATIONS

As discussed throughout this chapter, there are a large number of professional certifications available to IT auditors, depending on individual job requirements and skills. There is no one correct approach here, and IT audit professional certification depends on the auditor's needs and interests. The requirements for all certifications are similar, usually consisting of specified requirements to take the examination, pass it, and receive the designation, followed by continuing education requirements to keep the certification current.

A professional certification is a good way for an IT auditor to demonstrate that he or she has some unique and important professional skills. Professional certifications are important. The knowledge gained through obtaining a certificate allows an IT auditor to work more efficiently and effectively in service to management. Certification and in particular the CISA is important for all IT auditors, who should make the effort to become certified as CISAs and potentially CIAs. Individual internal auditors should use these certification examinations as a measure of their own professionalism. These are important indicators of knowledge, interests, and abilities. Both with an enterprise's internal audit function or moving beyond, certifications are measures of one's knowledge and interests in the profession. Every IT internal auditor should understand why a professional certification is important and should have a general knowledge of what it takes to achieve that certification.

 NOTE

1. www.microsoft.com/learning/en/us/certification/view-by-name.aspx contains a current list of Microsoft certifications.

CHAPTER THIRTY-ONE

Quality Assurance Auditing and ASQ Standards

I T AUDIT STANDARDS ESTABLISHED by the Information Systems Audit and Control Association (ISACA) and the Institute of Internal Auditors (IIA) are not the only ones that exist. Of course, Certified Public Accountant (CPA) external auditors have a major role in assessing IT controls, as do other audit professionals, such as U.S. federal government contract auditors. Another important group of internal auditors are called quality auditors; unlike many other internal and external auditors, these professionals typically do not work in corporate headquarters. Affiliated with the American Society for Quality (ASQ) professional organization, quality auditors are a unique internal audit–like professional group that has its own standards, codes of ethics, and professional certification designations. Quality auditors have responsibilities to review a wide range of International Organization for Standardization (ISO) standards relating to compliance, work simplification, and quality-related processes, including IT. Quality auditors historically operated primarily on the shop floor in manufacturing or process-production enterprises and often have had little contact with the ISACA- or IIA-type internal auditors.

Today quality auditors are becoming closer to the classic internal auditor. More accurately, each of these internal audit professional groups is changing in terms of objectives and approaches in ways that bring them closer together. The classic ISACA or IIA audit professional should have an understanding of the activities of quality auditors and how their work fits in the overall environment of corporate governance.

This chapter reviews the role of quality auditors in an enterprise, their practices and standards, and how their activities apply to IT audit needs. There are many similarities between the activities of these auditors and IIA operational internal auditors. With a growing convergence of enterprise activities to improve governance and internal controls, we can expect to see these two internal audit groups become more closely aligned. Although our focus throughout this book is on ISACA-type of IT internal auditors, there is an IT audit need for a general understanding of the roles, responsibilities, and activities of quality auditors.

In addition, we also consider another aspect of IT audit: quality-assurance (QA) reviews of an IT audit function performed by members of the IT audit team or by contracted outside reviewers. The terminology can be confusing. A quality auditor is a separate professional who is a member of the ASQ. The term *QA* refers to a process practiced by many audit functions. IT audit functions can often bring some real value to themselves and to their enterprise as a whole by authorizing an independent quality review of their IT audit practices and operations, either by independent members of the internal audit group or by outside providers.

DUTIES AND RESPONSIBILITIES OF QUALITY AUDITORS

For many, this terminology can be a bit confusing. Some quality auditors may belong to the IIA, but they have their own separate professional organization, the Quality Audit Division (QAD) of the ASQ. Similarly, some quality auditors who are interested and specialize in IT audit issues may belong to ISACA and the IIA as well as the ASQ. At one time the ASQ professional organization, with responsibilities for many activities in quality management, referred to its QAD professional affiliates as quality auditors. Now the ASQ refers to its audit members as just internal auditors. Confusing? Yes. We will refer to the ASQ professionals discussed and described in this chapter as quality auditors. In addition, the ASQ has made no real provision to call or identify any of its members as IT audit specialists.

The ASQ is the leading proponent of the quality movement in the United States. It offers a wide range of publications, professional certifications, and separate divisions covering industries such as aerospace and pharmaceuticals as well as professional practices, such as the QAD. The ASQ is very involved with the ISO quality standards, discussed in Chapter 18, and its QAD is responsible for compliance audits using those ISO standards.

The QAD's stated mission is "to support auditors and other stakeholders by defining and promoting auditing as a management tool to achieve continuous improvement, effective communication, and increased customer satisfaction." Again, its use of just the term "auditor" causes some confusion regarding the roles of these quality auditors. In addition, the ASQ and its QAD recognizes and defines several activity levels of auditing:

- **Self-audits.** This is a quality audit performed within the enterprise to review compliance with ISO quality standards and the like.
- **Second-party audits.** Quality auditors often perform reviews to assess whether their suppliers are operating in compliance with some specified standards. A second-party audit occurs when an enterprise's own quality auditors visit a supplier to test compliance with some standards.

- **Third-party audits.** These are audits performed at the enterprise by an independent organization, such as one of the ISO registrars, discussed in Chapter 18, or an auditor from a government agency, such as the U.S. Department of Labor's Occupational Safety and Health Administration (OSHA) or from the Federal Drug Administration (FDA).

The terminology change from "quality auditors" to "auditors" today is a result of the ASQ broadening its professional designations. Exhibit 31.1 describes the classifications of quality audits, showing both outside customers, who need quality audit assurances, and suppliers. These areas of activity put quality auditors in a different framework from ISACA or IIA internal auditors.

Quality audit terminology can be even more confusing because the ASQ designates audit professionals as either internal or external auditors. An ASQ internal auditor reviews controls and standards within that auditor's enterprise or employer; an ASQ external auditor, in this context, performs third-party reviews at other enterprises to establish such matters as ISO certifications. Although a quality auditor also may be a member of the IIA or ISACA in addition to the ASQ, the designation *external* quality auditor has no relationship with the financial statement attest auditors, who as CPAs are members of the American Institute of Certified Public Accountants (AICPA). In this chapter, we generally use the term *quality auditor* to refer to these ASQ-background auditors to distinguish among IIA-sponsored internal auditors, ISACA IT auditors, and CPA-certified external auditors. When we refer to just an *internal auditor* in this chapter, we mean the ISACA- or IIA-heritage internal or IT auditors who has been the main focus of this book.

The IIA has its Certified Internal Auditor (CIA) professional designation and ISACA has its Certified Information Systems Auditor (CISA); the ASQ has the Certified Quality

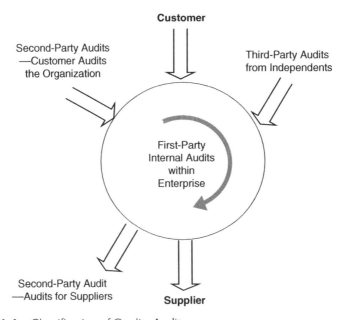

EXHIBIT 31.1 Classification of Quality Audits

Auditor (CQA) professional certification. Chapter 30 outlined these professional certifications. In addition to holding a CQA, a quality auditor may earn several quality audit specialty subdesignations, such as for hazardous analysis or biomedical auditing, among others. These certifications require designated levels of work experience and successfully passing a special additional examination. ASQ quality auditors are involved in similar professional activities and have standards similar to those of ISACA and IIA internal auditors. In addition, the ASQ has a series of special national meetings and conferences for ASQ quality auditors.

ROLE OF THE QUALITY AUDITOR

ASQ procedures, standards, and quality auditing guidance materials are similar to the standards used by ISACA IT or IIA internal auditors. Quality auditors follow many of the same general internal audit steps as ISACA- or IIA-sponsored internal auditors in their procedures for developing programs, reporting findings, and the like. However, quality auditors usually are not involved with audit issues such as reviews of financial internal controls; nor are they directly involved with audits covering many IT internal controls areas. Quality auditors follow published international industry standards, such as ISO 9000, and their audits tend to be much more quantitative and mathematical than the work of the typical ISACA- or IIA-heritage internal auditor. The work of quality auditors is often closely aligned with the classic tools used by manufacturing production quality-assurance specialists.

Quality audits include a set of terms that may be unfamiliar to many internal auditors and managers. For example, Exhibit 31.2 shows that quality audits can

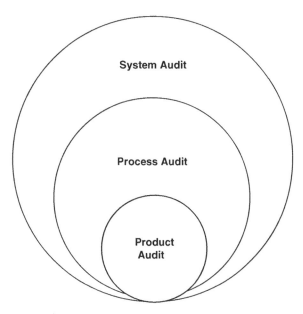

EXHIBIT 31.2   Types of Quality Audits

be designated as product, process, and system audits based on their scope and objectives.

- A *product audit* is an assessment of a final product or service and a review of its fitness for use against stated requirements or specifications. In a manufacturing sense, a product audit would be performed on some item that has just passed its final inspection and is ready for delivery to the customer.
- A *process audit* is the major type of audit performed by quality auditors. It is a review to verify conformance to standards, methods, procedures, or other requirements.
- A *systems audit* is *not* an IT-related systems review but one that covers all aspects of some type of control system. This type of review is conducted to verify, through objective evidence, that all aspects of management systems and organizational plans are implemented to adequately meet identified requirements.

Quality audits are typically more analytical in their approaches than many ISACA or the usual IIA internal audits. Because many quality auditors are more engineering technicians than IT specialists or accountants, they tend to make greater use of analytical tools and techniques in their workpaper analyses and audit reports. Perhaps because many quality audits are performed in process and manufacturing environments, they are more oriented to the production shop floor or an operations area than ISACA- or IIA-heritage internal or IT auditors. An explanation for this is that a quality audit function often does not report to the CAE and the audit committee but typically has stronger ties to production operations.

Quality audit tools and techniques are also often different from those used in many IT internal audits. An example might help explain such a typical quality auditor tool, technique, and approach. Exhibit 31.3 shows a Pareto chart, a common diagram used

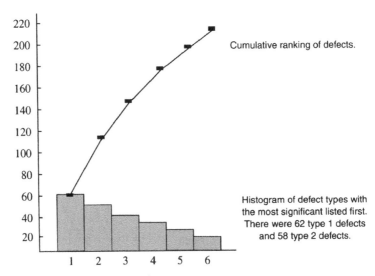

EXHIBIT 31.3 Pareto Chart Example

Source: Robert R. Moeller, *Brink's Modern Internal Auditing*, 6th ed. (Hoboken, NJ: John Wiley & Sons, 2005). Copyright © 2005, John Wiley & Sons. Used with permission of John Wiley & Sons.

in quality-related audit analyses. Such a chart ranks the types of errors or problems on the vertical axis with the most severe problems listed first. In this example, there were 62 cases of type 1 defect during the period reviewed. Similarly, there were 58 cases of type 2 defect with increasingly fewer cases for the other defects. The numbers of cumulative defects are plotted on the vertical axis. The line goes from 62 to (62 + 58 = 120) for the second point and continues. The idea behind a Pareto chart is to see which defects require the most attention. The fewer than 10 instances of type 6 defect shown should require less management attention.

Quality auditors traditionally have used tools such as Pareto charts to review quality defects and make recommendations. The recent worldwide movement to ISO 9000 quality standards, as discussed in Chapter 18, has very much changed the role of quality auditors. ISO quality standards call for management to conduct internal audits at planned intervals to determine whether the quality management system conforms to standard requirements and is effectively implemented and maintained. These standards also contain requirements for audit programs, management's responsibility, and other matters. Similar audit requirements exist for other quality management system ISO standards. For example, Section 6 of ISO 27001: 2000 is titled *Internal ISMS Audits*. The standard states, among other matters:

> The organization shall conduct internal ISMS audits at planned intervals to determine whether the control objectives, controls, processes and procedures of its ISMS:
>
> (a) conform to the requirements of this International Standard and relevant legislation or regulations;
> (b) conform to the identified information security requirements;
> (c) are effectively implemented and maintained; and
> (d) perform as expected.

The acronym *ISMS* stands for information system management systems. Any enterprise that is launching and seeking standards certification must establish a quality audit function.

Quality audit functions often are organized more informally than the audit committee connected ISACA- or IIA-trained internal audit functions. The next sections discuss the quality audit process. There are significant differences between quality auditors, who follow ASQ standards, and the IIA and ISACA IT audit professional standards discussed in Chapter 3. Over time, however, we may see a greater level of convergence between these auditing processes.

Quality auditors often are not that involved with IT-related issues, but based on their findings, their reviews emphasize areas for continuous improvement, including IT controls. To accomplish this continuous improvement, the data in a new review must be analyzed for trends and weaknesses. The quality auditor then compares results to goals and objectives, and analyzes process data to identify risks, inefficiencies, opportunities for improvement, and negative trends. The results may be recommendations for changes in procedures or in other areas of the process, such as improvements in acceptance criteria or methods of monitoring. Recommended changes in equipment or technology also may be among the quality auditor's recommendations for continual improvement. In many respects, quality auditors recommend more significant changes to an enterprise's process improvement cycle than either IT or operational internal auditors have done.

PERFORMING ASQ QUALITY AUDITS

Many business professionals understand that their internal and IT auditors follow established traditional internal auditing standards. The ISACA and IIA standards discussed in Chapter 3 provide a good overview for the overall profession of internal auditing. The ASQ-sponsored practice of quality auditing brings a somewhat different perspective to auditing. Although it has its roots in earlier quality-assurance and industrial engineering processes, quality auditing is particularly important for measuring compliance to ISO standards, where there are both internal and external components into this auditing practice.

ASQ-driven audits, quality audits, are reviews performed to assess regulatory compliance to rules or meet requirements for ISO standards registration or certification, as discussed in Chapter 18. They are also important because they are a key feedback loop in an enterprise's quality system to keep management informed about compliance with documented systems procedures. As discussed, quality audits are further divided into internal or self-audits and second- or third-party audits. Under these rules, a quality audit may be performed as a self-audit by persons very close to the actual process operations. Quality audits typically are not performed by a separate internal audit function but by persons in the enterprise who can demonstrate a level of objectivity.

Quality audits—whether they are internal or self-audit, second- or third-party—frequently take place in the ISO standards environment where an enterprise must check that its suppliers and others are in compliance with certain standards. Second-party audits occur when an enterprise performs a quality audit on one of its suppliers. A third-party audit occurs when an outside registrar or regulatory agency, such as OSHA or the FDA, performs an independent review. The concept here is that an enterprise must determine that its suppliers are in compliance with some standard through a second-party review. However, in order to show others that it is in compliance with a standard, such as ISO 90001, it must hire a certified independent registrar to certify that compliance.

Many quality auditing processes are based on the principles first established by Frederick Deming in Japan in the years following World War II. Deming's aim was to help repair and rebuild Japan's shattered manufacturing resources. He introduced many quality management techniques that soon led to very high-quality and innovative Japanese products, such as the offerings of Toyota and Sony. Deming's techniques initially were ignored by U.S. manufacturers.

A basic concept in Deming's work and a component of quality auditing activities is his plan/do/check/act (PDCA) cycle. Illustrated in Exhibit 31.4, this is a continuous improvement cycle where a team of quality auditors, among others, work to improve processes. They would use the PDCA cycle to review a process by following five steps:

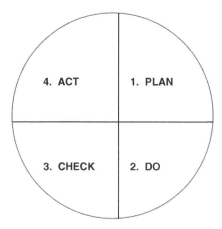

EXHIBIT 31.4 PDCA Cycle

Step 1: Plan. What are the objectives of a quality audit team? What changes are desirable, and what data is needed? What types of tests are needed? How will operations be observed?

Step 2: Do. What tests do we need to develop to assess compliance to these audit plans?

Step 3: Check. Observe the results of tests to develop preliminary conclusions.

Step 4: Act. Study all test results to assess what was learned and what can be predicted from the exercise. Based on these results, determine areas for process improvements.

Step 5: Repeat steps while gaining more knowledge.

This is a simple process for process improvement but is quite different from the traditional IT audit steps discussed in Chapter 5. The quality audit process is one of process improvement. Quality auditors do not just review an area and then report results through a formal audit report. Rather, they look at some area, evaluate their findings, and seek to return and improve the process. They often take the role of in-house consultants.

Although quality auditors often do not focus on IT security and control issues, the scope of their audits is often much more extensive than those of traditional ISACA- and IIA-heritage internal auditors. Quality auditors often are interested in compliance with applicable standards and aim to:

▪ Verify that the implemented system is working.
▪ Verify that the supporting quality assurance training programs are working and cost effective.
▪ Identify people or groups not following procedures.
▪ Provide evidence to management and others that processes are working as documented.

The quality audit process follows steps that are similar to the IT audit process described in Chapter 5, but quality audits often are not the more descriptive standards as

---

Pre-Audit Activities

1. Preparation for audit—establish audit objectives.
2. Plan for all audit activities.

The On-Site Audit

1. Opening meeting—meet with auditee and outline planned procedures.
2. Audit—activities will depend on the nature of the review.
3. Closing meeting—discuss findings and present draft report at end of fieldwork review.

Post-Audit Activities

1. Audit report—report on findings and recommendations.
2. Management review—discuss audit results with all levels of management.
3. Corrective actions—negotiate plan to correct audit findings.
4. Follow-up/corrective action audits.

EXHIBIT 31.5 Quality Audit Process Steps

---

described by the IIA or ISACA for performing their reviews. The quality auditing process is often much more analytical than IT and IIA-heritage internal audits. The Pareto chart in Exhibit 31.3 presents a typical procedure that quality auditors might use to develop their audit findings. Typical quality audits often emphasize statistical analysis and analytical techniques and often have a focus on manufacturing and production operations.

The process of launching and performing a quality audit, however, is very similar to the process used in IIA-heritage internal audits. Quality auditors start by developing an audit plan, then developing audit procedures, and finally writing the audit report to discuss their observations and recommended corrective actions. Exhibit 31.5 outlines these quality audit process steps. They are very similar to those used in ISACA and IIA audit standards. Perhaps a major difference here is that quality auditors are much more involved with correcting audit findings and launching corrective actions initiatives. In contrast to the audit professional standards discussed in Chapter 3, quality auditors assess control weaknesses and consult to help with the implementation of corrective actions.

As the importance of compliance with a growing number of ISO standards grows, the role of the quality auditor almost certainly will move to an enterprise's front office. Audit committees and management learn that ASQ-trained quality auditors and ISACA- and IIA-trained internal auditors have many common needs even though these professional groups often have had few contacts and little in common in the past, there is an evolving level of integration today with more traditional IT internal auditing and ASQ quality auditing.

As discussed, the term *quality auditing* is being replaced by just *auditing* in ASQ publications and in some ISO standards, and the terminology used in ISACA, IIA, and ISO standards is becoming increasingly consistent. For example, the ISO definition of an audit is a "systematic, independent and documented process for obtaining audit evidence and evaluating it objectively to determine the extent to which audit criteria are fulfilled."[1] The IIA's definition of internal auditing, discussed in Chapter 3, contains some quality-related words, such as: assurance, adding value, risk management, systematic, disciplined, control, and process orientation. Quality auditing and internal auditing terminology seems to be transitioning into a generic assessment and business process improvement model.

There probably will be a growing convergence of internal auditing and quality auditing over the upcoming years. An increasing number of enterprises worldwide are seeking ISO registrations, and ISO 9000 standards are becoming more process oriented, customer focused, and business driven. With an emphasis on "effectiveness," an ISO 9000–registered company must demonstrate its quality system effectiveness. In addition, there is a growing recognition of the ISO-like software standards released by the Institute of Electrical and Electronics Engineers in such areas as software acquisition processes and auditing software testing processes.

In some enterprises today, the chief audit executive (CAE) also is involved with an enterprise's quality audit function on at least a courtesy level. In the future, IT and other internal audit functions almost certainly will become more acquainted with their quality auditors and should give consideration to sharing resources. Although their historical roots are different, both audit functions should become involved with value-added audit functions for the enterprise. ISACA- and IIA-heritage internal auditors should develop a greater understanding of quality audit procedures. If there are separate quality and internal audit functions in an enterprise, the two groups should build some regular and ongoing communication links. Although each group has a different approach and objectives, there may be some value to sharing ideas and even doing some joint review work.

QUALITY ASSURANCE REVIEWS OF IT AUDIT FUNCTIONS

IT auditors have a special role in their service to the management through their assessments of IT security and controls. They visit an IT-related unit or component of an enterprise, review its controls, and make recommendations for improvements. An IT auditor should use the standards described in Chapter 3 as well as the supporting practices and procedures discussed throughout this book. Other members of the enterprise, and potential auditees, should understand that IT auditors will be following good practices when they perform their reviews. However, beyond a high-level review of overall internal audit activities by external auditors, no one regularly "audits their internal auditors" to see if they are following good practices and their own professional standards.

The effective internal audit function should look at itself from time to time to determine if all of its components are following good internal audit practices and procedures. This is best accomplished if IT audit goes through an audit of the auditors over its own functions. ISACA's standards do not focus on quality in the IT audit function or department,but the IIA's *Standards for the Professional Practice of Internal Auditing* do refer to what are called quality-assurance reviews. IIA Standard 560 calls for the CAE "to establish and maintain a quality-assurance program" to appraise the quality of the audit work performed through ongoing supervisory reviews, reviews by internal audit of its own work, and reviews by external parties.

In addition, and perhaps even more important, the IIA's Standard 1312 "requires every internal audit department to have an external quality assessment at least once every five years by a qualified independent reviewer from outside the organization." In other words, in addition to its own internal quality-assurance review function, internal audit must arrange for another independent audit entity or should contract with an outside provider to assess the overall quality of the internal audit function. This is a key requirement for all internal audit departments

IT audit quality-assurance reviews are a special type of audit—more than a normal management assessment of operations. Although the IIA Standard 560 calls for three levels of review, this chapter focuses on reviews of IT audit performed by normal IT audit operations, including members of other enterprises or a specialized department within internal audit. These reviews allow an IT audit function to assess the quality of *its own* procedures and its compliance with both general internal audit and IT audit standards. The next sections describe the elements that should be included in an IT audit quality-assurance program and how IT audit can establish a program to perform these reviews.

Benefits of an IT Audit Quality-Assurance Review

IT audit departments sometimes are viewed as operating outside of the operational and financial internal audit function and other mainstream enterprise functions. IT audit reports to the audit committee through the CAE with close ties with very senior levels of IT and general management. However, as a very specialized function, IT audit or even all of internal audit is not always considered when other enterprise performance measurement policies and procedures are established. This is not to suggest that IT audit is ignored. However, the design of a new enterprise program of employee incentive pay, a major quality-assurance initiative, or some other employee benefit does not always consider the unique aspects of the overall internal audit function. These programs often focus on the enterprise's main functions, whether they are manufacturing, distribution, or financial.

As a key function in the enterprise, however, IT audit needs a way to measure itself and to establish incentives to do a better job. This is one of the real benefits of an IT audit quality-assurance review. Although IT audit itself is the prime beneficiary of these reviews, other stakeholders in an enterprise also benefit from a strong program of IT audit quality-assurance reviews. These reviews allow IT audit to demonstrate to management that it is doing a good job or taking corrective action to improve if necessary.

Quality Assurance Review Benefits to the IT Audit Function

The main beneficiary of any IT audit quality-assurance review program is IT audit itself. It and all of internal audit operate somewhat differently from many other functions in a typical enterprise and cannot measure themselves by such common measures of success as sales, production, or administrative efficiencies. An external reviewer who understands the IT audit process and who has had exposure to other enterprises can review IT audit operations to check both internal audit's compliance with professional standards and how its operations compare with other similar IT audit functions. A review of compliance with IT audit standards also is valuable. An IT audit function should have a program in place to follow these standards in all of its auditing activities; however, compliance with one or another specific standard may slip due to inattention or the pressure of completing audit projects. A quality-assurance review allows an outside reviewer to assess how good a given IT audit function is doing in complying with IT audit standards. This can be a valuable benefit.

The other area where IT audit can benefit from an internal quality-assurance review is the reviewer's comparison with other IT audit functions. IT audit management does not always know how well it compares to other IT audit functions in terms of such things as its use of computer audit automated tools and techniques (CAATT) procedures, efficiency in performing application audit tests, or even travel policies. CAEs can gather some of this information through their professional contacts at IIA meetings or other contacts. However, these contacts do not always provide the same level of objectivity that would be found through the work of an independent reviewer who has looked at several IT audit functions. Even though one-on-one professional contacts are valuable, professional peers in different enterprises may gloss over some faults or weaknesses when comparing their relative activities.

IT audit quality-assurance reviews that are performed by either outside parties or a specialized unit of a larger internal audit department, can add significant value to the IT audit department. The review may point to areas where some internal audits were performed in a manner not fully in compliance with standards or where efficiencies could have been achieved by using different audit procedures. For example, an IT applications review approach used in a given audit may not be appropriate for others. Although the audit's results were correct, different application architecture might have required much different procedures. As a result of such quality-assurance reviews, IT audit may be able to take the recommendations for improvements to benefit and improve its own overall operations.

Benefits to Management

Several levels of management, ranging from the managers directly responsible for the IT audit areas reviewed to the audit committee, are beneficiaries of IT audit quality-assurance reviews. Although an IT audit team certainly should not show its latest quality-assurance review report findings to management of its next scheduled IT audit project, the findings of a good program of quality-assurance reviews should result in better and more efficient audits. All members of management—and managers directly responsible for units audited, in particular—will benefit from an efficient and effective IT audit function. A program of IT audit-related quality-assurance reviews should help to ensure ongoing audit efficiency and affectivity.

The audit committee and senior management also should realize even greater benefits from a strong program of IT audit quality-assurance reviews. As has been discussed throughout this book, IT audit as an element of an internal audit function and a strong component in an enterprise's system of internal controls. Senior management and the audit committee should understand the overall principles of internal control, but they may not fully understand the technical nature and workings of the IT audit function. By sharing the results of an IT audit quality-assurance review with the CAE and various levels of senior management, an IT audit group will have a greater confidence in the quality of the reviews performed. This is a major benefit to the overall enterprise.

Elements of an IT Audit Quality-Assurance Review

An IT audit quality-assurance review is a formal process similar to many of the IT audit procedures outlined in other chapters. The review should be properly planned, follow a formal plan or audit program, and be performed by qualified reviewers who have an appropriate level of independence. Whether performed by a special unit of IT audit charged with performing such reviews or by an outside consultant, the review should follow the same standards of independence and objectivity required by any internal IT audit. The only significant difference here is that the quality-assurance review focuses on IT audit procedures. The establishment of these requirements is an important first step to launch an IT audit quality-review function. Although management may want to vary the content of any review to reflect local concerns within an enterprise and its IT audit function, the review should concentrate on compliance with ISACA and IIA standards.

The specific details behind how the quality of IT audit operations will be measured depends on many factors, including the size of the IT audit department, special technical activities, directions by the audit committee and senior management specifying more emphasis on one area over another, and others. Nevertheless, all IT audit activities should be measured against compliance with CobiT guidance and enterprise IT audit standards.

A quality-assurance review usually is initiated through a detailed review of compliance with IT audit procedures. This would include such matters as an evaluation of the risk-assessment planning process, reviews of other planning documents, staff assignment procedures, a review of selected workpapers and reports used in actual audits, and all other planning and administrative materials used by IT audit in the course of performing its audit assignments. The purpose of this review approach is to measure the overall quality of IT audit's own procedures. The specific procedures to be performed will vary with the size and activities of the IT audit department; Exhibit 31.6 outlines general procedures to be performed for an IT audit quality-assurance review. In addition to reviewing workpapers and administrative procedures, the quality-assurance review should focus on areas where IT audit has supported other internal audit reviews and on the auditees who either request reviews or have had reviews performed in their areas. An IT audit function contributes little to the quality of procedures in the overall enterprise if auditee management has serious concerns about the nature of the work performed, including the appropriateness of the audit conclusions and how those conclusions were communicated to management. The idea is not to determine that a representative group of auditees necessarily *likes* the IT internal auditors who performed a review in their area but to assess whether the reviews were performed in an appropriately professional manner.

Using these review procedures and auditee surveys, the quality-assurance reviewer should summarize the results and prepare a report for IT audit management and the CAE. Based on the report recommendations, a plan for improvement or corrective action should be established. In some cases, if reviewers found that certain completed audits did

1. Define the areas to be included in the IT audit QA review—whether the entire IT audit function or just a separate component, such as just CAATTs, a separate function such as data warehousing, or geographic area.
2. Define the time period for the audits to be included in the QA review—whether from the conclusion of the last QA review or for the 12-month period prior to the announcement of the audit.
3. Determine who will be performing the QA IT audit review, and ascertain that the reviewer understands ISACA and IIA standards as well as supporting internal audit department procedures.
4. If internal audit has not had such a QA review within the last 24 months, take steps to ensure that members of IT audit, the internal audit staff, and management understand the purpose and nature of the QA review.
5. If the QA review team plans to survey or interview auditees outside the internal audit department, such as the IT function, make some preliminary plans to inform all affected persons.
6. Based on IT audits completed and in process, develop a general strategy for the number and types of audits to be selected for review. If special knowledge areas are to be included, such as computer security or automated design, determine that appropriate resources have been allocated.
7. Select for review a portion of completed operational or financial internal audits where IT audit played a significant supporting role, and coordinate those review plans with appropriate internal audit management.
8. Decide if the QA review will be on a top-level basis, checking for compliance to general standards, or planned to include detailed reviews of selected audits, including workpaper reference checks or reperformance of tests.
9. If problems are encountered in the course of the planned QA review, such as audits requiring a more detailed review, procedures should be prepared to evaluate the QA review's scope or schedule.
10. If the QA review includes a selection of CAATTs developed to support the overall audit process, arrange for live demonstrations of those tools to review their controls and operating procedures.
11. Develop a general procedure for the format and nature of the QA final audit report.
12. Develop a strategy for reporting the results of the IT audit QA review to other members of the internal audit department and to selected members of senior management.

EXHIBIT 31.6   Procedures for a Quality-Assurance Review of IT Audit Activities

not follow good IT audit procedures, a program of ongoing review or corrective action should be established, often including steps to launch IT audit.

Who Performs the Quality-Assurance Review?

Because of the technical nature of many IT audits, an independent party often is needed to perform them. This is often fairly easy in a large, multiunit internal audit department; a team of centralized corporate internal auditors and others from different division units who have IT audit skill can perform quality-assurance reviews of other units. Although jealousy and nonobjective appraisals sometimes occur, an in-house quality review, if properly managed, can be performed inexpensively, effectively, and efficiently. For larger IT audit departments, in-house resources can even be devoted to performing periodic quality-assurance reviews.

Many IT audit departments, however, are either not large enough to perform a separate quality-assurance review or may face other challenges that prevents members of the enterprise from perform these reviews. A five-person IT audit group, for example, cannot realistically conduct a quality-assurance review with one member of the staff reviewing the other four. IT and internal audit management has two options here. They can develop a self-assessment type of review and have all members of the smaller staff evaluate themselves, or they can contract with an outside party to perform the review.

Outside parties that perform quality-assurance reviews include public accounting firms, consultants who specialize in such reviews, or internal auditors from other enterprises. As another option, the IIA has a review program where it will send a team of professionals to perform the review. However, ISACA does not have a similar function.

A larger IT audit department can perform IT quality-assurance reviews using designated members of the department. In many respects, an internal auditor who is familiar with the enterprise, its procedures, and industry—but also understands general IT audit procedures—is often the best, most qualified person to review IT audit operations. Just as IT audit performs a review of another function, such as a data warehouse operation, the data warehouse operation could review itself by assigning certain people from its group to perform this task. However, unless these department members have experience performing such self-assessments, the results of their review could be viewed as self-serving. IT audit has an advantage over here, as it regularly exhibits its independence through its standards and other review activities. A larger IT audit function can perform its own effective quality-assurance reviews if it can demonstrate to others, both inside and outside of internal audit, that it is acting as an independent party.

Larger internal audit functions also can establish effective quality-review programs by assigning certain members of the enterprise to perform quality-assurance reviews throughout the department. The IT audit function must be large enough to allow one auditor, or a small specialized group of auditors, to perform these reviews separate from normal audit activities. In a large IT audit department, there may be enough activity to justify a full-time quality-assurance function. In addition to the reviews, it could develop audit procedures and perform other functions. This internal review arrangement will not work if members of the regular audit staff are regularly pulled from their normal schedule and asked to review their peers.

Although internal auditing standards require them to act independently, quality reviews can be viewed by outsiders as either self-serving exercises or as programs to "get" someone in the audit department. As mentioned, the reviews are best performed by an independent function within IT audit and should otherwise follow normal IT audit procedures. That is, the internal audit quality-assurance function would schedule each of its reviews in the same manner as IT audit plans and schedules any normal audit. For example, if it were doing a quality review of a separate organizational unit's IT audit function, it would schedule and announce the review like any normal audit. Once the review was completed, the manager responsible for the unit reviewed would respond to the audit report as would any other auditee. Copies of the final report would go to the CAE, who could take further action as necessary.

This is a particularly effective way to organize IT audit quality-assurance reviews when the audit functions are distributed throughout the enterprise. An outside quality assurance reviewer probably would not get to all geographically remote units in the course of a single review. An in-house set of quality assurance reviewers could.

Self-assessment reviews are often the most realistic way for a very small IT audit group, perhaps with fewer than ten members, to review its own operations. The staff might postpone normal scheduled audits and block out time to perform the self-assessment review. Time could be allocated for this type of review when the staff is not busy with scheduled audits.

A self-assessment review by the same IT audit staff responsible for normal audit procedures almost seems as if the auditees are auditing themselves. However, many times this is the only way to review the quality of IT audit procedures in a smaller enterprise. Budget limitations usually prevent hiring outsiders to perform the review, and a small internal audit department could not justify the people resources. In this situation, staff members are asked to step back and review all of the procedures performed in the course of a series of audits, including planning, workpaper documentation, audit report content, and a variety of other matters.

Rather than writing a report about findings from the self-assessment review, the observations and conclusions often are best shared through a series of introspective review meetings. Here, IT audit management and all parties involved would take steps to improve operations based on the self-assessment review findings. For a smaller IT audit department, self-assessment is usually a cost-effective way to measure quality assurance. People are often their own best critics.

FUTURE DIRECTIONS FOR QUALITY ASSURANCE AUDITING

This chapter has looked at IT audit quality-assurance from two different dimensions: the separate quality audits that have been the domain of the ASQ, and quality assurance reviews as a means of assessing the standards and performance of existing IT audit departments. Although QA standards and practices are important for all internal auditors, we can at times lose track of our objectives in this area because too many use the term *quality assurance* without fully understanding it.

We began this chapter with a discussion of the role of ASQ members who once called themselves quality auditors and now just are called auditors. They are important members of the overall internal audit community, but because of their manufacturing and process industry heritage, they often operate separately from conventional internal and IT audit functions with only minimal contact with the CAE and audit committee. We have called this group quality auditors, to distinguish them from the ISACA- and IIA-heritage internal auditors. Even though the ISACA, IIA, and ASQ professional organizations do not have many formal connections at present, we can only expect these audit professions to grow closer in the future. ISACA- and IIA-trained internal auditors need to learn and use some of the analytical and statistical tools that are common to ASQ quality auditors, and the latter need some of the rigor and discipline of the IIA's internal auditing standards. CobiT, as reviewed in Chapter 2, contains effective guidance to better bring convergence.

Returning to our same terminology, internal audit QA reviews are methods that allow an IT audit department to measure how well it is performing. Internal auditors perform reviews in many other areas and freely make constructive suggestions, but they often do not take the opportunity to review themselves. A formal program of IT audit QA reviews, with reviews performed by a specialized function within internal audit, by various qualified outsider reviewers, or by means of a self-assessment survey, will allow IT audit to better assess its own performance. Who performs the review will depend on the size and enterprise of the IT audit department as well as on management's commitment to this type of review program.

In addition to reviewing how an individual IT audit department is doing and how well it is operating in compliance with IT audit standards, an internal audit department often needs to assess how it is performing compared to IT audit functions in other enterprises. This becomes even more important with the IIA standard requirement that every IT audit function must arrange to have an external quality-assurance review at least once every five years. Understanding these IT audit quality-assurance requirements and the steps necessary to perform an effective quality-assurance review is an important IT audit requirement.

 NOTE

1. *ISO CD2/ISO 19011* (Milwaukee: ASQ Quality Press, 2000).

Index